THE NORTHWEST SPORTSMAN
ALMANAC

EDITED BY TERRY W. SHEELY

Alaska Northwest Books™

Anchorage • Seattle

Library of Congress Cataloging-in-Publication Data
The northwest sportsman almanac.
  Bibliography: p.
  Includes index.
    1. Hunting—Northwest, Pacific. 2. Hunting—Alaska. 3. Fishing—Northwest, Pacific.
4. Fishing—Alaska. 5. Game and game-birds—Northwest, Pacific. 6. Game and game-birds—Alaska. 7. Outdoor recreation—Northwest, Pacific. 8. Outdoor recreation—Alaska.
1. Sheely, Terry W.
SK40.N69 1988   799.´.09795   88-16830
ISBN 0-88240-295-1
ISBN 0-88240-296-X paper

Edited by Terry W. Sheely
Design and cartography direction by Robert Chrestensen
Cover design by Sharon Schumacher
Cartography by David A. Shott

Contributors: Bob Brister, Erwin and Peggy Bauer, Neil G. Carey, Ethel Dassow, Bill Davis, David Engerbrettson, David Frazier, Darrell Gulin, Dewey Haeder, Mark Henckel, Milt Keizer, Ron Kerr, Tom Kitchin, Myron Kozak, Gerry Lamarre, Keith Lockwood, Bill Loftus, Mike Logan, Robert Merz, Brian O'Keefe, Doug Olander, Ed Park, Don Robertson, Terry Rudnick, Michael S. Sample, Joy Spurr, Hilary Stewart, John Thomas, Gary Turbak, Martin D. Waters, Doug Wilson, George Wuerthner

Acknowledgments
The broad sweep of reference material required to produce a comprehensive outdoor guide of this magnitude, in a setting as vast and diverse as the Northwest, requires incredible cooperation and coordination. More than 200 individuals, organizations and manufacturers in various outdoor recreational areas contributed illustrations and expertise to *The Northwest Sportsman Almanac*. We are grateful to them all, with special appreciation to: Dr. Loren Grey, Alaska Fish and Game Department, Alberta Fish and Wildlife Division, British Columbia Fish and Wildlife Branch, Canada Fisheries and Oceans, Canada Parks, Idaho Fish and Game Department, Montana Fish, Wildlife and Parks, Oregon Fish and Wildlife, Washington Fisheries Department, Washington Game Department, U.S. Fish and Wildlife Service, U.S. Forest Service, U.S. Park Service, U.S. Department of Interior, International Game Fish Association, Boone and Crockett Club, Pope and Young Club, Luhr-Jensen Sons, Federation of Fly Fishers, Oregon Marine Board, Martin Tackle, Sebastes, Uncle Josh, Washington Charter Boat Association, Wall Industries, *Northwest Mileposts™*, Remington Arms, Sturm Ruger, Federal Arms, Bear Archery, Gerten's Forge, Warshal's Sporting Goods, *Eugene Register-Guard*, O. Mustad and Son.

Disclaimer
The fishing and hunting license fee information in this book is current as of 1989. Fees may vary slightly in following years, so the reader may wish to contact individual state and province wildlife departments to confirm up-to-date fees.

Alaska Northwest Books™
22026 20th Avenue S.E.
Bothell, Washington 98021
A division of GTE Discovery Publications, Inc.

PRINTED IN HONG KONG

Antler velvet at dawn. By Dewey Haeder

Elk below Mammoth Hot Springs.
By Michael S. Sample

Table of Contents

Introduction

The Northwest is a flannel-shirted region of staggering complexity, stunning natural beauty, and exceptional wildlife. It is divided more by unfinished mountain ranges and ancient big game migration routes than political boundaries or transient governments; a complicated blend of topography and natural resources, of challenges and opportunities that allows its outdoorsmen to routinely live the adventures that others experience only as wistful dreams.

We take our weekends in spectacular surroundings doing what most sportsmen consider once-in-a-lifetime events — packing the horses up to snow to bugle for bull elk, bouncing a McKenzie boat through white-water steelhead rivers, challenging the tallest peaks in North America, or tackling the Pacific for salmon and giant bottom fish. Within a few minutes of metropolitan areas we can fill baskets with rich mushrooms, a dozen varieties of wild berries and salt-chilled shellfish. Our fishermen drift lures through North America's finest trout river waters, and in the fall we explore the nation's greatest concentration of wildernesses and hunt through mountains and prairies where big game records are broken.

Geographically the sportsman's Northwest is larger than most countries, with a concentration of wildlife, wilderness and ocean-to-desert diversity unmatched on this continent, perhaps the world. It is impossible to drop a pin at the point where the Northwest ends and the remainder of the world begins. From the east it starts somewhere downriver of the last paddlefish hole on the lower Yellowstone, and up from the south it's marked by the Shasta-Trinity blacktail country. On the north the boundary wavers on the shifting ice of the polar Arctic, and to the west it follows the warm blue water of the Japanese current where long-range charter boats troll feathers and steel for albacore.

Within that wobbly framework are the snowcapped mountain ranges of the northern Rockies, Cascades, Coast, Olympics, Wrangell, Alaska and Brooks with dozens of lesser ranges dropping into the Great Basin, Snake River Plain, Alvord Desert, High Line Plateau and Columbia Basin. The fish, game, wildlife and natural resources within the region follow the natural courses of the rivers and the lay of the land but are regulated by the governments of two countries and the states of Oregon, Washington, Idaho, Montana, Alaska, with large chunks of northern California, Utah and Wyoming, and the Canadian provinces of Alberta and British Columbia.

Between breakfast bacon and lunch the Northwest sportsman can travel from coastal beaches, through moss-draped rain forests, across undulating alder and conifer foothills to the hacksaw peaks and alpine basins where the snow stays year-round. He can drop through the semiarid ponderosa and rimrock country into irrigated wheat fields crowded with pheasants, sliding into the chukar scablands of sage and basalt. Fishermen are faced with choices ranging from the prehistoric sturgeon and paddlefish through salmon, trout and warm-water panfish to exotic and powerful saltwater species.

The diversity of land and water is reflected in the quality and quantity of the Northwest's wildlife and natural resources and the techniques demanded of those who expect to harvest a share of this wealth. It is also reflected in the attitude, appreciation, perspective and broad-based expertise of its sportsmen. The country and its wildlife wealth defies puristic single interests, encourages discovery and requires a certain amount of how-to instruction and esoteric appreciation before it permits understanding. Bass fishing in Oregon is different than bass fishing in Ohio; Montana whitetails aren't hunted with the same tactics that work in Texas, and Rivers Inlet chinook will scorn the lures that produce kings in Lake Michigan.

The originating concept of this publishing effort was to produce a book that reflects the stunning beauty, mystery and diversity of the Northwest, that answers the basic how-to, where-to questions of those outdoorsmen with their best days still ahead of them, yet will intrigue and inform those who have dropped their deer in the same run for the past 25 years, who know within a day or two when the first spring morels will push up between the cottonwood roots, and who have come to place equal value on their memories and plans for next season.

The effort required the combined talents, resources and expertise of dozens of experienced writers, photographers, editors, guides, fish and game managers, illustrators and sportsmen. The combination of their unique talents and deep-rooted appreciation for the Northwest will long stand as a reflection and guide to the lands and waters of the *Northwest Sportsman.*

Terry W. Sheely, Editor

Buffalo snow. American bison. By Thomas W. Kitchin

Olympic Peninsula mountain goat.
By Thomas W. Kitchin

The sunset rise. By Dave Engerbretson

Arctic Ocean

BROOKS RANGE

ALASKA RANGE

WRANGELL MTS.

COAST MO

Gulf of Alaska

ALEUTIAN RANGE

Bristol Bay

Pacific Ocean

ALASKA

ALBERTA

BRITISH COLUMBIA

MONTANA

WASH.

IDAHO

OREGON

Land of the
Northwest
Sportsman

Illustration by Robert Chrestensen

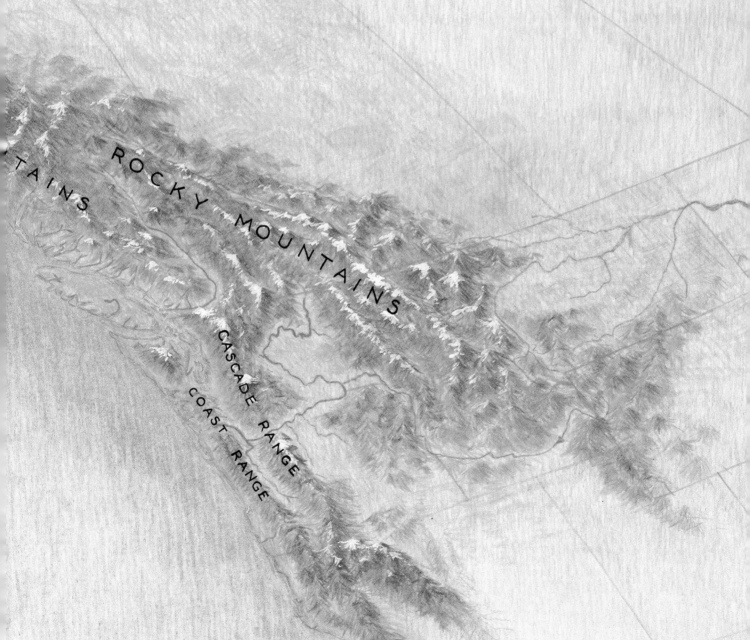

The Regions

Washington

From the razor clam beaches of the Pacific, east through mountains, sage, and irrigated wheat lands, to the dry and windworn hills of the Palouse, are 68,129 square miles of the most diverse hunting, fishing and outdoor recreational opportunities in the world. Washington is the smallest of the Northwest states and provinces, yet it offers the most outdoor recreation. Few residents will argue, beyond a shoulder-shrugging admission, that quantity and diversity sometimes surpass quality and solitude; negatives to be expected in the most populated region of the Northwest.

The wildlife and outdoor diversity is a product of the state's complex topography. Within a few miles it's possible to span marine beaches, coastal lowlands, mountain and desert. The ocean and its influence dominate the western part of the state. It begins with lonely coastal beaches, shaded from the morning sun by red-limbed cedars wrapped with tatters of pale green club moss. In swampy clearings small trees are rubbed barkless by rain forest elk and black-tailed deer. After dark, skitterish black bears prowl the beaches for tide-washed razor clams and stranded Dungeness crabs. The rivers with their famous runs of seagoing trout and salmon run to the hacksaw peaks of North America's two youngest mountain ranges, the Cascades and Olympics.

Hunting the foothills and mountains is not easy. The mountains are lung-searing steep, heavily timbered and etched with thousands of cascading streams. On the west slope, brush and trees are thick to impenetrable with towering sword ferns, moss-draped blow-downs and brush. Where timber companies have opened the forest canopy with clear-cuts the sun and rain have fertilized tangles of brush that defy description. Acres of thimble and salmonberry stalks,

Coyote, the Northwest's consummate hunter (left). By Mike Logan. Clear cutthroat trout creeks cascading into crystalline pools (above) are a common thread through Washington's coastal mountains. By Doug Wilson

Washington's ocean-to-desert diversity supports a sweeping variety of hunting opportunities, from the spectacular big game regions of Glacier Peak Wilderness Area (right) to the irrigated pheasant lands of the Columbia Basin (below). Basalt buttes and sage provide a strange, but incredibly productive setting for waterfowl hunters along the arid coulees of lower Crab Creek (far right). By Terry W. Sheely

blackberry tangles and blueberry bushes intertwine above a chaos of dropped, splintered trees. In some areas it is possible to fall and never hit the ground. Black-tailed deer slip like rabbits along knee-high tunnels through the tangles. Rabbit deer, the local hunters call them, appear and disappear in a blink, often less than a dozen feet away. Hunters gravitate to the easy paths, old logging and skid roads, hiking trails, alder ridges and streambeds.

Higher in the mountains there is less underbrush, the woods open and cross-country travel is easier, but no less steep. Between the peaks, are basins cooled with year-round snowbanks and scree slides descending into alpine trout lakes. There are more than 4,000 high lakes in Washington's mountains most rimmed with the purples and greens of high country heather and the clustered whips of mountain ash with their bright bunches of orange berries. This is mountain goat country, only British Columbia and Alaska have more. The creamy-white forms are easy to spot against the cliff rock, and tufts of white hair snagged on bushes above rounded hoof marks reveal their trails. The hollow hoots of bull blue grouse are heard here, along with the squeaks and whistles of pikas and marmots.

In the summer, trout fishermen follow topographical maps and an intricate system of U.S. Forest Service trails through these peaks carrying tiny break-down fly and spinning rods for cutthroat, rainbow, brookies and sometimes a golden or lake trout.

In September and October hunters pack into this vertical country afoot or horseback glassing the peaks, the basins and the dog-hair jackpine for goats, deer, elk and summer-fat black bear, and sometimes blue grouse and snowshoe hares. They'll be met with the first snows of winter. The country is steep and the hunting is hard but the game is there along with trout, lowbush blueberries, red or purple huckleberries, and dozens of edible mushroom species.

Puget Sound is nearly an inland sea, a saltwater area larger than all of the freshwater lakes, rivers and streams in Idaho and Washington combined. It dominates the northwestern slope of the Cascades. The sound's protected bays and points are heavily fished for salmon and prized bottom species. Dungeness and red rock crabs are caught in practically every bay of the sound. Shrimp, including giant spotted prawn, are pulled from deep-water traps. Oysters and abalone are plucked from submerged rocks.

The tidal marshes attract a wealth of shorebirds and waterfowl; mallards, wigeon, snow geese, snipe, rails and wild bandtail pigeons. Flocks of black

brant, a sea goose rare to most areas of the country, winter on the eelgrass beds of the north sound, and heavy-bodied black-and-white sea ducks mix with concentrations of divers. Some of the finest steelhead and salmon rivers in the Northwest drain into the sound.

The west slope climate is temperate in the lowlands. Lakes, rivers and salt water rarely freeze and fishing goes year-round. Snow is a once-or-twice-a-winter chaos in the lowlands, and rarely stays on the ground more than two weeks. A distinctive climatic break is from the mountains, however, where snow comes in late October, falls to world-record depths and stays until June. West slopers would rather go to snow when they want it, than have it come to them when they don't need it for tracking, skiing or snowshoeing. East of the mountains the climate runs to extremes of hot and cold, with summer temperatures soaring to 100 degrees and winters registering minus 30 degrees. Winter fishermen pack spud bars and sleds.

The central and eastern reaches are arid, the woods more open and bushwhacking easier. The fir and alder common to the coast, yield east of the crest to dryland pine and sage. Good hunting here for elk and mule deer, grouse and black bear. Beyond the mountains irrigated orchards and fields reach into the foothills from the Columbia River, replacing historical big game winter ranges with farmland pheasant and quail cover. Croplands bring down hundreds of thousands of ducks and geese, attracted by vast wheat fields and dozens of irrigated lakes and potholes. Where irrigation hasn't altered the natural landscape there is sage, basalt, cactus and rimrock; chukar and bighorn country.

On the far east side of Washington, the country north of Spokane turns from wheat fields to scrub pine and begins to climb into the Rocky Mountains — good trout and white-tailed deer country. In the southeast the country divides, with the rolling Palouse hills dropping into the Snake River canyon and the rest gradually ascending to the Blue Mountains. Fine country for pheasants, chukar, Hungarian partridge, mule deer, elk and bighorn sheep.

Washington Outdoor Information Sources

Washington's wildlife is managed by two state agencies with separate resource responsibilities. The **Department of Wildlife** regulates freshwater fish including anadromous rainbow (steelhead) and cutthroat trout in fresh or salt water, plus hunting and nongame wildlife management. The **Department of Fisheries** has responsibility for saltwater fish, including anadromous salmon, shad, smelt, sturgeon, carp and crayfish while in fresh water, plus saltwater shellfish.

Specific hunting, fishing and wildlife information, the locations of public hunting and freshwater fishing areas, and current regulations are available through the information sections of both departments at their Olympia headquarter offices. The Department of Wildlife also maintains six regional information offices.

Washington Department of Wildlife Headquarters: 600 N. Capitol Way, Olympia, WA 98504. Phone (206) 753-5700.

Region 1: North 8702 Division St., Spokane, WA 99218. Phone (509) 456-4082.

Region 2: 1540 Alder St. N.W., Ephrata, WA 98823. Phone (509)754-4624.

Region 3: 2802 Fruitvale Blvd., Yakima,

Washington Fish Game Management Zones
Regional Headquarter Locations

WA 98902. Phone (509) 575-2740.

Wenatchee District Office: 3860 Chelan Highway, Wenatchee, WA 98801. Phone (509) 662-0452.

Region 4: 16018 Mill Creek Blvd., Mill Creek, WA 90812. Phone (206) 775-1311.

Region 5: 5405 N.E. Hazel Dell Ave., Vancouver, WA 98863. Phone (206) 696-6211.

Region 6: 905 E. Heron St., Aberdeen,

WA 98520. Phone (206) 533-9335.

Washington Department of Fisheries (Salmon, Non-Trout Salt Water): 115 General Administration Bldg., Olympia, WA 98504. Phone (206) 753-6600. Free publications on saltwater fishing regulations, artificial reef location map, and saltwater fish records.

Washington State Parks and Recreation Office Headquarters: 7150

Highwood Lake, 9,127-foot Mount Shuksan. North Cascades National Park. By Doug Wilson

Cleanwater Lane, KY-11, Olympia, WA 98504. Phone (206) 753-2027; toll free in Washington (summer only), 1-800-562-0990. Information and free publications describing more than 100 state parks, winter snowmobile and cross-country skiing areas, public boating and marine facilities and horse trails are available.

Department of Natural Resources: Public Lands Bldg., Olympia, WA 98504. Toll free 1-800-562-6010. Regional offices in Chehalis, Colville, Sedro Woolley, Forks, Enumclaw, Ellensburg and Castle Rock. Provides free directory to more than 1,000 DNR camp and picnic sites, natural and multiple-use areas, and DNR managed public beaches and marine facilities.

Red Tide Hot Line: toll free 1-800-562-5632. Updated listing of beach areas temporarily closed to clam harvesting because of red tide, a natural and seasonal condition created by an outbreak of *Gonyaulax,* a microscopic red-celled organism ingested by clams that has a paralyzing affect on mammals. Shellfish beaches are closed by the state health department when a red tide is discovered in the area.

Steelhead Hot Line: phone (206) 526-8530. In operation from December through March, through NOAA, providing recorded reports on water levels, clarity and optimum fishing conditions on the state's major steelhead rivers.

Fish and Game Poaching Report Hot Line: toll free 1-800-562-5626.

Forest Fire Report Hot Line: toll free 1-800-562-6010.

Washington Outfitters and Guides Association: P.O. Box 397, Brewster, WA 98812. A listing of licensed hunting guides and outfitters providing horseback trips into mountain regions for fishing, hunting, photography, sightseeing or camping. Includes an outline of services offered by each outfitter or guide.

Washington State Charter Boat Association: P.O. Box 1066, Westport, WA 98595. Phone (206) 268-9485. Primarily Westport, Ilwaco, Strait of Juan de Fuca and Puget Sound members offering saltwater fishing trips for salmon, halibut and bottom fish plus spring whale watching and coastal excursion trips. Another partial listing of charter boats, fishing guides, tour and rental boats, is available from the Department of Commerce and Economic Development, Tourism and Promotion Division, 101 General Administration Bldg., Olympia, WA 98504. Phone (206) 753-5600.

August snow in the Tatoosh Range of the Cascade Mountains. By Terry W. Sheely

5

Oregon

For the outdoorsman, Oregon is a complicated land of overwhelming understatement, and distracting extremes wrapped around 96,981 square miles of some the finest hunting and fishing in North America.

Between the hard, alkaline desolation of the Alvord Desert country just up from Nevada and the soft drizzle on the shoulder of the Pacific Ocean, Oregon hunters, fishermen and weekend naturalists find a composite of Northwest topography and wildlife. Montana's big sky prairie and mule deer, Idaho's white-water rivers and trophy elk, Washington's steelhead and salmon fame, and the California waterfowl, stripers and sturgeon. Oregon has a share of the Northwest's best, and adds substantially to the regions legends and resources.

There are, it is claimed, 557 common forms of wildlife in Oregon. Ten big game species, 12 varieties of upland bird, 35 species of waterfowl, 17 different types of furbearers and 483 others not classed as game animals.

Oregon does not have an international reputation as a trophy-quality big game state, but it has the trophies. That it is overlooked by the general hunting world simply reflects Oregon's provincial foundation. State game and fish managers aren't opposed to nonresident hunters sharing the wealth, but they don't go out of their way to encourage them, either. Yet nonresidents who get wind of the Oregon big game potential, can expect a full measure of courtesy and cooperation. It's an attitude perhaps best reflected by Tom McCall's infamous gubernatorial decree that Oregon is a fine place to visit, but outsiders should not plan to stay.

Ironically, it was a nonresident who was among the first to worry publicly about the future of Oregon's vast resources, and in particular its magnificent rivers. International adventurer, outdoor writer and Western novelist, Zane Grey elected to spend his "home" days in the mid-1920s and early 30s on the Rogue and later the North Fork Umpqua, fly-fishing for steelhead, walking the hills for black-tailed bucks, and marveling at the great runs of salmon.

"The people of Oregon," Grey wrote in 1935, "and more especially those who live on or near the Umpqua, are as a whole deaf and blind to the marvelous good of this river, and if they do not wake up, its virtue and beauty and health will be lost to them." He later added, "I may be an outsider, but I love the Umpqua, and I know what it needs to be saved for Oregonians first and outsiders afterward."

A half century later Grey's private concerns have become public policy.

Oregon, like all the Pacific Rim regions, is a land of sharp topographic contrasts. Fifteen major rivers flow into the 400 miles of coastline, feeding lush

Ruffed grouse drumming (left). By Mike Logan. Ice-out brown trout at Oregon's Crescent Lake (above). By Ed Park

Flippers extended, California sea lions bask in a passive Pacific Ocean (top). By Tom Kitchin. The Eagle Cap Wilderness Area is popular with horse packers and big game hunters (above). By Ed Park

green mountains and foothills filled with trout streams, salmon rivers mixed with black-tailed deer, Roosevelt elk and black bear.

The Cascade Range crosses the state from Washington to California, a mile-high fence that catches ocean rain clouds and sharply divides the state into two regions. On the west it's wet, green and thick; on the east the state is dry, sunbrowned and open.

The central, northeastern and southeastern areas of Oregon are high desert. Hard, arid country burned by summer sun and frozen by incredible winter cold, separated by spring dust storms and fall hunting seasons. The land is split by several mountain ranges, rock gorges, lava fields and alkaline flats, yet it is incredulously stitched by some of the finest fishing rivers in the West. The Deschutes, John Day, Owyhee, Grand Ronde rivers and their tributaries and impoundments are meccas for trout and bass fishermen. Hunters find antelope, bighorn sheep and mule deer in the broken desert country, plus elk and bear where the pine trees mark the rise of mountains and water.

Chukar, Hungarian partridge, quail, sage hens and pheasants can be kicked out of the coulees, sage flats and fence lines. Chains of shallow lakes and tule marshes near Umatilla, Hart Mountain, Malheur and Warm Springs bring great goose and duck hunting to the desert.

West of the Cascade Range moisture-laden Pacific weather fronts, anchored to mile-high peaks, drop their loads of snow and "Oregon mist" on valleys and foothills thick with green brush and forests. The temperature swings are moderate and the climate mild and outdoor recreation runs every day of the year.

Most of Oregon's population is divided between small coastal towns strung together by U.S. Highway 101, and metropolitan areas in the Willamette River valley between Portland and Grants Pass along Interstate 5.

West side hunters find Roosevelt elk, black-tailed deer, black bear and cougar. Partridge and pheasants have been stocked in the Willamette Valley, band-tailed pigeons are dropped near the coast and ruffed grouse are kicked out of the alder bottoms and foothills. The giant blue grouse are found in the high country.

The broken coast lines of Washington, British Columbia and Alaska, with their protected deep-water bays, sounds and straits, smooth into miles of unbroken beaches in Oregon, open to the sea and unguarded from the weather.

Running the Rogue River for salmon and steelhead. By Erwin & Peggy Bauer

Sport and commercial fishermen launch for salmon, halibut, lingcod and rockfish from protected moorage in harbors carved from the estuary mouths of rivers.

The 18-foot kickerboats, common workhorses of the northern salmon fishing sport fleet are rarely used in Oregon, where sportfishermen challenge the open ocean and boats must be seaworthy enough to handle both the Pacifc and the often turbulent sandbars that divide the harbors from the ocean.

Still, saltwater fishing is popular and nearly every coastal town with a suitable bay or river estuary boasts a fleet of sturdy charter boats that book fishing space for between $35 and $55 a day, including tackle and bait. Most of the charters boats are between 40 and 60 feet long, with heated cabins, heads and a kerosene stove that keeps a kettle of tea water and pot of coffee warm.

Few ocean charters operate during the stormy coastal winters. Most book fares for day fishing trips from May into September. In May and June fishermen may find themselves sharing the coast with gray whales, migrating north from southern California to summering grounds in Alaska.

The bays are popular with crabbers trapping Dungeness and the sweet-meated red rocks, and clammers wearing splattered hip boots probing the tide flats for empires and hard-shells.

Steelhead, cutthroat and salmon run nearly every coastal flow, and the lower reaches of most Columbia River tributaries. There's not a month of the year when steelhead and salmon aren't running somewhere in the state, and during the summer, Oregon offers outstanding stream fishing for large rainbow and brown trout, plus bass and panfish.

The most northerly run of striped bass on the west coast is fished in Oregon's rivers. Guide Denny Hannah put this typical striper in the boat on the lower Umpqua River. By Erwin & Peggy Bauer

Oregon Outdoor Information Sources

Oregon's fresh and saltwater fishing, coastal shellfishing, hunting, wildlife and nongame birds and animals, are managed by the Oregon Department of Fish and Wildlife. The state police enforces fishing and hunting regulations. Annual hunting, fishing and shellfishing regulations, including maps, seasons, wildlife areas and license requirements are available by contacting the information office at the department's Portland headquarters office. The department also maintains seven regional offices including one concerned strictly with marine subjects. (All area codes are 503.)

Oregon Department of Fish and Wildlife Headquarters: 506 S.W. Mill St., P.O. Box 3503, Portland, OR 97208. Phone 229-5403.

Northwest Region: Route 5, Box 325, Corvallis, OR 97330. Phone 757-4186.

Southwest Region: 3140 N.E. Stephens, Roseburg, OR 97470. Phone 440-3353.

Central Region: 61374 Parrell Road, Bend, OR 97702. Phone 388-6363.

Northeast Region: Route 2, Box 2283, La Grande, OR 97850. Phone 963-2138.

Coastal sea stacks and beaches hold clams and bottomfish. By Erwin & Peggy Bauer

Southeast Region: Box 8, Hines, OR 97738. Phone 573-6582.

Columbia River Region: 17330 Evelyn St., Clackamas, OR 97015. Phone 657-2000.

Marine Region: Marine Science Drive, Bldg. 3, Newport, OR 97365. Phone 867-4741.

Oregon State Marine Board: 3000 Market St., NE 505, Salem, OR 97310. Phone 378-8587. Provides a 48-page guide to boating Oregon's coastal waters, including descriptions of bays, bars and river mouths. Another excellent publication from this department is a 32-page listing of boating facilities, *Oregon Boaters Handbook*. Both publications are free.

Oregon Parks and Recreation: 525 Trade St. S., Salem, OR 97310. Phone 378-6305. Provides listing and description of state parks, facilities and campsites.

Oregon Coast Charter Boat Association: 10188 Donald Road N.E., Aurora, OR 97002. A directory listing of charter boats operating from Oregon coastal harbors, plus a guide to when to fish, what to bring and who to contact. The directory lists charters for salmon, bottom fish, tuna, whale watching and sightseeing.

Oregon Guides and Packers Association: P.O. Box 3797, Portland, OR 97208. Phone 234-2173. Reference index for member guides and the areas they cover, plus information on river and mountain adventure, fishing and hunting trips.

Rogue River Guides Association: P.O. Box 792, Medford, OR 97501. Listing of guides and information on fishing, sightseeing, boating and camping on the legendary Rogue River, and neighboring steelhead, salmon, trout rivers in southern Oregon. The Rogue is one of the Northwest's most famous fishing and whitewater rivers.

Poaching Hot Line: toll free 1-800-452-7888. Report violations of fishing, hunting and general wildlife regulations.

Oregon Hunter's Association: 2150 N.E. Division, Suite 1, P.O. Box 6618, Bend, OR 97708. Phone 382-4058. A nongovernmental sportsmen group and reference source for Oregon hunting information.

Oregon Fish Game Management Zones
Regional Headquarter Locations

NORTHWEST
COLUMBIA RIVER
•Portland
•Clackamas
•La Grande
NORTHEAST
WILLAMETTE
Newport•
•Corvallis
CENTRAL
•Bend
•Hines
•Roseburg
SOUTHWEST
SOUTHEAST

Idaho

The trail is a narrow winding path of dusty pine needles and deer tracks that switchbacks along a mumbling creek to a small alpine lake a little west of the Continental Divide. In four miles the switchbacks climb 2,700 feet, mostly under the shaded canopy of Douglas fir and lodgepole pine. A few hundred vertical feet below the ridge top is tree line, where the mountain breaks into heather meadows and clusters of lowbush blueberries. A slide of loose scree runs from the summit into the back of the lake. The horizon is a jagged serration of hazy peaks.

"Idaho — A State With Room To Roam." That's what a local promotional brochure claims and that may be an understatement. Seventy percent of Idaho's 83,577 square miles, including portions of 15 national forests, is owned by a government agency, and open to hunting, fishing, hiking and camping. Big game animals outnumber human inhabitants, and there are trout lakes and streams that see less than a dozen fishermen in a year.

Either direction from this mountaintop is diverse country, divided by three major rivers into a complex of mountains, deserts, plains and prairie. These three drainages, the Clearwater, Salmon and Snake, effectively carve out the major hunting and fishing areas, with a diversity of wildlife and topography.

In the north, from the Clearwater River to Canada, most of the land is mountainous, heavily timbered, brushy and well watered. Storms born on the plains of eastern Washington are caught and drained by the Selkirk and Bitteroot mountains of northern Idaho. Lakes and streams are plentiful and the water is generally cold — good for native trout.

The largest lakes in the state are found in the north, the area known as the Panhandle. Lake Pend Oreille, the largest at 180 square miles, and the deepest at 1,158 feet, and sprawling Lake Coeur d'Alene and their tributaries are rich resources. Lake Pend Oreille produced the world-record landlocked rainbow trout, 37 pounds, and bull trout (landlocked Dolly Varden char) at 32 pounds. Both lakes and their tributaries hold bass, panfish and salmon as well as trout and are fine waterfowl hunting areas.

White-tailed deer, elk, black bear and mountain grouse are plentiful. Elk hunters stand a better chance of taking a 5-point or better bull in the St. Joe River drainage than perhaps anywhere else in the country.

The Salmon River — a powerful white-water sluiceway local Indians respectfully labeled "The River of No Return" — dominates the central part of the state. The Salmon begins in the creeks above Ketchum and flows north and west across the belly of the state to meet the Snake River at the downriver

Western Idaho mule deer country (left). By Dewey Haeder. Backtrail of a coyote tracked on the frozen surface of Arrowrock Reservoir, South Fork of the Boise River (above). By David R. Frazier

Henrys Fork of the Snake.
By David R. Frazier

Idaho Outdoor Information Sources

Fishing, hunting, wildlife management and enforcement in Idaho is directed by the Idaho Department of Fish and Game. Specific hunting and fishing regulations, seasons, license requirements and information on public wildlife areas is available from the information department at the IDFG headquarters office in Boise. Seven regional offices are scattered throughout the state to provide specific local information. (All area codes are 208.)

Idaho Department of Fish and Game Headquarters: 600 S. Walnut, P.O. Box 25, Boise, ID 83707. Phone 334-3700.

Region 1: 2320 Government Way, Coeur d'Alene, ID 83814. Phone 765-3111.

Region 2: 1540 Warner Ave., Lewiston, ID 83501. Phone 743-6502.

Region 3: 109 W. 44th St., Boise, ID 83704. Phone 334-3725.

P.O. Box 905, McCall, ID 83638. Phone 634-8139.

Region 4: 868 E. Main St., Jerome, ID 83338. Phone 324-4350.

Region 5: ISP Bldg., S. Fifth Ave., Pocatello, ID 83201. Phone 232-4703.

Region 6: 1515 Lincoln Road, Idaho Falls, ID 83401. Phone 522-7783.

P.O. Box 1336, Salmon, ID 83467. Phone 756-2271.

gateway to Hells Canyon. It carries the world's longest steelhead run, an 896-mile migration that begins at the Pacific Ocean and ends in the Sawtooth Mountains — a range sometimes called the American Alps.

Chinook salmon climb this river through some of the finest elk and bighorn sheep country in the Northwest. Dozens of outfitters book hunting trips and white-water float junkets on the Salmon, most headquartered in Salmon, Mackay or Riggins. The Sawooth, White Cloud, Lemhi and Lost River mountain ranges are dramatic challenges for hunters and fishermen packing their camps on their backs. Idaho has more than 200 peaks that exceed 8,000 feet and the tallest — Mount Borah at 12,662 feet — lies north of Mackay along the Big Lost River, a fine trout stream.

Forty percent of Idaho's 53 million acres are covered by trees, more than any other Rocky Mountain state. Nearly all of the treeless percentage is in the arid south along the Snake River plain. The Snake is the third major river dividing Idaho's topography and wildlife. It flows from the forested peaks of the Teton Range on the Wyoming border south and west through some of the driest, desolate country in the Northwest, before sweeping north to the Columbia River.

The Snake is locked into a series of dam impoundments through southern Idaho, heavily exploited for irrigation water and hydroelectricity. Near the river, irrigation canals and pipes carry water to lush agricultural fields that support fine pheasant and waterfowl hunting. The stilled waters behind the dams are fished for bass, crappie, catfish and sometimes trout.

Beyond the irrigation pipes the land is hard. Summer temperatures hold in the 100s for days at a time and in the winter the snow is freeze-dried into powder by months of below freezing temperatures. Sagebrush and cheat grass are the tallest nonrocks on the horizon.

The Snake River plains support the Gem State's major antelope and sage grouse populations and the dry mountains are rich in the minerals that develop trophy-sized deer antlers. Southern Idaho mule deer are potential record book bucks. The Owyhees, Payette, Boise mountains and scattered ranges in the southeastern corner along the borders of Wyoming and Utah are famous for high-racked mule deer.

Idaho sets aside 10 percent of its controlled-hunt permits for nonresident hunters, except for moose permits which are allotted to residents only.

Guides aren't required, but are recommended for most big game because of the remote hunting country and scattered concentrations.

Most hunting areas have general seasons for deer, elk, black bear and mountain lion with backcountry hunts opening in September and general seasons in October. There is no limit on the number of nonresident licenses available for general hunting seasons. Permits for controlled hunts for elk, bighorn sheep, mountain goats, antelope and deer are selected by computer.

The general fishing season runs from the Saturday before Memorial Day holiday through November, with local exceptions.

Idaho's unique geography, and outstanding wildlife resources attract sportsmen from throughout the world, and in some areas nonresident hunters and fishermen frequently outnumber residents.

Middle Fork of the Salmon River cuts through remote southcentral Idaho wilderness in a stairstep of placid runs and roaring whitewater. By Dave Engerbretson

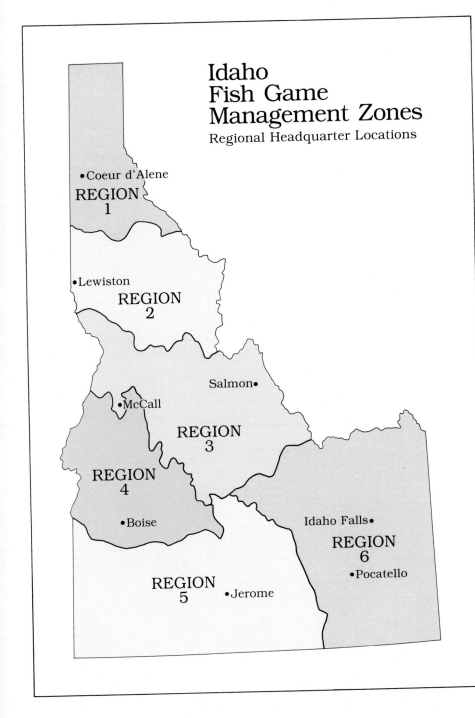

Idaho Fish Game Management Zones
Regional Headquarter Locations

• Coeur d'Alene
REGION 1

• Lewiston
REGION 2

Salmon •
• McCall
REGION 3

REGION 4
• Boise

Idaho Falls •
REGION 6
• Pocatello

REGION 5
• Jerome

Idaho Outfitters and Guides Association: P.O. Box 95, Boise, ID 83707. Provides a free 100-page directory of licensed hunting and fishing guides, outfitters, horse packers, white-water rafting companies and guest ranches.

Idaho State Parks And Recreation: 2177 Warm Springs Ave., Boise, ID 83702. Phone 334-2154. Listings, locations, facilities and descriptions of 22 state parks and campgrounds.

Idaho Travel Committee: Statehouse, Boise, ID 83720. Toll free 1-800-635-7820; in-state 334-2470. Provides free *Vacation Planner* magazine-style directory of recreational and travel services including public parks, fish and game offices, guides and outfitters, federal land, campgrounds, restaurants, skiing, historic sites, highway information and regional events.

Idaho Parks Foundation: 1020 W. Franklin St., Boise, ID 83702. Publishes free regional "adventure guides" to Idaho, listing county, state and federal camping areas, attractions and recreational opportunities.

Idaho Campground Owners Association: Anderson's Camp, Route l, Eden, ID 83325. Phone 733-6756. Listing of private campgrounds and facilities.

Poaching Hot Line: toll free 1-800-632-5999. Twenty-four-hour report system for reporting on fishing, hunting and general wildlife regulation violations.

15

Montana

The Northwest begins in the wind and sage of eastern Montana, evolving from a casual, Midwestern wave-of-the-hand direction into a specific region of climatic confusion and topographical diversity. It rises from the sharp meandering lines of a dryland antelope track to the glacial-scoured peaks of the Rocky Mountains and the dog-hair forests of the Pacific Coast.

Montana is a 550-mile-wide transitional zone, where the land, the rivers, the climate, the wildlife and even the attitudes of those who live here change remarkably when compared to the other three corners and the corn-fed midsection of America. Montana is the fourth-largest state, a dimension required to reflect the diversities of the Northwest; diversities that both multiply and complicate the hunting and fishing, the terrain and water, elevation and climate, seasons and weather. Except for the moderate temperatures and lush vegetation of the marine zones west of the coastal mountain ranges, Montana exemplifies the Northwest country.

Here an outdoorsman can get a taste of Alberta's bighorn sheep country, British Columbia's legendary trout and moose, the wild white-water rivers of Idaho and its high-racked mule deer, Washington's cliff-hanging mountain goats, black bear and bird shooting, and Oregon's high desert antelope and lowland bass lakes.

Montana's role as a reflection and introduction to neighboring superlatives is a minor standing, overshadowed by the state's own wealth of outdoor recreation, which some say is the best to be found in the Lower 48 states. Montana is the last of the contiguous states to allow hunters a chance for grizzly bear, the only state where anyone can hunt bighorn sheep without competing in special drawings and encompasses the finest collection of landlocked trout rivers in North America.

Nearly all of Montana's rivers spring from high mountain trickles, running down either side of the Continental Divide, east to the Atlantic, or west to the Pacific. At one spot high in the mountains of Glacier National Park, at a place called Triple Divide, a bucket of spilled water can run to the Gulf of Mexico and the Atlantic, down the Columbia River to the Pacific or north to Hudson Bay, and the Atlantic a little below the Arctic Circle. The headwater streams of the Missouri River pour from the treeless peaks of the southwestern mountain ranges to create the longest river running entirely within the United States and all of it fishable.

Typically, Montana rivers, east of the Divide, begin as fast, clear trout streams, bubbling with white water and eddying into classic western pools, their banks

In the Northwest the changing of the seasons is more often a matter of elevation differences than specific time periods. Typically, winter blankets the high country peaks with snow while in the valley of the Yellowstone River (above), an angler, wearing a short-sleeved shirt casts to summer trout. Far left, Mount Gould blocks the fury of a September snowstorm, shielding Lake Josephine from winter for another week or two. By Michael S. Sample

Granite Peak in the Montana Rockies.
By Michael S. Sample

tracked by trout fishermen carrying fly rods or light spinning tackle. In the first major valley a road swings alongside the rivers and follows them downstream to the plains where they broaden, deepen, warm and the trout are replaced by warm-water species, walleye, sauger, bass, northern pike and paddlefish. Anglers remove their waders and climb into boats, their tackle turns to medium and heavy action spinning or casting rods with trolling or bottom-bouncing bait rigs.

One of the first discoveries "outsiders" make shatters the popular Montana fly-fishing myth. If you are an outdoorsman living in Kansas City or Pasadena, and you read, your impression of a Montana fisherman is probably a lean figure, clad in $200 neoprene waders, in the shade of a $120 Stetson, pointing at $300 low-modulous graphite rod with a rosewood reel seat, at the form of a trout made visible in the depths by $25 polarized sunglasses. An imposing, if not intimidating sight. These folks exist, and some of them are actually residents. Most, however, are from Los Angeles or Baltimore or some such place, and the average Montana fisherman actually looks a lot like the average Kansas City fisherman, who may cast with a delicately tied fly or he may bang the bottom with a nightcrawler and marshmallow or troll a spoon sweetened with a slab of sucker meat. There are 16,000 miles of streams and rivers, and another 3,400 or so lakes in Montana — room enough for all types of anglers, as long as they show good river manners and pack out their leavings.

The Northwest was the first region to establish wild stocks of Chinese pheasants in North America, and they have adapted well to the irrigated farmlands and wild-grass river bottoms. By Erwin & Peggy Bauer

The name Montana is Latin for mountainous, yet two-thirds of the state is prairie and sageland, "Big Sky" country as described by Montana novelist A. B. Guthrie. Good country for mule deer, pronghorn. Pheasants, sharp-tailed grouse and sage hens live in the plains and irrigated croplands. In the river breaks and bottomlands, white-tailed deer populations are swelling, spilling into traditional mule deer ranges, and in the open, arid timber on the north side of Fort Peck Reservoir an elk herd is rapidly expanding.

The mountains, except for the Little and Big Belt ranges near Lewistown, and a few scattered upliftings, are confined to less than a third of the state, generally from the Missouri River west.

The Rocky Mountains drop south from Canada in a series of spectacular secondary ranges. The tallest peaks, and generally the steepest, are in the southwest corner in the Gallatin, Absaroka, Beartooth, Madison and Spanish Peaks ranges. The state's highest peak, Granite, is located here, near Cooke City and it measures 12,799 feet. The western mountains are timbered, ribbed with streams and generally accessible by logging road. Most of the mountain area, above the valley ranch lands, is public, part of the 17 million acres of national forest land in the state.

A dozen designated wilderness areas are set aside for foot or horse travel, and those who figure such things have determined that 20,000 miles of improved trails wind through the Montana mountains.

Mule and white-tailed deer, bighorn sheep, mountain goat, black and grizzly bear, cougar, moose, elk and some say wolves live in these mountains — as many big game species as you're likely to find anywhere south of Alaska.

The first hunting seasons generally begin in September, with the early hunts in the high country, and most general seasons follow in mid-October. Guides and outfitters and well-equipped locals pack hunting camps into the mountains throughout the season, setting up in remote backcountry ranges where only pack strings go: Pack strings and deer and elk and bear and moose, and maybe a wolf or cougar.

Weather runs to extremes, blistering hot in the open plains during summer, deadly cold in the mountains in winter. It can snow during any month of the year in Montana's higher elevations or it may melt the film in your camera. Dress accordingly and be ready to change.

Montana Outdoor Information Sources

Hunting, fishing, wildlife management and state access sites are directed by the Montana Department of Fish, Wildlife and Parks. Specific hunting and fishing regulations, seasons, license requirements, campsite facilities, and general information are available by contacting the department's headquarters office in Helena. Seven regional FWP offices, including information officers, are scattered across the state and can provide specific information about fishing and hunting opportunities in their regions. (All area codes are 406.)

Montana Department of Fish, Wildlife and Parks: Headquarters, 1420 E. Sixth Ave., Helena, MT 59620. Phone 444-2535.

Region 1: 490 N. Meridan Road, Kalispell, MT 59901. Phone 755-5505.

Region 2: 3201 Spurgin Road, Missoula, MT 59801. Phone 721-5808.

Region 3: 8695 Huffine Lane, Bozeman, MT 59715. Phone 586-5419.

Region 4: Route 4041, Box 243, Great Falls, MT 59405. Phone 454-3441.

Region 5: 1125 Lake Elmo Dr., Billings, MT 59105. Phone 252-4654.

Region 6: Route 1-4210 59230, Glasgow, MT 59230. Phone 228-9347.

Gardner River spawn-run brown trout. By Michael S. Sample

Region 7: Box 430, Miles City, MT 59301. Phone 232-4365.

Poaching Hot Line: toll free 1-800-847-6668. Twenty-four-hour report violations of fish and game regulations.

Department of Commerce: Promotion Division, 1429 Ninth Ave., Helena, MT 59620. Phone 444-2654. Out-of-state toll free 1-800-548-3390. Publishes free directories and guides to public and private campgrounds, resorts, ranches, and motels, plus general travel, camping and recreational information.

United States Forest Service: Northern Region, P.O. Box 7669, Missoula, MT 59807. Phone 329-3711. Request the *Outdoor Recreation Guide*, a free pamphlet providing the geographic locations, names and addresses of the 15 national forests in Montana, sources of local information, including detailed maps of each national forest, ranger districts and 15 designated wilderness areas.

Bureau of Land Management: P.O. Box 36800, Billings, MT 59107. Phone 657-6561. Maps and information on lands managed by the BLM.

National Park Service: Grant Kohrs Ranch National Historic Site, P.O. Box 790, Deer Lodge, MT 59722. Phone 846-2070. Informational pamphlets on NPS facilities and lands in Montana.

Montana Outfitters and Guides Association: P.O. Box 631, Hot Springs, MT 59845. Listing of hunting and fishing guides licensed by the state with membership in the MOGA. Sporting goods stores often arrange guided fishing trips in all areas of the state.

Fishing and Floating Outfitters Association of Montana: P.O. Box 1320, Livingston, MT 59047. Directory of licensed outfitters and guides providing fishing or white-water float trips.

Montana Fish Game Management Zones
Regional Headquarter Locations

Glacier National Park

Kalispell•

REGION 1

•Missoula

REGION 2

•Butte

REGION 3

REGION 4

•Great Falls

Helena

•Lewiston

•Havre

REGION 6

•Glasgow

REGION 5

•Billings

•Miles City

REGION 7

Yellowstone National Park

Antlers sheathed in velvet, a Montana bull elk finds relief from summer heat and flies by standing belly-deep in trout water. By Dave Engerbretson

Alberta

The great, flat grain plains of North America's midsection punch into southern Alberta bringing fields that roll to the horizon, roads bedded north and south, and weather that runs to extremes. In the morning, on a clear day while the sun is low in the east and climbing out of Saskatchewan, the light paints the prairie into quilted squares of pastel farm ground.

From the windshield-level perspective of a bruised pickup truck heading north on Canada Highway 4 from Sunburst, Montana, to Lethbridge, Alberta, the land appears dry and endless; wheat fields blending into parched patches of sagebrush and clusters of seedy wild grass. The perspective is narrow and perhaps misleading, and for a more accurate picture you climb into the right-hand seat of a red and white single-engine plane and spiral a few thousand feet into the air. With every increase in elevation there is a corresponding decrease in the illusion of perpetual prairie. Land that appears to be dry to the horizon is divided by rivers, creeks and occasional coulees. Splashes of blue materialize out of the dry ground marking irrigation reservoirs, lakes and ranch ponds. Good country to fish for walleye or nothern pike, jump thickets for white-tailed bucks, flush sharp-tails and ringnecks, or hunker in pit blinds while geese and mallards circle the spread.

To the north, above Yellowhead Highway 16, the plains fade into a remote land of low mountain ranges, divided by major rivers, huge lakes and dense woodlands. Moose and caribou country. The northern reaches of Alberta have been described by provincial boosters as, "a vast land of rugged forests, teeming lakes and untamed rivers. The outdoorsman and fisherman are king, with some of the world's finest fishing lakes set in the midst of unspoiled wilderness."

On the west, the patchwork plains end abruptly in the rugged upheaval of the Rocky Mountains. The Alberta Rockies are steep and by any measure spectacular. Much of the southwestern Alberta mountains are preserved in the chain of national parks on the British Columbia border, Jasper, Banff, Willmore and Waterton Lakes. In the parks where they are protected, and in the mountains outside the parks where they are hunted, are some of the largest bighorn sheep in North America. Broom-horned trophies that share the mountain country with mountain goats, elk, mule deer and wolves.

The land mass of Alberta is tremendous, covering more than a quarter million square miles, yet its entire population of 2.3 million could stand shoulder-to-shoulder on the 74-acre grounds of the Seattle Center. Nearly all of that population is scattered on the flatlands from Edmonton south to the Montana border. North of Edmonton the country rapidly reverts to wilderness. Only three

White-tailed deer (left) are thriving in Alberta's southern agricultural areas. By Thomas W. Kitchin. Above, sharp-tailed grouse are the dominate upland bird of the prairies. By Mike Logan

The lightly-populated potholes and wheatfields of southcentral Alberta attract thousands of ducks and geese, many unhunted. Wolves hunt the Alberta Rockies and the remote reaches north of Edmonton. By Thomas W. Kitchin

highways continue north each following wide valleys along the Athabasca, Loon and Peace rivers: Major route for big game hunters.

Alberta is a transisition zone, where the prairies meet both the mountains and the tracts of remote wilderness that lead eventually to the Arctic. The topographical collisions create a diversity that can challenge the most demanding outdoorsman.

The mountain ranges support quality big game hunting. Of the common northern trophies, only caribou are missing. Several herds of caribou are found in the northern third of Alberta, but they are protected and unhunted. Moose are common, and the bear hunting in the Athabasca country is almost legendary. Alberta's bighorn sheep are among the largest in North America, and in recent years bow hunters have found the sheep to be among the most accessible.

The southern mountains are good for mule deer, and the creek bottoms and coulees in the prairie/farmlands are hunted for white-tailed deer and pronghorns. Bird hunters walk the wheat stubble and bottom-brush for sharp-tailed grouse, Hungarian partridge and pheasants. Birds are plentiful in some areas and limits normally generous. Landowners are generally generous in opening their lands to considerate, polite hunters, especially in the areas far from major cities.

Duck and goose hunting is excellent in the fields in October, before freezeup sends the flocks into the United States. Goose hunting is especially productive. For many flocks of migrating geese the plains of Alberta are the first stop in a hunting zone. They drop into Alberta decoy spreads young and dumb. When the survivors arrive in the Lower 48 they have become incredibly wary, decoy-shy wraiths.

In the past few years Alberta's fishing has begun to attract national attention, primarily because of the uncompromisingly productive trout fishing in the lower Bow River — a river occasionally described in the national press as Canada's finest big trout river, and one of the finest anywhere. The Bow cuts a cool ribbon of trout water through the warm-water fishery of Alberta's midlands flowing from icy headwaters in Banff National Park through Calgary and the farm country. South of Calgary, outfitters and guides float anglers to large rainbow and brown trout.

Walleye, northern pike, perch and goldeye are also taken in the southern lakes and rivers, while char and trout dominate the mountain lakes and rivers of the West and North Country.

Nonresident hunting and fishing pressure is not nearly as intense in Alberta as in its neighboring states and provinces, but its wildlife wealth is being discovered. Outfitters and guides are available in nearly every major hunting area, and the number of fishing guides is growing.

Lightly populated and blessed with a topographical and wildlife diversity that combines the best of the American West and the Canadian North, Alberta stands to be a major hunting and fishing destination.

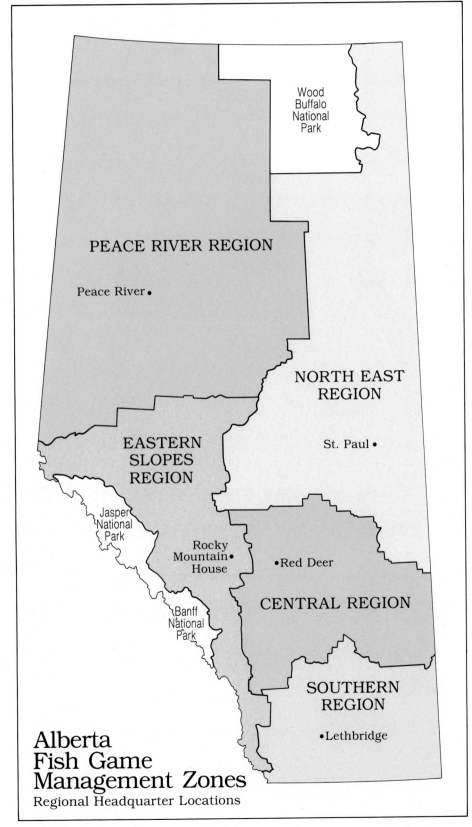

Wood Buffalo National Park

PEACE RIVER REGION

Peace River •

NORTH EAST REGION

St. Paul •

EASTERN SLOPES REGION

Jasper National Park

Rocky Mountain• House

•Red Deer

Banff National Park

CENTRAL REGION

SOUTHERN REGION

•Lethbridge

Alberta
Fish Game
Management Zones
Regional Headquarter Locations

Alberta Outdoor Information Sources

(All area codes are 403.)

Alberta Fish and Wildlife Division Headquarters: Fish and Wildlife Division: 9945 108th St., Edmonton, AB, Canada T5K 2C9. Phone 427-3590.

Northeast Region: P.O. Box 1450 El Dorado Bldg., St. Paul, AB, Canada T0A 3A0. Phone 645-6212.

Southern Region: Sun Centre, 530 Eighth St. S., Lethbridge, AB, Canada T1J 2J0. Phone 329-5266.

Central Region: Third Floor, 4901 48th St., Red Deer, AB, Canada T4N 6M4. Phone 340-5142.

Peace River Region: Bag 900, 38th River Drive Mall, Peace River, AB, Canada T0H 2X0. Phone 624-6246.

Eastern Slopes Region: P.O. Bag 388, Provincial Bldg., 4919 51st St., Rocky Mountain House, AB, Canada T0M 1T0. Phone 845-5357.

Travel Alberta: 14th Floor, 10065 Jasper Ave., Edmonton, AB, Canada T5J 0H4. Request *Alberta Adventure Guide,* a colorful booklet listing all registered Alberta big game hunting, fishing guides and outfitters, resorts, guest ranches and river rafting companies.

Also provides general information on the province's see-and-do opportunities, recreation and highway systems.

Canada Map Office: 615 Booth St., Ottawa, ON, Canada K1A 0E9. Provides topographic maps of the national parks wilderness areas, including elevations, creeks, roads and trails.

Map Distribution and Sales Centre: 9945 108th St., Edmonton, AB, Canada T5K 2C9. Can provide, for a fee, detailed maps showing ownership status in the province, plus provincial and federal forests maps.

British Columbia

There are only a few countries, some estimate about 30, larger than the province of British Columbia, a vast, often spectacular land of geographic enormities and fishing and hunting superlatives. To write of the fishing and hunting opportunities in British Columbia is to risk the accusation of boosterism, but it is difficult, perhaps impossible to avoid.

Simply reporting the size of the province appears grandiose. At the southern border, its narrowest, British Columbia sweeps past the entire northern borders of Washington, Idaho and western Montana. The European countries of France, West Germany, the Netherlands, Belgium and Austria, lumped together, would fit inside the borders of this third largest Canadian province. It reaches from Montana to Alaska and from the Rocky Mountains to the Pacific Ocean.

Nowhere, perhaps, is the topographical and climatic diversity of the Northwest typified more than in British Columbia. The contrasts of British Columbia, often within sight of each other, are striking. Big game hunters leading packhorses through mountain country can turn in the saddle and see the ultramodern skyscraper skyline of Vancouver. The world's largest natural salmon runs (up to 10 million returning spawners) are in the Fraser River which pours from the backbone of the Rocky Mountains on the west-central Alberta border across the belly of British Columbia to salt water in the Strait of Georgia between Vancouver and the Washington border.

Floatplanes lift off the mouth of the Fraser at Vancouver International Airport bound for legendary northern fishing lodges where the only way in is by plane or boat. Some of the pontoon planes follow the fjord-carved coastline north along the jagged white peaks of the Coast Mountains to salmon waters. Others swing northeast across the peaks carrying light-tackle fishermen to emerald green trout lakes in the timbered hills of the Cariboo and Kamloops regions. For all of its metropolitan glitter and congestion, Vancouver sits on the threshold of wilderness.

Geographically, mainland British Columbia is divided by mountain ranges running northwesterly. On the west is the Coast Mountains crowned by 13,176-foot Mount Waddington, on the east the Rocky Mountains and 12,972-foot Mount Robson. In between are scattered plateaus, and mountain ranges including the St. Elias, Skeena, Cassiar, Omineca, Stikine, Muskwa, and Shuswap mountains. The far northern corner is lowlands, an extension of the Great Interior Plains, and the southcentral is hot, dry ranch and orchard country.

There are more than two dozen wilderness-recreation areas, plus five national and 320 provincial parks featuring glaciers, volcanoes, forests, lakes and moun-

Flyfishing for steelhead on British Columbia's productive Bulkley River (left). Chicken Of The Woods (above) is one of more than two dozen varieties of edible mushrooms in the B.C. forests.
By Myron Kozak

The all-white Kermode bear (top), perhaps the rarest color phase of the common black bear, is found only in northwestern British Columbia near Kitimat, Terrace and Hazelton. The population is estimated at between 2,500 and 3,000, and hunting is prohibited. By Myron Kozak. Even more famous than its hunting, is British Columbia's salmon fishing, encouraged by catches similar to this pair of 30-pound plus tyees (above) from Vancouver Island's Alberni Inlet. By Terry W. Sheely.

tains. There is no hunting in the parks. The coastline is broken into thousands of islands, fjords, coves and inlets serviced by 28 marine parks, most in the sheltered coves between Vancouver Island and the mainland.

The inlets, islands and fjords are rich with salmon, bottom fish and shellfish, much of it accessible only to boaters wandering the maze.

Chinook and coho salmon and prize bottom fish species such as halibut (seasonal restrictions), lingcod, rockfish, and cod are caught year-round on the British Columbia coastline. Hard-shell steamer clams, oysters and crabs can be taken without a lot of effort. Steelhead and sea-run cutthroat move into the rivers in late summer and early winter. Inland, trout fishermen have long praised the wealth of small lakes in the Cariboo-Chilcotin-Kamloops regions. More than 4,000 lakes are found in the forests here, supporting kamloops, an acrobatic, hard-fighting strain of rainbow trout, plus brook trout, kokanee, lake trout and bull (Dolly Varden) trout.

Farther north, in the Peace River drainage, arctic grayling and northern pike are lightly fished. North of Yellowhead Highway 16 there are few roads and even fewer people. Excellent hunting country for mountain goat, bighorn sheep, grizzly and black bear, caribou and moose. There are also moose, elk, whitetail, blacktail and mule deer in most areas of the province. Some of the densest concentrations of wolves and cougars in the Northwest are found on Vancouver Island.

In most instances there is no shortage of guides or outfitters for hunting or fishing trips. Nonresident big game hunters are required to have a licensed British Columbia guide. Handguns and automatic weapons are strictly prohibited throughout the province. Fishermen will find separate licenses are required for fresh- and saltwater fishing, and a specific fishing license is required in the national parks of Canada. Sportsmen planning to enter British Columbia by private boat are to contact a regional Canadian customs agent.

British Columbia Outdoor Information Sources

Ptarmigan are plentiful in B.C. mountains, frequently providing a diversion and dinner for big game hunters. By Mike Logan

(All area codes are 604.)

British Columbia Fish and Wildlife Branch, Headquarters: Ministry of Environment, Parliament Bldg., Victoria, BC, Canada V8V 1X5. Phone 387-4573.

Vancouver Island: 2569 Kenworth Road, Nanaimo, BC, Canada V9T 4P7. Phone 758-3951.

Lower Mainland: 10334 152A St., Surrey, BC, Canada V3R 7P8. Phone 584-8822.

Thompson-Nicola: 1259 Dalhousie Dr., Kamloops, BC, Canada V2C 5Z5. Phone 374-9717.

Kootenay: 310 Ward St., Nelson, BC, Canada V1L 5S4. Phone 354-6333; 106 Fifth Ave. S., Cranbrook, BC, Canada V1C 2G2. Phone 426-1450.

Cariboo: 504 Borland St., Williams Lake, BC, Canada V2G 1R8. Phone 398-4530.

Skeena: Bag 5000, 3726 Alfred Ave., Smithers, BC, Canada V0J 2N0. Phone 847-7303.

Omineca-Peace: Plaza 400, 1011 Fourth Ave., Prince George, BC, Canada V2L 3H9.

Phone 565-6135; 10142-101 Ave., Fort St. John, BC, Canada V1J 2B3. Phone 787-3200.

Okanagan: 3547 Skaha Lake Road, Penticton, BC, Canada V2A 7K2. Phone 493-8261.

Guide-Outfitters Association of British Columbia: P.O. Box 759, 100 Mile House, BC, Canada V0K 2E0. Phone 395-2438. Can provide a 95-page booklet of the licensed big game hunting and fishing guides, and outfitters in British Columbia. Request booklet *Guided Wilderness Tours* which includes a listing of the services, facilities and trips each guide-outfitter offers or specializes in.

Fishing Camp Operators Associa-

tion: Box 3301, Kamloops, BC, Canada V2C 6B9. Provide a listing and brief description of freshwater fishing camps and resorts facilities in the interior region, primarily in the Cariboo, Kamloops and Williams Lake regions. Request the *Fresh Water Sport Fishing Pamphlet*.

Ministry of Tourism, Tourism British Columbia: 1117 Wharf St., Victoria, BC, Canada V8W 2Z2. Can provide general information on the province, plus specific listings of saltwater resorts, salmon and bottom fishing charter boats, steelhead and trout fishing guides, and lodges throughout the province. British Columbia is divided into nine regions and each region has an independent Tourism Office that can provide specific hunting, fishing and resort information in that region.

Regional Tourist Associations:

Vancouver Island: #608, 620 View St., Victoria, BC, Canada V8W 1J6. Phone 382-3551.

Southwestern: P.O. Box 94449, #2-5760 Minoru Blvd., Richmond, BC, Canada V6Y 2A8. Phone 270-6801.

Okanagan/Similkameen: Jubilee Pavilion, 185 Lakeshore Dr., Penticton, BC, Canada V2A 1B7. Phone 492-6611.

Kootenay Boundary: P.O. Box 172, Nelson, BC, Canada V1L 5P9. Phone 354-4831.

Thompson Country: P.O. Box 298, Salmon Arm, BC, Canada V0E 2T0. Phone 832-8028.

Cariboo: P.O. Box 4900, Williams Lake, BC, Canada V2G 2V8. Phone 392-2226.

B.C. Yellowhead 16: 1277 Main St., Smithers, BC, Canada V0J 2N0. Phone 847-5277.

Peace River/Alaska Highway: #14-9223 100th St., Fort St. John, BC, Canada V1J 3X3. Phone 785-2544.

Rocky Mountain: P.O. Box 10, Kimberley, BC, Canada V1A 2Y5. Phone 427-7469.

British Columbia Fish Game Management Zones
Regional Headquarter Locations

REGION 7
Fort St. John

REGION 6

REGION 5
Williams Lake

Smithers

Prince George

REGION 3
Kamloops

REGION 4
Cranbrook

REGION 2

REGION 8

Nelson

REGION 1
Surrey
Penticton
Nanaimo
Victoria

Alaska

Alaska covers more than 580,000 square miles, much of it wilderness, most of it spectacular, some of it magnificent. There is a tendency to be overwhelmed by the outdoor recreational opportunities of a state so large that it could cover 10 of the other 49 states, support 12 species of big game animals and the world's greatest salmon runs, produce 11 fish and game world's records, have 3 million lakes, 3,000 rivers, and measure 2,400 miles east to west, with 47,300 miles of tidal shoreline touching two seas and two oceans.

Alaska is a land of startling contrasts, a feature in common with the rest of the Northwest, ranging from lush, nearly impenetrable forests in the coastal Southeast to treeless tundra in the Interior and permanent pack ice in the North. Of the 20 highest mountains in the United States, 17 are in Alaska including the tallest in North America — the south peak of Mount McKinley at 20,320 feet. Moose, grizzly bear, caribou, mountain goats, Dall sheep, wolves, elk and deer are hunted in 39 separate mountain ranges varying from the diminutive Waring Mountains at 1,800 feet to the jagged four-mile-high spires of the Alaska Range.

Balancing the superlatives, Alaska also challenges sportsmen with some of the harshest conditions in the world. Temperatures can touch the upper 90s or plummet to minus 50. Black flies and 25 varieties of mosquitoes can arrive in clouds of madness and torment. Hunters can become the hunted in the land of the Great Bear, and wild rivers can suck in a steelhead fisherman's boat and blow it into a logjam 10 miles downstream. Pacific storms bank against the peaks and the rain and fog can keep you pinned down for a week or more. Bush pilots and floatplanes are the standard taxis for backcountry travel in this roadless (only 15,315 miles of highway in more than a half million square miles of land) tract and flying between the peaks is not without its memorable moments.

Fishermen and hunters come to Alaska for adventure and once-in-a-lifetime trophies, and with a lot of luck perhaps a world's record. Alaska is where world's records are set. The largest steelhead ever caught came from Alaskan waters, along with four of the five Pacific salmon, and halibut.

Of the 29 North American big game species scored by Boone and Crockett, Alaska has title to six No. 1 positions — brown bear, walrus, moose, barren ground caribou, mountain goat and Dall sheep.

Hunters and fishermen, resident or nonresident, expert or cheechako, have an equal responsibility to become familiar with the diverse geographical features and the climatic extremes of Alaska before setting out — whether it's for an afternoon of fly-fishing or two weeks in the Wrangells for Dall rams.

Full-curl Dall ram (left), North America's only white sheep. By Thomas W. Kitchin. Above, one of the most common scenes in Alaska, a solitary figure in a small boat fishing waters protected by towering mountains. By Doug Wilson

The largest land carnivore in North America is the Alaskan brown bear, a variety of grizzly that dominates southern coastal areas. By Erwin & Peggy Bauer

Weather is all-important to a hunter. When a hunting party invades North Country wilderness, it must be prepared to withstand extremes in wind, temperature and precipitation, whether it be rain or snow. Choice of proper clothing, tent, stove and sleeping bags not only makes the difference between comfort and discomfort, it can make the difference between life and death. The wise hunter will study the climate of the specific region in which he intends to hunt, and he will prepare for any eventuality. He must be cautious about forming opinions based upon a short visit or what is considered "usual" conditions. Some winters have remarkably mild conditions with temperatures in the 40s and 50s for several days or weeks. However, an annual temperature spread of 160 degrees is not uncommon in some areas of the North.

North Country winds can be frightening and dangerous. A storm track normally brings weather from the southwest across the North Pacific, and from Siberia and the Bering Sea for northern Alaska. Winds of more than 50 mph are not uncommon during all but summer months, and even during summer such winds are possible. Near mountain passes and on the weather side of mountains, velocities approaching 100 mph are not unusual.

High winds can be expected within several miles of the face of any large glacier, in high mountain passes and on both sides of all low-altitude mountain passes.

"Williwaw" is the name given to the violent wind which frequently occurs on the leeward side of the mountains of the Aleutian Islands, the Alaska Peninsula, the Kenai Peninsula, in Prince William Sound and in southeastern Alaska. This is an especially dangerous wind due to the suddenness of its occurrence, as well as its violence. It occurs when wind pressure builds up on the windward side of a mountain, then spills over the crest as an overwhelming surge.

Williwaws commonly flip small planes and collapse tents that are pitched where there is no shelter. They have been known to overturn commercial salmon fishing boats. Experienced hunters in williwaw country pitch tents in the middle of dense alder patches, fill floats of small planes with water to anchor them and keep small boats in sheltered coves where possible.

Permafrost: The northernmost parts of Alaska, Yukon Territory and Northwest Territories are underlaid by permanently frozen ground, which requires a mean annual temperature below freezing to form and to remain.

Permafrost is intermittent through the central part of Alaska and not found in most of southcentral Alaska and the southern coastal portions, including southeastern Alaska, the Alaska Peninsula and the Aleutian Islands.

Areas affected by permafrost are generally low in annual precipitation, but permafrost creates wet ground conditions which must often be dealt with in the same manner as those in a high-rainfall area.

Alaska is mostly a magnificent, beautiful, but often lonely wilderness of forests, tundra, glacier-studded mountains, lakes and streams. Of the 500,000 people living here — fewer than found in many of the country's larger cities — about one-sixth are Eskimos, Indians and Aleuts; descendants of the original inhabitants.

There are also about 25 modern or semimodern towns of 1,500 or more people mostly located in the southcentral coastal area and southeastern Alaska.

Four major physiographic regions reflect four major climatic zones in Alaska.

The Maritime includes southeastern Alaska, the south coast and the southwestern (Aleutian) islands. Here coastal mountains, sometimes of great height, couple with plentiful moisture to produce precipitation up to 150 inches a year in the panhandle of southeastern Alaska, and up to 200 inches along the north Gulf Coast. These amounts are reduced to near 60 inches on the southern side of the Aleutian Range on the Alaska Peninsula, and to about 30 inches along the Aleutian chain. Temperatures are moderated by the influence of the sea. Winter extremes of below zero are uncommon. Summers are cool, with temperatures generally in the 60s.

Alaskan rainbow trout are characteristically heavily-spotted with broad pink lateral stripes. By Brian O'Keefe

Number of Licensed Hunters and Fishermen
(Based on 1986 U.S. Fish and Wildlife Service Data)

	Total License Holders	Tags, Permits Residents	Tags, Permits Nonresidents	License Fees Paid
Alaska				
Fishing	304,487	180,936	133,051	$ 3.9 Million
Hunting	103,322	185,202	26,471	$ 4.2 Million
Idaho				
Fishing	424,127	305,588	164,079	$ 4.2 Million
Hunting	238,288	512,167	51,834	$ 7.6 Million
Montana				
Fishing	349,595	303,891	270,464	$ 5.6 Million
Hunting	250,376	802,712	194,616	$ 8.8 Million
Oregon				
Fishing	725,591	922,584	193,360	$10.4 Million
Hunting	355,729	980,370	21,171	$10.7 Million
Washington				
Fishing	821,612	1,046,889	109,888	$11.3 Million
Hunting	271,016	628,113	4,336	$ 9.8 Million

Uncommon outside of Alaska, the harlequin drake is a strikingly-colored duck; one of several fairly rare waterfowl species found in Alaska's under-rated marshes.
By Erwin & Peggy Bauer

The Transition zone lies between the moist marine and the dry continental influence. This is generally a narrow band along the southern part of the Copper River, the Chugach Mountains, Cook Inlet, Bristol Bay and the coastal regions of the west-central part of the state. Here precipitation is generally less than 50 inches annually. Winter temperatures are somewhat less than the maritime. Summer temperatures are moderate, usually in the 60s, with highs in the 70s or 80s at times. Rainfall occurs mostly in August and September.

The Continental zone includes the rest of the Copper River drainage, the Nelchina basin and the Interior basin. Precipitation in this area is generally less than 29 inches. Winter temperatures may plunge to -50° or -60°F. Winter days are short, summer days long, with temperatures in the 70s and 80s and extremes to the 90s. August and September may be rainy, with snow above 3,000 or 4,000 feet.

The Arctic zone, north of the Arctic Circle (or above the most northerly bend of the Yukon River), has 10 to 15 inches of precipitation. Winter temperatures may be extreme, dipping to -50° or -60°F. Daylight hours during spring, summer and fall are extremely long. In the heart of the Brooks Range, for example, it is possible to fly a small plane, hike in the mountains and read ordinary print without artificial light nearly 24 hours a day from June to about mid-August. Winter days are short; in the northerly part of this zone, the sun doesn't rise above the horizon from mid-November until mid-February. Summer temperatures in sheltered mountain valleys may be high, but the coastal plain is often plagued with fogs and cold winds that blow from the pack ice in the Beaufort Sea. The mean temperature for the North Slope is 10°F.

Freezeup: Alaska's rivers and lakes usually start to freeze over by October,

depending upon how northerly and how far from the coast they are. Freezeup in the high Alaska Range and in the Arctic may last well into May, with ice on some lakes remaining into July.

Arrigetch Peaks, in the remote Gates of The Arctic National Park. Courtesy *The ALASKA WILDERNESS MILEPOST®*.

The Land

Alaska has vast stretches of treeless land in the Arctic, on the Alaska Peninsula, and in above-timberline areas of its abundant mountains. There are thousands of square miles of tundra, also without trees or with trees sparse. There is scarcely a spot in the entire state out of sight of towering mountains. The dense rain forests of southeastern Alaska are made up of huge fir, spruce, cedar and hemlock. Interior and subarctic forests include white and black spruce, birch, aspen and cottonwood.

Alaska includes 12 large river systems, of which three are major tributaries to the great Yukon. Four of Alaska's major rivers have their headwaters in Canada.

Many of the major rivers (including the Yukon) are silty, or muddy. Streams that originate in glaciers are also muddy, or at least milky. As a result many of the streams in the glacially active Alaska Range and Coast Mountains appear turbid. Streams from the almost glacier-free Brooks Range are generally clear.

Denali National Park and Preserve, formerly Mount McKinley National Park, is open from about June 1 to Sept. 10. There are campgrounds available on a first-come, first-served basis; commercial lodges and campgrounds are located nearby. No fishing license is required. Glacier Bay National Monument is open

May through mid-September and offers wilderness camping, boating and fishing. Accommodations are available at private lodges and aboard charter craft. An Alaska fishing license is required. Katmai National Monument is open June to September, has a free tent campground and a private lodge. An Alaska fishing license is required. *No hunting is allowed in the monuments or the park.*

Monuments administered by the National Park Service with no sport hunting allowed include: Yukon-Charley, 1.72 million acres along the Yukon and Charley rivers near the Canadian border; Gates of the Arctic, 8.22 million acres in the central Brooks Range; Noatak, 5.8 million acres in northwestern Alaska; Kobuk, 1.71 million acres in northwestern Alaska; Cape Krusenstern, 560,000 acres near Kotzebue; Bering Land Bridge, 2.6 million acres; Denali, 3.89 million acres in Denali National Park; Wrangell-Saint Elias, 10.95 million acres in southcentral and southeastern Alaska; Kenai Fjords, 570,000 acres on the outer Kenai Peninsula; Lake Clark, 2.5 million acres at base of Alaska Peninsula; Katmai, 1.37-million-acre addition to existing monument; Aniakchak, 350,000 acres on the Alaska Peninsula; and Glacier Bay, 550;000-acre addition to existing monument.

Monuments established to be administered by the U.S. Fish and Wildlife Service with sport hunting allowed include: Becharof Lake, 1.2 million acres on the Alaska Peninsula; and Yukon Flats, 10.6 million acres along the Yukon River in central Alaska. Monuments to be administered by the U.S. Forest Service with hunting allowed include: Admiralty Island, 1.1 million acres; and Misty Fiords, 2.2 million acres in southeastern Alaska.

The 16-million-acre Tongass National Forest in southeastern Alaska is the largest in the United States. The 4.7-million-acre Chugach National Forest, the second largest in the United States, is found on the north coast of the Gulf of Alaska, rimming Prince William Sound and the Kenai Peninsula.

Both of these national forests have a large variety of fish and game and are open to hunting, fishing, camping, hiking and other recreational uses. State hunting and fishing regulations apply. The Tongass provides good deer and goat hunting; wolves, coyotes and wolverines are present. Brown bear are particularly plentiful on the "ABC" islands (Admiralty, Baranof, Chichagof), but they are also abundant near Yakutat, where a part of the Tongass is found. There are also black bear, moose and a variety of small game species.

The Chugach Forest provides good hunting for all species found in the Tongass, plus elk, found on Afognak Island, and Dall sheep, found on the Kenai Peninsula.

There are more than 130 public cabins in the Tongass Forest and more than 30 in the Chugach Forest, all erected and maintained by the Forest Service. Reservations are necessary to use the cabins, with a fee of $15 a day (for the cabin, regardless of the size of the party) and varying limits of time allowed, depending upon cabin and time of year. Most cabins can be reached by chartered aircraft, although some are within hiking distance of highways, and others may be reached by boat from major cities in southeastern Alaska.

Cabins are equipped with bunks, stoves (either wood or oil) and pit toilets. Visitors must provide their own camping gear, food and utensils. None of the cabins has electricity. Skiffs are provided at most of the lakeside cabins in the Tongass Forest, and some users take small outboard motors with them. The Forest Service usually provides cut wood at cabins, but there is usually a saw available at the cabins for you to cut your own wood if necessary.

Bedding, a lantern, food and cooking and eating utensils are about all that is needed to move into and be comfortable at one of these well-built cabins.

All species of game for which there are open seasons within these forests can be hunted from various cabins. For information on specific cabin locations

Surrounded by peaks, sport fishermen prepare to take off from a base camp resort for a floatplane trip to a more remote trout lake, a common system in Alaska.
By Dave Engerbretson

and game available at them, write to Tongass National Forest, P.O. Box 1628, Juneau, AK 99802, and request the free brochure on available cabins. For the Chugach Forest, write to Chugach National Forest, Pouch 6606, Anchorage, AK 99502, and ask for the Chugach National Forest brochure.

Each brochure includes a map showing cabin location and a table indicating what game and fish species can be found at each cabin, plus method of access. Instructions are given on procedure in making reservations for their use. These cabins are popular, and reservations must be made in advance.

Alaska's State Parks are large areas designated as parks, and are protected as such. Hunting and fishing are allowed in these parks, which include the Chugach State Park and Denali State Park near Denali National Park and the Kachemak Bay State Park and Kachemak Bay State Wilderness Park near Homer on the lower Kenai Peninsula.

(Condensed, in part, from ALASKA HUNTING GUIDE, *Alaska Northwest Publishing Company.)*

Alaska Outdoor Information Sources

Fishing and hunting in Alaska is managed by the Department of Fish and Game. Regulations and seasons are based on current conditions and subject to midseason revision and closures.

In addition to the Juneau headquarters office, the DFG maintains regional field offices in 32 communities throughout the state. (All area codes are 907.)

Alaska Fish and Game, Headquarters: Box 3-2000, Juneau, AK 99802. Phone 465-4190.

Anchorage: 333 Raspberry Road, Anchorage, AK 99501. Phone 344-0541.

Bettles: Box 69, Bettles, AK 99726.

Big Lake: Box 79, Big Lake, AK 99687. Phone 892-6342.

Cantwell: General Delivery, Clear, AK 99704. Phone 832-5430.

Cold Bay: Box 127, Cold Bay, AK 99571. Phone 532-2419.

Cordova: Box 669, Cordova, AK 99574. Phone 424-3215.

Craig: General Delivery, Craig, AK 99921. Phone 826-3263.

Delta Junction: Box 218, Delta Junction, AK 99737. Phone 895-4681.

Dillingham: Box 199, Dillingham, AK 99576. Phone 842-3811.

Dutch Harbor: c/o Standard Oil Dock, Dutch Harbor, AK 99685. Phone c/o RCA Unalaska.

Fairbanks: 1300 College Road, Fairbanks, AK 99701. Phone 452-1531.

Glennallen: Box 47, Glennallen, AK 99588. Phone 822-3309.

Haines: Box 304, Haines, AK 99827. Phone 766-4511.

Homer: Box 234, Homer, AK 99603. Phone 235-8594.

Hoonah: Box 917, Hoonah, AK 99829. Phone 945-3361.

Juneau: Headquarters, Subport Bldg., Juneau, AK 99801. Phone 465-4190 (game).

Regional: 188 S. Franklin St., Juneau, AK 99811. Phone 586-6700.

Ketchikan: 208 State Court and Office Bldg., 415 Main St., Ketchikan, AK 99901. Phone 225-519.

King Salmon: Box 37, King Salmon, AK 99613. Phone 246-3340.

Kodiak: Box 686, Kodiak, AK 99615. Phone 486-5754 (game); 486-3318 (sport fish).

Kotzebue: General Delivery, Kotzebue, AK 99752. Phone 442-3644.

McGrath: Box 61, McGrath, AK 99627. Phone 524-3322.

Nome: Box 862, Nome, AK 99762. Phone 443-2825.

Palmer: Box 1794, Palmer, AK 99645. Phone 745-3178.

Petersburg: Box 667, Petersburg, AK 99833. Phone 772-4221 (sport fish); 772-4237 (game).

Sand Point: Box 187, Petersburg, AK 99661. Phone 383-2066.

Seward: Box 936, Seward, AK 99664. Phone 224-3017.

Sitka: Box 499, Sitka, AK 99835. Phone 747-8488.

Soldotna: Box R, Soldotna, AK 99669. Phone 262-4525.

Tok: Box 305, Tok, AK 99780. Phone 883-2972.

Valdez: Box 428, Valdez, AK 99780. Phone 835-4357.

Wrangell: Box 200, Wrangell, AK 99929. Phone 874-3822.

Yakutat: Box 68, Yakutat, AK 99689. Phone 784-3255.

Fish and Game Poaching Report: Toll-free phone, ask operator for Zenith 3377.

Department of Commerce: Division of Guide Licensing and Control Board, Pouch D, Juneau, AK 99811. Will provide a complete list of master and registered guides for a $5 handling fee.

U.S. Fish and Wildlife Service: 1011 E. Tudor Road, Anchorage, AK 99502. Will provide information on federal wildlife refuges in Alaska.

Bureau of Land Management: 701 C St., Anchorage, AK 99501. General information on lands and wildlife managed by the BLM.

Tongass National Forest, U.S. Forest Service: P.O. Box 1628, Juneau, AK 99802. Information and maps on the Tongass NF, including information on the $15 per day USFS cabin rentals in popular fishing and hunting regions. For detailed information on the Tongass NF, see *The ALASKA WILDERNESS MILEPOST®*, published by Alaska Northwest Publishing Co.

U.S. Geographic Survey: 508 Second Ave., 108 Skyline Bldg., Anchorage, AK 99501; and USGS office, 441 Federal Bldg., 709 W. Ninth St., Juneau, AK 99802. Will provide, for a fee, contour maps of specific hunting, fishing and hiking areas in Alaska.

Alaska Division of Tourism: Pouch E, Juneau, AK 99811. Will provide maps and information on recreational and accommodation facilities.

Alaska Fish Game Management Zones — Regional Headquarter Locations

The jagged pinnacles of the Arrigetch Peaks is one of the most spectacular regions of the Brooks Range.
Courtesy of *The ALASKA WILDERNESS MILEPOST*®

National Forests

Within the serrated, sometimes disjointed borders of the Northwest's 37 national forests lies the greatest concentration of public outdoor recreational land remaining in America. Roughly 81.5 million acres of federal land open to hunting, fishing, hiking, camping, foraging, boating, skiing, walking, looking and feeling good.

The national forests are managed by the U.S. Department of Agriculture, and in the Northwest — with few exceptions — these lands overlay the timbered mountainous regions; the areas richest in big game animals, native trout waters and centerfold scenery. The forests are divided into specialized segments including areas set aside as multiple use, wilderness, primitive, and scenic. All are open for public use, with hunting, fishing and trapping controlled by the local state fish and game agencies.

National forests are truly federal entities, tracking — like the migrating deer and elk — the geographic lay of the land along prominent mountain ranges and river valleys, unencumbered by contrived and imaginary boundaries posted by local states and municipalities.

Most of the mountainous terrain in Montana, Idaho, Oregon and Washington is national forests land, set aside for recreation and timber harvests. Thousands, if not hundreds of thousands of miles of duff-covered hiking trails and unpaved switchback roads provide access to the heart of spectacular mountain and wildlife country in the ranges of the Rocky, Cascade and Coast mountains.

Campgrounds are scattered throughout the major recreational areas; less than half, only those with water or other services, require a fee. Backcountry roads are littered with unimproved Siwash sites where a camper can be parked or tent pitched without a crowd. Boat launches, loading ramps and corrals for horsepackers, cross-country ski and snowmobile routes, picnic shelters, amphitheater, and even swimming areas are maintained in most forests.

Alaska's Tongass and Chugach national forests also have a unique cabin rental program, offering $15 per day rentals on rustic cabins located in prime hunting, fishing and boating ares. The 17-million-acre Tongass National Forest provides 142 cabins in remote southeastern Alaska locations. The 6.2-million-acre Chugach has 36 cabins in southcentral Alaska. Most have wood or oil stoves, will sleep six people and some even provide skiffs. Nearly all of the cabins require floatplane or boat access. For specific requirements write to the respective national forest headquarter offices.

In all of the national forests colorful maps are available illustrating and identifying the road and trail systems, including facilities, points of interest, mountain and geographic names, elevations, waterways and campgrounds. The maps are available for a handling fee of $1 by writing to the headquarters office of specific national forests. Regional ranger stations sometimes also have maps available. Maps of specific wilderness or primitive areas, and larger scale ranger districts, within the national forests are also available through the appropriate forest service office.

Left, a pack train picks its way between a clear mountain lake and a long drop in the roadless Eagle Cap Wilderness Area of Umatilla National Forest, northeast Oregon. By Ed Park. Mountains in and around Jasper National Park on the Alberta-British Columbia border are spectacular combinations of rugged peaks and lush valleys, supporting deer, elk, sheep, goats and moose. Above, Mount Kitchener is reflected in the placid Sunwapta River. By Thomas W. Kitchin

Continues on page 44

MAJOR OUTDOOR RECREATION REGIONS

National Forests
Wilderness Areas
National Parks

ALASKA

Misty Fjords National Monument

Chugach National Forest

Tongass National Forest

Wrangell-St. Elias National Park

Yukon Charley Rivers National Park

Glacier Bay National Park

Admiralty Island National Monument

Gates of the Arctic National Park

Noatak National Park

Kobuk Valley National Park

Cape Krusenstern National Park

Denali National Park

Lake Clark National Park

Kenai Fjords National Park

Chugach National Forest

Katmai National Park

Bering Land Bridge National Park

Aniakchak National Park

Athabasca Forest

Lac La Biche

Wood Buffalo National Park

Slave Lake Forest

Footner Lake Forest

Peace River Forest

Grande Prairie Forest

BRITISH COLUMBIA

Stone Mountain Provincial Park

Prince George Forest Region

Gwillim Lake Provincial Park

Carp Lake Provincial Park

Monkman

Muncho Lake Provincial Park

Kwadacha Wilderness Park

Spatsizi Plateau Wilderness Park

Tatlatui Provincial Park

Prince Rupert Forest Region

Mount Edziza Provincial Park

Tweedsmuir Provincial

Atlin Provincial Park

Naikoon Provincial Park

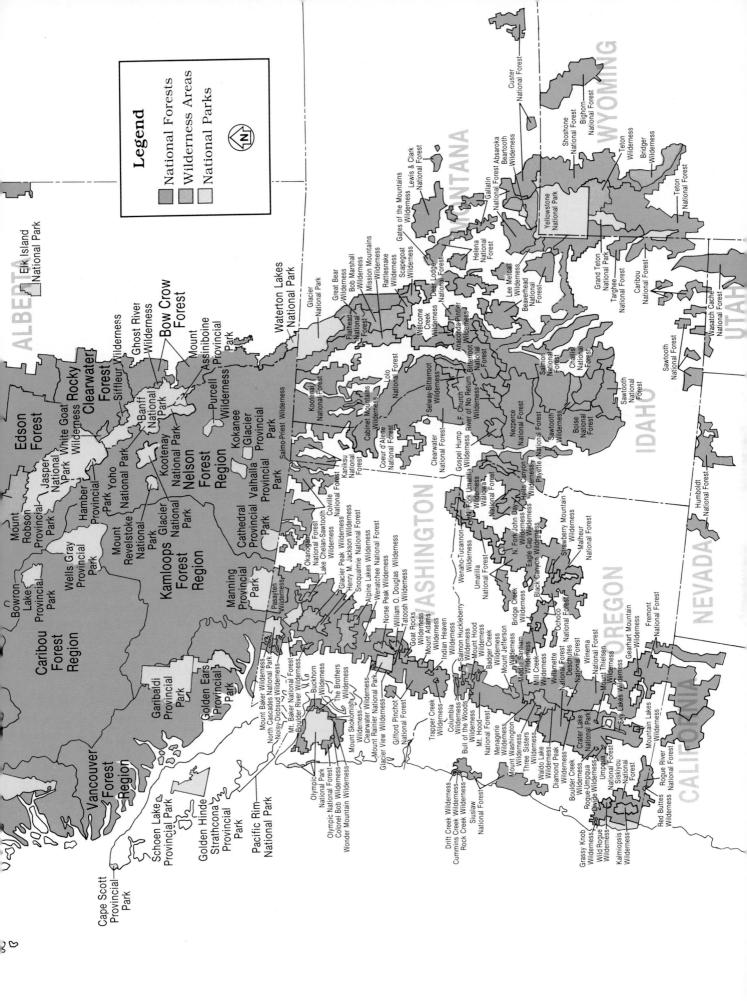

Legend

National Forests
Wilderness Areas
National Parks

N

An ever-growing number of Northwest
sportsmen are clamping on snowshoes or
cross-country skis to extend the hunting
and fishing seasons in high-elevation areas
where winter comes early and stays late.
This is Jackson Lake in Teton NP.
By Erwin & Peggy Bauer

The more than three dozen national forests of the Northwest have been parcelled
out to five regions for management; overseeing administration of forests in the Pacific
Northwest, Pacific Southwest, Northern, Intermountain and Rocky Mountain regions.
Questions about a specific national forest should, however, be directed at the appropriate
headquarters office and not the regional office.

Addresses and telephone numbers of the national forests headquarters are listed
separately.

Unlike the central and eastern reaches of the country where public land is scarce,
in the Northwest nearly two-thirds of the land is held by government agencies and
open to the public for recreational use. National forest lands account for much of this
public acreage and free access.

In Idaho, the forest service controls 61 percent of the state, 20.3 million acres. In
Montana 18 percent of the state, 17 million acres belongs to the Forest Service. The
U.S. Forest Service controls 25 percent of the land in Oregon which amounts to 12
million acres, and 20 percent of Washington with 9 million acres. Alaska has only
two national forests, both along the southern coast, but they total 23.2 million acres
and are the largest and second largest national forests in the nation.

Fishing and hunting opportunities are nearly unlimited in the national forests of the
Northwest. Streams, rivers and lakes support cutthroat, kamloops, brown, rainbow,
Dolly Varden, brookies, steelhead, kokanee, chinook, silver, pink, chum and sockeye
salmon, sturgeon, whitefish, bass, grayling, pike and panfish.

Big game animals include black, grizzly and brown bear; elk, mule, black-tailed and
white-tailed deer; mountain sheep and goats, cougar, coyote, wolves, pronghorn, moose
and birds, including ruffed, blue, sharp-tail, and spruce grouse, turkeys, ptarmigan and
band-tailed pigeons.

State hunting and fishing regulations and restrictions apply on the federal land.

Hurricane Ridge trail, Olympic NP.
By Thomas W. Kitchin

Pacific Northwest Region

Colville NF: (1,021,071 acres) Federal Bldg., 695 S. Main St., Colville, WA 99114. Phone (509) 684-3711.

Deschutes NF: (1,852,282 acres) 1645 N.E. Forbes, Bend, OR 97701. Phone (503) 388-2715.

Fremont NF: (1,710,580 acres) 34 North D St., P.O. Box 551, Lakeview, OR 97630. Phone (503) 947-2151.

Gifford Pinchot NF: (1,379,298 acres) 500 W. 12th St., Vancouver, WA 98660. Phone (206) 696-7500, (503) 285-9823 (Portland number).

Malheur NF: (1,540,761 acres) 139 N.E. Dayton St., John Day, OR 97845. Phone (503) 575-1731.

Mount Baker-Snoqualmie NF: (Mount Baker 1,312,120 acres; Snoqualmie 1,557,676 acres) 1022 First, Seattle, WA 98104. Phone (206) 442-5400.

Mount Hood: (1,108,285 acres) 2955 N.W. Division, Gresham, OR 97030. Phone (503) 666-0700.

Ochoco NF: (978,547 acres) P.O. Box 490, Federal Bldg., Prineville, OR 97754. Phone (503) 447-6247.

Okanogan NF: (1,536,961 acres) 1240 Second Ave. S., P.O. Box 950, Okanogan, WA 98840. Phone (509) 422-2704.

Olympic NF: (715,676 acres) Federal Bldg., P.O. Box 2288, Olympia, WA 98507. Phone (206) 753-9535.

Rogue River NF: (685,926 acres) Federal Bldg., P.O. Box 520, 333 W. Eighth St., Medford, OR 97501. Phone (503) 776-3600.

Siskiyou NF: (1,163,944 acres) 200 N.E. Greenfield Road, P.O. Box 440, Grants Pass, OR 97526. Phone (503) 479-5301.

Siuslaw NF: (835,279 acres) 4077 Research Way, P.O. Box 1148, Corvallis, OR 97333. Phone (503) 757-4480.

Umatilla NF: (1,511,139 acres) 2517 S.W. Hailey Ave., Pendleton, OR 97801. Phone (503) 276-3811.

Umpqua NF: (1,029,275 acres) 2900 N.W. Stewart Parkway, P.O. Box 1008, Roseburg, OR 97470. Phone (503) 672-6601.

Wallowa-Whitman NF: (Wallowa 1,604,634 acres; Whitman 1,311,545 acres) P.O. Box 907, Federal Office Bldg., Baker, OR 97814. Phone (503) 523-6391.

Wenatchee NF: (1,904,247 acres) 301 Yakima St., P.O. Box 811, Wenatchee, WA 98001. Phone (509) 662-4335.

Willamette NF: (1,796,866 acres) Federal Bldg., P.O. Box 10607, 211 E. Seventh Ave., Eugene, OR 97401. Phone (503) 687-6522.

Winema NF: (1,086,056 acres) Post Office Bldg., P.O. Box 1390, Klamath Falls, OR 97601. Phone (503) 883-6714.

Northern Region

Beaverhead NF: (2,198,806 acres) P.O. Box 1258, Dillon, MT 59725. Phone (406) 683-2312.

Bitterroot NF: (1,653,319 acres) 316 N. Third St., Hamilton, MT 59840. Phone (406) 363-3131.

Clearwater NF: (1,759,502 acres) Highway 12 & 126th St., Orofino, ID 83544. Phone (208) 476-4541.

Coeur d'Alene NF: (806,267 acres) 1201 Ironwood Dr., Coeur d'Alene, ID 83814. Phone (208) 765-7223.

Custer NF: (1,278,218 acres) P.O. Box 2556, Billings, MT 59103. Phone (406) 657-6361.

Deerlodge NF: (1,355,783 acres) P.O. Box 400, Butte, MT 59703. Phone (406) 496-3400.

Flathead NF: (2,629,075 acres) P.O. Box 147, Kalispell, MT 59901. Phone (406) 775-5401.

Gallatin NF: (2,149,552 acres) P.O. Box 130, Bozeman, MT 59715. Phone (406) 587-5271, Ext. 4233.

Helena NF: (1,164,289 acres) P.O. Drawer 10014, Helena, MT 59626. Phone (406) 449-5201.

Idaho Panhandle NF: (2,945,019 acres — includes Coeur d'Alene, Kiniksu and St. Joe NF) 1201 Ironwood Dr., Coeur d'Alene, ID 83814. Phone (208) 765-7223.

Kaniksu NF: (1,845,194 acres) 1201 Ironwood Dr., Coeur d'Alene, ID 83814. Phone (208) 765-7223.

Kootenai NF: (2,143,750 acres) R.R. 3, Box 700, Libby, MT 59923. Phone (406) 293-6211.

Lewis & Clark NF: (1,999,212 acres) P.O. Box 871, Great Falls, MT 59403. Phone (406) 727-0901.

Lolo NF: (2,617,286 acres) Bldg. 24, Fort Missoula, Missoula, MT 59801. Phone (406) 329-3557.

Nez Perce NF: (2,258,374 acres) Route 2, Box 475, Grangeville, ID 83530. Phone (208) 983-1950.

St. Joe NF: (1,076,773 acres) 1201 Ironwood Dr., Coeur d'Alene, ID 83814. Phone (208) 765-7223.

Intermountain Region

Ashley NF: (1,405,609 acrea) 437 E. Main, Vernal, UT 84078. Phone (801) 789-1181.

Boise NF: (2,959,719 acres) 1750 Front St., Boise, ID 83702. Phone (208) 334-1516.

Bridger-Teton NF: (1,744,630 acres) Forest Service Bldg., 340 N. Cache, P.O. Box 1888, Jackson, WY 83001. Phone (307) 733-2752.

Caribou NF: (1,085,961 acres) Federal Bldg., Suite 294, 250 S. Fourth Ave., Pocatello, ID 83201. Phone (208) 236-6700.

Challis NF: (2,487,549 acres) Highway 93, P.O. Box 404, Challis, ID 83226. Phone (208) 879-285.

Dixie NF: (1,967,187 acres) 82 N. 100 E., P.O. Box 580, Cedar City, UT 84720.

Fishlake NF: (1,525,686 acres) 170 N. Main

St., P.O. Box 628, Richfield, UT 84701. Phone (801) 896-4491.

Humboldt NF: (2,680,441 acres) 976 Mountain City Highway, Elko, NV 89801. Phone (702) 738-5171.

Manti-Lasal NF: (1,337,790 acres) 599 W. Price River Dr., Price, UT 84501. Phone (801) 637-2817.

Payette NF: (2,425,545 acres) 106 Park St., P.O. Box 1026, McCall, ID 83638. Phone (208) 634-2255.

Salmon NF: (1,794,276) Forest Service Bldg., Highway 93 North, P.O. Box 729, Salmon, ID 83467. Phone (208) 756-2215.

Sawtooth NF: (1,898,150 acres) 1525 Addison Ave. E., Twin Falls, ID 83301. Phone (208) 733-3698.

Targhee NF: (1,688,825 acres) 420 N. Bridge St., P.O. Box 208, St. Anthony, ID 83445. Phone (208) 624-3151.

Toiyabe NF: (3,378,072 acres) 111 N. Virginia St., Room 601, Reno, NV 89501.

Uinta NF: (889,531 acres) 88 W. 100 N., P.O. Box 1428, Provo, UT 84603. Phone (801) 377-5780.

Wasatch NF: (1,072,025 acres) 8226 Federal Bldg., 125 S. State St., Salt Lake City, UT 84138.

Northern Region Headquarters

USDA — Forest Service, P.O. Box 7669, Missoula, MT 59807. Phone (406) 329-3511.
Northern Region: Federal Bldg., P.O. Box 7669, Missoula, MT 59807. Phone (406) 329-3011.
Rocky Mountain Region: 11177 W. Eighth Ave., P.O. Box 25127, Lakewood, CO 80225. Phone (303) 234-3418.
Intermountain Region: Federal Bldg., 324 25th St., Ogden, UT 84401. Phone (801) 625-5182.
Pacific Southwest Region: 630 Sansome St., San Francisco, CA 94111. Phone (415) 556-0122.
Pacific Northwest Region: 319 S.W. Pine St., P.O. Box 3623, Portland, OR 97208. Phone (503) 221-2877.

Alaska Region

Chugach NF: (5.9 million acres) 201 E. Ninth Ave., Suite 100, Anchorage, AK 99501. Phone (907) 261-2599.
Tongass NF: (17,000,000 acres) Forest Service Information Center, Box 1628, Juneau, AK 99802

Alberta

Provincial Headquarters: Alberta Forest Service, Forest Land Use Branch, Recreation Section, 9915-108 St., Edmonton, AB, Canada T5K 2C9.
Athabasca Forest: 168 Airport Road, Fort McMurray, AB, Canada T9H 4P1.
Bow/Crow Forest: 8660 Bearspaw Dam Road N.W., Calgary, AB, Canada T2M 4L8.

In late summer, the brilliant red bodies and green heads of sockeye salmon appear in many national forests spawning streams. By Ron Kerr

Edson Forest: Box 1420, Edson, AB, Canada T0E 0P0.
Footner Lake Forest: Postal Bag 90, High Level, AB, Canada T0H 1Z0.
Grande Prairie Forest: 10811-84 Ave., Grande Prairie, AB, Canada T8V 3J2.
Lac La Biche Forest: Provincial Bldg., Box 450, Lac La Biche, AB, Canada T0A 2C0.
Peace River Forest: Postal Bag 900-39, Peace River, AB, Canada T0H 2X0.
Rocky/Clearwater Forest: Box 1720, Rocky Mountain House, AB, Canada T0M 1T0.
Slave Lake Forest: Postal Bag 390, Box 8, Slave Lake, AB, Canada T0G 2A0.
Whitecourt Forest: Postal Bag 30, Whitecourt, AB, Canada T0E 2L0.

British Columbia

Ministry of Forests Regional Offices:
Vancouver: Ministry of Forests, 4595 Canada Way, Burnaby, BC, Canada V5G 4L9. Phone: (604) 660-7608.
Prince Rupert: Ministry of Forests, Bag 5000, Smithers, BC, Canada V0J 2N0. Phone: (604) 847-7425.
Prince George: Ministry of Forests, 1011 Fourth Ave., Prince George, BC, Canada V2L 3H9. Phone: (604)565-6193.
Kamloops: Ministry of Forests, 515 Columbia St., Kamloops, BC, Canada V2C 2T7. Phone: (604) 828-4137.

Nelson: Ministry of Forests, 518 Lake St., Nelson, BC, Canada V1L 4C6. Phone: (604) 354-6286.
Cariboo: Ministry of Forests, 540 Borland St., Williams Lake, BC, Canada V2G 1R8. Phone: (604) 398-4420.

National Parks
British Columbia, Alberta

Pacific Rim: (511 square km) P.O. Box 280, Ucluelet, BC, Canada V0R 3A0.
Mount Revelstoke: (263 square km) P.O. Box 350, Revelstoke, BC, Canada V0E 2S0.
Glacier: (1,349 square km) P.O. Box 350, Revelstoke, BC, Canada V0E 2S0.
Yoho: (1,313 square km) P.O. Box 99, Field, BC, Canada V0A 1G0.
Kootenay: (1,406 square km) Box 220, Radium Hot Springs, BC, Canada V0A 1M0.
Waterton Lakes: (526 square km) Superintendent, Waterton Lakes, Waterton Park, AB, Canada T0K 2M0.
Banff: (6,642 square km) Box 900, Banff, AB, Canada T0L 0C0.
Jasper: (10,878 square km) Box 10, Jasper, AB, Canada T0E 1E0.
Elk Island: (194 square km) Site 4 R.R. 1, Fort Saskatchewan, AB, Canada T8L 2N7.
Wood Buffalo: (44,807 square km) Box 750, Fort Smith, NT, Canada X0E 0P0.

Snow geese. By Thomas W. Kitchin

Northwest National Wildlife Refuges

The ocean, coastlines, deserts, mountains, plains and marshlands of the Northwest support more than 50 national wildlife refuges, including hundreds of thousands of acres of key wildlife habitat.

Nearly all of the refuges are open to some type of hunting or fishing, especially waterfowl. The Northwest refuge system supports the greatest concentrations of ducks and geese in the Pacific and Central flyways. In the off-hunting months the refuges often offer fishing, excellent wildlife photography ranging from bighorns and buffalo to ruddy ducks and sage grouse, plus camping, picnicking, hiking, boating, and bird watching.

The refuges are strategically located in prime habitat for wildlife, emphasizing wetland management for duck and goose production, and in some areas endangered wildlife species.

Refuges vary in size from small prairie tracts up to entire mountains and giant lake/marsh complexes. Not all refuges emphasize waterfowl. Some are primarily for big game animals in areas with a blend of mountains, deserts and grasslands supporting deer, elk, mountain sheep, pronghorn, bison and a host of small game animals and upland birds.

All of the major, and many of the minor refuges, include interpretative centers and field stations with displays of wildlife, recreational and seasonal information and maps of the areas.

The Northwest is divided into two refuge management areas, the Pacific Region which includes Washington, Oregon, California, Nevada and Idaho; and the North Central and Rocky Mountain Region, an eight-state area including Montana, Wyoming and northern Utah. All are administered by the U.S. Fish and Wildlife Service.

Drake pintail. By Darrell Gulin

Pacific Region Headquarters
(Washington, Oregon, Idaho, California, Nevada)

U.S. Fish & Wildlife Service, Lloyd 500 Bldg, Suite 1692, 500 N.E. Multnomah St., Portland, OR 97232. Phone (503) 231-6121.

Pacific Region

Ankeny NWR: To reach Ankeny NWR from Interstate 5 exit 10 miles south of Salem at the Ankeny Hill. Follow Wintel Road west (toward Sidney) about two miles, where you enter the refuge.

Primary objective for the refuge is the protection and management of wintering habitat for endangered dusky geese, a smaller cousin of the Canada goose. The refuge is heavily used by waterfowl, and nearly 200 other species of wildlife. Grebes, herons, hawks, vultures, quail, band-tailed pigeons, shorebirds, woodpeckers, and a variety of songbirds use the refuge. Red fox and black-tailed deer are also found here.

The habitat includes 2,796 acres of Willamette Valley agricultural bottomland. Numerous hedgerows, thickets of Oregon ash, isolated Douglas firs and crops of grasses and grains dominate the area. For recreation there is wildlife observation, and photography; waterfowl and upland bird hunting.

Access to the refuge is limited between Nov. 1 and April 15 and refuge personnel are not always in the office. Normal office hours are 7:30 a.m. to 4 p.m.

Ankeny NWR, Route 1, Box 198, Jefferson, OR 97352. Phone (503) 327-2444.

Baskett Slough NWR: Located two miles west of Rickreall, Oregon, on State Highway 22.

Baskett was created as a protected wintering area for endangered dusky geese, but also supports several other species of waterfowl, grebes, herons, hawks, quail, shorebirds, band-tailed pigeons, mourning doves, woodpeckers, and a variety of songbirds. Thirty species of mammals, including red fox and black-tailed deer, eight types of amphibians and 10 species of reptiles can be found also.

The habitat covers 2,492 acres typical of Willamette Valley's irrigated hillsides, oak-covered knolls and grass fields. Also included is Morgan Lake and the Baskett Slough.

It's a popular duck, deer and small game hunting area in the fall and offers good wildlife photography during the off months.

Access to the refuge is limited from Oct. 1 to April 30, and refuge workers are not always in the office. Normal office hours are 7:30 a.m. to 4 p.m., Monday to Friday.

Baskett Slough NWR, 10995 Highway 22, Dallas, OR 97338. Phone (503) 623-2749.

Bear Lake NWR: The Bear Lake Refuge has an office in Montpelier, Idaho. The refuge is located six miles south of Montpelier. Drive south on U.S. Highway 89 from Montpelier to St. Charles, Idaho, then east on the causeway along the north shore of Bear Lake which borders the south boundary of the refuge. This is a good wildlife observation route.

Especially important as a nesting area for Great Basin Canada geese, this refuge is also a nesting, resting and feeding area of ducks, greater sandhill cranes and a variety of water and shorebirds.

There are 17,597 acres of marsh, open water and grasslands at an elevation of 6,000 feet in the mountain-ringed Bear Lake Valley. The marsh is drawn down severely for agriculture in late summer and is covered with ice for about 4½ months of the year.

Recreation includes wildlife observation, and photography; waterfowl and upland game hunting. North Beach State Park on the south boundary of the refuge offers picnicking, swimming and boat launching facilities.

Bear Lake NWR, P.O. Box 9, 370 Webster St., Montpelier, ID 83254. Phone (208) 847-1757.

Camas NWR: The Idaho refuge is northwest of Interstate 15 at Hamer. Signs identify Camas NWR headquarters.

This refuge is the nesting, resting and feeding area for ducks, geese and other birds. There are 10,656 acres of marshes, meadows and uplands. Recreation includes waterfowl and resident game hunting; wildlife observation, study and photography.

Camas NWR, Hamer, ID 83425. Phone (208) 662-5423 or 662-5424.

Cape Meares NWR: Located on a coastal headland just south of Tillamook Bay about eight miles west of Tillamook, Oregon, adjacent to Cape Meares State Park.

Band-tailed pigeons and black-tailed deer are in the timbered areas of the refuge. On the coastal side, common murres, tufted puffins and pelagic cormorants nest on the cliff faces, and seals and sea lions are occasionally spotted near the beach.

The NWR is 139 acres of rocky Pacific Ocean headlands and dense coastal forests of shore pine and Sitka spruce. Wildlife can be observed, studied and photographed, but not hunted.

Willamette Valley and Oregon Coastal Refuge Complex, Route 2, Box 208, Corvallis, OR 97330. Phone (503) 757-7236.

Clear Lake NWR: Located 15 miles southeast of Tulelake, CA, follow Highway 139 to Clear Lake Reservoir Road. Roads are often impassable during wet weather.

Primary wildlife includes white pelicans, cormorants, pronghorn antelope, sage grouse and waterfowl. The 33,440-acre refuge includes a 20,000-acre lake surrounded by dry grasslands. Recreation includes wildlife observation, study and photography, waterfowl and antelope hunting.

Klamath Basin NWR, Route 1, Box 74, Tulelake, CA 96134. Phone (916) 667-2231.

Cold Springs NWR: Located seven miles east of Hermiston, Oregon. Cold Springs is a resting and feeding area for a large concentration of Canada geese and ducks during the winter; pheasants, quail and mule deer are common. The habitat covers 3,117 acres of open water, marsh, sagebrush, grasslands and trees around the lake.

Wildlife observation, study and photography, waterfowl hunting and warm-water fishing. This area is superimposed on a Bureau of Reclamation reservoir.

Umatilla NWR, P.O. Box 239, Easton P.O. Bldg. (S.E. corner Sixth and I streets), Umatilla, OR 97882. Phone (503) 922-3232.

Columbia NWR: The refuge headquarter office is in downtown Othello, Washington, but the refuge is located in the treeless arid country of central Washington about 10 miles northwest

National Wildlife Refuges

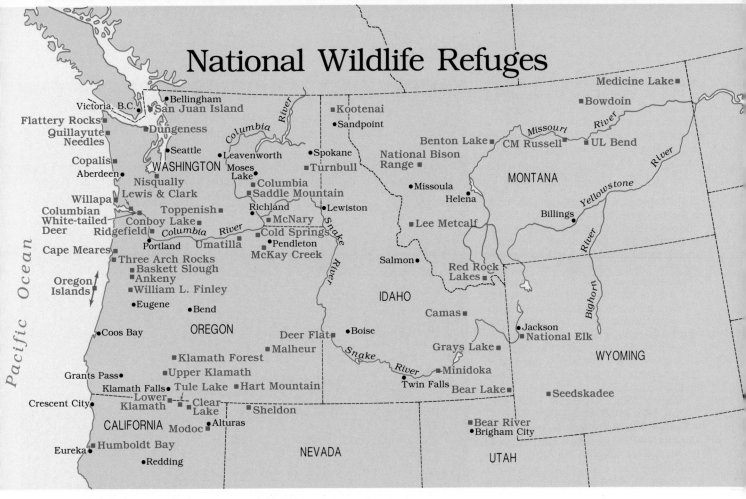

of Othello, south of O'Sullivan Reservoir. There are several access roads. Write for map.

A wintering area for an average population of over 100,000 ducks (mostly mallards) and Canada geese. Some mallards, blue-winged and cinnamon teal, scaup, ringnecks, pintails and Canada geese nest on the refuge along with song, water, marsh, shorebirds, hawks and owls.

The 28,952 acres in the famous channeled scablands of the Columbia River Basin includes more than 50 seep lakes ranging from less than an acre to more than 100 acres and 15 miles of streams surrounded by sagebrush, coulees and basalt buttes. Crab Creek cuts through the heart of the lakes area, which adjoins state land to form one of the largest and most productive hunting and fishing areas in Washington.

The area offers excellent fishing for rainbow, and brown trout, bass, panfish, walleye and white fish, upland game and waterfowl hunting, and trout and warm-water fishing. Mule deer are occasionally seen, along with coyotes, pheasants and some chukar. There is primitive camping. Hiking trails thread between the lakes and much of the area is off-limits to motorized vehicles. This is also prime terrain for rattlesnakes.

Normal office hours are 7:30 a.m. to 4 p.m., Monday to Friday.

Columbia NWR, 44 S. Eighth Ave., P.O. Drawer F, Othello, WA 99344. Phone (509) 488-3831.

Columbian White-tailed Deer NWR: From Cathlamet, Washington, drive west on State Highway 4 for two miles to refuge entrance. Follow signs to the refuge headquarters.

Islands in the refuge are only accessible by boat. The refuge is on both the Oregon and Washington sides of the Columbia River.

This is a critical habitat for the last remaining herds of Columbian white-tailed deer, an endangered species that in 1930 was believed to be extinct. A few surivors were later discovered on the unfarmed islands near the mouth of the Columbia. Columbian whitetails were thick along the riverbanks when Lewis and Clark explored the region, but failed to adapt when critical river bottomlands were put to the plow. Less than 400 of the animals are believed to exist now, most on this refuge. The refuge is also a prime wintering area for whistling swans, dusky and Canada geese, mallards, wigeon and pintails.

The habitat covers 4,798 acres of river floodplain and islands encircled by dikes. Pasture lands are separated by blocks of trees, brushy thickets and numerous sloughs and channels.

The Columbian whitetails are often seen and photographed from the county road which encircles the mainland portion of the refuge — evenings or mornings are the best times. Limited duck and goose hunting is permitted. The Columbia provides sturgeon, steelhead, cutthroat trout and salmon fishing and largemouth bass and panfish are common in the islands' sloughs and backwaters.

Office hours are 8:00 a.m. to 4:30 p.m., Monday to Friday, except 7:30 a.m. to 4:00 p.m. during the spring and summer months.

Columbian White-tailed Deer NWR, Route 1, Box 376C, Cathlamet, WA 98612. Phone (206) 795-3915.

Conboy Lake NWR: The marked turnoff to this southwest Washington refuge is approximately seven miles southwest of Glenwood, on the Glenwood-Trout Lake Road (Washington Highway 158).The refuge office is located one mile southeast at the end of a graveled road.

The refuge is open all week from sunup to sundown, but refuge personnel are not always in the office. The refuge is a one-time mountain lake bed including 6,729 acres of marsh, meadows, upland and forests with a seasonal lake. There is primitive camping, and limited fishing for trout and bullheads. Hunting in designated areas for black-tailed deer, ruffed grouse, black bear and ducks and geese.

Conboy Lake NWR, P.O. Box 5, Glenwood, WA 98619. Phone (509) 364-3410.

Deer Flat NWR: This 11,586-acre NWR is five miles southwest of Nampa, Idaho. Lake Lowell Road leads to refuge headquarters.

Lake Lowell, a Bureau of Reclamation reservoir on the refuge, is a wintering area for ducks, mostly mallards, and Canada geese and fishing area. Bald eagles and other raptors often feed on refuge waterfowl. Nesting marsh and water birds include the western grebe, eared grebe, great blue heron, and black-crowned night heron. California gulls, ring-billed gulls, and double-crested cormorants are commonly seen.

Annual irrigation water drawdown exposes mud flats where extensive stands of swart weed grow and attract large numbers of shorebirds. Sagebrush flats and riparian woodlands are also present.

Deer Flat NWR, P.O. Box 448, Nampa, ID 83651. Phone (208) 467-9278.

Dungeness NWR: This prominent

49

Washington refuge is located on the southern shore of the Strait of Juan de Fuca, off U.S. Highway 101, west of Sequim, adjacent to a state and county park. The refuge centers on a seven-mile-long peninsula, designated as the world's longest natural sand spit. A protected bay is inside the spit.

The bay is a key wintering and spring gathering area for 40,000 Pacific black brant and 275 species of waterfowl and birds. There is also excellent crabbing, area salmon fishing, horseback riding, hiking trails, waterfowl and black-tailed deer. Occasionally killer (Orca) whales, harbor and elephant seals and sea lions are seen. Nearby state lands are hunted for pheasants and waterfowl. The refuge includes 573 acres of sand spit, tidelands and woods.

Refuge recreation includes wildlife observation and photography, saltwater fishing, clamming, crabbing and beachcombing.

Dungeness Spit and neighboring Ediz Hook are the only land formations of this kind in North America. Public access to the refuge is by foot or horseback only.

Nisqually NWR, 100 Brown Farm Road, Olympia, WA 98506. Phone (206) 753-9467.

Flattery Rocks, Quillayute Needles, and Copalis NWR: The refuge is a series of small islands and sea stacks on the Pacific coast of Washington, inaccessible except by boat.

The islands extend for over 100 miles along the largely undeveloped Washington coastline. The refuge office is located 13 miles north of Ilwaco on U.S. Highway 101.

Approximately 150,000 pelagic birds nest annually on these islands, including Leach storm petrel, rhinoceros auklet, tufted puffin, fork-tailed storm petrel, common murre, glaucous-winged gull, western gull, Brandt's cormorant, pelagic cormorant, Cassin's auklet, black oystercatcher, pigeon guillemot, double-crested cormorant, and the hybrid glaucous-winged western gull. Other migrating birds sometimes swell the population to over 1 million Marine mammals use the islands for resting and feeding.

There are 870 islets, rocks and reefs along the Washington coastline from Cape Flattery south to Copalis — some islands support salmonberry, salal, grasses and even stunted conifers.

Landings on the islands require a special use permit. The refuge is designated a wilderness area.

Willapa NWR, Ilwaco, WA 98624. Phone (206) 484-3482 (Naselle).

Grays Lake NWR: Grays Lake NWR is north on Highway 34 from Soda Springs, Idaho. Refuge sign one mile west of Wayan. Access to the refuge is limited much of the year and refuge personnel are not always in the office.

Grays Lake is a nesting area for 700 migratory Great Basin Canada geese and a variety of diving and puddle ducks. A flock of endangered whooping cranes is being established from eggs imported from other whooper flocks and slipped into the incubating nests of greater sandhill cranes. Having sandhills hatch whooping crane eggs is apparently succeeding.

Columbian whitetail, an endangered species. By Thomas W. Kitchin

Some of the foster-egg whoopers have migrated and returned to Grays Lake since this experiment began in 1975. This habitat includes 17,385 acres of high mountain marsh at the foot of Caribou Mountain.

For recreation there is wildlife observation, photography and waterfowl hunting.

Grays Lake NWR, Wayan, ID 83285. Phone (208) 547-4996.

Hart Mountain National Antelope Refuge: Located 68 miles northeast of Lakeview, Oregon. From Lakeview drive north, then east on State Highway 140 for 22 miles. Turn north at the Plush/Hart Mountain Refuge junction for 20 miles to Plush. At the north edge

of Plush turn east on the Frenchglen/Hart Mountain Refuge road for 25 miles to the refuge field station. No gas is available at Plush or Hart Mountain.

Pronghorn antelope, Califonia bighorn sheep, mule deer, wild horses, pelicans, chukars and sage grouse are among the more common species found on this isolated range. Hart Mountain's steep west side is one of the best bighorn areas in Oregon, coming back on the success of transplant projects begun in 1954, after native animals were exterminated.

The refuge covers 241,104 arid acres of diverse habitat located at elevations between 4,500 and 8,065 feet. Sagebrush, juniper and native bunch grasses are the predominant vegetation, with aspen and pine groves present in canyons and along steep, precipitous and spectacular beautiful rims.

Wildlife photography, big game hunting, hiking, and limited stream fishing; and primitive camping facilities are available.

Office hours are 8 a.m. to 5 p.m., Monday to Friday.

Sheldon-Hart Mountain-Modoc NWR Complex, P.O. Box 111, Room 308, U.S. Post Office Bldg., Lakeview, OR 97630. Phone (503) 947-3315.

Humboldt Bay NWR: Access to this small refuge is limited. An important wintering area for the Pacific black brant and other migrating waterfowl and thousands of shorebirds.

There are 130 acres of tidal flats, salt marshes and bay, and when complete, the refuge will encompass 8,600 acres.

Outside the acquired land but within the approved refuge boundary there is wildlife observation, study and photography, waterfowl hunting, saltwater fishing and clamming.

San Francisco Bay NWR Group, P.O. Box 524, Newark, CA 94560. Phone (414) 792-0222.

Klamath Basin NWR: Refuges administered are Clear Lake, Klamath Forest, Lower Klamath, Tule Lake and Upper Klamath.

Klamath Basin NWR, Route 1, Box 74, Tulelake, CA 96134. Phone (916) 667-2231.

Klamath Forest NWR: Located 25 miles north of Chiloquin, Oregon, and seven miles east of U.S. Highway 97 on the Silver Lake Highway.

This refuge is an important nesting area for the greater sandhill crane and waterfowl. It covers 15,427 acres of a large natural marsh, and is a favorite with duck and goose hunters during the fall, plus summer fishermen.

Klamath Basin NWR, Route 1, Box 74, Tulelake, CA 96134. Phone (916) 667-2231.

Kootenai NWR: Kootenai NWR is 18 miles south of the Canadian border in the Kootenai Valley of Idaho. From Bonners Ferry drive west on the dike road along the south shore of the Kootenai River for five miles to the refuge; continue another 1.5 miles to refuge headquarters on Westside Road.

Numerous species of ducks use the refuge during the spring and fall breeding and migration periods. Mallards and goldeneyes are the principal nesters, while mallards, wigeon and pintails are principal migrants. Canada geese may number 2,500 in the fall and whistling swans are common spring migrants. Larger mammals using the refuge include both mule and white-tailed deer, black bear, coyote and occasionally an elk or moose.

The refuge comprises 2,764 acres of ponds, grasslands, cultivated croplands, shrubs and a timbered west edge.

For recreation there is wildlife to see and photograph, an auto tour road and hiking trails; hunting for deer, bear, upland game and waterfowl and fishing.

Kootenai NWR, Star Route 1, Box 160, Bonners Ferry, ID 83805. Phone (208) 267-3888.

Lewis and Clark NWR: Located in Oregon along the lower Columbia River, the refuge consists of numerous small islands accessible only by boat. Some of the islands are visible from Oregon Highway 30, five miles east of Astoria.

The islands provide wintering areas for 3,000 whistling swans, 2,000 dusky geese, 50,000 ducks and various shorebirds. Estuarine water provide vital food resources for juvenile salmon when they are becoming acclimated to salt water.

The refuge covers 8,313 acres of islands and sand bars in the lower Columbia River, and another 35,000 acres mostly of tidelands or open water. Good duck and goose hunting and wildlife photography, plus fishing for salmon, trout, sturgeon, bass and panfish.

Office hours are 8 a.m. to 4:30 p.m. (7:30 a.m. to 4 p.m. during the spring and summer months).

Columbian White-tailed Deer NWR, Route 1, Box 376C, Cathlamet, WA 98612. Phone (206) 795-3915.

Lower Klamath NWR: Located on the California-Oregon border 24 miles south of Klamath Falls, Oregon, this refuge has several entrances. Write for map. The primary wildlife includes over 1 million waterfowl at the peak of fall migration and a wide variety of marsh and waterbirds as well.

The refuge encompasses 21,459 acres of water, marsh, agricultural crops and uplands. There is wildlife observation, study and photography, an auto tour, waterfowl, and pheasant hunting.

Klamath Basin NWR, Route 1, Box 74, Tulelake, CA 96134. Phone (916) 667-2231.

Malheur NWR: An outstanding hunting and fishing area, this desert-country refuge is reached by driving two miles east of Burns on Highway 78, then south on Highway 205 for 24 miles, then east on a county road for six miles (paved except the last half mile). Write for map showing other entrances.

Managed primarily for ducks and geese, but also attracts thousands of marsh birds, including greater sandhill cranes, and raptors. There is a resident population of trumpeter swans. A 183,484-acre area of natural marshes, meadows and artificial ponds surrounded by sagebrush and juniper uplands.

Offers wildlife observation and photography, self-guided auto tour, museum with mounted bird and mammal exhibits (open 6 a.m. to 9 p.m. daily), photographic blind at headquarters, waterfowl hunting, trout fishing, upland game hunting, historical site interpretation, and archery deer hunting. Mule deer are often in the Frenchglen area at the foot of Steens Mountain and pronghorns are common in the sage plains along the Blitzen River. Bighorn sheep can be found on Steens Mountain, a 9,720-foot upheaval in the floor of the Alvord Desert southeast of Malheur. Wild horses are seen near Steens Mountain.

Lodging and meals available at Malheur Field Station four miles west of headquarters, April to August. Trailer hookups available. Call ahead

Drake mallards. By Darrell Gulin

for reservations for meals or lodging. The refuge office is open daily 8 a.m. to 4:30 p.m. from the first weekend in April through Labor Day weekend, and closed weekends the rest of the year.

Malheur NWR, P.O. Box 113, Burns, OR 97720. Phone (503) 493-2323.

McKay Creek NWR: From Pendleton, Oregon, drive five miles south on U.S. Highway 395. Turn left (east) at refuge sign.

Attracts tens of thousands of Canada geese and ducks during spring and fall. Ringneck pheasants are common in this 1,837-acre blend of open water, marsh and grasslands.

A fine area for wildlife (including bald eagles) observation and photography, waterfowl hunting, trout, bass and panfish angling and boating. The area is superimposed on a Bureau of Reclamation reservoir.

Umatilla NWR, P.O. Box 239, Easton Post Office Bldg., (S.E. corner Sixth and I streets), Umatilla, OR 97882. Phone (503) 922-3232.

McNary NWR: The office is located on the refuge, five miles southeast of Pasco, Washington, accessible from Highway 395. Cross the Snake River, continue southeast on Highway 395 for about one mile to the refuge sign, turn east (left) one-quarter mile to the office.

McNary is a major lower Columbia River migration staging area for thousands of waterfowl. Canada geese, mallards, wigeon and pintails along with lesser numbers of whistling swans, snow geese, green-winged teal, shovelers, canvasbacks, redheads, ring-necked ducks and lesser scaups. The waterfowl population peaks in November. Long-billed curlews and the white pelicans are summer residents.

Measuring 3,629 acres, this refuge includes 865 acres of marsh, 950 acres of croplands and 1,816 acres of grass and trees.

Recreation includes waterfowl observation and photography, a self-guided hiking trail, waterfowl and upland bird hunting and fishing for largemouth and smallmouth bass, catfish, crappie and carp.

McNary NWR, P.O. Box 308, Burbank, WA 99323.

Minidoka NWR: Six miles northeast of Rupert, Idaho, on Highway 24 via Acequia, then east six miles on County Highway 400

51

North. The south boundary of the refuge lies adjacent to the old U.S. Highway 30 North and Interstate 15 West on the extreme eastern end near Raft River.

Up to 250,000 ducks and geese are present during spring and fall migrations. Migrating whistling swans can be seen in spring in shallow bays and shores of the lake. Bald eagles, golden eagles, hawks, owls, and over 70 species of birds are frequently seen. Mule deer are year-round residents and antelope are occasionally seen on the north side of the river.

The habitat covers 25,630 acres including 11,000 surface backwater acres of the Bureau Of Reclamation, Minidoka Dam (Lake Wolcott). Weeds cover the surface of small bays and inlets of the lake. Surrounding uplands are sagebrush and grassland range.

Sportsmen find the refuge excellent for wildlife observation, and photography, plus fall waterfowl hunting and spring and summer trout fishing.

The Bureau of Reclamation manages a picnic area and boating facilities near the dam and refuge headquarters.

Minidoka NWR, Route 4, Rupert, ID 83350. Phone (208) 436-3589.

Modoc NWR: The refuge is located southeast of Alturas, California, approximately 3½ miles. Signs at the south end of town will direct the motorist to the refuge.

Large concentrations of waterfowl include Canada geese, mallards, cinnamon teal; wigeon and pintails are the most common. Whistling swans stop during migrations, sandhill cranes nest on the refuge and white pelicans are seen throughout the summer. Mule deer and pronghorn antelope are present.

The refuge includes 6,283 acres of ponds, cereal grain croplands, and sagebrush upland, at an elevation of 4,300 feet.

Recreation includes wildlife observation, study and photography, waterfowl hunting, fishing and a picnic area.

The office is open from 8 a.m. to 5 p.m., Monday to Friday.

Sheldon-Hart Mountain-Modoc NWR Complex, P.O. Box 111, Room 308, U.S. Post Office Bldg., Lakeview, OR 97630. Phone (503) 947-3315.

Nisqually NWR: The 2,760-acre refuge is located on the southeastern edge of Puget Sound about 10 miles northeast of Olympia, Washington, slightly north of Interstate 5. Exit Interstate 5 at Nisqually Exit 114, north under the highway, then right on the Brown Farm Road.

The refuge is a unique combination of estuaries, tidal flats, and freshwater marshes, preserved as a wintering area for waterfowl. Nisqually River running from the flanks of Mount Rainier, and McAllister Creek on the refuge host steelhead and cutthroat trout and several varieties of salmon. There is also a diverse population of raptors, shorebirds and songbirds.

Recreation includes wildlife observation, photography, hiking, crabbing, and duck and goose hunting. Facilities are few, although the state maintains a boat launch and public pier at the southern edge of the refuge. No camping. Foot and boat access to the refuge only. The Nisqually Delta is one of the largest remaining undisturbed estuaries in western Washington.

Nisqually NWR, 2625 Parkmont Lane S.W., Bldg. A-2, Olympia, WA 98502. Phone (206) 753-9467.

Oregon Islands NWR: Refuge is comprised of 56 islands and sea stacks totaling only 367 acres, located at various points along the 300-mile-long Oregon coast set aside for nesting seabirds and wildlife such as seals and sea lions. Public access is prohibited.

These rocks and islands provide habitat for countless seabirds and mammals. The entire refuge is included in the National Wilderness Preservation System. Boats must stay at least 200 yards offshore.

Willamette Valley and Oregon Coastal Refuge Complex, Route 2, Box 208, Corvallis, OR 97330. Phone (503) 757-7236.

Ridgefield NWR: The refuge headquarters is located in downtown Ridgefield, Washington, and the access entrances are located just south and north of city limits. Write for map.

The refuge, in southwestern Washington, is a major wintering area for dusky geese. Year-round wildlife includes great blue herons, red-tailed hawks, coots, crows and killdeer. Ridgefield is a popular bird-watching area with 200 species. Included is 3,017 acres of Lower Columbia River floodplain, dikes and croplands.

Recreation includes wildlife, photography, self-guided interpretive trail, waterfowl hunting and limited fishing for steelhead, salmon and largemouth bass in the nearby Columbia River.

Ridgefield NWR, 305 N. Third, P.O. Box 457, Ridgefield, WA 98642. Phone (206) 887-4071.

Saddle Mountain NWR: The refuge was developed for wintering waterfowl and nesting Canada geese, in the sagebrush land of southcentral Washington. It is located within a nuclear reactor control area at Hanford and is closed to all public use.

The refuge covers 30,810 acres of semiarid desert and includes one 730-acre lake, also closed to the public.

Columbia NWR, 44 S. Eighth Ave, P.O. Drawer F, Othello, WA 99344. Phone (509) 488-3831.

San Juan Islands NWR: The refuge consists of 84 small islands within the San Juan archipelago of northern Puget Sound. Access is by boat from Anacortes or Friday Harbor. A map is available from the Nisqually NWR.

Most smaller islands are nesting and loafing sites for seabirds including glaucous-winged gulls, cormorants, scoters, guillemots, puffins, auklets, oystercatchers and shorebirds. Harbor seals loaf and feed on some islands.

The combined land mass of all 84 islands amounts to only 458 acres, most of it categorized as reefs, rocks, grassy islands, or small woodlots.

Wildlife observation, study and photography are allowed on Matia, Turn, and Jones islands.

All other refuge islands may be viewed from boats, but are closed to public access.

The three accessible islands have considerable public use and are managed by cooperative agreement with Washington State Parks. On Matia Island, only five acres are considered Marine State Park with the remaining 140 acres being in the wilderness preservation system.

Sheldon NWR: Part of the Hart Mountain national antelope range complex, Sheldon NWR includes more than half a million acres located in northwest Nevada on the Oregon border about 45 miles northeast of Cedarville, California and 75 miles southeast of Lakeview, Oregon. Highway 140 bisects the northern portion of the range. Refuge roads are inaccessible much of the winter.

Established for the preservation of pronghorn antelope and also supports mule deer, California bighorn sheep, sage grouse, coyotes, bobcats, wild horses and burros, and numerous species of migratory birds. There are 536,955 acres of high desert wildlands with occasional reservoirs and creeks. The NWR is used as a wintering ground for antelope migrating south from the Hart Mountain summer range in Oregon.

For recreationists the refuge offers wildlife photography, hunting and limited fishing. Primitive camping facilities are located in designated areas.

Sheldon-Hart Mountain-Modoc NWR Complex, Room 308, U.S. Post Office Bldg., Lakeview, OR 97630. Phone (503) 947-3315.

Three Arch Rocks NWR: A group of rocky islands located about one mile offshore from Oceanside, Oregon (west of Tillamook).

Large numbers of nesting common murres, tufted puffins, Brandt's and pelagic cormorants use the area. Northern and California sea lions and harbor seals are also here. The refuge covers 17 acres of rock islands included in the National Wilderness Preservation System. Public access to the islands is not permitted.

Willamette Valley and Oregon Coastal Refuge Complex, Route 2, Box 208, Corvallis, OR 97330. Phone (503) 757-7236.

Toppenish NWR: Headquarters are on McNary NWR near Pasco, Washington. A subheadquarters is one mile from the turnoff on U.S. Highway 97, six miles south of Toppenish, Washington. Other units of the refuge are separated by more than 20 miles. Write for map.

The refuge is a major wintering and migrating area for northern ducks and geese. Up to one-quarter million migrating waterfowl use the 1,763 acres of brushy creek bottoms, wet meadows, sagebrush uplands and croplands located along Toppenish Creek.

Excellent duck and goose hunting in October and November along with pheasants, quail and some partridge. Off-season there is wildlife photography, hiking and bird watching.

Toppenish NWR, Route 1, Box 1300, Toppenish, WA 98948. Phone (509) 865-2405.

Tule Lake NWR: Located south of the Oregon-California border southwest of Highway

Refuges are excellent subjects for wildlife photographers. By Thomas W. Kitchin

139, this refuge has several entrances. This refuge supports peak waterfowl concentrations of over 1 million birds on the 37,617 acres of open water, marshes and croplands. Recreation and education include wildlife observation, study and photography; auto tour route, waterfowl and pheasant hunting.

The Bureau of Reclamation leases cropland to area farmers and the Fish and Wildlife Service plants about 2,000 acres of crops as "butter strips" around the borders of the water areas to provide food and cover for wildlife, and help reduce waterfowl depredations on adjacent agricultural lands.

Klamath Basin NWR, Route 1, Box 74, Tulelake, CA 96134. Phone (916) 667-2231.

Turnbull NWR: Located near the Washington-Idaho border the refuge is reached from Cheney, Washington, by driving south on Cheney-Plaza County Road (Badger Lake Road) to the access road, then two miles east to the headquarters.

As many as 50,000 ducks, and geese move onto the refuge in fall. Canada geese are numerous and trumpeter swans are becoming established. White-tailed deer, coyotes, beaver, racoons, muskrats and mink and numerous other small mammals are found here. Redheads and other diving ducks are the principal nesting species.

Chains of small lakes and marshlands provide 15,565 acres of game land, interspersed with ponderosa pine forests.

The refuge is open for wildlife observation and photography, auto tour route, and hiking trails. Special features: Two research natural areas have been established on the refuge. The Turnbull Laboratory for Ecological Studies (operated by Eastern Washington University) is located on the refuge. The office is open 7:30 a.m. to 4 p.m., Monday to Friday.

Turnbull NWR, Route 3, Box 385, Cheney, WA 99004. Phone (509) 235-4723.

Umatilla NWR: Located on the Columbia River in the vicinity of Boardman, Oregon, and Paterson, Washington, Umatilla is one of the greatest waterfowl production and hunting areas on the Columbia River. The refuge includes eight wildlife areas on both sides of the Columbia River. There are several access routes; write for map.

Roughly 90,000 Canada geese, a few hundred snow geese and 200,000 ducks winter here, including practically all species of ducks found in the West, except sea ducks. Pheasants and valley quail are common. Long-billed curlews, egrets, herons and other marsh and water birds nest on the refuge. Animals include mule deer, coyote and many smaller species. Steelhead, salmon, sturgeon, walleye, largemouth and smallmouth bass and panfish are caught in refuge waters.

The refuge comprises 29,370 acres of marshes, sloughs, open water, cropland and sagebrush uplands. Recreation includes wildlife watching and photography, hunting for deer, waterfowl and pheasant fishing, and boating.

Nearby state park and public campgrounds are located on Oregon and Washington sides of the Columbia River. There is no overnight camping in the refuge.

Office hours are 7:30 a.m. to 4 p.m., Monday to Friday.

Umatilla NWR, P.O. Box 239, Easton Post Office Bldg. (S.E. corner Sixth and I streets), Umatilla, OR 97882. Phone (503) 922-3232.

Upper Klamath NWR: Located 35 miles northwest of Klamath Falls, Oregon, at the north end of Upper Klamath Lake. Access is by boat only from Rocky Point Resort and Malone Springs, one mile east of Highway 236.

The marsh provides excellent habitat for several species of ducks, Canada and snow geese as well as white pelicans, herons, egrets and other nongame birds. Recreation at this 12,457 acres of marsh and water, is wildlife observation and photography, duck and goose hunting, boating and fishing for trout, bass and panfish.

Klamath Basin NWR, Route 1, Box 74, Tulelake, CA 96134. Phone (916) 667-2231.

Willapa NWR: The refuge is divided into segments near Willapa Bay on the southern

Washington coast. Headquarters is 13 miles north of Ilwaco on U.S. Highway 101. The Long Island segment is accessible only by boat and only during high tides. Other units are separated by up to 24 miles of driving. Write for map.

Wintering waterfowl, include black brant, Canada geese, canvasback, scaup, bufflehead and scooters. Up to 245 bird species use the areas, and the 43 mammals include black bear, deer and elk. The refuge covers 9,608 acres of uplands, sand dunes, beaches, flats, steep canyons and hills. Vegetation is thick, and grows around stands of shore pine, strand, Sitka spruce, western hemlock and western red cedar forest.

Recreation includes, wildlife photography, beachcombing, fishing, clamming and crabbing in Willapa Bay and tributary streams. Boat camping is allowed at seven Long Island sites. Hunting for ducks and geese, upland game, plus bow hunts for elk and deer.

Willapa NWR, Ilwaco, WA 98624. Phone (206) 484-3482.

William L. Finley NWR: South of Corvallis on Highway 99 West about 10 miles. West two miles to refuge office. Access is limited from Nov. 1 to April 15.

The primary objective for the refuge is the protection and management of wintering dusky geese. In addition to geese, other migratory and resident animals use the refuge lands. Several species of ducks visit the refuge during migration and wood ducks and hooded mergansers are common summer nesters. Blue and ruffed grouse, ringneck pheasants and California and mountain quail are present. The black-tailed deer is common as are many species of small birds and mammals.

A variety of habitats are encompassed on the 5,325 acres — Oregon oak and maple woodlands, Oregon ash thickets, second-growth fir, bushy hedgerows, marshes, meandering creeks, open meadows, pastures and cultivated fields.

For recreation and education there is wildlife observation, study and photography, self-guided interpretative trail, and fall hunting for ducks, geese, upland birds and deer.

Office hours 7:30 a.m. to 4 p.m., Monday to Friday.

William L. Finley NWR, Route 2, Box 208, Corvallis, OR 97330. Phone (503) 757-7236.

North Central and Rocky Mountain Region Headquarters
(Montana, Wyoming, Utah)

U.S. Fish and Wildlife Service, P.O. Box 25486, Denver Federal Center, Denver, CO 80225.

Rocky Mountain Region

Bamforth NWR: A 1,166-acre refuge located 11 miles northwest of Laramie, Wyoming, established as a waterfowl area.

Drake cinnamon teal. By Darrell Gulin

Bear River Migratory Bird Refuge: The headquarters, located 15 miles west of Brigham City, Utah, is open daily from 8 a.m. to 4:30 p.m., includes a small picnic area and a 12-mile self-guided wildlife drive through the refuge.

The 65,030-acre refuge is one of the most important waterfowl areas in North America. The refuge produces about 15,000 ducks and 1,500 Canada geese annually, supports tens of thousands of migrating waterfowl, and hosts 20,000 to 30,000 whistling swans during migration.

Fishing is permitted in designated areas, and a portion of the refuge is open to waterfowl hunting.

Bear River Migratory Bird Refuge, Box 459, Brigham City, UT 84302. Phone (801) 723-7001.

Benton Lake NWR: Established in 1929, this 12,383-acre refuge is located 12 miles north of Great Falls, Montana, a large man-made marsh surrounded by grasslands. It is an important production and hunting area for ducks and geese and supports numerous other water birds.

Graveled roads wind around the marsh pools and provide excellent waterfowl viewing opporunity during the spring, summer and fall. Part of the refuge is open to waterfowl hunting. The refuge also administers 16,000 acres of waterfowl production areas.

Benton Lake NWR, Box 450, Black Eagle, MT 59414. Phone (406) 727-7400.

Bowdoin NWR: The refuge and headquarters are located seven miles east of Malta, Montana, on old U.S. Highway 2. Established in 1936, this 15,437-acre refuge has approximately 8,000 acres of marsh, ponds and grassy uplands, centered around Bowdoin, Dry, Drumbo and Lakeside lakes.

It is a major nesting and migratory stop for geese, ducks and a fall hunting area. Other prominent birds, include nesting colonies of white pelicans, herons, cormorants and gulls. Pronghorns and white-tailed deer are year-round residents.

Recreation includes a 15-mile self-guided tour for bird-watchers and photographers. Hunters try for Canada geese, mallards, pintails, canvasbacks, teal, wigeon, redheads, and upland birds, including pheasants, sage grouse, Hungarian partridge and sharp-tailed grouse.

Bowdoin NWR, Box J, Malta, MT 59538. Phone (406) 654-2863.

The Bowdoin headquarters can also provide information on an additional 11,000 acres of refuge land at **Black Coulee NWR,** located in Blaine County; **Creedman Coulee NWR** and **Lake Thibadeau NWR**, both located in Hill County; and **Hewitt Lake NWR** in Phillips County.

Charles M. Russell NWR: This is the largest refuge in the Northwest and a prime eastern Montana hunting area for waterfowl, upland birds and big game. The refuge headquarters is located in Lewistown, Montana, with substations at Fort Peck, Roy, and Jordan. A 20-mile self-guided tour begins at the Sand Creek substation located 20 miles north of Roy, Montana.

Named for the famous Great Falls cowboy artist, this 1,094,301-acre wildlife refuge was created in 1936 and straddles the Missouri River below Fort Peck Reservoir. Although over 100 miles long, the refuge is relatively narrow and includes a portion of some of the last remaining unaltered sections of the Missouri River. This is an area of scenic, rugged beauty with gently rolling grassy plateaus and breaks that slope abruptly to the river.

The area provides excellent habitat for a variety of plains wildlife including mule and white-tailed deer, pronghorns, bighorn sheep, and elk as well as sage grouse, turkeys and sharp-tailed grouse. The refuge also provides

Drake wigeon (baldpate). By Darrell Gulin

a limited amount of grazing for livestock, and is generally open to seasonal hunting and fishing. Primitive camping is allowed and there are a few developed campsites in the region. The country is game rich, but remote from population centers and hunting pressure is lighter than in most areas. There is a lot of Big Sky between service facilities and good roads, however.

The Missouri River breaks afford fine pronghorn and mule deer hunting and attract thousands of migrating ducks and geese. Fort Peck Reservoir, 134 miles long, offers walleye, northern pike, perch, lake trout and sauger.

Charles M. Russell NWR, Box 110, Lewistown, MT 59457. Phone (406) 538-8706.

UL Bend NWR: Established in 1967, this 55,530-acre northern Montana refuge is designed for ducks, geese, cranes and other migratory birds. Improvements are in the early stages and the refuge is still dominated by grasslands and sagebrush with a few small waterfowl marshes and ponds. Hunters find pronghorns, mule and white-tailed deer, thousands of ducks and geese, pheasants, sage and sharp-tailed grouse, Hungarian partridge and turkey.

The refuge and a series of four smaller waterfowl refuges are administered from the C.M. Russell NWR headquarters at Lewistown.

Located in the Missouri River breaks, the UL Bend adjoins and complements the Charles M. Russell NWR, at the western end of giant Fort Peck Reservoir. Approximately 20,819 acres of the area has been designated as wilderness. Trails into the refuge and regional roads are often impassable during wet weather and winter months.

The smaller waterfowl refuges are the 2,240-acre **Hailstone NWR** and the 3,097-acre **Halfbreed NWR** in Stillwater County; the 18,692-acre **Lake Mason NWR** in Musselshell

County; and 2,192-acre **War Horse NWR** in Petroleum County.

Hutton Lake NWR: This 1,968-acre refuge is located 12 miles southwest of Laramie, Wyoming, in Albany County and established as a waterfowl area.

Lee Metcalf NWR: Established in 1964, this 2,628-acre refuge is located near Stevensville, in western Montana, and developed as a migratory waterfowl refuge. Osprey and many other water-loving birds are common, and the refuge is becoming noted as a place for nature study and wildlife observation. Waterfowl hunting is also permitted.

Lee Metcalf NWR, Box 257, Stevensville, MT 59870. Phone (406) 777-5552.

Medicine Lake NWR: Established in 1935, this 31,457-acre refuge, primarily open water, marsh, and grass, is located two miles south of the town of Medicine Lake in the extreme northeast corner of Montana. A headquarters is located on the refuge, which is divided into two sections, and includes seven major lakes and dozens of small ponds. Largest lake is Medicine Lake at 8,700 acres.

The refuge is primarily a nesting, resting and feeding area for puddle ducks, Canada geese, colonial nesting birds, and native upland game birds, including sharp-tailed grouse. In addition to the waterfowl, hunters find abundant white-tailed deer, pronghorns and a few mule deer.

The refuge is also a "hot spot" for nothern pike up to 20-pounds, plus panfish, smallmouth and largemouth bass. Maps of the fishing and hunting areas are provided at the refuge. A 14-mile self-guided tour begins at the refuge headquarters.

Also managed from Medicine Lake NWR are the 800-acre **Lamesteer NWR** and 16,800 acres of Waterfowl Production Areas in northeastern Montana. These latter areas are wetlands purchased or leased by the service to

conserve prairie wetland nesting habitat for waterfowl. They are open to the public for such activities as hunting, bird watching and nature study.

Medicine Lake NWR, Medicine Lake, MT 59247. Phone (406) 789-2305.

National Bison Range: A 18,540-acre range 47 miles north of Missoula in western Montana along the Flathead River. A big game exhibition area of white-tailed deer, elk, pronghorn, bighorn sheep and bison, is adjacent to the headquarters and open year-round. The range, established in 1908, was instrumental in saving America's native bison herds. Bison raised from 41 breeding animals collected from Montana, Texas and New Hampshire, provided the nucleus for a herd that now provides buffalo for many other areas of the country.

While hunting is not permitted, the National Bison Range is an excellent wildlife viewing and big game photography area. Roughly 400 bison, 100 elk, 200 mule deer, 200 white-tailed deer, up to 100 bighorn sheep and 100 or more pronghorns roam the enclosure. There are also blue and ruffed grouse, pheasants, Hungarian partridge, beaver, bobcat, coyotes, mink and badger.

The range, consisting of rolling grasslands and partly timbered hills, is devoted primarily to the perpetuation of the American bison. An interpretive visitor center tells the story of American bison, refuge wildlife, and refuge management. A self-guided auto tour is available during the summer months.

National Bison Range and WMD, Moiese, MT 59824. Phone (406) 644-2211.

National Elk Refuge: This 23,861-acre refuge is located in scenic Jackson Hole, one mile east of Jackson, Wyoming, against the jagged Teton Range. Headquarters is on the refuge.

Established as winter range for elk the refuge is internationally famous for winter concentration of up to 7,500 elk. It also supports moose, deer, coyote, and the relatively rare trumpeter swan. In winter a concessionaire offers sleigh rides to the elk herds.

No camping is available. Fishing is permitted in certain areas and a special elk hunt is permitted in season on a limited area.

National Elk Refuge, Box C, Jackson, WY 83001. Phone (307) 733-9212.

Ninepipe NWR: Located in western Montana's Flathead Valley, Ninepipe NWR is within a few miles of the National Bison Range, is centered around 2,000-acre Ninepipe Reservoir, located on reservation land.

The refuge is administered from the headquarters at the bison range. It was created in 1921, as a 2,022-acre waterfowl refuge. Fishing is permitted for panfish and largemouth bass. A special tribal fishing permit is required. Up to 80,000 ducks and geese use the reservoir's shallow marshes in the fall, and although the refuge is closed to hunting, public hunting for ducks, geese and pheasants is permitted on adjacent Montana Fish and Game Commission lands.

Limited vehicle access, but walking trails,

This muskrat is one of several dozen incidental species benefiting from refuges established primarily for waterfowl. By Thomas W. Kitchin

picnic areas and photography are encouraged. Boats are not allowed on the lake.

Pablo NWR: Established in 1921, this 2,542-acre waterfowl refuge and fishing area surrounds Pablo Reservoir 15 miles northwest of the Ninepipe NWR, and is managed from the National Bison Range.

The refuge is closed to hunting, but open to fishing for rainbow trout. Adjacent lands are managed by the state for public hunting of ducks, geese and pheasants. The most common ducks are puddler varieties, mallards, pintail, wigeon, teal, gadwall, plus a few redheads. Good numbers of Canada geese use the refuge.

There are also several waterfowl production areas just east of Charlo, including Montgomery, with 80 acres and Herak at 400 acres. Some 4,000 acres of duck and goose hunting are managed in the Flathead Valley as well as the **Swan River NWR.**

Pathfinder NWR: A 16,807-acre refuge located on Pathfinder Reservoir near Casper, Wyoming, established for waterfowl habitat. It supports mule deer, pronghorns and sage grouse. Camping is permitted. Trout fishing, and hunting is permitted.

Bamforth, Hutton and Pathfinder NWRs are managed by Arapaho National Wildlife Refuge, Box 457, Walden, CO 80480. Phone (303) 723-4717.

Red Rock Lakes NWR: Located in a high sage-covered valley between Monida and West Yellowstone, Montana, along the base of the towering Centennial Mountains, at an elevation of 6,600 feet. Headquarters is on the 40,301-acre refuge.

Approximately 32,350 acres of the refuge are designated as Wilderness Area. The area includes about 13,000 acres of shallow lakes, marshes and meadows, some of it opened to hunting.

Although established mainly for the protection and propagation of the trumpeter swan which remains here the entire year, it also supports large numbers of ducks and geese, plus deer, pronghorns, and Shiras moose. Elk roam the nearby timber. Grayling and trout are found in the lakes and streams throughout the refuge.

The refuge is an excellent area for wildlife viewing. Fishing, big game, and waterfowl hunting are permitted. Waterfowling is permitted in designated areas only, where this recreational activity will not adversely affect protected species of wildlife.

Red Rock Lakes NWR, Monida Star Route, Lima, MT 59739. Phone (406) 276-3347.

Seedskadee NWR: This 14,285-acre refuge lies along the Green River in Wyoming, 30 miles north of the town of Green River in

Sweetwater County. Headquarters is located on the refuge. Established to provide nesting habitat for ducks and geese, it also supports sage grouse, mule deer, moose and pronghorns.

Recreational uses along the refuge's 35 river miles include fishing, primitive camping, canoeing, hunting for deer, pronghorn, moose, grouse and waterfowl. The adjoining Green River provides excellent trout fishing.

Sedskadee NWR, Box 67, Green River, WY 82935. Phone (307) 875-2187.

Alaska

Alaska Maritime NWR: Operations Manager South, 1011 E. Tudor Road, Anchorage, AK 99503.

Alaska Peninsula NWR: Operations Manager South, 1011 E. Tudor Road, Anchorage, AK 99503.

Arctic NWR: Refuge Manager, Room 226, Federal Bldg. & Courthouse, 101 12th Ave., Fairbanks, AK 99701.

Becharof NWR: Refuge Manager, P.O. Box 211, King Salmon, AK 99613.

Innoko NWR: Operations Manager North, 1011 E. Tudor Road, Anchorage, AK 99503.

Izembek NWR: Refuge Manager, Pouch 2, Cold Bay, AK 99571.

Kanuti NWR: Operations Manager North, 1011 E. Tudor Road, Anchorage, AK 99503.

Kenai NWR: Refuge Manager, Box 2139, Soldotna, AK 99669.

Kodiak NWR: Refuge Manager, Box 825, Kodiak, AK 99615.

Koyukuk NWR: Operations Manager North, 1011 E. Tudor Road, Anchorage, AK 99503.

Nowitna NWR: Operations Manager North, 1011 E. Tudor Road, Anchorage, AK 99503.

Selawik NWR: Operations Manager North, 1011 E. Tudor Road, Anchorage, AK 99503.

Tetlin NWR: Operations Manager North, 1011 E. Tudor Road, Anchorage, AK 99503.

Togiak NWR: Operations Manager South, 1011 E. Tudor Road, Anchorage, AK 99503.

Yukon Delta NWR: Refuge Manager, Box 346, Bethel, AK 99559.

Yukon Flats NWR: Refuge Manager, Room 226, Federal Bldg. & Courthouse, 101 12th Ave., Fairbanks, AK 99701.

Alaska National Monuments and Preserves

Aniakchak National Monument & Preserve: Superintendent Katmai National Park & Preserve, Box 7, King Salmon, AK 99613.

Bering Land Bridge National Preserve: National Park Service, P.O. Box 220, Nome, AK 99762.

Cape Krusenstern National Monument: National Park Service, P.O. Box 287, Kotzebue, AK 99752.

Denali National Park & Preserve: National Park Service, Denali, Park, AK 99755.

Gates of the Arctic National Park & Preserve: National Park Service, 201 First Ave., P.O. Box 74680, Fairbanks, AK 99707.

Glacier Bay National Park & Preserve: National Park Service, P.O. Box 1089, Juneau, AK 99806.

Katmai National Park & Preserve: National Park Service, P.O. Box 7, King Salmon, AK 99613.

Kenai Fjords National Park: National Park Service, P.O. Box 1727, Seward, AK 99664.

Kobuk Valley National Park: National Park Service, P.O. Box 287, Kotzebue, AK 99752.

Klondike Gold Rush National Historical Park: National Park Service, P.O. Box 517, Skagway, AK 99840.

Lake Clark National Park & Preserve: National Park Service, 701 C St., Box 61, Anchorage, AK 99513.

Noatak National Preserve: National Park Service, P.O. Box 287, Kotzebue, AK 99752.

Sitka National Historical Park: National Park Service, P.O. Box 738, Sitka, AK 99835.

Wrangell-Saint Elias National Park & Preserve: National Park Service, P.O. Box 29, Glennallen, AK 99588.

Yukon-Charley Rivers National Preserve: National Park Service, P.O. Box 64, Eagle, AK 99738.

The primary purpose of the 50 Northwest refuges is the preservation of wildlife habitat with a secondary goal of managing game bird and animal populations through sport hunting. Most refuges offer hunting opportunities, especially those established primarily for waterfowl, like this Idaho snow goose. By Erwin & Peggy Bauer

Sport Fish of The Northwest

Trout, Char

Cutthroat Trout: Cutthroat trout are named for the bright red-orange streak in the fold under the jaw. The slash is used as a defense when the trout opens its mouth and flashes the red streak at fish it wants to drive away. Cutthroat are the native trout of the Western mountain and foothill streams. There are several varieties, the most popular are the Yellowstone, black-spotted, Lahontan and sea-run. Landlocked cutts are heavily spotted on the back and tail. Sea-runs are generally

silvery. Coloration varies substantially in different regions and water conditions. They range from Prince William Sound in Alaska, south to northern California.

Photo by Michael S. Sample

Artwork courtesy of Alberta Fish and Wildlife Division

Cutts prefer colder waters than other trout, spawn in the spring, which may be as late as early July in high mountain streams. They are frequently found in fast, white-water streams, but also adapt well to alpine lakes, beaver ponds and upland lakes. They are commonly caught on artificial flies, small spoons, small spinners, and bait. Cutthroat are not leapers and when hooked usually put up a strong, bulldogging fight occasionally wallowing to the surface.

The world-record cutthroat is a 41-pound fish caught in Nevada's Pyramid Lake on a cold December day in 1925. That fish was of the Lahontan strain, a subspecies being introduced to highly alkaline lakes in several areas of the Northwest. In most cutthroat areas they average between 1 and 3 pounds.

Coastal areas of northern California, Oregon, Washington, British Columbia and Alaska support a sea-run variety of cutthroat also known as bluebacks or harvest trout. Sea-runs are caught near gravel beaches in the salt water usually close to shore, and in the spring and fall migrate upstream into freshwater rivers, where they are caught on light spinning or fly-fishing tackle.

Rainbow Trout: Rainbow are the most important and widely distributed freshwater game fish in the cold-water rivers and lakes of the Northwest. They average between 1 and 5 pounds, commonly grow to more than 20 pounds and one monster — a 56-pound 'bow — was netted in 1913 in Jewel Lake, British Columbia. Like nearly all of the common Northwestern game fish, rainbow are not native to the region.

Coloration varies widely area-to-area, but is generally olive green with heavy black spotting over the length of the body. The adult fish has

a broad reddish stripe along the lateral line, from the gills to the tail. Their tail, caudal fin, is squarish and only mildly forked. Rainbow trout in lakes are usually more silvery colored than the dark, richly colored river-caught fish.

Rainbow are widely distributed throughout the Northwest from the heavily spotted trophies of southeastern Alaska to put-and-take waters in northern California. They are easily raised in hatcheries and the favorite of game department stocking programs. Like the cutthroat, there are numerous varieties and subspecies of rainbow, ranging from the standard hatchery-fare to the exotic Kamloops of northern Idaho and British Columbia. Anadromous rainbow are known as steelhead.

Wild rainbow trout spawn in the spring, but fish culturists have developed fall spawning races. These races allow fish hatcheries to raise young fish over the winter so they can be released at a catchable size in the spring. Rainbow are strong, acrobatic fish when hooked, often leaping clear of the water, while launching sizzling runs. They are great sport on light tackle, especially flies or small spinners or spoons, and one of the first trout to become active in the spring. Winter fishermen have also been discovering that rainbow are excellent targets for ice fishing.

Lake Trout: The lake trout, sometimes called mackinaw, is the least colorful of the cold-water game fish. Lakers are char, not trout, identified by the white edging on the front of the belly fins that mark all char. It is a gray fish with irregular white spots. During the fall spawning season, the fins near the tail become a pale orange.

Lakers are native to many of northern Canada and Alaska's deep cold lakes, and have taken hold in many of the Lower 48's largest lakes and reservoirs. Montana's Flathead Lake, Idaho's Priest Lake, Washington's Deer and Loon lakes and Oregon's O'Dell Reservoir are famous for their mackinaw action. Best catches in these lakes are immediately after ice-out when the big fish are near the surface. In summer they follow the cold water to the bottom. Lake trout grow slowly, but to large sizes, often exceeding 25 pounds. The world's record is a 65-pounder caught in 1970 in Great Bear Lake. Lake trout are long-lived with the larger ones reaching 25 years. Young lake trout feed on freshwater shrimp and other aquatic invertebrates. Larger lakers are predators, and primarily feed on other fish, mostly whitefish, tullibee and kokanee.

Lake trout feed near the surface of a lake when the water is cold (spring and fall). During the summer the cold water sinks to the bottom of the lake and the trout follow it down. Fishermen who seek this fish during the summer months often use wire lines, 5-inch plugs and heavy weights or downriggers to fish up to 150 feet deep. In northern rivers, and cold lakes where they are shallow, they are often taken with large weighted spoons.

Golden Trout: Relatively rare in the Northwest, goldens are olive green on the back and bright red-to-gold sides and belly. In the spring spawning season, the colors are extremely intense. They are the most colorful of the trouts. Goldens are native only to a few small lakes and streams at high elevations in the Sierra

Nevada mountains of California. They were introduced in a few alpine lakes in the mountains of southern Alberta, Idaho, Montana, Wyoming and Washington. Golden trout are very specialized for their particular environment, and do not adapt well to lower elevation streams and lakes.

The short growing season of the high mountain lakes does not allow this trout to grow fast and most golden trout are small. However, they are highly prized by the adventurous angler. The world's record is only 11 pounds and was caught in Cooks Lake, Wyoming, in 1948.

Brown Trout: Brown trout are golden brown in color with large black and red spots, some with pale halos. They are the only trout with both red and black spotting. A native to Europe, Asia and North Africa, brown trout were introduced into Northwest waters. They are now fairly common in the lower, slower sections of many major rivers east of the crest of the Cascade Range. Only a few lakes west of the Cascades support brown trout. In the arid regions, however, hundreds of lakes in all states and Alberta, offer browns. Only a couple of streams support browns in British Columbia.

Brown trout are more tolerant of silting and warm water than rainbow and cutthroat and tend to concentrate in the valleys and plain areas. They are also more wary and difficult to catch than other species. Brown trout are often stocked in areas that have been disturbed by man and where there is heavy fishing pressure.

While the recognized world's record is 35 pounds, 15-pound browns raise eyebrows in the Northwest and most are under 6 pounds.

Young brown trout feed on insects and other invertebrates, but the larger fish are active predators of other fishes, including young brown trout, although they will rise to the fly. Larger brown trout will also feed on small animals that fall in the water. In the summer browns usually do not become active and feed until the late afternoon or early evening, and are notorious night feeders. Brown trout are caught with artificial flies, spoons and bait, such as worms, grasshoppers or slices of sucker meat.

Brook Trout: The brook trout is one of the most colorful cold-water fish. Despite its name, brookies are members of the char family and not trout at all. They are easy to identify with their dark, green backlines, wormlike vermiculations and lines on the leading edge of their fins. Their sides and underbellies are often bright orange and heavily spotted. The sides sometimes have a purple sheen with blue-haloed red spots. There are no black spots on this char.

Originally native to the East Coast, the brook trout was introduced into Northwest waters around 1900. They now dominate many foothill streams, mountain lakes and lakes where the low concentration of oxygen does not favor other species of trout.

Brookies spawn in October and the eggs hatch in the spring. They can first spawn when they are 18 months old and only 2⅓ inches long. This feature causes many brook trout populations to overcrowd their habitat resulting in lakes filled with brookies stunted at a maximum growth of 6 to 10 inches. The world-record brookie is 14 pounds, 8 ounces, caught in Ontario. That record has stood since 1916. Few brookies in the Northwest exceed 5 pounds.

They are primarily insect feeders living on invertebrates (aquatic insects, shrimps, etc.), and occasionally other fish. Brook trout can be taken with all types of fishing lures, flies and bait and are especially susceptible to worms. They tend to hug bottom more than most trout.

Bull Trout (Dolly Varden)**:** Until a few years ago bull trout and Dolly Varden were considered one species. Today, however, biologists have divided the species by location. The landlocked variety is now recognized as a bull trout and the sea-run fish a Dolly Varden. A char, Dollies were named after Miss Dolly

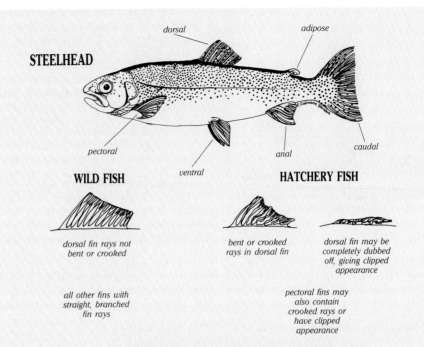

STEELHEAD

dorsal   *adipose*

pectoral   *ventral*   *anal*   *caudal*

WILD FISH   **HATCHERY FISH**

dorsal fin rays not bent or crooked

bent or crooked rays in dorsal fin

dorsal fin may be completely dubbed off, giving clipped appearance

all other fins with straight, branched fin rays

pectoral fins may also contain crooked rays or have clipped appearance

Varden, a colorfully dressed character in Charles Dicken's story, *Barnaby Rudge.* Dollies freqently have pink spots and show orange and red on the sides. The largest ever caught was a 32-pound fish from Lake Pend Oreille, Idaho. Today that fish would be called a bull trout.

Sea-run Dollies can be caught from Oregon north to Alaska generally in saltwater estuaries or upstream in tributary rivers. Dollies follow the salmon upriver and feed heavily on surplus eggs wafting downstream from spawning redds. Sea-runs are silvery colored with fainter markings than landlocked fish. They are generally slender, with large heads — some call them snaky. The bull trout is generally more vividly colored, and thicker through the body. The fish is usually gray in color with pale yellow or orange spots along its sides.

Bull trout are found in nearly all the river systems with headwaters in the Rocky Mountains, and some on the east drainages of the Cascade Range. They are a native char with the largest natural distribution in Alberta, British Columbia and Alaska. Northern Montana and Idaho also have many bull trout fisheries.

Bull trout are usually found in pools or backwater areas, instead of fast-moving riffles and rapids. They grow slowly in their preferred cold-water areas, and they spawn at a much later age than other fish. Spawning is in the early fall in small creeks. Spawners are usually large (over 12 inches), and vulnerable to bears, ospreys and man. Dollies and bulls are predators feeding heavily on other fish and may take small animals that fall into the water. Bull trout can be caught on most types of fishing lures and are very susceptible to bait, such as worms or meat. According to folklore a squirrel leg is excellent bait.

Arctic Grayling: These fish have a colorful, sail-like dorsal fin, much larger than that of any other cold-water fish. Grayling have large scales with black spots behind the gill cover. They have a black line in the fold under the mouth. The largest arctic grayling populations are found in fairly slow-moving streams of Alberta, British Columbia and Alaska. Only a few waters in Washington, Idaho and Montana support grayling. Small fish, grayling favor slower water currents for spawning and rearing than most other cold-water fishes.

Grayling are excellent sport fish, easily caught and therefore their populations are vulnerable

Wild or Hatchery?
How to Identify Native Steelhead

Recognizing the difference between a native steelhead that has spawned in the natural gravel of a river bar from a steelhead that got its start in the protective concrete confines of a hatchery tank is becoming as important to Northwest steelheaders as learning how to read water, tie nail knots or wade cross-current on a bed of moss-slick, rolling round river rock.

Not too many years ago, packing home a dime-bright native steelhead was a seasonal high point for many Northwesterners, an angling accomplishment praised along the riverbank and at the dinner table. Carry that same wild steelhead away from many rivers this winter and it's likely to attract scorn, derision and possibly a hefty court fine.

Opposition to catching and keeping native steelhead has gained the philosophical support of many sportfishermen, and the backing of strict state regulations coupled to a public relations push promoting the qualities of steelhead hatched and reared in the protective confines of state and federal hatcheries. Fisheries managers in the major steelhead regions of British Columbia, Washington, Oregon and Idaho are encouraging if not requiring the release of native steelhead spawned in the wild, while scrambling to resurrect depressed runs of wild fish in specific river systems or to maintain a quality catch-and-release steelhead fishery.

These hatchery-only steelhead regulations are forcing sport anglers, with no formal training in fish identification, to immediately determine if a steelhead is a native or hatchery fish, sometimes under adverse weather conditions, always during the confusion and excitement of landing a trophy-size trout, all without injuring the fish or destroying the delicate protective film that protects it from bacterial infection, so that it can be released alive if it's a wild fish.

The most reliable and rapid way of identifying protected wild trout is a quick check of the dorsal, that dominating sail-like fin in the center of a trout's back. The supporting rays in a wild steelhead's dorsal fin are straight with sharp crisp edges. The dorsal fin on steelhead developed in hatcheries are crooked, with wavy rays deformed by continual contact with the rough concrete runways, and in some instances the dorsal may be nearly dubbed off by hatchery workers attempting to make the identification chore easier. Most steelhead with dorsal fins measuring less than 2 inches high are hatchery-produced fish. If a dorsal fin check is not conclusive, biolgoists recommend checking the pectoral fin, located slightly behind and below the gills, for deformities created by hatchery handling.

Trout fishermen also find the bent fin system to be a handy way of finding out if their catch should be credited to nature or the government. It is also becoming commonplace for biologists to remove an adipose or ventral fin to identify hatchery-produced salmon and steelhead implanted with microscopic wire codes.

(Courtesy of Northwest Living*)*

to heavy fishing pressures. Arctic grayling can be caught on most types of flies, small spoons, spinners or baits but are fairly small. The world's record stands at 1 ounce under 5 pounds. Most are 1 to 2 pounds. They are thick in many northern British Columbia and Alaska streams.

Whitefish (Mountain, lake)**:** There are two varieties of whitefish in the Northwest, one for the rivers and one for the lakes. The river fish is the **mountain whitefish** recognized with large silvery scales, no spots and small underslung mouths. The general body color is a bronze white or greenish white. They are native to most rivers in the Northwest, concentrating in large schools in pools. Adult mountain whitefish undertake spawning migrations in the fall and feeding migrations in the spring.

These fish are more flexible in their environmental requirements than other cold-water sport fishes. They have maintained large populations in many streams. Large hydroelectric reservoirs often provide suitable habitat for these fish, and large populations are often present. Mountain whitefish are primarily bottom feeders and most anglers fish for them with maggots and small pieces of earthworm bounced downstream in the current, near bottom. A few skillful fishermen catch them with artificial flies and small spinners. Best fishing is in the winter when the fish are concentrated in tremendous schools. While not nearly as popular as trout, whitefish are fine fighters and are attracting new fishermen each year. They are not large fish, rarely exceeding 3 pounds.

The **lake whitefish** is even less popular with anglers although numerous Northwest lakes have excellent, but nearly untapped populations them. Lake whitefish are similar in appearance to mountain whitefish but much larger. Three- to 5-pounders are common and they have been caught to 14 pounds. Best action is in the spring when the lake schools concentrate near the mouths of tributary streams. Worms, leadhead jigs or clusters of salmon eggs are popular baits. Bony fish, whitefish are usually smoked or pickled. They have a good flavor.

Pacific Salmon

Chinook: Largest of the salmon, chinook can grow to more than 100 pounds and run under several aliases. The most common misnomer is king, a fitting title, for the giant of the species. In British Columbia, kings are called tyees unless they're under 30 pounds and immature at which stage they are referred to as springs. In Washington, those young fish are called blackmouth.

The blackmouth label refers to the black-colored inside of a chinook's mouth and gumline, a distinguishing feature in commonly indistinguishable species. The four other Pacific salmon have whitish mouths.

Chinook are spawned in major rivers and spend from two to seven years at sea. The largest, those incredible Kenai River, Alaska, 70-pounders, and Rivers Inlet, British Columbia, 50-pound trophies, also spend the longest time at sea, feeding in the rich pastures of the Pacific. Rarely do the 50-pound-plus chinook come back to fresh water before five years, where the average 10- to 20-pounder spends less than two years in the salt.

The rod-and-reel record is 97 pounds and was set in the spring of '85 on the Kenai. While the big kings grab the headlines and attract the traveling salmon chaser, there are actually more chinook spawning streams south of British Columbia in Washington, Oregon and California. Smaller salmon dominate most of the northern spawning rivers. Chinook are bottom dwellers, and they prefer a rocky ledge line 90 to 200 feet down. In fjordlike areas it is not unusual to find large kings within a few feet of the bank, and 90 feet down. Most of the

best king fishing areas in the Northwest are less than a mile or two offshore and often within a rod's length of a cliff face.

There are subspecies of chinook, some returning to spawning streams late in the summer, others in the spring and a few late fall or early winter. The largest return is late in the summer, in July and August. By September, most kings have moved well upstream in the fresh water, dodged the hooks of low-river lure slingers, spawned and by early October died. In fresh water, the cold steel silver of an ocean king fades to brown and finally black. The pea-sized black spots on the back and tail remain. Like all Pacific salmon, chinook die shortly after spawning.

Coho: Sometimes called silvers or hooknose salmon, they are the most intensively fished salmon, if not the most popular. They have white gum lines, few spots on a back the color of polished gun metal, and an aggressive disposition that endears them to sportfishermen. Coho run shallow, usually less than 60 feet and often just below the surface. They follow the tide rips and are usually a mile or more away from shore, often following the shipping lanes.

They are smaller than the kings, much smaller. The world's record is only 31 pounds and a typical silver will weigh from 5 to 15 pounds. They are fast, however, and take their fight to the air, often cartwheeling across the surface.

Silvers return to fresh water about a month later than the kings, coming back in August and September and swarming into spawning streams in October. Unlike kings that spawn in mainstream rivers, silvers spawn in tributaries, sometimes trickles so shallow that their backs stick up above the water as they fan a spawning redd in the gravel.

Coho originate in streams from California to western Alaska, but the heaviest concentrations are between the Columbia River and Cook Inlet. In British Columbia it is estimated that coho spawn in more than half the coastal

streams. They are fished in the offshore rips, near the estuaries and followed upstream by anglers with spinning rods and hip boots. In fresh water, the males become red and develop vicious-looking hook jaws. The females lack the hook and become a reddish gray. In the salt, they are brilliantly silver, exceptionally streamlined and small-mouthed.

Chums: One of the most underrated salmon, chums are hard-fighting, aggressive and delicious. It has a low fat content that makes it one of the finest smoking salmon, and a penchant for belting spoons in late fall. Chums are also called dog, calico and fall salmon. Dogs because many northern Indian tribes used them extensively as dog food; calicos because of the patchwork coloration of its spawning colors and fall because it is the last of the salmon to return to the rivers in the fall — often not appearing until November.

They aren't big fish (the record is 27 pounds), averaging between 10 and 25 pounds and few are ever taken in salt water by sportfishermen. Most chums are taken in nets, or by sport anglers casting into spawning streams. Chums are scrappers. A river fish will literally melt line off a reel spool and a saltwater catch will run and leap in step with the hardest fighting silver.

In salt water chums are identified by tight, small scales, a lack of spots and small head. In fresh water, the males develop an incredibly wicked-looking hook jaw, and both sexes appear splotched with dark colors.

Chums will be found from Oregon north to the Mackenzie River with the major spawning grounds between Puget Sound and Kotzebue, Alaska. They spend the least amount of time in fresh water of any salmon, leaving for the sea within days of hatching and returning late in the season to scoot upstream and spawn. They spend just two, sometimes three, years at sea.

Sockeye: Streamlined, finely scaled and rarely larger than 7 pounds, sockeye are a northern fish, rarely found south of the Columbia River. In Alaska, sockeye are usually called "red" salmon. They are the first salmon to greet the commercial fleet in Alaska and British Columbia and are primarily a canner. They can be caught in salt water, but are

usually passed up in favor of the more coveted silvers and kings which share the same water. One of the heaviest spawning runs of sockeye in the world takes place late each summer in British Columbia's Fraser River system, with other major runs developing in the larger rivers north to Bristol Bay.

They run shallow, like a silver, and can be caught on flasher and squid rigs, but rarely are. A few anglers have taken to catching the smallish acrobats on fly or spin tackle in spawning streams, especially in southeastern Alaska. They are protected in streams of Washington, but sometimes exceptionally popular sport fisheries are approved in Lake Washington near Seattle and Lake Wenatchee, a little west of Leavenworth.

Sockeye spend between two and three years at sea and return as four-year-olds after spending up to two years in freshwater rivers before migrating out. When they return to spawning streams sockeye become brilliantly red with green heads.

Pinks: Humpies, most anglers call them in deference to the camel-like back developed by the male at spawning. They are the most numerous salmon in British Columbia and Yukon River waters and the least important from a sportfishing standpoint.

They are small salmon, 3 to 10 pounds, with the eccentric trait of returning to spawning rivers every other year. In British Columbia's Fraser River and all Washington waters, pinks return to freshwater rivers only in odd-numbered years. In the Queen Charlotte Islands they spawn during even-numbered years and in some of the areas in between, both odd and even runs overlap. Both runs, however, have just a two-year life span, spending 18 months at sea.

A few pinks are taken on trolling gear, but most are swept into commercial nets. They are largely plankton feeders and rarely caught on bait — although artificals can trigger a strike response.

Common Saltwater Bottom Fish

(Illustrations courtesy of Oregon Fish and Wildlife)

The variety, size and table quality of bottom fish, a misleading misnomer, available in the Pacific will meet the demands of nearly any angler. Bottom fish is a collective term applied to any nonsalmonoid, and lacks any pretense of accuracy. Some species are caught on the surface, others at mid-depths, and some actually on the bottom.

The most common varieties important to sportfishermen include two dozen subspecies of rockfish, another dozen flatfish, plus cod, greenling and perch. They are a colorful group of fish, with different species varying from brilliant orange to deep blue. Weights can vary from 1 to 400 pounds, and, depending on species, are caught at the surface, mid-levels or belly to the bottom. Some have large, thick scales and others, particuliary the cods, are smooth skinned. All have a delicate, white flaky meat, fight stubbonly with hard short runs and head shakes and with just a few exceptions are found in large dense schools.

Rockfish

By far the most plentiful, diverse and frequently caught of the ocean "bottom fish" varieties, the Northwest rockfish family includes two dozen species. They are also prone to inaccurate and misleading regional misnaming such as sea bass, red snapper or rock cod, East Coast names erroneously applied to West Coast fish. There are no rock cod, snapper or sea bass in the Northwest.

As the name implies, rockfish generally prefer areas with rough broken bottoms, reefs, pinnacles or rocky islands. They are found in the open ocean near offshore pinnacles as well as the protected inshore inlets, sounds and coves.

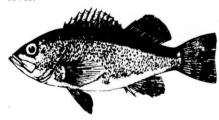

Black Rockfish: Common along the Pacific coastline and inside waters. Often called sea bass. Large schools. Coloration is dark black to gray on the back. Grow to 24 inches and can weigh up to 11 pounds. Often found near surface, or stratified at mid-depths. The dominant catch on Washington ocean charter boat trips. Excellent sport on spinning or fly tackle. In inside waters blacks seek the protection of jetties, log booms, piers and rock piles. Abundant.

Blue Rockfish: Nearly identical in size, range and coloration to black rockfish. Body color dark blue, nearly black. Common.

Brown Rockfish: Prefers shallow water, often near kelp beds. Brown, splotchy back coloration, with some pink on fins. Large schools. Grows to about 20 inches and 5 pounds. Common.

Yellowtail Rockfish: Often found in large schools stratified at mid-depths. Coloration is brown to greenish on the back and sides with yellowish fins. Sometimes exceeds 24 inches and 6 pounds. Common along coast.

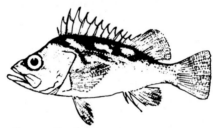

Copper Rockfish: Often found near shore and over rocky reefs in inside waters. Back coloration is mottled dark green, yellow and brown. Grows to 20 inches, 10 pounds. Common.

Quillback: Bottom dweller, rarely larger than 15 inches and 3 pounds. Often called rock cod. Coloration is mottled brown and yellow which extends up the spines. Dorsal spines are prominent, sharp and mildly toxic. Abundant near inshore reefs.

China Rockfish: Usually found in open ocean areas near pinnacles. Small, rarely exceeding 15 inches and 5 pounds. Mostly black with a dominant yellow stripe running from the middle of the dorsal fin to the tail. Rare.

Yelloweye Rockfish: Probably the most coveted of all rockfish, yelloweyes, commonly called red snapper, have been caught that weighed 50 pounds and were up to 36 inches long. Rarely found more than a few feet above bottom, usually deeper than 150 feet. Brilliant orange to red coloration, with a bright yellow eye. All soft-ray fins are tipped with black. Common in ocean and Strait of Juan de Fuca. Fairly rare in inside waters.

Canary Rockfish: Another bright orange fish, canaries are commonly confused with yelloweyes, but lack the black fin markings and the backs are generally more mottled with gray. Canaries also have three bright orange stripes radiating from the eye to the gill cover. Abundant in the ocean and most larger straits, rare in inside waters.

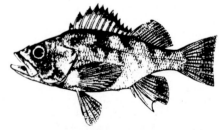

Vermilion Rockfish: A scarlet-red coloration splotched with black on the sides. Fins normally edged in black. Rarely caught less than 100 feet deep, weigh up to 15 pounds, 25 inches long. Fairly rare north of the Columbia River, but common in Oregon and northern California catches.

Tiger Rockfish: Found in deep water, on the bottom usually near caves. The color is pinkish red, with five black tiger stripes running from the dorsal fin down the sides. Maximum length 24 inches, weight 5 pounds. Rare.

Greenstripe Rockfish: Caught on the bottom in deep water. Red on back and sides, white belly with a distinctive green stripe on the sides. Length 15 inches, weight rarely more than 2 pounds. Rare south of Vancouver Island.

Rosethorn Rockfish: Probably the rarest of all rockfish. Found on offshore Pacific banks. Rarely longer than 12 inches and less than a pound. Bright orange-red color with white to tan splotches along spine.

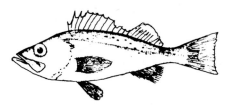

Bocaccio: Deep-water denizen, rarely caught shallower than 300 feet. Grows to more than 25 pounds, 36 inches. Color is tannish red, fading to pink along the sides. Mouth is disproportionately large. Rare.

Greenlings

With one exciting exception, the half-dozen species of greenling in the Northwest don't figure prominently in sportfishing.

The exception is the lingcod, a badly named prize that grows to exceptional size in the Northwest, fights hard, and rates near the top of the list for table quality. Members of the greenling family are recognized by a long, continuous soft-rayed dorsal fin, notched slightly at the midpoint. They are generally green to bronze colored, and soft featured. Except for lingcod, greenling are generally small fish, commonly caught in fairly shallow, rocky water. They are palatable, bite well, and those too small to eat, make excellent bait for larger lings or rockfish.

One of the most peculiar traits of greenlings is the color of the meat, which can vary from typical white to a blue green. The blue meat is created by a chemical imbalance and doesn't affect the flavor or quality of the meat. When cooked the meat loses the off-color and fades back to white.

Lingcod: For many bottom fishermen, lingcod are the top prize. The trophy catch for the sport. The name is a total misnomer, because lings are neither related to the freshwater ling (a burbot) or the codfish family, but is the largest of the greenlings. Sportfishermen have caught lings more than 6 feet long, weighing more than 80 pounds. Lings are believed to grow to more than 100 pounds in rarely fished remote areas of British Columbia and Alaska. Lings are caught as shallow as 20 feet and as deep as 200. The largest are females. Males rarely exceed 20 pounds. Lings prefer rocky areas, with strong tidal flows and feed heavily on other fish. They are long, green and brown splotched fish with a flat head and mouthful of inwardly slanted canine teeth. Ling are extremely agressive predators and some of the largest are caught when they swallow a hooked rockfish or greenling as it is being brought to the boat. Giant lings have been known to swallow 12-pound lings whole as they are being brought to the surface. Few anglers, however, use 12-pound ling as bait, preferring smaller rockfish or greenling. It's not unusual for lings to follow hooked rockfish to the surface where they can sometimes be netted without actually being hooked.

Lings require stout tackle, to keep them from returning to their rocky lairs. They fight hard and have a tendency to nose into rock crevasses where they are impossible to dislodge. Common on ocean pinnacles and rocky inside headlands and reefs.

Kelp Greenling: A fine shallow water fish, kelp greenling are caught on light tackle near kelp and eelgrass beds, or rock breakwaters. They grow to about 24 inches and weigh up to 5 pounds. Males are a dull bluish color with bright blue halos on the head. Females are golden bronze with brown spots on the sides. They can often be caught from piers or shore casting small jigs to kelp lines. Common.

Painted Greenling: A tiny fish, best used as bait for lingcod, painted greenling rarely grow to a foot in length. They are gray with seven red tiger stripes. Common near shore.

White-spotted Greenling: Grow to 15 inches and weigh up to 3 pounds. Thick white spots on the sides with a coloration varying from brown to green. Fairly rare in sport catches.

Rock Greenling: Perhaps the rarest greenling, rocks are distinguished by a fleshy appendage above the eyes. Coloration runs from dark green to brown with red mottling, and two blood red lines extending from the eye across the gill cover. Sometimes reach 24 inches and 4 pounds. Rare.

Codfish

There are four major members of the codfish family in Northwest waters, but only two, the true cod and walleye pollock, are of any importance to sportfishermen. Cod are most often caught during the winter spawning months and are highly valued on the table. The meat is white, in large flakes and extremely delicate. Cod should be immediately chilled and bled to avoid softening the meat.

Cod are easily identified by their smooth gray skin, three dorsal fins and a single chin barbel. Cod are nearly always found in large schools, often measuring several acres wide, stacked 20 to 100 feet deep in the water column. Most fishermen pound their lures against the bottom to attract the attention. Best fishing is generally at depths from 150 to 200 feet although cod are caught anywhere from 20 to 600 feet deep. They range throughout the Northwest, feeding on small fish, worms, crabs and shrimp. They are not fighters, but require substantial tackle to hoist out of the depths; 25-pound line, short stout rods, squidding reels, and weights between 6 and 16 ounces are standard. Most cod are caught on cod jigs, plastic worms or chunks of baitfish, most likely herring.

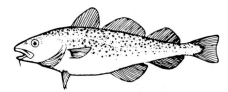

Pacific Cod: Also called gray cod, true cod, this is the largest of the Northwest codfish, sometimes reaching 40 inches in length and 25 pounds. Common at 3 to 10 pounds. Prefers deep water, and is highly valued for its table quality. Limit catches are common when a school is located. Abundant.

Walleye Pollock: Similar in physical appearance to the Pacific cod, but smaller and more slender, with a distinctively large eye and a small or nonexistent chin barbel. Generally found in large schools, during the winter, at depths of between 50 and 300 feet. While the meat is not equal to the Pacific cod, it is good if kept chilled. Jigs and baitfish are the most productive lures. Measure 18 to 24 inches, averaging 1 to 3 pounds. Abundant.

Two codfish relatives, of little value to sportfishermen, are the **Pacific hake** and **tomcod.** Hake are commercially netted by foreign fleets. They average 1 to 3 pounds, are extremely bony, silvery in color, with large teeth. Often caught at night and travel in large schools. Tomcod are small, usually less than 10 inches, and can be found from 20 to 600 feet deep. Only in their northern range are they deliberately sought, then usually as a food fish caught through the ice.

Sablefish: Also known as black cod, sablefish are handsome compared to their deep-water neighbors, with slate black backs, fading to greenish gray along the sides and belly. They are found on the bottom in water up to 600 feet deep, and have been reported weighing as much as 125 pounds. Most catches, however, are 3 to 20 pounds. Common in the ocean, less common in inside waters. In the winter sport-fishermen frequently find them in central Puget Sound, the Strait of Juan de Fuca and near Vancouver Island and the Strait of Georgia. They have an oily meat and are excellent smoked. Common.

Cabezon: The only species in the 36-member sculpin family deliberately sought for food and sport. Distributed from Mexico to southeast Alaska, cabezon have very large heads and fins, are heavily mottled with green, browns and grays, changing color patterns to match their habitat. They can reach lengths of 30 inches and weights of 30 pounds, but are commonly caught in the 2- to 10-pound range. Found on the bottom in rocky areas from shore to 150 feet. Feed almost exclusively on crabs, and are considered excellent table fare. The roe, however, is toxic. Hard fighters on light tackle. Common.

Flatfish

More than a dozen species of flounder, sole, sanddabs and halibut are caught in Northwest waters, all bottom dwellers, most the size of a large dinner plate shaped like a ping-pong paddle. Often found in sandy bottom areas where they lay flush on the bottom or even burrowed into the sand. They are typically dark brown, gray or greenish on the upside, and white on the downside. The eyes are located on the dark side.

Smaller, younger fish are found near shore, with the largest caught on the bottom in water 60 to 200 feet deep. They have been found as deep as 900 feet. Easily caught on small pieces of baitfish, or jigs fished flush against the bottom. Excellent eating. Abundant.

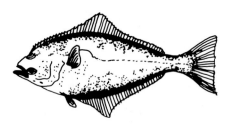

Pacific Halibut: Largest and most coveted of the flatfish, halibut can weigh up to 500 pounds, and stretch out to 8½ feet, with the largest coming from Alaska waters. Typical catches weigh 30 to 60 pounds. Powerful fish known to wreck the inside of boats if landed fresh. Most anglers dispatch their fish with a gun before bringing on board. Caught on large baitfish, or leadhead jigs weighing up to 3 pounds. Body is thick, powerful. Rarely caught in inside waters, preferring banks rising from the bottom of the open Pacific. In Alaska, and Washington's Strait of Juan de Fuca small boats frequently work the halibut grounds. Charter boats can be booked exclusively for halibut. A delicacy on the table. Common in coastal areas, rare in inside waters.

Soles, Flounders: Involves nearly a dozen bottom-dwelling species, all with both eyes on

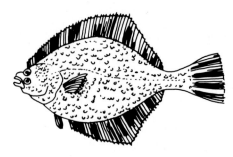

one (dark) side of the head, colored dark brown, gray or green on the back, and white on the belly. Included are, C-O, English, Rock, Butter, Sand, Flathead, Dover, Rex, Petrale, and Starry. Have been caught up to 20 pounds, but more common between 1 and 3 pounds. Prefer sand or gravel bottoms, often caught from shore or fishing piers, in coves, river mouths and along soft-bottomed peninsulas. Favorite baits are shrimp, pieces of herring, clam necks or pile worms fished on the bottom. Excellent table fare. Abundant.

Perch

The six varieties of sea perch in the Northwest are the panfish of saltwater fishing. They are common from Baja, Mexico, to southeastern Alaska, and nearly always found within a few yards of shore, both in inland sounds and along the ocean coast. Perch have typically small mouths, stout bodies, broad flat sides and sharp dorsal spines.

Sea perch are one of the few fish to give live birth. The young are well developed and immediately independent of the parent. They are not large fish, generally 6 to 17 inches long weighing up to 3 pounds. Found in shallows along the beach, pilings, bulkheads or rocks. Favorite bait is a tidbit of mussel gathered locally, followed by sand shrimp, slice of clam neck or pile worms. Excellent fighters on light tackle. Abundant.

Pile Perch: Largest of the perch, reaching 17 inches, greenish gray on the back, silvery along the belly, with a faint tiger stripe around the center. Deeply forked tail. Found primarily around pilings.

Striped Perch: Probably the most abundant perch, stripes prefer rocky shorelines and

Ocean Sunfish

Few Northwest fish are stranger than the ocean sunfish. Unlike the familiar freshwater sunfish, which is measured in inches, ocean sunfish are up to 10 feet long, weighing up to a ton. They are ponderous fish, often seen in the ocean bobbing on the surface. Sunfish move slowly, propelled by the dominant pectoral and anal fins. They feed on jellyfish, seaweed and crustaceans, and their meat is considered inedible. They do not take fishing lures or bait, and when spotted, sunfish are usually laying on their sides, floating apparently helpless in the current, a large baleful eye staring aimlessly.

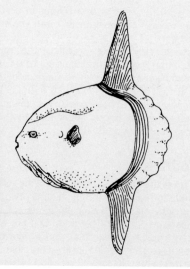

jetties. They are very colorful fish, with a bronze body, streaked with 15 brilliant blue horizontal lines along the side. Grow to 15 inches and hunt in large schools.

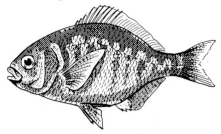

Redtail Surfperch: Abundant along sandy ocean beaches. Grows to 16 inches, is bright silver in color with dark tiger strikes radiating from the spine. The lower fins are red. This is the favorite target for most surf fishermen along the coast.

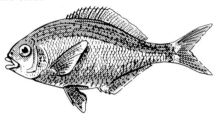

White, Kelp, and Shiner Perch: Small or uncommon and unimportant to the sport fishery.

Unclassified Game Fish

Albacore: Commonly called tuna, albacore may be the hardest fighting fish in the Northwest. They follow the warm waters of the Gulf Stream as it passes along the coast, annually swinging near the coast of northern California and Oregon in late summer. On some years they are fished by charter boats ranging 50 to 150 miles off the coast of Washington and British Columbia. Shaped like a torpedo, albacore are colored electric blue along the back, and mint bright silver on the sides. Weigh 15 to 30 pounds. Heavy tackle and nearly exclusively a charter boat fishery. Trolled with feathered jigs or caught on live baitfish. Rare.

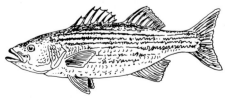

Striped Bass: Not found north of the Columbia River, Northwest stripers were introduced in 1879 from the East Coast and are

Sharks of Northwest Coastal Waters

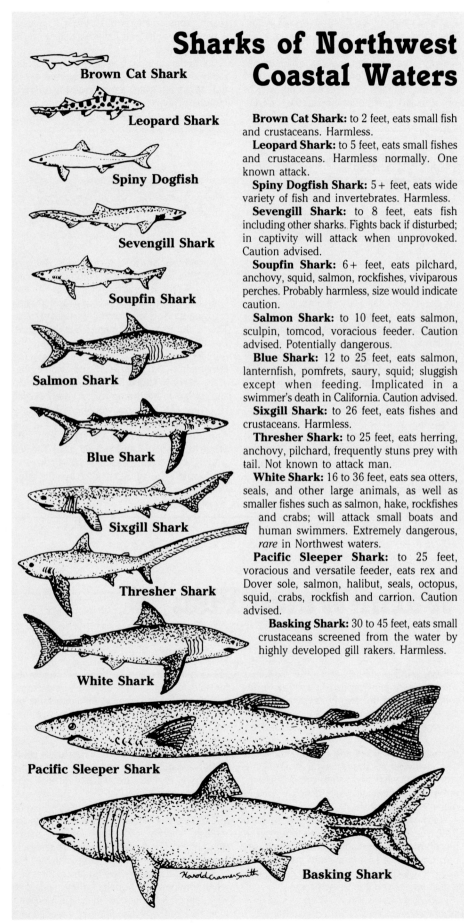

Brown Cat Shark: to 2 feet, eats small fish and crustaceans. Harmless.

Leopard Shark: to 5 feet, eats small fishes and crustaceans. Harmless normally. One known attack.

Spiny Dogfish Shark: 5+ feet, eats wide variety of fish and invertebrates. Harmless.

Sevengill Shark: to 8 feet, eats fish including other sharks. Fights back if disturbed; in captivity will attack when unprovoked. Caution advised.

Soupfin Shark: 6+ feet, eats pilchard, anchovy, squid, salmon, rockfishes, viviparous perches. Probably harmless, size would indicate caution.

Salmon Shark: to 10 feet, eats salmon, sculpin, tomcod, voracious feeder. Caution advised. Potentially dangerous.

Blue Shark: 12 to 25 feet, eats salmon, lanternfish, pomfrets, saury, squid; sluggish except when feeding. Implicated in a swimmer's death in California. Caution advised.

Sixgill Shark: to 26 feet, eats fishes and crustaceans. Harmless.

Thresher Shark: to 25 feet, eats herring, anchovy, pilchard, frequently stuns prey with tail. Not known to attack man.

White Shark: 16 to 36 feet, eats sea otters, seals, and other large animals, as well as smaller fishes such as salmon, hake, rockfishes and crabs; will attack small boats and human swimmers. Extremely dangerous, *rare* in Northwest waters.

Pacific Sleeper Shark: to 25 feet, voracious and versatile feeder, eats rex and Dover sole, salmon, halibut, seals, octopus, squid, crabs, rockfish and carrion. Caution advised.

Basking Shark: 30 to 45 feet, eats small crustaceans screened from the water by highly developed gill rakers. Harmless.

fished primarily in northern California, Coos Bay, and Umpqua and Smith rivers of Oregon. They weigh up to 125 pounds and are commonly caught between 10 and 40 pounds. Usually fished in river mouths and estuaries on trolled plugs, or jigs, occasionally streamer flies. Hard fighters. Stripers are long, narrow fish with dark green coloration on the back and distinctive black stripes with a white underside. Rare.

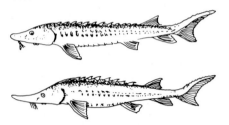

Sturgeon: Two species of sturgeon inhabit salt water in the Northwest, the giant white and the green. The white is the primary sportfishing target, living in large slow coastal rivers of British Columbia, Washington, Oregon and California. It is also caught in Idaho's Snake River system. Grows to more than 1,300 pounds, but the larger, brood stock are now protected in most waters. Catches are typically limited to fish between 3 and 6 feet long. Caught with bait, smelt, sand shrimp, herring, on the bottom of deep holes, frequently at river bends or along piling rows. The Columbia and Fraser rivers are the most productive sturgeon waters, although the Chehalis, Snohomish, Coos, Smith, Umpqua, Rogue, Klamath and Tillamook rivers can also provide action. White

sturgeon are hard fighters, known for long searing runs and tarponlike leaps. The meat is boneless, white and flaky. Excellent on the table. Common.

The green sturgeon is smaller than the white, rarely exceeding 7 feet, and spends most of its time in the salt water, rarely entering the river mouths. The meat is not as delicate or as appreciated as the white. Caught on same baits as the white. Rare.

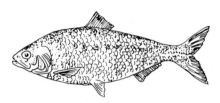

American Shad: The Chehalis River in Washington is approximately the northernmost range of these anadromous fish in any abundance, although they appear in small concentrations north to southeastern Alaska. The Columbia, Willamette, Sandy, Coos, Coquille, Siuslaw and Umpqua rivers are the primary range. Shad are introduced species, arriving from the East Coast, and is a member of the herring family. It ranges into the ocean and spawns in freshwater rivers. Rarely exceed 30 inches and normally weigh 2 to 6 pounds. Best fishing is during the spring spawning run, April through early July. A great fighting fish, prone to acrobatics and searing runs. Tackled with light to medium tackle, small spoons and shad darts. The meat is bony but flavorful. Common.

Smelt: A small fish, rarely exceeding 12 inches, there are two types of smelt in the Northwest; an anadromous smelt that moves up freshwater rivers in the spring to spawn, and beach spawner. The anadromous are netted with long-handled dip nets in selected river systems, while surf smelt are either scooped out of the breakers in A-frame nets or jigged with gangions supporting up to a dozen tiny golden hooks dressed with red or yellow thread. Runs arrive in rivers and beaches in late February and March. Some of the best beach netting is at night on high tides. Oily fish popular smoked or fried. Common.

Herring: Most often used for salmon or bottom fish bait, but large horse herring, 10 to 15 inches are popular for pickling or smoking. Herring are common in protected waters and can be caught on tiny-hooked herring jigs, scooped into small mesh dip nets or impaled on rakes festooned with dozens of tiny, sharp teeth. Balls of herring are commonly seen boiling to the surface, often forced up by fish feeding below.

Warm-Water Fish

Bass, panfish, catfish and other so-called warm-water or spiny-ray fish didn't swim Northwest waters until the late 1800s when fertilized fish eggs and fingerlings were shipped overland across the mountains from the Midwest. Less than a century later, warm-water species dominate many lakes and impoundments in the Northwest, in some instances displacing native trout, char and salmon and in others thriving in temperate water unsuited for the native cold-water fish.

Warm-water fish are still rare in most of British Columbia and Alaska, but thrive in the neighboring province and states. Where it was once impossible to find warm-water fish, it is now next to impossible to find a geographic region where you can't catch them.

Fish classed as warm-water species include several varieties with distinctive physical differ-

ences and one common bond — a tolerance for water temperatures warmer than most trout, salmon or char can tolerate. Although some are scaleless and soft bodied, most warm-water fish are protected by armorlike, large, transparent scales that have to be removed before the fish can be eaten. Their fins are supported by solid, sharply pointed tines, spearlike appendages that have earned this variety of fish the misnomer, spiny-rays.

The meat of most fish in this category is white and moderately dry, a flavorful contrast to the reddish, slightly oily meat of the native salmonoids. The flavor, however, is generally regarded as excellent. Many prefer it to the taste of native trout. Warm-water fish are at their best when trimmed into boneless fillets, sprinkled with pepper, rolled in corn meal and fried with a gentle hand in a hot skillet at the edge of a

lake. The meat is delicate and there is a tendency to overcook it.

There's another bonus for fishermen. As a rule, spiny-rays are school fish. Find one and you've found enough for a good mess. They have a stronger preference for the warm, shallow, brushy water than most trout, and favor submerged weed beds, brush piles, downed timber, docks or pilings. Because they school, are not especially selective about what they eat and can often be caught on simple freshwater fishing tackle, warm-water varieties are excellent targets for beginners. Action, except in the poorest of areas, is fast enough to hold the attention of impatient minds.

Live bait is the best lure, with earthworms, crickets, grasshoppers, small frogs, and minnows, where legal, leading. They also respond well to artificial action lures as small as $\frac{1}{32}$ ounce up to 6-inch plugs. Some of the standard artifical lures include small weighted jigs, ¼ ounce spinners, wobbling spoons, plastic worms and grubs from 1 to 8 inches long, and plugs designed to imitate baitfish or amphibians such as frogs. Except for the catfish family and to a lesser degree bass, warm-water fish are also excellent targets for winter ice fishermen.

While generally classified as warm-water or spiny-rays, these fish can be further divided into classifications of panfish, bass, perch and catfish.

Panfish

A physically descriptive classification for a variety of generally small, flat-sided fish that vaguely resemble the shape of a frying pan. There are several dozen species and subspecies of so-called panfish in North America. The ones of serious interest to sportfishermen include, bluegills, sunfish and crappie.

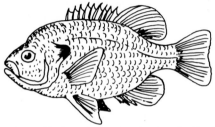

Bluegills have been described as the No. 1 sport fish in America, but that doesn't hold true in the Northwest where they are far less plentiful. Sometimes called brim, bream, or sunnies, "keepin' size" bluegills are between 5 and 8 inches long, narrow across the back and about two-thirds as wide as they are long. Their name comes from a deep blue tab at the rear of the gill flap. Gills are great sport on light tackle, are usually found less than 10 feet deep suspended around structure and bite readily on tidbits of bait such as worms or crickets on No. 8 bait hooks. They are also great sport on fly rods, and are rarely, if ever, selective. Nearly any No. 10 to 6 wet or dry fly will attract bluegills. Look for these school fish around shoreline lily pad beds over soft bottoms. Success is often best in May and early June when water temperatures near 60 degrees and the fish spawn in shovel-size depressions dug into the bottom, laying up to 50,000 eggs. They can be caught throughout summer. After the spawning period, evening fishing is usually best. Because bluegills are so prolific they often overpopulate lakes with stunted, undesirable

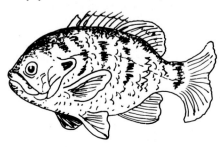

fish. If you catch a bluegill keep it. This is not a fish that benefits from catch-and-release management.

Common but less desirable cousins of the bluegill include **green** and **redear sunfish** and **pumpkinseeds** — which rarely grow longer than 5 inches. Green sunfish have a distinctively large mouth, and vivid green, orange and blue coloration. Their primary importance is as food for larger predator fish and they contribute little to the sport fishery.

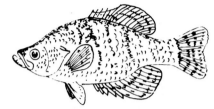

In the Northwest, it can be argued that the most popular panfish are not bluegills, but **crappies,** both black and white varieties. Crappies are larger than bluegills, averaging between 8 and 14 inches, with some of the rich desert country lakes in eastern Oregon and Washington kicking out crappie weighing 2 or more pounds. They are a whitish colored fish marked with black speckles, have a wide, paper-thin mouth with an underslung jaw and their favorite prey is minnows. Minnows, where legal, are the favorite bait, followed by red, yellow or white weighted jigs and streamer flies — all designed to imitate minnows.

Crappies are often in large schools and stratify at specific depths around submerged brush, stickups or weed beds. The big trick to catching them is to locate the precise depth where the school is holding. They are often voracious and easily caught, but can be selective and fickle. Crappie fishermen have found that if the bite dies on one lure, say a yellow jig, it can be refired by switching to another color, or different type of lure, perhaps trading the jig for a Colorado spinner sweetened with a fleck of white pork rind. Crappie spawn in May and June. Best fishing is generally early in the spring when the fish group in large schools before spawning. After spawning the schools break up into smaller units and the fish tend to go deeper.

Crappie are especially plentiful in the lowland lakes of Washington, Oregon and Idaho, and are not very numerous in lakes farther north, or at elevations above 3,000 feet.

Bass

Bass are at the top of the warm-water species in nearly everyone's estimation. They are hard-fighting, challenging to catch and respectable on the table. While still not as popular a game fish as they are in the East and Midwest regions, bass fishing popularity is exploding in the Northwest, especially in northern California, Oregon, Washington and Idaho. Bass fishing in Montana, British Columbia and Alberta is concentrated at far fewer fishing areas and attracts much less interest.

There are several varieties of Northwest bass, all introduced in the late 1800s and early 1900s.

In size, the **largemouth** is No. 1, growing to a maximum weight of about 12 pounds in Northwest waters. A respectable fish, but far lighter than the 17- to 20-pound records that come out of the warm bass waters of the southern United States. Three- to 5-pounders are relatively common. Several strains of largemouth have been introduced into Northwest waters, as biologists struggle to grow a larger largemouth, but it appears that the short warm weather seasons of the Northwest will continue to keep the growth of these warm-water fish in check.

Most bass fishermen concentrate on shoreline brush, docks and similar cover, points of land, flooded creek channels, weed beds, islands or underwater humps to find largemouth. Popular tackle includes 6- to 15-pound spinning and casting tackle, throwing rubber worms, leadhead jigs trailing pork rind, weedless spoons, neutral-buoyancy diving plugs, surface popping plugs and skirted spinner baits. Live bait fanciers prefer crayfish, nightcrawlers, small frogs and, where legal, large minnows suspended below a bobber.

Unlike the smallish largemouth bass, Northwestern **smallmouth** bass are among the largest in the nation. Washington's state-record smallmouth, 8 pounds, 12 ounces, is the largest in the Northwest and within 3 pounds, 3 ounces of the 11-pound, 15-ounce world-record smallmouth taken in 1955 at Tennessee's Dale Hollow Reservoir. Fishing experts have predicted the next world-record smallmouth will come from the Northwest, probably Washington, where fish managers are continually expanding the range of the fish.

Unlike warm-water loving largemouth, smallmouth bass thrive in the cooler lakes and rivers of the Northwest. The Snake and Grand Ronde rivers, shared by Washington, Oregon and Idaho, are among the finest and most productive in the country. The John Day, Columbia, and Okanogan are also good smallmouth waters. Although smallmouth thrive in the moving currents of rivers, the largest specimens generally come from upland lakes or lakelike river impoundments.

While largemouth tend to concentrate in slow, warm, sometimes discolored water, smallmouth prefer clear water at rocky points swept by current or wave action, rock ledges and gravel bars. Their favorite prey is crayfish, an excellent bait, along with nightcrawlers, grasshoppers and crickets. Most smallmouth fishermen use artificial lures such as, ¼-ounce spinners, leadhead jigs, small plastic worms, and diving plugs. Lure size is usually larger than those used for trout and smaller than standard largemouth lures. Fly-fishermen do well throwing streamers to imitate minnows or large nymph patterns. Smallmouth share the trout's appetite for insects.

Smallmouth fight hard, are prone to aerial acrobatics and have good stamina. They are, perhaps, the finest most challenging fighters of all the Northwest warm-water fish.

Smallmouth or Largemouth

Novice bass fishermen often find it difficult to recognize the difference between a largemouth bass and its smaller cousin, the smallmouth. Both are prominent in the Northwest.

Although smallmouth prefer moving, rocky water and largemouth favor slow, weedy areas, their ranges often overlap. As a general rule, largemouth are greenish colored with a prominent dark green lateral line along the side. Smallmouth are dark green, sometimes almost brown, with dark tiger stripes faintly appearing along the backline.

The accompanying diagram illustrates other identifying features.

Largemouth

Dark lateral stripe. Upper jawline extends beyond the eye. A clear separation between the spiny and soft portions of the two-humped dorsal fin.

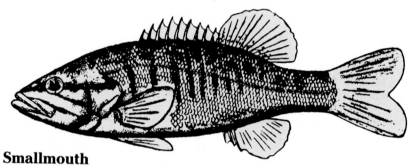

Smallmouth

Upper jawline ends at eye. Faint vertical tiger stripes along back. Spiny and soft portions of the dorsal fin. No separation between spiny and soft portions of dorsal fin.

perch is a trophy in nearly all Northwest waters. They are common to lowland lakes throughout the states and the southern regions of British Columbia and Alberta.

Perch collect in large schools and almost without exception are caught within an inch or two of the bottom. Earthworms, minnows where legal, and small pieces of cut baits or perch eyes are the best natural baits. They are also caught on ⅛-ounce or smaller leadhead jigs and small spinners. They are not hard fighters, but are fun fish to catch. The edges of weed beds are always good prospects for perch fishermen.

These little fish are easy to catch, especially good fish for novice anglers, and often available to shorebound fishermen watching tightlines from docks or along the shoreline. They spawn in May east of the Cascade Range and in June on the west side. The bite holds up well all summer and traditionally the biggest fish are caught in the fall when the schools move into deep water for the winter.

Yellow perch are excellent table fare when deep-fried. It's easiest to fillet the fish, removing the rib bones and skin the fillets to eliminate the need to scale.

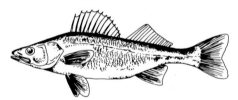

In addition to the largemouth and smallmouth action, bass fishermen also discover a few **rock bass** and fewer still **spotted bass.** Rock bass are dark fish with deep red eyes, rarely more than 10 inches long. They resemble a panfish with a large mouth and eyestrain, and are usually found in the same cover as largemouth bass. They are relatively rare throughout the Northwest. In this region, spotted bass are confined almost exclusively to northern California lakes. Sometimes called Kentucky bass, spotted bass are larger than rock bass, but smaller than smallmouth of the same age. A 3-pound fish is large.

A newcomer to the Northwest is the **white bass,** beginning to show up in catches in eastern Montana and California. White bass are

exciting school fish, with a decided prejudice for fast-moving lures that imitate frightened minnows. Darting streamer flies and small spinners are productive. These fish are generally small, averaging between 8 and 17 inches. Whites have not been reported in the Washington, Oregon, Idaho or Canadian regions.

White bass are streamlined fish, with silver flanks and dark pinstripes, closely resembling a miniature version of the anadromous striped bass found in coastal rivers of northern California and Oregon.

Perch

In the Northwest the perch family is represented by the popular and often overabundant little yellow perch, world-record class walleye, and sauger.

The most common are **yellow perch,** recognized by their green color, yellow and black stripes and bright orange fins. Perch are pan-sized fish averaging between 8 and 12 inches wherever they are found. A 2-pound

The giant cousin to the yellow perch is the **walleye,** a fairly recent import that is thriving in the Northwest, especially in the lower Columbia River area. Walleye have distinctive marble-sized eyes, green backs with dark splotches with a double hump of dorsal fins along the back and canine-type predatory teeth.

Walleye are well established in the lower Missouri, Yellowstone and Columbia rivers. They were practically unknown west of the Continental Divide before the late 1960s, when they mysteriously turned up in the Columbia River near Spokane, Washington. They have since spread throughout the Columbia and have demonstrated incredible growth, especially in the impoundments between Oregon and Washington. Fish managers have caught walleye in test nets near Biggs, Oregon, that exceeded the current world-record 25-pound walleye, and the number of 10-pound-plus fish commonly turning up in creel checks is attracting national attention.

Southern Alberta has a good population of walleye and so does central and eastern Montana. The lower Yellowstone River below Billings is walleye country. Some of the best fishing is in the Missouri River drainage at Fort Peck Reservoir and Lake Elwell. In Oregon these predator fish are confined to the Columbia River and Idaho has restricted the range to two outletless lakes, fearing the fish will spread into trout waters where they can't be controlled. In Washington, walleye have been distributed throughout the central and eastern lakes via irrigation water diverted from the Columbia River. Because they are predators, preying heavily on other fish, the walleye is being viewed by state agencies as a potential threat to native trout and salmon. Evidence appears slim, however, that walleye have much of an effect on salmonoids, yet state fisheries managers are not actively attempting to expand the walleye's range.

Walleye are bottom dwellers, with a preference for rocky reefs and boulder gardens. Fishing tackle is designed to bump along the bottom, and includes leadheaded jigs, Colorado spinners, large billed diving plugs and spoons. These lures are nearly always sweetened with nightcrawlers or strips of perch meat.

A close cousin of the walleye is the **sauger,** a fish similar in appearance, but generally smaller than a walleye. The Yellowstone River downstream from the Bighorn River to the Missouri River is probably the best sauger area in the Northwest. Few, if any, sauger are caught in Washington, Idaho, Oregon, California, British Columbia or Alaska. They are smallish fish, commonly weighing 1 or 2 pounds, and respond to the same lures as walleye.

Pike

The largest member of the pike family in the Northwest, **northern pike** are praised in the

central and eastern regions of North America as great game fish, but get short shrift in most of the Northwest, and more often viewed with alarm than praise. The best northern fishing takes place in the northern reaches of Alberta, British Columbia and interior Alaska. The Northwestern states try to discourage the spread of these predators fearing a detrimental impact on native salmon and trout populations. Montana has a spreading population of northerns in the Thompson Lakes area in the northwest corner and in Fort Peck Reservoir, Lake Elwell and the lower Milk River. Idaho supports a northern pike population in Lake Coeur d'Alene and tributaries and a few have managed to work their way into eastern Washington via the Coeur d'Alene drainage, an arrival the state Game Department views with more alarm than enthusiasm. Oregon does not list northern pike as an available sport fish.

Northerns are green lanky fish, with a long snout and teeth of a predator. They live almost exclusively on a diet of fish, but have also been known to clobber swimming mice, frogs and

ducklings. They fight viciously and are excellent targets for light tackle. Weighted wobbling spoons are the No. 1 lures.

Northerns are caught near weed beds and shallow shelves where they can ambush prey. Strange as it may seem, the best northern pike fishing in this region is in the land of salmon and char — Alaska. Northerns range from Alaska Peninsula streams pouring into Bristol Bay north to the Arctic coast. The Minto Lakes and Tolovana River near Fairbanks are excellent pike producers. Other good waters are Innoko River, Lake Minchumina, Kantishna River, Selawik Lake and the Kobuk River. Alaska northerns grow big. The state record is more than 38 pounds.

A smaller look-alike of the northern, **chain pickerel,** are rare in the Northwest. Washington acknowledges a few in the far eastern lakes, but generally these fish are unnoticed and unfished. Pickerel have ribbon-thin bodies usually less than 24 inches long, with the typical pike head, teeth and coloration.

Muskellunge, largest member of the pike family, are not found in the Northwest. Hybrid tiger-muskies have been introduced in Montana.

Catfish

Five species of catfish have been introduced in Northwest waters south of the Canadian border, and although acknowledged as powerful fighters and excellent tablefare, their popularity is generally confined to specific waters where a local following has developed.

All catfish have eight fleshy barbels (whiskers) near the mouth, and smooth, scaleless bodies, and generous but toothless mouths. Strong sharp spines are located on the leading edge of the pectoral and dorsal fins.

The most common catfish are bullheads, identified by coloration. The most plentiful is the **brown bullhead,** rarely getting larger than a pound in most waters, and often over-populating lakes, especially in western Washington, Oregon, and California to the extent of stunting growth to where they no longer interest anglers fishing for the pan. Brown bullheads have rounded tails, brown mottled backs and yellowish bellies. Less common, but similar species of bullheads, include the **yellow** and the **black** which are found in all of the Northwestern states except Alaska. Bullheads are usually caught at night on bait that includes dead fish, nightcrawlers, liver, and commercial scent baits.

The king of the Northwest catfish is the **channel catfish,** a strong adversary that grows to more than 30 pounds in the Northwest and is fast-growing in popularity. Channel cats are distinctly different from bullheads in appearance and character. Channels have a deeply forked tail, a smooth scaleless body that

is slate gray to silver with black specks. It's a streamlined fish that is more likely to be found in good trout water than in sluggish depths frequented by its bullhead cousins. They prefer cold, fairly clear water and have been caught on such decidedly uncatfishlike lures as Mayfly imitation dry flies, bucktail spinners, plastic worms and diving plugs. They will also gobble down a cluster of nightcrawlers, salmon eggs, crayfish, frogs or minnows. Where legal, live chub minnows suspended just above bottom are excellent channel catfish attractants. The Snake River is one of the best channel cat slots, but the lower and impounded reaches of most large rivers in the noncoastal areas have fishable populations. The fast, free-flowing streams draining directly into coastal waters do not support channels.

Idaho and eastern Oregon also have catchable populations of **flathead catfish,** but flatheads are relatively rare in the rest of the Northwest. They can weigh up to 40 pounds (100 pounds in the southern states) in the Northwest and are usually caught on bait in deep, muddy-bottomed areas in the slow, impounded lakes on major river systems. The Snake River in the vicinity of Brownlee Reservoir is one of the finest regional flathead fisheries.

Uncommon Freshwater Fish

The Northwest has several freshwater fish common only to specific regions, but very popular in those regions.

Perhaps the most unusual is Montana's **paddlefish,** a scaleless survivor of the dinosaur period, growing to more than 140 pounds. The paddlefish's most prominent physical characteristic is a flat snout, similar in shape to a paddle, roughly a third as long as the body. These fish are plankton feeders and in the Northwest are found only in the lower Missouri River near Fort Peck Reservoir and the lower Yellowstone River near Intake in eastern Montana where they are snagged during the annual late spring, early summer spawning run. The Yellowstone fishery at the Intake diversion dam is the most popular and state fish managers estimate that angler success runs as high as 75 percent.

Perhaps the ugliest freshwater fish in the Northwest, is the **burbot,** commonly called freshwater lingcod, lawyer, cusk, eelpout and occasionaly lush. They are smooth-skinned homely fish with brown mottling along the back and a white belly. The head is flat, with a single chin barbel, with a ridge of soft dorsal and anal fins that extends to the tail. They are found throughout the Northwest and the largest are usually caught in Alaska where 20-plus-pounders are frequently caught. Most burbot weigh less than 5 pounds. They are sluggish and caught primarily for food. Where legal, anglers often use multiple-hook setlines or trotlines baited with chunks of meat, nightcrawlers or fish. Winter is normally the best fishing.

Another uncommon freshwater game fish is Alaska's **sheefish,** a giant member of the whitefish family, not found outside of Alaska or extreme northern Canada. Sometimes called

inconnu (meaning unknown fish), shee, cony or shovelnose. Sheefish weigh up to 60 pounds and are commonly caught in the 10- to 20-pound class. Sheefish are slender with long tapering heads and a bright silver coloration that may appear purple immediately after being

caught. Scales are large, the mouth is thin skinned and herringlike. These features combined with the sheefish's penchant for spectacular leaps and line-searing runs have earned it the nickname "northern tarpon." In winter, sheefish collect in large schools and migrate slowly upstream to spawning areas, although they don't spawn until September. They are aggresive fish and will smash artifical lures out of irritation and hunger. Large spoons, spinners and bucktail streamer flies are popular. The meat is white and delicate. The best sheefish action usually requires floatplane access.

Paddlefish

One of the strangest fisheries in the Northwest takes place each spring in the roily waters of the lower Yellowstone and Missouri rivers. Fishermen stand shoulder-to-shoulder hurling large treble hooks into the murk hoping to snag a smooth-skinned relic of the dinosaur age.

The targets are paddlefish, prehistoric-appearing plankton feeders that along with sturgeon are among the oldest and strangest fish in the Northwest. The dominating features of a paddlefish are its size — Montana's state record is 142½ pounds — and the oarlike snout. The spatula-shaped snout is rigid, up to 2 feet long and serves as a specialized antenna that locates concentrations of food in the murky water it prefers. Paddlefish skin has been compared to a shark's — smooth, tough and scaleless, except for the upper lobe of the tail where a trace of primitive diamond-shaped scales are found. Paddlefish are boneless, with a cartilaginous skeleton (similar to sturgeon and shark) and the toothless mouth funnels plankton into comblike rakers.

They're a slow-growing fish. Males don't mature sexually until they're seven years old,

females 12 to 14 years old. Biologists know that paddlers can live more than 30 years, and while they haven't confirmed it, they believe some may live twice that long.

Paddlefish may be the oldest big animals surviving in North America, according to the Montana Fish, Wildlife and Parks Department. Fossil remains reveal that paddles lived in Montana for millions of years. The skeletal remains of a paddlefish were found trapped inside the rib cage of a large duck-billed dinosaur unearthed in 1938 in McCone County, Montana. The dinosaur skeleton was 65 million years old. Scientists believe the dinosaur died in the water and the paddlefish, along with a sturgeon, swam inside the remains, became trapped in the rib cage and along with the dinosaur were buried by silt. The Montana skeleton is the world's oldest paddlefish.

Today, paddlefish live in only two parts of the world; the Mississippi River drainage of North America and the Yangtze River drainage of China.

Several areas have emerged as prime paddle-fishing waters during the spawning run in May,

June and July. The major snagging area is a short stretch of the Yellowstone River near Glendive at the Intake Diversion Dam. Yellowstone paddlers are also taken at the mouths of the Tongue and Powder rivers and the Forsyth Diversion Dam. In these areas they are snagged with heavy treble hooks. In the Missouri River the top spots are near Fort Peck Reservoir in the Fred Robinson Bridge area 70 miles southwest of Malta, and the dredge cuts near Park Grove Bridge just below the small town of Fort Peck. In the Fort Peck dredge cuts some paddlefish fanciers are using bows and barbed fishing arrows to shoot paddlers in the shallows.

Paddlers are also taken in the Nashua-Wolf Point area of the Missouri River.

Paddlefish meat, a boneless white meat, is compared to the taste of swordfish and considered excellent by most standards. The trick is to remove the red muscular tissue that surrounds the meat and to withdraw the notochord from the cartilaginous spinal column. The notochord, an elastic ropelike substance, will taint the meat if severed.

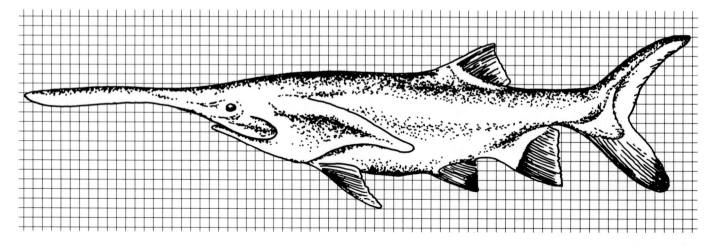

Northwest Sturgeon

Strong enough to drown a wide-eyed harness horse or sink a cedar fishing boat, Northwest river sturgeon are legends growing from a bloodline running straight to the age of dinosaurs.

Giant white sturgeon have been caught in Northwest waters for centuries, first by nomadic Indian tribes, later by pioneer settlers who used their horses to drag the behemoths out of the water and up the muddy riverbank. More than one legend tells of these powerful fish winning the tug-of-war, dragging the slipping, thrashing horse into the river.

Sturgeon have changed little since their cousins swam with prehistoric animals, and if anything, are a more popular sport fish today than ever. The largest white sturgeon on record is an 1,800-pound Snake River fish. It is doubtful that any that size exist today, but there are a lot of Northwest sturgeon that will bottom-out a 200-pound scale and stretch a tape measure well past 10 feet. According to the Washington Department of Fisheries, some reach 20 feet.

In the early days of Northwest river settlements, sturgeon anglers commonly hauled out "river monsters" weighing a half ton and state historical groups pridefully publish turn-of-the-century photos of felt-hatted boatmen dwarfed by giant sturgeon reposing in buckboards or suspended from sturdy block-and-tackle rigs. Sturgeon can be anadromous, migrating to and from salt water, and nearly all of the giant sturgeon stories flow from rivers draining directly into the Pacific Ocean.

The most famous sturgeon river is the Snake which even today can produce tremendously large sturgeon, all of which are released.

Anglers on the Columbia River are restricted to keeping only sturgeon between 3 and 6 feet long. Larger fish are kicked back to guarantee spawning. The Columbia is the most productive catch-and-keep river in the Northwest. In 1985 nearly 30,000 white sturgeon were caught by sportfishermen, mostly between Bonneville Dam and the Megler-Astoria bridge. Other famous sturgeon rivers include Oregon's Umpqua, Tillamook, Rogue and Klamath; Washington's Chehalis, Willapa, Grays and Naselle; and British Columbia's Fraser and Thompson.

Sturgeon are not only the largest freshwater fish, and one of the oldest, but also one of the gentlest. Whites are strictly bottom feeders, vacuuming mud and silt with a powerful suctioning mouth in search of crustaceans, mollusks and insect larvae.

White sturgeon are famous table fare, producing a delicate white meat that can be smoked, fried, poached or baked . . . there is no wrong way to prepare sturgeon. Another culinary plus with these giant fish is the lack

632 pounds, 10-feet 11-inches. Idaho Historical Society

of wastage. Their bodies are formed around a cartilaginous skeleton. No bones to bother with.

On sporting tackle, sturgeon are powerful, surprising fish, sometimes startling newcomers by cartwheeling out of the water like a salmon and then exploding on reel-searing runs.

Whites aren't the only Northwest sturgeon. The green sturgeon is occasionally caught in brackish estuary areas. Greens are smaller than whites, not as flavorful and rarely enter river systems.

Northwest anglers may no longer be dragging giant fish out of the river with teams or harness horses, and the 20-footer may be the rarest fish in the region, but white sturgeon continue to run the powerful Northwest rivers and, if anything, are attracting more attention than ever before. In Washington alone, anglers annually catch 44,000 legal-size sturgeon and the idea of tackling a monstrous survivor of the dinosaur era is spreading every year.

Sportfishing

Fishing Washington

International angling authority A.J. McClane once described the rich fishing resources in Washington as, "an angler's dream come true." There are few who would argue. In a few hours an angler can tackle the giants of the Pacific Ocean, wade a white-water steelhead river, drop a dry fly on the surface of a snow-fed mountain lake, troll sprawling reservoirs for giant char, flip plastic worms to bass, jig for world-record walleye, fill a bucket with perch, lock line with a sturgeon, fillet a true cod, net smelt, challenge giant catfish, brawl with hook-jawed browns, snag shad, trap crabs, rake clams, cast to rising rainbow. . . .

The list could continue almost indefinitely, changing as often as the terrain, the climate and the angler's inclination and ability. There are few fishermen who travel Washington's highways a second time without a fishing rod and enough lures to take advantage of spontaneous opportunties.

With a topography that ranges from coastal rain forest to densely wooded foothills, snow-crowned alpine basins to sage and sand deserts, there are dozens of salt- and freshwater species of game fish and literally hundreds of different fishing techniques. There are few angling demands that can't be satisfied in Washington.

Fishing, here, is a 365-day proposition. On the west side of the state anglers can ply open water every day of the year. Low-lying trout and spiny-ray lakes in the foothills of the Cascades and Olympics rarely freeze in the moderate winter temperatures, steelhead rivers run clear, and the protected reaches of Puget Sound salt water offer 12 months of fine salmon and bottom fishing. Some of the best salmon fishing in the sound occurs in December and January — traditionally the coldest months. East of the Cascades, where winters can be severe, ice fishing is popular and the rivers that are ice free offer steelhead and mountain whitefish.

A generally observed opening and closing date continues to be enforced for certain lakes and streams, but an increasing number of waters are being converted to year-round fisheries. The traditional "opening day" for freshwater lakes is the third Sunday in April. The historic western Washington river opener takes place on Memorial Day weekend, with closures occurring at the end of November. In the last few years, however, fish managers have aimed at designing specific regulations for specific waters, slowly abandoning the generalized statewide management program, resulting in more year-round fishing waters.

Washington's fishing seasons, tackle restrictions, bag limits and regulations are among the most complicated in the country. It has also become customary in the past few years for the

Winter steelheader (left). Charterboat fisherman (above) bound for Pacific salmon cross the Westport Bar. By Terry W. Sheely

By Dave Engerbretson

Why?

"Why do you do it?" I ask him. "Why do you spend almost every day fishing?"

"Well," he said, "I wrote it down once. I'll go find it and say it for you if you'd like." He did, and it went like this:

"I fish because I love to. Because I love the environs where trout are found, which are invariably beautiful, and hate the environs where crowds of people are found, which are invariably ugly. Because in a world where most men seem to spend their lives doing things they hate, my fishing is at once an endless source of delight and an act of small rebellion. Because trout do not lie or cheat and cannot be bought or bribed, or impressed by power, but respond only to quietude and humility, and endless patience. Because I suspect that men are going along this way for the last time and I for one don't want to waste the trip. Because, mercifully, there are no telephones on trout waters. Because only in the woods can I find solitude without loneliness. Because bourbon out of an old tin cup always tastes better out there. Because maybe one day I will catch a mermaid. And finally, not because I regard fishing as being so terribly important, but because I suspect that so many of the other concerns of men are equally unimportant and not nearly so much fun. Amen."

Judge John Voelker, author Trout Madness

state to enact so-called emergency regulations in midseason, superceding regulations printed in the seasonal rule summary. These emergency rule changes are sometimes posted at fishing access sites but don't depend on it. If in doubt, ask.

Freshwater Fishing

The most popular sport fish are trout; rainbow, brook, brown and cutthroat. **Rainbow** are heavily stocked throughout the Evergreen State. East of the Cascades rainbows are stocked in lakes and streams, while on the west side of the state trout plants are restricted primarily to lakes. The state's best rainbow fishing is generally acknowledged to be from the east slope of the Cascades across the Columbia Basin to Idaho. The fertile lakes in the Okanogan and Spokane regions offer excellent catches of husky rainbow. Action is best in spring and early summer, but rainbow can be caught all summer and fall. Most rivers in Washington offer rainbow, but the best and biggest fish are taken from lakes. There are a few good rainbow rivers, however. Chief is the Yakima paralleled by Interstate 90 and Interstate 82. Also good are the Wenatchee, Icicle, Nason, Chiwawa, Naches, Colville, upper Spokane, Touchet, Tucannon and Palouse.

Two clusters of productive rainbow lakes attract considerable angler attention in the spring at Sun Lakes Recreation Area just north of Ephrata on Highway 17 and in the Desert Lakes Recreation Area between Othello and O'Sullivan Reservoir. Dozens of small trout lakes are trapped in rocky coulee walls at both areas, and rank as some of the most productive trout waters in the state, especially in March, April and May.

In western Washington planted rainbow are generally, but not always smaller than east side trout, and are confined largely to the hundreds of lakes dotting the foothills, most only a few hundred acres or less in size. The lakes planted on a put-and-take basis are often "fished out" by the middle of May; however put-and-take programs are being phased out in favor of fry-planting, midseason supplemental stocking programs and year-round fishing seasons maintaining a better summer-long fishing program. Western Washington streams are reserved for native rainbow and cutthroat, sea-run cutthroat and anadromous salmon and steelhead. Anadromous salmon, steelhead and sea-run cutthroat dominate the lower reaches of all rivers running directly to salt water on the west side of the Cascade Range and Olympic Peninsula. Resident rainbow and cutthroat are confined to those rare streams isolated from salt water by impassable dams or falls. Only a few western Washington streams are stocked with catchable rainbow and most of these are located in the upper Cowlitz River drainage.

The state can produce large rainbow. The Washington record is a 22-pound, 8-ounce monster caught in Waitts Lake. Roosevelt, Moses, O'Sullivan, Washington, Soda and many other lakes regularly produce 5-pound-plus rainbow.

Washington boasts some of the finest and varied **cutthroat** fishing in the West, with five varieties of these slash-jawed trout represented. Coastal streams and rivers support good populations of the sea-run variety; Lahontan cutthroat have been stocked in several high-alkaline lakes in the eastern part of the state; Montana black spots and Yellowstone cutthroat inhabit any of the thousands of remote high mountain as well as lowland lakes; and the Crescenti, a giant of the species, lives only in Lake Crescent west of Port Angeles. Sea-runs are silvery and the famous bright red throat slash may be faint. There is excellent sea-run cutthroat fishing in the southwest rivers in the spring and again in the fall during and after the salmon spawning runs. The best sea-run rivers are on the Olympic Peninsula and along the coast in the Grays Harbor, Willapa

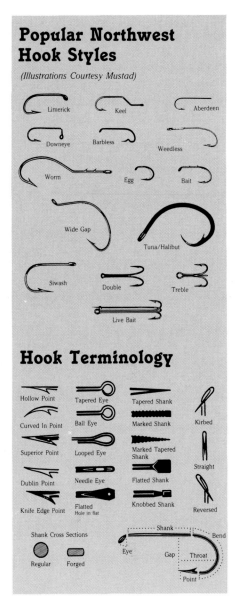

Popular Northwest Hook Styles

(Illustrations Courtesy Mustad)

Limerick — Keel — Aberdeen
Downeye — Barbless — Weedless
Worm — Egg — Bait
Wide Gap — Tuna/Halibut
Siwash — Double — Treble
Live Bait

Hook Terminology

Hollow Point — Tapered Eye — Tapered Shank — Kirbed
Curved In Point — Ball Eye — Marked Shank
Superior Point — Looped Eye — Marked Tapered Shank — Straight
Dublin Point — Needle Eye — Flatted Shank
Knife Edge Point — Flatted Hole in flat — Knobbed Shank — Reversed

Shank Cross Sections
Regular — Forged

Shank — Bend
Eye — Gap — Throat
Point

Upper Rivord Lake in the Glacier Peak Wilderness is typical of the hundreds of alpine cutthroat lakes in Washington's Cascade Mountains. By Terry W. Sheely

77

Washington's Main Fishing Rivers & Lakes

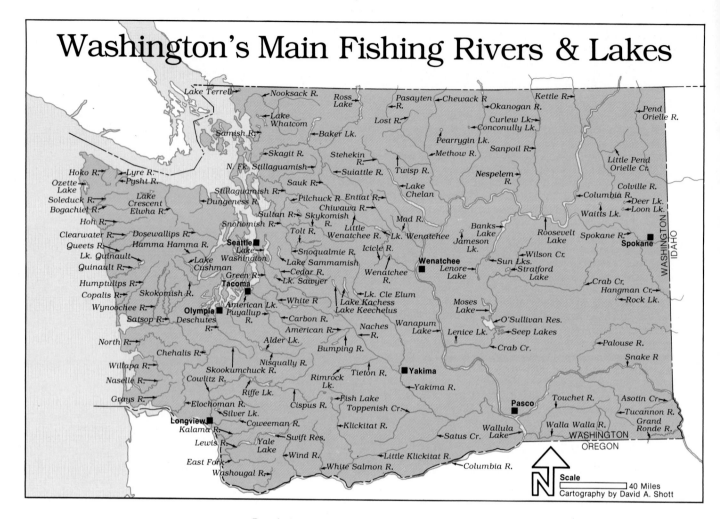

Lake Terrell
Nooksack R.
Ross Lake
Pasayten R.
Chewack R.
Kettle R.
Pend Orielle R.
Lake Whatcom
Samish R.
Baker Lk.
Lost R.
Okanogan R.
Curlew Lks.
Conconully Lk.
Little Pend Orielle Cr.
Pearrygin Lk.
Skagit R.
Stehekin R.
Methow R.
Sanpoil R.
Hoko R.
Lyre R.
Pysht R.
N. Fk. Stillaguamish
Suiattle R.
Twisp R.
Nespelem R.
Colville R.
Ozette Lake
Sauk R.
Lake Chelan
Columbia R.
Deer Lk.
Soleduck R.
Lake Crescent
Stillaguamish R.
Pilchuck R.
Entiat R.
Loon Lk.
Bogachiet R.
Elwha R.
Dungeness R.
Chiwawa R.
Banks Lake
Waitts Lk.
Hoh R.
Sultan R.
Skykomish R.
Little Wenatchee R.
Lk. Wenatchee
Jameson Lk.
Roosevelt Lake
Spokane R.
Spokane
Clearwater R.
Snohomish R.
Tolt R.
Mad R.
Dosewallips R.
Hamma Hamma R.
Seattle
Lake
Icicle R.
Wenatchee
Wilson Cr.
Queets R.
Snoqualmie R.
Sun Lks.
Lk. Quinault
Lake Washington
Lake Sammamish
Wenatchee R.
Lenore Lake
Stratford Lake
Quinault R.
Cushman
Cedar R.
Lk. Sawyer
Crab Cr.
Green R.
Tacoma
Hangman Cr.
Humptulips R.
White R.
Lk. Cle Elum
Moses Lake
Rock Lk.
Copalis R.
Skokomish R.
American Lk.
Lake Kachess
Lake Keechelus
Wynoochee R.
Olympia
Puyallup R.
Carbon R.
Wanapum Lake
O'Sullivan Res.
Satsop R.
Deschutes R.
American R.
Naches R.
Lenice Lk.
Seep Lakes
Palouse R.
North R.
Alder Lk.
Bumping R.
Crab Cr.
Snake R.
Chehalis R.
Nisqually R.
Willapa R.
Skookumchuck R.
Tieton R.
Yakima
Naselle R.
Cowlitz R.
Rimrock Lk.
Touchet R.
Asotin Cr.
Grays R.
Riffe Lk.
Cispus R.
Fish Lake
Yakima R.
Tucannon R.
Elochoman R.
Toppenish Cr.
Pasco
Walla Walla R.
Grand Ronde R.
Silver Lk.
Klickitat R.
Longview
Coweeman R.
Satus Cr.
Wallula Lake
WASHINGTON
Kalama R.
Swift Res.
OREGON
Lewis R.
Yale Lake
Wind R.
Little Klickitat R.
East Fork
White Salmon R.
Columbia R.
Washougal R.

WASHINGTON
IDAHO

Scale
40 Miles
Cartography by David A. Shott

Bay drainages. Action can be outstanding for anglers with fly rods and light spin tackle, yet this is one of the most ignored fisheries in the state. The best sea-run rivers are several hours driving time from the major Washington metropolitan areas and during the peak of the sea-run migration most local anglers are concentrating on catching the much-larger salmon.

One of the most exotic cutthroat is the Lahontan strain, a colorful, fast-growing fish that is thriving in heavily alkaline lakes. Native of Nevada's Pyramid Lake, Lahontans can tolerate water that is too alkaline to support other trout. They have been introduced in several barren alkaline lakes, most notably Lenore and Grimes, north of Ephrata, where trophy fisheries have developed. Five- to 10-pounders are not uncommon in Lenore. Buoyed by the success of the Lenore plant, biologists are stocking the Lahontan strain in other lakes throughout the state. The state cutthroat records stand at sea-runs, 6 pounds and Crescenti, 12 pounds.

Brook trout, char actually, are plentiful but usually small. Many high lakes are overpopulated with stunted 5- to 8-inch brooks, and they have worked their way into most of the state's stream systems. The biggest brook trout are caught in the northeastern part of Washington above Spokane. The record is a 7-pound, 5-ounce brookie caught in Goose Lake, but in most areas a 3-pounder is considered a trophy catch.

Until the mid-1980s **brown trout** were restricted to a few select lakes in central and eastern Washington, but an ambitous stocking program has seen the range of these legendary fighters extended throughout the state, including Green Lake, in the heart of Seattle. The state record is a 22-pound brown caught at Sullivan Lake in the remote northeast corner of the state. Some of the best brown trout fishing now is in the lakes of Dry Falls, Fish (near Leavenworth), Soda, Rock, Waitts, Wannacut, Silver (near Tacoma) and Lacamas. The Palouse, Pend Oreille, Colville, Touchet and Tucannon rivers and Crab Creek also boast fair populations of brown trout. While not yet widespread, the range of the brown trout is expanding in Washington.

The state's largest inland trout is actually a char, the **lake trout,** commonly called mackinaw. Macks are not widely distributed in Washington and the best fishing is restricted to just two lakes, Loon and Deer, both northwest of Spokane. Loon holds the state record, a 30-pound, 4-ounce trophy. Macks are commonly caught near the surface before Memorial Day but drop to the deepest spot on the bottom during warm weather. Macks are also caught in Lake Chelan, Bead, Bonaparte, Isabel, Eightmile and Cle Elum lakes.

The rarest trout is the **golden,** imported to a few remote high mountain lakes in the Cascade Range, and rarely caught by sportfishermen. Almost as rare as goldens are **grayling,** which

Winter steelheading on the Tolt River (left). Rainbow trout (above) are the most popular gamefish in Washington.
By Terry W. Sheely

are now found only in one lake, Granite in Skagit County and are fully protected by state law. The colorful coastal **Dolly Varden** and its landlocked cousin the **bull trout** can be caught in many areas of the state. The best area for sea-going dollies is north of Seattle, and rivers draining the west slope of the Olympic Peninsula. The Skagit River and a major tributary, the Sauk, are excellent Dolly Varden producers during the salmon spawning season. The Stillaguamish and Skykomish also produce these spotted char, and September is considered the best month. The state record Dolly Varden, in fact, was caught in the Skykomish and weighed 10 pounds. On the Peninsula, good catches of dollies are boated in the Hoh, Bogachiel, Queets and Quinault rivers.

Landlocked Dolly Varden are now recognized as bull trout, and the record here is 22 pounds, 8 ounces — a Tieton River catch. Cle Elum Reservoir, Kachees and Keechelus reservoirs on Interstate 90 near Snoqualmie Pass, plus Lake Wenatchee, White River, Wenatchee River, Rimrock Lake and the Tieton River are good places to try for bull trout. In recent years, however, the number of bull trout has dropped and special restrictions are sometimes imposed to limit the catch.

Trout-sized landlocked salmon, **kokanee** (sockeye) and **silvers** (coho) are favorite targets for lake fishermen. Caught by trolling small red spoons or bait behind strings of attractor blades or by still-fishing with tiny bits of worm or fly larvae, these salmon are hard fighters, notorious school fish and outstanding table fare. Best action is from late May through August. Silvers and kokanee have been stocked in nearly every large lake and dozens of smaller waters.

Some of the most popular are Washington, Stevens, Summit, Alder, Samish, Yale, Merwin, Bead, Banks, O'Sullivan, Deer, Loon, Rimrock, Chelan, American, Whatcom, Goodwin, Mayfield, Riffe, Wenatchee, Sawyer, Baker and Ross. Most kokanee and silvers average 8 to 14 inches. The state record is only a little over 4 pounds. There is, however, a bonus limit in effect on many lakes allowing anglers 16 fish per day, double the normal limit. Chumming with bait eggs or specially prepared feeds is generally banned in Washington, but is allowed at some of the more prominent salmon lakes.

Until 1880 panfish, perch and bass were unknown in Washington, but they are rapidly making up for lost time. Panfish are now more popular than trout in many lakes. Smallmouth bass and the most recent introduction, walleye, are attracting national interest. Largemouth bass have spread throughout the state, and northern pike are beginning to show up in the Spokane and Snake river drainages.

Yellow perch and **white and black crappie** are the most popular panfish with excellent distribution statewide, especially in those lakes open on a year-round basis. The No. 1 perch and crappie producer is Potholes (O'Sullivan) Reservoir south of Moses Lake. Anglers routinely haul buckets of panfish out of the lake and into the freezer here year-round.

Bluegills, often billed as the most popular fish in the United States, are strangely in short supply in the panfish-rich Everegreen State. Anglers in western and central Washington have to look long and fish hard to fill a platter with Washington bluegills. Most spiny-ray lakes have a fair supply of stunted sunfish, but not their more desirable cousin. The best spots for big bluegill include Moses Lake, Potholes, Eloika, Silver (near Longview), Pend Oreille River and Long Lake on the Spokane River. Even less important than bluegills to panfishermen are the crappie-sized **warmouth** and **rock bass** found in only a handful of panfish lakes and usually caught incidentally by crappie or bass anglers.

Quick, Scaleless Fish Fillets

A. Using a sharp knife with a thin, flexible blade, cut behind gill cover down to backbone.

B. Turn blade toward tail and cut along the backbone with knife point skimming top of the rib cage.

C. When knife passes last rib, push the blade completely through fish, exiting near anal passage and continue to follow backbone to tail. Cut fillet free.

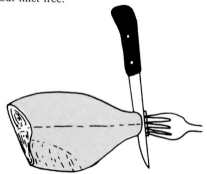

D. Lay fillet skin-side down, secure tail end of skin to cleaning board with a fork or fingernail and skin by sliding knife between skin and flesh and pushing toward head while slightly angling blade.

(Artwork courtesy of Idaho Fish and Game Deptartment)

The spiny-ray fish making the biggest splash in Washington, however, is the **walleye,** a fairly recent arrival that appears to grow unusually large in Northwest waters. It has attracted national angling attention with reports of 18-pound-plus fish. Walleye weren't even classed as game fish in Washington until 1970 and limits weren't imposed until 1974 when the Department of Wildlife received complaints of some fishing parties catching up to 300 fish per trip. Now carefully regulated, walleye are a premier game fish, with the biggest fish coming from the Lake Celilo reach of the Columbia River near the Highway 97 bridge. Distribution of walleye follows the winding course of the Columbia River, and excludes nearly all of western Washington. Walleye have spread through the Columbia from Lake Roosevelt west of Spokane downstream to Bonneville Dam and beyond. Popular Columbia walleye areas are at the mouth of the Spokane River through Lake Roosevelt and Rufus Woods Lake to Rock Island Dam. The midsection of the Columbia between Rock Island and McNary is generally poor walleye water, but from McNary downstream to The Dalles Dam anglers enjoy some of the finest walleye action in the world.

Walleye are not limited to the Columbia, however. Good walleye catches are also reported in I-82 Pond near Yakima, Soda Lake, Potholes Reservoir, Moses Lake, Billy Clapp Lake, Banks Lake and Pend Oreille River. Guided fishing trips are offered in the top areas.

In the past 20 years bass fishing has also taken a firm grip on Washington, once the exclusive domain of trout and salmon sport. **Largemouth bass** are widely distributed, but generally smaller than those caught in more southerly western states. The state record is just 11 pounds, 9 ounces, only half as big as the world's record, but anglers will find plenty of 2- to 6-pound largemouth. The best largemouth waters are in the Columbia Basin east to the Spokane area. The cooler waters of western Washington support plenty of largemouth in hundreds of lakes, but they average a tad smaller than those in the arid, warmer regions. The west side exceptions are shallow, fertile Silver Lake north of Longview and the Columbia River sloughs near Vancouver.

East of the Cascades, standout largemouth waters include, Potholes Reservoir, Moses, Banks, Eloika, Long, Newman, Liberty, Scootenay and numerous ponds in the Desert Lakes Recreation Area north of Othello. On the west side of the Cascades, excellent largemouth lakes include Patterson, Long, Mason, Duck, Sawyer, Washington, Sammamish, Kapowsin, Big, Campbell, Black, Goodwin and sloughs along the Chehalis River. Lowland lakes with largemouth outnumber those exclusively devoted to trout and probably the quickest way for travelers to get the lowdown on good nearby largemouth waters stop at the local tackle store or call the regional game department information office.

While Washington's largemouth bass may not earn national ranking, its **smallmouth bass** fishery does. The state record smallmouth weighed 8 pounds, 12 ounces — just 3 pounds lighter than the world's record. Smallmouth are well distributed, especially in the Columbia and Snake river drainages. The Snake River reservoirs above Pasco are well-endowed with excellent smallmouth areas. Concentrate on Lower Granite, Lake Bryan, Lake Sacajawea, Lower Monumental and Lyons Ferry. Other excellent smallmouth prospects are Potholes and Banks Lake, Osoyoos, Moses, Island, Okanogan River, Samammish, Mayfield, Palmer and Washington. Smallmouth thrive in the cool water and pea gravel environment that typifies many of Washington's low lakes and their range is being steadily expanded. Bass guides are relatively rare in Washington, but are available in a few of the premium spots.

Probably the most overlooked of Washington's freshwater fish are the catfish. Good numbers of foot-long **brown bullheads** (not to be confused with bullhead sculpin) can be caught in many western Washington lakes by bait fishermen. Although they are reasonably abundant in all year-round lakes and many so-called "trout only" waters, few anglers fish for these tasty bottom dwellers. More popular but not nearly as widespread are the **channel catfish.** The state record is 31 pounds. The state's best channel catfish area is in the Pasco-Richland-Kennewick area. The Snake, lower Walla Walla and Yakima rivers attract three-quarters of the state's channel catfish pressure. The best area to catch a channel is in the Walla Walla just above the confluence with the Columbia at Wallula.

The No. 1 river fish in Washington is the legendary **steelhead,** a sea-going rainbow trout common to all western Washington, Olympic Peninsula and many eastern Washington rivers.

Steelhead are hatched in fresh water, migrate to the fertile Pacific to grow and return to the natal streams two to three years later as 6- to 30-plus-pound adults ready to spawn. Unlike salmon, steelhead do not necessarily die after spawning, although the number that survive the rigors of adjusting from salt to fresh water, predator attacks, infection or injury and spawning stress is only from 1 to 6 percent.

Washington steelhead can be caught any month of the year, depending on what river you're fishing. There are two basic steelhead; those that return to spawning rivers in winter and those that come back in summer. Some of the southwest rivers also have a so-called "spring" steelhead that returns after the winter fish and before the summer-runs. Both summer and winter fish are found in most of the rivers of Puget Sound, the Olympic Peninsula and southwest counties. Steelhead seasons spelled out in the regulations booklet are structured to take advantage of the peak of the runs.

Steelhead also can be challenged in eastern Washington tributaries of the Columbia. The Snake, Yakima, Methow, Wenatchee, Touchet, Walla Walla, Okanogan, Naches, Icicle and Entiat are the most popular. Steelhead in eastern Washington rivers are all summer-runs, but it's usually late fall or winter before they reach their home rivers.

Summer steelheading on the Green River east of Seattle. By Terry W. Sheely

The state tabs the annual sport catch at roughly 175,000 steelhead, split 115,000 winter-runs and 60,000 summer fish — more than any other Northwest steelhead producer. Commercial gill nets manned by treaty Indian tribes accounted for another 100,000 steelhead trout.

Steelhead are notoriously wary, difficult to catch, and require fairly specialized tackle and techniques. Inexperienced anglers often book river float trips with licensed guides who operate either double-ended McKenzie-style drift boats, or flat-bottomed, shallow-draft boats called sleds powered by outboards equipped with jet propulsion units. Jet sleds are used on the larger rivers, while the smaller and often rougher rivers are fished from drift boats.

The 10 most productive winter rivers include the Cowlitz, Puyallup, Green, Elochoman, Skagit, Skykomish, Hoh, Bogachiel, East Fork Lewis and Elwha. Top 10 summer-run producers are the Snake at Lower Granite, Methow, Columbia at Ringold, Wells, Kalama, North Fork Lewis, Skykomish, Big White Salmon and East Fork Lewis.

Winter-runs begin showing in western Washington rivers in November and are heavily fished through February and in many cases March and April. Summer-runs usually begin appearing about Memorial Day and the heaviest catches are registered in July, August and September. River access along steelhead streams is rarely a problem since most of the main rivers are paralleled by roads, and offer state or county access sites and improved boat launches.

Saltwater Fishing

With 3,026 miles of tidal coastline, Washington boasts some of the finest and most diversified saltwater fishing in North America, a recreational resource complemented by outstanding shellfishing opportunities, and serviced by an excellent charter and resort industry. Excellent salmon, bottom fishing, crabbing and shellfishing takes place within sight of the lights of Seattle, Everett and Tacoma.

Essentially the state is divided into five recreational regions, the Columbia River mouth, Pacific coastline (including Willapa Bay and Grays Harbor), the Strait of Juan de Fuca, Puget Sound (including Hood Canal) and the San Juan Islands. In those five regions are miles of open ocean, sand-swirled beaches, heaving surf, quiet bays, rock-walled islands, surging straits, protected points, sheltered harbors, complex estuaries and plunging fjords.

A gangion of bottomfish shrimp flies.
By Terry W. Sheely

Washington License Requirements

Fishing: If, when and where you need a fishing license in Washington depends on how old you are and what you're fishing for. Fresh- and saltwater license requirements vary with the species of fish and age of the angler. Freshwater and salmon fishing licenses are renewable on Jan. 1. Steelhead punch cards expire April 30.

A Department of Wildlife fishing license is required of all fishermen over 15 angling in fresh water except in Mount Rainier and Olympic national parks, where unlicensed fishing is allowed. A state fishing license is necessary, however, in North Cascades National Park, and steelhead punch cards are required when steelheading in Olympic National Park. Steelheaders are required to carry a Department of Wildlife general fishing license plus a steelhead punch card. (Only the punch card is required inside Olympic National Park.)

A license is required to fish in salt water. A Department of Fisheries salmon punch card is required to catch chinook, coho, chum, sockeye and pink salmon in salt and fresh water. The punch card is free to fishermen inside Olympic National Park, and anglers under 16 and over 70. The Department of Wildlife requires all fishermen, regardless of age, to have a general fishing license plus a steelhead punch card to steelhead in either salt or fresh water. Sea-run cutthroat in salt and fresh water require a general fishing license from the wildlife department. The Department of Fisheries requires licenses to trap Hood Canal spotted shrimp, and dig razor clams on ocean beaches. Licenses are required to catch saltwater bottom fish, but not dig hard-shell clams, crabs and non-Hood Canal shrimp.

Freshwater fishing licenses, salmon and steelhead punch cards are available in hundreds of sporting goods outlets, bait shops, resorts and charter offices. In recent years quite a few sporting goods stores have quit selling licenses because of the clerical time required, but most can direct you to the nearest license outlet. Regional offices of the Department of Wildlife do *not* sell hunting or fishing licenses, although nonresidents may order licenses directly from the Olympia headquarters office.

Department of Fisheries (Salt Water) License Fees			
	Annual	3-Day	1-Day
Salmon Stamp			
Resident	$ 3	NA	$1
Nonresident	$ 3	NA	$1
Nonresident Fresh Water	$10	$5	NA
Food Fish			
Under age 16	Free	NA	NA
Resident 16-69	$ 3	NA	NA
Hood Canal Shrimp			
Resident	$ 5	NA	NA
Nonresident	$15	NA	NA
Razor Clams			
Resident	$ 2.50	NA	NA
Nonresident	$10	NA	NA
Sturgeon			
Resident	$ 3	NA	NA
Nonresident	$ 3	NA	NA

To understand the magnitude of Washington's saltwater recreation consider that Puget Sound has more than 1.6 million surface acres. That's more fishing and boating water than in all of the combined freshwater rivers, lakes, ponds and creeks in Washington and Idaho. That expanse is fed by 10,217 rivers and creeks that pour into Puget Sound, and another 3,738 rivers and streams wash into the 506 miles of saltwater shoreline along the Pacific coast.

Fishermen can enjoy the challenge and power of the Pacific or the protection of Puget Sound. Fish from 60-foot charter boats, 10-foot dingies or cast from the beach. Rake Puget Sound pea gravel for butter clams, probe the coastal sand for razor clams, set deep-water pots for Dungeness crabs, drop a star trap into the shadow of a public pier for red rock crab and squirm into diving gear for a try at abalone. The variety of marine recreation offered on Washington's "wet side" is staggering.

Charter skipper Bill Aldrich displays one of Washington's most coveted catches, a 20-pound plus Puget Sound yelloweye rockfish. By Terry W. Sheely

Department of Wildlife
Fishing License Fees

Resident Hunt/Fish Combination	$24
Resident Fish	$14
Resident 3-Day	$ 7
Nonresident Annual Fish	$40
Nonresident 3-Day	$14
Steelhead Punch Card	$15
Conservation	$ 8

Catch, Bag Limits
(Regional and season exceptions)

	Daily Limit	Minimum Size
Trout (all trout and char)	8	NA
Grayling	Protected	NA
Sea-run Cutthroat	2	12 inches
Dolly Varden	1	Varies
Kokanee Salmon	8	NA
Steelhead	2	NA
Bass	10	NA
Walleye	5	18 inches
Whitefish	15	NA
Panfish, Catfish, Pike	None	NA
Chinook, Ocean	2	24 inches
Chinook, Puget Sound	2	22 inches
Coho, Ocean	3	16 inches
Coho, Puget Sound	3	NA
Pinks	3	NA
Chums	3	NA
Sockeye	3	NA
Rockfish, Puget Sound	5	NA
Rockfish, Ocean	15	NA
Bottom fish, Cod	15	NA
Lingcod, Puget Sound	1	22 inches
Lingcod, Ocean	3	NA
Halibut, Ocean	2	NA
Halibut, Puget Sound	1	NA
Sturgeon, Snake R.	2	48 inches
Sturgeon	2	48 inches
Smelt/Herring/Scallops	20 pounds	NA
Crabs, Dungeness	6 males	6¼ inches
Crabs, Rock	12	NA
Shad/Carp	None	NA
Perch, Ocean	None	NA
Perch, Puget Sound	10	NA
Clams	Varies	Varies
Oysters	18	NA
Shrimp	10 pounds	NA

Dwarfed by the hacksaw peaks of the Olympic Mountains, kicker-boat anglers mooch for Puget Sound salmon. By Doug Wilson

Ocean-going charter fishing boats at Westport (which bills itself as the salmon fishing capital of the world), Ilwaco and Neah Bay operate summers only. Charter operators fish year-round in Puget Sound, San Juan Islands and from Port Angeles east in Juan de Fuca Strait. Anglers who book on charter boats can expect to try for salmon, plus a variety of bottom fish including cod, rockfish, ling and halibut. Charter services can provide full tackle and bait.

Saltwater fishing is a year-round sport, and the No. 1 target is salmon which can be caught in the shadow of Seattle's skyscrapers, or on some wave-tossed boat far up the remote coast of the Olympic Peninsula. Five varieties of Pacific salmon are caught in Washington waters — chinook, coho, chum, sockeye and pink — and they can range from two-handed 70-pounders that can test stout trolling rods to ambitious 1-pounders tackled on the surface with fly rods or 2-ounce spinning wands.

Chinook are the premier fish for sportfishermen. Also commonly called kings, blackmouth, springs and tyees, chinook are the largest of the Pacific salmon, growing to 70 pounds in Washington waters. Ten- to 25-pounders are common in June off the coast at Westport and Ilwaco and in July and August when the mature ocean fish begin migrating toward inland spawning streams. During the balance of the year, especially November through March, anglers take excellent catches of immature chinook called blackmouth, weighing between 5 and 20 pounds.

Chinook are caught in all saltwater areas, and attract considerable attention from the charter and trailer boat fleet, especially in midsummer during the peak of the run. Right behind the chinook in popularity is the **coho.** In most seasons Washington fishermen catch three times more coho than chinook. Frequently called silvers, coho lack the size of chinook, but double their fighting abilities, waging an explosive, acrobatic surface battle. Coho are caught year-round in Washington's inside waters, but the peak is in late summer and early fall.

Ocean fishermen begin hitting coastal coho as early as June, 2 to 20 miles offshore between the Columbia River and Grays Harbor, but it's not until September and October that the big fish enter Puget Sound rivers. June coho weigh about 5 pounds, growing to a maximum of 10 to 20 pounds by October. Small-boat fishermen do well trolling for coho. While chinook can be difficult to catch in fresh water, silvers are more aggressive and provide a popular river fishery in major tributaries during October and early November. Ocean salmon fishing seasons vary.

In recent years a popular light-tackle spring fishery has developed for the l- to 3-pound immature resident coho feeding heavily in the placid waters of south Puget Sound near Olympia and Tacoma. In March, April and May fly rodders and spin fishermen casting light trout tackle from small boats catch the abundant feeders in the shallows of Hale Pass, Carr Inlet, Case Inlet, Johnson Point and north in Possession Sound.

While substantial number of pink, sockeye and chum salmon spawn in Washington's waters, more are caught incidentally by anglers after chinook or coho. **Pinks,** also known as humpies, return to Washington waters only during odd-numbered years. They are a small fish, rarely weighing more than 7 pounds, but stack in large schools off the mouths of spawning rivers providing a brief and regionally important target for sportfishermen. During peak run years the state opens a season for pinks to be caught in rivers, usually the Snohomish, Skagit and Nooksack systems. Many of the pinks caught in Washington are bound for British Columbia's Fraser River, one of North America's premier pink rivers.

Sockeye return to only a few Washington rivers. When the run is heavy with surplus fish the state opens special sockeye seasons on Lake Washington in Seattle and Lake Wenatchee west of Leavenworth. The seasons are extremely popular and usually occur in July and August. Weighing 3 to 10 pounds, and basically plankton feeders, Washington sockeye are difficult to

Armed with boots, buckets and long-handled sweep nets, thousands of Northwest sportsmen follow the spring runs of smelt up western Washington and Oregon rivers. This catch was made on the lower Cowlitz River where smelt are regarded as seasonal delicacies.
By Terry Rudnick

catch in lakes and are protected in rivers. Between coho and kings in size, **chums** are hard fighters, yet nearly ignored by sport anglers. Also called dog salmon, chums are the last ocean salmon to arrive in Puget Sound often not hitting freshwater streams until November or December.

Weighing 20 to 200 pounds, **halibut** are the most-prized bottom fish in Washington. The best halibut fishing is in April, May and June with hot spots at Port Angeles, Neah Bay, mouth of the Lyre River and near Sekiu. Charter boats are available for halibut trips at Neah Bay and Port Angeles. Few halibut are caught inside Puget Sound or in the ocean.

Lingcod thrive in the rocks on the coast at Westport, north at Neah Bay and wherever there are rock piles or reefs in the Strait of Juan de Fuca. The deep reefs in the San Juan Islands produce lings that would bottom out a 50-pound scale. Lings are occasionally caught from shore in the rocky jetties and breakwaters of the coastal communities, especially at Westport. In Puget Sound lings have been overfished by commercial boats but are making a strong comeback in the sound, especially in the Tacoma, Possession Bar and Admiralty Inlet area at the mouth of Hood Canal.

True cod and **pollock** are popular targets in fall and winter when large schools mass in the eastern end of the Strait of Juan de Fuca and inside Puget Sound. Charter boats operating from Tacoma, Seattle and the Everett area often put visiting anglers into incredibly heavy catches of cod, a fish with a minimum of fight, but maximum table value. **Rockfish,** looking much like a freshwater bass, are exciting targets in the spring and summer along the coast. Thousands of black rockfish weighing 3 to 8 pounds arrive in dense, ravenous schools and are great sport on light freshwater tackle. Charter boats at Westport book trips for these voracious feeders. Several varieties of rockfish from the diminutive and calico-colored **quillback** to the husky **yelloweye** — a brilliant reddish-orange fish that can weigh 20 pounds or so — are caught year-round in Puget Sound, the Strait of Juan de Fuca and around the San Juan Islands. Several varieties of **sea perch** are caught near shore throughout the sound, strait and coast. An added bonus for pier fishermen is the winter **squid** fishery. From November to February undulating schools of spawning squid mass at night around piers and other lighted areas. They are snagged with small jigs and are considered a delicacy by many, and salmon bait by others. They are sold in local restaurants as calamari. While Puget Sound's squid are small, its **octopus** are the largest in the world, with tentacles reaching a dozen feet. Most of the octopus harvest goes to scuba divers.

Rental boats are available in all resort towns although rental outboard motors may be difficult to find. There is an excellent charter boat fishing fleet in nearly every city or town fronting salt water and public fishing piers are available at Everett, Edmonds, Seattle, Des Moines, Dash Point, Redondo, Tacoma and Westport. Salmon, rockfish, flounders, cod, crabs and squid are commonly caught on the piers.

Some of the finest **white sturgeon** fishing left in North America occurs in Washington. These giant throwbacks to the era of dinosaurs can be caught on sand shrimp or smelt baits in the Chehalis River near Aberdeen and in the lower Columbia River. From Bonneville Dam downstream is the most popular sturgeon fishing region in the state. Guided fishing trips can be arranged at White Salmon, Cathlamet, Megler and Ilwaco. Shore fishermen also take a share of the sturgeon action. Sturgeon are also in the Snake, and upstream areas of the Columbia, in a few of the larger lakes, and in the Grays, Naselle, Willapa and Snohomish rivers. Another variety of sturgeon, the green, prefers salt water and are caught in the bays near the mouths of these same rivers. In June and July **American shad** attract hundreds of light-tackle anglers to the Columbia just below Bonneville Dam. A few of these acrobatic herring are also caught in the Chehalis below the confluence of the Skookumchuck River and in the lower Willapa River.

Fishing Oregon

Oregon has been endowed with some of the most outstanding fishing opportunities and adventures in the country. Salmon, steelhead and trout hide in the shadows of mroe than 50,000 rivers and creeks, quiet-water fishermen have more than 1,600 lakes and ponds to choose from and the relentless Pacific pounds out salmon, tuna and bottom fish lairs along 400 miles of public coastline world famous for spectacular sea stacks, snow-white dunes and hard-packed sand.

Almost every river draining into the ocean or Columbia River attracts heavy seasonal runs of salmon, steelhead, smelt and shad. Sturgeon are found in several river systems, along with the northernmost populations of striped bass. Trout are heavily stocked or native to nearly all rivers and lakes in the Beaver State, and large and smallmouth bass share hundreds of lakes with crappie, perch and catfish. Atlantic and kokanee salmon can be tackled along with lake trout and walleye.

The bays, estuaries and miles of saltwater coastline provide excellent open-water salmon trolling, plus eye-popping catches of rockfish, lingcod and halibut. The coast is paralleled by U.S. Highway 101 and nearly every major city offers charter fishing and rental boat opportunities. Boats aren't necessary to fish the Oregon coast. In some areas the cliffs and jagged sea stacks can be fished from shore for lingcod and rockfish, while in more gentle country miles of rolling gravel beaches accommodate surf casters trying for broadsided ocean perch. Occasionally a salmon can be picked from the beach or jetty near a river mouth. Crabs are trapped in the bays and estuaries and low tide will reveal the gravel and mud bottoms that hold bay clams.

Oregon, like all the Pacific fronts, is a land of topographic contrasts. Fifteen major rivers flow into the 400 miles of coastline from dense green mountains that rise abruptly from the ocean. Most of the rivers are ice free in the winter when steelheading is at its peak. The most popular fishing seasons are from July through November when chinook and coho salmon head inland and again from November until March when winter steelhead and sea-run cutthroat trout are caught.

Some coastal rivers, especially the larger ones like the Rogue, Umpqua and Coquille, also offer summer runs of steelhead. There are tackle-testing striped bass in meandering channels of the lower Umpqua River at Charleston and Coos Bay and in Winchester Bay. Suction-mouthed sturgeon strain tackle in the lower Umpqua, Rogue and Coquille rivers. Offshore and bay salmon angling peaks in August all along the coast, from Astoria to Brookings. Surf and jetty fishing, as well as clam digging and crabbing is year-round sport in most river-mouth towns, and the Oregon Dunes reach is famous for big bass lakes. Siltcoos and Tahkenitch lakes between Reedsport and Florence are two of the best.

The wide Willamette River valley, paralleled by Interstate 5, runs between the green, timbered mountains of the Coast and Cascade ranges, supporting hundreds of small trout streams, lowland trout and panfish lakes, steelhead in the Willamette, McKenzie and Santiam rivers, and sturgeon in the lower Willamette. Spring chinook fishing is famous in the lower Willamette inside Portland's city limits in May and June.

The Washington and Oregon sides of the Columbia River gorge are heavily fished for salmon and steelhead, plus largemouth bass in the sloughs and backwaters below Portland. From January through May and August through December, chinook salmon are caught in the Columbia. Below Bonneville Dam bank and boat fishermen catch sturgeon, large and smallmouth bass, king and silver salmon, steelhead, and in June, American shad. The Sandy River is a favorite with Portland anglers after winter and summer steelhead, spring and fall chinook and coho salmon and in March and April, a run of smelt appears.

Farther south the upper Rogue and Umpqua rivers are famous for steelhead, salmon and resident trout. Rainbow fishermen do well on the upper portions of the Rogue and the North Fork Umpqua, especially the 35-mile section of the North Fork reserved for fly-fishing. Rogue River

Umpqua River striped bass (left). By Erwin & Peggy Bauer. Above, flyrod popping bugs are a favorite with lily pad bass fishermen. By Terry W. Sheely

More than 50,000 creeks and rivers
challenge Oregon anglers. By Brian O'Keefe

tributaries, the Illinois and Applegate, are popular salmon, steelhead and trout waters between
Grants Pass and the ocean.

More than 100 lakes and the famous Deschutes River make the west-central part of the state
along the eastern slope of the Cascades, a mecca for sportfishermen. The area runs the threshold
between where the Cascade Range drops into the arid, desert country common to the eastern
part of Oregon.

The Deschutes is regionally famous for summer and winter steelhead, and a run of "red-sides,"
a resident rainbow that attracts hundreds of light-spin and fly-fishermen each year. Steelhead
guides and white-water rafting companies float the Deschutes regularly from bases in the Dalles
or Bend. The June salmon fly hatch on the Deschutes is nearly as famous and popular as the
salmon fly hatch on Montana's Madison, Big Hole and Yellowstone rivers. Several companies
and ranches along the river provide a shuttle service for floaters, driving tow cars and boat trailers
to downstream pullout spots.

The Deschutes flows north from the central Cascades for more than 200 miles before entering
the Columbia west of Hood River. In April and June the river is heavily fished for spring chinook,
tapering into a July to November run of summer steelhead. Above Bend most of the fishing
pressure is directed at rainbow, brook and brown trout. The Metolius River, a major tributary,
is renown for fly-fishing quality.

The dry, sagebrush country in the Northeast corner is not without angling possibilities. The
John Day River is becoming an incredibly productive smallmouth bass producer, with anglers
also catching chinook in the spring and some steelhead in the fall. The Snake River runs through
this country bringing with it sturgeon below Hells Canyon Dam, channel catfish, smallmouth
bass, rainbow and crappies. The Wallowa and Blue mountains hide dozens of picturesque alpine
lakes where backpackers and day hikers fish for rainbow trout. Outfitters lead horse pack trains
into these mountains after trout, mule deer and elk. Many of the streams hold brown and rainbow
trout in the LaGrande and Baker areas.

The little town of Biggs on the Columbia River is rapidly gaining national attention as a premier
walleye producer, delivering both the Washington and Oregon state records within the past couple
of years. It has been estimated that more 10-pound-plus walleye are caught in the Biggs areas
than in any other area of the country. Guides are available.

Oregon's largest lakes will be found in the vast, arid desert of the southeast part of the state.
Lightly populated, this corner of the Beaver State can kick out surprising catches of trout.

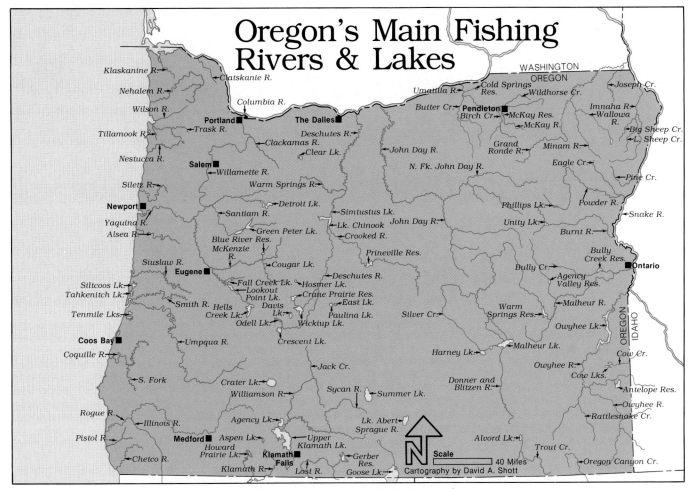

Oregon's Main Fishing Rivers & Lakes

WASHINGTON
OREGON

Klaskanine R.
Clatskanie R.
Nehalem R.
Wilson R.
Columbia R.
Portland
The Dalles
Trask R.
Tillamook R.
Deschutes R.
Clackamas R.
Clear Lk.
Nestucca R.
Salem
Willamette R.
Siletz R.
Warm Springs R.
Newport
Detroit Lk.
Santiam R.
Simtustus Lk.
Yaquina R.
Green Peter Lk.
Lk. Chinook
John Day R.
Alsea R.
Blue River Res.
Crooked R.
McKenzie R.
Siuslaw R.
Cougar Lk.
Prineville Res.
Eugene
Deschutes R.
Siltcoos Lk.
Fall Creek Lk.
Hosmer Lk.
Tahkenitch Lk.
Lookout Point Lk.
Crane Prairie Res.
Smith R.
Davis Lk.
East Lk.
Tenmile Lks.
Hells Creek Lk.
Odell Lk.
Paulina Lk.
Silver Cr.
Wickiup Lk.
Coos Bay
Umpqua R.
Crescent Lk.
Coquille R.
Harney Lk.
Malheur Lk.
Jack Cr.
S. Fork
Crater Lk.
Sycan R.
Summer Lk.
Donner and Blitzen R.
Williamson R.
Rogue R.
Illinois R.
Agency Lk.
Lk. Abert
Pistol R.
Sprague R.
Medford
Aspen Lk.
Upper Klamath Lk.
Howard Prairie Lk.
Klamath Falls
Gerber Res.
Alvord Lk.
Trout Cr.
Chetco R.
Klamath R.
Lost R.
Goose Lk.
Oregon Canyon Cr.

Umatilla R.
Cold Springs Res.
Wildhorse Cr.
Joseph Cr.
Butter Cr.
Pendleton
Birch Cr.
McKay Res.
Imnaha R.
Wallowa R.
McKay R.
Big Sheep Cr.
L. Sheep Cr.
Grand Ronde R.
Minam R.
Eagle Cr.
N. Fk. John Day R.
Pine Cr.
Phillips Lk.
Powder R.
John Day R.
Unity Lk.
Snake R.
Burnt R.
Bully Creek Res.
Bully Cr.
Ontario
Agency Valley Res.
Warm Springs Res.
Malheur R.
Owyhee Lk.
Cow Cr.
Owyhee R.
Cow Lks.
Antelope Res.
Owyhee R.
Rattlesnake Cr.

OREGON
IDAHO

Scale
40 Miles
Cartography by David A. Shott

The vast high desert plateaus and canyons are splotched with sprawling irrigation impoundments that provide excellent fishing in the spring and fall. Summer temperatures in this region can be brutally high and the fishing success falls because of it.

In the high dry country of Steens Mountain there is brook trout and rainbow fishing in Fish Lake. Owyhee Reservoir, the largest lake in eastern Oregon, is one of the hottest crappie producers in the state, delivers channel catfish to 15 pounds and is a fine largemouth bass spot. The Williamson River is well known as a sturgeon producer and the upper Wood River is considered a premier fly-fishing stream for trout. Native rainbow to 5 pounds and some very large brown trout can be caught in this small, picturesque stream.

The Wood eventually flows into the fertile waters of Upper Klamath Lake, at 64,000 acres the largest lake in Oregon, and a premier waterfowling area.

The Oregon coast is the northernmost range of striped bass which are popular trophy fish in the Coos, Umpqua and lower Coquille river regions. These black-striped warm-water fish weigh from 15 to 60 pounds and are concentrated in the bay areas at Coos Bay and Reedsport. Best striper catches are in April, May, July, August, September and October, although the fish are taken year-round. Striper guides and rental fishing boats are available in both areas, and local bait shop operators can point the way to good bank fishing spots.

While every major river mouth or coastal community supports a resident chinook and coho salmon fishing fleet, during the summer months, there is none as personalized or adventurous as the Cape Kiwanda dory fishery off the mouth of the Nestucca River.

Double-ended dory boats, 18 to 22 feet long, are launched from trailers directly into the breaking surf from hard-packed sand beaches near Pacific City without the protection of a breakwater wall or a shielding river mouth. The dory fleet is unique to the northern Oregon coast. Salmon and bottom fishing trips can be chartered on these legendary craft at Pacific City.

The small fleet of charter boats at Depoe Bay work some of the richest bottom fishing waters on the coast, mixing good catches of halibut and rockfish with their salmon action. Depoe Bay boasts of being the world's smallest harbor, and the charters head to sea through a 30-foot cleft in the rock. North of Gold Beach and the mouth of the Rogue are excellent surfperch areas, but few anglers can be pried away from the Rogue's legendary salmon and steelhead runs to try for the little Pacific panfish.

The jagged black rocks reaching into the surf as breakwalls and jetties at Brookings, Bandon, Waldport, Newport and Coos Bay are fine places for spring and summer shore fishermen to

89

Shad fishing on the Umpqua.
By Erwin & Peggy Bauer

Oregon's World-Record Largemouth Bass

One of the least known legends in the Northwest is the credible report of a lower Columbia River largemouth bass 13 pounds heavier than the legendary 22-pound, 4-ounce world-record largemouth caught in 1932 in Georgia's Lake Montgomery.

The mysterious Northwest bass was swept up with a catch of salmon five years after the end of World War I, and reported by cannery workers unloading salmon in Portland, Oregon. According to several published reports, most recently the *Comprehensive Guide To Western Gamefish*, the episode took place in 1924.

According to reports, a warden for the Oregon State Game Commission was summoned to a Portland salmon processing plant to identify a mysterious fish mixed in with a load of salmon.

The warden immediately identified the fish as a giant largemouth bass. It was weighed on the scales at the fish plant. The needle plunged down to 35 pounds, according to witnesses, demolishing any recognized world's records, and weighing at least 25 pounds heavier than any largemouth bass ever reported in the Columbia River.

Reports of the giant bass apparently never traveled beyond the local region and national recognition or verification was never sought. Still, while there is more than a little room for doubt, there are those who note the warden had ample credentials for identifying fish and quietly believe that Oregon, as unlikely as it may seem, may have produced the largest largemouth bass ever known.

catch rockfish, occasionally a lingcod, and sometimes salmon. Generally fishing pressure is light. In downtown Bandon and Winchester Bay a network of public piers and breakwalls is well used by crabbers dropping baited star and ring traps for Dungeness and red rock crabs.

Adjacent to the Oregon Dunes National Recreation Area are two of the finest largemouth bass and panfish lakes in the Northwest. Siltcoos and Tahkenitch lakes adjacent to U.S. Highway 101 between Reedsport and Florence are dream waters for bass fishermen. Countless coves with sunken trees and tule marshes support good numbers of largemouth bass and panfish, while trout fishermen do well in the open water. Rental boats are available at both lakes, along with resort facilities and campgrounds.

There are few places in Oregon where you can't find good stream fishing for trout. Some of the best rainbow and cutthroat river action is on the upper Deschutes, Clackamas, Molalla, McKenzie, Rogue, Umpqua and Santiam. The Metolius, Little Deschutes and Crescent are favorites with fly-fishermen, and the Williamson River near Klamath Falls holds large numbers of large resident rainbow.

Some of the largest trout are caught by lake fishermen. The best time to fish lakes is in the spring when the fish are prowling the shoreline, but deep-water fishing techniques pull fish all summer — especially in the higher elevation waters which tend to run cooler than lowland lakes.

A sampling of outstanding trout lakes includes East, Diamond, Big Lava, South Twin, Paulina, Elk, Sparks, Woods, Morgan, Crane Prairie, Wickiup, Prineville, Detroit, Malheur, Haystack, Ochoco, Howard Prairie, Upper Klamath and Ana Springs.

Kokanee, trout-sized landlocked sockeye salmon, are gaining popularity throughout the state. Caught mainly by boat fishermen trolling with small lures and attractor blade strings, or still-fishing with fly larvae or small bits of earthworm, kokanee are hard-fighting fish with a well-deserved reputation for excellence on the table. Good kokanee waters include Odell, Big Cultus, Wallowa, Lost, Suttle, Elk, Crater, Davis, Crescent, Crane Prairie, Wickiup and Fourmile.

Odell Lake, as well as being possibly the most productive kokanee lake in Oregon, is the No.1 mackinaw producer. These lake trout average 14 pounds, and 35-pounders have been caught. Odell is a large mountain lake abut 65 miles southeast of Eugene in the rich cluster of picturesque trout lakes passed by Oregon Highway 58 between Interstate 5 and U.S. Highway 97. Macks are caught throughout the season.

Bass and panfish anglers find plenty of action. The Snake, Dalles, John Day, Owyhee and Columbia rivers are good for smallmouth bass and crappie. Best warm-water fishing lakes would have to include Tenmile, Garrison, Tahkenitch, Siltcoos, Cullaby, Loon, Mercer, Sutton and Devils. In most of these lakes, largemouth bass, perch, crappie and bullhead catfish are the primary targets.

Steelheaders pound the coastal rivers of Oregon year-round, working such legendary waters as the Nehalem, Wilson, Trask, Alsea, Siletz, Big Nestucca, Umpqua, Rogue, Chetco, Coquille, Sixes, Illinois, North Fork Umpqua and Siuslaw. Coastal rivers normally produce their best catches in December and January. The Columbia River tributaries are also well stocked with steelhead. The two best Columbia rivers are the Deschutes, which is famous for its summer-run fishing, and the Willamette which passes through Portland. Other good Columbia steelhead tributaries include Clackamas, North Fork Santiam (summer-fish only), Sandy, McKenzie, John Day, Grand Ronde, Umatilla and the main Columbia. Steelhead fishing in the Columbia River tributaries is usually better from February through April than in coastal rivers.

In late summer, July through October, the lower Rogue River hosts one of the most prominent summer-run steelheading fisheries in the West. Called half-pounders, these Rogue summer fish actually weigh 2 to 8 pounds, a little smaller than winter-runs. These aggressive fish are excellent fly-rod targets in the low clear summer water.

Current fishing information and conditions or guide service can be obtained at sports shops in Gold Beach on U.S. Highway 101 or Grants Pass on Interstate 5.

Oregon License Requirements

Fishing: All anglers 14 years old and older need a fishing license for all freshwater fish and anadromous saltwater fish, including salmon, mullet, shad, striped bass, and sturgeon. Licenses *are not* required to fish for albacore or most so-called saltwater bottom fish, including cod, rockfish, halibut, lingcod, cabezon, flounder, sole, greenling, perch; or to dig clams, trap crabs, gather oysters or collect mussels. A fishing license is also not required inside Crater Lake National Park north of Klamath Falls.

Steelhead and salmon fishermen, except for daily angler license holders, regardless of age, are required to have a steelhead-salmon punch card in salt and fresh water. Both Oregon and Washington licenses are valid when fishing for salmon in the ocean within 5 miles north and south of the Columbia River mouth.

Licenses are available at hundreds of sporting goods outlets, including resorts and charter operations, and directly from the main office of the Oregon Department of Fish and Wildlife.

Oregon Fishing License Fees

	Annual	1-Day	10-Day
Resident	$12	$3.50	NA
Resident Fish/Hunt	$19	NA	NA
Juvenile (14-17)	$ 4	NA	NA
Salmon/Steelhead	$ 5	NA	NA
Nonresident	$30	$3.50	$18
Sturgeon tag	$ 5	NA	NA

Catch, Bag Limits
(Regional and season exceptions)

	Daily Limit	Minimum Size
Trout	5	6 inches
Salmon	2	24 inches
Steelhead	2	20 inches
Jack salmon	10	15 to 24 inches
Bass	5	None
Catfish, Perch, Crappie, Sunfish	None	None
Whitefish	None	None
Walleye	15	None
Sturgeon	2	36 to 72 inches
Shad	25	None
Striped Bass	3	16 inches
Mullet	10	None
Ling, Rockfish, Sole	25	None
Halibut	2	None
Cabezon, Perch	25	None
Greenling, Flounder	25	None
Herring, Smelt	25 pounds	None
Abalone	3	8 inches
Razor Clams	24	None
Bay Clams	20	None
Soft-shell Clams	36	None
Dungness Crab (males only)	12	5¾ inches
Red Rock Crab	24	None
Mussels	72	None
Shrimp	20 pounds	None
Scallops	24	None
Crawfish	50	None

Oysters (protected, no sport harvest)

In southcentral Oregon springs well from the slopes of the Cascade Mountains giving rise to numerous trout-rich spring creeks typified by this scene. By Dave Engerbretson

Fishing Idaho

Fishing in Idaho is as simple as floating a bobber and dunking a worm in a roadside borrow pit, or as complicated as trolling for 20-pound rainbow with computer-controlled down-riggers and electronic fish-finders. It's as accessible as the nearest irrigation reservoir or as remote as a two-week backpack deep into alpine wilderness areas. As exciting as arrowing a fly into tiny pockets of holding water from a wildly bouncing drift boat on the River Of No Return or as sedate as wind-drifting for whatever's biting in the warm waters of Lake Lowell.

Idaho is almost as famous for its fishing as its potatoes, and the angling action is as diversified as you would expect from a state that runs from desert to rain forest, with elevations soaring from a mere 720 feet above sea level at the confluence of the Clearwater and Snake rivers to the rocky summit of 12,662-foot Mount Borah dominating the northern skyline above Mackay.

The general fishing season, with local exceptions, is from Memorial Day weekend through Nov. 30. The exception is the Panhandle region where streams close Oct. 31, lakes and reservoirs can be fished year-round for warm-water species, but not for trout, char or grayling before the last weekend in April. Opening and closures are managed on a regional basis, in some cases water by water and current fishing regulations should always be consulted before fishing unfamiliar waters.

The Gem State is perhaps best known for its trout fishing — nine varieties; and for producing the largest freshwater fish in North America — giant white sturgeon weighing up to 1,800 pounds. The quick, clear rivers of Idaho are the easternmost spawning grounds of Pacific steelhead and salmon, 900-plus miles inland from the Pacific through several mountain ranges, deserts and dams.

Idaho, especially the arid southern section where rainfall is as light as 10 inches a year, is also earning a reputation for warm-water species. Large and smallmouth bass, crappie, perch, channel catfish, bluegills and bullhead catfish are popular targets along the Snake River system, and in the large northern lakes near Sandpoint and Coeur d'Alene. Landlocked sockeye salmon called kokanee and their coho cousins, usually measuring 10 to 15 inches, are heavily stocked in major reservoirs. Some lakes have been experimentally stocked with Pacific salmon, and the marshy lakes in the Coeur d'Alene chain are well known as the westernmost (Alaska excluded) home of good northern pike fishing.

Trout fishing is No. 1 in Idaho for residents and tourists alike, much of it hatchery originated. Twelve hatcheries pump out trout, mostly rainbow, but also cutthroat, browns and Kamloops. The few goldens in the state originated in California and are now found in a handful of high lakes in the upper Salmon and Payette river drainages and in the alpine lakes of the North Fork Clearwater River. The state also produces char, primarily mackinaw which grow to 57½ pounds in Priest Lake; and brookies perhaps most famous in Henrys Lake where the state record, a shade under 6 pounds, 13 ounces, was caught in 1972.

Brookies have been extensively stocked in high lakes and are especially plentiful in the Sawtooth, Lost River and White Cloud mountains in the southcentral part of the state. The most brookie water is found north of Interstate 90 in the northern Panhandle region.

Idaho holds the world's record for landlocked rainbow trout caught on rod and reel — a 37-pound Kamloops caught in 1947 by Wes Hamlet at Lake Pend Oreille. Rainbow, including Kamloops, are the most popular fish in the state, with anglers catching upwards of 12 million a year, compared to 4 million warm-water fish and 2 million landlocked kokanee salmon. By contrast the state-record steelhead catch was just 32,200 fish bagged in 1983.

There are very few waters in Idaho where you can't catch a trout, beginning at the Canadian border where the Moyie River attracts fly-fishermen during late summer and ending in the southeastern corner with native cutthroat in the Bear River on the Utah border.

The Panhandle, squeezed between Montana and Washington, supports hundreds of excellent trout streams and lakes. Lake Pend Oreille, the largest lake in the state at 180 square miles

Left, typical setting of a central Idaho trout stream, semi-arid woodlands, winding through mountain valleys. By Dave Engerbretson. While trout will probably always be the number one gamefish in Idaho, panfish are rapidly gaining popularity. This angler (above) found the flyrod and float tube, staples of trout fishermen, equally effective for ranchpond crappie. By David R. Frazier

Fly-fishing float trip down the wild Middle Fork of the Salmon River. By Dave Engerbretson

with a maximum depth of 1,158 feet, is famous for its Kamloops trout, but also delivers fine catches of brookies, cutthroat and browns along with record-book Dolly Varden, plus kokanee, bass and panfish. Best fishing months are May, October and November.

North America's biggest char, mackinaw, have made Priest Lake famous. The state-record 57½-pounder was caught here and 20-pound-plus fish are taken each year. The best time to catch a mack is in May and November when the big fish are cruising near surface. Trollers dredging the bottom will manage a few macks in the heat of summer. Priest is also a good bet for kokanee, cutthroat and Dolly Varden. South of Priest Lake anglers enjoy trout and bass fishing at Spirit, Twin, Hauser and Hayden lakes, plus the Coeur d'Alene River and chain lakes. In the early spring, just after ice-out, northern pike up to 10 pounds are caught in the Coeur d'Alene chain lakes. The St. Joe River south of Couer d'Alene is an outstanding trout river after spring runoff.

Swinging south, anglers reach the confluence of the Snake and Clearwater rivers at Lewiston, the one point every sea-run steelhead and salmon in Idaho must pass en route to upriver spawning rivers. The confluence is one of the most heavily fished steelhead holes in the state. Idaho's No. 1 steelhead producer (14,400 caught) is the Clearwater River. Steehead seasons are generally scheduled from January through April.

Upriver on the Clearwater, above Dworshak Dam and the steelhead run, is some of the state's finest wilderness-area trout fishing. The North Fork Clearwater, the Lochsa and the Selway rivers are excellent trout producers, but don't expect much until mid-June after spring runoff clears. Backpackers will also find a wealth of high lakes in this mountain country which is part of the Selway-Bitterroot Wilderness Area.

Jet boats from Lewiston climb the rapids upstream on the Snake River for steelhead, sturgeon and smallmouth bass fishing. The mouth of Grand Ronde and Salmon rivers are popular steelhead and smallmouth bass areas. Rainbow trout and an assortment of spiny rays are caught in several nearby lakes — Manns, Waha, Blue and Spring Valley Reservoir. Big Dworshak Reservoir on the Clearwater is excellent kokanee trolling water during June and July and provides outstanding spring smallmouth fishing.

Grayling are found in about six high mountain lakes in the state. Several are in the upper Clearwater and St. Joe national forests, high lakes near McCall and in the headwaters of the Salmon River. Attempts to establish grayling in the Henrys Fork of the Snake above Island Park Reservoir and in the South Fork Payette River appear to have been unsuccessful.

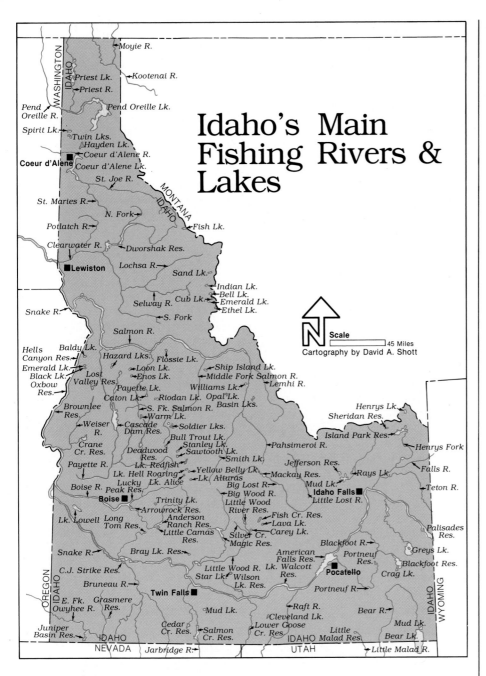

Idaho's Main Fishing Rivers & Lakes

Moyie R.
Priest Lk.
Priest R.
Kootenai R.
Pend Oreille R.
Pend Oreille Lk.
Spirit Lk.
Twin Lks.
Hayden Lk.
Coeur d'Alene
Coeur d'Alene R.
Coeur d'Alene Lk.
St. Joe R.
St. Maries R.
N. Fork
Potlatch R.
Fish Lk.
Clearwater R.
Dworshak Res.
Lewiston
Lochsa R.
Sand Lk.
Indian Lk.
Bell Lk.
Selway R.
Cub Lk.
Emerald Lk.
Ethel Lk.
Snake R.
S. Fork
Salmon R.
Baldy Lk.
Hells Canyon Res.
Hazard Lks.
Flossie Lk.
Emerald Lk.
Loon Lk.
Ship Island Lk.
Black Lk.
Enos Lk.
Middle Fork Salmon R.
Oxbow Res.
Lost Valley Res.
Payette Lk.
Williams Lk.
Lemhi R.
Caton Lk.
Riodan Lk.
Opal Lk.
Brownlee Res.
S. Fk. Salmon R.
Basin Lks.
Henrys Lk.
Weiser R.
Warm Lk.
Sheridan Res.
Cascade Dam Res.
Soldier Lks.
Crane Cr. Res.
Bull Trout Lk.
Island Park Res.
Deadwood Res.
Stanley Lk.
Pahsimeroi R.
Henrys Fork
Payette R.
Sawtooth Lk.
Lk. Redfish
Smith Lk.
Jefferson Res.
Falls R.
Boise R.
Lk. Hell Roaring
Yellow Belly Lk.
Mackay Res.
Rays Lk.
Lucky Peak Res.
Lk. Alice
Lk. Alturas
Big Lost R.
Mud Lk.
Teton R.
Boise
Big Wood R.
Idaho Falls
Trinity Lk.
Little Wood River Res.
Little Lost R.
Lk. Lowell
Arrowrock Res.
Fish Cr. Res.
Palisades Res.
Long Tom Res.
Anderson Ranch Res.
Lava Lk.
Greys Lk.
Little Camas Res.
Silver Cr.
Carey Lk.
Snake R.
Magic Res.
Blackfoot R.
Blackfoot Res.
Bray Lk. Res.
American Falls Res.
Portneuf Res.
C.J. Strike Res.
Little Wood R.
Lk. Walcott Res.
Pocatello
Crag Lk.
Bruneau R.
Star Lk.
Wilson Lk. Res.
Twin Falls
Portneuf R.
E. Fk. Owyhee R.
Grasmere Res.
Mud Lk.
Raft R.
Bear R.
Mud Lk.
Juniper Basin Res.
Cedar Cr. Res.
Salmon Cr. Res.
Cleveland Lk.
Lower Goose Cr. Res.
Little Malad Res.
Bear Lk.
Jarbridge R.
Little Malad R.

Scale
45 Miles
Cartography by David A. Shott

The Salmon River is one of the West's greatest rivers. Indians described it to Lewis and Clark, somewhat fearfully as the "River Of No Return."

The Salmon pours into the Snake just below the Washington-Oregon border after a 300-mile romp through some of North America's wildest primitive areas. Much of the Salmon is accessible only by foot, pack train or boat. It is a favorite float stream and can provide excellent fishing for steelhead, cutthroat, rainbow, Dolly Varden and in some years chinook salmon. The Salmon is the second most productive steelhead water in Idaho and the most heavily fished, ranking slightly behind the Clearwater in production.

Best trout fishing in the Salmon comes after runoff, June through September. Registered outfitters, rafting companies and fishing guides are numerous on the Salmon. Float permits are required on certain wilderness sections. Anyone intending to float the legendary River Of No Return must make arrangements months in advance. The Salmon slices across Idaho's midsection between the towns of Riggins on the west and Salmon on the east, where it swings south through the Lemhi and Lost River mountain ranges to headwater streams tumbling from basins in the spectacular Sawtooth National Recreation Area.

Below the mouth of the Salmon, the Snake River pours from Hells Canyon full of crappie, smallmouth bass, and a few rainbow trout. The best trout fishing is farther up the canyon where the pools are deeper, colder and shadowed by towering cliffs. The canyon, at 6,600 feet deep, is the deepest river gorge in the world, and during the heat of summer it is one of hottest.

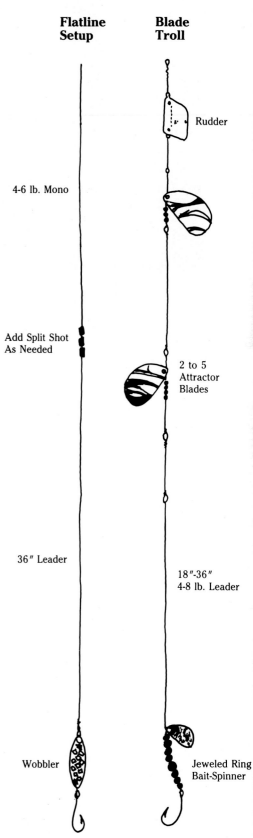

Trout, Kokanee Trolling Rigs

Flatline Setup

4-6 lb. Mono

Add Split Shot As Needed

36" Leader

Wobbler

Blade Troll

Rudder

2 to 5 Attractor Blades

18"-36"
4-8 lb. Leader

Jeweled Ring Bait-Spinner

Hooked. By Brian O'Keefe

Numerous float companies, and a few fishing guides, provide jet boat and raft trips between Hells Canyon Dam and Lewiston. Riggins, Lewiston and Salmon are headquarters for dozens of float companies boating the white-water rivers of central Idaho.

Private parties floating the Snake River in Hells Canyon between the middle of May and first week of September are required to make reservations and obtain a federal permit. Applications are available from the Hells Canyon National Recreation Area, 3620-B, Snake River Ave., Lewiston, ID 83501. Private powerboats must also be registered.

Above Hells Canyon Dam, smallmouth bass and crappie fishermen do well in Brownlee Reservoir. Crappie, smallmouth and channel catfish are prime sport in all the upriver impoundments of the Snake especially between Brownlee and Swan Falls. Twenty-pound-plus channel catfish are occasionally taken in the Weiser section of the Snake. From the State Highway 45 bridge upstream to Glenns Ferry is excellent sturgeon fishing, although the behemoths must be released.

Possibly the most popular trout and salmon fishing lake in these parts is at 24,000-acre Cascade Reservoir on the Payette River. Trollers find plenty of rainbow, kokanee, coho and perch. Fly-fishermen have long loved the fast action on the Middle Fork Payette River. Nearby Payette

Idaho License Requirements

Fishing: All anglers 14 and older must have a license to fish all Idaho waters. Nonresident children younger than 14 must be accompanied by a licensed adult when fishing, and their fish must be counted as part of the adult's daily limit.

Children, under 14, who are residents of Idaho can fish without a license and without an adult. Idaho licenses are also valid while fishing from boats on the boundary waters of the **Snake River** between Idaho, Oregon and Washington, and **Bear Lake** which straddles the border with Utah.

Steelhead and salmon fishermen need a general fishing license plus separate steelhead and salmon permits. Children, including nonresidents, under the age of 14, are exempt from buying steelhead permits, if accompanied by licensed adults. The children's catch, however, must be counted against the adult's bag limit.

Licenses are available at more than 500 sporting goods stores, resorts and marinas and expire Dec. 31.

Idaho Fishing License Fees

	Annual	1-Day	10-Day
Resident	$10.50	$5.50	NA
Resident Fish/Hunt	$15.50	NA	NA
Res. Juvenile Fish (14 to 17)	$ 6.50	NA	NA
Res. Juvenile Fish/Hunt	$ 9.50	NA	NA
Nonresident	$35.50	$5.50	$17.50
Steelhead Permit	$ 5.50	NA	NA
Salmon Permit	$ 5.50	NA	NA

Catch, Bag Limits
(Regional and seasonal exceptions)

	Daily Limit	Minimum Size
Trout, Char, Grayling	6	None
(Only 2 over 16 inches)		
Brook Trout	10	None
Bass	5	
(Only 2 over 17 inches in Region 1. Only 3 over 17 inches in Regions 2, 3, 4, 5, 6.)		
Landlocked Salmon (Kokanee, Coho, Chinook	25	
(Only 2 over 16 inches)		
Walleye	5	None
Whitefish	50	None
Burbot (Ling)	2	None
Bullfrog	12	None
Sturgeon	Catch-and-release only	
Steelhead	Varies by river	
Salmon	Varies by river	
Panfish (Crappie, Perch, Bluegill, Catfish)	None	None

Lake is one of only five lakes in the state where anglers catch mackinaw. The other four are Priest, Pend Oreille, Bear and Palisades. The beautiful mountain and timber country near McCall has a wealth of trout streams, creeks and lakes to challenge. McCall is a headquarters area for many of the outfitters and guides working the nearby wilderness areas.

Southern Idaho can be blistering hot in the summer and fishing peaks early in the spring, just after runoff and again in the fall. In the summer concentrate on the dawn and dusk hours and sleep during the day.

Impoundments on the Boise River are heavily fished and normally not as productive as the more remote lakes in the region. Lucky Peak Reservoir provides rainbow, coho and kokanee, as well as perch and smallmouth bass. Arrowrock Reservoir also kicks out kokanee and rainbow while Anderson Ranch still provides some very large trout, just not a lot of them. Lucky Peak is probably the best of the Boise reservoir bunch.

The Boise River's North, Middle and South forks offer fair action for trout fishermen, especially fly anglers, but watch for rattlesnakes, which seem to have a special fondness for guarding the few large trout in the rocky canyon on the South Fork. In the cool higher elevations of the

How To Rig Salmon Egg Bait

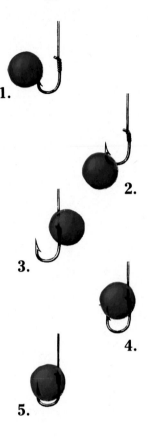

Whitefishing on the upper Snake River.
By Erwin & Peggy Bauer

Brown trout rising. By Michael S. Sample

Besides their obvious appeal to a game fish's appetite, there's a second reason why grasshoppers make excellent late-season bait. They are naturally buoyant, and when fished with a slip sinker, will float above the tops of bottom weeds that frequently foul late-season fishing tactics.

Sawtooth Mountains northeast of Boise, the fishing holds up well into the summer.

Good trout fishing spots along the Snake River downstream from American Falls Reservoir include Minidoka Dam, between Twin Falls and Hagerman and in the spring C.J. Strike Reservoir is good. The Magic Valley region can be surprising. Many of the lakes near towns in the valley have been stocked with brood-stock rainbow up to 10 pounds. Some of the better spots include Rock Creek, Dierkes Lake, Sumner gravel ponds, Emerald Lake and Dog Creek Reservoir.

Silver Creek below Hailey is world famous for quality fly-fishing and large trout. The spring creek is an oasis of cold meanders in a hot, dry valley and the slow swirling eddies are, at times, alive with dimpling rises. Bring your waders, and your best patterns. These trout have seen the finest flies and fly-fishermen. Big Wood River is good trout fishing throughout the season and excellent in September and October. The headwaters of the main branch of the Big Lost River are excellent for trout and Mackay Reservoir is a favorite with trollers in the spring. Magic Reservoir north of Shoshone is one of the most popular fishing holes in southern Idaho.

The best trout fishing on the upper Snake River is in the Island Park area, in the mountain and tree country above the near-desert harshness of the Snake River plain. Henrys Lake and Island Park Reservoir offer several varieties of trout and are fine destinations for boat fishermen. The Henrys Fork of the Snake is legendary among fly-fishermen, especially the Railroad Ranch section. Twelve-pound trout are fought in this stretch after runoff in late June and early July. There's no shortage of camping, cabins or fishing guides.

In the southeastern corner of the state, the standout fishing waters include Blackfoot Reservoir and Blackfoot River just above and below the lake. Other regional favorites are Soda Springs, Malal, Daniels, Montpelier, Bear River, Treasureton Lake and the Portneuf River below Pocatello. In Idaho Falls good fishing is often no further away than the greenbelt marking the course of the Snake River through town; urban rainbow and brown trout in the city. Twelve miles east of Idaho Falls, Ririe Reservoir is good for coho, rainbow and brown trout.

Stream fishing is also good in this area. The Buffalo River is a regional trout-fishing favorite. If you favor small streams try Medicine Lodge, Birch or Beaver creeks. Pan-sized bows and trout big enough to brag on are frequently caught from streams and small ponds along the Teton Scenic Route between Swan Valley and Ashton.

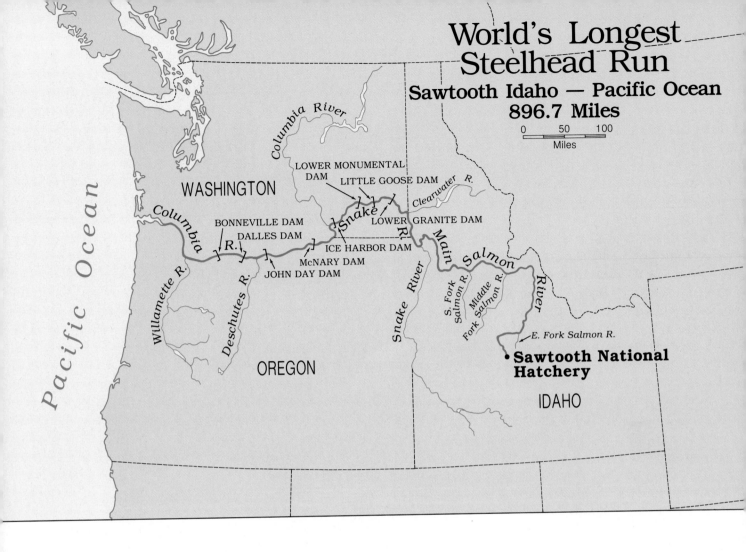

World's Longest Steelhead Run

Sawtooth Idaho — Pacific Ocean
896.7 Miles

World's Longest Steelhead Run

By David R. Frazier

The Indians called it "The River of No Return," but thousands of steelhead trout make it back to central Idaho each year, after an 1,793.4-mile journey to the Pacific Ocean and back, the world's longest steelhead migration.

The journey ends at the Sawtooth Fish Hatchery on Idaho's Salmon River, 896.7 miles up the Columbia, Snake and Salmon rivers from the Pacific Ocean. Most of the steelhead began life in the hatchery, built to resurrect salmon and steelhead runs nearly decimated by downstream dams and commercial fishing. The hatchery appears to be working, with thousands of steelhead returning to waters that until a few years ago were practically barren of sea-going trout. The hatchery and revitalization of the world's longest steelhead run has been a bonanza for Idaho fishermen, who along with biologists feared the run would become extinct, along with the prized chinook salmon return.

The new Sawtooth hatchery is designed to raise both steelhead and salmon.

At a popular steelhead hole near Sunbeam, anglers begin as early as 4 a.m. climbing down a steep, rocky path by lantern light to stand in the predawn cold trying their luck at "the big one." Idaho Fish and Game officers have counted as many as 80 fishermen in that hot spot and are amazed at the lack of problems.

About 477,000 steelhead were released in April 1984 at the new Sawtooth hatchery on the upper reaches of the Salmon River. They began to return in March 1986, and Idaho Fish and Game hatchery chief Evan Parrish said about 1 percent or 4,500 adult fish are expected to return to that stretch of water based on return rates at similar facilities.

The $35 million project is a joint effort of Idaho Fish and Game, the U.S. Army Corps of Engineers, and the U.S. Fish and Wildlife Service. Funding comes from the Corps of Engineers as compensation for eight hydro-electric dams which were responsible in part for nearly eliminating salmon runs up the Columbia, Snake and Salmon rivers.

Shoulder-to-shoulder Salmon River steelheaders try for sea-run fish near the end of their record migration. By David R. Frazier

Fishing Montana

Trout fishermen are hard-put to find better water than the challenging 17,000 miles of rivers and streams that roll through Montana. The mountainous western third of our fourth-largest state is the finest example of world-class trout fishing in the Northwest and possibly the country.

The area brims with superlatives. The Missouri, longest river in the nation at 2,475 miles, starts at Three Forks in the tailwaters of the Jefferson, Madison and Gallatin, three of the West's best trout rivers. The bounding riffles of the Madison have been hailed as "the nation's best trout stream," and the 678-undammed miles of the Yellowstone River attract international angling interest. The last major population of river grayling in the Lower 48 states holds in the cold waters of the upper Big Hole, and the wilderness forks of the Flathead River are famous with float fishermen targeting heavily spotted cutthroats and powerful bull trout.

Most first-time Montana fishermen are surprised at the quantity and quality of Big Sky angling beyond the nationally acclaimed blue-ribbon waters. Stillwater, Bitterroot, Smith, Prickly Pear, Boulder, Ruby, Lolo, Red Rock, Jocko, Blackfoot, Burnt Fork, Sun, O'Dell, Yaak, Flint, Kootenai, Thompson, Fisher — just a few of the prime Montana trout streams that have escaped the national fanfare and heavy nonresident fishing pressure. Most nonresident anglers also think of Montana in terms of river fishing, although the Department of Fish, Wildlife and Parks claims that resident anglers divide their time equally between stream and lake fishing.

Montana is not widely recognized as a lake-fishing state, but its 3,400 lakes include some real jewels. Canyon Ferry Reservoir, a 25-mile-long Missouri River impoundment outside of Helena, is the most popular fishing spot in a state that boasts the Madison, Yellowstone and Big Hole rivers. The reservoir earns its ranking with 5-pound rainbows, 10-pound browns, dense schools of kokanee, millions of perch, and 10 campgrounds and marinas. Georgetown Lake near Anaconda, is one of the finest rainbow producers in the state; little Lake Mary Ronan is excellent for kokanee, rainbow and bass; giant Flathead Lake supports an incredible variety of fish ranging from 42-pound state record mackinaw to pesky perch; Thompson Lake is alive with northern pike; Ninepipe Reservoir is a mecca for bass fishermen; Hebgen Lake is heavily fished for foot-long rainbows and record-class browns; and Clark Canyon Reservoir may well be one of the most consistent producers of big rainbow and brown trout.

Surprisingly, most of the prime big fish areas of the state are easily accessible by paved road, many within sight of major highways.

Once the highlight of summer, fishing is fast becoming a year-round sport in nearly all of Montana. The Department of Fish, Wildlife and Parks not too long ago opened all lakes to year-round fishing, and many lakes now support an enthusiastic population of ice fishermen. The general stream and river fishing season is from the third Saturday in May to November, but regional exceptions and special winter seasons have been approved in many areas to take advantage of whitefish and potential trophy trout fisheries.

For regulation purposes, Montana is divided into three regions; the Western Region includes everything west of the Continental Divide, the Central Region stretches from the divide to Lewistown and Billings and the Eastern Region continues to the Dakotas. Seasonal restrictions and daily bag limits within those three regions are set on a water-by-water basis, producing one of the most complex sets of fishing regulations in the country. As a result, it's nearly impossible to fish in Montana, confident that you are within the law, without checking for specific variances enforced at each stream or lake you fish. For your own peace of mind, keep a copy of the current fishing regulations handy as you look for new fishing water.

While few traveling anglers can convince themselves to pass up an opportunity to fish the famous blue-ribbon waters, like the Missouri and Madison, Yellowstone, and Big Hole, the fishing is often just as productive in the smaller creeks and rivers that rarely enjoy the attention of national magazines or suffer the sometimes-overwhelming fishing pressure. While the most famous

Jordan Lake, Beartooth Mountains (left). By Erwin & Peggy Bauer. Fall float for browns and mallards on the Yellowstone River south of Livingston (above). By Michael S. Sample

Montana's Main Fishing Rivers & Lakes

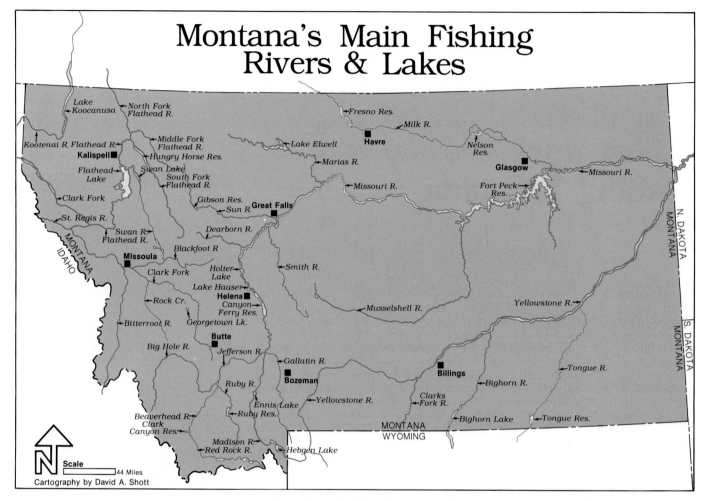

Lake Koocanusa
North Fork Flathead R.
Fresno Res.
Milk R.
Kootenai R. Flathead R.
Middle Fork Flathead R.
Lake Elwell
Havre
Nelson Res.
Kalispell
Hungry Horse Res.
Flathead Lake
Swan Lake
South Fork Flathead R.
Marias R.
Glasgow
Missouri R.
Clark Fork
Gibson Res.
Sun R.
Great Falls
Missouri R.
Fort Peck Res.
St. Regis R.
Swan R. Flathead R.
Dearborn R.
Blackfoot R.
Missoula
Holter Lake
Clark Fork
Lake Hauser
Helena
Smith R.
Musselshell R.
Yellowstone R.
Rock Cr.
Canyon Ferry Res.
Georgetown Lk.
Bitterroot R.
Butte
Big Hole R.
Jefferson R.
Gallatin R.
Billings
Tongue R.
Ruby R.
Bozeman
Bighorn R.
Beaverhead R.
Ennis Lake
Yellowstone R.
Clarks Fork R.
Clark Canyon Res.
Ruby Res.
MONTANA WYOMING
Bighorn Lake
Tongue Res.
Madison R.
Red Rock R.
Hebgen Lake

MONTANA IDAHO

N. DAKOTA MONTANA

S. DAKOTA MONTANA

N
Scale
44 Miles
Cartography by David A. Shott

rivers have the credentials to live up to their reputations, the trout can be finicky and difficult for the unschooled. Smaller, less intensely fished waters, by contrast, are often forgiving and reasonably generous. They are excellent places to take the family fishing, warm up for a try at the Madison or soothe away defeat on the Big Hole. Often these little waters parallel the road, and where they don't, most sporting goods dealers can steer you toward a likely target.

Probably the biggest misconception about Montana fishing is that everyone is a fly rod purist and probably an expert. This is untrue. Fly rods are popular and fly-fishermen account for most of the national press, but spinning rods outnumber fly wands several times, especially among resident fishermen.

Trout are not the only game fish in Montana, although they are definitely the most popular, according to a survey by state fish managers, which declares that rainbow trout are the No. 1 summer game fish in the state, providing more than 30 percent of the Montana catch. Next are cutthroat at 13 percent, followed by brook trout and browns at about 10 percent, kokanee with almost 9 percent and whitefish at 7.5 percent.

The most popular nontrout game fish are yellow perch, which supply thousands of firm fillets and about 4 percent of the state's sport fish catch, followed by walleye at 2.5 percent and largemouth bass at 2.2 percent. Grayling and northern pike contribute less than 2 percent each to the state's total summer catch. Rainbows continue to dominate the winter catch, but perch and whitefsh are winning an enthusiastic winter following.

Summer fishing waters in western Montana come in two landscapes — cool mountain green or sweltering sagebrush brown. The rivers and many of the finest fishing lakes start in the forested mountains and drop into timberless valleys bordered by either scabland rock and sage or irrigated agriculture. The biggest fish are, as a rule, taken from the slower, more fertile stretches of the lower rivers, but taking good catches from these valley waters in the heat of summer can be difficult.

The best valley fishing is during spring, early June usually, just after snow runoff clears, and again in September when cold nights and cool mornings drop daytime and water temperatures. Between those seasons, expect to be on the water at dawn and dusk. During the heat of most summer days, you'll work hard for a meager catch, although overcast periods, storm fronts and insect hatches can provide exciting exceptions.

Every major river supports an annual series of fly hatches that spur frenetic trout feeding sprees and attract intense fishing pressure. The most famous hatches are the giant stoneflies, locally

called salmon flies, that erupt on the Big Hole and Madison rivers during late June and early July. Salmon flies are 1 to 2 inches long and winged, with light tan to orange bodies. The hatch triggers a major feeding spree that begins just after peak runoff, in the lower rivers and gradually works its way upstream. Salmon fly hatches occur on virtually every major river in the southwestern corner of the state, but the intensity of the hatches varies from water to water and season to season.

Most sporting goods dealers, especially those offering fishing guide service, have drawn up listings of those dates when specific hatches are expected on the rivers in their areas. Others display a chalk board marking the geographic progress of specific hatches.

A southwestern Montana grayling makes a final run (top) before being netted. The last naturally spawned river grayling in the Lower 48 are in the upper reaches of the Big Hole River. The fish are distinctively gray, with black stitched lines and a sail-like dorsal fin. By Mike Logan

Picking a place to fish in Montana is not as difficult as it used to be, because of a computerized rating of stream fishing developed by the DFWP, to replace the once-popular blue-ribbon ranking which was discontinued in 1965. The new map, available from the DFWP Helena office, classifies more than 3,000 sections of various streams according to their sportfishing potential. Factors entered into the evaluations include fish densities, angling pressure, public access and aesthetics.

In recent years the top 11 rated river sections, with the best combination of these factors include: **(1) Beaverhead** from Clark Canyon Dam 12.5 miles downstream; **(2) Big Hole River** from

Yellowstone River below 10,960-foot Emigrant Peak. By Michael S. Sample

Montana License Requirements

Fishing: All anglers 15 years of age and older must have a general fishing license. Nonresidents under 15 don't need a license if they fish with a licensed adult, and the youngsters' fish are counted against the licensed angler's limit. Resident anglers between 12 and 14 must have a conservation license to fish. No license is needed for resident fishermen under 12.

All anglers must buy a conservation license as a prerequisite to a fishing or hunting license, or special permits. The only supplemental fishing permit required is for paddlefish snagging in the Yellowstone River. All other game fish can be tackled with a general fishing

license. State fishing licenses are available at sporting goods stores and many resorts and marinas, as well as all FWP offices. Licenses are valid from March 1 through Feb. 28.

All lakes in the state and many major rivers are open to fishing year-round and streams and rivers are open from the third Saturday in May through November. Free national park fishing permits are issued upon request at the entrance gates to Glacier and Yellowstone national parks. Fishing on Indian tribal land is controlled by the administering tribe, and permits, if available, can be purchased on the reservations.

Montana Fishing License Fees

	Annual	2-Day
Resident	$ 9	NA
Nonresident	$ 35	$8
Conservation License	$ 2	NA
Paddlefish Permit	Two for $3	Two for $10
(Yellowstone River)		(nonresident)
Resident Combination	$ 36	NA
(Includes fish, conservation, 1 deer,		
1 elk, 1 black bear, game birds)		
Nonresident Combination	$450	NA
(Includes conservation, fish, birds,		
1 deer, 1 elk, 1 black bear.		
Available from Helena FWP office only.		
Annual quota 17,000)		

Catch, Bag Limits
(Regional exceptions, water-by-water variations.
Consult state regulations.)

	Daily Limit	Minimum Size
Trout (rivers)	1 to 10	NA
Trout (lakes)	10(or 10 pounds)	
Landlocked Salmon	10	NA
Salmon Snagging	20	NA
Whitefish	100	
Brookies (special areas)	10 to 20	NA
Bass	5 to 20	NA
Northern Pike	15	NA
Walleye	2	NA
Paddlefish	16-pound maximum	
White Sturgeon	Catch-and-release	NA
Catfish, Burbot, Panfish	No limit	NA

Six-pound Missouri River brown.
By Mike Logan

Divide to the Jefferson confluence and from Wise River to Divide; **(3) Blackfoot River** from Clearwater to the Clark Fork; **(4) Flathead River** from the mouth of the South Fork for 23 downstream miles; **(5) Gallatin River** from Spanish Creek to Gallatin Gateway Bridge; **(6) Kootenai River** between Libby Dam and Kootenai Falls; **(7) Madison River** from inside Yellowstone Park to the Missouri River; **(8) Missouri** from Canyon Ferry Dam downstream to Fort Peck Reservoir (best for trout from Canyon Ferry to Cascade); **(9) North Fork Flathead River** from Canada to Camas Creek; **(10) Rock Creek** from the forks to the Clark Fork; **(11) Yellowstone River** its entire length (concentrations of trout above Livingston and warm-water species, including sauger and paddlefish in the slow, lower river).

As a rule, the rivers in the southwest part of the state are dominated by rainbow and brown trout with many of the smaller creeks and brushy beaver ponds supporting brook trout. The northwestern streams, especially in the Flathead and Kootenai drainages, are basically rainbow and cutthroat water, again with small brook trout in trace creeks and beaver ponds. Warm-water fishing is confined almost exclusively to still-water lakes and impoundments. In western Montana, warm-water fishing is concentrated, with a few regional exceptions, in the northwestern corner, north of the Flathead Valley and Ninepipe Reservoir.

Ironically, this area also supports the largest cold-water fish species caught in Montana — mackinaw. Commonly called lake trout or macks, these giant char have been caught at weights of up to 42 pounds in Flathead Lake. The peak of the mackinaw action is just after spring ice-out when the fish feed near the surface. As the weather warms, they move deeper, gradually drifting to the bottom, a hundred feet or more down, for the summer.

How To Rig A Plastic Worm

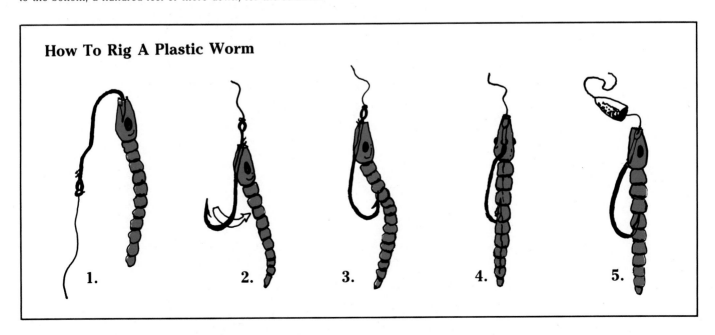

1.   2.   3.   4.   5.

Fishing British Columbia

The 366,266 square miles of British Columbia support the richest sportfishing cache in the Northwest. A rugged 600-mile coastline peppered with plunging saltwater fjords and islands, most accessible only by floatplane, others within sight of glass-walled skyscrapers, and nearly all alive with bottom fish, salmon and shellfish. Rivers spill through coastal mountain valleys supporting legendary runs of salmon, steelhead, sea-run cutthroat, and Dolly Varden, while thousands of interior lakes deliver memorable catches of tail-walking Kamloops rainbow which are measured by the pound not the inch. Some of the southern lakes are earning reputations for perch, smallmouth, largemouth bass and walleye but warm water species are fairly rare and lightly fished.

Northern reaches of the province above the trans-provincial Yellowhead Highway, are broken into ragged mountain ranges, separated by rivers and glacial lakes with untested schools of char, grayling and rainbow. Much of the northern waters, and a surprising number of the southern lakes, are nearly virgin, accessible only by floatplanes, pack trains or foot.

The coastal side of the province is a narrow strip of land, trapped between the Pacific Ocean and the jagged snow-crowned peaks of the Coast Mountains. Tides heaving in from the ocean and floods washing down river valleys from the incredibly steep mountains have combined to corrugate the land with countless inlets, islets, straits and sounds. There are trophy-size fish here that have never had an opportunity to scorn a baited hook. **Lingcod** that will bottom-out a 75-pound scale, **halibut** weighed by the hundred-pound, and exotic **rockfish** rarely found in more heavily fished waters. On a choice feeding tide it is not only possible, but nearly routine to catch a fish on every cast or drift. In most of the province the so-called bottom fish are nearly ignored by resident anglers, and are often stacked in dense schools on pinnacles, bars, kelp lines, rocky points and tide-washed reefs where they can be caught from small boats and, if you enjoy a good fight, with medium to light-action freshwater tackle. The exception is the Strait of Georgia between Vancouver Island and the mainland where bottom fishing is popular.

There are areas along the coast, including the west coast of Vancouver Island, north to Alaska, where bottom fish, especially the many varieties of basslike rockfish, can be easily caught with a minimum of effort. A small boat is a tremendous asset, and most smaller communities offer rental kicker boats plus charters and most have tackle that can be rented for a nominal fee. In areas where there are log booms, jetties or rocky shores, casting weighted jigs with plastic worms or wobbling spoons from shore will produce several meals worth of rockfish in short order. In British Columbia waters rockfish, sculpins, **perch, greenling** (excluding lingcod) and **flatfish** (including halibut) are now protected by daily catch limits.

The bottom fish potential ignored in British Columbia would be the pride and joy of most coastal states. Here it receives almost incidental attention and the reason is the overshadowing quality of salmon fishing available in these same waters. British Columbia salmon action is world renown, attracting anglers from as far away as Australia.

There are few, if any areas where one of the five Pacific salmon species common to the Northwest can't be caught. Seasonal runs of chinook, coho, pinks, chums and sockeye surge into the inside waters throughout the summer and well into fall. In the so-called off-season, November through May, there are resident coho locally called **bluebacks** and immature chinook referred to as **springs.** The best of the big fish action falls in the summer, however, with July and August heavily weighted with giant **chinook,** which when they exceed 30 pounds are recognized as tyees, a Siwash Indian word for "chief."

Chinook and coho are the dominant sportfishing targets, favored for their size, fight, flavor and catchability over chums, pink and sockeye. British Columbia once held the rod-and-reel world's record for chinook with a 92-pounder caught in 1959 in the Skeena River east of Prince Rupert. Fifty-pounders are now considered trophy-class chinook and many 20- to 30-pounders

River rainbow (left). By Erwin & Peggy Bauer. Bowron Lake (above). By Myron Kozak

Brilliant red bodies, olive green heads identify freshwater coloration of male sockeye salmon. By Brian O'Keefe

are caught each summer. Springs, also known as feeder chinook, are immature and smaller averaging between 5 and 20 pounds. The peak of the chinook run varies depending on what area of the coast is being fished, but the normal high point is between mid-July and mid-August. Chinook fishing trips can be as simple and inexpensive as pitching a one-man dingy into Vancouver's Howe Sound, hiring a guide boat at Campbell River, reserving space on a multipassenger charter boat at Saanich or as complicated and expensive as booking a floatplane charter trip to a luxury lodge in a remote area famed for big fish.

Chinook are caught just about anywhere there is salt water in British Columbia, and some spots are world-famous for their trophy potential. Among the best are Rivers Inlet, Campbell River, Knights Inlet, Howe Sound, Alberni Inlet, Bella Coola, Bamfield, Cowichan, Barkley Sound, Telegraph Cove, Queen Charlotte Strait and Prince Rupert. The Gulf Islands, which are an extension of the San Juan archipelago off the southeastern tip of Vancouver Island, are excellent chinook producers throughout the year. The Gulf Islands share the luxury of calm, protected winter fishing enjoyed by the neighboring San Juans across Haro Strait in Washington. Both island groups are in the protective shadow of the towering Olympic Mountains which catch and milk out most of the storm clouds pushing inland from the Pacific producing a banana-belt environment for comfortable year-round fishing. The towns of Cowichan, Saanich and Sidney are salmon fishing centers for the Gulf Islands.

Coho, while physically less than half the size of the brawny chinook, are highly prized for their reckless, acrobatic fighting ability, and their sheer numbers. Nearly every stream spilling into the salt water off the British Columbia coast hosts a spawning population of coho which return later than the chinook, usually peaking in mid-September and October. Expect, however, to find excellent coho fishing from spring through fall, especially in the summer thanks to an ambitious and successful hatchery propogation program.

At spawning maturity coho weigh 8 to 15 pounds but they can get bigger. In fact the only Pacific salmon rod-and-reel world's record not owned by Alaska, is the 31-pound coho caught in 1947 in Cowichan Bay north of Victoria. Summer coho will average 5 to 7 pounds, and grow rapidly before peaking in the late summer or early fall.

Some of the best coho areas are Cowichan Bay, Barkley Sound, Campbell River, Rivers Inlet, Prince Rupert, Comox, Nanaimo, Powell River, Howe Sound, and just outside Vancouver Harbor. It is nearly impossible, however, to find an area that doesn't offer coho fishing in the summer.

Most of British Columbia's salmon fishing is concentrated in the protected waters either inside Vancouver Island or in major inlets along the coast. An exception is the recent development

British Columbia License Requirements

Fishing: Freshwater and saltwater fishing licenses are required of all anglers 16 and older. Both licenses are renewable on March 31. Saltwater licenses are available in more than 600 outlets, mostly along the coast, including sporting goods, hardware and resort, and marine recreational fishing service operations.

Freshwater permits are available in nearly all sporting goods, resort, or hardware stores in the province. Special permits are required for steelhead and for nonresidents fishing lakes and streams classified as "Special Waters," generally trophy-class fishing opportunities. A basic general license is required in order to buy a steelhead or special waters supplemental permit. Fishing is generally open in nontidal waters year-round, however many lakes and streams have temporary closures and a few are permanently closed. Consult current regulations for specific closures. Saltwater areas are subject to regional restrictions by season and species of fish. Consult a current copy of the *British Columbia Tidal Waters Sport Fishing Guide* for closures. Emergency midseason closures sometimes occur and it is wise to investigate locally before assuming a season is open. British Columbia residents over 65 are entitled to a nontidal annual license for $1. Provincial licenses are not valid in national parks.

Ice fishing for yellow perch is attracting popularity in the lower Okanagan lakes region. By Doug Wilson

Nontidal Fishing License Fees

	Annual	6-Day	Steelhead	Special Waters
Resident	$15	$ 8	$ 7	$150
Canada Resident	$17	$ 9	$17	$ 17
Nonresident	$25	$13	$42	$150

Daily bag and size limits are established by region and in many instances by specific streams, rivers and lakes, which are listed in the current regulations booklet. The localized limits are too numerous to allow accurate capsulization. Refer to a current regulations booklet for specific limits and restrictions.

Toll-free Information: Spot closures for salmon are available on a toll-free phone number, 1-800-663-9333. For other marine information phone (604) 666-0383 during weekday business hours.

Tidal Water Fishing License Fees

	Annual	5-Day	4-Day	3-Day	2-Day	1-Day
Canada Resident	$10	NA	NA	NA	NA	$3.50
Nonresident	$35	$17.50	$14	$10.50	$7	$3.50

The tidal water license is required to fish for all saltwater fish, but not clams, crabs, shrimp or crustaceans. Licenses are not required for anglers under 16.

Daily Tidal Water Catch Limits
(Local exceptions possible)

	Daily Limit	Minimum Size
Salmon (non-chinook)	4	30 cm
Chinook (varies)	2 to 4	45 cm
Trout	8	30 cm
Sturgeon	1	100 cm
Halibut	2	NA
Sole, Flounder	8	NA
Lingcod	3	NA
Clam (limits vary from 3 to 75 by species)		
Shrimp	12 kg	NA
Crabs (area limits)	2 to 6	NA
Red Rock Dungeness	115 mm	165 mm
Oysters	15	NA
Octopus	1	NA
Rockfish, Sculpins	8	NA
Abalone (varies)	6 to 12	10 cm

Winter rainbow trout anglers at Lake Williston near Mackenzie. By Ron Kerr

of a charter fishing industry at Ucluelet and Bamfield on opposite sides of on Barkley Sound on the southwest side of Vancouver Island.

Most of the areas that provide good coho action also host a more limited fishery for **pinks, sockeye** and **chum,** although these fish are generally regarded as commercial salmon lacking the concentrated sportfishing pressure and popularity of coho and chinook.

One of the least recognized but most exciting light-tackle fisheries on the coast is for **sea-run cutthroat** near river and creek mouths. These anadromous trout are most plentiful in April, May and June and again in September, October and November. They migrate upstream in November and stay to spawn in late winter. Sea-runs, also known as harvest trout or bluebacks, weigh between 1 and 5 pounds, and school near cover, such as log rafts, pilings and overhanging trees.

The No. 1 freshwater fish in British Columbia is the **rainbow trout,** which is ideally suited to British Columbia's chilly waters. The best rainbow fishing is east of the Coast Mountains in the Kootenay, Okanagan, Kamloops, Quesnel and Williams Lake areas. While some streams support moderate populations of native rainbow, the best fishing is reserved for lakes inhabited by the Kamloops strain of rainbow, an agressive silvery trout famous for its acrobatics and strength. Kamloops are favorites with fishermen in the Kootenay, Kamloops and Okanagan region where anglers find hundreds of picturesque and reasonably remote light-tackle lakes tucked into the rolling green hills.

If your reason for traveling to British Columbia is trout fishing, the area within a 150-mile radius of Kamloops will provide all that you want. The area hosts the heaviest concentration of resorts, fish camps and angling lodges in the province. Many of the outlying resorts provide access to chains of small lakes that usually offer excellent light-spin and fly-fishing. The camps and lakes are frequently far removed from the beaten path, accessible by floatplane, 4-wheel drive or special arrangements. A directory of interior resorts is available from the: B.C. Interior Fishing Camp Operators Association, Box 3301, Kamloops, BC, Canada V2C 6B9.

Most rainbow in British Columbia average 1 to 2 pounds, with innumerable lakes holding 10- to 20-pound trout. There are also giants in these waters. The world's largest documented rainbow, a 56-pound fish was netted during a 1913 spawn-taking operation in Jewel Lake.

The second most popular interior fish in British Columbia is the **kokanee,** a landlocked sockeye salmon weighing 1 to 3 pounds, common to nearly all the large, easily accessible lakes in southern British Columbia. Kokanee are school fish, with reputations for finicky feeding habits and excellent table flavor. The kokanee's slightly oily meat is excellent smoked or baked. A few streams host kokanee runs, but 90 percent of the fishing is in lakes where they are caught by trolling strings of attractor blades rigged with small fluorescent red or pink spoons or baited with fly larvae, kernels of white corn or tiny pieces of fish worm. In some locations still-fishing with these tidbit baits is as popular as trolling. Some of the best kokanee lakes are Koocanusa, Kootenay, Okanagan, Woods, Echo, Lac La Hache, Shuswap and the Bowron Lake chain. There is no limit on these tasty troutlike salmon, and the peak action is usually in May and June.

Although few anglers are aware of it, there is some pretty fair but limited **brown trout** fishing in British Columbia. Unfortunately this fine game fish is limited to sea-locked drainages on Vancouver Island. Browns are reported in the Cowichan and Qualicum rivers, where they were initially planted in the early 1930s, and in Niagara Creek. The best brown trout fishing is reported in the upper reaches of the Cowichan where 5-pound fish have been caught.

Brook trout were not stocked in the province until about 1900, and they have never contributed much to the sport fishery. Most are small fish, 6 to 10 inches. Anglers find them on Vancouver Island in the Cowichan drainage, Spectacle, Semenos and Round lakes. They are also caught near the borders of Alberta and Montana and in the southern Okanagan Highlands.

While rainbow and salmon dominate sportfishing south of Williams Lake, the north country is the home of the chars. Mackinaw and Dolly Varden are in excellent supply and grayling are present in many of the streams. **Mackinaw,** also called lake or gray trout, are creatures of large deep lakes, and weigh up to 60 pounds although 10- to 30-pounders are more likely. Best lake trout fishing is north of the Yellowhead Highway in the Yukon lakes, Skeena, Omineca and Fort St. John region. Some of the most productive mackinaw lakes include Babine, Morrison, Stuart, Quesnel and Fraser.

Dolly Varden can be caught throughout the province, except in the Okanagan River drainage. Anadromous dollies can be caught in nearly all coastal rivers especially in the spring and fall, as well as interior rivers draining into the Columbia, Thompson, Stikine and other major drainage systems. Some of the better northern waters include the Bella Coola, Babine and Skeena. Chars are not spectacular fighters, preferring a dogged run and dive struggle that does not endear them to sportfishermen enamored with the slash, dash and leap battle of a true trout. Perhaps the best known Dolly Varden producer in the province is giant Lake Kootenay east of Nelson, where dollies to 22 pounds have been caught, usually by trollers working large salmon-style plugs. In the early spring before the water begins to warm, mackinaw and dollies can be caught within inches of the surface. While casting can be productive, trolling minnow-imitating plugs is the favorite technique at most lakes. This is the favorite fishing period for most anglers, before the big fish drop into the depths, often 100 feet or more, for the summer.

While saltwater fishermen hail British Columbia's excellent salmon potential and light-tackle devotees praise the explosive Kamloops, it is the **steelhead** that often attracts international

Purcell Mountains cutthroat lake.
By Myron Kozak

angling attention. The coastal rivers of British Columbia nurture some of the finest steelhead trout water in the world. Skeena, Bella Coola, Babine, Kispiox, Thompson, and Dean are river names as familiar in Europe as Vancouver. Unfortunately, nearly all of British Columbia's steelhead are found in just a few rivers.

Nearly every coastal drainage hosts a run of these sea-going rainbow trout, including streams spilling off Vancouver Island. Most of these runs, however, are small and almost inconsequential from a sportfishing standpoint, because the drainages are small, steep watersheds, blocked by waterfalls and low in nutrients that could support fingerlings during their year in fresh water before migrating to the ocean. The major rivers of British Columbia do not host nearly the number of steelhead found in major rivers spilling from the mountains of Washington, Oregon and northern California.

Ironically, British Columbia and neighboring Washington were the last regions of the Northwest to be inhabited by steelhead. According to biologists, a massive ice sheet covered British Columbia 10,000 years ago. Steelhead survived in the neighboring areas of Alaska, Oregon, California and northern Mexico. As the ice sheet retreated, steelhead moved into Washington and British Columbia waters which now produce the best steelhead fishing in the West.

Although summer-run steelhead are available in a few streams, most notably the Dean, Seymour, Capilano, Coquihalla, Silver and Thompson rivers, steelheading in most of the province doesn't develop until about October at the earliest and in many cases not until December. It is basically a winter sport, endured by hearty anglers between November and April when the trout return to their natal streams to spawn. Unlike salmon which die after spawning, a low percentage of steelhead survive both the rigors of spawning and natural predators, to spawn a second and even third time, which — along with sometimes intense fishing pressure — has prompted the province to encourage catch-and-release steelheading in many areas, especially rivers that are either heavily fished or boast a quality run of native (nonhatchery produced) steelhead.

Some of the best rivers to try for a British Columbia steelhead in the southern portion of the province include: Brem, Dean, Babine, Bella Coola, Powell, Thompson, Nahatlach, Chilcotin, Coquitlam, Alouette, Nahatlach, and Vedder.

Northern provincial steelhead standouts include: Skeena, Kispiox, Morice, Telkwa, Bulkley and Copper rivers. Vancouver Island visitors can try the Ash, Stamp, Cowichan, Campbell, Nimpkish, Qualicum and Nanaimo. Even the offshore Queen Charlotte Islands offer steelhead. Favorite waters include the Tlell, Yakoun, Hancock and Copper. Some of the fly-in salmon fishing lodges are also beginning to offer winter steelhead fishing especially in the Rivers Inlet, Knights Inlet and Bella Coola headwaters. Rivers feeding these famous salmon fishing inlets also host steelhead in the fall and winter, but rarely see a sportfisherman.

While standard spin, cast and fly tackle can be pressed into service for steelheading, equipment requirements are fairly specialized. Casting and spinning rods are 7 to 10 feet long, with enough backbone to beach a 30-pound river fish, yet stiff and sensitive enough in the tip to detect a bite sometimes as subtle as a premonition. Fishing lines test at least 10 pounds, sometimes 20, and lures are designed to bounce along the rocks on the bottom. Steelhead like their bellies in the gravel and unless a lure is banging bottom it isn't working. Popular lures include "drift bobbers" designed to imitate drifting egg spawn, weighted spinners or spoons, and wide-billed diving plugs intended to provoke strikes by irritating lethargic steelhead. Guide trips are available on most of the more popular rivers and are the best way for a newcomer to the sport to learn the game and hook a fish. Rates are generally in the neighborhood of $40 to $50 per day per angler. Steelhead fishing can be complicated and confusing, and an inquiry at local sporting goods outlets can save hundreds of wasted hours.

Fishing Alberta

Left, prairie lakes perch and crappie.
By Terry Rudnick. In late summer, the
rainbows rise for 'hoppers (above).
By Brian O'Keefe

The horizon-to-horizon prairies, wind-brushed wheat lands and disjointed mountain ranges of Alberta support a surprisingly diverse sportfishery, opportunities often overlooked by anglers mesmerized by the international reputations of neighboring provinces and states for their excellent trout, salmon and steelhead fishing.

Alberta is an enormous land, nearly 255,300 square miles (almost twice the land mass of Montana) streaked with 13,000 miles of streams and puddled with 6,500 square miles of year-round lakes. Cut off from the anadromous salmon and trout runs of the Pacific Ocean by the Continental Divide, Alberta's waters are devoted to resident populations of cold- and warm-water species. It has been estimated that 40 percent of the provincial waters are suited for trout and char, while 60 percent is dedicated to warm-water species.

This breakdown roughly corresponds with the provincial topography as it climbs from the sun-warmed plains — where they troll large spoons and spinners for northern pike and walleye or toss wet flies and small spinning lures to goldeyes — upstream to the cold-water lakes and streams of the mountains with their grayling, trout and whitefish.

The warm-water species, walleye, northern pike, yellow perch and goldeye, dominate the prairie lakes and lower river fisheries, although an extensive rainbow stocking program is rapidly expanding the trout range.

The most widely distributed of these species is the **northern pike,** a voracious predator that thrives in nearly all the nonmountainous regions of the province. The provincial record is a 38-pounder taken in 1983 at Keko Lake north of Lethbridge. Northern pike are caught on large dead baitfish (chubs, suckers), Dardevle-type spoons, bucktail spinners and sometimes streamer flies measuring several inches long.

Trolling is the most popular technique, although casting to weed beds, logjams or other natural cover is very productive. Best fishing is in the spring just after ice breakup. Pike are long, narrow fish with multiple rows of vicious-looking teeth, with reputations as both hard acrobatic fighters and poor table fare. The meat is white and not unpleasant, but extremely bony and difficult to prepare.

Some of the most famous northern pike waters are St. Marys, Keko, Park, McGregor, Pinehurst, Moose, Skeleton, Beaver, Calling, Cold, Winagami, Wabamun, Lac la Nonne, Chestermere and Lac la Biche.

The most prized of Alberta's warm-water fish is the **walleye.** A table delicacy, the walleye is a bit more elusive than the northern pike, but does well in the Alberta prairie country. The provincial record is 14 pounds, 10 ounces, from the Athabasca River. Other good walleye waters include Sturgeon, Fawcett, Smoke, Wolf, Moose, Helena, Elinor, Seibert, Ironwood and Baptiste lakes and the slow, lower sections of the Athabasca, Peace, South Saskatchewan, Red Deer, Beaver and Pembina rivers. They are caught on weighted jigs, spinners, plugs and spoons trolled or bounced along the bottom. All walleye lures can be improved dramatically by tipping the hooks with bait, usually worms or a strip of baitfish several inches long.

The province's favorite panfish are **yellow perch** and **goldeye.** Perch are excellent table fare, usually abundant and easy to catch. Perch can be found in just about all warm-water lakes. Standout lakes include Beaver, Elkwater, Moose, Kehiwin and Sturgeon. Goldeyes are important commercial as well as sportfishing target. They are confined primarily to the lower, slower sections of the major rivers — Athabasca, North and South Saskatchewan, Peace and Red Deer. Few goldeyes exceed 1 pound but they are hard fighters, tend to jump a lot and an excellent target for light spinning tackle using wet flies ahead of split shot, small spinners or bait.

Some very fine trout fishing can also be found here. Rainbow are the most widespread, but anglers will also find browns, goldens, cutthroat, plus the popular northern char, brookies, Dolly Varden and mackinaw, and the northern rivers teem with grayling.

Mackinaw. By Doug Wilson

The Bow River downstream of Calgary is the best rainbow river in the province and one of the finest in the Northwest. Professional outfitters and guides routinely float-fish this rich river where there is a *maximum* size limit of 16 inches and all larger fish must be released. Rainbow in the Bow routinely run 4 to 6 pounds. Guided trips can be arranged through Calgary sport shops.

Rainbows have been stocked heavily in most small potholes and lakes in the province. Some of the best producers are Schuman, Tyrrell, Henderson, Stubel, Mitchell, Star, Chichako, Two, Reesor and Beauvasi. They are also plentiful in the Oldman, Athabasca and Smoky rivers. Streams spilling from Jasper National Park are also good for rainbow. The trophy is a 20-pound, 4-ounce trophy caught in 1980 at Maligne Lake.

Cutthroat are caught primarily in the southern region between Cardston and Bow River. Perhaps the best cutthroat river in Alberta is the Ram River southwest of Rocky Mountain House. Good cutthroat fishing is also found in the Oldman, Livingstone, Racehorse Creek, Castle River, Daisy Creek, Vicary Creek and Dutch Creek. Largest cutthroat ever recorded in Alberta was only 8 pounds, 15 ounces and it came from the Lower Kananaskis Lake more than 30 years ago. Alberta has one of the most northerly populations of **brown trout** on the continent. They have been successfully introduced in the central part of the province, with the best brown trout fishing found in the Raven River, Beaver, Stauffer, Fallen Timber, Alford, Dogpound and Shunda creeks. Browns can also be found in Athabasca, Peace and Waterton river systems, and some lakes. The provincial record, in fact, was taken from Swan Lake in 1983 and weighed 15 pounds, 14 ounces. **Golden trout,** imported from mountain lakes in California's Sierra Range, have been stocked in a few high mountain lakes in the Pincher Creek drainage, but they are rare catches and the largest ever reported was a 4-pound, 4-ounce golden pulled out of the Barnaby Ridge Lakes in 1965.

Alberta offers several excellent areas for char. The most popular are the **brookies,** which were heavily planted throughout the province and now provide good fishing in hundreds of lakes and streams especially in the remote northern waters. Prime brookies waters include these rivers or creeks: North and South forks of Prairie Creek, Upper Stony, Lookout, Williams, Alford; and the lakes of Rat, Elbow, Muskiki and Bovin. Some of the largest brookies in the Northwest are caught in the waters of Wood Buffalo National Park which produced the provincial record of 12 pounds, 14 ounces.

The biggest of the char, **mackinaw** (lake trout) are confined primarily to the northern reaches. Trollers list the best mack lakes as Cold, Grist, Namur, Margaret, Wentzel, Peerless, Swan and Rock. Most of the mackinaw fishing is found north of Athabasca. The provincial record is a 52-pound, 8-ounce monster caught in Cold Lake in 1929. It's the oldest unbroken fish record in the province.

Selecting Lure Colors, Depths

Just how important the color of your fishing lure is, depends on how deep you'll be fishing. Water filters out sunlight and reduces the color spectrum, so that different colors are eliminated at varying depths.

A salmon plug that's colored red at the surface, will appear gray at 30 feet, while a green-colored plug will retain its color down to nearly 100 feet. Knowing how deep the color of your lure is retained is an important consideration if color is a major factor in a lure's appeal.

The accompanying chart, prepared from data compiled by Martin Tackle Co., illustrates at what depths the major lure colors are retained. Beyond those depths the colors fade to gray.

Approximate Penetration of Light Rays

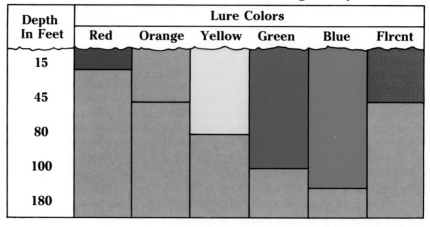

Depth In Feet	Lure Colors					
	Red	Orange	Yellow	Green	Blue	Flrcnt
15						
45						
80						
100						
180						

The strike. By Brian O'Keefe

Dolly Varden are plentiful in the cold-water streams and river systems from Lethbridge north to Peace River. The largest dollies are caught in the Muskeg, Cardinal, Widhay and Berland rivers. The Muskeg owns the provincial record, a 25-pound, 13-ounce dolly caught in 1947. Dollies are not considered to be prime game fish by resident anglers so the fishing pressure is not as intense as it is for the more popular trout. These fish give an excellent account of themselves, however, and wage the *dogged,* nonacrobatic fight typical of chars.

The provincial **grayling** fishery is a good one. Grayling can be caught in streams and rivers along well-traveled highways in the North, the western mountains and in remote, fly-in reaches. Best grayling waters lie in the headwaters of the Peace, Athabasca and Smoky rivers. They are also commonly caught in the Swan, Wapiti, Freeman, Kakwa, Cutbank, McLeod, Berland, Marten and Christina rivers along with Kinky Lake, Christmas, Two, Marsh Head, Trout, Pembina, Pinto and Sunday creeks.

Names and addresses of professional guides providing fishing, big game hunting, white-water float trips, horse packing and outfitting are available by requesting the free publication, *Alberta Adventure Guide,* distributed by Travel Alberta, 14th Floor, 10065 Jasper Ave., Edmonton, AB, Canada T5J 0H4. Nonresident big game hunters are required to be accompanied by an authorized guide.

Fish and Wildlife Headquarters, 10361 108th St., Edmonton, AB, Canada T5J 1L8; Information Centre, Main Floor Bramalea Bldg., 9920 108th St., Edmonton, AB, Canada T5K 2M4. Phone (403) 427-3590. Hunting and fishing regulation pamphlets, including license fee schedules and seasonal restrictions available upon request from the department's information office.

Regional offices: The province is divided into five hunting and fishing management regions — Northeast, Southern, Central, Peace River and Eastern Slope — and subdivided into 62 local offices. Locations and phone numbers of the 62 local offices are printed in the hunting and fishing regulation packets for specific local reference.

Alberta License Requirements

Fishing: Licenses are required of all anglers over 16 years old, except Alberta residents 65 or older, and are valid from April 1 to March 31. Licenses are available at Fish and Wildlife division offices and from private vendors, usually sporting goods dealers. Trophy lake licenses are required of all anglers on designated trophy lake waters. Angling is permitted year-round, 24 hours per day, subject to specific closures listed in the regulations pamphlet. Alberta licenses are valid in provincial parks but invalid in national parks of Canada.

Daily Catch Limits (Refer to regulations for local exceptions)

Trout	5
Golden Trout	2
Dolly Varden (bull), 16 inches	2
Lake Trout (mackinaw)	5
Grayling, 12 inches	5
Perch	30
Northern Pike	10
Goldeye, Mooneye	10
Walleye, Sauger	5
Whitefish	10
Sturgeon (per year)	2

Alberta Fishing License Fees

Resident; Canadian nonresident	$ 7
Nonresident Season	$12
Nonresident 3-day	$ 5
Trophy Lake	$ 5
Sturgeon	$ 5

Size Limits

Sturgeon, minimum 39 inches.
Trout, Bow River from Highway 22X bridge in Calgary to Carseland Weir, maximum length 16 inches.

Fishing Alaska

North Country fishing is top quality. **Southeastern Alaska** offers primarily salmon and trout. Both are found in salt water and in the numerous streams and lakes. Saltwater bays abound with herring, and **king** and **silver salmon** feed heavily on them. Use herring for bait, fasten it to your hook so it will twist and turn as if it were swimming and crippled, and troll it slowly or work it as it drifts. If you are in the right place at the right time you'll catch king salmon or silver salmon. You can also catch these fish by casting from the beach, or in saltwater lagoons.

King salmon fishing is prohibited in all drainages from Dixon Entrance to Cape Fairweather (this includes all of southeastern Alaska) — thus restricting fishing for king salmon to salt water in Alaska's panhandle.

The average weight of commercially caught king salmon is about 20 pounds, with fish up to 80 pounds not being unusual. Silver salmon average about 9 pounds, with the current Alaska record at 26 pounds.

Pink salmon also take a lure, and great schools of these fish move in from the Gulf of Alaska, starting in June and continuing through August. Weights are usually from 2 to 5 pounds.

Southeastern Alaska is also the home of **cutthroat trout,** a speckled cousin to the rainbow. Sea-run cutthroat are from 15 to 20 inches long, and hit a spoon, a fly or a spinner. Best fishing for them is at mouths of rivers or on grassy tidal flats.

Steelhead trout are found in most streams from Ketchikan to Yakutat. The Situk River at Yakutat is one of the best, and fishing is good in June. The Karta River on Prince of Wales Island is good, as is the Naha River north of Ketchikan. The big Stikine near Wrangell or Petersburg Creek near Petersburg are good for steelhead.

Dolly Varden, a cousin to the eastern brook trout, are found virtually everywhere in southeastern Alaska — in the rivers and in the lagoons and in the sea. There are Dolly Varden found invariably where salmon spawn. Usually Dollies will take a fly, a spoon, a spinner or a wobbler. Best bait is fresh salmon roe.

Best months for fishing in southeastern Alaska are from May to September, with July and August offering the most action in both salt and fresh water.

Heavy saltwater spinning gear is popular for king and silver salmon fishing; or trolling rods, saltwater type, with big star-drag reels are commonly used.

Lighter weight spinning tackle is often used on cutthroat, Dollies and steelhead. The fly rod fisherman will enjoy southeastern Alaska, and a fairly heavy fly rod, perhaps 5 to 6 ounces, with a variety of wet and dry flies will fit fishing in most of the large or small streams, and will even work well in salt water.

Southcentral Alaska, which includes Cook Inlet through Prince William Sound and the arc south of the Alaska Range, offers good fishing for all five species of Pacific salmon that spawn in Alaska. Some of the king salmon are taken by trolling in Prince William Sound, and from the clear water of lower Cook Inlet. Anglers also take kings from the spawning streams of the Susitna drainage, using salmon roe, spoons and spinners.

Lower Cook Inlet streams annually fill with king salmon, silver salmon, pink salmon and Dolly Varden. This is the northern limit of the steelhead's range, and good steelheading is available from September to November (weather permitting) in Anchor River, Deep Creek and Ninilchik River.

Grayling are available in Crescent Lake on the Kenai Peninsula, and rainbows and grayling can be taken in the Talachulitna River, a tributary of the Susitna. On even-numbered years hundreds of thousands of pink salmon are found in the tributaries of the Sustina during late July, August and into September.

Good **rainbow** fishing is available in the lakes and streams of the northern Kenai Peninsula. Dozens of lakes, with connecting streams, can be negotiated by canoe.

Alaskan anglers (left). By Dave Engerbretson. In the salmon rivers (above) it's red flies and stout leaders. By Brian O'Keefe

Rigging for southeast rainbows.
By Dave Engerbretson

The network of clear gravel-bottomed streams at the headwaters of the Copper River offers excellent grayling fishing. Lakes in this area are full of **lake trout,** up to 30 pounds.

Much good fishing can be had along the highways of this part of Alaska. A few hikes of short distance can take the fisherman into areas that are seldom fished. Local inquiry or a check with the Department of Fish and Game will often reveal streams and lakes that are not visible from the highway and fishermen should be sure to obtain necessary licenses and the latest information on stream openings, limits, etc.

Local airplane charter pilots know of good fishing, and most will be happy to drop you off at a cabin, or with camp gear, where the fishing is good. Most charter services have their own special places to take fishing clients.

Interior Alaska, that 250-mile-wide swatch that runs from the Yukon Territory boundary to the Bering Sea, is dominated by the Yukon River and its tributaries. A paralleling stream, the Kuskokwim, runs a shorter distance than the Yukon, but the mouths of the two big rivers empty into the Bering Sea not many miles apart.

Streams in the Interior tend to be slow-flowing and winding, although there are a few foaming, dashing-type cataracts. There are many lakes, both large and small, in this region.

Main species are grayling, **pike,** lake trout, **sheefish** and **arctic char.** The grayling favors clear-water streams and cool lakes. Pike are found in muddy as well as clear streams, and shallow tundra ponds often hold surprising numbers of pike. Lake trout favor the deep and cool lakes. Sheefish, some reaching 50 and 60 pounds, are found in the entire Yukon and Kuskokwim drainages, where they migrate in fall.

On the northern edge of the Interior you'll find arctic char, a cousin to the Dolly Varden, where it lives in the cold waters of the Brooks Range.

Good fishing is available in virtually every clear-water tributary to the Yukon River. Best way to reach most of them is by small aircraft on floats, although boats are usually available at most villages along the Yukon. You usually can hire an Indian or Eskimo boatman and his craft for a fairly reasonable figure.

Be prepared to camp if you go into any of the villages. Few have hotels or accommodations for visitors. Take food too, because food is often scarce and expensive.

In this area you can fish for grayling that may weigh 2 or 3 pounds, or lake trout that may weigh 30 pounds, or sheefish to 50 pounds. Favorite type of fishing tackle is spinning gear, although many fly rod enthusiasts can catch all species found in the region without difficulty. A variety of flies, plugs, spoons and wobblers will work for virtually all species.

Bristol Bay and the **Alaska Peninsula** offer probably the best freshwater fishing in Alaska. The clear-water streams and lakes in the arc around Bristol Bay abound with huge rainbow trout, lake trout, Dolly Varden, grayling, salmon of all five species, pike and arctic char.

This is the region that produces the largest run of **red salmon** in the world. In some areas these reds can be taken with wet flies fished close to the bottom, but as often as not, red salmon ignore the sportsman.

The largest **grayling** in Alaska are found in Ugashik Lake on the Alaska Peninsula. Bristol Bay holds Alaska's "Wild Trout Area," so designated by the Alaska Board of Fisheries. Limits on streams here are small, and it is illegal to use helicopters to fly to them to fish. The idea is for fishermen to enjoy the fishing and not take from the area too many of the deep, heavy rainbows, leaving fish for others to enjoy.

There are a number of fishing lodges in the Bristol Bay region, and air taxi services will take fishermen to various lakes and streams for drop-off and pickup; or a day of varied fishing can be arranged — a pilot will fly a fisherman from lake to river to lake for a day of some of the finest fishing in the world.

Arctic Alaska is a vast region where few sportsmen have fished. Only in recent years, since the great oil strike at Prudhoe Bay, has there been any considerable study of the sportfishing potential of this remote region.

The Brooks Range dominates **Arctic Alaska.** Clear-water streams drain north, south and

Lower Cook Inlet in the northernmost range of the Northwest's premier freshwater gamefish, the steelhead trout. By Brian O'Keefe

Alaska License Requirements

Fishing: A sportfishing license is required, with exceptions, of anglers 16 years and older to fish or dig razor clams. The exceptions are residents more than 60 years old, residing in the state for more than one year.

Limits and seasons are managed locally, vary considerably from region to region and are listed in the *Alaska Sport Fishing Regulations Summary,* published annually and distributed free at license sales agencies. Licenses are available at all Alaska Department of Revenue field offices and most sporting goods stores.

Supplementary changes in seasons and regulations are frequently made in midseason, and notifications are available at regional offices of the Fish and Game Department.

A fishing license is not required in Denali National Park.

Alaska Fishing License Fees

	Annual	3-Day	14-Day
Resident Sport	$10	NA	NA
Resident Blind	25¢	NA	NA
Resident Fish/Hunt	$22	NA	NA
Resident Fish/Hunt/Trap	$32	NA	NA
Nonresident Fish	$36	$10	$20
Nonresident Fish/Hunt	$96	NA	NA
Resident Military Fish	$10	NA	NA
Resident Military Fish/Hunt	$22 (small game only)		

Catch, Bag Limits
(The accompanying limits are generalized guidelines. Actual limits vary by fishing area, size of the fish and season. Consult regional regulations for specific daily catch and possession limits.)

	Daily Limit
Adult Salmon	2 to 6
Rainbow Trout	2 to 5
Cutthroat	1 to 5
Steelhead	1 to 2
Brook Trout	5 to 10
Dolly Varden	2 to 10
Grayling	10 to 15
Halibut	2
Burbot	15
Char	5 to 10
Rockfish	5 to 10
Others	10

The largest Alaskan grayling are challenged on the Alaska Peninsula. By Dave Engerbretson

west from this vast, rugged wilderness range of mountains. Countless lakes and thousands of miles of clear-water streams are found in Arctic Alaska, and few of them have been fished.

Grayling, lake trout, arctic char, sheefish, whitefish and pike are the major species. Grayling are found in virtually every cool, clear lake, stream and river. They readily hit a variety of spoons, plugs, flies or wobblers — and at times, even a shiny bare hook. Lengths to 20 inches are found, with the usual length being in the 16- to 18-inch size.

Lake trout are usually small — to perhaps 15 to 18 pounds. In spring, just as the ice goes out, they can be found around the edges of many lakes, feeding near the surface. They'll hit a variety of flies, spoons, spinners or plugs.

Sheefish arrive in the **Koyukuk** drainage in the fall, with Hughes being one center of abundance. Sizes to 50 pounds are known. These fish are great fighters and will hit spoons, wobblers and plugs; some people claim they hit well on streamer flies.

Pike are found in the lakes and in some of the slower flowing streams of the southern slope of the Brooks Range. They're the same pike found in the northern states and Canada and they will hit almost any bright, flashing lure. A wire leader is needed on lures to prevent the sharp teeth of the pike from cutting the lure free.

Arctic char are found in the north and westward-draining systems of the **Brooks Range,** with a few being found in the headwaters of southward-flowing systems. They're usually small — up to 15 inches. They are active, hard-fighting fish and will hit flies, various types of spoons and spinners.

Major jump-off points to Alaska's Arctic are Fairbanks and Anchorage. From the international airports at both of these cities there are numerous daily scheduled flights of modern aircraft into the Arctic — to Nome, Kotzebue, Barrow, Fort Yukon, Bettles Field.

Secondary jump-off points from the central and eastern Arctic are Bettles Field and Fort Yukon; for the western Arctic, Kotzebue, Nome, or Barrow.

Top streams in the western Arctic are the Kobuk and Noatak. The Koyukuk that flows out of the central Brooks Range and south into the Yukon is a fine, clear stream, with tributaries that hold many good fishing holes. In the eastern section, the Coleen, the Chandalar, the Sheenjek are all clear-water streams that offer good fishing.

Clam digging is a popular activity along much of the coast of Alaska and British Columbia. Paralytic shellfish poisoning is known to occur in blue mussels and in hard-shell clams in some areas and caution is advised. For the present, the attitude of the health officials of the state of

How, Where and When To Catch Fish In Alaska
From Alaska Dept. of Fish and Game, "Alaska Sport Fishing Guide"

Fish Species	Best Bait or Lure	Max. Size	Time of Abundance				
			Southeast	Southcentral	Westward	Interior	Kodiak
Arctic Char	Spoon, Eggs	20 lbs.	Absent	June-August	June-Sept.	July-Sept.	Absent
Arctic Grayling	Flies	5 lbs.	July-Sept.	May-Sept.	May-Sept.	May-Oct.	Absent
Burbot	Bait	30 lbs.	Absent	All Year	All Year	All Year	Absent
Chum Salmon	Spoon	15 lbs.	July-Sept.	July-August	July-August	July-Sept.	July
Cutthroat Trout	Bait, Spin., Flies	7 lbs.	May-Sept.	June-Sept.	Absent	Absent	Absent
Dolly Varden	Bait, Spin., Flies	15 lbs.	May-Oct.	All Year	All Year	Absent	May-Oct.
Brook Trout	Eggs, Spin.	5 lbs.	May-Sept.	Absent	Absent	Absent	Absent
Halibut	Octopus, Herring	300 lbs.	May-Oct.	All Year	All Year	Absent	May-Sept.
King Salmon	Herring, Spoon	100 lbs.	April-July	May-July	May-July	July-August	June-July
Kokanee	Spin., Eggs	2 lbs.	May-Sept.	All Year	All Year	Absent	Absent
Lake Trout	Spoon, Plug	45 lbs.	Absent	All Year	All Year	All Year	Absent
Lingcod	Herring	80 lbs.	All Year	All Year	All Year	Absent	All Year
Northern Pike	Spoon, Spin.	30 lbs.	Absent	All Year	All Year	All Year	Absent
Pink Salmon	Sm. Spoon	10 lbs.	July-August	July-August	July-August	Absent	July-August
Rainbow Trout	Flies, Lures, Bait	20 lbs.	May-Sept.	All Year	All Year	All Year	All Year
Red Salmon	Spoon, Flies	15 lbs.	June	June-July	June-Aug.	Absent	June-July
Rockfish	Herring, Spin.	20 lbs.	All Year	All Year	All Year	Absent	All Year
Sheefish	Spoon	50 lbs.	Absent	Absent	May-Sept.	July-Oct.	Absent
Silver Salmon	Herring, Spoon	25 lbs.	July-Oct.	July-Sept.	July-Sept.	All Year land-locked	Sept.-Nov.
Steelhead Trout	Spoon, Eggs	45 lbs.	April-June Oct.-May	May-June Aug.-Oct.	May-June Aug.-Oct.	Absent	April-May Sept.-Nov.
Whitefish	Flies, Eggs	10 lbs.	All Yr. Haines	All Year	All Year	All Year	Absent

Alaska is that no hard-shell clams are safe to eat. Polluted beaches in British Columbia are usually posted with warning signs.

Generally razor clam beaches are safe (you need a sportfishing license to dig razor clams in Alaska). Razor clam beaches are found along Cook Inlet (both east and west sides) and along beaches of the Alaska Peninsula near the Katmai National Monument. Beaches between Cordova and the Copper River are also famous for their fine razor clams.

Wild berries are abundant in many regions of the North. Visitors enjoy picking and sampling the many varieties peculiar to specific areas.

(Condensed from ALASKA HUNTING GUIDE*)*

Fishing The National Parks

All of the national parks in the Northwest provide sportfishing, but the quality and quantity of that fishing is as varied as the parks themselves. Some parks are generous with their fish, some stingy and some have few fish to offer.

The National Park Service generally manages the fishing resources in most national parks with reluctance and indifference, and the park's ability to provide quality fishing experiences depends more upon its inherent resources than modern fisheries management. In some areas the NPS has allowed mountain lakes to become completely depleted of trout rejecting requests to restock the waters, by citing national policy to eliminate or eradicate all non-native wildlife or introduced species. That policy extends, they say, to mountain lakes originally barren of trout, often because of extended snow or ice cover or lack of spawning areas.

Some national park waters, however, are incredibly productive. Most famous of them all is Yellowstone National Park, which affords some of the most outstanding trout fishing in the nation. National parks in the Rockies and Cascade mountains generally provide trout, while on the coast, trout plus salmon, steelhead, panfish, bass, and saltwater species are caught.

General fishing information, regulations and requirements are available by writing directly to each park.

Yellowstone National Park, P.O. Box 168, Yellowstone Natl. Park, WY 82190. Despite the crowds and publicity, Yellowstone National Park continues to be a mecca for anglers. Heavy fishing pressure is generally confined to the areas within sight of pavement, and solitude is nearly always just a short walk away from the road. Even where fishing pressure is intense, restrictive regulations keyed to catch-and-release fishing have provided a wealth of large trout.

Yellowstone Lake and Yellowstone River receive the heaviest fishing pressure. The 88,000-acre lake attracts fully half of all the fishing pressure in the park, yet shore anglers can drop a fly into the shallows within sight of one of the major lodge facilities and expect to catch several 1- to 3-pound cutthroat. Boats are used, but are far from necessary on the big cold lake. Fly-fishermen often wade hip deep into the lake along the gravel shoreline and cast to schools of cutthroat feeding along the shore.

On the river, the average fish caught is more than 15 inches long. Most are heavily spotted Yellowstone cutthroat, but mackinaw, brookies and grayling are occasionally caught. There are more than 120 streams and lakes in Yellowstone National Park and nearly all of them are rated excellent for trout fishing, including the headwaters of the Madison, Gallatin, Firehole, Yellowstone, Lamar, Lewis, and Gibbon rivers. Tackle dealers in West Yellowstone and Gardiner on the west and north borders of the park keep track of fishing conditions and hot spots within the park. Yellowstone is one of the few national parks where a high percentage of the vacationers are attracted by the fishing potential.

Glacier National Park, West Glacier, MT 59936. Glacier National Park on the Alberta/ Montana border is better known for its spectacular peaks, grizzly bears, mountain goats and bighorn sheep than trout, yet the fishing potential is excellent.

Few people come to Glacier exclusively for the fishing, but perhaps more should. Jagged peaks scoured smooth during the ice age, 50 glaciers, meadows carpeted with wildflowers and sprawling canopies of rich green conifers provide perhaps the most scenic fishing arena in America. Yet it has been estimated that fewer than 10 percent of the park's 1.5 million visitors fish.

There are more than 200 lakes in Glacier National Park, and at least 50 of them qualify as waters with excellent fishing promise. Most of the fishing in Glacier is concentrated on the lakes, nearly all of which require a hike of from two to 20 miles. Bring a day pack for tackle and gear. Most of the fish are native cutthroats, although bull trout, kokanee, rainbow, whitefish and even northern pike can be caught. A few waters support grayling.

Lamar River, Yellowstone NP (left). By Mike Logan. Above, the Olympic NP is well known for its winter and summer steelhead fishing rivers. By Doug Wilson

Some of the finest fishing occurs in October and November, when the vacation crowds have left, and the brown trout spawning run peaks. By Mike Logan

Ideal Fishing Water Temperatures

To a large degree, water temperature controls the activity levels of game fish. Certain species of fish, according to fisheries biologists, are more active and more inclined to feed when the water temperature is at a specific mark.

The accompanying chart lists the optimum water temperatures (measured in Fahrenheit) that provoke maximum feeding activity for several species of game fish. Find water in this temperature range and you'll find feeding fish.

Rainbow trout	61-68
Brook trout	58
Lake trout (mackinaw)	41-55
Brown trout	61-68
Steelhead	50
Kokanee	55
Grayling	50
Chinook	54
Coho	54
Chum	57
Sockeye	55
Pinks	49
Smallmouth bass	67
Largemouth bass	60-73
Crappie	65
Bluegill	69
Perch	68
Channel catfish	80
Bullhead catfish	83
Northern pike	60-80
Walleye	55-70

The rivers within the park are generally fair to poor prospects, running fast and low in nutrients. The better rivers, generally tributaries of the Flathead, are often closed to protect spawning runs of bull trout and cutthroat.

One of the lakes in the park, Red Eagle, produced the Montana state record cutthroat in 1955, a 16-pound trophy. Other potentially good fishing lakes include Swiftcurrent Lake, noted for its rainbow, brook trout and kokanee. Kintla Lake is popular for bull trout and Two Medicine Lake has brookies and rainbow. Hidden Lake, the highest fishing lake in Glacier, is a three-mile hike above Logan Pass and is a spectacular setting for cutthroat up to 20 inches.

McDonald Lake, nine miles long and the largest lake in the park, dominates the southwest side of Glacier, and is famed for its kokanee salmon. In the fall the little salmon jam McDonald Creek which parallels Going-to-the-Sun Road in a spectacular spawning run that attracts hundreds of eagles, and thousands of spectators to the Apgar area.

One of the surprises of the park is the northern pike population in Sherburne Lake, a lanky stretch of water on the east side of the park north of St. Mary. St. Mary Lake is trolled for mackinaw, rainbow and bull trout, but is not one of the park's best waters.

While a few fishing lakes can be reached at roadside or with trailerable boats, most require day hikes or overnight backpacking trips. A few anglers pack in light inflatable rafts, but most get by fishing from the bank with light spinning or fly gear.

Glacier is the only national park where it is possible to fish in waters draining to three oceans, the Pacific, Atlantic and Arctic.

Grand Teton National Park, P.O. Drawer 170, Moose, WY 83012. Fishing opportunities in Grand Teton National Park, just south of Yellowstone, are confined to a few specfic areas. Cutthroat are the primary targets and the rumbling swirl of the upper Snake River attracts most of the serious angling attention. Guides can be hired to work the Snake although freelance anglers also do very well in this rich, productive fishery. A highway parallels the river. The Buffalo River forks are prime trout waters but more inaccessible, requiring a backpack trip or horse ride to the best water. The best fishing usually occurs in early summer after runoff from winter snows subside.

The main fishing lakes in the park are Jackson Lake, 26,000 acres, and the much smaller Jenny and Leigh lakes at the south end of Jackson Lake. Jackson is a full-service lake with guides, boat rentals and tackle shops and produces cutthroat, mackinaw and brown trout. The average Jackson Lake fish measures about 18 inches. Best fishing is early in the spring immediately after ice-out. Jenny Lake is a favorite fishing water, located adjacent to a paved road, while providing good catches of cutts, brookies, rainbows and mackinaws. Leigh Lake is at the end of a one-mile trail hike and like Jenny can deliver good to incredible action for cutthroat averaging nearly 16 inches.

The distinctive jagged peaks of the Teton Range also shelter numerous high lakes that can provide backpackers or horseback anglers with quality light tackle or fly-fishing. A few of these lakes, especially those in the upper Buffalo River area harbor golden trout, a rarity in the Northwest.

North Cascade National Park, 800 State St., Sedro Woolley, WA 98284. Straddling the Cascade Range in Washington, just south of the British Columbia border, North Cascade National Park is largely undeveloped. Most of the fishing is targeted at a trio of large lakes, Ross and Diablo on the west and Chelan on the east, and on hike-in mountain lakes.

The Skagit River, famous in its lower reaches for runs of salmon and steelhead, runs along the western flank of the park, and is impounded to create Ross, 12,000 acres, Diablo, 910 acres

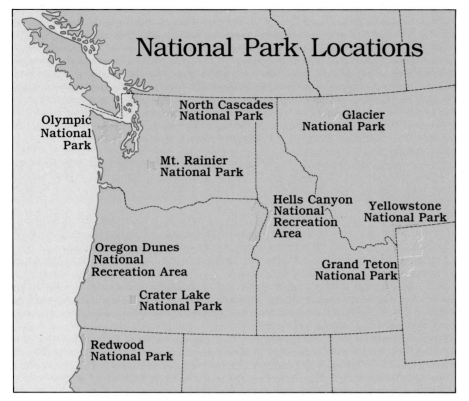

National Park Locations

Olympic National Park

North Cascades National Park

Glacier National Park

Mt. Rainier National Park

Hells Canyon National Recreation Area

Yellowstone National Park

Oregon Dunes National Recreation Area

Grand Teton National Park

Crater Lake National Park

Redwood National Park

and 210-acre Gorge lakes. The river is generally a poor fishing prospect in the park. Ross Lake, however, is a very good producer of fairly large rainbow, cutthroat, Dolly Varden and kokanee, but anglers with trailerable boats are forced into Canada and down a 39-mile gravel road to find a launching ramp on the 24-mile-long mountain lake. The trout in Ross are all native and the best action is normally near creek mouths.

Hiking trails lead to numerous alpine trout lakes in this steep, mountain country, but information is generally sketchy. Nearly all of the lakes have cutthroat, rainbow or brook trout, and most are located on trail systems.

Lake Chelan touches the southern tip of the park and nearly all of the developed facilities are beyond the borders. Lake Chelan is 1,500 feet deep, roughly 50 miles long, and generally difficult to fish. The Stehekin River flows into the north end and can provide some fine, remote trout fishing. The lake is not intensively fished but can provide fair to good catches of land-locked salmon, rainbow and burbot.

Mount Rainier National Park, Tahoma Woods, Star Route, Ashford, WA 98304. Dominated by the overwhelming mass of snow-crowned Mount Rainier, 14,410 feet, this dramatically scenic park offers little for the fishing family. The 378 square miles of peaks and valleys supports a lot of water but few fish. Most streams are fast, fairly infertile and the few fish that are caught are generally small. A 10-incher is often a trophy.

Lakes are victims of the National Park Service's no-stocking policy, depending on natural reproduction to replenish trout population despite unnatural fishing pressure. Most of the easily accessible lakes are closed to fishing and in the backcountry trout anglers are encouraged to catch-and-release. Small cutthroat, rainbow and brook trout dominate.

Glacial melt during the summer fills many of the streams with a white silt that inhibits fishermen, if not prohibiting success. The Ohanapecosh River, a small pool and riffle stream, runs clear year-round, and is restricted to fly-fishing only, but again the trout are generally small and few.

Anglers camping in the park, are wise to prospect streams, and lakes in the adjacent national forests outside the park boundaries. The fishing is markedly better there.

Crater Lake National Park, P.O. Box 7, Crater Lake, OR 97604. Crater Lake is a 1,932-foot-deep lake formed 6,000 years ago when 12,000-foot-high Mount Mazama imploded and collapsed. The crater slowly filled with water, much of it from the 50-foot annual snowfall, creating the second deepest lake in North America.

Until 1888 the crater water was barren of fish, but a stocking program — with fish hand-carried in buckets up the mountain — resulted in a stable and reproducing game fish population. Today's angler will find large rainbow, kokanee salmon, cutthroat and a few Dolly Varden, brook trout and browns. The lake is no longer stocked and private boats are not allowed. Rental boats are available. Best fishing is usually in the shallows near Wizard Island. Crater Lake rainbow have a reputation of being large, 17 to 35 inches, but lethargic fighters.

Steep banks impede shore fishermen, although anglers often fish from the shore of Wizard Island, reached by a tour boat.

National Park Fishing Permits

Fishing permits are required in most national parks of the Northwestern states and Canada. Some parks charge a fishing fee, others issue free permits and some don't require any licenses or permits.

Each park enforces independent fishing regulations, seasons and restrictions governing specific park waters, including daily limits, tackle restrictions and closed fishing waters. Permits and regulations are available upon request at the entrance toll booths or visitor information stations in the parks. The regulations are not normally provided and must be specifically requested upon entering the parks.

Angling in the **Canadian National Park** system requires a $4 fishing permit valid in all national parks of Canada. In western Canada that includes Alberta's national parks; **Waterton Lakes, Banff, Jasper** and **Elk Island national parks.** Also, British Columbia's **Pacific Rim** (freshwater areas) **Mount Revelstoke, Glacier, Yoho** and **Kootenay.**

Fishing in Northwestern United States national parks is generally free with several notable exceptions. Some parks, although they don't charge a fee do require anglers to possess a free park fishing permit.

The no-fee exceptions include the **Olympic National Park** in Washington where anglers fishing for sea-run steelhead trout must have a $15 Washington steelhead card and a valid Washington fishing license. A state license is not required to fish for other species in Olympic National Park.

A Washington State fishing license is required to fish the creeks, streams and lakes of **North Cascade National Park,** and a California license is required in fresh- and saltwater areas of **Redwood National Park.**

Another exception is **Grand Teton National Park** in northwestern Wyoming where anglers are required to buy a Wyoming fishing license.

Yellowstone and **Glacier national parks,** both renown for excellent trout fishing, do not charge a fee but require anglers to possess an angling permit, available at the park entrance stations.

Washington's **Mount Rainier** and Oregon's **Crater Lake national parks** do not require licenses or permits, and regulations must be requested from park officials.

Hells Canyon NRA. By Terry Rudnick

Redwood National Park, 1111 Second St., Crescent City, CA 95531. The 56,201-acre northern California park is one of the few to offer a combination of fresh- and saltwater fishing, and the only one to shelter anglers with towering 2,000-year-old redwood trees.

Salmon and steelhead fishing highlight the two major river systems. In the Klamath and Smith rivers summer steelhead, known as half-pounders, are agressive trout extremely popular with sportfishermen. They actually weigh between 3 and 5 pounds and fly-fishermen find them to be one of the most responsive runs of steelhead. Best half-pounder action is from August through October. The Klamath also hosts a good population of sea-run cutthroat near Panther Creek, Dad's Camp and Requa Resort. A few sturgeon are also taken in this area.

Excellent runs of spring and fall chinook salmon, winter steelhead and sea-run cutthroat are reported. The Smith has produced the last two California record steelhead — the largest a 27½-pounder. Winter steelheading is best from December through April.

The two major rivers, plus nearly all of the smaller creeks in the park, support good salmon runs, which are caught in the creeks where allowed or occasionally in the ocean off the mouth before they move into the fresh water. The runs of mature salmon are in the rivers from October to January.

Estuary lagoons visible from U.S. Highway 101 are fished for trout, and occasionally salmon or steelhead that move into the ponds on high water. When coastal rivers and streams are swelled by rain these lagoons offer an excellent alternative for salmon or steelhead anglers.

Freshwater Lagoon and Lagoon Creek are stocked with trout and provide fair to excellent catches of thick, 12- to 15-inch rainbow trout.

Surf fishing is popular for red-tail surfperch and in the spring hordes of smelt wash up on the beaches where they are scooped up or netted. Along the sandy beaches off the mouth of Redwood Creek, Gold Bluff Beach, and False Klamath Cove is some of the best surfperch fishing, along with sea trout, cabezon and lingcod.

Olympic National Park, 600 E. Park Ave., Port Angeles, WA 98362. Olympic National Park occupies 1,400 square miles of hacksaw mountain peaks and lush rain forests in the heart of Washington's Olympic Peninsula. Spilling from those peaks are the headwater streams of some of the finest steelhead and salmon rivers in the Lower 48 states. Most of the good steelhead and salmon fishing is outside the park in the adjoining checkerboard of national forests and timber company lands, but not all. Fine cutthroat, steelhead and salmon fishing takes place inside the park in the upper reaches of the Soleduck, Hoh, Queets, Quinault, Dosewallips and Bogachiel rivers. The small town of Forks is the unofficial headquarters for guides and fishermen working the anadromous species.

Rivers and streams support most of the fishing in Olympic National Park. The steep peaks of the Olympic Mountains protect several dozen high lakes, reached by hiking trail, but fishing varies from poor in the most popular lakes to fair in the more isolated ones. The Park Service does not allow the lakes to be restocked if they are incapable of sustaining natural reproduction and that includes nearly all of the higher lakes. The result is that the trout population is being depleted in many of the lakes. The best areas to find lakes with spawning trout are below 4,000 feet elevation.

Steelhead and salmon run year-round in the peninsula rivers, with late summer and fall producing most of the salmon and cutthroat runs. Steelheading is best winter, spring and summer. Several streams can provide reasonable success for resident trout. The upper Elwha, Hamma Hamma and Dosewallips are worth exploring.

Two large lakes attract fishing interest, but pressure is usually light. Lake Quinault is on Quinault tribal lands at the western edge of the park and tribal permits are required to fish. The lake supports schools of freshwater sockeye salmon, trout, Dolly Varden, plus migrating schools of steelhead and salmon moving from the Pacific to upstream spawning beds.

Lake Crescent, on the northern side of the park, supports remnant populations of two unique species. Crescenti and Beardslee cutthroat evolved here and grow to 15 pounds. The lakes also have kokanee salmon, cutthroat and rainbow trout. Both lakes have resorts, rental boats and campgrounds.

While technically outside the park boundary, the nearby saltwater fishing areas offer some of the finest salmon and bottom fishing action in Washington. Full saltwater sportfishing facilities are available on the waterfront in Neah Bay, Sekiu, Port Angeles, Port Townsend and Sequim. Excellent salmon and bottom fishing exists off the coast at La Push, but this area is controlled by regional tribes and frequently closed to nontribal sportfishing.

Coves, bays and boat harbors along the Strait of Juan de Fuca are also excellent for crabbing. Hood Canal follows, at a few miles distance, the eastern boundary of the park and is well known for clams, crabs and oysters as well as salmon and rockfishing. Information on the canal fishing and shellfishing opportunities is available in Hoodsport.

Hells Canyon/Oregon Dunes. While not part of the national park system, Hells Canyon and Oregon Dunes national recreation areas hold considerable sportfishing promise.

Hells Canyon is an incredibly rugged 20-mile gorge carved by the Snake River on the boundary of Idaho between Washington and Oregon. Commercial guides tackle the wild white-water rapids, and only veteran boatmen should consider running the canyon.

Smallmouth bass, crappie and rainbow trout are the most popular targets in the canyon, although channel catfish and sturgeon are caught. Most successful fishing is from drift boats, rafts or jet

Surf fishing, Oregon.
By Erwin & Peggy Bauer

boats. The river previously produced trophy-sized rainbow trout, but the fishery has suffered from nitrogen supersaturation created by the upstream dams and the number of trophy fish is down. Rainbows average 12 to 15 inches and the best trout fishing is in the first few miles below Hells Canyon Dam.

The most popular fish is the smallmouth bass averaging between 1 and 3 pounds. It's not unusual to tangle with half a dozen or more at each stop, especially in the bass-rich lower canyon. The sturgeon fishery is popular and exciting, although it is strictly catch-and-release. Both Idaho and Oregon fishing licenses are valid.

For fishing, camping and floating information, maps, and a list of outfitters providing Hells Canyon float trips contact, Hells Canyon National Recreation Area Headquarters, Wallowa-Whitman National Forests, P.O. Box 490, Enterprise, OR 97828. Regional offices are also located in Riggins; Lewiston, Idaho; and Baker, Oregon.

The Oregon Dunes National Recreation Area encompasses some 32,000 acres of central Oregon's Pacific coastline between the Coos and Suislaw rivers. Ironically the best fishing is in large and small freshwater lakes pocketed between the famous saltwater sand dunes.

Lake Tahkenitch is stocked annually with rainbows, but along with nearby Lake Siltcoos is best known for largemouth bass fishing. Some argue that these two lakes are the best bass lakes in Oregon. There is also panfish, and anadromous cutthroat, steelhead and salmon. The Umpqua River, second largest river on the Oregon coast, is fished heavily for striped bass, chinook, coho, steelhead, sturgeon, shad, smelt, perch and sea-run cutthroat.

The Siuslaw River and bay offers Dungeness crab, the largest sea-run cutthroat fishery in the world, shad, chinook and coho salmon, steelhead, smelt, pinkfin perch, lingcod. Offshore is for salmon and bottom fish.

Maps of the Oregon Dunes NRA, general fishing, hunting and camping information, is available by contacting Area Manager, Oregon Dunes NRA, Siuslaw National Forest, 855 Highway Ave., Reedsport, OR 97467.

Fly-fishing Yellowstone Lake cutthroat.
By Terry W. Sheely

Fishing Yellowstone

By Michael S. Sample

No doubt about it, Old Faithful, the Grand Canyon of the Yellowstone and the impressive parade of wildlife headline the attractions of Yellowstone National Park. That Yellowstone has some of this country's best trout fishing, has been an open secret for 50 years.

Crowds? Except in a few spots, anglers will find all the undisturbed solitude they could desire. This immense park, larger than some states, encompasses more than a hundred superb trout streams and subalpine lakes, many surprisingly lightly fished.

Fishing in the park has actually been improving over the past 15 years since a major revision of fishing regulations in 1970 aimed at protecting the fishery and the extraordinary ecosystem. Today, Yellowstone Park has some of the most restrictive and successful regulations in the country, including local and seasonal closures to protect spawning fish, elimination of bait fishing, size and creel limits, catch-and-release areas, and fly-fishing only.

The regulations are complicated but the results have been more fish, a greater diversity of fishing opportunities, and more anglers taking advantage of these opportunities. The percentage of successful anglers has risen, and in many waters, average fish size is increasing. Park policy has shifted away from consumptive fishing toward a fish-for-fun philosophy that seems to be working.

Yellowstone Park is divided into six fishing zones, each with unique fishery characteristics and regulations. Opening day varies from May 28 to July 15, depending on the zone. Creel and size limits vary from zone to zone, as do catch-and-release or fly-fishing-only waters, so check the regulations. No matter where in the park they fish, however, all anglers must obtain a free fishing permit, available at the entry gates.

Fishing in the park is limited to single-hook, artificial flies and lures. (Treble hooks are considered a single hook under the regulations.) Fish mortality, particularly in the catch-and-release waters, has significantly declined with the elimination of bait fishing.

A wide variety of flies and lures are effective in the park. Standard dry flies used on lakes or smooth-surfaced streams include the Adams, Blue Dun, Ginger Quill and Light Cahill. Royal Wulffs, Humpies, Elk-hair caddis and hoppers bring the best dry fly action in the fast, broken water stretches. Salmon fly patterns are good in season on the Yellowstone River. Wet flies worth

Yellowstone National Park
Fishing Areas

Madison River. By Michael S. Sample

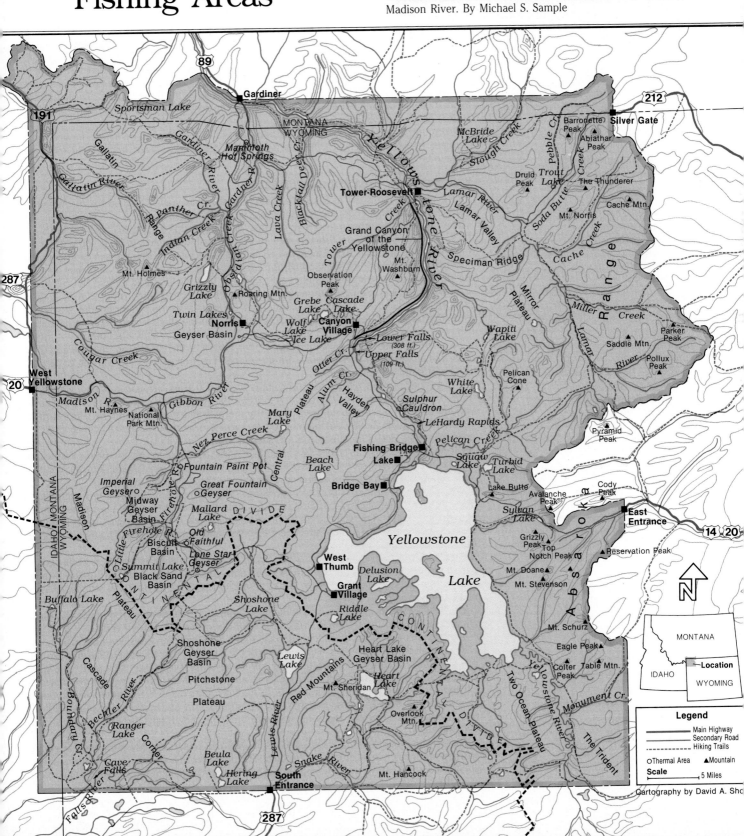

Streamside Ethics

Treat the fisherman on the other side of the river as though he were on yours.

If you are unsure of the movements of an angler it may be wise to have a word with him and adjust your movements to be compatible with his.

Fish so as to cause as little disturbance to water or fish as possible. Take precautions to keep your shadow from falling on the pool.

Allow the fisherman at the hole to fish through it without interference.

After a reasonable time on a pool a fisherman should either invite a waiting angler to join him, to pass through and fish the upper or lower water, or should vacate the pool entirely, leaving it to the other angler.

When sharing a pool or riffle allow fellow fishermen room so casts, drifts and the fish are not disturbed.

Yield enough water to the angler who has hooked a fish to permit him to play it without interference.

Do not impose yourself roughly on other anglers. Wait a polite time and then, if necessary, request permission to fish through.

Never tie up a pool indefinitely.

Practice the Golden Rule. Ask yourself, would I find it offensive if some----?

Take care not to crowd other anglers on a drift. Adjust your progress to those preceding you.

Fish a riffle progressively. Avoid standing in one spot.

Always allow an angler you meet on a stream to fish through.

When entering an occupied drift move in behind the other angler or wait until he has fished it out.

When in doubt ask the other anglers permission.

If you wish to converse with another angler wait quietly aside until he has fished out the pool or preferable, time your finish with his.

(Courtesy of Federation of Fly Fishers)

trying include Wooly Worms, Muddler Minnows, and a variety of dark-colored streamers. In the park, Hamilton Stores has helpful clerks and supplies of fishing gear. Outside the park, West Yellowstone and Gardiner are amply supplied with fishing shops that can provide up-to-date information for specific waters. They also have guide services for park fishing.

Lures are particularly successful in the park's lakes but can be used effectively in many rivers and streams as well. A selection of spoons, and spinners should provide good action. On rivers, a fly and bubble on spinning gear may prove the most successful for the spin fisherman.

The fishing potential in Yellowstone Park is almost limitless. The kind of fishing preferred or the species of fish desired will influence where one chooses to fish. Yellowstone Park fisheries biologist Bob Gresswell believes that "the best fishing in the park is found in catch-and-release areas for cutthroat trout. There are good populations of nice-sized fish in these waters, and the fish are catchable." By comparison, brown and rainbow trout fisheries in the park, such as the Madison River, provide tough fishing for the average fisherman, with a substantially lower average catch rate. Brook trout fishing is fast, but the fish are small. The percentages of fish caught per species reflect these conditions: 70 percent cutthroat, 10 percent rainbow, 7 percent brown, and 7 percent brook trout. An amazing 50 percent of the fish caught in Yellowstone exceed 14 inches.

Some 24 waters receive over 95 percent of angler use in Yellowstone Park. These provide the best combination of good fishing and easy access. Most are accessible from park roads and require little or no walking.

Backcountry lakes and streams require permits, available at any ranger station, for overnight camping. Remember, Yellowstone is home to black and grizzly bears, both of which can be dangerous.

Yellowstone's Most Popular Fisheries

Yellowstone Lake is the most popular fishery in the park, and with good reason, Whether fishing from shore or boat, anglers enjoy amazingly consistent results.

The pure native cutthroat fishery in the lake has had its ups and downs over the years. In 1975, the Park Service established a regulation which allows anglers to keep fish only up to a maximum of 13 inches. The fishery has responded magnificently. The average cutthroat now measures 14.6 inches and, for the first time in many years, a few go over 20 inches. Due to the shrimp diet, these cutthroats have the rich pink flesh so treasured around the campfire.

Anglers hoping to enjoy trout for dinner sometimes have a happy problem — all the fish they catch measure over the 13-inch maximum limit. There is a solution — for boating anglers at least. The bigger fish tend to hang out closer to shore in the shallow water. To catch smaller fish, move away from shore and fish deeper — that's where the little ones are.

Yellowstone Lake opens later than some other waters in the park. From the opening date to the end of July, catch rates generally are sensational. Thereafter, the fish spread out, go deeper, and become harder to find.

A huge body of water with a surface encompassing 88,000 acres surrounded by over a hundred miles of sandy beaches, rocky breaks and forested shorelines, Yellowstone Lake has a general weather pattern anglers should heed. The early morning hours usually find the lake's surface wonderfully smooth, but by late morning, the breezes have started up at least a light chop. Afternoon often sees violent thunderstorms and sudden high winds with large waves that can swamp small craft. Even during the hottest days of summer, these bone-chilling waters pose the immediate threat of hypothermia — survival time is short. Anglers should keep constant watch on the weather and stay within easy reach of shore. And be sure to check boating regulations.

Virtually the whole lake offers excellent fishing. The south and southeast arms have reputations for even better angling, but they are miles from the nearest road and have some restrictions on boat motors. The whole north shore parallels park roads, while hiking trails reach remote sections on the east and south. Public boat launches and marinas at West Thumb and Bridge Bay offer convenient services.

Flies work well early in the season when cast to rising fish. Spoons and spinners bring results almost any time. The most popular lure is Jake's Spin-a-Lure, a heavy metal lure about the size of a domino with red spots on its side. Small to medium sizes work best. Lures with more than one cluster of hooks are illegal.

The Yellowstone River ranks as one of the nation's premier trout streams. Thousands of anglers annually wade into the river and think they have discovered heaven on earth.

The river actually begins in wilderness to the south of the park and flows north to Yellowstone Lake through the Thoroughfare, a wild section of the park far removed from civilization. When it flows into the Southeast Arm of the lake, it is already a river of substantial size. People who value wilderness experiences trek to the Thoroughfare to enjoy these trout-laden waters in solitude.

The river is more convenient for anglers, as it gently flows out of Yellowstone Lake through several miles of pines and meadows, past the Sulphur Cauldron, and across the tranquil, wildlife-rich Hayden Valley before cascading violently into the picturesque Grand Canyon of the Yellowstone.

The Hayden Valley stretch is closed to all fishing, but anglers can ply the waters at either end provided they release any fish they catch. The upper end, between Fishing Bridge and the Sulphur Cauldron, draws the most anglers and has been called the most intensively fished reach of wild trout population in the United States.

The fishing begins spectacularly on opening day July 15, when the resident river cutthroat and some of their lake cousins are just concluding their spawning in the river below the lake. Stacked along the banks, behind logs and rocks and across the gravel bars, the thousands of fish are readily visible to even casual observers. Although not in the best condition after their recent strenuous activity, these beautifully colored fish readily take flies and lures in the first days after opening. Landing rates are sometimes fantastic; some anglers consider this cutthroat fishing at its finest.

As the weeks pass, river fishing becomes progressively more difficult as the lake's cutthroat move back to the lake, which opens June 15, leaving the resident river fish more room and less urgency to feed.

Except briefly at LeHardy Rapids, the river is one smooth glide from the lake outlet to the bridge just above the Upper Falls. Bank fishing is very good along this stretch; wading is even better. Floating is prohibited.

Spinners and spoons do catch fish here, but most anglers tie on flies, even if they have only a spinning rod and reel. With a bobber and a little lead, spin anglers who have never used a fly before often surprise themselves by catching plenty of fish.

This section of the river has an inconsequential salmon fly hatch about July 15, mostly near the LeHardy Rapids. Plentiful mayflies and some caddis and baetis round out the hatches. Experienced angler Mike Brady watches especially for a big gray mayfly, the gray drake. He also notes that some fine hatches of small mayflies come off the water during and after stormy weather. And for attractor flies, Brady singles out the house and lot fly, sometimes known as the hair wing variant, as a must to keep on hand.

From the Lower Falls down through the Grand Canyon, past Tower Junction, through the Black Canyon, and on to Gardiner, the river continues to offer outstanding fishing. Except at a bridge near Tower Junction, anglers must hike several miles down to the river, then climb steep trails back out.

Still, there are several attractions to the fishing here. Because the river is more remote and anglers must expend considerable effort just to reach it, the crowds do not fish here. Incredible as it may seem to some, an angler could walk an hour to the river, fish all day in one of the finest trout fisheries in the country, and hike out without seeing another angler.

Yellowstone River below Fishing Bridge. By Michael S. Sample

Hatch matching can be critical.
By Michael S. Sample

This section of the river has some of the best fast-water fishing in the park. For example, anglers can fish Seven Mile Hole, or the bottom three miles of the canyon. The remainder of the Grand Canyon is off-limits due both to the dangers of climbing in the canyon and to bear closures.

This section also has the attraction of a late and often very good salmon fly hatch. Salmon fly patterns produce excellent results in July and sometimes early August, even after the hatch is over. Thereafter, the fishing holds up well through the season. The best fly patterns are often caddis imitations, attractors, grasshoppers, and short streamers. Sometimes the Muddler Minnow is the most enticing fly for this section.

From Knowles Falls to Gardiner, the river has a more varied population of game fish. In addition to the dominant cutthroat, anglers can also find a few brookies, good numbers of browns and rainbow, and some rainbow-cutthroat hybrids with interesting color variations. Since the trout are not fished much, they tend to be less selective and sophisticated than most, but on the hook, they are scrappy fighters.

The **Bechler River,** located in Yellowstone's southwest corner, runs its course in an area of beautiful waterfalls and large meadows far from the sight of most of the fishing public. A road well off the usual tourist routes runs from Idaho into the Bechler ranger station, with a spur to the Cave Falls picnic area near the mouth of the Bechler. Because mosquitoes by the zillions use the Bechler's soggy meadows for their breeding grounds, most anglers avoid wetting a line in the Bechler until the end of the summer.

Most of the larger trout in the Bechler swim in the lower end of the river, from its junction with the Falls River up to Bechler Falls. Most of the rainbow and cutthroat average 10 to 12 inches, but a few of the rainbow grow considerably larger, especially in the meadow sections of the stream — deep pools and undercut banks provide excellent cover. Anglers use a wide range of flies and lure effectively, but trying a grasshopper imitation can be dynamite.

The **Falls River** runs along the southwest border of the park. The river can be reached by road from Idaho into the Cave Falls picnic area. Fishing is excellent for rainbow and cutthroat averaging 11 inches. Trails provide some access to the upper reaches.

The **Firehole River** is one of Yellowstone's nationally famous trout streams. It is also the fourth most popular fishery in the park. The river's 30 miles are restricted to fly-fishing. The Firehole is one of the most picturesque rivers in the park as it winds through meadows dotted with geysers. Some geysers erupt literally into the Firehole. Bison and elk are commonly seen grazing along the river.

Unless the weather has been unusually cold, anglers should try other waters in July and August. Much of the Firehole's water comes from thermals and summer water temperatures sometimes reach 85 degrees, which puts trout into a feeding funk. Local anglers save the Firehole for early and late in the season. In June, provided the river is not too turbid, modest-sized nymphs and streamers generally work best. Toward the end of June use dry flies — perhaps mayfly imitations, but more likely caddis.

In autumn, most experienced anglers regard the Firehole as a spring creek and fish accordingly. With long, fine leaders and size 18 flies such as Quill Gordons and blue wing olives, anglers stalk the spooky trout. These rainbow and browns average about a foot in length, but a few large fish haunt the Firehole.

From Biscuit Basin downstream to the mouth is the most popular fishing stretch and has the best fish habitat. Wading is easy on the Firehole, but watch for occasional deep pockets. Geyser activity keeps the water warm enhancing the wading. There is good road access along the entire river.

The **Gallatin River** has its beginnings in the park, but most of the fishing takes place outside park boundaries. The upper reaches of the Gallatin run through big meadows. Undercut banks and deep holes punctuate the meandering, easily wadable stream. With no trees to hinder backcasts, the upper Gallatin is an excellent place to teach kids how to fly-fish. Lots of aggressive pan-sized trout and whitefish keep the attention level high.

The **Gardner River** runs almost its entire course within the park, joining the Yellowstone River just outside the border at the town of Gardiner on the north edge of the park. This is a classic pocket-water stream. The fast current is broken by an abundance of rocks that provide terrific holding water for fish.

Osprey Falls in Sheepeater Canyon divides the river. The upper eight miles above the falls has mostly 9- to 10-inch brookies and a few small rainbow. The lower 23 miles has brown, rainbow, and brook trout averaging 9 to 12 inches. Almost all the larger trout caught in the Gardner come from the lower end of the river, which is warmed by the runoff from Mammoth Hot Springs. Most of the lunkers here have migrated out of the Yellowstone River. The Park Service protects some of the spring and fall spawning with seasonal closures. But when the season is open, this beautiful, rushing trout stream can provide excellent fishing.

The **Gibbon River** is another of Yellowstone's famous and scenic fishing streams. Much smaller than the Madison or Yellowstone, the Gibbon provides superb fly-fishing. The Gibbon flows for 37 miles from its headwaters at Grebe and Wolf lakes to Madison Junction, where it joins the Firehole to form the Madison River, perhaps the most famous trout river in the Northwest. The river above the delicate veil of 84-foot Gibbon Falls was originally barren of sport fish, but now supports a good population of brook, brown and rainbow trout. The meadows around Elk

Park, Gibbon Meadows, and Norris Basin feature fine fishing when a hatch is on and the fish are rising.

Below the falls, the river provides fairly good fishing for brown trout and some rainbow and brook trout. There are lunker browns in here, but they're not easy to catch. This water is restricted to fly-fishing only. Attractor flies work very well in the broken water, as it meanders through meadows. This is one of Yellowstone's more heavily fished waters, although the success rate is only fair compared to most of the park's fisheries. It just takes a little more skill to outwit the Gibbon River trout.

Grebe Lake, about a 3.5-mile, level hike near Canyon, provides good catch-and-release fishing for beautiful pan-sized and larger grayling. Cutthroat-rainbow hybrids, running from 10 inches on up in size, provide another attraction. Anglers have a very good success rate here and consider Grebe Lake one of the most satisfying fisheries in the park. Grizzly bears occasionally graze on the area's succulent meadows in the early summer.

Heart Lake is a backcountry lake about eight miles in from the trailhead on the south entrance road. Though not a difficult hike, the lake receives only moderate pressure, especially considering its attributes. Spectacular scenery, interesting vegetation, and geyser activity add significantly to the pleasures of fishing this beautiful lake, the fourth largest in the park. Both the native cutthroat and the introduced lake trout grow large. The lake trout average 18 to 20 inches. The cutthroat average 16 to 18 inches, but a few monsters in the 2- to 8-pound category swim in this lake.

Heart Lake has special restrictions protecting the cutthroat. Best fishing for lake trout is in the fall, when they are in shallow waters for spawning.

Indian Creek is a small stream flowing northeast for 13.5 miles to join the Gardner River. The stream has very good fishing for 7- to 10-inch brookies. Indian Creek is remarkably popular for its size.

The **Lamar River** flows for 66 miles across the northeast section of the park to its junction with the Yellowstone River. One of the longest rivers in Yellowstone Park, the Lamar also provides some of the best fishing. The lower third of the river, easily accessible, is now catch-and-release only for cutthroat trout. The Lamar features excellent fishing for cutthroat; rainbow (including a few large rainbow in the lower reaches); and occasionally, beautifully colored rainbow-cutthroat hybrids. Anglers heavily pressure the obvious, easily accessible spots, but much of the Lamar sees few fishermen. Even a short, mile-long hike increases the success rate considerably. The Lamar is one of the premier terrestrial waters in the park. From mid-July through August, fish hopper imitations along the banks and at the riffle-corners. By early September, the water drops and the fishing slumps.

Lewis Lake, near the south entrance, is the third largest lake in Yellowstone. This popular fishing lake features road access, a boat launching ramp, and a 100-unit campground on its shore. Originally barren, Lewis Lake now supports a good population of brown and lake trout and a rare big brook trout, but these fish are hard to catch. Lewis Lake has a reputation for trophy-sized trout.

During the summer, boat fishermen have significantly better success than the shore angler. The best times to try for lake trout are just as the ice comes off in June, and in the fall, when they are in shallower water for spawning. At other times, anglers must get their lures very deep.

The **Lewis River** flows south out of Shoshone Lake through Lewis Lake to its junction with the Snake River just south of the park. Marshy swamplands along the river below Lewis Lake provide excellent habitat for moose.

The most popular section of river is the catch-and-release water below Lewis Falls, providing good fishing for 10- to 12-inch brook trout. Some lunker brown trout in the Lewis River prove very hard to catch. The river through the canyon is mostly inaccessible. The channel between Shoshone and Lewis lakes is a popular fall fishing spot, despite the requisite five-mile hike and unpredictable weather. A broad, slow-moving stream that can be canoed during the summer, this channel is normally only a moderate fishery, but in the fall, the upper half of the river is a major spawning ground for brown trout averaging 18 inches and ranging up to huge. The river is shallow, crystal clear and difficult.

Only 14 miles of the famed **Madison River** flow in Yellowstone Park. Nonetheless, this section of river catches more fishing pressure than any other waters in the park except Yellowstone Lake and Yellowstone River. Part of this attention is due to the location of a major campground at Madison Junction, where the union of the Firehole and Gibbon rivers gives the Madison its beginnings.

Without doubt, the Madison in the park is superb, but anglers new to this section should keep in mind two qualifications. First, stating that the river is superb does not mean it is easy to catch fish. In fact, fully half the anglers who try the Madison do not catch any. The entangling weed beds, glassy water, and shaky banks swing the odds in favor of the trout.

Second, because roughly a quarter of its water comes from thermal areas along the Gibbon and the Firehole, Madison trout suffer from heat stress in July and August, feeding on a midnight to 4 a.m. shift. Action is usually desultory except during a cold spell.

As with the Firehole, most knowledgeable anglers hit the Madison either in June, when the water is still cool or in September and especially October. And like the Firehole, the Madison has a fly-fishing-only restriction. Again, most anglers use either small dry flies or modest-sized

The Madison is most productive in June, September and October. By Michael S. Sample

133

Yellowstone Park waters are at their best in the spring for rainbows and in the fall for browns. By Mike Logan

nymphs and streamers. Mostly nymphs in the spring; perhaps pale morning duns from June 15 to July 7, soft hackle flies in September, and Maribou Muddlers and Spuddlers in October.

Due to conducive water temperatures, prodigious amounts of food, excellent cover, and protective restrictions, the Madison supports a large number of trout. The fall spawning runs of rainbow and brown add excitement to the already extraordinary experience of fishing the Madison. Anglers return year after year to try their skills again. During the runs, fish in the 20-inch range become common and a true monster trout might be the next to take the hook.

One night a Montana Fish, Wildlife and Parks Department (FWP) biologist set four gill nets in Hebgen Lake and the next day found a brown of at least 10 pounds in each net. Also, a 20-pounder was caught in June 1982 in Hebgen Lake. These fish spawn in the Madison.

Anglers can easily reach most of the Madison from the road that parallels the river. Some incredibly mucky bogs guard the river in spots above the seven-mile bridge. The music of bugling elk often accompanies fall fishing here.

Nez Perce Creek flows for about 15 miles from Mary Lake into the Firehole River. It is bordered by forest and meadows and is a popular area to see bison. The Mary Mountain Trail follows the creek most of the way to Mary Lake.

Nez Perce Creek has 10- to 11-inch brown and rainbow trout, but the fishing is only fair. The most popular area of river is the lower end, accessible by car.

Obsidian Creek is a small stream bordered by the road between Mammoth and Norris. It flows for nearly 16 miles, ending in the Gardner River. There is good fishing for small brook trout that provide great action for kids of all ages.

Pelican Creek extends for 52 miles from its mouth on Yellowstone Lake east of Fishing Bridge. Pelican, a broad, slow-moving creek, flows through willowy swamplands at its lower end. This is a likely area to see moose. The road crosses Pelican Creek, but you can reach the fishable portions of the creek only by trail.

Pelican Creek is the second-largest tributary to Yellowstone Lake and provides critical spawning grounds for the lake's cutthroat trout. There is also a sizable population of resident cutthroat. Because of spawning, the lower end of the creek is closed to fishing. The remainder is catch-and-release. The season does not open until July 15. The creek offers some of the finest fishing in Yellowstone Park. The cutthroat run 14 to 16 inches and are very catchable. Anglers give Pelican Creek the best overall rating for quality of fishing. This is also good bear country, so be on guard.

Riddle Lake is located just south of Grant Village. A two-mile hike is necessary to reach the lakeshore, which is bordered by large meadows west and south. Riddle Lake has good fishing for foot-long cutthroat. Check the regulations for special restrictions.

Shoshone Lake is the second-largest lake in Yellowstone, covering 12 square miles, and reportedly the largest lake in the United States without road access. Restricted to motorless craft, the lake is fished from canoes or inflatables. It is easily accessible by trail either from the north via the DeLacy Creek Trail (3.1 miles) or from the south at the north end of Lewis Lake. Despite the hike, this is a rather popular fishing spot.

Yellowstone Area Hatch Schedule

(Hatch Research Courtesy Jacklin's Fly Shop)

	May		June			July				August			September		
	22	1	8	15	22	1	8	15	22	1	8	15	22	1	8	15	22

Henry's Fork, Idaho — Box Canyon: SALMON FLY; GOLDEN STONE; CADDIS

RR Ranch: GREEN DRAKE; FLAVILINEA; TERRESTRIALS; BROWN DRAKE; BLUE WINGED OLIVE; INFREQUENS; TRICOS

Montana — Madison River (Below Quake Lake): SALMON FLY; GOLDEN STONE; TERRESTRIALS; CADDIS

Madison River (Above Hebgen Lake): TRICOS; BAETIS; CALIBAETIS; SALMON FLY; GOLDEN STONE; TERRESTRIALS; CADDIS

Yellowstone Park — Yellowstone River: SALMON FLY; GOLDEN STONE; BAETIS; CADDIS

Madison River: INFREQUENS; TRICOS; BAETIS

Firehole River: PALE MORNING; CADDIS; TRICOS; BAETIS; BLUE WINGED OLIVE

Originally barren of fish, Shoshone now has a good population of big lake trout, some brown trout, and a few brook trout. These browns are lunkers averaging 16 inches, with brook trout only slightly smaller. Boat fishermen get most of the lake trout, while bank fishermen do better for browns and brookies. The lake trout generally hang out in deep water (requiring special rigs) until October and November, when they move into shoals to spawn.

Slough Creek, in the northeastern corner of the park, is one of the most highly rated fisheries in Yellowstone. Approximately 16 miles of the stream are within the park, but this stretch is accessible only by trail for all but the lower end, where a campground provides access.

Since the introduction of catch-and-release-only regulations in 1973, cutthroat size has increased, and the trout now average a healthy 14 inches, with a respectable number exceeding 16 inches.

Slough Creek also has a small population of rainbow and rainbow-cutthroat hybrids in its lower reaches. Anglers frequently use terrestrial patterns such as Joe's Hopper and attractors such as the Royal Wulff, as well as the usual nymphs, small streamers, and small mayfly and caddis imitations.

Despite its limited access, this is one of the more-popular fishing streams in the park. It provides outstanding fishing in a pristine setting. In its lower end, Slough Creek has a rocky bottom and riffly water interspersed with large boulders. Upstream a few miles, it opens into the meadows of Slough Creek Valley, where the water is exceptionally quiet.

The **Snake River** extends for 42 miles along the southeastern boundary of the park before leaving Yellowstone at the south entrance. This is a moderate fishery for cutthroat, brown, rainbow, brook and lake trout.

Much of the Snake River has limited access. There is road access at the south entrance, but the majority of the river requires hiking. The first 10 miles of trail are good, but from there the going gets rough. The Snake is a deep river with wide gravel streambeds. It runs through scenic canyons intermixed with peaceful meadows.

Soda Butte Creek is bordered by the park road from the northeast entrance near Cooke City. It is a popular stream, providing good fishing for 10- to 11-inch cutthroat and a few rainbow trout in a valley of magnificent scenery.

Sylvan Lake is a popular roadside fishery, complete with picnic tables, located on the road between Fishing Bridge and the park's east entrance. Anglers do well hooking 12-inch cutthroat trout. Due to the heavy pressure this 28-acre lake was receiving, it has been designated catch-and-release fishing only. Sylvan Lake now has one of the highest catch rates in the park.

Editor's note: *Until the mid-1970s fishing was not heavily restricted in the park and limit catches, while not encouraged were tolerated, to the detriment of perhaps the finest concentration of pristine fishing in the contiguous United States. For the past decade, however, restrictions have been tightened to protect spawners, discourage "meat" fishing and to encourage catch-and-release. Now the vast park is divided into regional management areas, many of the trophy trout areas are protected with catch-and-release regulations and fishing success is coming back strong. Surprisingly, the number of fishermen in the park is few compared to the legendary hoardes that visit each summer. It's not at all difficult to find quiet fishing room, with large trout in a postcard setting.*

Seven Steps to Basic Fly Casting

The Grip

Wrap your fingers around the cork grip and position the thumb on top of the grip for support and better control. The grip must be firm, yet comfortable.

The Stance

Position feet directly in line with shoulders for balance. The foot opposite the rod hand should be slightly advanced. Casting with the right hand, move the left foot forward.

The Casting Clock

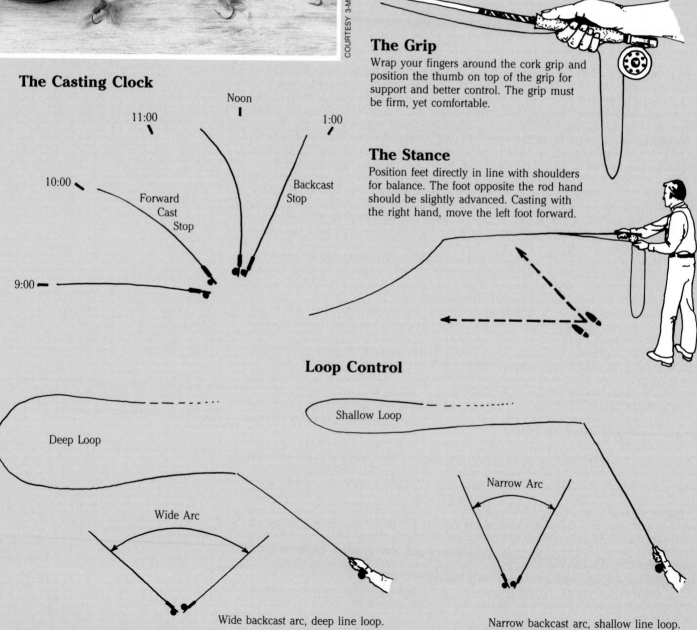

Noon

11:00

1:00

10:00

Forward Cast Stop

Backcast Stop

9:00

Loop Control

Deep Loop

Shallow Loop

Wide Arc

Narrow Arc

Wide backcast arc, deep line loop.

Narrow backcast arc, shallow line loop.

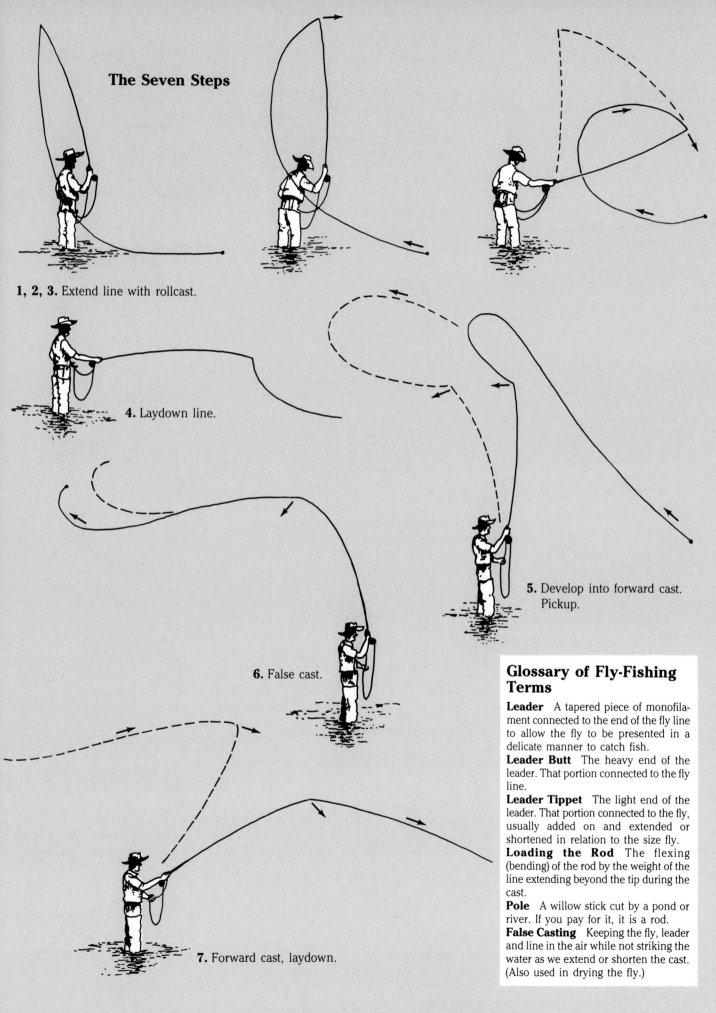

The Seven Steps

1, 2, 3. Extend line with rollcast.

4. Laydown line.

5. Develop into forward cast. Pickup.

6. False cast.

7. Forward cast, laydown.

Glossary of Fly-Fishing Terms

Leader A tapered piece of monofilament connected to the end of the fly line to allow the fly to be presented in a delicate manner to catch fish.

Leader Butt The heavy end of the leader. That portion connected to the fly line.

Leader Tippet The light end of the leader. That portion connected to the fly, usually added on and extended or shortened in relation to the size fly.

Loading the Rod The flexing (bending) of the rod by the weight of the line extending beyond the tip during the cast.

Pole A willow stick cut by a pond or river. If you pay for it, it is a rod.

False Casting Keeping the fly, leader and line in the air while not striking the water as we extend or shorten the cast. (Also used in drying the fly.)

Knots

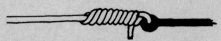

3. Pull standing line and lure in opposite directions, seating and locking the wraps into neat tight spirals. Be careful that one wrap does not overlap another. Trim tag end tight to knot.

Arbor Knot
(Attach Line To Reel Spool)

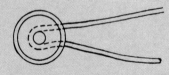

1. Pass line over and around reel arbor (spool).

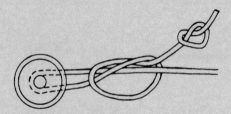

2. Tie a single overhand knot around the line.

3. Tie a second overhand knot in tag end.

4. Moisten and snug down against spool arbor.

Improved Clinch
(Line to Lure Connection)
Knot Strength 95-100%

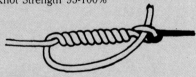

1. Insert tag end of line through hook or lure eye and double back, paralleling standing line. Allow at least 4 inches of tag line for easy handling. Wrap tag end around standing line a minimum of five times.

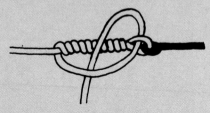

2. Insert tag end through loop between first wrap and hook eye. Pull through and insert through large loop. Pinch tag end against standing line with your fingers.

Palomar Knot
(Line to Small Lures, Flies)
Knot Strength 100%

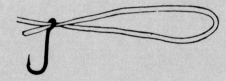

1. Pass line through hook eye front-to-back. Bring tag end back through eye, back-to-front, forming loop twice as long as hook, fly or lure.

2. Hold hook and line at eye. Pass loop around standing line and tag end on opposite side of hook eye. After wrapping around lines, run loop back through itself, creating an overhand knot.

3. Pull loop down and over hook so that loop legs come up on either side of hook shank.

4. Pull on line to seat knot against eye. Trim tag end.

Egg Loop
(Snell Loop For Holding Soft Baits On Hook)
Knot Strength 100%

1. Strip out 24 inches of leader. Insert it through the eye of the hook, front to back, and hold tag end flush against hook shank.

2. Using leader in front of hook eye, take eight wraps around shank and tag end, working front to rear.

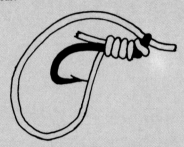

3. Run end of leader back through hook eye, going back-to-front, creating a large loop around the shank of the hook.

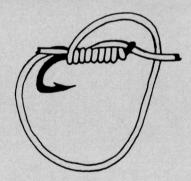

4. Hold leader below wraps against the shank and continue wrapping line against hook shank.

5. Continue holding wraps with fingers to avoid unraveling and pull steadily on leader until loop closes. Be sure loop is between hook shank and original tag end when it closes.

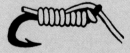

6. Finished knot should look exactly like this. Make certain no wraps overlap and cut into another. They should form a perfect spiral.

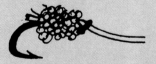

7. Fresh fish roe, shrimp or other soft baits can be inserted between loop and shank and held to hook by tension on the line.

Snell
(Leader to Hook Connection)
Knot Strength 95-100%

1. Pass one end of leader through hook eye until it reaches hook barb.

2. Pass the other end of the leader through the eye in the opposite direction and let it extend 2 inches beyond the eye, creating a large loop.

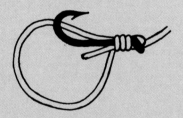

3. Hold the two tag ends against the shank. Grasp the leg of the loop nearest the eye and wind a tight, spiral coil around the shank and the two tag ends. Wind from the eye toward the gap.

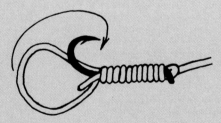

4. Take 15 turns around shank. Hold wraps tight with fingers. Grasp the leader end protruding from the eye and pull steadily until the entire leader has passed under the coil and out the eye.

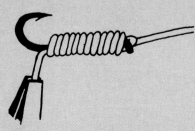

5. Grasp the remaining tag end with pliers and pull solidly to seat and lock wraps.

Blood Knot
(Joining Two Lines)
Knot Strength 90-95%

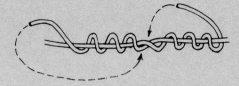

1. Place two 6-inch pieces of line parallel to each other, head-to-tail. Hold lines at midpoint. Take five turns around standing line with tag ends in both directions from midpoint.

2. Insert tag ends between midpoint segments, running one tag in from bottom and second tag end down from the top so they point in opposite directions.

3. Moisten strands and simultaneously pull both standing lines in opposite directions. The wraps will pull into loops as the knots pull together. Clip ends close to the knot.

Buffer Loop
(Nonslip Loop For Line/Lure Connection)

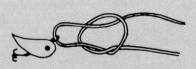

1. Tie a loose overhand (shoelace) knot in line leaving 6 inches of excess tag end.

2. Run tag end through lure eye. Tie a second overhand knot above first knot, using tag and standing line.

3. Tighten overhand knot nearest lure eye. Tighten second knot firmly against the first knot. Snip off tag end.

Two-Hook Sliding
(Two-Hook Baitfish Rig, Adjustable)

1. Run leader through eye parallel with shank. Pinch against shank.

2. Take leader above the eye, double back and wrap shank three times.

3. Pass leader end back through eye, creating a loop.

4. Wrap loop around shank below top knot. Tuck final loop beneath spur.

5. Place fingers over knot to maintain wraps and pull leader tight.

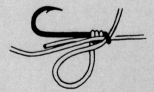

6. Using separate leader, duplicate first knot on top hook.

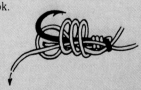

7. Run main leader through loop wraps parallel with shank, passing through hook eye.

8. Position at desired distance from bottom hook and snug.

139

The Uni-Knot System

One knot that can be varied to meet just about any situation common to fresh and saltwater angling . . . that pretty much describes the Universal Knot System, developed by Vic Dunaway in the early 1970s.

Of all knots, the Uni ranks as a favorite, a position earned by excellent knot strength, ease of tying, lack of complications, and incredible versatility. With one knot, you can join two lines, snell hooks, connect lures, devise dropper loops, etc., etc. If you can commit only a few knots to memory, one of those should be Uni-Knots.

Uni
(Joining Two Lines)
Knot Strength 85-95%

1. Lay two line ends parallel in opposing directions with about 6 inches of overlap. With one end form a 2-inch Uni-Knot circle.

2. Make six wraps around the two lines, and pull end to seat wraps.

3. Tie a duplicate knot with the other tag end. Moisten with water, and pull the two lines against each other, sliding two knots together. Trim close to knots.

Uni
(Hook Snell)
Knot Strength 100%

1. Thread line through eye and pull out 6 inches of line. Hold line against shank and form Uni-Knot circle.

2. Make six to 12 wraps through loop around line and hook shank. Pull tag end to close and seat wraps.

3. Pull standing line and hook in opposite directions to tighten snell.

Uni
(Line To Lure, Hook)
Knot Strength 90-100%

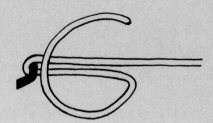

1. Run 6 inches of tag end through eye. Hold two lines together, then double back the end, forming a circle.

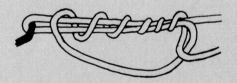

2. With tag end make six wraps around both lines above the eye, working from the lure up the line.

3. Pull tag end to seat wraps. Be careful not to let turns overwrap. Pull standing line to slide knot firmly against eye. Trim tag end close to knot.

Deciphering Fly Line Codes

The most common problem encountered by novice fly-casters, according to the Federation of Fly Fishers (FFF), is mismatched, or unbalanced equipment. The delicate, splashless presentation of a nearly weightless fly is the result of precisely matched rods, lines and leaders.

Fly rods are rated to handle specific weight lines, measured in grains. To avoid confusion, however, the various size lines are identified by numbers. The higher the number, the heavier the line.

Selecting a fly line that balances with the rod is mandatory for balance. Most rods have the number of the matching line stamped on the butt. There are numerous types of fly lines and weights, some sink, some float, some have most of the weight in the forward end, some have no taper. Each serves a different purpose. Most beginning anglers select one floating and one sinking or sinktip line.

In sporting goods stores fly lines are coded. Selecting the right line requires the ability to decipher the code. The accompanying chart, prepared by the FFF, illustrates and defines the code system.

Line Shape	Symbol
Level	L
Double Taper	DT
Weight Forward	WF
Single Taper	ST
Shooting Head	SH

Line Type	Symbol
Floating	F
Sinking	S
Intermediate	I
Fast Sinking	FS
Hi Density	HD

Line Number	Weight in grains First 30' of line
4	120
5	140
6	160
7	185
8	210
9	240
10	280

Typical Description
5DTS or DT5S = Line Number — 5, Line Shape — Double Taper (DT), Line Type — Sinking (s)

Conventional spin-cast (left) and
open-face spinning reels.
Courtesy Wright & McGill Co.

Mastering the Spinning Rod

To cast using spinning tackle, follow these steps:

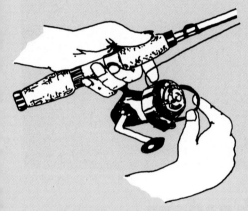

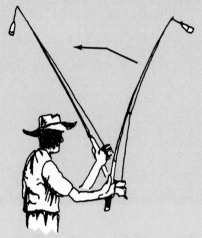

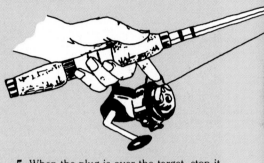

1. Grasp the rod's handle, placing the reel "stem" between your second and third fingers. Place your thumb on top of the handle and extend your forefinger to touch the spool cover. With other hand, rotate reel spool until line roller is directly beneath your extended forefinger. Pick up line in front of roller with forefinger and open, or cock, the reel's bail with your other hand. (Note: Some new reels have a lever so you can grasp the line and open the bail in one motion.)

3. Swiftly and smoothly, using just one motion, bend your casting arm at the elbow and raise your casting forearm so your hand is almost at eye level.

5. When the plug is over the target, stop it by touching the top edge of the reel's spool with your forefinger.

If the lure landed close in front of you, your forefinger released the line too late. If the plug went more or less straight up, you released your forefinger too soon.

Don't be discouraged if your first casts don't go as planned. In casting — no matter what kind of fishing tackle you use — timing is critical for long, accurate casts, and you will improve with practice.

(Developed by the American Fishing Tackle Manufacturers Association)

2. Face the target area with body turned at slight angle — about a quarter turn. The arm holding the rod handle should be closest to the target. Aim the rod tip toward the target at about eye level.

4. When the rod is almost vertical, it will be bent by the weight of the practice plug. As the rod bends, move your forearm forward with a slight wrist movement.

When the rod reaches eye level, straighten your forefinger to release the line. As the plug nears the target, slow it gradually by touching the line coming off the reel with your forefinger.

By Doug Wilson

A winter-run in its prime. By Doug Wilson

Steelhead, Steelheaders, Steelheading

By Milton L. Keizer

Each summer and winter in the Pacific Northwest, silver streaks of muscle and speed come in from the ocean, nose into freshwater rivers then plunge upstream. The steelhead are coming home and their arrival quickens the spirits of fishermen up and down the coast. Once you've tightened a fishing line against the power and determination of a steelhead you're never again the same person.

There is a mystique peculiar to steelhead that generates strange thoughts and eccentric behavior among steelheaders. For instance — one night a few years back I had a dream so vivid that it awoke me at 3 a.m. with an undeniable urge.

It was a vision of a large steelhead crashing through the emerald surface of Washington's Green River, the giant trout's body arcing against the background of a fishing hole that I knew well. The fish, a hen, stood out so clearly in my dreams that there could be no more sleep until I found out if the dream was a promise or just a wish. I gulped breakfast, hung my business suit on a hanger in the car, threw fishing gear in the trunk and set off for that hole on the Green, following my dream.

The Green is a beautiful, winding river tumbling from the crest of the Cascade Range, to pour into Puget Sound in Seattle's prominent Elliott Bay. It's one of the best steelhead rivers in Washington and one of the most heavily fished. Three hours of hard fishing later, the cold reality of a February dawn had pretty well dissolved the silver outlines of my dream steelhead and I was down to the "10 more casts and I've got to go to work" stage. On the seventh cast, the spoon stopped below a jutting tree root that in the past had hidden other steelhead. When I struck, the rod bowed and the dream came alive.

A big female steelhead came out of the water in a fountain of spray. She somersaulted identical to the way she looked in the dream just a few hours earlier and hit the water with a resounding "thwack!" No one can persuade me that 16-pound steelhead didn't call through my sleep. It's part of the steelhead mystique that captures nearly a million anglers from northern California to Alaska.

That 3 a.m. inspiration and success was more than a dream come true, however. The dream led me to the fish, but I managed to hook it because I followed the "basics" of fishing for *Salmo gardneri*, the Pacific Northwest's most-prized freshwater game fish. Steelhead fishing techniques have been cloaked in mystery and confusion that can distract a novice and inhibit a beginner. Steelheading is not really that difficult if approached with an open mind and a willingness to pay attention and learn. Like all good skills there are techniques that work for beginners and techniques best left to those anglers with a lot of years of experience at the river's edge.

Simple, steelhead-fishing fundamentals instruct: to catch steelhead, you have to fish a stream that has a good run of steelhead; you'll have the best success in a spot you know how to fish and are first to fish that spot with proven tackle.

A course of basic Steelheading 101 starts with the question, "What is a steelhead?" and finishes with "How do you catch one?" A steelhead is a descendent of the common ancestor to salmon and char, a rainbow trout spawned in freshwater rivers, that migrates to saltwater oceans to feed and mature, then returns to fresh water to spawn, nearly always in the same river where it was hatched, often within a few yards of the natal redd. This ability to survive in both fresh and salt water includes the steelhead in a select pack of coastal fish known as anadromous species. Perhaps the best known anadromous fish are salmon. Unlike the salmon, however, which spawn and die, a reasonably high percentage of steelhead survive the rigors and predators of ascending white-water spawning streams. Biologists estimate that between 10 and 17 percent of all steelhead spawn twice and some a third time.

Steelhead begin their odysseys in fresh water, holding in streams for 12 to 18 months before yielding to instinct and migrating downstream to the estuary at the river mouth where salt and fresh water blend. In the estuary, steelhead develop their saltwater tolerance and finally slip into the ocean where they will feed and wander for a year, sometimes two. In the river, during their downstream migration, these troutlike fish are known as smolts, and unfortunately many are creeled by trout fishermen who mistakenly confuse the silvery transients with the more colorful resident rainbow.

Steelhead migrate in the open ocean for two to three years, feeding on krill, shrimp and bait fish. Exactly where their ocean travels take them is pretty much conjecture and one of the best mysteries of the sea. They have been caught in commercial nets near the Arctic Ocean and Japanese longliners report catching Northwest steelhead within 200 miles of Tokyo. It's pretty much accepted that when they enter the ocean, most steelhead turn north toward the rich waters in the Gulf of Alaska.

In salt water these seagoing rainbow trout increase in weight from about 10 ounces to between 6 and 40 pounds at maturity when they return to freshwater spawning rivers. Steelhead wear the colors of saltwater salmonoids — deep blue along the back, metallic chrome sides and cream white along the bellyline. The difference in coloration is striking between the sea-run rainbow and the multihued, dark markings of a resident rainbow. They are also typically sleeker and larger than resident fish. The world-record steelhead is 42 pounds, 2 ounces, caught at Bell Island, Alaska, on June 22, 1970, by David White.

An average steelhead, in most river systems, will weigh less than 10 pounds. Between 10 and 20 pounds they rank as "good" fish and above 20 pounds are considered trophies. As a rule, the farther north the bigger the steelhead are, beginning in northern California where steelhead average less than 5 pounds to southeastern Alaska where 12-pound-plus fish are common. Typically, hatchery-produced steelhead are 25 to 50 percent smaller than steelhead hatched in the wild, and the average size in many river systems has decreased as declining wild fish are replaced by hatchery stocks. Perhaps a little late, most state fish managers now are implementing seasons and regulations directed at increasing wild fish runs by protecting native fish, and emphasizing hatchery catches.

Some rivers and specific runs of steelhead are based on unusually large fish. The Snake and Clearwater rivers of central Idaho have reputations for producing exceptionally large trophy-class steelhead including both Washington and Idaho state records. Washington's Skagit, Cowlitz and Lewis rivers, plus British Columbia's Fraser and Thompson river systems share this reputation.

When steelhead first come into fresh water from the coastal salt water, they are dime-bright in color, a trait that has earned them the nicknames chromers, mint or bright fish. The longer the fish are in fresh water, the darker their coloration becomes, a chameleon affect affording the spawners some protection from predators by allowing them to better blend into the bottom of shallow spawning rivers.

Females, typically called hens, become gray and the males known as bucks develop the rainbow-hued side stripe and olive-green back common to nonmigratory rainbow trout. Both sexes reach the darkest stage of their coloration at spawning peak. During this so-called "dark" period, the meat is soft and considered less palatable. Veteran steelheaders frequently release "dark" fish to complete their spawning cycle. Shortly after spawning, both hens and bucks begin to regain their ocean colors, losing the rainbow hues to silver and dark blue. As they move downstream from the spawning grounds, back to the ocean, empty of eggs and milt, steelhead are referred to as "spent" or "downstreamers." They rapidly regain their silvery bright coloration as they near the ocean.

There are few if any months when steelhead can't be caught somewhere in the Northwest, with most rivers supporting several separate runs of the big trout, each run arriving in the river

Steelheading demands quality tackle and concentration to detect the light pickups of a winter fish. Rod tip at 10 o'clock, reel palmed, and arm braced to strike, this Washington angler displays excellent form drift fishing bobber and eggs through a deep, sullen run. By Terry W. Sheely

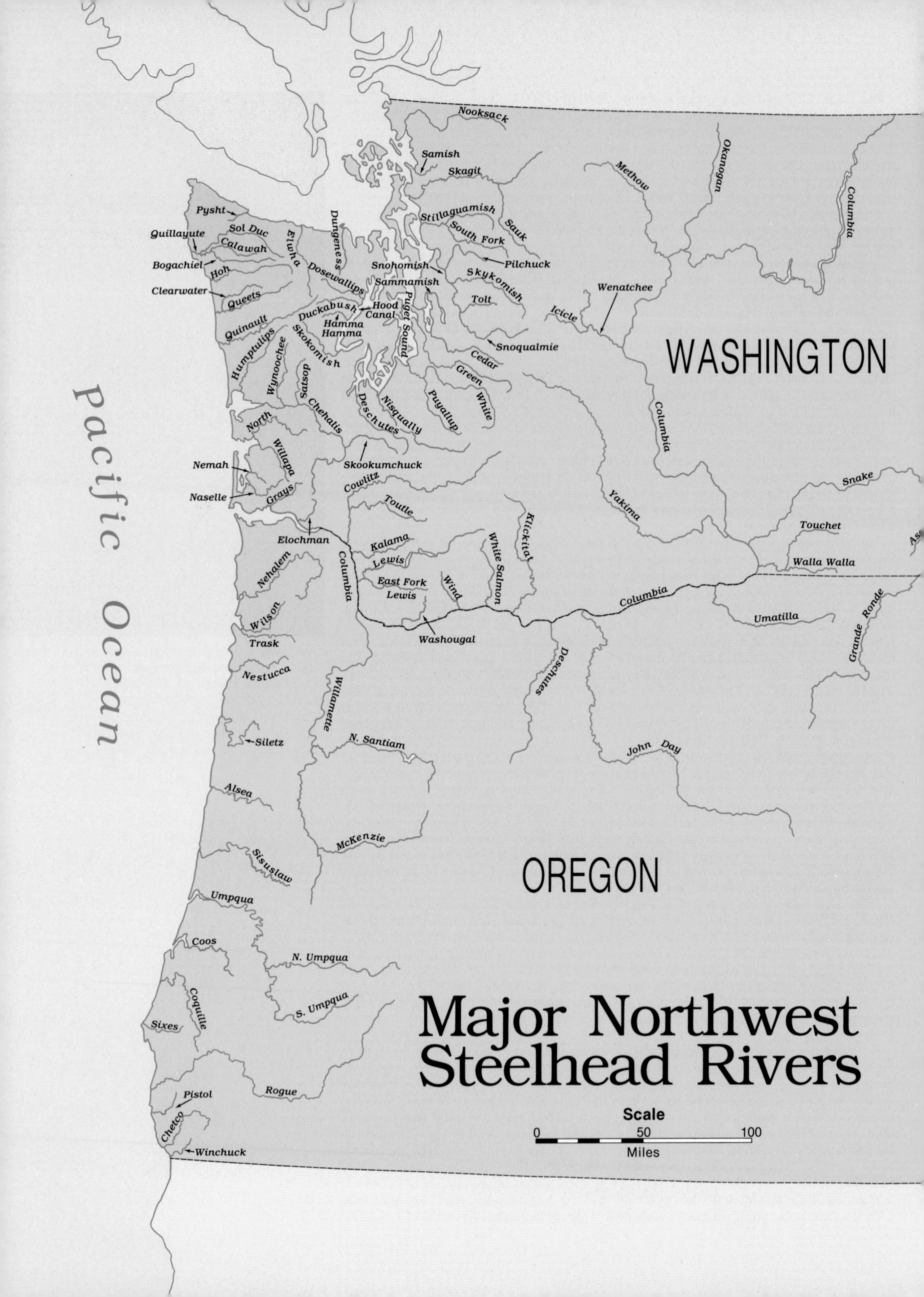

Pacific Ocean

WASHINGTON

OREGON

Major Northwest Steelhead Rivers

Scale

0   50   100

Miles

Nooksack
Samish
Skagit
Methow
Okanogan
Columbia
Pysht
Stillaguamish
Sauk
South Fork
Guillayute
Sol Duc
Calawah
Dungeness
Elwha
Pilchuck
Bogachiel
Hoh
Dosewallips
Snohomish
Skykomish
Wenatchee
Clearwater
Sammamish
Queets
Tolt
Icicle
Quinault
Duckabush
Hood
Canal
Hamma
Hamma
Puget Sound
Snoqualmie
Humptulips
Skokomish
Cedar
Wynoochee
Satsop
Green
White
WASHINGTON
North
Chehalis
Deschutes
Nisqually
Puyallup
Nemah
Willapa
Skookumchuck
Columbia
Naselle
Grays
Cowlitz
Toutle
Klickitat
Snake
Elochman
Kalama
Yakima
Touchet
Nehalem
Columbia
Lewis
White Salmon
Walla Walla
East Fork
Lewis
Wind
Columbia
Wilson
Washougal
Umatilla
Grande Ronde
Trask
Deschutes
Nestucca
Willamette
Siletz
N. Santiam
John Day
Alsea
McKenzie
Sisuslaw
Umpqua
Coos
N. Umpqua
Coquille
S. Umpqua
Sixes
Pistol
Rogue
Chetco
Winchuck

Brightly colored egg-shaped bobbers and fluorescent yarns are standard winter steelhead attractors. Some steelheaders prefer to match their yarn and bobber colors while others select opposing colors that clash to provoke strikes.
By Doug Wilson

during separate times of the year. Essentially, however, there are two major waves of sea-runs, those that return during the low-water months of summer and those that come back during the winter. Summer-run steelhead enter their home rivers between April and October and don't spawn until January or March. Summer-run steelhead feed occasionally and are generally considered the most acrobatic and aggressive of the two.

Winter-run steelhead move into freshwater spawning rivers between October and March, usually coming in on high-water flows. They dig their redds (nest) in gravel flats between February and April depositing up to 3,000 eggs in each redd. The redds are slight depressions in the gravel bottom which the hen creates by alternately wallowing and sweeping with her tail. After the eggs are fertilized both hens and bucks protect it for a short period from marauding resident trout, Dolly Varden, sculpins, squawfish, crayfish and other predators.

Winter-runs undergo internal body changes during their spawning runs that render them nearly incapable of feeding. Eggs and milt sacs swell until they displace the stomach tract. Although they can't feed, they still have the urge, picking up bright objects bouncing along the river bottom,

Steelhead, Salmon Drift Sinker-Rigs

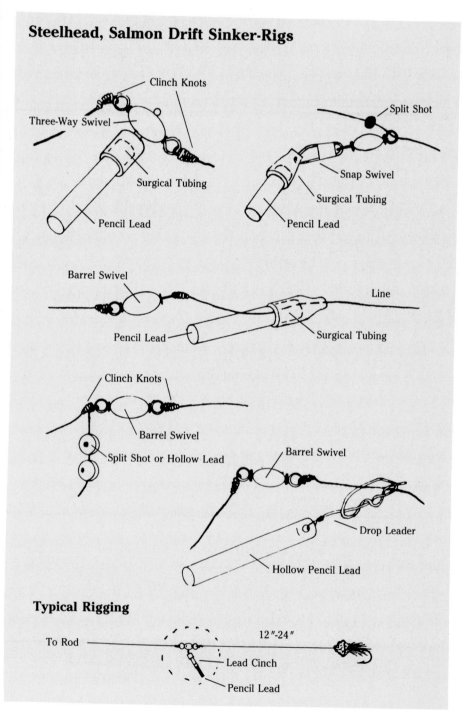

Typical Rigging

146

Bright, 16½-pound winter-run hen.
By Doug Wilson

clearing material from redds and attacking predators. Except for the defensive attacks against what appear to be predators (spoons, spinners, plugs) which are often powerful and savage, the strike of a trophy-sized steelhead can be deceptively light, almost imperceptible. These are, however, the traits that allow steelheaders to catch a fish that doesn't feed.

Learning to fish for steelhead is a matter of research, beginning with the state catch counts that show the number of steelhead taken each month from each river in the state. It helps to keep a log of fishing trips, listing success or lack of it, the height and color of the river, even the air and water temperatures.

After determining when the most steelhead are caught in a given month from a particular river, pinning down the exact spot on the riverbank is hardly any more difficult. Steelhead follow essentially the same paths within the riverbed upstream year after year, and the sunken boulder or deep slot that produced one year will hold fish again the next season, barring any major physical change in the streambed. If you've never fished the river before, follow the footprints of other anglers. Literally. Good fishing spots get a lot of wear from hip boot clad fishermen, and spilled bait, mashed cluster eggs, and worn paths left by a succession of anglers stick out like a sore thumb.

Step into that spot and look for the obvious place to cast, a place where a predator-conscious steelhead would feel comfortable. A place it can hide. White water spilling from a riffle, a sunken log, a patch of boulders, overhanging cedar boughs, a slight depression in the bottom, a rock ledge. The river surface provides clues, long, smooth flows generally indicate deep holes that steelhead often favor. Be alert for deep troughs where the current is moving three to five miles per hour. The color of water often reveals its depth. Generally, the darker the deeper. A narrow run of rough, choppy water 3 to 4 feet deep also is a good choice for anglers. The broken surface gives fish the cover — protection from predators — they instinctively seek. As a rule steelhead will hold on the downstream side of cover. The structure breaks the river current providing a pocket of protection and a little rest, and creates a surface turbulence that shields the fish from the sharp eyes of ospreys, otters, bears and other land-based predators. Steelhead also show a decided preference for "edge" water, that narrow area where the main current abuts the slow water on the fringe of the channel.

The riffled head and tail-out of a pool are usually far more productive than center where the current is most placid. A longtime steelheading practice is to fish the tail of a pool in the morning and evening for newly arrived and slightly disoriented steelhead, then concentrate on the head during midday for fish that have moved up the pool and are waiting for the right conditions before climbing the white-water section into the next pool.

Steelhead often move upriver as high off-colored water begins to drop and clear. When you can catch a stream with a dropping water level, coming off a high discolored (near flood) period, with a foot or two of depth visibility you've caught perhaps the finest conditions that can exist for catching steelhead. Steelhead will be on the move, aggressive and more responsive to lures than at any other time during their migration.

Steelhead can be caught with spinning, bait-casting and fly rods and reels. The tackle is usually factory modified to meet the demands and conditions of steelheading. Several specific lure presentation techniques have also evolved, including a tight-line fishery known as plunking, a bottom-bouncing variation referred to as drift-fishing and a back-trolling tactic Northwesterners call plugging.

The third largest steelhead to be caught in British Columbia's Thompson River was boated by Buzz Ramsey of Hood River, OR, on Nov. 5, 1984. It weighed 30 pounds, 5 ounces. By Luhr Jensen

In each case, the idea is to get the lure to the bottom. There's a time-worn, but accurate steelheading cliche that warns, if a steelhead lure isn't bouncing bottom and snagging rocks it isn't down where the fish are. Often steelhead won't move 2 feet to bang a lure (although at times they'll career completely across the river to strike) and if a lure doesn't smack them right on the nose they don't bother to hit it. These fish aren't feeding and the only reason they have to pick up a lure is to satisfy their curiosity or defend their lie. Unless the lure passes within a few inches of them it doesn't provoke either of these instincts.

Steelhead fly patterns: Deschutes Skunk (left), Deschutes Demon, Doc Gillis. By Ed Park

Fly-Fishing

Fly-fishing is an effective, but challenging technique. Because of the difficulty in adjusting to a steelhead's specialized requirements fly-fishing attracts the least number of participants of any common technique. The recent development of high-tech fly rods and lines, however, has made getting a fly down to a bottom-hugging steelhead a little easier and a few more anglers are taking up the challenge of the long rod each year.

Fly-casters often prefer to first spot their steelhead, by using polarized glasses, then casting wet fly, nymph, or streamer patterns to that specific fish until it strikes or spooks out of reach. Fly rods are fairly stout, 8 to 9 feet long. Graphite is a favorite blank material, designed to handle a No. 8 to 11 full-sink or sink-tip line, knotted to a short tapered monofilament leader. Leaders are trimmed to as little as 4 feet (adjust to conditions) so the sinking fly line can hold the leader and fly to the bottom where steelhead live. Fly leaders have a normal breaking weight of 6- to 8-pound test.

Most steelheaders prefer a single-action reel as opposed to an automatic. Single actions usually spool more line and backing than automatic models, a major consideration when tackling a fish as powerful as a steelhead, and are easier to control with finger pressure. A few anglers invest the extra cost of a multiplier reel, but most settle for the conventional, and relatively inexpensive, single-action models. Very few steelhead are caught on dry flies — a feat reserved for the most persistent and masochistic steelheaders who delight in coaxing a nonfeeding bottom-hugger to the surface in pursuit of a morsel that it can't digest. The exception, of course, are summer-run fish which do occasionally feed and can be coaxed to a well-presented dry fly. Dry fly-fishing for winter-run steelhead is one of the most difficult challenges in freshwater fishing.

Most fly lines, then, are selected for subsurface fishing. Get a fly deep, down to the bottom where the rocks are. Full sinking lines were common before the late 1970s when they began to be replaced by less cumbersome and more effective sink-tip models where only the first 10 to 15 feet of line sinks. Weight forward or sink tip lines are preferred by most steelhead fly-fishermen.

Picking a fly pattern can generate some heated arguments on which is best — bright attractor pattern flies designed to arouse a steelhead's curiosity or provoke its defense instincts, or imitators that duplicate the physical appearance of a natural insect, such as caddis or stone flies. As a rule, more imitator patterns are used in the summer for the sometimes-feeding summer-runs while bright attractor patterns dominate the winter fishery. The exceptions are flies that imitate fish eggs, bright dabs of red or orange color that both summer and winter fish find hard to resist.

Fly casting presentations, as with all steelhead lures designed to be cast into flowing water, are pitched in a quartering upstream pattern, that allows the lure or fly to sink to the bottom as it drifts directly opposite the angler, continuing to drift downstream along the bottom at the end of a tight line for the length of the cast. All casts to structure (rocks, logs) should pitch in above the lie so the lure is kissing bottom when it reaches the holding water. Lures that land exactly in the holding water will drift downstream, beyond the fish before sinking deeply enough to attract interest.

Another casting rule is to fish the closest water first. Initial casts are short, and the length of each succeeding casts is extended slightly until progressively every foot of holding water is covered by the sweeping lure. This pattern offers the lure to every foot of potential holding water and holds true whether you're flinging flies, spinners, spoons or bait.

Plugging

Plugging is an extremely productive steelhead technique so effective that most Northwest fishing guides rely on it to produce steelhead for rank beginners or during difficult weather and river conditions. Strikes on a plug are dramatic and often as not the fish hook themselves.

The heart of the technique is a broad-bill floating plug that dives deeply when held against the current. The most popular plug in the Northwest is the Hot Shot, a squat little floating plug that has been used so long that the terms plugging and Hot Shoting are synonymous among steelheaders. The plugs are brightly colored and vibrate wildly as they dive, forced down by the current pressing on the flat, elongated surface of the diving bill. The gyrations appear to trigger a predatory or "first strike" reaction in steelhead and they usually attack the intruding lure with a vicious strike.

Most steelhead plugs are 3 to 5 inches long, with rounded, streamlined bodies, leading from a flat-surfaced diving bill to a trailing treble hook. As a rule, bright metallic blue and green plugs are used in clear water, more solid or fluorescent colors such as white, red, or black when the water is somewhat colored.

Although a few steelheaders cast plugs from the bank, or work them from planing devices, the most common technique is back-trolling downstream from a drift or jet boat held against the flow so current pressure against the bill of the plug forces it deep.

The plugs are free-spooled downstream 35 to 40 feet below the boat. When the plugs are positioned and diving the boat is allowed to gradually drift downstream, held against the current by motors or oars, maneuvered slowly side-to-side across the river so the plug sweeps slowly across and downstream thoroughly covering the holding water. The plugs advance through the holding water bearing down on steelhead like invaders. Some steelhead immediately strike the threatening lure, others allow it to back them down the hole and only strike when their tails are against the wall of shallow water. When fish decide to slam that lure jittering in front of their noses it pays to have stout rods with 17-pound or higher test monofilament.

Spinners/Spoons

Steelhead will grab lures fished by casting devotees that appear to imitate bait fish or predators invading their holding areas. Spoons weighing ⅓ to ⅝ ounce, or No. 2, 3 and 4 spinners are the most common "hardware" lures. Nonbuoyant, metal spoons and spinners are fished with both spinning and casting rods by casting slightly upstream and drifting downstream on a tight line, retrieving just enough to take up the slack created by the current and variances in bottom depth. There's a fine line between holding a spoon or spinner just off bottom where a steelhead can hammer it, and embedding that lure in the bottom. It takes a while to develop the touch and the lessons mean breaking off a few $2 lures.

Novice steelheaders often favor spoons and spinners because steelhead strikes are more pronounced than when using bait or bobber/yarn drift rigs, which often evoke a gentle, difficult to detect pickup. Steelhead generally smack intruding spoons and spinners hard enough to hook themselves requiring only a slight "rod set" to drive hooks home and then hang on for the wild battle.

Both spinning and casting rods make fine steelhead sticks. Spinning rods generally are 8½ to 9½ feet long, and have a sensitive tip for detecting light pickups and a backbone stout enough to handle a big fish. The butt is exceptionally long to provide maximum leverage against a fish. Spinning reels are loaded with monofilament line testing from 8 to 12 pounds with spools that will hold at least 250 yards of line. A good spool drag system is a major consideration.

Drift Tackle

In many areas the so-called steelheading standard is a bait casting rod and reel combination. Most steelheaders favor casting rods from 7½ to 9½ feet long with the extended butt. The favorite blank material is graphite with its high level of sensitivity, although graphite/fiberglass composites are popular mainly because they are cheaper to buy.

Casting rods are equipped with level-wind reels that have been outfitted with high-speed multiplying gears supplying 4-to-l retrieve ratios. Star drag systems are standard. The spools are loaded with monofilament line testing between 8 and 20 pounds, and leaders slightly lighter than the main line. The combination is ideal for a technique known as "drifting" bait or buoyant artificial lures a few inches above the bottom, through steelhead holding runs and lies.

Natural baits that entice steelhead are cluster eggs, shrimp, nightcrawlers, pieces of shelled crayfish tails, single salmon eggs, and even grubs, garden worms, meal worms and maggots. Maggots are a popular bait for whitefish and many a whitefisherman, with his tiny tackle has been surprised with a rampaging steelhead.

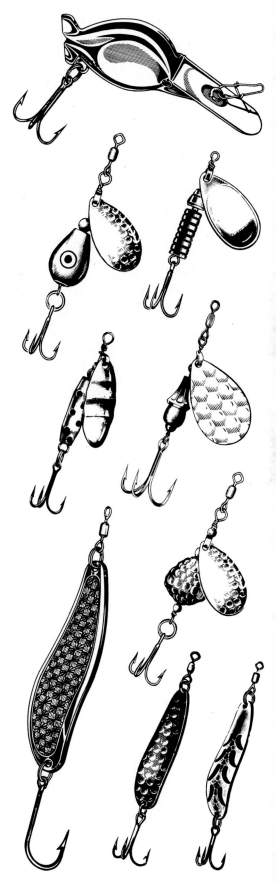

On the fly. By Brian O'Keefe

Artificial lures that work well often imitate natural baits, especially single and cluster eggs. Round, knobby and winged bobbers, with tufts of colorful yarn or curly plastic tails, are standard in the Pacific Northwest. These drift rigs may be fished alone or sweetened with bait or scents that attract fish and mask the odor left on terminal gear by L-Serine (carried in perspiration) from an angler's hands.

These baits or lures are fished by "drifting" with the current, weighted to the bottom with pencil lead sinker weights. The weights are cut from bulk spools of soft lead with the diameter of a small pencil, to match current flow and water depth. The object is to cut a lead heavy enough to bounce along the bottom but light enough not to snag on the bottom. The elongated pencil shape of this type of weight doesn't wedge in the rocky bottoms of Northwest steelhead rivers as easily as rounded split shot or bell sinkers. There are numerous ways of attaching the lead.

A three-ring, snap or barrel swivel connects main line and leader and serves as a connection for attaching the pencil lead. One of the most common methods for attaching the lead is with inch-long sections of elastic surgical tubing. One end of the tube is secured to the swivel with wire or by piercing it with the open end of a snap swivel. The lead is squeezed into the opposite end of the tubing, held firm by the elasticity, but capable of being pulled free when it snags on the bottom, saving the lure. Some anglers tie the main line to the ring on a snap swivel, spike the snap through the side wall of the surgical tubing, and tie the leader to the bottom loop of the swivel. Others slip a snap swivel's upper loop on the main line, add barrel swivel, tubing, lead and leader, and allow the weight to freely slide on the main line. Three-ring swivels are tied with one end of the T top to main line and the opposite side to leader, with pencil lead in surgical tubing hung from the bottom of the T. Other anglers leave a long piece of main line extending from the swivel knot and pinch on split shot or hollow pencil lead. A few simply run the line through the tubing, and squeeze in a piece of lead pinching the line between the lead and tubing to secure it.

Leaders normally measure between 14 and 18 inches from the lead. Longer leaders allow the buoyant bobber lures to float up out of a steelhead's strike zone.

The lead should bounce bottom every foot or two throughout the drift, a good indication your offering is down where steelhead lie, next to and almost in the main current. When steelhead pick up the hook in their mouth a pulsation, small tugs, or feeling of sudden weightlessness is transmitted up the line . . . your cue to slash back with the rod, strike hard enough to cross their eyes, then strike them again the first time the fish settles down and faces upstream. If you strike when the fish is head-on to the rod, it's easy to pull the hooks free. Strike hard, there's a reason they call these big trout steelhead.

Learning to sense or detect these light pickups is the hardest part of steelheading, and every angler sets the hook on plenty of rocks before connecting with the real thing. The best advice is to set the hook whenever the lure stops or bangs something solid. At the least, those who follow this advice lift their lures off potential snags, and at the best, they lift the hook into a steelhead's jaw. It helps to hold the rod tip high, about the 10 o'clock position, to keep as little line as possible in the water and provide maximum sensitivity. Water and slack line absorb the gentle impact of light bites, and the less of both the better.

Plunking

Of all the ways to catch steelhead, plunking is the least taxing, most relaxing and steeped in the most tradition. It generally takes place in the lower rivers where current flows are too slow to drift and the river rocks are sheathed in silt. Plunkers often use the same rods, reels and lures as drift fishermen, but use heavier weights — often pyramid sinkers — that pin the lures to the bottom. Unlike drift fishermen who depend on the moving lure to find stationary fish, plunkers expect moving fish to find the stationary lure. They fish when the water is high and brown or low and clear, and all stages in between. They like the high water best, because that's when fresh runs of steelhead are moving upriver.

Plunkers favor winged bobbers and globs of cluster eggs or shrimp, tied on 20 to 30 inches of leader, suspended just off bottom by buoyant bobbers, knotted on the main line a foot or two above 2 to 6 ounces of weight that pins the rig to the bottom.

Plunkers lob the heavy rigs into known steelhead paths, cradle their rods in forked sticks, hang a small signal bell on the tip as a strike indicator and gather around a warming fire to swap fish tales with other plunkers, drink coffee, and wait for a bite. At some of the longtime plunking areas, fishermen waiting for a bite have pitched weathered shacks, unpainted and sagging but stout enough to ward off the winter rain and buffet the chill of a light wind.

Many veteran steelheaders, whether plunking, drifting or spinning, keep a light reel drag, stopping line slip during the strike by pinning the line to the spool with finger or thumb pressure, then releasing tension as the fish runs. Play a hooked steelhead with light drag tension to compensate for searing runs, acrobatic leaps, or stubborn head shakes, and better control the battle.

Steelhead often come to the bank or boat early in the fight while still green and fresh, and when they see the fisherman they streak away. They may repeat this tactic several times before finally coming to net. If the reel drag is screwed down tight during these bursts of speed, the line — regardless of its strength — will often snap. It's common for many steelheaders to back off the drag as the fish nears the net, controlling line tension with a finger or thumb riding on the reel spool.

Handling the Catch

In some rivers wild steelhead are protected and only hatchery-produced fish, identified by clipped or missing fins, can be taken home. If there is a chance the steelhead is to be released keep the fish in the water. The less a steelhead is handled the better are the odds it will fully recover when released. With needlenose pliers grab the hook and twist. If the fish is exhausted, grasp it around the peduncle (just in front of the tail) and holding the fish upright, rock it to and fro in the water forcing water into the gills, until it regains strength to swim. Try not to remove the protective slime covering.

Fish that are to be kept should be cleaned quickly. There is no finer eating that a fresh steelhead properly handled. As soon as the fish is on the bank, sever a gill arch and pause for a minute while the fish bleeds out, then a sharp crack with a billy at the top of the skull, just above and behind the eyes, will kill it quickly. Slit the belly from anal opening to the gills, remove the viscera, scrape the blood vein along the backbone clean and cut out the gills. Store in a cool, well-ventilated area. Never store in a plastic bag without ice. Heat and blood are the two biggest spoilage culprits. Do your best to eliminate both.

Accessories

Every steelheader requires a certain amount of specialized equipment. Novices can jump in with a minimum of the tackle, baits and lures described, but, as skill and experience develop there are some accessories that become downright essential.

Waders or hip boots top the list. Quality, insulated boots or waders allow you to wade through mud and wet gravel, cross side streams and reach the best casting positions. By getting closer to the steelhead, slack line is reduced providing better feel, lure control and casting angles. Felt soles or metal cleats provide firm footing on the treacherously slick river rocks in most rivers.

Next in line is rainwear. A winter trip to a coastal river can end in soggy, shivering disappointment and possible hypothermia without good rain gear. Parkas or good rainsuits are worth their weight in gold when you have to choose between leaving willing steelhead and being drenched. Sturdy, breathable rain gear is best and naturally more costly. Buy the best you can afford, and select drab colors. A flame-orange parka will scare the bejabbers out of a steelhead trying to hide in a low, clear stream. Wide-brimmed, waterproof hats keep the rain off your neck. Scandanavian-style wool stocking hats will absorb water but retain body heat.

Fingerless wool gloves keep the hands warm, yet provide the finger dexterity required to cast, unravel backlashes and tie knots.

Summer-runs respond better to flies than winter fish. This fish is in prime condition and is about to be released.
By Dave Engerbretson

Leader Selection

Unlike most fishing line, leader material is rated by the diameter of the line, not the breaking strength as measured in pounds. The change can be confusing to anglers accustomed to selecting their line by breaking strength.

The accompanying chart illustrates the breaking strength, as measured in pounds, of most common leader sizes. Example, a 1X leader equals 9-pound test line.

Size	Tip Dia.	Butt Dia.	Test Lb.
0X	.011	.021	10
1X	.010	.021	9
2X	.009	.021	7
3X	.008	.021	6
4X	.007	.021	5
5X	.006	.021	4
6X	.005	.017	3
7X	.004	.015	2
8X	.003	.013	1

Examples of Standard Fly Styles

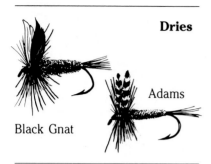

Dries

Black Gnat

Adams

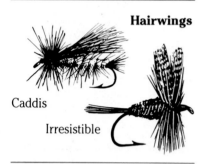

Hairwings

Caddis

Irresistible

Terrestrials

Grasshopper

Ant

Nymphs

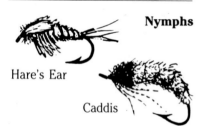

Hare's Ear

Caddis

Wets

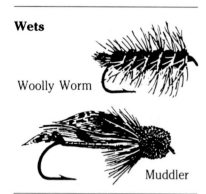

Woolly Worm

Muddler

Streamers

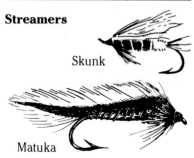

Skunk

Matuka

Developmental stages of steelhead Top to bottom: alevin, fry, smolt, adult sea-run, spawning male and female. By Fisheries and Oceans, Canada

Multipocketed fishing vests are specifically designed to hold the leads, bobber and fly boxes, leader spools, yarn packets, spinner containers, spoons, sinkers, tubing and assorted odds and ends a steelheader needs. The vest of a well-equipped steelheader may weigh between 10 and 20 pounds when loaded for a day fishing. Pick a stout one, with double or triple stitching. Some substitute a shoulder satchel for a vest. Few veteran bank fishermen operate out of tackle boxes.

Bait anglers require a bait box, a belt to hang it from, and a hand towel to clean the hands after handling a glob of juicy eggs or shrimp. Tighten the belt on the outside of chest waders.

Other handy accessories include a collection of small plastic boxes that fit the vest pockets and keep tackle from tangling. Needlenose pliers with side cutters for sizing pencil lead, folding scissors to trim yarn lures, nail clippers to clip knot tags, leader dispensers with several different strength lines, polarized glasses, spare match case, small plastic bag for packing steelhead eggs, hook file, scent masks, an extra length of surgical tubing, assorted swivels, snaps, and a selection of hooks from No. 4 to 3/0. A folding gaff, hand scales, lunch, camera and even a small vacuum of coffee are packed into a vest.

These are the basics of Steelheading 101 but to graduate Steelheader cum laude require years of practical application and field trips to the banks of a Northwest steelhead river. There is an old saying that the hardest steelhead to catch is that first one. It's true. But after that first silver streak from the Pacific unloads its lightning on you, you'll be caught in the mystique of Pacific Northwest steelheading. And, maybe, one night you'll see a silver streak dancing and splashing in your dream. A wishful delusion or visonary promise? You'll not rest 'til you know.

Steelhead roe skeins.
By Terry W. Sheely

The Best Bait

By Bill Davis

If a poll of veteran fishermen was taken to select the best natural bait for steelhead, big trout and river salmon around the Northwest, the winner would no doubt be cluster eggs. Sand shrimp would get many votes, but the use of these fragile beach-dwellers as river bait is relatively new, dating back only a dozen years or so. The ubiquitous egg cluster has been catching fish for over half a century.

There are several ways to prepare cluster eggs, and each has its share of advocates. Many longtime steelheaders swear that how the eggs are prepared is as important as how they are fished. In these days of increasing competition for a decreasing resource, I don't believe that is true.

Cluster eggs are obtained from several species of mature female fish. After trying them all, I prefer sockeye salmon and winter steelhead to all others. Coho, chinook, pink and chum salmon eggs will also work very well, as will mature skeins from sea-run cutthroat and late summer steelhead. Some rivers receive summer steelhead as late as December and I like the eggs from these late, bright fish as well as any I have used.

Good bait egg skeins combine firmness with the right amount of juiciness. Immature eggs will not milk properly and tend to dry excessively when cured. Eggs that are too mature separate from the skein easily and should be fished as "berries" rather than clusters.

When cutting egg skeins into cluster baits, consider the target fish. Fall chinook prefer a healthy 50-cent-size gob of eggs, while the low, clear water of late summer will find steelhead more receptive to nickel-size clusters. Dolly Varden and cutthroat, being smaller than salmon and steelhead, will also prefer smaller baits.

Egg clusters targeted at steelhead and salmon are usually fished in combination with a strand or two of fluorescent yarn under normal to low water conditions, and when rivers are up and dirty, a small drift bobber such as the Cube, Okie Drifter or Corky may be added. On rare occasions, when streams are low, clear and the fish are spooky, I've had to remove the yarn and fish bait to connect consistently.

Over the years, egg clusters have gained the reputation of being the bait of "pros," reportedly because fish bite eggs so gently the take is almost impossible to detect. Baloney! Summer steelhead, trout and coho salmon, in particular, grab eggs with no hesitation and the bite is unmistakable. Even with winter steelhead and chinook, both of which tend to be a bit more delicate in their approach, I've had many fish jerk the rod tip down fiercely.

Why do anadromous fish like steelhead and salmon bite egg clusters, which have never entered their realm of experience before their return to the river? There are many theories. The point is, steelhead, salmon and trout *do* respond to cluster eggs.

Rig your clusters by pushing over the hook point and cinching in an egg loop. I use as little lead as I can so the eggs will drift naturally along the bottom, following the current. Remember that eggs are nonbuoyant and will tend to settle to the bottom (another reason many anglers fish eggs along with a drift bobber is to add flotation). If the drift sort of stretches to a halt and the feeling is one of unyielding weight at the end of the line, you are probably hung on the bottom. You can often free your gear losing nothing but an egg cluster with a few upward bounces of the rod (followed by a direct, steady pull if the first tactic doesn't work).

A typical bite will occur as your bait drifts downstream followed by your lead sinker. You will feel the "bump, bump, bump" of the lead, then your gear will pause and several small tugs will follow. Upon occasion, there will be a sharp jerk or two followed by the surge of a fish. This kind of bite is not too hard to detect, obviously. Let the fish pull the bait a few times before setting the hook. Fish tend to stay with eggs, rather than to reject them after a second or two as they do with plain bobbers or other hard lures. Remember . . . it may not feel like a big fish, but it it *tugs*, give it a second or two and *set the hook*.

Curing Eggs

There are three basic methods used for curing cluster eggs; borax, sodium sulfite and salt, listed in order of their popularity. For about five years, I have been using sodium sulfite almost exclusively.

Borax Cure: Wrap skeins in paper towels and refrigerate overnight. This dries the eggs a bit, and the towels soak up excess moisture.

The next day, put several layers of newspaper on the table and pour a mound of powdered borax on the paper. Roll the skeins in the borax, coating thoroughly. Cut the skeins in half lengthwise, then again to form long, narrow strips. Cut strips into walnut-sized clusters (or to suit your needs) and roll pieces in borax.

Pack the clusters in containers alternating layers of fresh borax and eggs, topping with a layer of borax. Mark the container with date and type of eggs (e.g. "mature coho," etc.), refrigerate four to five days to let cure take effect, and freeze.

Sodium Sulfite Cure: Mix one part sodium sulfite with two parts granulated sugar. Sodium sulfite resembles sugar or salt — a white, granular substance. Be careful not to leave the egg cure where

153

it could be mistaken for sugar or salt by family members. I keep my sodium sulfite cure in a large seasoning salt bottle — with a shaker top, remove the manufacturer's label and mark it plainly as egg cure.

If egg skeins are fairly mature, wrap in paper towels and refrigerate overnight. If the skeins are tight and not overly juicy, you can waive the drying period. Hold the egg skeins over newspaper or the sink, with the membrane side down. Sprinkle with sodium sulfite cure, making sure to get some of the cure between each layer of eggs. *Don't overdo it* or the eggs will dry excessively.

Put skeins in containers and refrigerate. After 24 hours, pour off juice. Keep refrigerated four to five days, then freeze. To use, thaw the day before your fishing trip and cut into clusters. If you cut them before freezing, the eggs will become "soupy," and be fairly messy to handle.

Salt Cure: Use plain (uniodized) table salt or the slightly coarser kosher, or canning salt. Pour salt on a pile of newspapers and place skeins on the salt. Cover with more salt, then more newspapers. Place a weight on top of the papers, such as a heavy book. Leave for 24 hours. Pack eggs and salt in sealable plastic bags, freezer cartons, etc., and place in the freezer. Because of the high salt content, the eggs will never freeze solid and will thaw quickly. They may become almost like a red gumdrop in texture. Cut into clusters before fishing. These eggs, like eggs cured in sodium sulfite, milk very well and all types of trout and salmon seem to take them eagerly.

While carefully tended boraxed eggs work very well indeed, you can see that the sodium sulfite and salt cures are much faster in terms of preparing the eggs. This time savings becomes significant when you are putting up a lot of skeins at one time.

There are other choices of curing methods for cluster eggs, but these will cover just about any of the very favorites with a few variations. One popular alteration to the straight borax cure calls for adding about one part of flavored gelatin (cherry, raspberry or strawberry are the favorites) to each three parts of borax. Flavored gelatin not only adds a fruity aroma to your bait, but it helps to preserve the color.

Some sodium sulfite cures I have seen add salt to the mixture. This is okay, but it can dry the eggs excessively if not used with care.

Whatever you do, don't use iodized salt as a cure. It imparts a metallic, undesirable flavor that fish reject.

Borax Cure

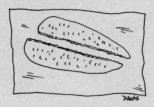

A. Remove skeins from fish. Wipe clean with a damp cloth, wrap in paper towels and refrigerate overnight.

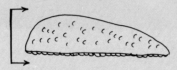

B. Cut skein in half lengthwise, roll sections in powdered borax. Do not use Boraxo or Borateam.

C. Again divide skeins in half lengthwise. Roll strips in borax.

D. Cut strips into walnut-sized clusters. Drop clusters into a container of borax and tumble until well coated.

E. Pack eggs in freezer cartons or jars. Pack in alternating layers of eggs and borax until full. Top with a layer of borax. Date and mark containers. Refrigerate for four or five days to cure, then freeze.

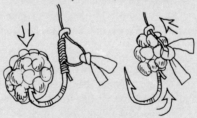

F. Push hook point through the center of membrane. When cutting clusters, always leave some of the membrane attached to each one.

G. Slide cluster up hook shank, turn and secure under leader loop. Yarn tied to leader loop adds attractive color and makes it easy to pull out loop to change bait.

Sodium Sulfite Cure

A. Wrap skeins in paper towels, refrigerate overnight. Hold skein with membrane side down and sprinkle with cure. Work cure between each layer of eggs. Don't overdo it or eggs will dry excessively.

B. Pack whole skeins in jars and refrigerate for about 24 hours, pour off juice. Refrigerate for one week, then freeze. Cut into cluster sizes as used.

Berries

A. Use 3-inch squares of red, pink or orange maline mesh, or wedding veil material. Pack eight to 12 single eggs in center of material.

B. Fold corners to center and tie with a piece of fluorescent yarn. Trim ends of yarn and excess maline. Use loose eggs left after handling skeins while boraxing or using sodium sulfite.

C. Push hook through the center of the berry. Slide it up the hook shank, turn and secure knot under egg loop in leader. The bait rides high on the hook with the point well exposed.

British Columbia's Barkley Sound provided this 28-pound chinook salmon, a typically thick-bodied, stout fish caught in its prime. By Doug Wilson. Below, streamer-style flies are strolled for coho and chinook salmon and jigged for bottomfish. By Terry W. Sheely

Salmon

By Terry Rudnick

The Pacific salmon has played an important part in Northwest history, and even though some of "our" salmon have done well in other places where they have been transplanted — most notably in the Great Lakes — the roots of sport salmon fishing are here.

Salmon attract anglers from all over the world, and even nonanglers are familiar with the names of some of the more popular fishing ports, places like Rivers Inlet, Campbell River, Sekiu, Neah Bay, Westport, Astoria, Newport and Brookings. And for every one of these world-famous fishing areas, there are a dozen smaller, less known but often equally productive spots, places with colorful names like Blubber Bay, Hat Island, Devil's Head, Chinook and Garibaldi. Hundreds of good salmon fishing spots are scattered along the coast from British Columbia to northern California, and with so much fishing opportunity available, it's easy to understand why the Pacific salmon is such an important part of the heritage of the Pacific Northwest.

There are five species of Pacific salmon, some of which are more important to sportfishermen than others. They have many things in common, such as a life history that sees them spending the first part of their lives in fresh water, migrating to sea to spend one to four years gorging on the Pacific's rich bounty, then returning to fresh water as adults to spawn and die. But there are many differences between the five — differences in size, feeding habits, migration routes and fighting ability — that separate the more prized species from those that are less dear to the hearts of Northwest anglers.

Salmon Trolls

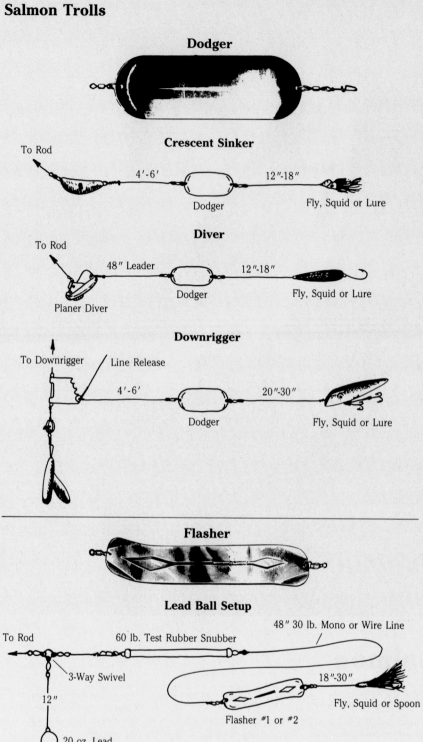

Dodger

Crescent Sinker

To Rod

4'-6'   12"-18"

Dodger   Fly, Squid or Lure

Diver

To Rod

48" Leader   12"-18"

Planer Diver   Dodger   Fly, Squid or Lure

Downrigger

To Downrigger   Line Release

4'-6'   20"-30"

Dodger   Fly, Squid or Lure

Flasher

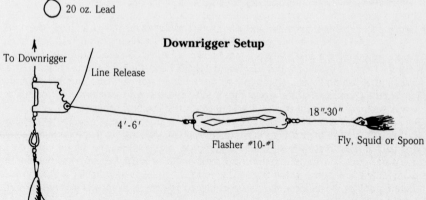

Lead Ball Setup

48" 30 lb. Mono or Wire Line

To Rod   60 lb. Test Rubber Snubber

3-Way Swivel   18"-30"

12"   Flasher #1 or #2   Fly, Squid or Spoon

20 oz. Lead

Downrigger Setup

To Downrigger   Line Release

4'-6'   18"-30"

Flasher #10-#1   Fly, Squid or Spoon

Les Anderson of Soldotna, Alaska is dwarfed by his number one world record chinook salmon. The 97-pound, 4-ounce king was caught May 18, 1985 in the Kenai River.

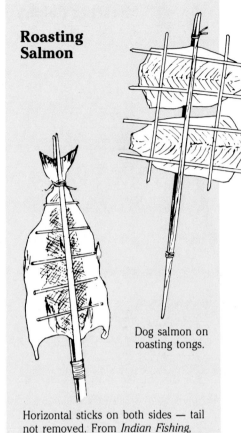

Roasting Salmon

Dog salmon on roasting tongs.

Horizontal sticks on both sides — tail not removed. From *Indian Fishing*, by Hilary Stewart.

Winter blackmouth caught on candlefish-style jig. By Terry W. Sheely

Most people know the chinook as the king salmon, and, although it may be called a tyee, a spring, a blackmouth or a jack salmon at various times of its life and in various places, the title "king" really is most appropriate. It's the biggest of the Pacific salmon, and the most highly prized by anglers. An adult chinook may weigh 50, 60, 70 pounds or more, it's an active biter that will strike a variety of baits and lures, and when hooked it provides the kind of reel-screaming, never-say-die battles that produce campfire stories of legendary proportions.

The chinook is widely distributed from northern California to the Bering Sea, and in some places — like the protected waters of Washington's Strait of Juan de Fuca and the east side of Vancouver Island — it's available to anglers throughout the year. But the chinook of winter and spring, known as blackmouth in Washington and springs in British Columbia, are the "little guys" of the chinook world, immature fish of "only" 5 to 20 pounds. The chinook fisherman's real prize, the adult king or tyee, is a fish of summer and early fall, one that is intercepted as it makes its way from the vast feeding grounds of the Pacific to the freshwater stream where it was hatched several years earlier.

As if a victory over one of these monarchs weren't reward enough for any angler, the person who catches a big king is also treated to perhaps the best meal anyone has a right to expect.

157

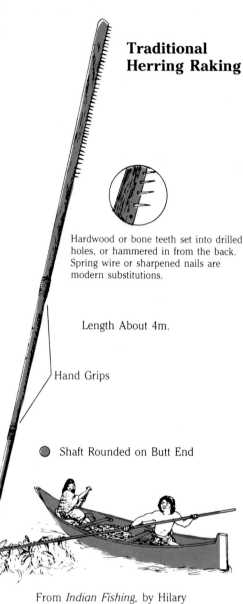

Traditional Herring Raking

Hardwood or bone teeth set into drilled holes, or hammered in from the back. Spring wire or sharpened nails are modern substitutions.

Length About 4m.

Hand Grips

Shaft Rounded on Butt End

From *Indian Fishing*, by Hilary Stewart.

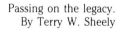

Passing on the legacy.
By Terry W. Sheely

The rich, red flesh of a well-fed chinook is second to none in the hearts and stomachs of seafood gourmets.

The coho, whose most popular nicknames are "silver" and "silversides," is somewhat smaller but generally more abundant than the chinook. In many areas of the Northwest it is the mainstay of the sport salmon fishery from June to September. The coho's popularity among anglers, though, isn't due to only to the fish's abundance. Silvers are eager biters, and their willingness to gobble any bait or lure that looks like an easy meal sometimes makes for fantastically wild fishing.

A typical Northwest coho will weigh in at 5 to 15 pounds, occasionally topping 20, and when they feel the sting of a hook they put every ounce of their weight into play. A sizzling, 50-yard run just beneath the surface may be capped by a series of twisting jumps, as one of these acrobatic fighters attempts to throw the hook. A typical coho doesn't quit fighting until it has been brought over the side and stashed safely in the fish box.

Like the chinook, the coho's carrot-orange flesh is among the best that the food-rich Pacific has to offer, and a freshly baked coho fillet is a just prize for anyone who has out-slugged one of these worthy opponents.

The pink salmon is a fairly important part of the sport fishery in many areas of British Columbia, quite common in Washington's Strait of Juan de Fuca during odd-numbered years, but rare south of the central Washington coast. The fish's most common nicknames, "humpback" and "humpy," come from the large hump that forms on the back of a male pink as it reaches maturity. Pinks, which typically weigh 3 to 6 pounds, can be identified by their extremely small scales and by the large, oblong, black blotches on their tails. Although their diet consists mostly of small, marine creatures, pinks aren't above taking a swipe at the baits and artificial lures offered by Northwest anglers, a habit that tends to shorten their life expectancy but which endears them to fishermen who would otherwise be unaware of the pink salmon's existance. The flesh of a pink is usually softer, lighter and has a more delicate flavor than that of chinook and coho.

Sockeye are known as red salmon in some areas — a name that comes from the fish's deep-crimson spawning color — and blueback in some of its more southern range. Although millions of these fish return to some river systems to spawn, anglers catch relatively few of them in salt water. A fairly successful sockeye sport fishery has developed in Seattle's Lake Washington, but for every sockeye caught by Northwest anglers, hundreds are caught commercially or escape harvest entirely and manage to make it back to freshwater spawning areas. A typical adult sockeye weighs 5 to 10 pounds.

Chum salmon are often the last of the five salmon species to return from their oceanic odyssey each year, sometimes arriving as late as January or February. Their nickname is "dog salmon," a title that doesn't do much for their reputation among anglers. They are, however, one of the largest Pacific salmon, sometimes topping 20 pounds, and they put up a strong, stubborn battle when hooked on sport tackle. Sportsmen, though, hook far too few of them for chums to be considered an important part of the sport salmon fishery.

Just as there is more than one way to skin a cat (although one would seem to be enough), there is certainly more than one way to catch a salmon. There are, in fact, four distinctly different fishing methods, with dozens of local or personal variations on each.

"Mooching" is the term most salmon anglers use to describe still-fishing for salmon with bait. The bait usually is a whole herring or anchovy or a herring that has been "plug-cut" by slicing its head off at an angle. A typical mooching rig consists of a crescent-shaped sinker of 1 to 6 ounces and a 3- to 6-foot leader of 8- to 20-pound test. A pair of size 1 to 5/0 hooks are tied, in tandem, to the business end of the leader, with the top hook about 3 inches above the second.

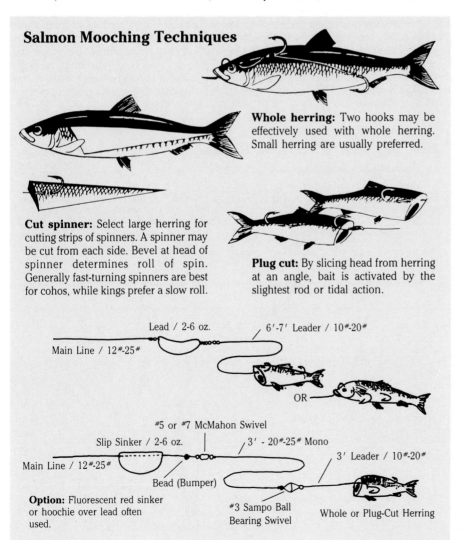

Salmon Mooching Techniques

Whole herring: Two hooks may be effectively used with whole herring. Small herring are usually preferred.

Cut spinner: Select large herring for cutting strips of spinners. A spinner may be cut from each side. Bevel at head of spinner determines roll of spin. Generally fast-turning spinners are best for cohos, while kings prefer a slow roll.

Plug cut: By slicing head from herring at an angle, bait is activated by the slightest rod or tidal action.

Lead / 2-6 oz. 6'-7' Leader / 10#-20#

Main Line / 12#-25#

OR

#5 or #7 McMahon Swivel

Slip Sinker / 2-6 oz. 3' - 20#-25# Mono

3' Leader / 10#-20#

Main Line / 12#-25#

Bead (Bumper)

Option: Fluorescent red sinker or hoochie over lead often used.

#3 Sampo Ball Bearing Swivel

Whole or Plug-Cut Herring

The Right Way To Release Fish

How a game fish is caught, played and released determines if that fish will survive to be caught again, or die within a few hours. When a fish is to be released it should be landed as quickly as possible. The fish will need its strength to recover.

Avoid touching the fish or letting it come into contact with a net or the boat. The scales on immature fish are loosely attached and can be wiped away with a stroke of the hand. Removal of scales allows dehydration of the fish and 25 percent scale loss can prove fatal.

Keep the fish in, or at least over, the water to reduce handling and increase its chance of survival.

Some form of hook releaser is helpful to free lightly hooked fish without touching the fish. The most basic device is a straightened coat hanger with one end looped to form a handle and the other bent into a small U-shape. Some anglers use long-nosed pliers or a gaff as a hook releaser.

At times it is best to flatten the barb or cut the hook to avoid severely wounding the fish. A hook that is swallowed, gill-caught or eye-caught is often best left in the fish. Unless the hook is stainless steel, it will soon rust away, with little harm to the fish.

When a fish is caught on a two-pronged or treble-pronged hook considerable handling may be necessary to release it. The opposing tensions make it difficult to free the fish without tearing a great deal of tissue.

Whenever possible, fish with single-pointed, corrodable hooks, particularly when trolling. Many fishermen find single-pointed hooks more efficient than treble because the three points of a treble hook can prevent adequate barbing.

Fish caught by anglers and played to the boat usually are in a form of shock and, if released, may need some seconds to recover. Unless a fish is active enough to dart away upon being unhooked, it should be held gently upright in wet hands and moved fore and aft, swishing water through the gills. Although grasping active fish with dry hands tears vital scales loose, and restraining active fish with wet hands requires too much squeezing of vital organs, a dazed or unconscious fish must be gently held in water with wet hands and moved to and fro until it is conscious and can swim off under good power.

Sinker weight depends on the depth you want to fish, while leader strength and hook size may be determined by water clarity and the size of the bait used.

When mooching, the idea is to hook the herring or anchovy so that it spins in the water, giving it the appearance of crippled baitfish. To give it that tempting spin, hook the bait near the head end with the top hook and sink the bottom hook farther back, near the tail. Drop it slowly to the desired depth, then work it up and down with the rod tip or the reel to keep it spinning. Mooching is extremely popular along the Washington coast and in Puget Sound, with different variations used everywhere throughout the Northwest.

Some anglers use the boat rather than the rod and reel to keep their bait moving. "Motor mooching" means kicking the motor in and out of gear while the baited hooks hang in the water. The bait spins to life and climbs toward the surface as the boat moves forward, then drops back toward the bottom when the motor is disengaged and the boat drifts to a stop.

The same rigs used for mooching can be used for trolling with bait, which takes the whole process one step further than motor mooching. A majority of anglers from Ilwaco, Washington, to Brookings, Oregon, troll bait for their salmon. If two or more anglers troll from the same boat, they usually use the same size sinkers and often leave their fishing rods in holders to keep the lines apart and avoid tangling while covering as much salmon water as possible.

Anglers can troll for salmon with something other than bait. A variety of artificial plugs, streamer flies, plastic squid and wobbling spoons have proven effective for Pacific salmon. These lures are usually trolled fairly near the surface for coho and pink salmon, somewhat deeper for chinook. Getting a trolled lure down to 50 feet or more for chinook may require the use of special diving devices or downriggers that incorporate heavy lead balls and special break-away connectors to keep the lure at the desired depth.

Jigging, usually called "drifting" in British Columbia, has really caught on with Northwest salmon fishermen in the past 10 years. Anglers jig with a wide range of metal, baitfish-imitating lures to catch everything from 2-pound pinks and coho to 50-pound kings. Jigging is especially popular in Washington's Strait of Juan de Fuca and along the southern British Columbia coast and east side of Vancouver Island.

Whatever fishing method a salmon angler may decide upon, he'll want to choose a rod, reel and line that's appropriate for the job. A typical salmon rod will be an 8- to 10-footer with a medium action and a tip that's sensitive enough to help an angler detect those light strikes. Canadian fishermen prefer a rod 1 to 2 feet longer than most American salmon anglers use. Fishermen north of the border also prefer large, single-action reels to the smaller, multiplier level-winds used in United States waters. Whatever the reel, it should be large enough to hold at least 150 yards of line. That line can range from 8- to 30-pound test, and should be a premium-grade monofilament that is "hard" to be fairly abrasion-resistant.

How to Use a Wire Hook Releaser

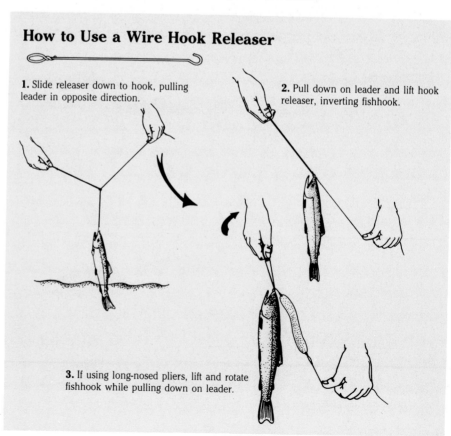

1. Slide releaser down to hook, pulling leader in opposite direction.

2. Pull down on leader and lift hook releaser, inverting fishhook.

3. If using long-nosed pliers, lift and rotate fishhook while pulling down on leader.

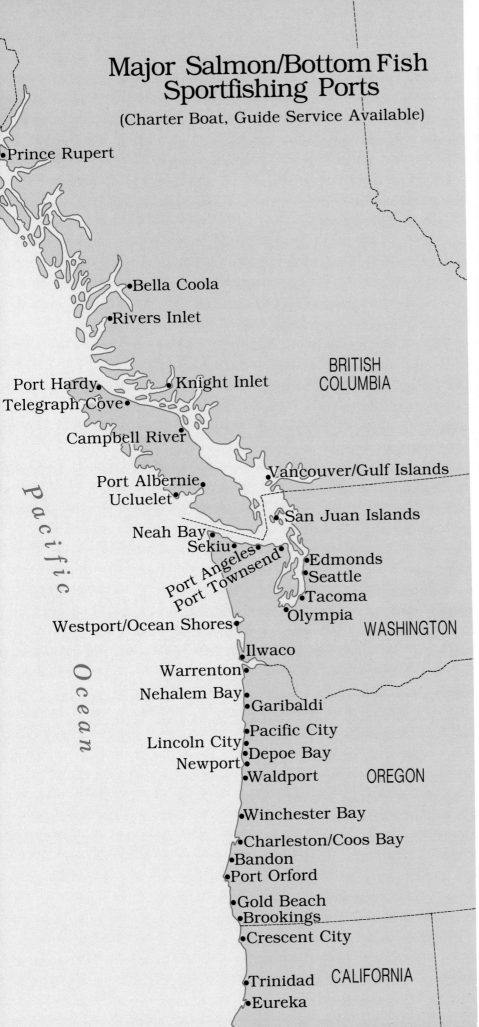

Major Salmon/Bottom Fish Sportfishing Ports

(Charter Boat, Guide Service Available)

•Prince Rupert

•Bella Coola

•Rivers Inlet

BRITISH
COLUMBIA

Port Hardy•
Telegraph Cove•   •Knight Inlet

Campbell River•

Port Albernie•
Ucluelet•   •Vancouver/Gulf Islands

Neah Bay•   •San Juan Islands
Sekiu•
Port Angeles• •
Port Townsend•   •Edmonds
                    •Seattle
                    •Tacoma
Westport/Ocean Shores•   •Olympia   WASHINGTON

Pacific Ocean

•Ilwaco
Warrenton•
Nehalem Bay•
            •Garibaldi
            •Pacific City
Lincoln City• •Depoe Bay
Newport•
            •Waldport   OREGON

•Winchester Bay

•Charleston/Coos Bay
•Bandon
•Port Orford

•Gold Beach
•Brookings

•Crescent City

•Trinidad   CALIFORNIA
•Eureka

Plug-cut herring rigged, a Puget Sound
angler hits the water at first light,
traditionally one of the best periods for
feeding chinook salmon. By Doug Wilson

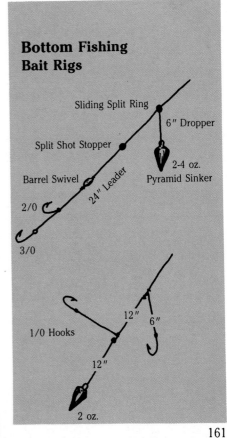

Bottom Fishing Bait Rigs

Sliding Split Ring
6" Dropper
Split Shot Stopper
2-4 oz.
Pyramid Sinker
Barrel Swivel   24" Leader
2/0
3/0

1/0 Hooks   12"   6"
              12"
             2 oz.

Shellfish

The saltwater shoreline of the Northwest is among the finest shellfishing regions of the world. Northern Washington, British Columbia and Alaska is a labyrinth of remote inlets, sounds, islands, bays, coves and beaches. On even the most minor low tides of the year, the dropping water uncovers rich beds of soft- and hard-shell clams, and oysters. Several varieties of crab and shrimp are lured to baited pots and abalone, octopus, scallops, and sea urchins are bagged by divers. The water is generally cold and fairly clear and the pickings are easy.

On the ocean coast of Washington the sprawling expanse of sand beaches at Ocean Shores, Copalis, Moclips, Kalaloch and Grayland support a resurging population of **razor clams,** the only clam with a season and license requirement. The warm-water incursion of El Nino in the early 1980s spawned a bacteria that nearly wiped out Washington's razor clam population, but the resiliant mollusks are making a dramatic comeback. During minus tides razor clam beaches are packed with diggers and it is easily one of the most popular recreations on the coast. The sand beaches of Alaska and the ocean side of Vancouver Island are also probed for razor clams, although in British Columbia the beaches are frequently closed by health officials concerned with paralytic shellfish poisoning (PSP).

In Oregon, the beaches are entirely public, but the better clamming is inside from the ocean, on the bottoms of boat basins, harbors and bays where low tides reveal the large empire and soft-shell clams that do so well in chowders and fritters.

Most of the public beach areas on Puget Sound, especially those relatively distant from major population centers, can provide a limit of hard-shell clams on any low tide. The most common finds are **littlenecks, butter,** and **cockles**. Soft-shelled **gapers** and **horse** (eastern) **clams** can be dug on most mud-bottomed tide flats, especially the expansive Skagit River flats. The state's most famous clam, the **geoduck** (gooey duck) is relatively rare in the shallows of most public beaches. Sometimes clusters of these giant clams will be revealed by extreme minus tides, but most are gathered by scuba divers.

Crabs can be trapped in bays, off piers and occasionally are scooped out of the shallows throughout Puget Sound and the Strait of Juan de Fuca. In recent years the ocean crab catch, including Grays Harbor and Willapa Bay, has been down. Numerous species of crabs can be caught, but the two most popular on the table are the **Dungeness** and **red rock crab.** Rock crabs are often caught in the shallows around breakwaters, dikes and marinas. There is no size or sex restrictions on rock crabs. Dungeness are larger than rock crabs, and generally more desirable. Only hard-shelled males are legal. Minimum sizes vary regionally. Crabbing is usually better in the bays, harbors and north part of Puget Sound, along the Strait of Juan de Fuca, the southern end of Hood Canal and north into British Columbia's protected sounds and fjords. They are caught in traps, picked off the bottom in shallow water, snared in fishing line or lured into collapsible mesh. In Alaska, king and tanner (snow) crabs are pulled from deep water but even here the Dungeness is popular.

Shrimping usually requires a boat, specialized trap and enough rope to reach a bottom 200 feet down. Puget Sound, Strait of Georgia, Alberni Inlet, and Hood Canal can provide several varieties of **shrimp.** The most popular is the spot shrimp, generally recognized as prawns. In Washington these giant shrimp are caught primarily during a brief and stiffly regulated season in Hood Canal. A few are taken in the San Juan Islands. In Hood Canal, prawns are protected by seasons and a license is required. Consult the fisheries regulation booklet for details. Several varieties of smaller shrimp can be taken without a license, and most are taken in the northern reaches, including the San Juan Islands.

Shellfishing is regulated by seasons and bag limits in each state and province, and copies of current regulations are available at sport and bait shops.

The clamming, shrimping, crabbing and general shellfishing in the Northwest is outstanding by any measure, and possibly one of the most closely guarded secrets.

Left, kelp barnacles at Grayland, WA. By Keith M. Lockwood. Northwest delicacies, Dungeness crab, spot shrimp, hardshell clams (above). By Terry W. Sheely

163

Spot (Prawns) shrimp. By Washington
Department of Fisheries

Shrimp

Found in song, salad and deep water, shrimp are first a delicacy and second a creature of mystery. There are several varieties, most too small and delicate to be considered for dinner tables.

The five most popular, edible Northwest shrimp include the **spot shrimp** (prawn), **coonstripe, sidestripe** and two species of **pink shrimp.**

Pinks most frequently are found in the ocean and are taken largely by the commercial trawl industry. The most popular sport shrimp is the spot shrimp, commonly called a prawn. This large shrimp can attain a body size of 8 inches and is the favorite for deep-frying or boiling. Large coonstripes and sidestripes also are considered to be prawns, while the average size, 3 to 5 inches, of these species are used for cocktails and salads.

If eating fresh shrimp is, as most addicts devoutly believe, a grand exercise, then catching your own shrimp is the ultimate exercise, lacking neither mystery, challenge nor reward.

On the sport level, shrimping calls for the use of pots. Deep-water commercial fishermen lean toward large trawls requiring large craft and a lot of muscle. Pots are light, easy to handle and can be set and pulled from a small boat or skiff. The only requirement regarding the boat is that it be large enough to handle the water in your trapping area.

Shrimp pots come in a variety of designs and sizes. In general, however, most pots consist of a frame covered with fiber netting or a welded, galvanized-wire mesh cloth pot rigged to be self-supporting without a frame. If mesh pots are purchased or made (unless vinyl coated), they should be tarred to preserve the life of the mesh.

Most pots have two to four entrance tunnels sloping inward to a circular opening of about 3 inches. The mesh size varies from ½ to ⅞ inch square.

For years, the best shrimp bait has been fish-flavored cat food available on supermarket shelves.

Puncture the cans on sides and ends so the oil and bits of food will filter out, attracting shrimp over a wide area. It's best to position the pot upcurrent from the area you intend to trap so the chum line will flow over a wide area. Place the can near the center of the trap and strap it into place with a cut section of inner tube rubber. Some natural baits, such as fresh or frozen fish carcasses, clams and oysters also can be used. These baits should be placed into a porous container such as plastic bag or nylon stocking.

Pots are fished on the bottom at depths ranging from 100 to 400 feet and generally are rigged one to a line, although some shrimpers run a ground line sporting several pots spaced 20 to 50 feet apart. Mark the trap with a sturdy buoy (commercially marketed urethane buoys are tops) connected with a ⅜-inch braided nylon rope. The rope should be 100 feet longer than the depth set to compensate for tidal pull and wave action. The upper 25 feet of buoy line must be weighted to prevent it from floating near the surface as a hazard to boaters.

The pots should be weighted to prevent them from washing away. Because some species of shrimp are most active at night and appear in the shallows at that time, most shrimpers leave their pots out for extended periods, checking them two or three times a day. It's generally a good idea to check the traps about midmorning and again in the late afternoon.

The most popular method of cooking shrimp is to boil them in salt water, either water taken from the sea or by adding ¼ cup of salt to each quart of fresh water. Bring the water to a boil and add the shrimp. When the water resumes boiling, allow the shrimp to cook for another three to eight minutes, depending on the size. Remove the shrimp from the water, cool, peel away the shell and remove the dark entrail streak from the back.

Littleneck clams. By Doug Wilson

Clams

Razor: Big, extremely meaty and a prized delicacy, razor clams are the number one attraction of our coastal beaches. Minus tides attract thousands of clammers to the sandy shoreline from Oregon to Alaska.

The best razor clam digging usually occurs in April and May when clams are preparing to spawn, when they are the fattest and in the best condition for eating. The most rewarding period for digging (especially in early spring) is on a minus tide. The lower the tide, the better the digging and the more beach available. Extremely low tides will uncover razor clam areas that normally are out of reach. Divers have located razor clam populations in water as deep as 30 feet. It's not unusual to find diggers wading as far out in the receding water as they can and still see the bottom, exploring for unexploited populations.

Razor clams grow from a length of ½ inch their first fall to 3½ inches the second. A two-year-old clam averages 4½ inches and weighs up to three times as much as the younger clams.

Razor clams have a reputation for outdigging clam diggers, ie., digging their way through the sand faster than the clammer can. Not true. But razors are the speedsters of the clam world, submerging at the rate of up to 9 inches a minute in soft sand. Diggers get a false impression of the razor clam's speed by mistaking the rapid retraction of the neck for actual movement. A razor clam's neck is often stretched when it's discovered, but the disturbance usually causes it to retract rapidly, giving a false impression of speed.

Razor clam "shows" are slight depressions or oval-shaped holes in the sand. These depressions are formed when the tip of the clam's neck, which is near the surface of the sand when feeding, is retracted, causing the sand to settle. Razors sometimes can be made to create shows by stamping your feet or whacking the sand with the flat of the shovel. The best place to spot shows is near the surf line. The bigger the show, the bigger the clam. If a razor's siphon is above the sand it often will create a V wake on the sand.

The two main tools for razor clam digging are the **clam shovel** and **tube.** The shovel, sometimes called a clam gun, is a rather specialized affair, with a short, stout handle and a long, slender, curved blade. Both are available at most sporting goods departments.

When you've discovered a clam *show,* insert the blade of the shovel into the sand 4 to 6 inches away from the show on the *seaward* side. Drive the blade *straight* into the sand. If you angle the blade toward the clam there is an excellent chance of crushing the thin shell or severing the neck. Lift the sand out of the hole (it may take four or five scoops before you locate the critter), grasp the clam by the shell or neck and pull it smoothly out of the sand. Refill the hole with sand.

Butter: The sweet flavor of a butter clam justifies the extra effort it sometimes takes to locate and dig these husky, thick-shelled delicacies. Beginners sometimes confuse butter clams with the more abundant and smaller littleneck clams. This mix-up can be blamed on the excellent flavor of both clams. The name butter clam sounds so sweet and succulent that diggers sitting down to a platter of littlenecks figure than anything tasting that good must be a butter clam. Butter clams, however, are much larger than little necks, growing up to 5 inches in length with extremely heavy, thick shells.

Butter clams sometimes are difficult to locate because of their penchant for burrowing 8 to 14 inches deep. The best place to look is low on the beach, adjacent to or in the water. The

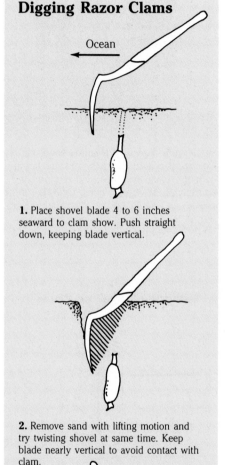

Digging Razor Clams

1. Place shovel blade 4 to 6 inches seaward to clam show. Push straight down, keeping blade vertical.

2. Remove sand with lifting motion and try twisting shovel at same time. Keep blade nearly vertical to avoid contact with clam.

DON'T Pry Back On The Handle.

3. Succeeding shovelsful expose the clam enough to reach down and grasp its shell. Razor clams move rapidly downward, but never horizontally.

165

Razor clam digging is a family sport on Northwest coastal beaches, and this father-daughter team have the right equipment and technique. Razor clams, right, are thin-shelled and easily broken. The undug clam on the left is purging its digestive tract of sand. By Thomas W. Kitchin

Using the "Pipe" or "Tube"

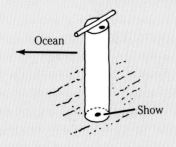

Ocean

Show

1. Facing the ocean, check impression of tube in sand, then center the clam tube.

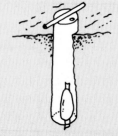

2. Slant the top of the tube toward the sand dunes. Work the tube in carefully with a rocking or twisting motion. Place thumb over air vent, pull up core. Do this 1 to 3 times.

lower the tide the better, because butter clams concentrate in the lower intertidal and shallow subtidal zones. Beds of butter clams have been found in up to 69 feet of water.

Butters prefer a pea-gravel beach but frequently are found on sandy stretches. One of their favorite lairs is in a patch of gravel between large, protective rocks. One of the nice things about butter clams is that they usually come in bunches . . . find one and you'll find more. The best tools are sturdy shovels (strong enough to move rocks) and clam forks, an L-shaped tool with strong, curved tines used to rake gravel.

Normally, you'll find the small clams close to the surface and the large specimens below them.

Littleneck: There are two distinct species of littleneck clams, the **native** littleneck and the **Japanese** (sometimes called **Manila**) littleneck.

These tiny, round clams are the foundation of Northwest sport harvest and the Japanese littleneck makes up more than half of the annual commercial harvest of hard-shelled clams.

Littlenecks are abundant throughout Puget Sound and British Columbia fjords. They also can be harvested along the coastline wherever there are gravel beaches. Unlike butter clams, littlenecks rarely are found on sand beaches.

Nearly every firm, gravel beach has a harvestable population of littlenecks, and the small, white to chocolate-colored brown shells usually are evident in the debris marking the high tide line. Another major factor in their extreme popularity is the ease with which they are harvested.

Unlike the larger clams that require extensive digging, littlenecks usually are found just below the surface where they can be located by raking the surface with clam forks down to a depth of several inches or by scraping away the surface gravel with shovels. Littlenecks also are fond of hiding beneath large rocks and it often pays to uproot these boulders and check out the bottom of the hole.

These clams are small, with a 2½-inch-wide specimen considered well above average. The shell color varies, but is normally a creamy-white, gray or mottled brown. The outside of the shell is marked with concentric rings and ridges, sometimes giving the appearance of a cross-hatch design.

Both natives and Manilas are in the peak of condition and flavor during spring and early summer when they are preparing to spawn. The preferred way to eat littlenecks is to steam the clams until the shell opens, extricate the meat and dip it into hot butter.

Gaper: These big, thin-shelled clams are rated only so-so as a main entree on the dinner table, but as a chowder clam they are great. Because they are not as delicate and flavorful a clam as some of the more popular species, the clam's popularity with diggers sags somewhat, actually resulting in underharvesting. This has proven to be a bonus for clammers who have discovered the clam's claim to chowder fame. In some areas they are called Empire, mud or horse clams.

They are large clams, frequently measuring 8 inches across the shell. The shell is rather thin and usually is colored white (sometimes a yellow white) with splotches of brown periostracum, a leatherylike substance that grows on the outside of the shell. They are dug almost exclusively from sandy, gravel areas and rarely found higher on the beach than one-third of the way above the low tide mark. They can be tough to dig because the large siphon allows this clam to burrow 15 to 20 inches deep. It's usual to find horse clams mixed in with butter clams in areas with

166

overlapping habitat conditions. Horse clams are abundant and widespread in Puget Sound and encourages increased harvest.

When preparing these clams for chowder, remove the tough skin which covers the siphon. The amount of edible meat from a horse clam is low compared to this husky clam's total weight, but the flavor is excellent when chowdered. It's fairly common to find small pea crabs living inside horse clam shells. Pea crabs are white, soft-shelled and absolutely harmless to man. Simply discard them with the shells.

Cockle: The tan, fan-shaped shells of the cockle clam are much more responsible for its popularity than its food value. The meat is coarse and tough by comparison, although it makes a good chowder when thoroughly diced.

The shell, however, is sought by collectors and beachcombers. It is distinctive from other hard-shell clams, with a rounded, fanlike shape, deeply corrugated and runs from light tan to red in color. Cockles average about 3½ inches wide and often are found on the surface or just below it, where they are easily harvested by hand or with a stiff-tined garden rake. These clams are unique in their lack of a foot that can anchor them on the bottom against wave action or allow them to move across the bottom. Cockles have been known to jump 2 feet underwater.

They prefer sand and mud beaches. Small clams may be washed high onto the beach by heavy tides, but the larger cockles will be located near the low tide line.

Soft-shell: Once thought to have been accidentally imported from the East Coast, eastern soft-shell clams are one of the few shellfish that prefer a touch of fresh water around their shells. Recent studies have produced evidence that soft-shells are native to the Pacific Coast, but that apparently hasn't been enough to convince Northwesterners that they're good for the table. They are one of the least popular clams, yet on the East Coast they are considered a delicacy.

Soft-shells are large, measuring up to 6 inches long, with fragile, easily broken shells. The shells have rounded edges and are an off-white to gray color. These clams prefer mud flats, especially those at the mouths of freshwater rivers. They are a fine clam to collect during moderate tides because they are most abundant above the half-tide mark (level of tide between high and low levels). They frequently are concentrated near river mouths and the heads of bays where the salinity of the water is lowest.

As their size indicates, soft-shells can bury themselves deeply and often are located between 8 and 14 inches below the mud. A standard clam gun or garden spade is used to harvest.

Geoduck: The average geoduck (gooey-duck) clam weighs a meal-size 2½ pounds and bigger specimens are common.

The Washington Department of Fisheries describes this unique bivalve as "the most impressive hard-shell clam in the Pacific Northwest." Its impressiveness extends beyond its size and onto the gourmet table. They are such a popular clam that areas regularly accessible to diggers are dug dry and only on the lowest minus tides (minus 2 feet) of the year are the unexploited beds accessible. Normally, extreme minus tides occur only about 20 times a year, restricting the sport harvest. But don't get the idea these delicacies are endangered. They aren't. It's estimated that the geoduck population between Olympia and the San Juan Islands is well over 114 million. Unfortunately for clam diggers (fortunately for the clams), most major geoduck beds are located below the lowest tide mark, accessible only to scuba divers.

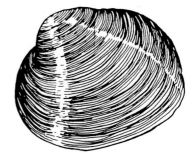

Butter Clam
Shell-fine concentric lines of growth

Littleneck Clam
Shell-radiating ribs, lack deep scalloped edge of cockle

Gaper Clam
(Blue, Empire)
Large gape where the neck protrudes

Cockle
Scalloped fan shell, evenly spaced ridges (ribs)

The inelegant siphon of a giant geoduck is a thing of beauty to clam diggers picking through kelp fronds in search of the elusive, giant clam. By Doug Wilson

The name geoduck is believed to have originated from an Indian language. It also is spelled *goiduck* and *gweduck*.

They prefer an area with a soft sand and mud bottom and their shiny, smooth siphons sometimes can be seen protruding through sloughs of seaweed on the beach.

The average (5-year-old) geoduck shell is 5.6 inches in length, but the siphon (neck) often extends up to six times that distance. Since geoducks have a 20-year lifespan, there are a lot of clams that exceed those measurements, most in unexploited offshore beds.

Diggers often spot the siphon neck extending above the surface only to discover (half a ton of mud later) that the body of the clam is 18 inches to 4 feet down. Muddy shirt sleeves and saturated pants are the mark of a dedicated geoduck digger.

Geoducks spawn once a year, usually in May or June. They have been found in Puget Sound from the beach all the way out to depths of 200 feet. They are strictly a clam of the inshore region however, because the geoduck embryo cannot tolerate the high degree of salinity found in the open ocean and along the coast.

How To Dig

Digging out a geoduck is plain hard work. The main requirements are a long-handled shovel, a strong back and set-jawed determination.

For shovel slingers, the best way to tackle a geoduck is by digging a trench beside the clam. Leave a wall of sand between your trench and the clam. When you estimate you're close to the shell, knock down the separating wall and probe carefully.

Another system involves a geoduck can — an open-ended, canlike affair measuring at least 18 inches across and 4 feet long. The can prevents the sand or soft mud from collapsing into the hole as you dig. Force the can as far down around the siphon as you can, then dig the clam out. Never pull on the siphon . . . it will break off.

Blanch the whole clam in boiling water for 10 seconds. With a paring knife, separate the clam from the shell. Remove the viscera from the neck and breast. Peel the skin off the siphon and breast. Thoroughly wash. Split the siphon by inserting the knife into the lower siphon hole where the viscera were removed and cut lengthwise. Wash the siphon, eliminating sand and grit. Split the breast meat down the median line and cut into small lengths. The breast, sans skin, is tender.

The main requirements for a well-equipped geoduck digger are a good shovel, old clothes, a strong back and set-jawed determination. The giant clams can be as deep as 4 feet, and weigh up to 3 pounds. They are considered a Puget Sound delicacy. By Doug Wilson

The siphon, however, should be cut into sections and tenderized with a kitchen mallet or back of a heavy knife. Tenderizing is not necessary if the meat is to be used as chowder or pressure-cooked.

Cleaning Clams

Cleaning clams is less complicated than it would appear. The most important step is to make certain that all grit and sand is removed before cooking. The most popular treatment is to place the clams in a tub of cold salt water for between four and eight hours, depending on the size and number of clams. The live clams will expel most of the sand and grit from their systems while soaking. A trick sometimes used, but rarely necessary, is to add cornmeal to the water. The clams expel the sand and replace it with the cornmeal.

After soaking, larger clams should be removed from the shell. Razors, large butters, horse clams and soft-shells are cut away from the shell with a sharp knife. Remove all black areas and the glands which appear as greenish, wormlike appendages. Rinse the body in running fresh water. Skin the necks and flatten for frying. Eliminate the black tip of the neck.

In large clams the necks may be tough. These can be diced or finely chopped and make excellent chowder.

Smaller clams, cockles, littlenecks and small butters are best eaten directly from the shell, after being steamed open. Using a double boiler, steam the clams until they open, pull out the meat, dip into hot melted butter and eat. Everything is edible. When steaming clams, however, the most important factor is to make certain there are no dead clams in the pot. Dead clams frequently are filled with sand, which gets into the good clams when they open. Clams and melted butter are superb. Clams and sand grit aren't.

To get the most flavor from clams they should be kept alive as long as possible. There probably are as many ways to accomplish this as there are clam diggers. Some work, some don't.

Among those that usually don't are the ones that require keeping bivalves in salt or fresh water. Clams use oxygen rapidly and often suffocate. Fresh water will kill clams within an hour or two.

Place the clams on a screen or rack that will allow excess moisture to drip away. Space the clams so they don't smother each other. Cover the clams with a burlap bag (or similar fabric) soaked in salt water. Some clammers recommend placing the clams on a nest of sea weed. Every few hours resoak the bag in salt water. The clams should stay fresh for several days.

Dungeness males. By Doug Wilson

Crabbing

Dungeness: From Mexico to the Aleutian Islands of Alaska, the Dungeness crab is widely sought for its thick, white meat. Despite the high harvest officials say the protection of females and young crabs and the high (more than 2½ million) number of eggs produced by each female keep the population stable.

Mating takes place in May and June along the coast between hard-shelled males and molted soft-shell females. Few females ever reach 6 inches, but males usually exceed 6 inches by their fourth birthday.

Giant males that measured 10 inches across have been hauled from the offshore grounds, but these are incredibly rare. The average size of the harvested male is 7 inches and less than 1 percent exceed 8 inches.

Because a crab's exterior skeleton is rigid, it can grow only by shedding (molting). This usually occurs in June or July. Crabs captured during the molting stage are soft, generally regarded as inferior table fare, and must be released according to fisheries regulations.

The best depths to set crab pots vary with the season. In the Pacific there is a general migration of adult male legal crabs from deep (200 feet or more) into shallow water (20 to 50 feet) from January to June. During the last six months of the year they retreat to deeper water. Dungeness crabs are highly migratory critters. One was tagged at Westport, Washington, and wound up in a trap at Tillamook Bay, Oregon, an 80-mile jaunt. Tagging studies have shown that crabs tagged and released 20 miles offshore in 50 fathoms of water usually are harvested within five miles of the coastline.

Possibly the most popular and efficient crab trap is the round wire crab pot usually carried in most near saltwater sporting goods stores.

The pot is flat on the bottom and top, with rounded sides and two funnellike openings to admit the crabs. Some "gates" are guarded by a trigger that prevents the crab from climbing out the same way it climbed inside.

These pots generally are lightweight and adequate for Puget Sound and protected coastal areas. If you intend to attempt the open ocean, however, a commercial-weight (150 pounds) or anchored pot is recommended because of strong tidal flows.

The pot has a hinged lid that allows easy extraction of crabs. These traps require baiting. Contrary to what Uncle George probably told you, crabs are not underwater garbage collectors. They want their bait fresh (fresh frozen is fine) and are repulsed by putrid or decaying bait. There are a few commercial crab baits on the market, but most crab seekers rely on their own larder and imagination. Popular and productive baits include clam necks, chicken backs, fish and salmon carcasses, or skinned squid. (Note: Octopus makes a good bait when skinned, but because octopi and crabs are natural enemies, crabs will flee from an unskinned one.)

The bait should be wired to the bottom in the center of the trap to force the crabs to enter the trap to reach the tidbit. Unwired baits drift to the side and can be nibbled out of existence by crabs reaching through the side of the pot.

Meat taken from fresh fish (and frozen) also works. Be sure to wire the bait up before freezing so that it can be attached to the trap without thawing. It's almost impossible to secure a frozen bait if it wasn't wired when fresh.

Since crabs usually are attracted to a trap by the scent line, it's a good idea whenever possible to position the trap so the entrance faces directly down-current. This permits the crab to enter immediately and not waste time climbing around the outside looking for a way inside.

Light, easy to use and efficient ring traps are popular with pier crabbers. This catch was made in Bandon, OR, near the mouth of the Coquille River, a popular crabbing spot. By Terry W. Sheely

Where To Set

Dungeness crabs prefer a sandy bottom in an area with a minimum of tidal flow, eelgrass beds, bays, backwaters and sand spits are prime areas. Pots can be set as shallow as 10 feet or as deep as 200, but the average is 20 feet to 150 feet.

The sunken pots are marked by a buoy leading from a ⅜-inch braided poly rope, twice as long as the depth of set. The buoys are sufficiently large to float the rope and be visible in low light or rough water.

Crabs, like most bottom dwellers, lie low and hold on tight during strong tide changes. They forage and move when the tide is the weakest. That makes the best crabbing hours from one hour before to one hour after slack tide. In bays and marinas where tidal action is low, crabs are taken every hour.

The ring net is simply a collapsible basket that lies flat on the bottom. A fresh bait is secured in the center of the trap and when a crab falls to the feast, a handline is pulled, elevating the mesh sides of the net and trapping the crab as it is hauled to the surface.

These rigs are best used in fairly shallow water and are especially effective from docks, piers or anchored boats where you can see the bottom and watch for crabs arriving at the bait.

Similar in operation to ring nets, pyramid pots are collapsible, lightweight traps with hinged folding sides. The sides fold upward tepee-style to meet in the center.

The trap is baited and dropped to the bottom, where the sides fold out to lay flat. When the trap is retrieved, usually after a 10- to 15-minute wait, the retrieval rope folds the sides up, trapping crabs that are on the bait. This solid-sided pot has the advantage over the ring trap of closing completely, preventing crabs from spilling out the top during a careless retrieval. These also are used in fairly shallow water and are ideal for docks, piers or small boat use inside marinas.

Dip nets are also used. The nets usually have a diameter of 15 to 20 inches and sport short, compact net bags. Most crab netters concoct their own nets, sometimes attaching a typical trout net to 8- to 12-foot handle. Metal handles are easier to control in deeper water than buoyant wooden ones.

Dip nets are used from boats drifting over shallow water or by waders picking their way across the bottom. In either case, the action usually is fastest on a low tide when there is maximum bottom visibility.

Many boatless crabbers, restricted to piers and backwaters, haul in crabs every year with their saltwater rods and reels.

Forget about a hook . . . it isn't necessary. What is necessary is a sturdy roll of heavy monofilament fishing line, 15- to 20-pound test. Take 10 to 15 feet of the line and tangle it into that

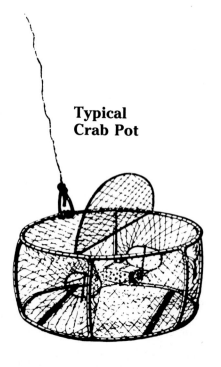

Typical Crab Pot

infamous bird's nest that cartoonists have made famous. The bird's nest should measure 15 to 20 inches across. For casting and anchor weight, attach a spark plug (or similar junkyard expendable) securely to the ball of line. Tie your main line to the weight. In the center of the bird's nest tie in a fresh bait . . . fish heads or small carcasses are good.

Simply cast the rig, allow the anchor to get a good bite on the bottom, crank out slack line, prop the rod against a tackle box or forked stick and wait for a bite. Crabs will crawl into the mono mess, tangle their legs in the line and jerk the line like a biting fish. Reel in, rebait and catch more. This is an excellent way for nonboaters to crab from beaches, jetties or piers.

Red Rock: Similar in appearance to the Dungeness, but smaller, the red or rock crab, as it is sometimes called, is a good eating crab with fewer legal size restrictions.

Rock crabs usually measure less than 6 inches across the back and are far less meaty than Dungeness. The claws generally are large in relation to body size, and the rock crab can be distinguished from the Dungeness by the presence of black on the tips of the pincers and a red body coloration.

They usually, but not always, are found near rocky areas, whereas the Dungeness prefers a sandy bottom. Crabbers working near breakwater retaining walls frequently catch rock crabs near the structure and Dungeness crabs farther away.

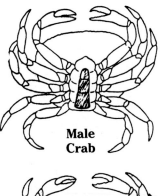

Male Crab

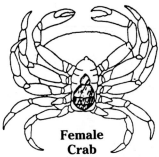

Female Crab

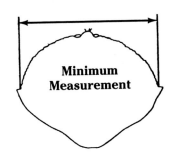

Minimum Measurement

Shucked oyster shells, Willapa Bay, WA.
By Terry W. Sheely

Oysters

Oysters require fairly warm (for this region) water temperature in order to reproduce. The ideal temperature, according to shellfish biologists, is 65°F, a factor that limits oysters to the protected, shallow confines of bays and harbors where water temperatures can be increased by the heat of summer.

Oysters are scattered throughout Washington and British Columbia inside saltwater areas and pehaps the biggest problem is sorting out the public oyster beds from the fervently protected private beds maintained by commercial growers. Many of these commercial beds are unmarked. Washington is the leading producer of oysters on the Pacific Coast, contributing about 10 percent of the total United States oyster production.

Oysters are rich in proteins, vitamins and such trace elements as iron, iodine, copper, phosphorus, cobalt and manganese . . . the ingredients that support a healthy human. The key to enjoying the best flavor is turned by the calendar . . . not by preparation. Oyster shuckers generally can rely on winter oysters for the best flavor. Beginning in November oysters are prime. The peak condition lasts until May, sometimes June if the water remains fairly cold because of a slow, cold spring. Pearls found in Northwest oysters have no commercial value, except to dentists repairing cracked teeth.

The best size oyster for quaffing raw is between 2 and 3 inches . . . while the internal organs still are small enough to be ignored. Larger oysters hit the taste buds a little sweeter if they're deep-fried, steamed or chopped and smoked.

To store oysters, place them in a bucket and cover with a burlap bag that has been drenched with salt water. Keep out all fresh water, including rain. Stored in this manner, oysters have been kept for more than a week. If you are staying near salt water, place the oysters in a mesh bag (onion sack) and suspend them just below the low tide mark, well above the bottom. If oysters are kept on the bottom there's a good chance they will be attacked by star fish, crabs, skates, ducks, snails, worms or other natural enemies.

The two main shucking tools are an oyster knife and a heavy, protective glove. The glove belongs on the hand that will hold the oyster, rounded shell down on a cutting board. Insert the rounded point of the knife (the end of the blade should be sharp for easier penetration) between the shells near the hinge. Push the blade into the cavity and at the same time twist the knife so the handle moves up and the blade down to cut the abductor muscle near the hinge. When this muscle separates, the shell will open. Remove the meat by cutting away the top abductor muscle.

Gooseneck barnacles often completely blanket saltwater pilings. By Neil G. Carey

Mussels

Of the several species of mussels found in the Northwest salt waters, the most available and most sought for the table is the small **blue or bay mussel** *(Mytilus edulis)*. The secondary mussel, **California mussel** *(Mytilus californianus)*, is considerably larger but mostly found on rocky, tough-to-reach spots along the coast. They are not considered nearly as sweet and flavorful as the blues. The blues are prolific and easily harvested from backwaters and bays, attached to pilings, piers, rocks, jetties, permanent floats and abandoned or sunken boats. Typically, there will be dozens of mussels densely crowded into a single area. Mussels are at their prime during the winter and spring months. Summer mussels are extremely thin, soft and bland. Steam for 15 minutes to eat.

Scallops

Scallops are the jetsters of the beach set, a unique swimming bivalve (clamlike) which literally jets through the water. It moves by quickly closing its valve and ejecting a stream of water through a small hole. Scallops are harvested mostly on a commercial basis by large trawls dragging deep water, but they can be found in shallow water, especially on low tide. They can sometimes be seen "jetting" just below the surface in ankle-deep water, although they frequently rest in the sand, blending in well and difficult to spot. The best way to locate scallop areas is to search the tide line for pieces of broken scallop shells washed up after the speedster has expired.

The world's largest octopus are found in the Northwest. By The Washington Department of Fisheries

Octopus/Squid

The Northwest offers one of the most prolific octopus and squid populations in North America. Both are edible and in some circles highly prized as a delicacy.

Northwest squid *(Loligo opalescens)* are only 6 to 10 inches long and sport ten arms. Often seen at night in Puget Sound, swimming in large schools. They are caught by snagging with specialized jigs, usually from lighted piers.

Octopus *(Octopus dofleini)* are giants by comparison, frequently growing to more than 120 pounds. Puget Sound octopus are the largest in the world. Octopus have eight arms and can be found in all the saltwater areas. The meat is white and comes both from the arms and the body. It has a clamlike flavor but many find it tough, requiring tenderizing.

The octopus generally is found in a crevice or cave in rocky areas with a good tidal exchange. Every now and then a bold octopus will be found on the bottom well away from cover. It can be found in water ranging from knee-deep to over 100 feet, but most are harvested by divers between 30 and 60 feet down. The entrance to an octopus den usually is marked with broken crab shells, clams or bones of consumed fish.

Abalone

The least abundant and naturally most delectable shellfish is the **northern abalone** sometimes called pinto abalone.

Full-grown pintos are 4 to 6 inches long, much smaller than the commercially harvested abalone of California.

Abalone are taken almost exclusively by sport divers from 10 to 40 feet below the surface. Their preferred habitat is a smooth rocky surface near kelp beds. They are pried loose from the rocks with a blunt wedge called an ab-iron.

To separate the meat from the shell, insert a flexible knife between the shell and body and sever the attachment at the top of the shell. The large foot is the edible portion and is cleaned by removing the dark, soft visceral material from the white muscular foot. Cut into thin pieces, tenderize with a meat mallet, coat the meat with a breading mixture and fry in hot oil in a shallow skillet.

Sea Cucumber

Sea cucumbers are edible, if you can force yourself beyond their warty appearance. The skin is a reddish color. Slit the skin and you will find five bands of light-colored muscle. Peel the muscle away from the skin. They normally are prepared for the table by dicing for chowder or deep-frying.

Left, purple sea urchins in the Queen Charlotte Islands. By Neil G. Carey. A freshwater shellfish (below), crayfish are abundant in lakes and rivers during the summer. By Washington Department of Fisheries

Sea Urchin

Sea urchins are enclosed in a heavy shell armored with hundreds of spines. Very few are taken by recreational gatherers, but they are considered a delicacy and compared to caviar. There are three species in the Northwest. The **red urchin** *(Strongylocentrotus)* is found in the San Juans and Strait of Juan de Fuca. The **green urchin** *(S. drobachiensis)* is abundant in Puget Sound. The **purple urchin** *(S. purpuratus)* frequently is found in tidal pools and shallow coves. They are at their peak of edibility in the fall and early winter. Growth and reproduction is slow. The shell is cracked, revealing five yellowish-orange sections of roe, the edible portion. Gently remove, wash, eliminate connecting tissue and eat raw. They can be cooked, breaded and spread on crackers.

Crayfish

In recent years there has been an upswing in the popularity of this freshwater lobster. Crayfish (also called crawfish and crawdad, or erroneously crab) are strictly freshwater creatures. The ones found in the Northwest *(Astacus pacifastacus)* are considered among the most delectable in the country.

They are fairly large, reaching 6 inches in length, and resemble a small lobster. They can be captured by hand beneath logs, rocks or piers or by dangling a piece of fish or meat bait and setting a crayfish trap. Cook by boiling in plain or salted water or in a boiling stock consisting of five quarts of water, onions, carrots, lemon, parsley sprigs, pepper, salt, bay leaves. Boil 20 at a time, for five minutes or until bright red. Dip in melted butter or a seafood sauce. Crayfish are most active during the summer and almost never are found in the winter. They become totally inactive when water temperature drops to 38 °F.

Hunting

Hunting Washington

Washington is the most unheralded hunting region in the Northwest, yet its 68,129 square miles support one of the most diverse wildlife populations, and an equally complex hunting ground.

Just 360 miles wide and 240 miles deep, Washington is the smallest of the Northwest regions and the most densely populated. The latest census puts the population figure at 4.3 million. Eighty percent, however, live in metropolitan areas, leaving vast tracts of coastal forest, mountain high country and rolling sagebrush hills for wildlife. Fifty percent of the land in Washington is publicly owned and open for the 307,000 licensed hunters.

The state is a complex mix of climate and topography. Sprawling coastal marshes thick with geese rise into black timber stitched with elk trails, sharply climbing to rugged snowcapped peaks where mountain goats look down on high-racked mule deer in glaciated alpine basins. Bighorn sheep can be found on the barren, rocky ridges overlooking the desertlike sagebrush flats and ranch lands of the Columbia Basin, home of some of the finest pheasant and waterfowl hunting in the country.

It is one of the few places where hunters can bag three kinds of deer, two species of elk, four types of quail and five varieties of grouse. Although bear numbers are steadily falling, Washington continues to have the greatest concentration of black bears in the United States, except for Alaska, plus a healthy population of cougar and a growing herd of moose. Of the West's common big game hunting animals, only the pronghorn is missing. There are a few in the state, confined mostly to the sage lands near Yakima. Antelope, along with grizzly bears, caribou, wolves, wolverines, fishers and squirrels are protected. All squirrels enjoy complete protection in Washington, and the woods are full of the noisy Douglas squirrel variety. Protection of the rodents, popular hunting targets in most areas of the country, apparently comes from Washington's close ties with the timber industry and the role squirrels play in distributing cone seeds, a natural tree planter.

Although elk are the state's premier big game animal, more hunters track deer than any other big game animal. Hunter success is 25 to 30 percent with a harvest of 50,000 to 70,000, regionally split between mule deer, blacktails and whitetails. Most hunters bag a mule deer, with blacktails running a strong second, followed by whitetails which account for 10 percent of the state harvest.

Figures put together in 1986 by the Department of Game reveal 91 percent of the state's deer are bagged with rifles, 7 percent with bows and 2 percent with muzzle loaders. Success in 1985 ran 23 percent for riflemen, 21 percent for archers and 41 percent for muzzle loaders.

There are roughly 250,000 **mule deer** in Washington, ranging from the crest of the Cascade Range east to Idaho. U.S. Highways 2 and 97 slice through some of the best mule deer areas in the state. The heart of the mule deer country is in the northern ranges in the Okanogan National Forest, but they are likely to be seen anywhere east of the Cascade crest. Mule deer hunting centers include Winthrop, Omak, Republic, Twisp, Clarkston and Teanaway.

Alberta bull (left). By Thomas W. Kitchin. Western Washington's dense conifer and alder forests (above) are laced with creeks and beaver ponds that attract both puddle and diver ducks and jumpshooters.
By Terry W. Sheely

Washington's major mule deer areas are in the semi-arid mountainous regions.
By Erwin & Peggy Bauer

The state produces some very nice 4- and 5-point racks, but is not known as a trophy state. No Washington mule deer is listed in the top 30 typical or nontypical Boone and Crockett records.

The world-record No. 1 **blacktail,** however, is a monster 5-point shot in 1953 near Chehalis, Washington. A close cousin of the mule deer, blacktails dominate western Washington. They spill into a few areas of eastern Washington, sharing the range with mule deer in the Cascade Range west of Yakima, near Cle Elum, and around Goldendale.

In the Cascades, blacktails frequently crossbreed with mule deer, but in coastal regions, including the Olympic Peninsula, mule deer are not found and the blacktail breed is pure. Blacktails are found only in the coastal areas of northern California, Oregon, Washington, British Columbia and Alaska. They are well-suited to the dense brush and thick timber of the coastal rain forests. Because of their penchant for hiding, sneaking and staring instead of bolting through the woods, blacktails are difficult and elusive game animals.

Blacktails can be found within the city limits of Seattle or the remote reaches of alpine wilderness areas. It is difficult to find a hunting area in western Washington where fair to good numbers of blacktail are not found. Some of the best hunting is in the Cascades around Morton, North Bend, Darrington and Rockport, as well as in the southwest near Raymond, Willapa Hills, Pe Ell and Shelton.

Although Washington has never contributed any trophy **whitetails** to the top ranks of the Boone and Crockett record book (the highest listing is 70th in the nontypical class for a 1981 Stevens County buck), these deer are making significant inroads.

The heart of the whitetail range is concentrated in the Colville and Kaniksu national forests north of Spokane and the Blue Mountains on the tri-state corner of Oregon, Idaho and Washington. Their famous white "flags" dominate the brushy hills north of Spokane, especially the Colville, Chewelah and Curlew regions of Ferry, Stevens and Pend Oreille counties. There is also evidence that whitetails are moving into the traditional mule deer country in the Okanogan, along Lake Chelan and the Columbia River breaks northeast of Wenatchee.

Washington Hunting Requirements

All hunting in Washington, except on Indian reservations, is managed by the Washington Department of Wildlife, 600 N. Capitol Way, Olympia, WA 98504. Phone (206) 753-5705. Hunting regulations booklets are mailed upon request. Resident and nonresident hunting licenses and stamps are available at most sporting goods outlets and some resorts. Licenses are not available at the six regional game department offices, but can be obtained at the Olympia headquarters office by mail or in person.

The state does not require hunter orange, but encourages its use during big game firearm seasons. Nonresidents are not required to hunt with licensed guides, and there is no minimum age for hunters. All hunters under 14 must be accompanied by an adult and hunters under 18 must pass a hunter education, safety program. A general hunting license is required before buying supplemental tags and stamps.

Big game hunting rifles cannot be lighter than .240 (6mm) caliber. Deer, bear and cougar, can be hunted with these handguns, .41 magnum, .44 magnum or .45 magnum. Handguns of any caliber can be used to hunt blue, ruffed, and spruce grouse except during supplemental or extended seasons when just shotguns are legal. Shotguns used to hunt game birds must be plugged to 3-shot capacity, 10-gauge maximum. Crossbows are illegal, and long, recurve or compound bows used to hunt big game must pull at least 40 pounds, at 28-inch draw.

Hunting seasons are set by species, region and hunting weapon. There is no limit on the number of big game licenses available with five specific exceptions. Permits for antlerless deer and elk, bighorn sheep, mountain goats, moose are limited and licenses are awarded by drawing. Applications for these special controlled hunts are available from the Department of Wildlife Olympia headquarters or most license agents. Deadline to apply for a special deer or elk permit is Aug. 1. Sheep, goat and moose tags are awarded in July.

Big game hunters, except those trying for bear, cougar and moose, are required to select a weapon before buying a hunting license. Deer, elk, sheep and goat hunters must choose to hunt with either a modern firearm, muzzle loader or bow. It is acceptable to select different weapons for different animals. Bear, cougar, deer, grouse, small game and waterfowl can be hunted statewide, but elk, sheep, goats, moose, upland birds (pheasant, quail, chukar, partridge) and turkey hunters are restricted to specific regions. Upland bird hunters can buy permits to hunt statewide but big game hunters are confined to a specific region.

There is some spring hunting for black bear in areas where tree damage is recorded. Fall hunting seasons begin Sept. 1 with ruffed grouse in the creek bottoms and alder groves, blue and spruce grouse on the mountaintops, band-tailed pigeons in the coastal foothills and doves in the sage and wheat lands of the Columbia Basin. It ends Feb. 28 with snowshoe and cottontail rabbits.

The first fall big game season is in mid-September when a high mountain, bucks-only backcountry hunt is held in the Pasayten, Alpine Lakes and North Cascade wilderness areas. General deer season begins in mid-October and runs into November depending on what area of the state you are hunting. Bow hunters can challenge elk during the September bugle season, but modern rifle seasons don't begin until after the rut, usually the final week of October through mid-November. Hunters are restricted to one deer or elk per season.

Regional management programs have scattered Washington's opening days across the calendar, but traditionally the acknowledged opener is the second Saturday in October when general deer season opens, along with eastern Washington upland birds and statewide duck and goose season. Big game hunters have no problem finding areas to hunt because of the vast tracts of state and federal lands in Washington. Upland bird hunters, especially pheasant seekers, will find the best shooting in central and eastern Washington on private ranches and farms requiring permission to hunt. Public hunting areas, stocked with pheasants, are located throughout the state. Hunters bag more than half a million pheasants a year, nearly a quarter of them in the Columbia Basin region of Grant County. Other prime pheasant areas are Yakima, Whitman, Franklin, Adams and Asotin counties. In western Washington 90 percent of pheasant hunting is for released birds.

Despite the variety of wildlife, Washington attracts fewer nonresident hunters than any other Northwest state or province and there has never been a shortage of nonresident licenses.

Hunting License Fees

	Resident	Nonresident
Hunt/Fish Combination	$ 24	NA
Hunt General	$ 12	$125
Deer	$ 15	$ 50
Elk	$ 20	$100
Bear	$ 15	$150
Cougar	$ 20	$300
Mountain Goat	$ 50	$150
Bighorn Sheep	$ 75	$300
Moose	$150	$300
Turkey	$ 15	$ 15
Upland Bird (East)	$ 8	$ 8
Upand Bird (West)	$ 15	$ 15
Falconry	$ 30	$ 30
Waterfowl	$ 5	$ 5

Bulls rut in late September and early October, challenging each other for dominance, losing some of their inherent wariness. By Thomas W. Kitchin

A special late-season hunt is held around Thanksgiving north of Spokane and is attracting a lot of hunting interest despite the distance from coastal metropolitan areas. Whitetails are the primary target, with game managers hoping to crop whitetails that eluded hunters during the general October seasons when hunters are handicapped by thick brush. Visibility in the woods and hunter success increases dramatically with the first heavy snows of early winter. A few mule deer, forced down from the surrounding mountains by snow, are also taken during the late hunt.

A rare, unhunted subspecies of whitetail is also found in Washington. The **Columbian white-tailed deer** once roamed all of southwestern Washington, northwestern Oregon and the Willamette River Basin, but is now classified as an endangered species and confined to a herd of about 300 on a 3,000-acre federal preserve of low brushy islands and riverbanks near Cathlamet and another herd of about the same number scattered on 2,000 acres near Roseburg in southern Oregon. Biologists believed Columbians were extinct until the late 1930s when a small herd of the slightly built swamp deer was discovered in a bog near Cathlamet. Columbians are slightly smaller than Northwest whitetails, shy and their antlers are generally more erect and slender.

A lot of big game animals call Washington home, but to most resident hunters big game means **elk.** No other animal commands the attention, generates as much enthusiam or accounts for as much vacation time as Washington's elk herds. Statewide there are more than 60,000 elk in Washington, restricted to seven major regions. The two major elk herds are in the mountains east of Yakima (12,000), and on the Olympic Peninsula (15,000). The other five areas are Willapa Hills (9,000), Wenatchee Mountains-Colockum (5,800), Blue Mountains (7,000), Mount St. Helens region (7,000) and Mount Rainier (3,500). A small herd of 500 elk are hunted along the Nooksack River east of Bellingham, and approximately 300 elk are in the northeast corner of the state around Sullivan and Kalispell creeks.

Two species of elk roam Washington's timbered mountains, and are generally separated by geography. The western Washington herd is primarily **Roosevelt elk,** a native to the Olympic Peninsula and southwest coastal region. Eastern Washington herds, plus Mount Rainier and Nooksack elk are **Rocky Mountain (or Yellowstone) elk,** the progeny of a 1912-13 release of 307 elk imported from Montana. Before that release, there were no elk in the Cascade Range and few in the Blue Mountains of southeastern Washington. Only the Olympic Peninsula herd of Roosevelts are native to the state. These elk are sometimes seen along U.S. Highway 101. Roosevelts are darker than Rocky Mountain elk and 5 percent larger.

Spikes and 2-points make up the bulk of Washington's bull elk harvest, but the Evergreen State has earned a place in the international record books. Kittitas County produced the Boone and Crockett club's No. 12 Rocky Mountain elk in 1957 and owns three of the top 10 Boone and Crockett positions in the Roosevelt elk classification. More big bulls are bagged in the rain forests of the Olympic Peninsula than in eastern Washington, but hunting is generally more difficult in the west side's thick timber and brushy creek bottoms.

Elk hunters must select a weapon (modern rifle, bow, muzzle loader) and a specific hunting area. In 1985, modern firearm hunters accounted for 69,620 licenses, while archers 9,998 and muzzle loaders 2,514. According to the Department of Game 85 percent of the elk are taken with rifles, 12 percent with bows and 3 percent fall to muzzle loaders. Success runs about 11 percent for rifle hunters, 8 percent for bowmen and 20 percent for muzzle loaders.

The state is divided into four elk zones; Blue Mountains, Colockum, Yakima and Western Washington, and separate seasons within these four areas are set by weapon choice and elk season. Regulations and hunting dates are more complicated for elk than any other big game animal.

"Many novice sheep hunters have heard and read of long-range shooting at wild rams. The truth is that sheep are easily stalked to within close or moderate rifle range. Hunters who bang away at rams at more than 300 yards are displaying their lack of hunting skill."

From Trophy Dalls Come Hard, *Tom Walker*

Some bow areas are open during the September rut when bulls are bugling, but generally firearm and primitive weapon seasons run from the last week in October to mid-November.

Washington's rugged mountains, timbered foothills and swampy coastal lowlands support a heavy concentration of **black bear.** In recent years, however, with increased hunting restrictions and a four-month reduction in the season, hunter success has fallen dramatically. Fewer than 2,500 bears are now bagged in Washington.

Black bears can be found in all mountainous and timbered areas of the state, but are rarely seen in the arid Columbia Basin. Heaviest concentrations of black bears, in order, are in the pie-shaped wedge of northeastern Washington between the Kettle and Columbia rivers, the heavily logged foothills north of Interstate 90 at North Bend, on the Long Beach Peninsula near Ilwaco and Long Island in Willapa Bay.

The state's **grizzly bear** population is believed to be limited to two small, remote areas where the big bears are fully protected. Grizzlies have not been extensively studied in Washington, and their numbers have been estimated at between five to 25. One group is located in the extremely rugged mountains of the North Cascade National Park north of Lake Chelan and the second group is cross-state in the Selkirk Mountains near the boundaries of Idaho and British Columbia. Occasionally grizzlies are reported, but unconfirmed, in the Mount Stuart area of the Wenatchee Mountains.

The steep, jagged peaks of the Cascade and Olympic mountains support the largest **mountain goat** population in the contiguous United States, and it's not unusual for travelers on U.S. Highways 2 and 20 and Interstate 90 to spot the creamy-white animals browsing in high basins or bedded on rocky outcroppings. Hunting is by permit only, with applications drawn in the summer by the game department. In the future the goats range may be limited to the Cascades and a few mountains on the Olympic Peninsula outside Olympic National Park. The National Park Service has launched a mountain goat eradication program designed to remove the 1,000 goats inside the 900,000-acre national park because they are not native to the Olympics.

Goats were introduced to the park peaks in the 1920s, and have never been hunted. Some of the Olympic goats are being captured and transplanted to other areas of the state, plus neighboring states.

In the open hunting units most goat hunters backpack into remote areas for their trophies. A few outfitters can arrange horse camps and pack service, but the majority of hunters are powered by shank's mare and live out of a backpack for several days.

Hunting success in Washington is usually around 50 percent, permits are allotted by region and there has been a substantial drop in the number of permits offered each year. In 1986 there were 325 mountain goat permits drawn; 203 for all weapon hunts, 93 for archery-only and 29 exclusively for muzzle loaders. The northern section of the Cascades supports the heaviest concentration of goats.

Washington is one of only a handful of states where hunters can challenge **bighorn sheep.** In the late 1960s the big game managers began to ambitiously reintroduce bighorns to the arid regions of the state. There are an estimated 600 bighorns in the state; 540 **California** bighorns and 60 **Rocky Mountain** bighorns, according to the Department of Game. Competition is stiff for the few permits available, applicants numbering between 2,000 and 4,000. In 1986 there

Lester H. Miller and his world-record black-tailed deer, taken in 1953 in Lewis County, Washington. The buck scores 182⅜ Boone and Crockett Points. Washington Department of Wildlife photo

Two of Washington's rarest game birds are the sage grouse (below) and turkey. Sage grouse numbers are rapidly dwindling as irrigated croplands replace native sagebrush, and turkey populations are expanding in response to relocation and release programs. Sage grouse photo by Ed Park. Turkey by Thomas W. Kitchin

were only 11 sheep permits authorized, down from the 30 awarded just a few years earlier. Six of the sheep permits are awarded to all-weapon hunters, four set aside for archery-only and one designated for a muzzle loader.

Bighorns are distributed in secluded bands, favoring broken, fairly treeless mountain country. In the north the Okanogan-Colville region has sheep at Vulcan, Hall, Hull and Aeneas mountains. In the central and southern Cascade Range sheep can be found in Swakane Canyon, Colockum Pass, and northwest of Yakima on Umtanum Ridge and Cleman's Mountain. There are three bands in the Blue Mountains. One on the upper Tucannon, another on Cottonwood Creek and small herd on Joseph Creek.

Moose are rare in Washington. The only established herd is scattered north of Spokane in the Kalispell Basin region of the Selkirk Mountains. Less than a half-dozen hunting permits are awarded each year and there has only been a legal season since 1977 when more than 3,000 hunters applied for three permits.

Waterfowl hunting is excellent in the state with hunters bagging nearly a million **ducks** and **geese** each season. The waterfowl season is among the longest in the nation running from mid-October to mid-January. The heavily irrigated Columbia Basin, with a network of canals, lakes, ponds and grainfields, is the best waterfowling in the state and in fact in several states. Nearly 200,000 ducks — mostly mallards and teal — and Canada geese are bagged in just Grant County, primarily on O'Sullivan (Potholes) Reservoir and Moses Lake. Some of the best duck and goose hunting in eastern Washington is found on state-controlled areas, especially, Sunnyside, Wahluke, Priest Rapids, Winchester Wasteway, lower Crab Creek, and Stratford, Banks, and Billy Clapp.

Federal wildlife refuges on the Columbia and Snake rivers are providing some of the finest waterfowling in the West, if not the country. The refuges produce a fine crop of local ducks, primarily mallards, and attract thousands of migrating fowl funneling south along the Columbia and Snake river drainages. National wildlife refuges with good shooting potential are Umatilla on the Oregon border, Columbia west of Othello and McNary at the confluence of the Snake and Columbia rivers.

The No. 1 western Washington duck and goose area is the Skagit Flats west of Mount Vernon where waterfowlers drop 90,000 birds a year, a good many of them snow geese, mallards and wigeon.

Most river valleys downstream from the mountains provide excellent jump and float shooting for mallards and assorted divers, mostly goldeneye, bufflehead, bluebills and ringnecks. River shooting is fast and humbling toward the end of the season, when ducks are forced off the thousands of lowland lakes and salt marshes by ice and retreat to the rivers before continuing south. Steel shot is required in the major waterfowl hunting areas.

Cackling ringneck rooster pheasants, 3 pounds of brassy feathers and deceptive speed blasting out of an irrigation ditch, disappearing into the next field faster than two barrels of No. 6 shot. That's the vision that puts between 90,000 and 125,000 hunters in the fields each year, pushing Labradors, springers, shorthairs and setters after **Chinese ringneck pheasants.**

Pheasants are the most popular upland bird in Washington and have been since the first season opened in 1897, just 16 years after the first imported ringnecks were released in Oregon. Washington received some of the Oregon birds in 1883 and heavy plants were made in western Washington in 1893 and in eastern Washington in 1898.

As irrigation brought water up from the Columbia and Yakima rivers to turn the arid sage country of the Columbia Basin into croplands, the eastern Washington pheasant population zoomed. The irrigated eastern part of the state soon became the top pheasant region. In western Washington nearly all of the pheasants bagged by hunters are planted birds, stocked on a put-and-take basis by the Department of Game. Some 40,000 pheasants are released in 60 western hunting areas, more than half of those in the lowlands on the east side of Puget Sound.

In eastern Washington nearly half a million ringnecks are dropped each fall, with the prime pheasant grounds following the irrigation systems that brought alfalfa, wheat and corn to the Columbia Basin, Yakima and Kittitas valleys. The daily limit reflects the quality of hunting, with two birds allowed west of the Cascades with three roosters a day east.

Pheasant hunters ocassionally roust Japanese greens, Reeves, and white-crested Kalij pheasants — remnants of earlier attempts to establish new game birds.

Upland bird hunting doesn't live and die with pheasants in Washington. Wing shooters have an abundance of targets matched by few other states. Six native grouse, five species of quail, three other varieties of pheasants, turkey, two patridge species, dove, snipe, and band-tailed pigeons.

Upland bird hunting is most popular on irrigated land of central and eastern Washington where they take 300,000 **quail** (mostly valley), another 300,000 **chukars,** 100,000 **Hungarian** partridge, 450 **sage hens** and about 200 **turkeys.** Sage hens are found primarily in Yakima and Douglas counties with a few bagged in Kittitas and Klickitat counties.

One of the saddest stories in Washington's game bird legacies is the fall of the sage grouse. In 1834 naturalist J.K. Townsend wrote, "we found these [sage grouse] birds so numerous in some places that at times we even made use of our riding whips to prevent them from being trodden to death by our horses." By 1986, sage grouse populations consisted of isolated flocks in small areas of Kittitas and Yakima counties, the hunting season was restricted to two days and the bag limit one bird per year.

Ironically, in order to expand its world-class shooting, for America's most popular imported game bird, the Chinese ringneck pheasant, Washington is eliminating perhaps its finest native prairie grouse.

The end for the native sage grouse is flowing in the irrigation pipes that allow the exotic ringneck pheasant to thrive. Irrigated cropland is replacing much of the state's old growth sage, a plant critical to sage grouse survival. As late as 1900 large flocks of sage grouse were kicked out of the brush near Ellensburg and Wenatchee. It is now confined primarily to the sage country in the rugged Columbia River breaks region.

A similar fate appears inevitable for the **sharp-tailed** grouse, which was orginally abundant in the open timber and grassland areas of eastern and central Washington. Today they are found in limited numbers in the grasslands of Lincoln, Okanogan and northern Douglas counties.

The grouse of the timbered mountains, however, are in good shape compared to their prairie cousins, and represent some of the finest, if not most difficult wing shooting in western Washington's foothills and the wooded mountains throughout the state. **Blue grouse** are the largest of the forest grouse and are found on both sides of the Cascades at higher elevations. **Ruffed grouse,** "native pheasants" to some old-time hunters, are found statewide in lowland timber, along logging roads, alder bottoms and along creek thickets. In western Washington the bird is reddish brown and in the east it's grayish. **Spruce grouse (Franklin's)** is smaller than the blue, but larger than the ruffed and considerably more colorful. This is the grouse they

How Long to Venison

Big game hunters in Washington put in a lot of hunting hours between shots. According to figures averaged from recent seasons, it took the average rifle hunter 21 days in the field to drop a deer and 60 days to find an elk in the scope.

Bow hunters put in 50 hours for a deer, and 85 hunting hours for an elk. The least amount of hunting time spent in the woods before putting venison steaks on the table was by muzzle loaders who hunted an average of 12 days per deer and 60 for elk.

Irrigation has transformed Washington's arid Columbia Basin from sage land into an agricultural mecca supporting the finest pheasant hunting in the Northwest.
By Erwin & Peggy Bauer

call "fool hen" because it often perches in trees, refusing to fly when approached by man. Spruce grouse are not nearly as widely distributed as the other mountain grouse, inhabiting lodgepole pine, subalpine fir and Engelmann spruce regions of the Cascades and Olympics.

Washington gunners also have a shot at five species of quail. The most numerous are **valley quail,** found through the agricultural and brushy areas on both sides of the Cascades. The male has a distinctive forward-curving topknot. **Mountain quail,** the largest member of the quail family, is found only in the logged areas of Kitsap, Thurston and Pierce counties and in a few river drainages in the southeast. There's also **Gambel's, scaled** and **bobwhite quail.**

There are four wild partridge in Washington all imported from overseas, including **Hungarian, French red-legged, chukar** and **bamboo.** The most popular are the chukars and Huns. Chukars were imported and released in 1938 in the Yakima Canyon between Ellensburg and Yakima. Huns were first brought in 1897 but not successfully released until the early 1900s. Today, they are found primarily in eastern Washington with small scattered flocks in prairie areas of western Washington. Best Hun hunting is in eastern Washington in the grassy benches and wheat lands of Asotin, Columbia, Garfield and Whitman counties.

Chukars prefer the wild, rocky breaks of the scablands along the Columbia, Yakima and Snake, Okanogan, Palouse and Grand Ronde rivers. Tough hunting in rough country, but one of the most popular seasons in the state. Red-legs and bamboo partridge are rare, never really took hold, and are occasionally dropped in the lower Yakima Valley near Grandview.

Turkey hunting is one of the newest and fastest growing sports in the Evergreen State. Nearly all of Washington's turkeys are the Merriams variety. Hunting seasons were first established in 1965 when a fall season was authorized and the first spring gobbler hunt wasn't held until

Annual Northwest Hunting Harvests

The number of big game animals and upland birds harvested annually in the Northwest varies widely region-to-region, divided by topography, climate and hunting pressure.

Comparing annual harvests numbers provides an overview guide to the comparitive hunting strengths of the four states and two Canadian provinces encompassed by the Northwest. The annual harvests figures vary each year, dependent upon hunting pressure, wildlife populations, regulations, weather and other seasonal considerations.

These figures are based on Fish and Game Department yearly averages.

Big Game Harvests
(NA = Not Available)

	AB	BC	ID	MT	OR	WA
Deer	38,058	70,048	49,000	169,649	81,696	40,616
Elk	3,330	13,554	15,550	18,478	20,371	9,047
Moose	9,820	34,381	295	565	—	4
Grizzly	45	734	—	14	—	
Black Bear	3,000	8,747	2,100	365	1,250	1,026
Mountain Goat	11	1,315	35	227	—	113
Mountain Sheep	486	1,137	80	297	36	4
Cougar	20	224	NA	NA	62	122
Pronghorn	3,950	—	2,440	33,413	1,023	—
Caribou	—	590	—	—	—	—

Upland Bird Harvests
(NA = Not Available)

	AB	BC	ID	MT	OR	WA
Quail	—	1,580	56,500	—	202,884	108,005
Chukar	—	1,176	30,800	446	134,305	46,218
Hungarian Patridge	29,500	325	17,000	34,768	27,305	27,546
Blue Grouse	—	25,971	73,400	21,564	39,719	47,078
Ruffed Grouse	60,050	64,410	combined	24,682	68,411	93,115
Pheasant	35,600	4,388	238,100	104,880	251,284	264,050
Dove	993	3,974	124,100	—	191,000	96,528
Band-tailed Pigeon	—	3,074	—	—	96,528	30,591
Turkey	—	—	75	429	55	84
Sage Grouse	NA	—	26,900	22,972	NA	162
Sharp-tailed Grouse	17,500	2,228	2,000	63,168	—	117
Ptarmigan	—	1,057	—	—	—	—

1970. Stable flocks are hunted in Klickitat, Yakima, Stevens and Kittitas counties, with flocks taking hold in 15 eastern and five western Washington counties.

By far the best turkey hunting is found in the scrub brush country of Klickitat County, along the Klickitat River, but is getting better in many areas of the central Cascade Range, Okanogan and north Spokane regions.

Band-tailed pigeons offer exciting shooting in September in the coastal areas, especially the foothills of the northern Cascades and the southern hills of the Olympic Peninsula. Band-tails are hunted from the first to the end of September, primarily in the mountains and foothills of western Washington where they gather at mineral springs, and feed heavily on cascara and mountain ash berries. Blue-gray birds with bright yellow bills and feet, the crow-sized pigeons are frequently found high in the mountains, sitting on the uppermost branches of pine and fir trees. Some hunters spot feeding flocks and stalk, while others locate a flight path (sometimes along salt marshes, often at low passes between mountains) and pass shoot during migration periods.

The hot September sun also shines on **mourning dove** shooters in grainfields of eastern Washington. The sight of a dove in western Washington is rare, in the grain-rich arid country east of the Cascades they are plentiful before the first cold snap drives the birds south. Dove hunters stake out fence rows, grainfields and watering holes in the Yakima Valley, Okanogan valleys, and along the lower Snake River. It's rare to find a mourning dove in Washington past Sept. 15.

Probably the least hunted of all Washington's game birds, and undeniably one of the toughest to find and hit, is the long-billed **Wilson's snipe.** Snipe belong to the sandpiper family and is normally found around water, especially marshes, irrigation overflows, ponds and sloughs. It's the Northwest's version of the woodcock only smaller, about robin size. It's long, needlelike beak and corkscrew flight pattern helps identify the brownish bird — a tough target fit to challenge the smuggest wingshots.

Washington also has its share of predators and rare animals. Nearly all of the 70 to 150 **cougars** shot in Washington each year are taken incidentally during big game seasons or with hounds. Stevens and Okanogan counties appear to have the heaviest concentrations of the big cats, but they can be found in any of the timbered, mountainous country, including occasional forays inside Seattle's city limits.

Wolves are protected and occur very rarely in Washington, usually reported in the Okanogan or Selkirks. **Caribou** are found only in the Selkirks, along with **wolverine. Coyotes** are plentiful throughout the state and hunters annually bag nearly 50,000 of the wild dogs.

Range of the imported Hungarian partridge is expanding. These birds have found a niche between the pheasants in the low crop lands and the chukars in the inhospitable rimrock. By Mike Logan

Hunting Oregon

Bighorns, bull elk, pronghorns and record book deer firmly establish Oregon's credentials as big game country, yet the Beaver State is perhaps best known as the place where ringneck pheasants, now the most popular upland bird in America, were first successfully released.

It happened in 1881 when Owen H. Denny shipped 21 Chinese ringnecks from Shanghai, China, to his brother's farm near Corvallis in the Willamette Valley. During the next few decades progeny of those 21 birds were used to establish flocks throughout the country. Thirty-seven states, plus much of southern Canada now hold pheasant seasons in agricultural and prairie areas, and the birds number in the millions.

Oregon's 96,981 square miles are shared by one of the most diverse topographies in the nation. Lush coastal mountains, sand dunes, miles of open beach, rich green river valleys, mile-high mountains, arid plains and harsh desert. More than half of the state is federally owned and open for public recreation, yet the population is just 2.6 million, about twice the size of Dallas. About 357,000 of those are hunters.

Like most western states, deer are the most popular big game animals. Oregon has three huntable species, the blacktails, common to the western coastal country, the mule deer of the arid eastern ranges, and a few whitetails are found in the mountainous country in the northeast near the Idaho-Washington border. A fourth species is fully protected. A subspecies of eastern whitetail, the Columbian whitetail is an endangered species found only on federal preserves near Roseburg and on swampy islands of the Columbia River near Cathlamet, Washington. The geographic division between blacktails and mule deer roughly follows the backbone of the Cascade Range, blacktails to the west, muleys on the east, with some cross-breeding in the center. Oregon deer hunters can't hunt statewide and must select licenses for either the west or the east regions.

Blacktail are the most popular targets, attracting about 64 percent of Oregon's 101,000 deer hunters. They are hunted in western Oregon from the sand dunes of the coast to the crest of the Cascade Range. There are few areas in western Oregon where you cannot expect to see a blacktail at any time of year. Excellent concentrations are found in the hills near Eugene, Roseburg and Grants Pass. The shoulders of the Williamette Valley are popular with blacktail hunters, partially because of the convenience to metropolitan areas and partially because of the number of large deer found there. Clackamas County, which includes Portland's southern suburbs and the state capital, Salem, has produced five of the top 10 blacktail trophies listed in the Boone and Crockett record book.

Mule deer have been hard hit in Oregon by severe winter storms and summer draught. Populations of these eastern Oregon deer are down and various areas have been closed or restricted to hunting to allow herds to rebuild. Muleys are found throughout eastern Oregon and occasionally crossbreed with blacktails, a genetic cousin, where their ranges overlap in the Cascades.

The most popular mule deer areas are on the east slope of the Cascades, roughly paralleled by U.S. Highway 97, and in the northcentral and eastern regions of the Blue, Wallowa and Elkhorn mountains — an area that has produced two top 15 Boone and Crockett record book bucks since 1982, and several high-ranking Pope and Young trophies for bow hunters.

Compared to blacktails and mule deer, the **white-tailed deer** take is almost negligible. It is concentrated in the northeast corner of the state, between Pendleton and the Hells Canyon Wilderness area. Most whitetails are taken incidentally by hunters looking for mule deer, where their ranges overlap.

In the early 1900s heavy market hunting almost pushed Oregon's elk herds into extinction. Herds have rebounded throughout the state and numbers have increased substantially. Elk hunters are required to choose between Roosevelt or Rocky Mountain elk. **Roosevelt elk** are native to the Coast Mountains, and some areas on the west slope of the Cascades. Prime hunting regions are near Tillamook and Clatsop counties and in the far south in the upper Coquille and Millicoma river drainages. An ambitious transplanting program has distributed Roosevelts to most of the mountainous areas on the west side of the state. Other favorite hunting areas include Stott Mountain, Trask River, Fall Creek, Randall Saddle, Crane Prairie, Wickiup Reservoir, Davis Lake and Broken Top Mountain.

Rocky Mountain elk prefer the arid, open climate on the east side of the Cascades. The best hunting is in the Blue and Wallowa mountains. Herds have pushed into northern Harney

Cascade Mountains cougar (left). By Thomas W. Kitchin. Eastern Oregon elk country (above). By Erwin & Peggy Bauer

and Malheur counties and west into the Ochoco Mountains of central Oregon. While these elk can occasionally be spotted wintering in sagebrush, they prefer the mountains where access is difficult enough to discourage casual travelers.

Favorite eastern Oregon elk areas include Grouse-Lick, Mount Emily, Ukiah, Walla Walla, Starkey, Wenaha and Catherine creeks, and the Steens Mountain region.

Oregon has fewer bears than its neighboring states but enough by most standards — there are just black bears now. The awesome grizzly bears that in 1843 harassed the scouts and hunters of Captain John Fremont's legendary expedition, are now extinct in Oregon.

Hunters take about 1,300 **black bear** a year from Oregon's brush and timber country, mostly with hounds in the coastal areas. Blacks can be found throughout the Coast and Cascade ranges and share the timbered elk range in the northeast quarter of the state. Few bears are found on the farm ground floor of the Willamette Valley between Portland and Eugene or in the high desert in the southeast corner.

While bears shun the desert, it is ideal habitat for **pronghorns.** Commonly called antelope, pronghorns are expanding in the arid southeast although winter losses have taken a toll recently.

Oregon Hunting Requirements

Oregon hunting is managed by the Oregon Department of Fish and Wildlife, P.O. Box 59, 506 S.W. Mill St., Portland, OR 97207. Phone (503) 229-5403. Hunting regulation booklets and special hunt permit applications are sent upon request. Resident and nonresident hunting licenses and stamps are available at most sporting goods stores.

Hunter orange is not required during firearm seasons, although it is recommended during deer and elk hunts. Hunters under 14 years old must be accompanied by an adult, and hunters less than 18 years old must have a Hunter Education Certificate. The minimum age for big game hunters is 12. General hunting licenses are required before applying for big game or controlled hunts.

Center-fire firearms for deer, elk and bear must be larger than .24 caliber, although deer and black bear can be hunted with handguns of .25 caliber, .40 caliber muzzle loaders and No. 1 or larger buckshot and slugs. Bows must pull at least 40 pounds for deer hunting and 50 pounds for elk. Shotguns for upland bird hunters must be plugged to restrict shell capacity to three.

Oregon hunting seasons are set by region, species, and in some instances hunting weapons, with special big game hunts set aside for muzzle loader and archery hunting. Permits for antlerless deer and elk, bighorn sheep, antelope, High Cascade early deer hunt and certain controlled regions are limited and awarded on a drawing basis. Applications for these coveted permits are available from the Oregon Department of Fish and Wildlife. There is a filing fee of $3 to enter each drawing.

Special regulation pamphlets are printed for antelope, bighorn sheep and cougar. Seasons are usually set in late March and the deadline for applying is the first week in May.

Elk, deer, antelope, bighorn sheep, gray squirrel, turkey and cougar hunters are restricted to specific areas of the state. Elk and deer hunters must select a specific hunting area, which in some areas includes weapon restrictions, before buying a license. Several elk areas, especially in the northeast region, are regulated by limited entry permits. Statewide hunting is permitted for bear, upland birds (including pheasant, quail, chukar, Hungarian partridge, ruffed, blue and spruce grouse, doves, band-tailed pigeons and snipe) waterfowl, rabbits and crows.

Annual hunting seasons in Oregon begin with special antelope permits the first week of August and windup in mid-January with duck and goose shooting. Bear hunting opens statewide the last week in August followed the first of September by dove, pigeon, crow, grouse, silver gray squirrel and mountain quail seasons.

General upland bird and waterfowl seasons begin the second Saturday in October, running until mid-November and mid-January respectively. Deer seasons in eastern and western regions get under way the last week in September and are generally wrapped up by the middle of November. The western Oregon Roosevelt elk season is divided into two segments and opens on the first Saturday in November and ends on the fourth Friday of the month. Rocky mountain elk also have two opening dates with the first becoming fair game in central and eastern Oregon the last week in October with seasons extending to the middle of November. There is a popular bow hunting season for Rocky Mountain elk from about the third week in August to the third week in September during the period when rutting bull elk are bugling and can be called.

Antelope seasons fall between the first weeks of August and September. Bighorn sheep are stalked during September and cougars are fair game in December and January. Hunters are restricted to one deer, elk, antelope and sheep per season.

Oregon Hunting License Fees

	Resident	Nonresident
Hunting	$ 9.50	$100.50
Hunt /Fish Combination	$19.50	NA
Juvenile Hunting	$ 2	NA
Deer	$ 7.50	$ 75.50
Elk	$19.50	$165.50
Black Bear	$10.50	$ 75.50
Antelope (Pronghorn)	$25.50	$125.50
Bighorn Sheep	$90.50	$900.50
Cougar	$50.50	$150.50
State Waterfowl Stamp	$ 5	$ 5
Game Bird Only	NA	$ 50.50
Turkey	$13	$ 13
Controlled Hunt Application	$ 3	$ 3
Daily Hunting Unit Permits (Waterfowl units and pheasant release sites.)	$ 5	$ 5

Twin coastal black bear cubs.
By Thomas W. Kitchin

Approximately 2,000 hunting permits are issued with 60 percent success. The largest number of permits go to the Steens Mountain, Beatys Butte and Owyhee areas. The highest Boone and Crockett ranking for an Oregon pronghorn is 18th, where ironically there is a four-way tie, that includes two Oregon animals, one from Lake County, the other from Baker County. Probably the best place to view these tan-and-white speedsters is at the National Antelope Refuge near Hart Mountain northeast of Lakeview in southcentral Oregon. Between 100 and 300 pronghorns use the refuge.

When cold weather sets in, most of the refuge antelope abandon the 6,000-foot plateau and migrate to milder winter range on the Charles Sheldon Antelope Range in Nevada. Nomadic resident herds are sometimes spotted from Highways 20, 78, 395 and 95 near Burns.

One of the real success stories in Oregon is its **bighorn sheep** enhancement and reintroduction program. Native Rocky Mountain bighorns in the Wallowa Mountains and California bighorns in the Modoc Lava Bed area on the border of northeastern California were nearly exterminated by pioneer settlers. The comeback started on a cold day in November 1954 when 20 California bighorns, trapped near Williams Lake, British Columbia, were released on Hart Mountain, a multipeaked tower rising above the scabland of Warner Valley to 8,065 feet. This herd now numbers about 100 animals and on a good day when the light is right, they can be spotted in their beds on the west face of the monolithic mountain. Eleven sheep from the Hart Mountain herd were transplanted to Steens Mountain south of Malheur Lake in 1960-61. Rocky Mountain bighorns were reintroduced to Oregon in 1981 when 40 Jasper National Park, Alberta, sheep were stocked along the Lostine River in the Wallowa and Snake River above Hells Canyon.

In 1965 the state had its first sheep hunt, a special permit-only hunt on Hart Mountain. Now, California bighorns are hunted at Hart Mountain, Steens Mountain, Leslie Gulch and Abert Rim. Forty-eight sheep permits were allocated last year and in 1984 hunters were issued 44 sheep permits. They bagged 17 Hart Mountain animals, five from Steens, six from Leslie Gulch at Owyhee Reservoir, two from Juniper and six from Hurricane Divide in the Wallowas. Rocky Mountain bighorns are now found in five areas of northeastern Oregon in the Lostine and Snake River country.

The highest position in the Boone and Crockett record book held by an Oregon bighorn is a three-way tie for 19th, held by a Wallowa County sheep shot in 1981. Sheep hunts are restricted to Oregon residents only. Seasons are held on Hurricane Divide in the Lostine River region, Aldrich Mountains, Leslie Gulch in Owyhee, Pueblo Mountains and Alvord Desert, Steens Mountain, Hart Mountain and on the Hart Mountain National Antelope Refuge.

Within 2 weeks in September 1985 Oregon bowhunters twice broke the world record for Roosevelt elk. The two now occupy the number one and two positions in the Pope & Young Record Book. Number one was taken by Dale Baumgartner (above) on September 21 six miles from his home in Beaver on Mt. Hebo in Tillamook County. The 6x6-point bull scored 356 6/8 points, making it one of the few bow records larger than the record for firearms. On September 7, Ken Adamson (right) of Estacada, briefly held number one with a 6x6 bull that scored 353 4/8. Now ranked number two, Adamson's bull was called to within 40 feet in thick timber 50 miles west of Portland.

Mountain goats are not native to the peaks of Oregon, apparently stopped in their southern drift by the Columbia River, the desert mountains of the Owyhee country and the sometimes blistering summertime temperatures south of the 45th parallel.

Goats, with their thick fleece undercoat and 8-inch guard hairs are creatures of the high cold country. Small herds are being established in northern Oregon with transplants from neighboring states, especially goat-rich Washington. There is no Oregon goat hunting season, yet.

The shaggy, creamy-white goats appear to have taken hold in the high Eagle Cap area of the Wallowa Mountains near Wallowa Lake where the state's first goat transplant was accomplished in 1950. Goats can be seen south of Enterprise, Oregon, above Hurricane Creek, on Sacajawea Peak and on the flanks of 10,004-foot Matterhorn Mountain. The most recent transplants moved Olympic National Park goats to the Elkhorn Mountains above Baker and on Tanner Butte near Bonneville Dam on the Columbia. The Elkhorn and Wallowa herds appears to be adapting well, but few of the Tanner Butte animals appear to be surviving.

Oregon hunters have placed three **cougars** in the top 20 of the North American record book, all taken in the mountains of northeastern Oregon in Baker and Wallowa counties. Cougars, also called panthers or mountain lions, prowl nearly all the timbered mountain country of Oregon, including the Coast and Cascade mountain ranges. The Wallowa, Blue and Elkhorn mountains are good cat country. Hunting pressure is light. Only 79 were reported taken in 1984, 42 of which were bagged in eastern Oregon. Twenty-one hunting areas are open for cougar and about 360 permits issued. Bobcats and a few lynx also hunt the Oregon country, but they are every bit as solitary and secretive as the cougar and spotting one without hounds is incredibly lucky. There are hunters who have spent 40 years in the woods without spotting any of the big cats.

Two color phases of **wolves** once roamed Oregon, the prairie wolf of the plains and timber wolf in the Cascades. Biologists doubt that any wolves now live in Oregon wilds. The state Fish and Wildlife Department hedges short of declaring the infamous howl of the wolf extinct in Oregon. They report that it would be improper to state for certain that there are no wolves left in Oregon, but if they do exist, they are extremely rare.

In addition to wolves and grizzlies, Oregon is the only Northwest state or province that does not have a resident herd of **moose** or **caribou.**

Oregon is a bird hunting state, a tradition that has continued since 1881, when the Chinese ringneck pheasants were first introduced.

During most seasons upwards of 96,000 upland bird hunters walk the woods, prairies and fields of Oregon, dropping about 1 million birds, and probably missing twice that many.

Chukar, red-legged and Hungarian partridge, turkey and bobwhite quail have also been imported, released and hunted. The imports complement a fine assortment of native birds — sage, ruffed, blue and spruce grouse, valley and California quail, doves and band-tailed pigeon.

In recent years **turkey** hunting popularity has soared as populations have exploded, to the point where some farmers have filed crop-damage complaints because of Ben Franklin's favorite fowl. (The Philadelphian lost a campaign to have the turkey, not the bald eagle, which he considered a scavenger, designated as the national emblem.)

Two subspecies of turkeys have taken to the Oregon oaks, Merriams and the Rio Grande, both of hearty Texas stock. Oregon game managers have been trying to establish turkeys since 1899, and the state now grants about 1,025 permits for mid-April to mid-May gobbler hunts in 12 hunting units.

The heaviest concentration is in Douglas County centered by Roseburg. Ranchers near the small town of Tiller along the upper Umpqua River have actually complained that wintering turkeys are creating crop losses. There is also good turkey shooting in the North White River region between The Dalles and Highway 97 along the Columbia River. Turkeys are also at Garrison Butte east of the Metolius River, foothills around Mount Hood, Wenaha Wildlife Area near Troy. They are also taking hold in the scrub oak country near Medford and around the Warm Springs Indian Reservation.

Ringneck pheasants have been transplanted to every county in the state. The best bird hunting is in agricultural areas in northern Malheur and Umatilla counties, and the Columbia Basin. Half the state's pheasant harvest comes from here. The Rogue River valley also produces good pheasant hunting, along with Wallowa, Union, Baker, Crook and Jefferson counties.

Other upland bird hunting includes statewide **valley** and **mountain quail, band-tailed pigeons** in the Coast Mountains, Willamette Valley and Hood River areas; **mourning doves** in the arid eastern agricultural lands and Willamette Valley. **Chukar** and **Hungarian partridges** are well established in the rimrock, butte and coulee country of eastern Oregon. Every county in eastern Oregon can offer partridge shooting, but the best is found in the Snake River breaks, Owyhee Canyon, Steens Mountain, Malheur River Basin and the lower sections of the John Day and Deschutes rivers.

Blue and **ruffed grouse** are plentiful in the timbered mountain ranges on both sides of the state. Heaviest concentration of blues is in the Wallowa Mountains.

Ruffs are in the alder along creek bottoms and just about any nonalpine wooded area. Nearly a third of the grouse hunters in Oregon concentrate on the late season in western Oregon, Hood River and Wasco counties.

Sage grouse are few and far between and the ones that are left are strutting in the sage lands of the Malheur National Wildlife Refuge at Foster Flat and at the Hart Mountain refuge. A few solitary flocks are in the vast treeless southcentral and eastern areas of the state. Harney, Malheur and Lake counties support some sage hens, and remnant flocks are found in Grant, Baker, Deschutes and Klamath counties. There is no hunting season.

On both sides of the Oregon Cascades, there is excellent duck and goose shooting. Waterfowlers drop 600,000 in an average year and probably miss three times that number. Oregon is the choke point for much of the Pacific flyway, the spot where the various windrows of migrating ducks and geese merge. There can be 6 million ducks and geese in the flyway and many of them come in low and fast across Oregon decoys.

On the west side and up the Willamette Valley, waterfowlers take their sport where they can find it — in river sloughs, ranch ponds, lowland lakes and grain fields. On the east, gunners concentrate on lakes and marshes.

The best duck and goose hunting, however, is found near several major wildlife refuge complexes. The Sauvie Island Wildlife Area (adjoining Washington's Ridgefield National Wildlife Refuge) on the Columbia River, northwest of Portland, is an outstanding example. Up to 75,000 ducks, 3,000 whistling swans and 2,000 sandhill cranes winter there.

The Umatilla National Wildlife Refuge on the Columbia River between Boardman and Umatilla is a complex of islands, sloughs and and backwaters where 90,000 Canada geese and 250,000 ducks winter. Mallards are the most plentiful. Much of the refuge is open to duck and goose hunting.

As impressive as those numbers are, however, they don't match the volume of ducks and geese that winter-over in the southern part of the state. Half a million ducks and geese swarm into the Klamath Basin complex on the California border. The Klamath and Tule Lake regions afford some of the finest waterfowl hunting in the northwest, attracting heavy concentrations of puddle ducks, snow and Canada geese.

There is some outstanding **duck** and **goose** shooting in eastern Oregon. The prime areas are along the Columbia River, especially between The Dalles and Hermiston. More good shooting can be found along the California border near Klamath Falls, Goose Lake, extending northeast to the cluster of lakes below Hart Mountain up to Warm Springs Valley and Malheur Lake. Coastal areas are also heavily hunted, especially the estuaries when winter storms force the ducks into interior waters for protection.

> "From my vantage point I could already begin to see and appreciate the bigness and ruggedness of this Oregon wilderness. It was a mountain stronghold such as I had never before looked into. All the hunters in the United States could not kill the game here. There never will come a time when bear, deer, cougar, wildcats, and foxes will be scarce in this part of the West."
>
> *From* Downriver, *Zane Grey, 1926*

Prickly pear cactus appears in the arid regions of the Northwest, extending well into southern British Columbia.
By Thomas W. Kitchin

Hunting Idaho

For most hunters Idaho, with its vast tracts of mountain wilderness and desert sage land, is synonymous with big game. Trophy-class whitetails, mule deer and elk attract thousands of hunters each fall, plus the Gem State hosts limited hunts for antelope, moose, bighorn sheep and mountain goats. Black bears are plentiful enough to allow hunters two per season, and cougars range throughout the mountainous country north of U.S. Highway 20.

Idaho is big country, 13th largest state, with more than 83,557 square miles, portions of 15 national forests inhabited by less than 1 million people — one of the sparsest populated states in America.

While it doesn't get the international recognition of big game hunting, Idaho is a fine state for bird shooters, especially in the irrigated farm country on both sides of the upper Snake River system rumbling through the arid flatlands of southern Idaho. Thirteen species of upland birds can be flushed; five species of grouse (blue, Franklin's, ruffed, sharp-tail and sage), four kinds of quail (valley, Gambel's mountain and bobwhite), two partridges (chukars and Hungarian), ringneck pheasants and turkey.

Turkeys have only been scratching the Idaho hill country since 1962 when Colorado birds were released near Riggins. Additional turkeys have been stocked along the Salmon, Payette and Boise rivers, in the Snake River/Hells Canyon country near Lewiston and in the heavily timbered hills south of Lake Coeur d'Alene around St. Maries. Flocks are now established in 31 locations and 150 spring hunting permits are authorized. The Idaho turkey hunt is growing and more permits will be allocated as the birds multiply.

Mule and white-tailed deer are the most popular big game animals in Idaho, sometimes overlapping ranges; mule deer browsing the mountaintops and the whitetails ranging brushy river valleys and foothills. It's nearly impossible to find an area of the state where deer don't exist, and 11,500 permits are set aside for nonresident hunters.

Deer have taken some severe licks from winter weather in recent seasons; winter kills that are reflected in lower hunting harvests. They are starting to come back. In 1985 deer hunters bagged 48,950 deer, 6,300 more than in 1984. The total kill figures include 1,300 bagged by archers and 600 by muzzle loaders. Much of the earlier dropoff was attributed to winter kills and blizzards that pinned down hunters during prime hunting periods and winter kills that spurred the Fish and Game Department into setting a bucks-only season in 29 southern Idaho regions.

There are more **mule deer** in Idaho than any other big game animal. They range throughout the state, dominating the southern section and sharing the range north of the Salmon River with whitetails. The best mule deer hunting areas, according to the state game managers, are in the Owyhees in southwestern Idaho, the Upper Payette and Boise river drainages in the Sawtooth and Salmon River mountain ranges, the Cassia, Sublette and Black Pine areas in extreme southcentral Idaho.

Less accessible, but a good place to find a trophy buck is the rugged, remote wilderness areas along the Middle Fork Salmon River and in the sparsely populated country near the Blackfoot and Bear rivers in the southeast corner.

Southern Idaho mule deer are trophy-class animals, especially the high-racked bucks in the mineral-rich Owyhee Mountains. The No. 2 typical mule deer trophy listed in the Boone and Crockett record book was taken in 1979 in the mountains of Idaho County in central Idaho, and the No. 3 Boone and Crockett nontypical muley was bagged in the heavily hunted area of Gem County northwest of Boise.

Idaho bow hunters have also done well, nailing down several positions in the Pope and Young record book including a 6x5 muley dropped in Boise County that was No. 2 in the nation in 1984.

The heavily timbered range of northern Idaho is shared by mule deer and **whitetails** but dominated by whitetails. They thrive in the timbered mountains and brushy creek bottoms north of the Salmon River. The farther north you travel from the Salmon the more dominate whitetails become.

Good whitetail hunting is always reported in the Snake-Salmon River country near Lewiston, Clearwater, Riggins and White Bird. Whitetails are also heavily hunted in the upper Clearwater, Lochsa, and Bitterroot Mountains, near St. Maries, east of Coeur d'Alene, and north through

River bottom ruffed grouse (left). By Dewey Haeder. Idaho has produced many nationally ranked mule deer trophies, and is a favorite hunting ground for nonresident hunters. By Thomas W. Kitchin

Most of Idaho's pronghorns range through the Snake River Plains. By Terry W. Sheely.

Sandpoint into the Bonners Ferry-Kaniksu country. Idaho's mountain whitetails, however, can't match the size of eastern whitetails and have not placed any racks in the firearm or bow hunting record books.

Deer may be the most popular big game animal in the state, but to most hunters Idaho means elk. **Rocky Mountain elk** range across all of Idaho except for the agricultural areas in the Snake River plain of southern Idaho. They are the No. 1 target for nonresident hunters and 10,500 nonresident licenses are granted; 90 percent of them for the central part of the state and the balance assigned units in the Panhandle.

Gem State elk herds have been thriving in recent years on a strict new management program enacted by the game department to head off serious problems that loomed late in the 1970s. The plan was to set seasons that allowed bulls to mature to near-trophy status, reduce hunter density, and to keep season lengths and specific hunts flexible enough to match changeable conditions. Success of the new program can be measured by hunter success.

There are 120,000 elk in Idaho, roughly the same as other Northwest states and provinces. Hunting pressure, however, is signicantly lower producing a better success percentage among hunters. The state also produces an unusually heavy percentage of trophy bulls. About 58 percent of the bulls taken in general seasons during the past five years have been 5-point or better.

Harvest figures show how the new elk management programs are succeeding. In 1976 the statewide elk kill was only 4,100. Less than a decade later, in 1984 Idaho's mountains gave up 15,600 elk to hunters, a whopping 23 percent gain over the 1983 hunt. That harvest figure held during 1985 when 15,550 elk were bagged. Bow hunters accounted for 500 elk in 1985 and muzzle loaders another 150, a fraction of the overall take. Idaho's post-season ratios of bulls to cows and branch-antlered to spikes is among the highest in North America.

Nearly all of Idaho north of the Snake River plains supports elk herds. Logging roads often provide vehicle access into prime elk country, a mixed blessing. There are vast tracts of mountain country in designated wilderness or primitive areas where horses or backpacks are the only way to hunt. Perhaps the best known elk area in the state is the rugged Chamberlain Basin between the South and Middle forks of the Salmon River.

Good elk country is also found in the upper reaches of the Clearwater River drainage, including the Selway, Lochsa and North Fork watersheds. The upper St. Joe River east of St. Maries is becoming a prime elk producer. You'll also find elk hunted in the Lemhi, Lost and Sawtooth mountains, plus the Bitterroots on the boundary with Montana and on the east side of the Panhandle in the Coeur d'Alene and Pend Oreille areas.

These are the hot spots. Elk are likely to be encountered in any of the timbered mountain ranges of the central and northern state. The backcountry and high-mountain elk areas open in mid-September to take advantage of fair weather and the bull elk bugle season. The general elk season begins about Oct. 1 for all of the state west of Mount Borah near Mackay, and in mid-October the areas east of Mount Borah open, including the Teton, Targhee and Caribou range along the Wyoming border.

Bighorns are making a comeback in Idaho, reintroduced to several areas where they had been driven to extinction by subsistence hunters, disease, and encroaching cattle and sheep herds. In 1985 hunters were allowed 165 bighorn permits, about 10 percent allocated to nonresident hunters. Hunter success runs a little better than 50 percent.

Two varieties of bighorns, Rocky Mountain and California, can be found in central and southern Idaho. Biggest concentrations are found in the arid Owyhee south of Boise and in the Salmon River mountains in the Challis National Forest.

More than 200 bighorns have recently been brought in from other states to create new herds or beef up breeding populations in the Little Lost River drainage, Craig Mountain Wildlife Manage-

General Hunting Requirements

Idaho hunting is managed by the Idaho Fish and Game Department, P.O. Box 25, 600 S. Walnut St., Boise, ID 83707. Phone (208) 334-3700. Hunting regulations, special hunt applications and resident hunting licenses are available at 500 sportings goods dealers throughout the state. Nonresident deer, elk and antelope archery tags are available only at IFGD offices. Nonresident general hunting licenses and tags for bear, cougar and turkey can be bought at sporting good stores.

Idaho's firearm and safety restrictions and requirements are among the most liberal in the country. Wearing of hunter orange is not required during any firearm season, hunters 15 years old and younger must pass a state-approved hunter safety program before applying for a license, and nonresidents are not required to employ a licensed guide to hunt big game.

The number of permits available to out-of-state hunters is limited for all big game except bears and cougars, and varies annually. In 1985 there were 11,500 deer tags and 10,500 elk tags set aside for nonresident hunters. Nonresidents are also allowed 10 percent of the permits available for bighorn sheep and mountain goats. In 1985 there were 165 sheep tags and 50 goat permits to be divided between resident and nonresident hunters. The state also allocates 350 moose permits, but restricts the sale to resident hunters only.

Big game hunters are allowed to use any caliber of rifle or handgun larger than .22 caliber rimfire cartridges. Crossbows are legal except during archery-only hunts and long bows must have a 40-pound draw at 28 inches for big game hunting. All shooting hours are one hour before sunrise to one hour after sunset. There is no shell-capacity restriction for shotguns used to hunt upland

bird and only the federal three-shot restriction for waterfowl.

Idaho hunting seasons are set by region, species and in some instances hunting weapon. Special big game hunts are set aside for muzzle loader and archery hunting. Controlled hunt permits for deer, elk, moose, sheep and goats are awarded on a drawing basis. Applications are available from the IFGD. There is a $3.50 filing fee.

Nonresidents may apply for controlled elk and deer hunts after first buying a general hunting license and then submitting the application form with the proper tag fee to the IFGD before June 30. A drawing is held Aug. 1. Deadline for applying for sheep and goat and moose permits is April 30 with June notification.

Except for controlled, permit-only hunts, deer, elk, bear, antelope, mountain lions, upland birds, waterfowl, grouse and small game can be hunted wherever there is a legal season statewide. The only fully protected animals in the Gem State are caribou,

gray wolves and grizzly bears.

Annual hunting seasons begin in mid-July with a special elk archery seasons and winds up with a mid-January closure of duck season. General deer, upland bird waterfowl seasons begin the second or third Saturday in October. Some general elk units open as early as mid-September but most fall within the first two weeks of October, with the more remote mountainous areas opening earlier to avoid heavy snows and take advantage of the bull elk bugle season. Grouse, quail and chukar seasons open the last week of September, and some 150 permits are allocated for a mid-April turkey hunt.

Black bears are hunted in the spring beginning April 1 and again in the fall after Aug. 31 in most areas. That's the same day moose, bighorn sheep and mountain goats become legal game for most permit holders. Hunters are restricted to one big game animal of each species a year, except for black bear where there is a two-bear limit.

Idaho Hunting License Fees

	Resident	Nonresident
Hunting	$ 6.50	$ 85.50
Juvenile (12-17)	$ 4.50	NA
Nongame (January to August)	NA	$ 10.50
Deer	$ 8	$ 90.50
Elk	$ 14	$235.50
Cougar	$ 10.50	$100.50
Black Bear	$ 6.50	$ 40.50
Turkey	$ 6.50	$ 25.50
Antelope	$ 32.50	$ 90.50
Antelope Archery	$ 27	$ 52
Archery Stamp	$ 5.50	$ 5.50
Muzzle Loader	$ 5.50	$ 5.50
Moose	$ 71	NA
Bighorn Sheep	$ 71	$500.50
Mountain Goat	$ 71	$500.50

The best sage grouse hunting remaining in the Northwest is found in southern Idaho. By Mike Logan

ment Area south of Lewiston, Cottonwood Creek southeast of Twin Falls, West Fork Bruneau River and the South Fork Owyhee River near Bruneau-Jarbridge. In 1986 22 Rocky Mountain bighorns were brought in from Oregon to start a new herd in the Beaverhead Mountains east of Leadore.

Rafters and float fishermen infrequently spot remote herds of bighorn sheep in the Salmon River breaks, Middle Fork Salmon and in Hells Canyon on the Snake.

The rarest big game animals in Idaho are **mountain goats,** those creamy-white, bearded cliff-climbers with ebony-colored dagger horns. Only 50 hunting permits are granted each season and those are on a once-in-a-lifetime basis.

Hunting success on goats runs about 70 percent. Spotting a mountain goat in Idaho is rare. They cling to remote mountaintops and are almost never visible from heavily traveled roads. The biggest concentration is in the southeast along the Wyoming border in the Caribou and Snake River mountains including Targhee and Caribou national forests.

Mountain goats are also found in the northern region in the upper drainages of the Clearwater, Lochsa and Coeur d'Alene river drainages, and along the Bitterroot Mountain border with Montana.

The desolate, arid plains of southeastern Idaho support the state's entire **pronghorn antelope** population, most of which is concentrated in the Snake River plain between Twin Falls and Rexburg. A little more than 3,000 permits are allocated for antelope hunters, 300 set aside for nonresidents. Hunting success runs high, however, with an annual kill of 2,440. The highest number of hunting permits are issued for the Little Lost River, Birch Creek drainages north of Arco and northwest of Idaho Falls.

The only big game animal hunted exclusively by Idaho hunters is **Shiras moose.** Idaho's moose herds browse in opposite ends of the state. The heaviest concentration is in the northern

Grizzly 3-Year-Old Male

Black Bear Brown Phase

Black Bear Black Phase

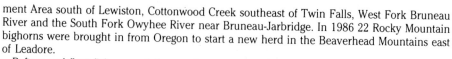

Black Bear or Grizzly?

Several color phases of black and grizzly bears roam the thick brush and mountains of the Northwest. In several regions their ranges overlap and being able to distinguish one from another becomes essential. Cases of mistaken identity are not uncommon, and occasionally lead to a licensed black bear hunter pulling the trigger on a grizzly, or a hiker crossing paths with a cinnamon-colored black bear and spreading a grizzly alert. There are several distinguishing differences.

Adult grizzly bears are found throughout Alaska, British Columbia and Alberta, with isolated populations in the mountainous regions of the northwestern states. Only Oregon does not report a grizzly bear population.

The largest concentration of grizzlies south of Canada is in Montana where they roam the north and west perimeters of Yellowstone National Park; the Bitterroot-Selway mountains on the border of Idaho; along the Continental Divide north of Interstate 90 through Glacier National Park; and in the Cabinet and Yaak mountain ranges west of Kalispell. Grizzlies may also be encountered in the Selkirk Mountains of extreme northern Idaho and northeastern Washington. A few of the giant bears are also found in the remote peaks of Washington's North Cascades between Lake Chelan and British Columbia.

In coastal areas of Alaska grizzlies are recognized as ''Kodiak'' or ''brown'' bears, while mountain or interior bears are identified as grizzlies. Biologically, they are the same bear, although the coastal ''brownies'' are considerbly larger. The brown variety is the largest living carnivorous land mammal in the world. (Polar bears grow larger, but spend most of their life offshore on drifting pack ice.) Alaska grizzlies have been measured that exceeded 9 feet nose-to-tail, weighing up to 1,500 pounds.

Grizzlies have long, brown to silverish-colored hair. The face is somewhat square and slightly dished above the muzzle which is often long and fairly pointed.

Black bears have evolved in several colors. Black is the most common phase, but brown or cinnamon-colored phases of the black bear are fairly common throughout the range and actually dominate several specific regions. In the Yakutat area of Alaska, there is a blue-colored phase known as a glacier bear, and in northwest British Columbia is found the all-white Kermode bear. The entire population of Kermode black bears is estimated at less than 3,000, all in the Kitimat, Terrace and Hazelton regions. They are protected.

Blacks generally have shorter hair than grizzlies, and a more roundish appearance, especially in the face. The muzzle is shorter and more roundish than a grizzly's and blacks lack the distinctive shoulder hump. A black bear's claws are shorter, rounder and less formidable looking than grizzly claws which are long, slightly curved and often yellowish white in color.

All color phases of adult black bears are considerably smaller than adult grizzlies. Adult blacks weigh from 100 to 400 pounds, with a few approaching 500. Most blacks average around 200 pounds, and measure 5 to 6 feet long nose-to-tail.

Panhandle region, with moose moving as far south as the Salmon River. The second concentration is along the Wyoming border in the upper Snake, Teton, Blackfoot and Bear river drainages.

Idaho offers resident hunters 350 moose tags (no nonresident moose hunting), allocated by drawing. In past years success for moose hunters has averaged about 85 percent, and the number of permits up for grabs has been steadily increasing, reflecting a growing herd.

Bow hunters have put Idaho moose in the Pope and Young records, with bulls from Fremont and Madison counties — both taken in 1983. An Idaho Shiras is also ranked No. 5 in the firearm records of Boone and Crockett, with an antler spread of 58⅛ inches. That moose was killed in 1981 in Idaho County.

Timbered mountain areas support an excellent and, in some areas, troublesome bear population. Only **black bears** are legal game and the remnant grizzlies in the state are fully protected and confined to a few isolated areas near the Montana border. Hunters are allowed up to two black bear a year and the annual kill has been climbing for the past few years. Still, the bear harvest is low compared to other big game, 2,100 in 1984. Blacks are likely to be encountered anywhere north of the Snake River plain and in the timbered mountains along the Wyoming border. The state schedules hunts for spring, summer and fall.

Grizzly bears are protected, and stay in the mountain backcountry. Grizzlies have been spotted along the Yellowstone National Park border in the Targhee National Forest, in the eastern Selway-Bitterroot Wilderness Area and in the Kaniksu National Forest below the British Columbia border.

"They'll come in high and wary, green necks craned, suspicious. Keep your face down, use the chuckle call when they circle, switch to the lonesome hen when they swing away from the spread. Talk 'em down. You can do it." By Mike Logan

195

Coyote on the hunt. By Dewey Haeder

The same areas that support black bear also have a **cougar** population, but spotting a cougar in Idaho without the help of a dog pack requires a great deal of luck. Cougars are secretive, wide-ranging animals roaming rugged terrain and most hunters track their cats with lion dogs.

No special permit is required, in addition to a general hunting license, but hunters are limited to one mountain lion a year. Hunting season on the big cats is generally from the end of August until the end of February. Idaho's highest ranking in the Boone and Crockett record book for cougar includes two cats in a five-way tie for 13th position. Those animals were bagged in Adams and Idaho counties in 1977 and 1982.

Probably the most controversial animal in Idaho is the **gray wolf.** The first part of the controversy is whether or not there are any wolves in Idaho.

It is estimated that in Idaho more gray wolves, and crossbred wolf-dogs now live in captivity than in the mountains. A recent report by the U.S. Fish and Wildlife Service put the total wild wolf population in the state at between seven and 15. Most reports are in the Bear Valley-Warm Lake area northeast of Cascade in the edge of the Idaho Primitive Area, and there have been reports of wolves in the Frank Church River Of No Return Wilderness Area of the Salmon River.

In 1978 a wolf was shot and verified near Lowman on the South Fork Payette River. There is a federal plan to designate a Central Idaho Wolf Recovery Area from the backbone of the Bitterroot Mountains near Lolo Pass, south nearly to McCall through the Selway-Bitterroot Wilderness, Salmon River Breaks Primitive Area, Idaho Primitive Area and the Frank Church Primitive Area. Smaller recovery areas are also proposed on the border near Yellowstone National Park. Although biologists would like to see the Idaho gray wolf population rejuvenated in remote regions, the effort is meeting considerble resistance from agricultural and wildlife groups.

Idaho's "big game" bird, the **wild turkey,** is still in limited supply and hunting is on a permit drawing basis. In 1986 there were more than 500 applicants for just 150 permits divided among 24 hunting units. Flocks of Merriams and Rio Grande turkeys are being established throughout

the state. The spring season runs from the middle of April until the middle of May in most units, and is restricted to male gobblers.

Most of Idaho's **upland birds** are concentrated in the arid sage flats and irrigated agricultural areas of southern Idaho and along the rugged walls of Hells Canyon on the Snake River. Forest grouse are in the timbered mountains, and sage grouse in the plains of the southeast.

In 1985 bird hunters in Idaho bagged: 238,100 pheasants, 30,800 chukar, 26,900 sage grouse, 73,400 forest grouse, 2,000 sharp-tailed grouse, 56,500 quail, 124,100 mourning doves, and 17,000 Hungarian partridge.

The **ringneck pheasant,** the No. 1 upland bird in Idaho, is the top hunting areas are in the farm lands along the upper Snake River from Payette east to Rupert. The best hunting, according to Department of Fish and Game managers is in farm fields between Burley and Twin Falls, west to Weiser. Although not as plentiful as the Snake River plain birds, pheasants are also in fair number in the brushy draws and wheat fields near Lewiston.

Chukars do well in the Owyhee and Hells Canyon country and the lower Salmon River breaks near Riggins. The Palouse hills surrounding Lewiston offer some of the finest **Hungarian partridge** shooting in the country.

Ducks and geese are hunted throughout the state, but the best shooting follows the Snake River through the agricultural and nesting areas between Boise and Rexburg. The late November and December action is often classed as outstanding, especially for Canada geese, at Island Park, Dingle Swamp near Bear Lake, Blackfoot Reservoir, Grays Lake, American Falls Reservoir, and the Snake River lakes from C.J. Strike Reservoir downstream to Weiser.

In the north, the best waterfowl hunting is in October on the Kootenai National Wildlife Refuge area near Bonners Ferry. The islands, sloughs and marshes lining the Pend Oreille River are good decoy areas. Goose hunters work the wheat fields near Lewiston.

A rooster ringneck pheasant glides into the swale cover of an irrigation ditch, prime habitat in the Northwest.
By Thomas W. Kitchin

"Remember that a moose is a big animal. A deer standing next to a moose would look like a dwarf next to Wilt Chamberlain. A moose that is 60 yards away will appear to be only half that distance to a bow hunter used to shooting at smaller game, and he will likely shoot low. The first time I went bow hunting for moose, I took a shot at a bull I estimated to be about 35 yards from me. The arrow fell short, and when I paced off the distance, I found it to be over 65 Yards."

From Alaska Hunting Guide, *Jay Massey*

In an average year Idaho waterfowlers bag 355,300 ducks, 56,800 Canada geese and another 4,100 snow geese.

Mourning doves are popular targets in early September in the Snake River grain country between Weiser and Pocatello with marginal hunting in the Coeur d'Alene and Lewiston areas.

Idaho is one of the few Northwest regions continuing to offer good **sage grouse** shooting with nearly 27,000 sage hens shot a year. Sage and **sharp-tailed grouse** are hunted in the southern and southeastern prairie country. Owyhee, Twin Falls, Bannock, Butte, Blaine, Minidoka, Custer and Lemhi counties are favorite areas. Numbers of these plains birds have been on the drop, seasons are generally short. The longest open season is in the Pahsimeroi, Lemhi and Big Lost river valleys.

Idaho also has a remnant and vigorously protected, woodland caribou herd that roams the high country of the Selkirk Mountains between Washington, Idaho and British Columbia.

Hunting Montana

"The whol [sic] face of the country was covered with herds of buffaloe, Elk and Antelopes."
On a mild April evening in 1805 on the wind-brushed plains of eastern Montana, Captain Meriwether Lewis penned that glowing description of Montana's legendary big game. Just three months later in the simmering heat of August, along the eastern slope of the Bitterroot Mountains, his desperate expedition was eating packhorses to ward off starvation.

One hundred and eighty years later that feast to famine experience continues to sharply define the bewildering contrasts that can confound hunters in a state as big as the empire of Japan. Overall, Montana is probably richer in big game today than when Lewis and Clark explored the region. It's one of the most popular destinations for big game hunters on the North American continent and has contributed a wealth of big game trophies to the North American record books.

Montana is the fourth-largest state in the nation — 147,138 square miles, 550 miles from Idaho to North Dakota, 325 miles fron Canada to Wyoming. Yet, there are fewer than a million permanent residents, leaving a lot of room to support wildlife. Ten varieties of big game animals are hunted, more than in any other of the contiguous 48 states. Montana offers the only grizzly bear season and unlimited bighorn sheep hunting south of Canada.

While most of the international attention is concentrated on Montana's enviable herds of big game animals, prairie and mountain grouse, upland birds and waterfowl hunting are popular with resident hunters.

The diversity of game animals is matched by the state's contrasting geography. The eastern region is largely flat or rolling treeless prairie, spotted with brushy river bottoms and vast tracts of sage land and ranches. The western third of the state is dominated by national forests, heavily timbered mountain ranges and steep-sided river valleys. Nearly 17 million acres of Montana is managed by the U.S. Forest Service, and another 8 million acres is controlled by the Bureau of Land Management. Half a million acres are set aside as national wildlife refuges, and another 1.1 million are classed as national park. Still, state biologists estimate that more than 50 percent of the hunting is on private property.

In eastern Montana leasing and fee hunting is becoming more common, but in the central and western parts of the state, permission to hunt is more commonly granted to well-mannered hunters.

The most popular big game animals in Montana are deer, attracting nearly 240,000 hunters and still managing to produce a statewide hunter success rate of 71 percent, better than any other region in the Northwest. In many of the central and eastern units hunter success for deer borders on 100 percent. Biologists expect the deer population to remain high through the decade.

Hunters pursue both **mule and white-tailed deer** in just about all areas of the state, and their ranges often overlap. Whitetails favor the brushy lowlands following the river and creek bottoms through ranch and farmland, while mule deer prefer the high mountains, remote valleys and open sagebrush prairies. In a few areas, however, one or the other will dominate because most of the habitat favors one variety. Whitetails dominate the northwestern counties north of Missoula and occupy most of the lowlands and river bottoms throughout the state.

The whitetail population is booming, spreading into new ranges and in a few areas displacing mule deer. Whitetails account for about 35 percent of the statewide deer harvest and 75 percent of the harvest in the heavily timbered country west of Kalispell and north of Missoula. Whitetails are also spreading into the northcentral and eastern parts of the state, as prairie land falls to the plows of agriculture. The more farms, it seems, the more whitetails and the less mule deer, which do much better on natural prairie lands than in tilled fields. In contrast with the expansion of the whitetail range, mule deer populations seem to be dropping slightly, a condition blamed on drought, prolonged cold and a down curve in the natural population cycle.

The prime mule deer regions are in central and eastern Montana, especially in the Missouri River Breaks country near Fort Peck Reservoir. The open hunting country near Billings produces its share of big mule deer bucks, and whitetails don't appear to be making the inroads here they are in other areas of the eastern region of the state. The Bridger Mountains near Bozeman and the Gallatin Range are also prime for big muley bucks. Other favorite areas include the high country of the Bitterroots, the Sapphires and the upper Whitefish mountain ranges. There are actually few areas of Montana where large mule deer bucks can't be bagged. According to

Left, tracks of winter on the banks of the Yellowstone River. By Michael S. Sample. Mountain valleys and creek bottoms of western Montana support most of Montana's ruffed grouse population (above). By Mark Henckel.

the state FWP, there are more mule deer per square mile in undeveloped prairie country than in the mountains, although in the high country geographic barriers tend to concentrate the animals more. Whitetails are heavily hunted in the northwest, but the biggest bucks nearly always come from the river valleys east of the Rockies. The Musselshell and Yellowstone river valleys, Little and Big Belts and Bull mountains are excellent for big whitetails.

Montana Hunting Requirements

Hunting in Montana, as well as management of the state's big game, small game, upland birds and nongame wildlife, is controlled by the Department of Fish, Wildlife and Parks, 1420 E. Sixth Ave., Helena, MT 59620. Phone (406) 444-2535. Hunting regulations, special hunt application forms and resident hunting licenses are available at several hundred license agents, mostly sporting goods dealers statewide. Nonresident big game combination licenses, as well as licenses for mountain lion, antelope, mountain goat, moose and bighorn sheep, can be purchased only from the department's Helena office. Other nonresident licenses can be purchased at sporting goods stores.

Montana is the only northwestern state or province requiring big game hunters to wear "hunter orange," requiring a minimum of 400 square inches above the waist. Bow hunters are excluded during archery-only seasons. Big game hunters will find there are no caliber limitations for hunting with rifles or pistols, although shotguns used for deer hunting must be loaded with slugs, O or OO buck. Crossbows are not legal.

Hunters younger than 18 years old must complete a certified firearm safety course and those younger than 12 are not eligible to purchase big game hunting licenses. Nonresidents are not required to employ a licensed guide to hunt big game.

Montana limits the number of big game combination licenses set aside for nonresident hunters after deer and elk to 17,000. These $350 tags are quickly snapped up by nonresident hunters. In 1985 all were sold within six days. Black bear and upland bird licenses are unlimited. Limited permits are also issued on a drawing basis for both nonresident and resident hunters after antelope (approximate number of permits, 39,000); deer B, 40,700; bighorn sheep, 300 although in some southwestern sheep areas permits are unlimited; mountain goat, 350; and moose, 650. The number of available permits varies each year.

What's the probability of being drawn for a permit? As high as 92 percent for Deer B licenses, and as low as 4 percent for moose. The odds change year to year, varying with the number of licenses offered and applications received. These figures from 1984 are reasonable yardsticks for estimating your chances of drawing a permit. Applicants have a 24 percent chance of getting one of the 19,000 antlerless or either-sex elk permits issued, 5 percent for bighorn sheep, 7 percent for mountain goat, and 56 percent for nonresident Deer A licenses. The deadline for applying for limited permits is June 1.

Montana is divided into dozens of small hunting districts and hunting seasons. Bag limits and the number of available permits are set according to the management requirements of each unit.

Excluding special spring seasons, hunting in Montana begins in the heat of Indian summer during the first week of September with archery hunts for antelope, deer and elk, and winds up in the windblown cold of a duck blind late in December. Special depredation-control hunts for elk, deer and buffalo are authorized during the winter, but on a permit-only basis.

General antelope firearm seasons open in mid-October and end in mid-November. Deer and elk are fair game for rifle hunters from late October through November. Special backcountry rifle hunts for deer and elk start on Sept. 15, the same day that most sheep, goat and moose hunting seasons open.

Doves, grouse and partridge become fair game in early September, but duck season doesn't open until mid-October and pheasant hunters have to wait until late in October to begin their hunts. Grouse, partridge and pheasant seasons wrap up early in December, and the final duck season ends late in the month.

Hundreds of big game animals have been outfitted with radio transmitting collars, neck bands or streamers. It is legal to shoot collared or tagged animals, but the radio equipment and markers must be returned to the Department of Fish, Wildlife and Parks. Hunters intending to bring in out-of-state horses or mules are required to obtain an animal health permit from the state Department of Livestock and submit their stock to brand inspection. Phone (406) 444-2043 for specific information.

Hunting License Fees

	Resident	Nonresident
Conservation	$ 2	$ 2
Sportsman's License (Includes 1 deer, 1 elk, 1 black bear, game birds, fishing)	$45	NA
Upland Bird	$ 6	$ 53
Turkey	$ 3	$ 13
Black Bear	$ 8	$120
Deer A (statewide)	$ 9	$200
Deer B (antlerless whitetail in specific units)	$ 8	$ 52
Elk	$10	NA
Big Game Combination Conservation (1 black bear, 1 deer A, 1 elk, upland birds, fishing. Available in Helena FWP office only. Annual quota of 17,000)	NA	$450
Bow and Arrow	$ 7	$ 6
Mountain Lion	$10	$320
Antelope	$ 8	$122
Mountain Goat	$52	$322
Moose	$52	$322
Bighorn Sheep	$52	$322

Despite its overall excellence as a deer hunters' mecca, Montana is not, however, a prime trophy deer state. Many broad-beamed, high-racked 4- and 5-point bucks are bagged in the Treasure State, but few ever make the Boone and Crockett record book for North American big game. The highest placed Boone and Crockett Montana mule deer (typical antlers) is 30th, a 6-by-6 dropped in Flathead County in 1980. A 1943 nontypical Montana buck with 29 total antler points is eighth place in that category. No Montana whitetails are listed in the top 100 of the typical antler category, but a Snowy Mountain buck with 28 separate antler points holds down the No. 2 spot in the nontypical class.

The undisputed king of Montana's big game is the **Rocky Mountain elk.** Massive antlers, large, strong bodies, exceptional wariness and the finest venison flavor to ever hit a plate have endeared elk to hunters throughout the West. Most of the elk hunting in Montana is west of Highway 191, but regional herds have become established in the Judith and Little Belt mountains near Lewistown and in the Missouri River Breaks near Fort Peck Reservoir.

Hunting success runs about 21 percent, high compared to most elk states, with an annual kill between 15,000 and 19,000. That success figure could be a little misleading, however, because it includes guided hunts, which have a much better success rate than most freelance hunters achieve. Success for the average hunter climbing out of a pickup truck to climb a steep mountainside in hopes of spotting an elk at the top, probably runs closer to 6 percent, according to some authorities. Up to 90,000 elk hunters comb the hills in the western third of the state from late October through November. That number is expected to exceed 100,000 by 1990.

Until the late 1960s, nearly all elk areas in Montana were open to elk of either sex. However, in the early 1970s general elk licenses were restricted to bulls only in most areas, with either-sex or antlerless hunts opened on a permit-only basis. Permits are awarded by public drawing.

Elk numbers are stable and possibly on the rise in some areas. About 80 percent of Montana's elk harvest takes place on public lands, principally national forest tracts, so hunter access is rarely restricted.

Elk are common to all mountain ranges in the western third of the state, with exceptionally popular hunting areas in the forks of the upper Flathead River drainage, and the Bob Marshall and Scapegoat wilderness areas. To the south, the best known elk areas include these mountain ranges: Bridger, Gallatin, Sapphire, Gravelly, Bitterroot, Absaroka, Big Belts and Pioneer. In the winter the state's southern elk population is bolstered by herds migrating to winter range in Montana from the protection of Yellowstone National Park. Special permit-only hunts are held to manage these herds.

Occasionally elk can be spotted grazing on mountainsides above highways or slipping out of thick timber to water in a trout stream, but they prefer rugged, remote country. The more inaccessible and less roaded an elk area is, the better the hunting will normally be.

Another very popular big game animal is the **pronghorn antelope,** a lightly built speedster common to the sage and prairie country. Hunters working the prairies of central and eastern Montana and a few of the arid high plains in the southwest bag about 30,000 pronghorns each year, a remarkable comeback for an animal that numbered less than 3,000 in 1924, virtually extinct when compared to the 2.5 million believed to have roamed Montana in the early 1800s. Modern antelope hunting in Montana didn't start until 1943 when just 750 permits were awarded. Despite recent summer drought conditions, Montana's "prairie goats" now appear to be stable, with slight decreases in specific areas.

Montana offers 39,000-plus antelope permits annually on a drawing basis. Sixty-five percent of the hunters who put in for an antelope tag are drawn, and hunter success runs over 70 percent most years. The bulk of the permits available are for either-sex pronghorns. The season runs about one month, beginning in mid-October.

The heaviest antelope concentrations are in the arid, eastern Montana prairie. Billings, Miles City, Lewistown, Glasgow, Broadus, Roundup and Harlowton are centers for antelope hunting.

Two of Montana's most popular big game animals are the pronghorn (left) and mule deer. The best pronghorn hunting is east of the Missouri River. By Gary Turbak. Mule deer are hunted statewide, sharing the prairie with pronghorns and the conifer-covered peaks with elk.
By Erwin & Peggy Bauer

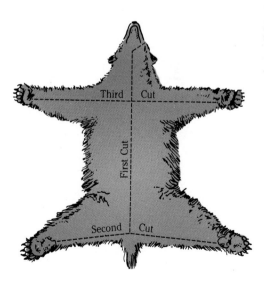

Three cuts for skinning an animal for entire hide.

The tan-and-white animals are also spotted occasionally in the broad river basins, traversing the southwestern corner of the state, the upper Madison River valley near Ennis, south of Dillon, in the Centennial Valley below Red Rock Lake. A few are in the Flathead Valley north of Missoula. The highest ranking of a Montana pronghorn in the Boone and Crockett record book is a five-way tie for 48th position. That animal was shot in 1982 in Big Horn County south of Billings.

The timbered mountain country west of Lewistown to the Idaho border is prime for **black bear** hunting during the spring and fall seasons. Hunters bag about 1,300 black bears a year. The most popular season is spring, beginning mid-April when the bears, fresh from winter hibernation, are spotted in mountain meadows feeding on fresh green grass. Baiting is illegal. Hunter success runs around 13 percent.

The top black bear hunting areas are in the Big and Little Belt mountains, in the upper Yellowstone River area, along the South and Middle forks of the Flathead Rivers, in the vicinity of Thompson Falls and in the Swan and Whitefish mountain ranges.

Montana is the last of the Lower 48 states to offer **grizzly bear** hunting licenses, but how many and for how long is always questionable and subject to emergency restrictions and closures. It is easily the most controversial hunt in the Northwest. Grizzlies prowl several rugged areas of the state. Most inhabit the mountains along the Continental Divide in the Flathead and Lolo national forests, the Bob Marshall and Scapegoat wilderness areas and the Mission Mountains rising on the eastern flank of the Flathead Valley. Grizzlies inhabit the mountains on the borders of Yellowstone and Glacier national parks. They also roam the Whitefish Mountain range north of Kalispell and the Cabinet Mountain Wilderness in the Kootenai National Forest near Libby.

Montana is also **cougar** country. The big cats range primarily in the same mountainous country favored by black bears, concentrating the population between Great Falls and the Idaho border. A few cats prowl the eastern prairie, and the deer-rich Missouri Breaks east of Great Falls support some cougars. Mountain lions have been reported in the Bighorn Mountains south of Billings, extending their range east along the Wyoming border. Only since 1971 have cougars been elevated from varmint to "game animal" status in Montana, and hunting pressure is generally light. Roughly 1,000 licenses are sold each year.

The sweeping horns of a **bighorn ram** are among the most coveted trophies in the world, and Montana has its share. Some would argue more than its share. It has been estimated that more than 3,500 bighorns range Montana. There are at least 11 major sheep herds, and in more than a dozen other areas, small herds are being established by transplant and relocation efforts. The last "unlimited" bighorn hunting in the contiguous 48 states takes place in the rugged peaks of southcentral Montana. The unlimited areas are bordered on the north by Interstate 90, on the south by Yellowstone National Park and the Wyoming-Idaho borders, on the west by the Madison River and on the east roughly along Highway 78. In 1985 the state set a quota of 21 bighorn rams from this area. An unlimited number of hunters are granted licenses to hunt, but as soon as the annual quota is reached the season closes. Hunting success in the unlimited areas runs less than 20 percent most years.

"The buck was fat and heavy — a four pointer around 135 pounds. I sat down on the ground and got the pack on my back, then twisted around on my knees to straighten up. I never yet met a hunter who loves this part of the hunt, and I still think the Alaska Indians had something good. When they killed a moose they moved the whole family to it, ate it, then moved on to the next one."

From The Spell of Old Baldy, *Sixten Johanson, 1950*

Another 720 licenses are granted for limited entry hunting units where licenses are awarded on a drawing basis. Hunter success is considerably higher in these units, often running from 60 to 90 percent. The odds of being drawn for a Montana sheep permit are 1 in 10, which is actually fairly good compared to most bighorn states, and better than the chances of being drawn for a Montana mountain goat or moose permit.

Promising areas to find bighorns include areas around the Sun River Game Range and Glacier National Park, West Rosebud Creek, Spanish Peaks, Stillwater River, Blue Mountains near Miles City, Gates of the Mountains Wilderness, Cabinet Mountains, Beartooth Mountains, Absaroka Mountains, Salish Mountains, Purcell Mountains, Bob Marshall Wilderness Area, and the Bridger Mountains. Also check the slopes near Nez Perce Pass in the Bitterroots, the Tobacco Root Mountains and the upper Rock Creek drainage in the Sapphire Mountains. Herds are also being reestablished in the Missouri River Breaks near Fort Peck Reservoir and on Wildhorse Island in Flathead Lake.

Despite its towering peaks and permanent snowfields, Montana does not have a large population of **mountain goats.** Annual harvest is around 200 and permits are awarded on a drawing

basis. In 1984, 351 goat licenses were issued and the odds of getting one were seven out of a 100. Mountain goats are high-country animals, ranging elevations from 5,000 to 11,000 feet. Hunters have a high success rate, often around 65 percent. The best hunting area is in the Bitter-root Mountains between Highway 12 and Highway 93. Goats also can be spotted above Highway 2 near Glacier National Park, inside the park, along the South and Middle forks of the Flathead Rivers, in Absaroka Mountains, and in the Cabinet Mountains near Libby. Goats have also been established in the Crazy Mountains, Big Snowys, Bridger Range, Sapphires, Pioneers, and Gates of the Mountains wilderness areas.

Both bighorn sheep and mountain goats are being enthusiastically transplanted to suitable range throughout the state and populations are increasing.

Montana is not a major **moose** hunting state, issuing between 600 and 700 hunting licenses a year, with an annual take of about 500 animals. The odds of being drawn are usually less than 5 percent. These are Shiras moose, the smallest subspecies of North American moose, and their range is largely confined to the northwestern and southwestern corners of the state. Moose are fairly common in the mountains of Beaverhead and Madison counties, ranging north to Missoula and the Little Belt Mountains. In the northwest, the Kalispell, Libby, Whitefish, and Swan Lake country is excellent for moose. Contrary to popular opinion, moose aren't confined to marshy, lowland river bottoms but are equally as comfortable in high mountain basins, sharing the range with elk and grizzly bear.

Wolves are protected in the Treasure State, and no one is sure how many still survive. Reports have established wolf populations in the mountains surrounding Yellowstone National Park and along the Continental Divide especially in the Flathead and Lolo national forests and the areas surrounding Glacier National Park. Even more rare than wolves in Montana are **caribou.** Hunting for caribou is not allowed, and the only reports of caribou in the state come from the Kanisku National Forest on the Idaho border, where a small herd of Selkirk Mountain caribou roam between British Columbia, Washington, Idaho and perhaps, Montana.

Montana is an outstanding state for upland game bird hunting. **Ringneck pheasants** occupy just about every acre of agricultural ground from Missoula to Glendive. In the western part of the state, pheasants are confined to valleys — the Flathead, Bitterroot, Beaverhead, Madison, Missouri. Excellent pheasant shooting can be found in the irrigated wheat lands north and west of Great Falls, along the length of the Missouri River and throughout the Yellowstone and Musselshell river valleys. Lewistown is a favorite destination for pheasant hunters, as well as

First frost in the high country will often trigger the rut, pitting bull elk against each other in a ritualistic contest for herd domination. By Erwin & Peggy Bauer

203

Mule deer strapped to the saddle, a pair of high-country hunters pack out of the Sun River country west of Great Falls. By Mike Logan

the river bottoms along the Marias and Milk rivers. The eastern areas that support pheasants also supply good **sharp-tail** and **sage grouse** shooting. Great Falls, Lewistown, Billings, Miles City are centers for eastern Montana sharp-tail hunters. The arid sage country of southwestern Montana also is hunted for sharp-tails, and most the valley area in the southwest counties offer sage grouse.

Blue, ruffed and Franklin grouse erupt in front of hunters in the timbered mountains of western Montana. Hunters find good shooting and lots of birds during most years.

Waterfowl hunting is excellent in the fall before freezeup. The Bitterroot and Flathead valleys offer outstanding waterfowling on the western side of the state. The Missouri River between Townsend and Great Falls also is good, and the Yellowstone, Musselshell and Bighorn rivers contribute a lot of ducks and geese to hunter's bags each year. Grainfields in the north, above the Missouri River and along the Fort Peck Reservoir, are outstanding waterfowl areas. Several major waterfowl refuges concentrate large flocks of geese which feed in surrounding fields. The Freezout Lake, Pablo-Ninepipe and Benton Lake areas are especially productive.

Turkey hunting is growing in popularity in Montana, keeping pace with an ambitious transplant program that is establishing flocks of these big birds wherever suitable habitat can be found. There are spring and fall hunting seasons in specific areas, but the number of open areas is on the rise. Now, nearly 1,000 turkeys are bagged by Montana hunters yearly, yet until 1954, when 13 Merriam's turkeys were planted in the Judith Mountain range, there were no turkeys in the state. Flocks of turkeys are now found in the woods along the Bitterroot and Clark Fork rivers near Missoula, in pockets of northwestern Montana, in the hills surrounding Helena, south of Great Falls along the Missouri River, north of Lewistown along the Judith River, near Roundup on the Musselshell River, along the Bighorn, in the area surrounding Miles City, on the banks of Fort Peck Reservoir and along the Missouri River breaks, and in the Medicine Rocks-Ekalaka region east of Miles City. Because of the state's growing turkey populations, it would not be surprising to find Montana listed among the best turkey states in the country within the next few years.

Quail, chukar, Hungarian partridge, doves, snipe — Montana has plenty of these birds, and hunting areas are not difficult to find. The best bet is to contact a regional FWP office, where information officers can recommend the best direction for your hunt.

Where the Game Animals Are

The Northwest is the most diversified hunting region in the country, encompassing a staggering variety of terrain, climate and wildlife. The hunting country includes coastal rain forests, foothill thickets, alpine mountaintops, desert and irrigated agricultural areas. Climates range from the moderate conditions on the Pacific Coast to the extreme high and low temperatures of the desert and mountains.

Hunters in the Northwest can select from more species of game animals than any other region of North America, an area that compares respectively with the best wildlife areas in the world. Multiple species of five of North America's most prominent big game animals can be hunted, including three subspecies of bear, two caribou, four deer, two elk, and five separate species of mountain sheep. Upland bird hunters follow the dogs to five species of grouse, four types of quail, three ptarmigans, and two species of partridges.

The accompanying tables list the major game birds and animals in each Northwest state and province, and where they are hunted.

Guide to Northwest Game Animals

* = No hunting season

	WA	OR	ID	MT	BC	AB	AK
Bear, black	■	■	■	■	■	■	■
Bear, brown							■
Bear, grizzly	*		*	■	■	■	■
Bison				■	*	*	■
Caribou, barren ground					■	*	■
Caribou, woodland	*		*		■	*	■
Cougar	■	■	■	■	■		
Coyote	■	■	■	■	■		■
Deer, black-tailed	■	■			■		
Deer, mule	■	■	■	■	■	■	
Deer, Sitka black-tailed							■
Deer, white-tailed	■	■	■	■	■	■	
Elk, Rocky Mountain	■	■	■	■	■	■	
Elk, Roosevelt	■	■			■		■
Goat, mountain	■	*	■	■	■	■	■
Moose	■		■	■	■	■	■
Musk-ox							■
Pronghorn	*	■	■	■		■	
Sheep, California bighorn	■	■	■	■	■		
Sheep, Dall					■		■
Sheep, Fannin					■		■
Sheep, Rocky Mountain bighorn	■	■	■	■	■	■	
Sheep, Stone					■		
Wolf	*		*	*	■	■	■
Wolverine	*		*	*	■	■	■

Guide to Northwest Game Birds

	WA	OR	ID	MT	BC	AB	AK
Chukar Partridge	■	■	■	■	■		
Doves, Mourning	■	■	■	■	■	*	*
Grouse, Blue	■	■	■	■	■	■	■
Grouse, Ruffed	■	■	■	■	■	■	■
Grouse, Sage	■	■	■	■	■		
Grouse, Sharp-tailed	■	■	■	■	■	■	■
Grouse, Spruce	■	■	■	■	■	■	■
Partridge, Hungarian	■	■	■	■	■	■	
Pheasant, Ringneck	■	■	■	■	■	■	
Pigeon, Band-tailed	■	■	■		■		*
Ptarmigan, Rock					■	■	■
Ptarmigan, White-tailed	*		*	*	■	■	■
Ptarmigan, Willow					■	■	■
Quail, Bobwhite	■	■	■				
Quail, Gambel's	■	■	■				
Quail, Scaled	■	■	■				
Quail, Valley	■	■	■				■
Snipe	■	■	■	■	■		■
Turkey	■	■	■	■			

Hunting British Columbia

Some of the finest wilderness wildlife areas in North America are found in British Columbia's glacial-scoured mountain ranges, miles of rolling black-timber forests and cedar-shadowed saltwater shorelines. The westernmost Canadian province is a land of sharp contrast and rich diversity, varying from the arid Okanagan highlands, to an ocean coastline drenched by seasonal Pacific storms, and lush river bottoms rising to sparse alpine crags.

Wildlife is as diverse as the topography and hunters rank the province with the finest big game hunting grounds in North America, attracting hunters from around the world. Four species of mountain sheep, mountain goats, grizzly and black bears, caribou, moose, cougars, wolves, elk, deer and wolverines inhabit the province, complementing some fairly respectable water-fowl shooting and nearly unhunted multitudes of forest grouse including blues, ruffed, spruce and Franklin. In some areas of the southeast there are huntable populations of pheasants, chukar, quail, Hungarian partridge and prairie chickens.

Upland bird hunting, however, doesn't compare with that offered in neighboring states, and is generally the localized sport of resident wing shooters. On the coast in September, band-tailed pigeons — a wild, migratory cousin of those popcorn-munching city park dwellers — can provide a tough challenge for shotgunners. The popularity of all bird hunting, however, places distantly behind the challenge of big game in the rugged terrain of British Columbia.

Only a small area of British Columbia's vast inland and coastal region is developed. The province is larger than the combined states of California, Oregon and Washington, yet the population is just 2.7 million, one-third of which live in the greater Vancouver area, and most of the rest centered around small communities in the 200 miles between Kamloops and the United States border. Only two major highways run north from the Kamloops region, the Alaska Highway (Highway 97) and Yellowhead Highway 5. Only the Alaska Highway continues north of Prince George completely through the province. The result is that nearly all of the province north of Kamloops is sparsely populated, heavily forested and nearly roadless. Ideal habitat for man-shy big game — grizzlies, caribou, mountain sheep.

Like all the Northwest, British Columbia has a good population of deer, concentrated primarily in the southern third of the province and rarely found north of Prince George. Provincial limits allow hunters two deer a year, but don't expect trophy animals because British Columbia deer generally sport smaller antlers than deer in other areas of North America. The province has placed only one deer in the top 25 of the Boone and Crockett Club records for black-tailed, white-tailed and mule deer. The single British Columbia record book entry is a mule deer (typical), shot in 1979 near Princeton and it ranks 14th.

What species of deer you spot depends on what area of the province you are traveling through. **Blacktails,** a lightweight cousin of the mule deer, thrive in the dense protection of the coastal region. They are found on the west slopes of the Coast Mountains from the United States border north to Stewart, and are easily recognized by their smallish physical features, stocky muzzle and wide black tail tipped with white. Their easternmost range is up the Fraser River valley as far as Hope. A few blacktails will be found along the Thompson River as far north as Cache Creek. Nearly all the islands off the British Columbia coast support heavy concentrations of blacktail, including Vancouver and the Queen Charlottes.

On the eastern slope of the Coast Mountains **mule deer** are the dominant species, inhabiting the timbered hills and mountain high country in the southcentral reach of the province. Mule deer are densest from Penticton north to Quesnel and from Merritt east to the Rocky Mountains. Small pockets of mule deer are scattered north of Quesnel. The mule deer's southern range, roughly from Kelowna south, and Osoyoos east, is shared with **whitetails** spreading into the province from a growing population in neighboring Washington and Idaho. Whitetails run the border country from Highway 97 east with the heaviest concentrations in the Okanagan region and in the Purcell Mountains along the upper Columbia River to the edge of Yoho National Park. A few whitetails are also found sharing the range with mule deer in the Chetwynd/Dawson Creek area which is about northern limit of their distribution in British Columbia.

Whitetails are easy to identify, with their light-colored streamlined bodies and distinctive white flag of a tail, which can be up to 15 inches long and 5 inches wide. When spooked, whitetails flash the broad white flag to alert other deer and distract predators. The best place to find a

Left, pintail on ice of the Fraser River estuary. By Thomas W. Kitchin. Curved claws of a black bear (above), a common track in British Columbia. By Gary Turbak

The finest mountain goat trophies are taken late in the season, when the thick creamy-white coat is the thickest, and beards the longest. By Erwin & Peggy Bauer

whitetail is in thickly timbered foothills or extremely brushy creek bottoms. In the summer they often appear almost reddish colored and are occasionally spotted feeding with range cattle near woodlines.

While British Columbia may not be the place for trophy deer, it owns the record book on **Canada moose.** Of the top 20 trophies in the Boone and Crockett records 15 are held by British Columbia moose, including the top three positions. Moose are the premier big game animal in British Columbia, attracting most of the nonresident hunters, and the heaviest resident pressure.

Regional herds are scattered throughout the timbered foothills and low mountains of the southern province, especially in the lake region surrounding Vernon and Kamloops. A pretty fair concentration of moose is found just north of the Montana border along the west slope of the Rocky Mountains, and in pockets of the Purcell Mountains. The biggest concentration, however, is in the north, above Williams Lake. The Skeena and Omineca mountains are excellent moose range. Travelers can expect to see moose in every significant river drainage north of Kamloops, and east of the Coast Mountains. Few moose are found on the western side of the Coast Mountains, including Vancouver and Queen Charlotte islands, according to the provincial wildlife managers. Trophy moose are taken in the areas of Grayling, Teslin, Prophet, Klappan, Frog, Graham, Fox, Toad and Iskut rivers. The Dease, Stewart, Scoop and Cold Fish lakes regions are also known for trophy-size animals.

Elk hunting is not as popular in British Columbia as in other Northwest regions, but it is a growing sport, especially in the southeast corner of the province in the Kootenay and Banff regions on the skirts of the Rockies. These are Rocky Mountain variety elk and additional herds can also be found north along the Alberta border in the Monkman Park and Tumbler Ridge region and north and west of Fort St. John.

Roosevelt elk are found on Vancouver and Queen Charlotte islands. The biggest concentration of Roosevelts is found on the north end of Vancouver Island south of Port McNeill. The area near Kelsey Bay had produced two record book Roosevelt elk, including the No. 3 and No. 8 Boone and Crockett heads. A smaller herd is sometimes seen near Port Alberni. The Queen Charlotte Island herd is concentrated on the east side of the main island in the Tlell River region north of Skidgate.

Except for a few regionally isolated herds, most of the **mountain caribou** in British Columbia are along the Rocky Mountains in the northern reaches of the province from Mount Robson Park on the Alberta border northwest along Williston Lake to the heart of the caribou range in the remote Cassiar and Omineca mountain ranges. Caribou are plentiful in the mountain country north of Yellowhead Highway 16. Smaller concentrations can be found in Tweedsmuir National Park and a famous few wander the high country of the Selkirk Mountains on the Washington-British Columbia-Idaho border. This herd of about two dozen is the most southerly herd of caribou in North America, and are protected. No British Columbia mountain caribou have made the Boone and Crockett trophy book minimum score.

Four species of **mountain sheep** are in British Columbia, including the southernmost range of the thinhorns; Dall, Stone and Fannin. Stocky, Roman-nosed Rocky Mountain **bighorns** are the most plentiful, however. Scattered populations of bighorns are found throughout the central region of the province, and there is a good opportunity to glimpse these high mountain recluses in the national parks along the Rocky Mountains. Yoho and Kootenay and Mount Robson national parks are prominent sheep viewing areas. Bighorns are also spotted above Highway 97 between Cache Creek and Kamloops, and just north of the Washington border in the Cathredal Park region. Many British Columbia bighorns are ranked in the Boone and Crockett record book including the No. 6 and 8 horns taken in Elbow and Simpson rivers country respectively. Trophy bighorns have also been bagged near Vaseux Lake, Mary Ann Creek and Lake Louise.

The No. 1 trophy sheep in British Columbia is the rare **Stone sheep.** Most of their range is in the remote northern section of the province with the Prophet and Muskwa rivers standing out. Other trophy areas include Townsley and Mile creeks, Dease and Tuchodi lakes, Racing and Gataga rivers. Stone sheep are rarely seen from a road or by casual observers.

The high peaks of the glaciated Coastal Mountains and the crags of the Rockies along the Alberta border support good numbers of creamy-white **mountain goats.** They are often seen from paved roads along the Rockies in Yoho, Mount Robson, Mount Assinboine, Hamber and Monkman parks. Most of the goats are found in the Coast range from Whistler just north of Vancouver north into Alaska and the Yukon. The rugged Stikine and Cassiar, Ominec and Skeena mountains are excellent goat regions. It is not unusual for the Skeena region to have more permits

British Columbia Hunting Requirements

Hunting in British Columbia is managed by the British Columbia Ministry of Environment, Wildlife Branch, Parliament Bldg., Victoria, BC, Canada V8V 1X4. Phone (604) 387-4573. Hunting regulations and restrictions are mailed upon request. Resident hunting licenses are available at all regional offices and many sporting goods stores, and there is a minimum age of 10. Nonresident hunting licenses are only available from regional and subregional Ministry of Environment offices, and the Wildlife Branch office in Victoria. Nonresident licenses are available by mail.

Non-Canadian residents hunting big game must be accompanied by a licensed British Columbia guide. Residents of Canada outside of British Columbia may hunt big game with a British Columbia resident instead of a licensed guide, if the resident has obtained a provincial permit. Guides are not required for nonresidents hunting small game, including waterfowl and upland birds. Handguns are not permitted in Canada. A $10 license is required to carry a firearm, plus there is a $3 surcharge earmarked for Habitat Conservation Fund on hunting, angling, trapping and guiding.

Hunting seasons are established by species and region. Big game seasons in the northern part of the province open in mid-August and most end by the last of October. In the southern portion of the province, big game seasons generally run from mid-September to mid-December. There are spring and summer hunts for grizzly and black bear, and many areas of the province black bear hunting seasons are being liberalized. In most cases big game bag limits are set at one animal, except for bear and in certain areas deer. On Vancouver Island hunters are allowed three blacktails, including one antlerless. While not specifically prohibited, hunters are discouraged from shooting moose, caribou, mountain goat, mountain sheep, blacks and grizzly bear deer, elk and wolves that have been collared and equipped with radio transmitters.

In mid-July there is a drawing for limited entry permits in special areas to hunt grizzly, caribou, deer, elk, mountain goat, mountain sheep and moose. Usually there are 19,500-plus permits with 70,700 applicants. The most popular special permits are for elk, with 8,228 available, and moose offering 6,253. More than 23,000 hunters apply in each of those two categories.

Nonresidents intending to hunt big game in British Columbia should make initial inquiries at least a year in advance through the guides association or the Victoria offices of the wildlife branch.

Hunting License Fees

	Resident	Nonresident Canadian	Nonresident Alien
Firearm	$10	$ 10	$ 10
General	$19	$ 19	$118
Migratory Bird	$10	$ 10	$ 10
Habitat Fund	$ 3	$ 3	$ 3
Black Bear	$ 8	$ 50	$ 50
Grizzly	$70	$320	$320
Caribou	$20	$120	$120
Cougar	$20	$120	$120
Deer	$ 8	$ 60	$ 60
Elk	$20	$120	$120
Moose	$20	$120	$120
Mountain Goat	$30	$130	$130
Mountain Sheep	$50	$300	$300
Wolf	None	$ 25	$ 25

Black bears often rip apart decaying logs, searching for ants and grubs to eat. This black is in prime condition.
By Erwin & Peggy Bauer

authorized than hunters interested. Manning Park on the Washington border also supports a fair population.

Hunters have put numerous British Columbia mountain goats in the record book, including the No. 3 and 4 goats which were taken at Mount Horetzky and in the Cassiars respectively. Other trophy areas include Kaza Lake, Mount Carthew, Telegraph Creek, Duti and Swan lakes, Tahtsa, Johnston lakes and Bingay Creek.

Black bears are found throughout the province and many areas support **grizzlies.** The southernmost reach of the grizzly is in the far southeast corner just above Glacier National Park. Grizzlies range primarily in the mountains on both east and west borders of the province and in the far northern reaches. Expect to be in grizzly country in the Purcell, Cariboos, Columbia and Hart mountain ranges on the east side of the province. Much of the Coast Mountain range is grizzly country and occasionally they are reported as far south as Merritt.

British Columbia has one of the densest **cougar** populations of any region in the Northwest. Vancouver Island supports an exceptional number of the big cats. These so-called mountain lions are also plentiful in the maze of inlets along the eastern shelf of Queen Charlotte Strait opposite Port Hardy. Just north of Vancouver good numbers of cougars are found in the Garibaldi Park region and just east in Manning Park and the upper Skagit River area. The Okanagan Highlands also have high numbers of cougars. Most of British Columbia's cougar population is in the southern section of the province and few of the cats are ever seen north of Quesnel.

Wolves are also plentiful in the province, with their mournful howling echoing across Vancouver Island and among the peaks on the western slope of the Coast Mountains. Most of the wolves in British Columbia are confined to the northern regions above Williams Lake.

The tendency on a steep downhill shot is to shoot high. Compensate by holding low on the target. The steeper the hill, the lower the sight hold.

Care Of Big Game

The proper care of game meat begins when you raise your rifle and ends with the final storage of the butchered meat. Between these two are a series of steps that will determine whether the result is a delightful addition to your table or an unpalatable collection of spoiled meat.

Preparation is essential. The hunter must know what steps and precautions are necessary for successful care of game meat, and carry with him enough equipment to be able to properly prepare the carcass.

A well-placed shot will save a great deal of trouble and wasted meat. Get as close as possible to your target: a shot just behind the front shoulder should penetrate the heart or lung and result in a quick kill with little damaged meat.

Equipment

- A 5- to 6-inch hunting knife and whetstone.
- A sharp belt ax or folding saw.
- About 20 feet of strong cord or rope.
- Some string or twine.
- Some blaze-orange cloth to be placed on animal when carrying it out of the bush.
- Muslin sacks or cheesecloth to wrap quartered meat.
- Plastic bag for heart and liver.

Prop carcass belly-up (rocks or brush may be used for support). At this point, musk glands may be removed or left until entire carcass is skinned. (If removing glands, make sure the knife is well cleaned before using it again.)

Split hide from tail to throat. Insert knife point under skin but do not cut into body cavity or puncture stomach. Hide may be peeled back several inches on each side to keep hair out of meat.

Cut through pelvic bone. Turning carcass downhill will cause viscera to sag into rib cavity. This will reduce the chance of puncturing viscera while chopping through bone. Large intestine can then be cut free from pelvic cavity but not severed from viscera.

Slide two fingers ahead of blade to keep knife from penetrating intestines.

Sever windpipe and esophagus as close to the head as possible. Tie string tightly around the esophagus and anus to prevent contents from escaping onto meat.

Heart and liver may be removed at this time.

Turn carcass head uphill. Free windpipe and esophagus and pull viscera toward rear, cutting

any parts that hold. An alternate method is to leave head downhill and strip viscera from rear, out over the head.

The hide can be left on to keep the meat clean while carrying the carcass out. However, remove the hide as soon as possible to promote cooling, if night temperatures above freezing are anticipated.

Wipe the body cavity clean with a damp (not wet) cloth. Do not wash the meat after a glaze has formed on the surface, since this glaze inhibits growth of bacteria and molds. Remove legs at knees. Carcass should now be hung, and if meat sacks are available, skinned and sacked.

After skinning, black pepper can be sprinkled on the exposed meat to keep flies away. Open chest cavity and spread the ribs to ventilate and speed up cooling. A cooling time of six hours before transportation is recommended by many hunters.

Open carcass by cutting through length of breastbone and neck into exposed windpipe. If head is to be mounted, stop cut between the front legs at the base of the breastbone. If using a knife, it may be easier to cut on either side of the breastbone rather than through it.

Do not remove evidence of sex: proof of sex must remain attached to the carcass.

(Courtesy of British Columbia, Ministry of Environment)

Recommended position for hanging carcass. Prop body cavity open to allow air circulation.

Basic Meat Cuts

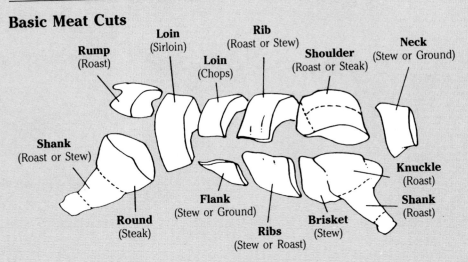

Rump (Roast)

Loin (Sirloin)

Loin (Chops)

Rib (Roast or Stew)

Shoulder (Roast or Steak)

Neck (Stew or Ground)

Shank (Roast or Stew)

Flank (Stew or Ground)

Knuckle (Roast)

Shank (Roast)

Round (Steak)

Ribs (Stew or Roast)

Brisket (Stew)

Hunting Alberta

Alberta is a hunter's mecca, a topographical mix of prairie and mountain terrain that supports every species of big game animal found in North America, along with quality waterfowl and upland bird shooting.

The province's sparse population of 2,344,700 is concentrated in the southcentral part of the province, squeezed into the wheat lands between the Montana border and Edmonton. Surrounding these grain and cattle ranches, crossroad communities and satellite subdivisions of Lethbridge, Calgary, Red Deer and Edmonton are rugged peaks jutting from the backbone of the Rocky Mountains, roadless wilderness areas, and in the north, vast tracts of lake country isolated except for the occasional floatplane.

The fields, fence rows, riverbanks and brushy draws of southcentral Alberta offer **ringneck pheasants, sharp-tailed grouse, Hungarian partridge** and **sage grouse,** and provide spring nesting sites and fall shooting areas for thousands of ducks and geese. This is fine goose shooting country, with early flocks of **snow, Canada, white-front** and **Ross geese** dropping into decoy spreads. The mountains harbor **ruffed, spruce** and **blue grouse** and north of Fort McMurray in the far northeastern corner of the province there are **willow ptarmigan.**

White-tailed ptarmigan walk the ridges of the Pelican Mountains, Swan Hills, and in Willmore, Jasper, Banff and Waterton, the national parks complex along the western border with British Columbia. (No hunting is permitted in the national parks.)

The plains, prairie and eroded river breaks south of Edmonton support some of the largest **white-tailed deer** in North America. Big-bodied, heavy-antlered deer that have gone largely unnoticed by the general hunting public until the last few years. The whitetails have extended their range northwest of Edmonton to the Peace River country through the Swan Hills.

The accessibility, physical size and abundance of whitetails is attracting more local and nonresident hunters each fall. Several Boone and Crockett Club ranked whitetails have come from the southeastern plains of Alberta. The areas around the towns of Castor, Drumheller, Brooks and Medicine Hat are very popular with whitetail hunters.

The only other big game animals common to the plains and prairie land are **pronghorn,** commonly called antelope. These brown-and-white speedsters are fairly rare in Alberta, and confined almost exclusively to the southeast corner of the province near Medicine Hat and Milk River. There have been some efforts to expand their range by capture and transplant programs.

The bulk of Alberta's big game animals are hunted in the mountainous regions along the western border and in the nearly roadless northern half of the province above Whitecourt, Athabasca and Medley. The southcentral and southeastern region south of Highway 28 and east of Highway 2 is ranch and prairie country given to upland birds, waterfowl and white-tailed deer.

Mule deer inhabit the western and northcentral part of the province and are most plentiful along the shoulders of the Rocky Mountains, especially the areas protected by Jasper and Banff national parks. In most of the foothills, mule and white-tailed deer ranges overlap, yielding exclusively to mule deer the higher you climb into the mountains.

The same mountainous areas that support mule deer are also home to **grizzly** and **black bear.** An Alberta grizzly shot in 1981 in the Muskeg River country near Willmore Wilderness Park is the sixth largest in the Boone and Crockett Club record book. Grizzly bears range north from the United States border following the Rockies through Waterton, Banff and Jasper national parks. Their range extends east of Peace River into the Buffalo Head Hills. Black bears can be found in all the timbered and hilly country, west and north of Edmonton.

Hunting has not been permitted for mountain and woodland **caribou** in Alberta since 1980, but there are still substantial herds in the northern reaches. There is another concentration in the lake country from Highway 67 east through Fort McMurray to the Saskatchewan border with smaller concentrations between the Buffalo Head Hills and Birch Mountains. Spotting caribou from a highway in southern Alberta is highly unlikely.

Canada moose are plentiful in the mountainous and wilderness areas of Alberta. The No. 1 Boone and Crockett record was killed in 1980 in the Sulphur Creek drainage. The Alberta moose range skirts the agricultural southeast corner of the province and is concentrated along the Rockies and northern mountain ranges. The prime moose range, according to provincial wildlife managers, is in the Far North, above Lesser Slave Lake. The Peace and Athabasca rivers snake through

The agricultural and prairie country of southeast Alberta supports the northernmost herd of pronghorns. By Terry Rudnick. Mountain goats (left) are found in the mountains on the western rim of the province. By Terry W. Sheely

213

Bighorns grazing above the Athabasca River. By Thomas W. Kitchin

excellent moose country. Travelers on Highway 93 through Jasper and Banff and Highways 43 and 2 near Grande Prairie are likely to spot moose browsing in brushy valleys and along creek bottoms.

Rocky Mountain **elk** will be seen in the western boundary national park system with much of the provincial hunting concentrated southwest of Edmonton in the hill country of the Brazeau River drainage. Highways 16, 40 and 47 cut through the heart of the central provincial elk range. The best elk range is southwest of Calgary between Waterton and Banff national parks. There are very few elk north of Grande Prairie. The only herd on the eastern side of the province will be found south of Medicine Hat in Cypress Hills Provincial Park. Alberta elk are famous for large, heavy racks, but strangely very few are entered in the Boone and Crockett record book. The highest-ranked Boone and Crockett Alberta elk places 11th and was bagged in the Red Deer River area north of Calgary.

Rocky Mountain bighorn sheep and the dagger-horned white **mountain goats** are hunted in the Rockies. Unless you are into strenuous backpacking, the best opportunity to see and photograph these elusive animals is in Banff, Jasper and Waterton national parks. The largest population will be found on the steep mountain border between Alberta and British Columbia south of Grande Cache on Highway 40. Only two zones are open to nonresident hunters.

Cougars are relatively rare in Alberta but are present in the Rockies south of Grande Cache. The haunting howl of **wolves,** however, is common to nearly all the timbered areas west and north of the agricultural plains south of Edmonton and east of Highway 2. The greatest concentrations occur in the sparsely inhabited northern reaches of the province in the Peace, Wabasca and Athabasca river drainages, and in Wood Buffalo National Park. Their range extends southward along the Continental Divide into Waterton-Glacier National Park on the Montana border. **Coyotes** can be found nearly everywhere in the southern half of the province, including backyards and city suburbs.

Alberta Hunting Requirements

Names and addresses of professional guides providing fishing, big game hunting, white-water float trips, horse packing and outfitting are available by requesting the free publication, *Alberta Adventure Guide*, distributed by Travel Alberta, 14th Floor, 10065 Jasper Ave., Edmonton, AB, Canada T5J 0H4. Nonresident big game hunters are required to be accompanied by an authorized guide.

Fish and Wildlife Headquarters, 9945 108th St., Edmonton, AB, Canada T5K 2C9. Phone (403) 427-6729. Hunting and fishing regulation pamphlets, including license fee schedules and seasonal restrictions available upon request from the department's information office.

Regional offices: The province is divided into five hunting and fishing management regions — Northeast, Southern, Central, Peace River and Eastern Slope — and subdivided into 62 local offices. Locations and phone numbers of the 62 local offices are printed in the hunting and fishing regulation packets for specific local reference.

Hunting in Alberta is managed by the Alberta Energy and Natural Resources, Fish and Wildlife Division, P.O. Box 2223, Edmonton, AB, Canada T5J 2P4. Phone (403) 427-3590. Hunting regulations and requirements are available upon request.

All hunters in this province are required to possess a Wildlife Certificate and Resource Development Stamp, $11,

to be eligible to purchase a hunting license or big game tag. The minimum age to hunt is 14, and hunters under 16 must be accompanied by parent, guardian or authorized person 18 or older.

Non-Canadians are required to hunt with a licensed guide or resident in big game zones. Canadians who are not residents of Alberta are required to be accompanied in the field by a resident in most big game areas. Big game includes wolves, black and grizzly bear, cougar, mule and white-tailed deer, elk, moose, sheep, mountain goats, antelope. Guides are not required for small game,

including waterfowl and upland birds.

General hunting seasons are held between September and December. There is a spring grizzly bear hunt for permit holders. Sunday hunting is not allowed for migratory game birds, and limited to specifically designated regions for big game and upland birds.

Drawings for special big game licenses are held in June and applications for nonresident trophy sheep permits must be made through a qualified outfitter by March 31. Nonresident license orders through the mail require a money order or certified check.

Hunting License Fees

	Resident	Nonresident Canadian	Nonresident Alien
Bow	$ 5	$ 10	$ 15
Black Bear	$10	$ 50	$100
Grizzly	$20	$125	$250
Cougar	$20	$100	$200
Mule Deer	$10	$ 75	$150
Whitetail	$10	$ 75	$150
Elk (general)	$10	$100	$200
Moose (general)	$10	$100	$200
Moose (bull)			
Zone 1, antlered	NA	NA	$100
Sheep (trophy)	$20	$250*	$250*
Pronghorn (trophy)	$20	$125	$125
Pronghorn	$10	NA	NA
Wolf	NA	$ 15	$ 25
Game Bird	$ 5	$ 20	$ 40
Pheasant	$10	$ 10	$ 10
Migratory Bird	$ 7.50	$ 10	$ 10
Wildlife Stamp	$11	$ 11	$ 11

*By special draw only

Hunting Alaska

An Alaskan big game hunt is the ultimate reward and challenge for most North American hunters. The wildlife, terrain and hunting opporties within this massive state compete, perhaps unfairly, with the world's finest hunting regions. Big game herds, with regional exceptions, are in good to excellent condition, hunting success is high, and bag limits often more generous than in most North American hunting regions.

While international attention focuses on Alaska's big and potentially dangerous game animals, the state's outstanding duck, goose and small game opportunities thrive in the shadows, enjoyed almost exclusively by local hunters. In a more populous area, Alaska's waterfowl hunting would be the celebrated pride of the state. In Alaska it is an also-ran, finishing far behind the popularity of big game animals: grizzly, the world's largest land carnivore; moose, the largest deer on earth; Dall sheep, the only all-white kind of its species; the United State's only huntable herd of barren ground caribou . . . the list continues and every entry is overwhelming competition for a l-pound ptarmigan, 12-ounce teal, or splay-footed snowshoe hare.

Alaska, despite its great resources, is not escaping the complications, controversy and pressures currently detracting from the traditional aesthetics of hunting everywhere. Game laws have become more complicated,and regimented if not more restrictive in the face of court decisions directed at political-social issues, often at the expense of natural resources, plus subsistence hunting, land development and increased hunting pressure. Still, the 49th state, an area larger than many countries with tremendous topographical diversity, continues to dominate North American hunting opportunities.

The first step for hunters anticipating an Alaskan season is to acquire a copy of the *Alaska Game Regulations* and the two companion supplements, *Registration Permit Hunts* and *Permit Drawing Hunts*. The permit supplements include more than 100 special hunts for grizzly, bison, Dall sheep, musk-ox, black-tailed deer, caribou, mountain goat, moose and elk.

The regulations booklets are generally available about July 1. Applications to enter the drawings for special fall hunts must be made during May, while applications for spring big game hunts are received from August to Dec. 31. An application fee of $5 to $10 depending upon species, is required.

Licensed guides are required for nonresident hunters after grizzly bear and/or Dall sheep. Resident hunters are not required to hire a guide, and need supplemental license tags only for grizzly bear, and musk-ox licenses.

Hunting seasons are managed primarily on a regional basis and often close prematurely when the prescribed harvest quota is reached. Hunters are generally advised to contact the regional game department office for conditions, closures and supplemental regional regulations.

Selecting a hunting area in the vast, and often trackless mountains and tundra of Alaska is often the most difficult part of the hunt, and guided or outfitted hunts are more common than in other Northwest regions. While statewide big game numbers are high, they can be scarce in specific areas, and abundant in the next drainage. Local know-how and experience is more valuable than luck in turning hunting success. There is not a moose behind every bush, a grizzly on every salmon stream, or a caribou where it should be.

Alaska moose, the largest of the three species of Northwest moose and the earth's largest deer, are the most popular big game animal in most areas of the state. Residents favor the moose because it is relatively common and a tremendous source of meat. These enormous animals are popular with nonresident hunters for the same reasons, plus a guide is not required.

Several areas are considered tops for moose, including Area 20A south of Fairbanks, in the flats of the Tanana River and the foothills of the Alaska Range. Moose are also found in scattered herds along the Chena River, Delta Junction and Minto areas. A wolf control program, according to ADFG spokesmen, in this region is seeing an increase in moose numbers. Other prime interior moose areas include the mountains of Area 19 where nearly 1,000 moose are taken each season.

In the southcentral region, the best moose area is in Nelchina Basin, although access is restricted to fly-in or ATV. The Kenai Peninsula, famed for other big game animals, is not considered good moose country, although a few are bagged each season. Surprisingly, the flat tundra country

The end of a wet day in the Bradley Lake area of the Kenai Mountains. By Chlaus Lotscher

215

Bull moose in the Alaska Range.
By George Wuerthner

of northwestern Alaska is supporting a steadily increasing number of moose. The state also reports fine moose hunting on the Seward Peninsula, along the western Arctic Slope, Some of the heaviest concentrations of moose will be found along the Noatak, Kelly and Kugururok rivers. Good northern moose hunting is also found along the remote Chandler and Colville rivers. Except for a few specific areas, moose hunting is only fair at best in the marine reaches of the southeast. The exception is the area around Yakutat.

In September, hunters begin searching for **barren ground caribou** in interior Alaska. Herds are prime in both the controlled and general hunting regions. Some of the best locations for interior caribou hunts include Yanert, and Area 20E north of Fairbanks. The central Arctic herd is reported expanding and is a popular target for fly-in drop hunts. The western Arctic caribou herd, in northwestern Alaska numbers more than 200,000 caribou. Hunters also work the north side of the Alaska Peninsula from King Salmon. Resident-only hunts are held in Area 13. In August, hunters stalk the Colville River drainages, up through the central portion of the Noatak River.

One of the most feared, respected and coveted trophies in the world, **grizzly bears** appear to be in good supply throughout their hunting range, including the southcentral and southeastern areas where the largest variety, those known as brown bear, are hunted. Biologists describe brown bear numbers as "abundant" throughout their range, and expect hunter success to remain high. Some of the finest brown bear trophies are taken on the west side of Cook Inlet, on Kodiak Island and the Alaska Peninsula. There are plenty of browns, some believe too many, on the islands of southeastern Alaska, especially the ABC islands, Admiralty, Baranof and Chichagof.

Away from the coast, the big bears are known as grizzlies, and their numbers appear to have stabilized at a high plane. Some of the finest grizzly hunting anywhere is found in Area 20A, throughout the Brooks Range, and in Areas 12, 20, 20E and 23K. In the northwestern areas of the state, the prime grizzly areas include the Noatak River, plus Areas 22, 23 and 26A.

Black bears are plentiful along the coast, and although they are not as coveted a trophy as grizzlies, they are fine trophy animals in their own right. It's tough to find an area in southeastern or southcentral Alaska where there aren't black bears, including several color phases. One area where there are no blacks is on the ABC islands which are dominated entirely by brown bears. Bag limits are generally generous statewide. Some of the favored coastal hunting areas include Prince of Wales Island, Susitna Valley, the Kenai Peninsula, Nelchina Basin. Blacks are also found in the interior regions. Highway 2 from Manley Hot Springs to the Yukon border bisects excellent black bear regions. In the Fairbanks area, Minto Flats, Toklat, Tanana and Chena river drainages are considered prime black bear areas.

On Aug. 1 of each year, the interior regions open to Dall sheep hunting. Their sweeping yellow horns and white coats make the Dall one of the most coveted big game trophies in North America. Nonresidents must be accompanied by a registered guide and in most areas a limited number of permits are allocated. There are areas, however, like Area 20A, where special permits are not required.

Sheep are creatures of the mountains and nearly every major range has a huntable herd. Sheep hunting is tough under the best of conditions, and success does not come easy. Areas famous for their Dall ram trophies include, the Wood River drainage, Delta River near Donnelly, the mountains surrounding Tok, Mentasta, the Wrangell and Chugach mountains. In the Brooks Range, the largest concentration of sheep is in the eastern mountains. The Kenai National Wildlife Refuge is hunted for Dalls and in the northwest, hunting takes place along the Noatak River. The largest trophy Dalls are in the Tok management area and Area 19.

Some of the largest **mountain goats** in North America are found on the cliffs of southeastern Alaska, and the farther south the better the hunting. The Chugach Mountains, the peaks on the Kenai Peninsula, the Alaska and Boundary mountain ranges are excellent goat country. In some areas, generally the more productive southeast areas, hunters are allowed two goats per year. By contrast, in most other areas of the Northwest, goat licenses are allocated by controlled drawings. Alaska hunters also draw for permits in the southcentral goat units. While plentiful, however, southeastern Alaska goats are traditionally found on the slickest rocks on the steepest cliffs and hunting is a challenge.

While deer are the backbone of most big game hunting states, in Alaska they are a distant also-ran. They are hunted only in the coastal southeast regions, and there is only one species, the **Sitka blacktail.** Best hunting is on the islands, especially Kodiak, Afognak, Admiralty, Prince of Wales, Baranof and Chichagof. The best of the lot is Kodiak Island. The mainland areas over-

Brown bear near Katmai National Park. A variety of grizzly, Alaskan brown bears are the largest land carnivore on earth.
By George Wuerthner

Alaska General Hunting Requirements

State hunting and wildlife management is administered by the Alaska Dept. of Fish and Game, P.O. Box 3-2000, Juneau, AK 99802. Copies of the complete hunting regulations and supplemental restrictions and permit applications are available through the Juneau office or from any of the regional Fish and Game offices.

Licenses may be obtained from any designated licensing agent, (generally sporting goods dealers, resorts or guide-outfitter companies) or by mail. For license information contact the Licensing Section, Alaska Dept. of Revenue, 1107 W. Eighth St., Juneau, AK 99801. Hunting licenses are not available at Fish and Game offices.

There are 26 game management units in Alaska, and because of the vast area, varied terrain and weather conditions hunting seasons and bag limits vary considerably. There are special regulations in each unit.

Except for nonresidents seeking grizzly bear or Dall sheep, guides are not required. Hunters must live 12 consecutive months in Alaska to qualify as residents. A list of registered guides is available for $5 from the Guide Licensing and Control Board, Dept. of Commerce, Pouch D, Juneau, AK 99811.

There is no "hunter orange" requirement or minimum hunting age. A hunting or trapping license is not required for resident hunters under the age of 16 or over 60 (if they have 30 years residency).

Anyone who has been airborne, in Alaska, may not hunt big game until 3 a.m. of the following day, except for several black-tailed deer and caribou hunting units.

Big game firearms are restricted to shotgun, muzzle-loading rifle, or pistols or rifles with center-fire ammunition. Crossbows are legal, except in bow-only areas, and shotguns are limited to 10-gauge or smaller. Arrows must be tipped with broadheads, have a combined weight of 437.5 grains and be unbarbed. Bows must be powerful enough to cast an arrow 175 horizontal yards.

Baiting is legal for black bears, more than one-quarter mile from a public road. Dogs are legal only for small game, upland birds and black bear hunting.

Hunting is allowed in some state parks and areas of national parks identified as preserves. Areas titled park or monument are closed to hunting, except for subsistence.

Hunting License Fees

	Resident	Nonresident
Trapping	$10	NA
Hunting	$12	$ 60
Hunt/Trap Combination	$22	$ 200
Hunt/Fish Combination	$22	$ 96
Hunt/Fish/Trap Combination	$32	NA
Black Bear	NA	$ 200
Grizzly Bear	$25	$ 350
Bison	NA	$ 350
Caribou	NA	$ 300
Dall Sheep	NA	$ 400
Deer	NA	$ 135
Elk	NA	$ 250
Moose	NA	$ 300
Mountain Goat	NA	$ 250
Musk-ox	$25	$ 1,100
Waterfowl (state)	$ 5	$ 5
Wolf	NA	$ 150
Wolverine	NA	$ 150

Alaska Range Dall rams.
By George Wuerthner

looking these islands, however, offer poor deer hunting as a rule. Annual deer harvest is about 13,000.

Alaska is also beyond the natural range of elk, and hunting is confined to two islands, Afognak and Raspberry, where **Roosevelt elk** were imported. There are five herds and the maximum counted population was 1,500. Herds are Raspberry Island, Afognak Lake-Raspberry Strait, Malina Lake, Interior and Tonki Cape. The island herds are descendants of eight Roosevelt elk transplanted in 1928 from Washington's Olympic Mountains. Hunting is limited to registration permits. These islands are extremely brushy and rugged and hunting is hard.

There is also limited hunting for musk-ox and bison. **Musk-ox** are an introduced species, numbering about 1,000. Permits are awarded by drawing. Alaska's musk-ox are descendants of 34 animals imported in the 1930s from Greenland and released on Nunivak Island in the Bering Sea. It has been estimated that the last native Alaska musk-ox was killed in the 1860s. Hunting is on Nunivak and Nelson islands.

Except for a disease control hunt held near Yellowstone National Park in Montana, Alaska is the only Northwest state to provide an opportunity for the public to hunt **bison.** Between 25 and 50 hunting permits are awarded each fall. Alaska has four bison herds, descended from 23 Montana bison released in 1928 in the Delta Junction area about 100 miles south of Fairbanks. There are herds at Delta, McGrath, Healy and Copper River.

Wolverines and wolves are classed as game animals and furbearers and can be hunted and trapped. Wolves are abundant in Alaska, ranging throughout the state except for the Bering Sea islands and some islands in the Southeast, Aleutians and Prince William Sound. Alaska is the only state with an open hunting season for wolverines, as well as trapping season. They are found throughout the state, and abundant on the Alaska Peninsula, Alaska, Brooks and Wrangell mountain ranges.

Fur animals that can also be hunted with firearms include coyote, blue or white arctic fox, red fox, lynx, and red squirrel. No hunting is allowed for beaver, marmot, marten, mink, weasel, muskrat, otter and flying squirrel.

Coyotes moved north into Alaska about the turn of the century and are now found in the upper Tanana River valley, southwest onto the Kenai Peninsula, in the Arctic, along the lower Yukon River and on the mainland of Southeast. **Red fox** are most abundant from Unimak Island east to the the Alaska Peninsula and in the Kuskokwim and Yukon rivers. They are rare in

"Matching a guide and the type of hunt he offers with the expectations of the hunter is an essential, although often lacking ingredient in producing a memorable hunt."

From Alaska Hunting Guide, *Dan Wetzel, registered guide*

southeastern Alaska. The north is the home of the **arctic fox** found in white or blue color phases. The white phase is found from the Kuskokwim River north to Point Barrow and east along the Arctic Ocean. They frequently are found on the ice pack, scavenging on polar bear kills. The **lynx** is the only wild cat in Alaska and is common throughout the state, except on the extreme Arctic Slope, the Aleutian Islands and some islands on the Alaska Peninsula. In the wooded areas, hunters will find **snowshoe hares** and in the open tundra country the giant **arctic hares** are jumped. Like the snowshoe, arctics turn white in winter, brown in summer. They are the largest hare in North America, weighing up to 15 pounds.

While Alaska bird hunters may never swing a double-gun ahead of a cackling ringneck pheasant, jump a covey of quail or shoot behind a flock of chukars, there are grouse and ptarmigan enough to soothe the loss.

Forest grouse include spruce, blue and ruffed varities. **Spruce grouse,** often called "fool hens," are common throughout the state and abundant near Bristol Bay on the Kenai Peninsula and the woods in the upper Kuskokwim, Yukon and Tanana rivers. **Ruffed grouse** are found mostly in the woods along the Yukon, Tanana, Kuskokwim, upper Copper, Taku and Stikine river drainages, plus throughout the Southeast. **Blue grouse** are the largest upland bird in Alaska, weighing up to 4 pounds, but are found only in the Southeast from Glacier Bay south. The rarest grouse in Alaska is the **sharp-tail,** with scattered flocks in the Yukon River valley, the upper Koyukuk, upper Kuskokwim, Tanana and upper Copper rivers.

The most common upland bird is the **willow ptarmigan** which thrive in wet places nearly everywhere in the state. The state bird of Alaska, willow ptarmigan are found near timberline. The **rock ptarmigan** are generally found at higher elevations than the willow variety in all major treeless areas of Alaska. In southcentral and southeastern regions the **white-tailed ptarmigan** is found. Smallest of the ptarmigan and grouse family, white-tailed ptarmigan are especially numerous near Juneau, Denali National Park, and along the Richardson Highway.

Alaska's waterfowl hunting does not get the recognition it deserves, and local hunters are just as happy it doesn't. Long recognized as an important breeding area for ducks and geese, Alaska's marshy lowlands can provide spectacular hunting early in the fall. It is a major area for **whistling swan, emporer, Canada, cackling, dusky** and **white-fronted geese,** and **black brant.** The most popular ducks include impressive numbers of **pintail, mallard, teal, wigeon, shoveler, greater scaup, goldeneye, spectacled, Pacific, Steller's,** and **common eider, old-squaw, harlequin** and several varieties of **saltwater scoters.**

The greatest waterfowl breeding area in Alaska is in the hundreds of ponds and potholes between the mouths of the Yukon and Kuskokwim rivers. Other important hunting areas are on the Fort Yukon flats, Innoko flats, Minto Lake and Copper River flats near Cordova.

In the south during the start of the migration, good duck and goose hunting is found at Egegik, Port Heiden, Port Moller, Izembek Bay, Chickaloon flats, Susitna flats and the Copper River flats near Cordova. In Southeast, the Stikine flats near Wrangell provide excellent duck and goose shooting.

While numerous, sea ducks, including several varieties of scoters and eiders, are rarely hunted in Alaska, a neglect shared by waterfowlers the length of the Northwest coastline.

Ptarmigan are the most abundant game bird in Alaska. This is the white-tailed variety, the smallest of the three subspecies, all of which have the ability to change plumage from summer browns to winter white. By Thomas W. Kitchin

Rocky Mountain bighorn ram.
By Erwin & Peggy Bauer

To Hunt The Unlimiteds

By Mark Henckel

There were times when Bruce Saunders was sure he'd never see a bighorn ram. They were ghosts, mythical spirits who flitted about the high peaks of Montana's Absaroka-Beartooth Wilderness and lured hunters onto the lung-sapping alpine plateaus of autumn.

But that was some years ago. Over the course of 16 hunting seasons and more than 300 days spent in the high country in search of bighorn rams, Saunders has begun to unravel the mystery of the Absaroka-Beartooth's unlimited districts.

These four unlimited districts south of Big Timber and the three that are clustered near the northwest corner of Yellowstone National Park are the only places in the Lower 48 where anyone can get a sheep permit simply for the asking. The season simply runs until a harvest quota is reached for each district.

But as Saunders, of Columbus, Montana, put it, getting an unlimited tag and getting the sheep to fill it are two different matters.

"The Beartooth is a place to go sheep hunting but people have to understand it's tough," he said. "Even today when I look back, I don't know how I made it through the misery, the frustrations, the times I thought I had it figured out and I didn't have anything figured out.

"Whoever comes to take a sheep is going to pay the price and not in money, but in self-esteem and in time."

To understand what it takes, you have to realize that Saunders' sheep hunting odyssey began back in 1970 when an outfitter enlisted his aid in getting some hunters into the high country.

"We hunted five days and never saw a sheep, never saw a ewe," he said. "At the time, I didn't have a clue. I didn't know winter range from summer range and didn't know the tracks. I didn't know as much as I thought I did."

But the trip was interesting enough that he came back for some sheep hunting on his own. And with the 1971 season, his litany of learning really began.

"In 1971, I hunted four days and it snowed 2 feet and we never saw a sheep track," he said. "After I was done with that trip, I was sure I didn't know anything. The sheep were lost as far as I was concerned. They didn't exist.

"In 1973, that was the year we finally saw a ram. We set up a hunt and got into some rough ground. We got into a snowstorm Sunday night and it snowed 2 feet in two days. On Tuesday

220

The older rams are the ones that tend to go real high. Snow won't necessarily bring them down, but it gets them out of the timber where you can see them.
By Michael S. Sample

it starts to clear and on Wednesday morning, we hunt and still see no sheep. I'm real discouraged, about ready to throw away the rifle and my brother Ralph is too. On Thursday morning, we went back in to a ridge and I spotted some sheep including a 5/8-curl ram with a collar on it, just short of legal. It was the first ram we'd seen and we were excited. But I still didn't know enough.

"In 1974, I didn't get much sheep hunting in, just 10 days. That was the year Ralph retired as a sheep hunter. Eight years later Ralph went back to the Beartooths to help his brother and the mountain nearly kept them both.

"In 1975, I spent about 25 to 30 days sheep hunting and didn't see any legal rams. I did see about 40 sheep in one day, though. One day, I had the whole herd run right through me. Some guy ran them off the mountain and they came past at about 30 yards. What a sight!

"In 1976, it was 35 to 40 days and I couldn't find any legal rams.

"In 1977, it was 40 days. I was still working on them at Thanksgiving. I was starting to mess around a little bit with showshoes and I was hunting later. I saw my first ram that was close to legal, about a half inch short. I saw tracks all over. The temperature averaged from 10 above zero to 10 below. But I saw sheep and I was pleased."

By that time, Saunders had reached a turning point in his sheep hunting career. His time in the high coutry had begun to pay off and his timing and methods had begun to develop and reap dividends.

"I stopped worrying about shooting a ram in 1978. That season and the next three years, I almost lived on the mountain. I averaged 35 to 40 days a season up there," he said.

"In 1978, I was beginning to realize that mountains have four sides and those sheep run around mountains. They might run literally. They might find a ridge and run to another mountain and run around it for a while."

Saunders began to sort out his hunting into time periods and found his greatest success just after equinox storms raked the high country and during the final days and weeks of the season.

"It's more difficult in September to find them. It's like a poker hand. All it takes is putting four aces together and you've got a ram. But the odds are against you," Saunders said. "In October, you can get into your equinox snows better. In October, you've got a better shot."

"November gets even better, if you can stay where you should. Weather is super-important. It's as critical as anything. November is the best time to hunt there is. It makes the sheep more accessible to your sight. It won't necessarily bring them down to you. Many times they go farther away, right to the top of the mountain. But it gets them out of the timber and in the open where you can see them.

"They start to move up toward the wind-blows on top," Saunders said. "The older rams are the ones that tend to go real high. By early December after the season is closed, they're solidly out on top."

Those late-season tactics led Saunders to his first crack at a legal sheep in 1981, a chance he muffed.

"I missed a full curl in 1981. It was a 400-yard shot and I just muffed it. It was a 45-degree angle down the slope and I shot over him. It was the sheep I had dreamed about taking and still dream about taking," he said. That season, he said, "I saw a full curl, a ⅞ and a ¾, all legal rams, and innumerable numbers of smaller rams."

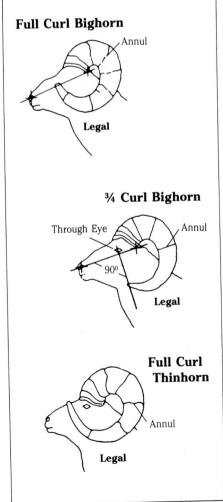

Full Curl Bighorn

Annul

Legal

¾ Curl Bighorn

Through Eye — Annul

90°

Legal

Full Curl Thinhorn

Annul

Legal

221

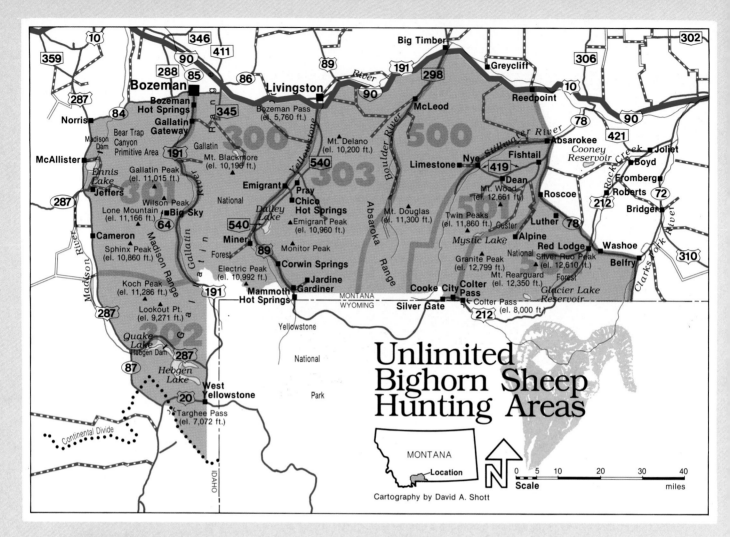

The map shows labeled locations including: Bozeman, Livingston, Big Timber, Greycliff, Reedpoint, Absarokee, Joliet, Boyd, Fromberg, Roberts, Bridger, Red Lodge, Washoe, Belfry, Luther, Roscoe, Dean, Nye, Fishtail, Limestone, McLeod, Norris, McAllister, Jeffers, Big Sky, Cameron, Miner, Emigrant, Pray, Chico Hot Springs, Corwin Springs, Jardine, Gardiner, Mammoth Hot Springs, Cooke City, Silver Gate, Colter Pass, West Yellowstone. Highway markers: 10, 346, 411, 90, 359, 288, 85, 86, 89, 191, 298, 302, 306, 78, 421, 287, 84, 345, 540, 64, 419, 212, 72, 212, 310, 20, 87. Elevations noted: Mt. Delano (el. 10,200 ft.), Bozeman Pass (el. 5,760 ft.), Gallatin Peak (el. 11,015 ft.), Mt. Blackmore (el. 10,196 ft.), Lone Mountain (el. 11,166 ft.), Wilson Peak, Sphinx Peak (el. 10,860 ft.), Koch Peak (el. 11,286 ft.), Lookout Pt. (el. 9,271 ft.), Electric Peak (el. 10,992 ft.), Monitor Peak, Emigrant Peak (el. 10,960 ft.), Mt. Douglas (el. 11,300 ft.), Twin Peaks (el. 11,860 ft.), Mt. Wood (el. 12,661 ft.), Granite Peak (el. 12,799 ft.), Silver Run Peak (el. 12,610 ft.), Mt. Rearguard (el. 12,350 ft.), Colter Pass (el. 8,000 ft.), Targhee Pass (el. 7,072 ft.). Also: Madison Dam, Bear Trap Canyon Primitive Area, Ennis Lake, Dailey Lake, Mystic Lake, Glacier Lake Reservoir, Cooney Reservoir, Quake Lake, Hebgen Dam, Hebgen Lake, Madison River, Gallatin River, Yellowstone River, Boulder River, Stillwater River, Rock Creek, Clarks Fork River, Absaroka Range, Madison Range, Gallatin Range, Continental Divide, Yellowstone National Park, Montana/Wyoming border, Idaho.

Unlimited Bighorn Sheep Hunting Areas

MONTANA — Location

Scale: 0 5 10 20 30 40 miles

Cartography by David A. Shott

If You Go

There is no finer, more coveted trophy in the Northwest than a full-curl bighorn ram. They live where the summers are blistering hot, the winters unbearably cold — where mountains are the highest, the snow the deepest and the terrain the toughest. They are a challenge, a test of mettle and mountain savvy and the odds are always long against the hunter.

The more difficult the hunt, the higher the obstacles and the longer the odds, the more coveted the trophy. Every state in the Northwest sets a limited bighorn season. Only one, Montana, offers an unlimited hunt for the ultimate mountain trophy. In the limited hunts the number of hunting licenses is few and those are awarded by drawing. The odds of getting a sheep tag are often several thousand to one. So prized are bighorn permits that some states withdraw one tag from the public allotment and auction it to the highest bidder as a fund raiser. In 1986, an Oregon hunter paid the state of Montana $79,000 for one permit. The year before, Nevada auctioned a bighorn tag for $67,500. Truly once-in-a-lifetime opportunities, except for the unlimited Montana hunt.

Here in one small, rugged area of southwestern Montana, everyone who applies to hunt bighorn rams gets a permit. As coveted as sheep permits are, it might be easy to imagine the area overrun with high-country hunters, flushed with sheep fever, running every canyon, glassing every mountain meadow. It doesn't happen that way. The mountains, the weather and the sheep control success and failure. The area is in the Beartooth and Gallatin mountains adjacent to Yellowstone National Park, an unforgiving land of 12,000-foot peaks, year-round snow and lonesome places. There are seven sheep hunting districts with a total hunting quota of 21 rams. The most rams allowed to be killed in any one district is four and when the quotas in each district are filled those districts are closed

with only 48 hours notice. The seasons open in early September and close in early November and December.

These are the last unlimited sheep mountains in the contiguous 48 states. The only place where anyone can hunt for bighorns. Hunting pressure is limited by the country, by the cold, by the steepness, and the miles between animals. This is where you come when it's time to hunt your sheep.

The deadline for buying a bighorn sheep permit in an unlimited area is Aug. 31 at the Montana Fish, Wildlife and Parks headquarters office in Helena. Cost of a permit is $50 for Montana residents and $300 for nonresidents. There are no refunds.

Unlimited Districts	Seasons	Ram Quotas
300	Sept. 1-Nov. 3	3
301	Sept. 1-Nov. 3	4
302	Sept. 1-Nov. 3	2
303	Sept. 15-Nov.3	2
500	Sept. 15-Dec. 1	4
501	Sept. 15-Dec. 1	3
502	Nov. 19-Dec. 15	3

(Quotas and seasons are reset annually and may vary.)

In 1982, he made another major assault on the mountain that accounted for 40 more days in the high country. And, finally, he shot a legal ram.

"I got a 4/5-curl ram in the first week of November," he said. "It was a good sheep, a nice ram, but not as good as the one I missed the year before."

In 1983, he put in another 25 days and took a mountain goat.

In 1984, Saunders, took along a friend, Tim Schaff of Park City, and spotted three legal rams. Schaff passed on a ¾-curl that year.

And in 1985, he hunted 10 days with his wife who had drawn a permit in a limited district near Thompson Falls, seeing their share of legal rams, but passing them all in search of a truly big one.

Saunder's tactics over the years, including the ones that led him to the sheep that now rests in a full-body mount in his father's home, have increasingly turned to the late season on the high ridges and plateaus.

He hunts on aluminum-framed showshoes, both to handle deep snow and to bridge his steps over boulder fields. He packs a windproof tent and polyester-fill sleeping bag capable of handling temperatures to 20 below. His boots are a plastic, waterproof mountaineering model with wool felt inserts. And much of the rest of his gear more closely resembles that of a winter mountaineer than standard hunting issue.

Even the sheep he took in 1982 nearly cost Saunders, his brother Ralph and a friend, Bill Johnston, their lives when they were caught in a subzero high-country blizzard on a 10,000-foot plateau while they were packing it out.

They made it out alive after leaving the meat behind and spending a freezing, miserable night jammed in a one-man tent until the storm blew itself out and they were able to find their way.

"If you're going to a high plateau area, make sure you are prepared," Saunders said. "I hunt from 8,500 feet clear up to the tops, 11,000 and 12,000 feet. Anybody who goes onto that mountain who isn't in good shape is crazy. Do realize that you can die. Mistakes can kill you," he warns, and he's serious.

Hunters should also realize that success in these districts comes with time. The more of it a person puts in to learn the sheep, the better their chance for success.

"At the start, I figured that I saw one ram for every 75 days I put in," he said. "Later on down the road, I got it down to one every eight days. I got it to the point where I could find a ram in an eight-day trip."

Saunders also pointed out that the bighorns that hunters are seeking here aren't the limited district variety that stand a good chance of making the Boone and Crockett Club's record book.

"Montana holds the biggest bighorn rams in the world. There is not another place in the United States that holds rams as big as Montana. But while the Beartooth is a place to go sheep hunting, it's not a place to shoot trophy rams," he said.

"There is only one ram I know of in Boone and Crockett that's come out of the Beartooths. It was [with horns that measured] 38 inches [long] with a good base. Thirty-one or 32 is a very nice ram in the Beartooths. He's better than average. Most that are shot are 28 to 30. You're not looking at the truly large rams."

Saunders added that the large expanses of rugged country with relatively few sheep scattered over it demand different tactics than those used in limited districts.

"You've got to watch for clues more. You look for tracks, fresh tracks, and track them more. When I learned to track rams, I started to find sheep," he said.

"You have to know what their manure looks like. There are areas in the Beartooths where you'll find lots of manure but no sheep. That's a winter range area. Summer range you'll find manure that's looser and in different spots. And you have to be able to read it to see if they're moving.

"They're heavy travelers. They'll come through the same areas every year and within a few days of the same time.

"You have to spend a lot of time looking and spend more time looking behind you than you do in front of you. Most of the time I see sheep behind me instead of in front of me. I've already walked past them. Where they are when I go by, I still don't know."

A former jockey standing 5 feet 7 inches and weighing just 105 pounds, Saunders also believes in putting in the miles.

"You walk five to seven miles a day and five miles is a long way in rough country. I started to cover a lot of country and not worry about not seeing them. Generally, most of the rams will give you a see if you do enough glassing."

And, he added, a hunter who truly wants a bighorn ram shouldn't be discouraged as the time in the high country begins to add up. "A lot of people go up there and get discouraged and give up. I can understand that. It takes time and lots of days," Saunders said. "There were a lot of days when I'd go up there and see nothing but squirrels. Squirrels were the best friends I had.

"Sheep are the toughest because of the land they live in. And to get one, you have to stick with it," he said.

"Time is the most important thing on sheep. If you're going to hunt them, you might as well throw everything else away. You'll live them, eat them, breathe them.

"You might be out there five or six or 10 days and not see anything, then have one walk right out and shake hands with you."

Clark's Nutcracker. Like the bighorn, and maybe a hunter or two, these gray birds turn their shoulders into the storms of early winter and ride it out. They'll stay in the high country after everything else has moved to low winter range.
By Thomas W. Kitchin

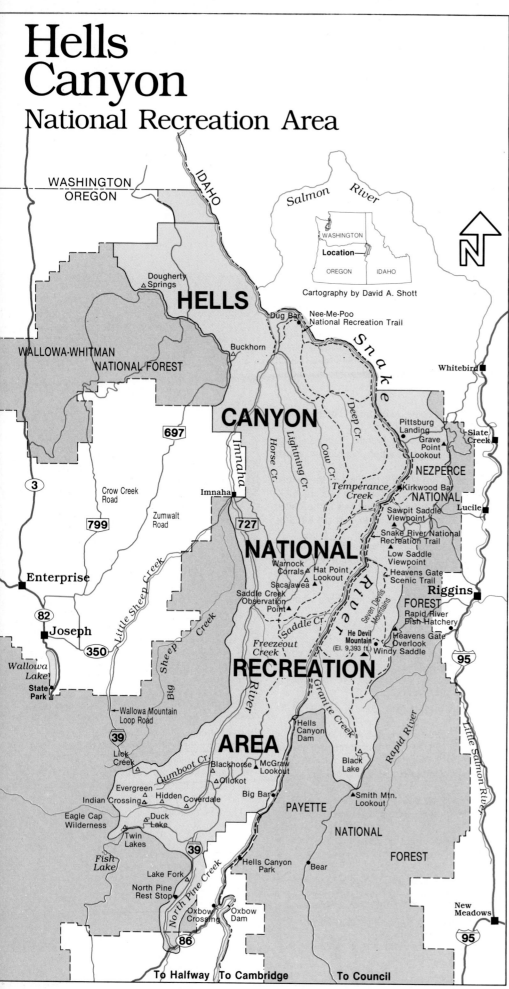

Hells Canyon
National Recreation Area

WASHINGTON
OREGON

IDAHO

Salmon River

Location

WASHINGTON

OREGON | IDAHO

Cartography by David A. Shott

HELLS

Dougherty
△ Springs

Dug Bar
Nee-Me-Poo
National Recreation Trail

Buckhorn
△

WALLOWA-WHITMAN
NATIONAL FOREST

Whitebird

CANYON

Snake

Deep Cr.

697

Pittsburg
Landing

Slate
Creek

Imnaha

Horse Cr.

Lightning Cr.

Cow Cr.

Grave
Point
Lookout

NEZPERCE

3

Crow Creek
Road

Imnaha

Temperance
Creek

Kirkwood Bar

NATIONAL

Lucile

799

Zumwalt
Road

727

Sawpit Saddle
Viewpoint

Snake River National
Recreation Trail

NATIONAL

Low Saddle
Viewpoint

Warnock
Corrals △ ▲ Hat Point
Lookout

Heavens Gate
Scenic Trail

Enterprise

Sacajawea
▲

Saddle Creek
Observation
Point ▲

Riggins

FOREST

Rapid River
Fish Hatchery

82

Little Sheep Creek

Saddle Cr.

He Devil
Mountain
(El. 9,393 ft.)

Heavens Gate
Overlook

Joseph

350

Big Sheep Creek

Freezeout
Creek

Windy Saddle

Seven Devils Mountains

Wallowa
Lake

RECREATION

95

State
Park

Wallowa Mountain
Loop Road

Imnaha River

Granite Creek

Rapid River

39

Lick
Creek

AREA

Hells
Canyon
Dam

Gumboot Cr.

Blackhorse △ ▲ McGraw
Lookout

Black
Lake

Evergreen
△

Hidden △

Coverdale
△

Big Bar

Ollokot △

Smith Mtn.
Lookout

Indian Crossing

Eagle Cap
Wilderness

Duck
△ Lake

Big Bar

PAYETTE

Little Salmon River

Twin
Lakes

39

NATIONAL

Fish
Lake

Lake Fork

North Pine Creek

Hells Canyon
Park

Bear

FOREST

North Pine
Rest Stop

Oxbow
Crossing

Oxbow
Dam

New
Meadows

86

95

To Halfway   To Cambridge   To Council

224

You'll earn your birds when you hunt the
rim of the deepest river gorge in the world.
By Dewey Haeder

Hells Canyon Chukar

By Bill Loftus

Hells Canyon. Any visitor can tell you this place is hot. Really hot — 100-degree afternoons are not rare. Yet chukar hunting, at times, is just as hot as the temperatures in this rugged, vertical Snake River canyon. Some hunters swear the name of this mile-deep cleft in the granite and basalt foundations of Idaho and Oregon is devilishly appropriate.

The canyon air is so hot late in the summer, when the hunters come for chukars, that rocks along the river seem to sweat. The desert varnish accumulated through the centuries, glistens and heat waves make the distance dance. As a rule, there are real reasons places become known for what they are: Hells Canyon follows that rule.

Consider the poor soul who rests for a moment after a morning of chukar chasing. Hot and sweat-soaked from struggling up lung-searing slopes, the hot lava rock on which he sits to catch his breath provides little comfort. The only breezes this seemingly desolate canyon offers are the faint downdrafts fanned in the dust by a departing covey of chukars flushing behind his perch, just out of range.

So it goes. The hunter after chukar must go to the birds on their terms, not his.

Those terms in this canyon, the continent's deepest abyss, can be unforgiving. Averaging 6,600 feet deep for more than 20 miles, Hells Canyon is one of the deepest river gorges in the world.

Chasing Hells Canyon chukar is not for the fainthearted. By Dewey Haeder

Rattlesnakes and poison oak are as common as cliffs that drop a thousand feet or more and some of the most awesome white-water rapids in the world. Hardly gentle country for bird hunters. Technically the canyon includes only the river's course from Spring Creek near Oxbow, Oregon, downstream to Idaho's Johnson Bar. But anything south of the mouth of Salmon River to Oxbow is commonly considered Hells Canyon. Flanked east and west by the towering Seven Devils and Wallowas mountain ranges, the canyon is a lesson in durability.

The basalt that has cloaked the granite peaks has worn into an intricate, but rumpled robe of ridges and valleys. Against these harsh eroded slopes of dry grasses and rough stone, shoe leather means little. A hunter can watch a seasoned pair of hiking boots wear away before his disbelieving eyes as he claws across the rocks and shale chasing chukar shadows.

Despite the canyon's ruggedness, or perhaps because of it, this is home to one of the Northwest's finest chukar concentrations. A dapper, hearty upland bird, chukars are halfway in size between a bobwhite quail and a pheasant. They are the color of the desert, tan and gray with bands of black and white. Their beaks are a distinctive red and their legs — legs that can run an English setter into the ground — are thin and pinkish colored. These birds would rather run than fly and they do both well. A gregarious bird, they run and fly in flocks numbering from a half-dozen to 50 or more and they signal each other with shrill little whistles that can drive you crazy, tease you into running madly up and down grades chasing ghosts whistles.

Chukars came to the United States and eventually this harsh canyon in the mid-1950s imported from Asia's Himalaya Mountains. They have adapted well to the scorching summers and bitter western winters. In some arid regions they thrive in conditions that kill other upland game birds. Hells Canyon is one of those regions.

Hunting the chukar in Hells Canyon means a lot of things. Chief among them are experiences like sharp cheatgrass seeds working their way into tender body parts and a lot of walking. But chukar hunting, like steelhead fishing, mornings in duck blinds and the smell of saddle leather, can be addictive. There are enough moments of grandeur to make the good days more than hold their own among memories. A hunter in good physical condition can return with a heavy game bag and good memories. Hunters who are a little soft and out of shape will also remember Hells Canyon.

A good hunting dog can be a valuable asset on a trip to the canyon. Watching a German shorthair pointer nose out singles from a scattered covey can be rewarding on any trip. Reaching down to take a chukar from a panting retriever (after a downhill shot) instead of sliding down the shale on your own wounded knees to fetch the bird justifies a year's worth of dog food.

But hunters with dogs should take extra precautions. Carrying water for both hunter and dog for the long pauses between draws is wise practice. A dog hunting hard for chukars can suffer heat stroke with tragic ease. Dog handlers also need to watch their charges for signs that the barbed seeds of cheatgrass have begun spiraling into foot pads, ears or even eyes. This is tough country on dogs and dog handlers alike.

A good hunter with good timing can improve the odds. In the early part of the chukar hunting season, which runs from mid-September to December, in both Oregon and Idaho hot weather prevails. Before the fall rains arrive, chukars are often concentrated close to water, and the only water around is often the Snake River. Boaters and rafters, if they listen and watch closely often will hear the chukar's grating call echoing off the hills, and sometimes see the white-barred flanks of the gray birds bobbing and weaving among the boulders along the shore.

The same observations can cut the number of steps between shots. Veterans of the Hells Canyon chukar front will tell you to find your birds before you hunt. Locate them by their calls and by sight. If you can't hear them or see them there's nothing left but plain persistent hunting. Walking the slopes above side streams or the river with a dog. It's tough but it can be productive for the hunter with good wind and a stout heart.

If chukar hunting is ever easy, which is debatable, the early fall season might qualify. That's when the birds can be found along the bars and occasional benches along the river.

The flush of a chukar covey is comparable to the eruption of a quail covey. Once the covey flushes and scatters, single birds will sit and hold for a dog or a boot. It's not too long before they begin reuniting the covey with short, crisp calls. That's where the similarity with flat-ground quail ends, because seldom do farmland quail take to running as enthusiastically uphill as a flock of chukars pushed by a hunter. Seldom do quail set their wings to glide a half mile across broken canyon walls to another ridge that will take three hours of up and down climbing to reach.

First shots count for a lot under such conditions. A double barrel shotgun provides quick second shots and for that reason are favored by many canyon hunters. Longtime Hells Canyon chukar chasers invariably attach leather rifle slings to their smoothbores, leaving both hands free to climb. Modified chokes are the rule. Clean, quick kills are vital because a wounded bird's wobbling 100-yard flight can mean a half mile of up and down walking and maybe a lost bird. High-base shells with No. 7½ shot are recommended. Like chukar everywhere, these birds invariably run uphill and fly down, a situation that means tough downhill shots, a strange direction for upland bird hunters more accustomed to topping birds on the rise. The first hundred or so you shoot at you shoot above and finally it dawns that to hit these dropping targets you hold below the bird, a foot or two below its belly feathers.

It is in the early fall when the river jet boat reigns as king among chukar hunting coveyances. A popular fall ritual for many chukar hunters is a jet boat trip into the canyon bouncing through the Snake's white-water rapids. Outfitters registered with the Hells Canyon National Recreation Area at Lewiston provide a ferry service for hunters not experienced as white-water rivermen. Hunters are dropped off along the banks and picked up at prearranged times either farther upstream or downstream. A fairly common tactic is to drop off the hunting party at one spot, the other half at another and have the two work toward each other, pincering the birds in the center. It can be effective, especially when the birds are flushing wild. The U.S. Forest Service manages the recreation area, authorizes outfitters and can provide information. The states set the hunting seasons and regulations.

Experience is required of boaters who plan to navigate the canyon. Even a relatively mild rapids on the scale of Temperance Creek is impressive and to be taken seriously. A white-water rapid on the scale of Rush Creek can be disastrous to the novice's boat and the novice. The major rapids are dangerous for even skilled boatmen.

For the more pedestrian hunters who like to keep both feet on the ground and their boots dry, there are roads that allow cars and 4x4s to reach the edge of the canyon and chukar country. Chief among the roads to the Oregon side of the river is a winding gravel road from Imnaha to Dug Bar. On the Idaho side the main portal is from Whitebird to Pittsburg Landing. This road can be both a scenic wonder and a holy terror as it switchbacks sharply down from Pittsburg Saddle to the Snake. Car travelers would be wise to check their brakes and the conditions of both roads and the many others along the canyon rim. Overheating is not uncommon for cars or trucks towing boats or campers.

After all the cautions and exertions of reaching the chukars in Hells Canyon, hunters might rightfully expect to deserve good wingshooting above the Snake. And in the future they will probably get it. During the past few seasons they didn't.

The great chukar crash of the early 1980s has been reversed, and in 1985 hunters found shooting worth coming back for. Five coveys of chukar provided an average day's hunt in 1985. During

Imported from the Himalaya Mountains in the 1950s, chukar partridge thrive in the arid basalt and cliff country of the Northwest. By Erwin & Peggy Bauer

the depths of the chukar decline there was a lot more miles and fewer birds between shots. Chukar numbers rebound quickly with good spring nesting seasons and favorable summer weather. Biologists, however, are not optimistic that the fantastic shooting days of the late 1960s and early 1970s will be repeated, as the population of the introduced birds begins to level out after peaking in the alien terrain.

A factor that makes Hells Canyon an optimstic target for the future is that simply, the terrain is ideal chukar country. Although flocks may fade from marginal areas, chukars are almost sure to remain in the canyon. Wet springs that spoil nesting may trim their numbers but even those setbacks will not eliminate this tough little bird.

And if a hunter becomes sated by covey after covey of the most difficult upland bird to rise from the rocks of the Northwest, there is other game in the canyon. Mule deer browse the draws and ridges. Elk hold in the forested fringes where the grass meets the trees and bighorn sheep are staging a dramatic comeback after annihilation by domestic sheep and hunters before World War II. It's not unusual to spot bighorns on the canyon walls. Even mountain goats are fair game to special permit holders in the Seven Devils Mountains high above the river where one of the few healthy herds in Idaho is found.

If you're tough enough, got a good dog, and can hit what you shoot at, this canyon is a helluva place to hunt one of the finest upland birds in the Northwest.

The Odds For Northwest Moose

Moose are hunted in every state in the Northwest, except Oregon, but the permits are few and the odds of being drawn are exceptionally long. Serious moose hunters book trips to Canada or Alaska where moose are plentiful and licenses are unlimited. In Canada's southwestern provinces licensed guides are required for nonresident hunters.

British Columbia and Alberta sell moose permits to nonresidents moose hunters, with British Columbia generally considered the better of the two. The nonresident moose license in British Columbia is $120, and $20 for residents plus general licenses.

In Alberta the moose hunting license is $10 for residents, $100 for nonresident Canadians, and $200 for non-Canadians.

In Washington, Idaho and Montana moose hunting permits are awarded by drawing and the odds are long against success. There are no moose reported in Oregon.

Montana provides the most moose tags, about 650, and the odds of being drawn for one are 5 percent — the best in the Northwest. Cost of a moose license is $52 for residents and $302 for nonresident hunters.

Idaho sets aside 350 moose permits and reserves them all for resident hunters, and still the odds of being drawn are astronomical. In 1984 0.47 percent of the 7,400 applicants drew a $71 moose tag.

Washington allows nonresidents to enter the moose tag drawing, doesn't require license guides and has a 100 percent success rate for moose hunters. However, with only five licenses available, only 0.4 percent of the number of hunters submitting applications are drawn. Licenses in Washington are $150 for residents and $300 for nonresidents. Permits are granted on a once-in-a-lifetime basis.

In Alaska guides are not required for moose hunters and the nonresident moose license is $300.

British Columbia Moose
By Ron Kerr

British Columbia moose are rarely easy.

Ordinarily, and especially when hunted, an adult moose is cunning and wary. While its sense of sight is not too keen, its ability to smell is excellent and the hearing phenomenal. Bulls frequently stand motionless for long periods behind a screening edge of timber. They stare across a marsh or meadow without moving their head or shifting their stance.

British Columbia has some of the greatest moose herds and finest hunting in North America. Hunters are attracted from around the world by the prospects of matching wits with these incredible animals. Moose are second only to deer in popularity with British Columbia hunters, but still, by Lower 48 standards the hunting pressure is light. In the mid 1980s there were only 35,000 moose hunters licensed in the province and they took about 9,200 moose.

Moose are the largest member of the deer family, up to 10 feet long and more than 6 feet high at the shoulder. They'll weigh from 800 to 1,300 pounds and the bulls carry a great, flat rack of palmated antlers that can spread 5 feet across.

Of the top 20 Canada moose in the Boone and Crockett record book, 15 were taken in British Columbia, including the top three listings. The No. 1 Canada moose in the record book was dropped in October of 1980 near the Graylong River. It had a 63-inch spread. The No. 2 moose had a greater spread, 66 inches, but fewer overall points. It was taken in 1982 in the Teslin River area.

Bow hunters have been just as successful as rifle hunters at putting British Columbia moose in the record book. Of the top 25 Canada moose trophies recorded by Pope and Young, 19 came from British Columbia, including the top six listings.

There are three subspecies of moose in the Northwest, the Shiras (Wyoming) that lives in Idaho, eastern Washington and the Rocky Mountains of Montana; the Canada moose of British Columbia and Alberta; and the Alaska-Yukon moose common to the Far North. Shiras are the smallest, and Alaska the largest.

During the rut, bulls often throw caution to the wind and stupidity blunts their senses. Normally no other animal of equal size can slip through brush and timber as noiselessly as a moose. But a lovesick bull barges through the blowdowns grunting and challenging all competitors.

The rut peaks between the last week in September and the second week of October. The woods change and spotting game is easier. Green willow pastures are transformed into stands of bare willow stalks, where a 1,000-pound moose is as prominent as a black bear in a cow pasture.

Getting into British Columbia's moose country generally requires time, effort, a hunting camp, and hunting partners. Nonresidents are required to use registered outfitters or guides. The methods of hunting are usually dictated by the area to be hunted and the technique of the guide or outfitter; stalking the animal on foot or horseback; hunting lake edges inlets, outlets and adjacent creeks with a canoe; sometimes by calling. A few outfitters are using wide-tired or tread-equipped ATVs to hunt the muskeg or bogs moose prefer.

In areas where large wooded tracts must be covered, guides often favor horseback hunting from a base camp in combination with stalking.

The most practical method of hunting on foot is to hunt during feeding periods — dawn and dusk — always into the wind and in the most likely places; meadows, muskeg and timber edges and lake shores where low brush grows. Moose also feed on water plants until lakes freeze. I've probably taken more moose at these dining areas than any other spot.

Bugling Alberta bull. By Erwin & Peggy Bauer

Elk Hunting

By Ed Park

Dawn slowly won its battle with night, and soon Mike and Randy could see details of that high mountain basin with its alpine meadow of lush grass. They grinned with the expectation that any moment a herd of elk could slip from the timber to feed.

Suddenly it happened!

Not 100 yards away, a huge bull elk with long, massive antlers, drifted into the meadow. Mike eased his rifle up, settled the cross hairs and squeezed off a shot. As the roar of his Magnum echoed from the surrounding ridges and faded into the valleys below, the mighty record-book bull of the Blue Mountains was his.

Similar stories appear frequently in outdoor magazines, and while it is enjoyable and instructional to read how others outwit trophy animals, we sometimes forget such experiences make good articles because they are exceptions. In truth very few record-class elk are taken, and when compared with the total number who try, hunters take relatively few elk of any size.

To return to reality, we merely need to remember just one figure — 17 percent — which is the average hunter success on elk in the Northwest, according to official figures. Expressed other ways, a hunter needs an average of six years to get one elk, or a camp of six average elk hunters will take one elk each year. However, the word is "average," and there are many ways any individual can improve his personal odds.

The best way to increase your chances is to hire a good guide, but to again face reality, although a guide is well worth the expense, most of us simply cannot afford it.

For any hunter, I offer the following suggestions, based on decades of hunting the Northwest: (1) Hunt good areas. (2) Gain hunting expertise. (3) Accumulate experience. (4) Become a crack shot. (5) Keep in top shape. (6) Be persistent.

To locate good hunting areas, begin with population and harvest figures from wildlife departments. Top areas will change from year to year as conditions change, but some areas always produce, including the Selway-Bitterroot Wilderness of Idaho, southwestern Montana and the east slope of the Rockies west of Great Falls, the extreme northwest and extreme northeast regions

The best elk hunting is generally found far from road's end, and pack animals are invaluable to serious elk hunters, packing in camps and carrying out game.
By Erwin & Peggy Bauer

of Oregon, and the Yakima area of Washington. Detailed information on better areas can be obtained by talking with wildlife biologists, foresters, ranchers and other hunters.

Gaining expertise and experience should go together, but some hunters spend years in the woods and never catch on. Experience helps only if used, and the best hunters make an extra effort to become familiar with the country and the species they are hunting, to learn how the animals react to weather, habitat and other hunters, and how to utilize good optics, terrain, wind direction, stealth, and patience to detect and then get within range of their quarry.

Once within range, the shot must be true. Year-round practice helps keep a hunter familiar with his firearm or archery gear. It is critical to become proficient at range estimation, so you'll know where to aim for all logical ranges.

Physical conditioning allows hunters to keep going, from dawn to dusk, day after day, in rough country and miserable weather. If the spirit is willing but the body can't hack it, the odds decrease rapidly.

Finally, persistence will eventually pay off, and hunters who keep at it do best.

To show how these factors work in actual practice, let me relate the true story of my 1981 elk hunt with brothers Mark and Scott Pine of Santa Cruz, California, and Ed Coleman of Bend, Oregon. Based on averages, we'd beat the odds a bit if just one of the four of us got an elk. Which one?

We were equal on having a good area. This was one of my few guided hunts, and I selected noted guide Cal Henry of Joseph, Oregon. Cal guides out of The Horse Ranch, deep within the Eagle Cap Wilderness Area. We had a top guide and were in one of the West's better areas.

For experience and expertise, all of us would rely on Cal's knowledge of elk and the area. Beyond that I was the most experienced of the four, although Ed Coleman is also experienced. The Pine brothers were on their first big game hunts, so what more can I say. The odds were leaning my way.

My rifle is a super-accurate, scope-sighted Remington .30-06, shooting Federal Premium cartridges with those superb Nosler Partition bullets, and has accounted for scores of big game animals over the past 30-plus years. I shoot it year-round. Ed Coleman was also shooting a familiar rifle, but unfortunately Mark and Scott Pine had new rifles. My odds were getting better.

Since I take physical conditioning seriously, I was also in the best shape. When the tough hunting began, I was sent up the highest, roughest ridges, where the big, trophy bulls were most apt to be. Finally, I also had the mental toughness, the persistence, to keep hunting in any kind of terrain or weather. More points for me.

That's the way I analyzed things as we assembled at The Horse Ranch. I stood the best chance, with Ed Coleman second. Mark and Scott Pine were great guys and fun to be with, but I hoped they wouldn't be too disappointed at going home empty.

So how did our 1981 hunt turn out?

The Pine brothers, along with wrangler Gene Wolf, left The Horse Ranch, headed for Cal's deluxe tent camp, an hour ahead of Ed Coleman, Cal Henry and me. When they arrived at camp there was still an hour of shooting light left, so Gene took the boys on a short hunt. As Ed, Cal and I rode into camp we heard a shot, rode out to check, and found the others dressing out Mark's 5-point bull elk. One hour of big game hunting; one elk. So much for hunting experience.

The second day Scott Pine got a shot — and a fat spike bull. At dinner Scott admitted his rifle was so new he hadn't had time to shoot it. The new rifle's first-ever shot downed an elk. So much for shooting experience.

Two days later I was again hunting superbly — slowly, carefully, as silent as fog. Every few steps I paused long minutes to study every shadow, in an effort to spot a leg, patch of hide, the flicker of an ear, or the glint of sun off an antler. If hunting skill pays, the next elk was mine.

Down the ridge out of sight, Ed Coleman tripped on a root, took a nasty fall, dropped his rifle, and cut his hand on a rock. He got up, brushed the crud from his rifle scope, took two more steps, and fell again, spraining his ankle. He sat there in pain, loudly cursing everything within sight. Then he spotted movement in the timber 75 yards below. He jerked his rifle up, found a 3-point bull elk in his scope, and dropped him. So much for silent, skillful hunting.

At least our party had exceeded the odds in grand style, with 75 percent success. The only problem was that I was the other 25 percent and my hunting theories were also taking a beating.

Another theory fell apart when some other hunters came through camp on their way out. Their success was right on average, with one elk for six hunters. Five hunters were tough, and had been hunting hard. The sixth, Robert Cole of Charlotte, Michigan, had severe heart trouble so was limited to short strolls near camp. The 5-point bull elk he took was standing in the trail, 60 yards from the tents. So much for physical conditioning.

In September rutting bulls will respond to a bugle call. Most northwest seasons, however, are scheduled after the rut, limiting bugle hunts to special hunts requiring a controlled permit or primitive weapon. By Erwin & Peggy Bauer

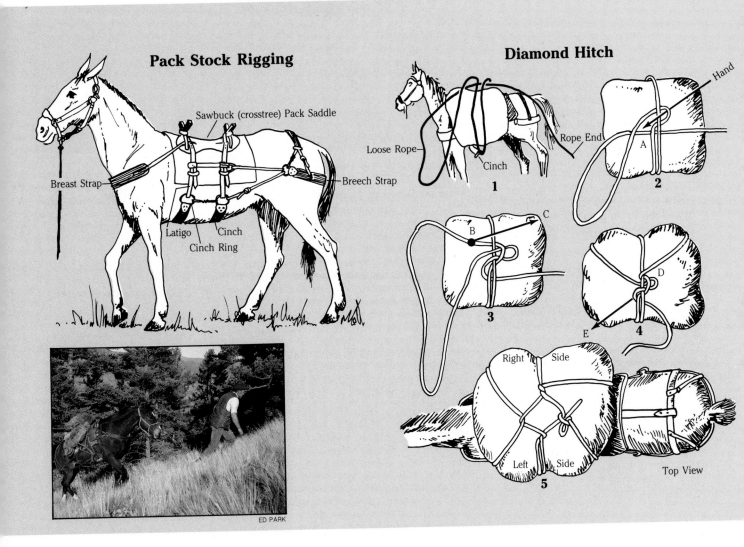

Pack Stock Rigging

Sawbuck (crosstree) Pack Saddle

Breast Strap

Breech Strap

Latigo

Cinch

Cinch Ring

ED PARK

Diamond Hitch

Hand

Loose Rope

Cinch

Rope End

1

2

A

3

B

C

4

D

E

5

Right Side

Left Side

Top View

Lacking the resources of a packstring, many Northwest elk hunters backpack into prime areas, a tactic that requires good physical conditioning and stout determination. Game is generally relayed out, a quarter at a time. By Erwin & Peggy Bauer

For current regulations, hunting statistics and reports on specific elk areas contact the information offices and big game division managers in these departments.

Northwest Wildlife Departments

Alberta Dept. of Energy & Natural Resources, Fish and Wildlife Division, Main Floor, North Tower, Petroleum Plaza, 9945 - 108 St., Edmonton, AB, Canada T5K 2C9.

British Columbia Ministry of Environment, Wildlife Management Branch, Parliament Bldg., Victoria, BC, Canada V8V 1X5.

Idaho Fish and Game Dept., P.O. Box 25, Boise, ID 83707.

Montana Dept. of Fish, Wildlife and Parks, 1420 E. Sixth, Helena, MT 59620.

Oregon Dept. of Fish and Wildlife, P.O. Box 59, Portland, OR 97207.

Washington Dept. of Wildlife, 600 N. Capitol Way, Olympia, WA 98504.

I still held to belief in persistence, so hunted many long, hard hours, climbing ridges, glassing carefully, still-hunting the thickets as silently as possible. The elk continued to elude me.

On the last evening of the season, Cal put me on an excellent stand. Although day was fading, there was still enough light to make out the details of that high mountain basin with its alpine meadow of lush grass. I grinned with the expectation that any moment a herd of elk could slip from the timber to feed.

Suddenly it happened!

I learned what you are now also learning, that realistic elk hunts aren't perfect.

But the results of one hunt prove nothing, and the hunter who expects to be successful will indeed follow the suggestions I outlined. Hunt good areas, gain expertise and experience, become a good shot, stay in top shape, and keep at it.

To further show the realities of elk hunting, I contacted the wildlife departments of Alberta, British Columbia, Idaho, Montana, Oregon and Washington, to obtain the latest data.

In 1985 British Columbia had the fewest hunters, 14,970, and they took 3,674 elk for a hunter success of 25 percent. Alberta sold 37,381 elk licenses and hunters took 3,330 elk, for a success of just under 9 percent. Idaho followed with total of 67,200 hunters, a harvest of 15,550, for a success of 23 percent. Montana was next with 86,443 hunters, a take of 18,478, and a success of over 21 percent. Washington had 82,200 hunters, who took 9,500 elk, for an average success of over 11 percent. Oregon was the top state in both number of hunters, at 133,676, and the harvest, at 20,371, for a hunter success near average, of just over 15 percent.

The totals for the six provinces and states are 421,870 elk hunters and a harvest of 70,903, for a combined hunter success of 16.8 percent.

Regardless of the numbers, elk hunting is one of the finest experiences available to those of us who live in the Northwest. Just being out and seeing all this magnificent scenery, sharing camp life with compatible friends, and escaping for a time the pressures of daily living, are worth the troubles. Add the opportunity to challenge those mountains and the weather, and to match wits with a superb game animal, and it is easy to see the figures are not the important part, but rather the chance to enjoy the entire experience of Northwest elk hunting.

By Mike Logan

Waterfowling

With two major flyways, the Pacific and the Central, vast water systems, and millions of acres of irrigated croplands, the Northwest is a tremendous waterfowl hunting area, a fact that often goes unnoticed in the shadow of its big game hunting.

Seasons are generally long and generous, in most regions running from October until mid-January. Fast-flowing rivers, saltwater estuaries and wind-lashed upland impoundments resist freezeup long after other areas of the country are locked in and their waterfowl migrated south. Despite the northern latitudes of most of this area, the temperate coastal climate proves suitable wintering areas for large numbers of ducks, geese and seabirds. The earliest seasons start in August in the marshes of Alaska and the last birds generally fall in mid-January in Washington and Oregon coastal regions.

The inventory of Northwest waterfowl runs long and thick, and includes some of the finest concentrations of premium puddle ducks to be found. The irrigated grainfields, with their attendant canals and reservoirs in the arid country between the coastal mountain ranges and the apron of the Rockies provide outstanding shooting for mallards, pintail and teal. Decoys early in the season, pit blinds carved into wheat fields when the ice comes. On the coast, snow geese, wigeon, mallards, divers and sea ducks take refuge from northern winds, piling into marshes, following the steelhead rivers upstream. What type of duck or goose appears over the bead of your shotgun usually depends on where and when you hunt.

Differences in size, shape, plumage patterns and colors, wing beat, flocking behavior, voice and habitat — all help to distinguish one species from another.

233

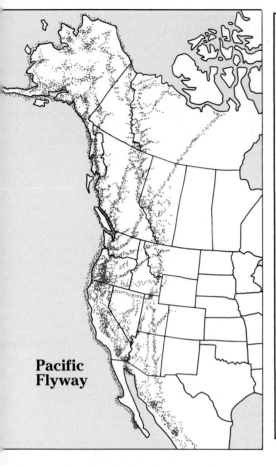

Pacific Flyway

HOW DUCKS RESPOND TO DECOYS

Species desired	Stools to	Other species attracted	Table fare	Decoy difficulty	Rig size (dozens)
Canvasback	self	divers	excellent	cautious	8
Pintail	self	dabblers	excellent	cautious	4
Goldeneye	self	redhead, ringneck	poor	easy	1
Mallard	self, dabblers	dabblers	excellent	cautious	4
Wigeon	self, dabblers	dabblers	good	cautious	4
Gadwall	self, dabblers	dabblers	good	cautious	4
Teal	dabblers	dabblers	excellent	easy	1
Wood duck	anything	probably none	excellent	seldom	1
Shoveler	dabblers	probably none	passable	easy	3
Redhead	most divers	ringneck	excellent	easy	4
Ringneck	anything	redhead	excellent	easy	1
Scaup	self, canvasback	divers	good	cautious	6
Coot	self, divers	wigeons	poor	seldom	3
Bufflehead	divers	probably none	poor	easy	2
Mergansers	divers	probably none	terrible	easy	1
Ruddy duck	self, divers	probably none	excellent	easy	1
Black duck	self	dabblers	excellent	cautious	4

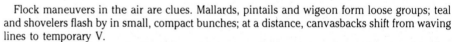

(Compiled by Idaho Fish and Game Dept.)

Flock maneuvers in the air are clues. Mallards, pintails and wigeon form loose groups; teal and shovelers flash by in small, compact bunches; at a distance, canvasbacks shift from waving lines to temporary V.

Closer up, individual silhouettes are important. Variations of head shapes and sizes, lengths of wings and tails, and fat bodies or slim can be seen.

Within shotgun range, color areas can be important. Light conditions might make them look different, but their size and location are positive keys. The sound of their wings can help as much as their calls. Flying goldeneyes make a whistling sound; wood ducks move with a swish; canvasbacks make a steady rushing sound. Not all ducks quack; many whistle, squeal or grunt.

Although not a hard and fast rule, different species tend to use different types of habitat. Puddle ducks like shallow marshes and creeks while divers prefer larger, deeper and more open waters.

Puddle Ducks

Puddle ducks are typically birds of fresh, shallow marshes and rivers rather than of large lakes and bays. They are good divers, but usually feed by dabbling or tipping rather than submerging.

The speculum, or colored wing patch, is generally iridescent and bright, and often a telltale field mark.

Any duck feeding in croplands will likely be a puddle duck, for most of this group are sure-footed and can walk and run well on land. Their diet is mostly vegetable, and grain-fed mallards or pintails or acorn-fattened wood ducks are highly regarded as food.

Diving Ducks

Diving ducks frequent the larger, deeper lakes and rivers, and coastal bays and inlets.

The colored wing patches of these birds lack the brilliance of the speculums of puddle ducks. Since many of them have short tails, their huge paddle feet may be used as rudders in flight, and are often visible on flying birds. When launching into flight, most of this group patter along the water before becoming airborne.

They feed by diving, often to considerable depths. To escape danger, they can travel great distances underwater, emerging only enough to show their head before submerging again.

Their diets of fish, shellfish, mollusks and aquatic plants make them second choice, as a group, for sportsmen. Canvasbacks and redheads fattened on eelgrass or wild celery are notable exceptions.

Since their wings are smaller in proportion to the size and weight of their bodies, they have a more rapid wing beat than puddle ducks.

Central Flyway

By Mike Logan

Comparative Sizes of Waterfowl

All birds on this page are drawn to the same scale.

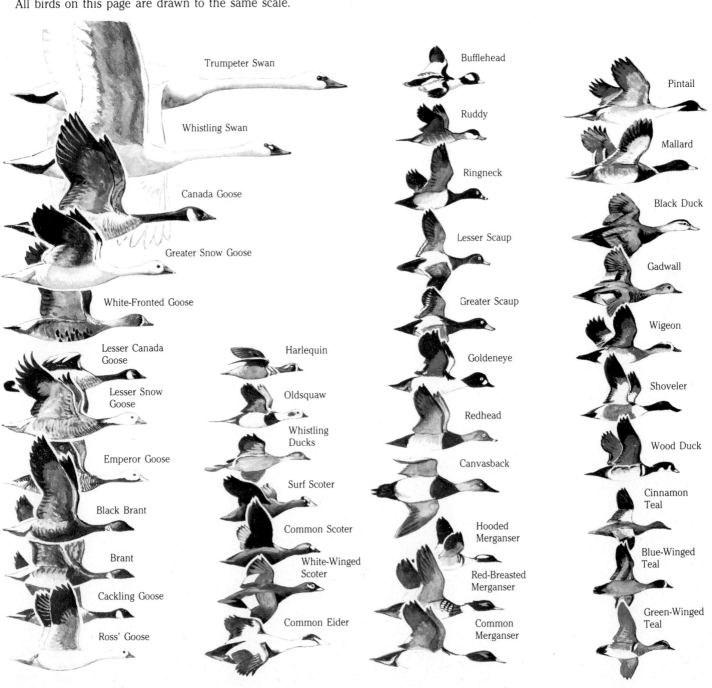

Trumpeter Swan

Whistling Swan

Canada Goose

Greater Snow Goose

White-Fronted Goose

Lesser Canada Goose

Lesser Snow Goose

Emperor Goose

Black Brant

Brant

Cackling Goose

Ross' Goose

Harlequin

Oldsquaw

Whistling Ducks

Surf Scoter

Common Scoter

White-Winged Scoter

Common Eider

Bufflehead

Ruddy

Ringneck

Lesser Scaup

Greater Scaup

Goldeneye

Redhead

Canvasback

Hooded Merganser

Red-Breasted Merganser

Common Merganser

Pintail

Mallard

Black Duck

Gadwall

Wigeon

Shoveler

Wood Duck

Cinnamon Teal

Blue-Winged Teal

Green-Winged Teal

Northwest Wildlife

Big Game

Moose: Moose are the world's largest member of the deer family. Three varieties are hunted in the Northwest, the **Shiras** found in Montana, Wyoming, Idaho and Washington; the **Canada** of British Columbia and Alberta; and the **Alaska moose.** The Alaska variety is the largest and the Shiras, also called Wyoming, the smallest. Bulls can weigh over 1,600 pounds, and stand 7½ feet at the shoulder. Cows average about 770 pounds. Moose coloration varies from dark brown to black. Other distinguishing features of both sexes are the broad bulbous nose, shoulder hump, and a loose fold of skin called a "bell" which hangs under the throat. Bulls have broad, palmated antlers that can measure as much as 6 feet from tip to tip, and together both may weigh up to 88 pounds.

Despite their bulk and ungainly appearance, moose can move through underbrush very

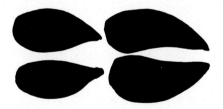

quietly. They have acute senses of smell and hearing, but sight is poor. The breeding rut usually occurs from mid-September to mid-October. Calves are born the following spring.

In Canada and Alaska moose are common in muskegs, brushy meadows and small groves of aspen or coniferous trees, particularly where such habitat adjoins lakes, ponds or streams. The Shiras is often found in high mountain meadows and elk parks. During the spring and summer, moose feed on aquatic plants and browse on the tender shoots of willow, birch and poplar. In the spring, moose also seek aspen bark, aquatic vegetation and minerals from natural salt licks. During the winter, moose browse near the edges of dense forests where there is less snow. In Washington, Idaho and Montana moose hunts are tightly regulated and the coveted licenses issued by drawing. Idaho restricts its licenses to residents only. The giant deer are more plentiful in Canada and Alaska and seasons are far more liberal.

By Mike Logan

Wildlife Illustrations courtesy Alberta Fish, Wildlife Division

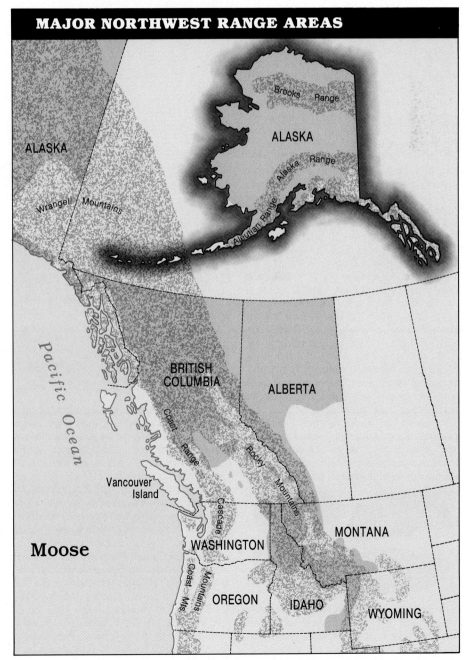

MAJOR NORTHWEST RANGE AREAS

Brooks Range

ALASKA

ALASKA

Wrangell Mountains

Alaska Range

Aleutian Range

Pacific Ocean

BRITISH COLUMBIA

ALBERTA

Coast Range

Rocky Mountains

Vancouver Island

Cascade

Moose

Coast Mts.

WASHINGTON

MONTANA

Mountains

OREGON

IDAHO

WYOMING

MAJOR NORTHWEST RANGE AREAS

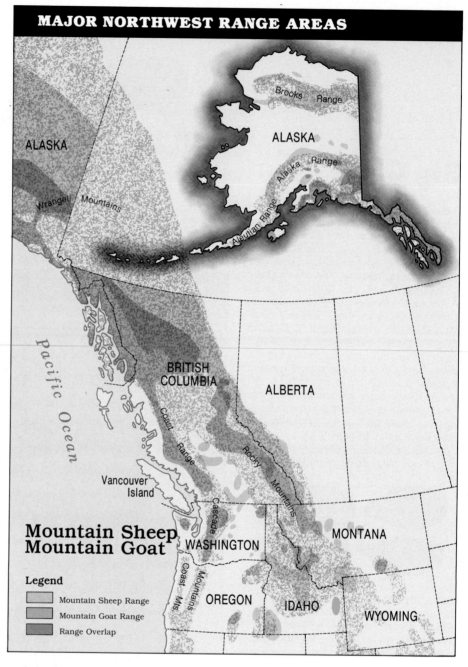

ALASKA

Brooks Range

ALASKA

Wrangell Mountains

Alaska Range

Aleutian Range

Pacific Ocean

BRITISH COLUMBIA

ALBERTA

Coast Range

Rocky Mountains

Vancouver Island

Cascade

Mountain Sheep
Mountain Goat

WASHINGTON

Coast Mts.

MONTANA

Legend

Mountain Sheep Range

Mountain Goat Range

Range Overlap

OREGON

IDAHO

WYOMING

Mountain Goat: Mountain goats are the only true North American relative of the antelope family. They have short, stocky bodies, rarely exceeding 4 feet at the top of the back, and creamy-white hair. Long guard hairs over the shoulders give it a hump-backed appearance. They have full white beard or chin hairs, black nose and pointed black horns 6 to 12 inches long. Their hooves are uniquely rounded, with hard outer edges for support and soft inner core for traction. Goats are slow-moving, but incredibly agile. Few hunters are willing to follow in a goats track. Both sexes have horns, but the females are generally more slender. Average males, called "billies," weigh from 190 to 300 pounds and the females, or "nannies" about the same. Older animals tend to have a yellowish cast to their hair, which they shed in summer. Hunters after long-bearded trophies wait until late in the season, generally the end of October.

Goats are found in the Rocky, Cascade and Coast mountains, plus the coastal ranges of Alaska. The biggest concentrations are in the steep Pacific front mountains including the Cascade Range of Washington and Coast Mountains of British Columbia, extending to the Alaskan ranges. They are also hunted in the Rockies of Alberta, Montana and Idaho. Successful efforts are under way to establish herds in eastern Oregon, primarily with goats transplanted from Washington.

Preferring high, windswept peaks and cliffs, goats feed on grass, lichens, sedges and forbs, and browse on dwarf willow and subalpine fir. Goats are powerful climbers and can cross difficult terrain with apparent ease. Their agility

is mainly due to the construction of their hoofs. These have soft bottom pads which are surrounded by a hard outer shell. Unlike other cloven-hoofed animals, the two parts of the

goat's hoof can move independently of each other. These features enable goats to grip rough and slippery surfaces when climbing. The rut occurs from November to December. Young (known as kids) are born the following spring. Goats remain in or near alpine areas throughout the year, moving only in winter to south and southwest facing slopes or to wind-swept ridges where snow cover is minimal. Mountain goats rarely venture to lower elevations except to visit salt or mineral licks.

Mountain Sheep: The Northwest is blessed with two species of mountain sheep, identified separately as bighorns and thinhorns. The bighorns include **Rocky Mountain, California** and **desert sheep.** Their horns are massive, tightly curled and usually broomed. Most sheep hunted from central British Columbia south are Rocky Mountain or

California bighorns. The thinhorns include **Dall** and **Stone sheep,** which graze the mountains north of the bighorn range from northern British Columbia into Alaska. Dall and Stone sheep are lighter colored and their horns are generally more delicately shaped, sweeping up and away from the animals head ending in a point. Horn brooming is not as common among thinhorns as bighorns.

Rocky Mountain bighorn sheep are the largest of all North American wild sheep. Adult rams weigh up to 300 pounds, ewes about 150 pounds. The short-haired coats are brown to grayish brown with light underparts, a white muzzle and distinctive white rump. Bighorns prefer rocky, rugged open country, either alpine or desert, where their acute eyesight can detect the slightest motion more than a mile distant.

Hooves of a sheep have a hard outer rim with soft centers providing excellent footing on the precarious ledges, although they are not as agile or as sure-footed as mountain goats. They can,

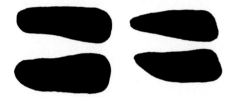

however, move quickly across the rough terrain. They are primarily grazers feeding on grass and forbs. During the heat of summer bighorns are found at the highest elevations in their range, rams and ewes grazing in separate herds. In winter they migrate to lowlands or southwest slopes where there is less snow. The rut occurs from November to December when the rams stage their classic head-banging battles for herd superiority. Sheep are hunted in all Northwest states and provinces. In Washington, Oregon, Idaho and most of Montana licenses are awarded on a drawing system. Montana has the only unlimited bighorn seasons remaining in the Lower 48. Alberta is becoming one of the most popular areas for trophy-sized bighorns, especially in the archery areas on the east slope of the Rocky Mountains.

Thinhorns dominate the northern country. The Stikine and Skeena river regions of northern British Columbia offer the finest Stone sheep hunting in North America. There are about 20,000 Stone sheep, all concentrated in the mountains of southern Yukon and extreme northern British Columbia. A cousin of the Dall, Stones are dark-colored sheep with white on the face and belly. Their horns are lighter colored than a bighorns but darker than the yellowish hue of a Dall. Stone sheep are slightly larger than Dalls, with a mature ram weighing about 250 pounds. Large Dalls weigh about 200 pounds. Both varieties are a little over 3 feet high at the shoulder, considerbly shorter than most novice hunters expect. Because of their restricted range, Stone sheep are one of the rarest trophies in North America.

Dall sheep, the only all-white sheep, live the high mountains of Alaska, Yukon, Northwest Territories and a small corner of northwestern

British Columbia. Approximatley 50,000 Dalls live in Alaska, more than any other hunting region. Their flared, yellow horns attract hunters from around the world, with an annual Alaskan harvest of about 1,200. Toward the southern edge of their range, some Dalls tend to have grayish saddle marks, producing a coloration halfway between Dall-white and Stone-brown. These sheep are called **Fannins** but are not recognized as a separate species.

Mule Deer: Mule deer get their name from their large, mulelike ears, and are the dominant deer of the high mountain and arid regions in the Northwest, east of the crest of the Cascade Range. Grayish brown in winter and reddish brown in summer, muleys are slightly larger than Western white-tailed deer. Mature bucks average about 220 pounds and does about 155 pounds.

Mule deer can be identified by their tails and antlers. The thin, brown tail has a black tip and is surrounded by a white rump patch. Where

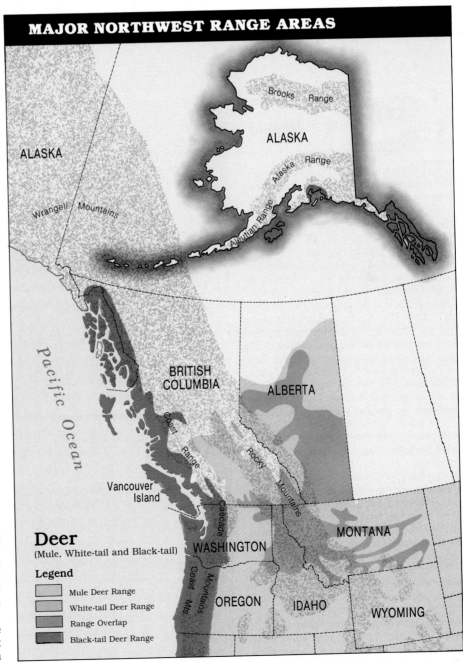

MAJOR NORTHWEST RANGE AREAS

Brooks Range

ALASKA

ALASKA

Alaska Range

Wrangell Mountains

Aleutian Range

Pacific Ocean

BRITISH COLUMBIA

ALBERTA

Coast Range

Rocky Mountains

Vancouver Island

Cascade Range

MONTANA

WASHINGTON

Deer
(Mule, White-tail and Black-tail)

Legend

	Mule Deer Range
	White-tail Deer Range
	Range Overlap
	Black-tail Deer Range

Coast Mts.

OREGON

IDAHO

WYOMING

239

whitetail antlers rise from a single beam, mule deer antlers expand in a series of Y forks, each tine dividing into another fork. They have acute senses of smell, sight and hearing. However, unlike the nervous, easily spooked whitetail, mule deer are often inquisitive. When jumped by hunters they sometimes stop for a last look before bounding out of sight. They exhibit a distinct, stiff-legged, pogo bounce when running.

There is ample evidence, however, that hunting pressure is forcing the mule deer to evolve the same wary senses as the whitetail, hiding instead of bolting into the open, sticking to cover, slipping secretly between hunters. The rut usually occurs in November, the bucks developing extremely swollen necks, and combative dispositions that blunt their natural suspicions. One or two spotted fawns are born to each doe in May or June.

A coastal cousin of the mule deer, **blacktail** are the dominant deer from the crest of the Cascade mountain range west to the Pacific. A biological cousin of the muley, blacktails combine many of the physical characteristics

of mule deer with the wary, secretiveness of the whitetail. The combination often makes them the most difficult deer to hunt.

Blacktails are smaller and stouter than mule deer, rarely exceeding 220 pounds. Does frequently weigh less than 100 pounds, and most bucks less than 175 pounds. They have a short, blunt nose, and distinctive wide white-and-black tail that more closely resembles the flag of a whitetail than the rope of a mule deer. Blacktails favor hilly country, thick with brush and timber. They have a maddening tendency to freeze statuelike until danger passes, or to slink into warrens better suited for large rabbits than small deer. The coast of northern California, Oregon, Washington, British Columbia and southeastern Alaska is the only area in the world where these deer are found. They can be found on the east slope of the Cascade Range, but do not extend their range into the arid prairie country beyond the foothills.

White-tailed Deer: The white-tailed deer's coloration changes from reddish brown in summer to grayish brown in winter. Western white-tailed deer are slightly smaller than mule deer. Bucks average about 170 pounds, does about 130. The largest whitetails are in the Midwest and East, and although the Northwest produces some very large animals, they are not regarded as trophy class.

White-tailed deer antlers have unbranched tines extending up from single beams. The broad flaglike tail is brown, fringed with white, and solid white underneath. When running, the tail is held erect, exposing its white underside. Whitetails possess excellent senses of sight, smell and hearing. They are extremely wary,

and when alarmed move rapidly, in smooth graceful bounds. The rut, or mating season, usually occurs in November. One or two

spotted fawns are born to each doe the following spring.

Whitetails are found in the wooded river flats and coulees of the prairies, inroading into mule deer range. Most of the prairie river bottoms in Montana and the broken edge country of northwestern Montana, northern Idaho and northeastern Oregon is dominated by whitetails. They are also found in extreme southern British Columbia and Alberta. Their range is expanding into former mule deer country throughout its range. They generally browse on brush and shrubs.

Caribou: Except for a remnant herd of 100 or so woodland caribou that range the high country of the Selkirk Mountains at the common border of Washington, Idaho and British Columbia, caribou exist only in the Canadian and Alaskan reaches of the North-

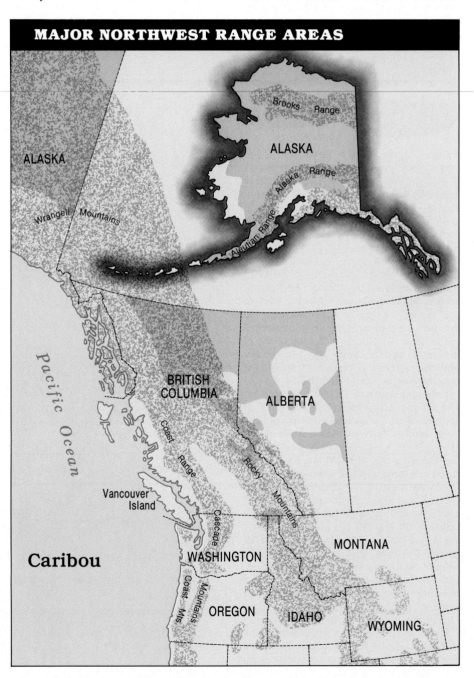

MAJOR NORTHWEST RANGE AREAS

Caribou

240

European settlers, who compared the animals to the moose of their homelands, which were called elk. North American elk are more accurately called wapiti — the Shawnee word for "white rump." This description refers to the prominent, cream-colored rump patch. There are two races of wapiti in the Northwest, the Yellowstone or Rocky Mountain and the Roosevelt also called Olympic. Yellowstone dominate from the Cascade Range east, while the Roosevelts are found in the dense rain forests along the Pacific coast. Elk are tan bodied, with a long dark brown mane over the head, neck and front legs. Bulls can weigh up to 1,500 pounds although most are between 500 and 700 pounds. The antlers of a mature bull are massive, carrying a single beam, with five to seven white-tipped tines. Immature bulls carry spikes or spindly 3-points. These antlers are used during the rut when bulls challenge each other for possession of cows. The elk is the only member of the deer family that collects a harem. The rut usually lasts through

west. The Selkirk herd is believed to be the southernmost herd in North America. British Columbia's southernmost herd, excluding the Selkirk animals, is in the Columbia Mountains north of Revelstoke above Highway 1. The farther north, the more abundant caribou become. They have been fully protected in Alberta since 1980. Bulls carry high, slightly palmated antlers that sweep back from the head, and then arc forward. One or two brow tines, called "shovels," extend over the face. Right and left antlers are usually different from each other and measure up to 4 feet long. Many

cows also carry antlers, generally much thinner and shorter than those of bulls. Caribou have wide hooves which enable them to travel easily over snow and soft ground. The rut occurs in mid-September. Calves are born the following May or June. Caribous are highly migratory, continually moving cross-country.

There are 13 subspecies of caribou. The animals are brown bodied, with a white neck, tail and rump. Woodland bulls average between 250 and 450 pounds, while cows are considerably smaller.

Another race, the mountain caribou, is generally larger, darker and has heavier antlers than woodlands. In Alberta, mountain caribou are now confined to the northern portion of Jasper National Park, Willmore Wilderness Park and its adjacent foothills.

A third subspecies, the barren ground caribou, is the smallest of the races, although mature bulls generally weigh between 350 and 400 pounds. It is an arctic animal and the dominant caribou of Alaska. It only enters forest in winter after migrating from the barren lands of the Arctic.

Elk: The large sweeping antlers on the dark brown head of a bull elk, sometimes reaching more than 6 feet long, distinguish it from all other deer. The name elk originated with early

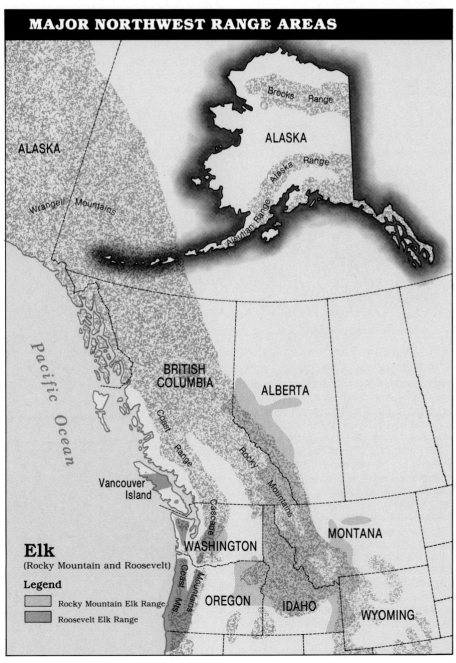

MAJOR NORTHWEST RANGE AREAS

Brooks Range

ALASKA

ALASKA

Alaska Range

Wrangell Mountains

Aleutian Range

Pacific Ocean

BRITISH COLUMBIA

ALBERTA

Coast Range

Rocky Mountains

Vancouver Island

Cascade Mountains

MONTANA

Coast Mts.

WASHINGTON

Elk
(Rocky Mountain and Roosevelt)

Legend

▢ Rocky Mountain Elk Range
▢ Roosevelt Elk Range

OREGON

IDAHO

WYOMING

September with spotted calves born the following spring.

Elk prefer areas of woodland mixed with open grassland. Such habitat is found at forest edges and in mountain meadows. Elk usually graze on forbs and grasses, although they will browse on aspen bark and twigs in winter when

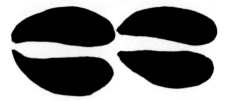

food is scarce. These animals are found mainly in the foothills and mountains, although they were originally prairie animals. They migrate seasonally from summer ranges high in the mountains to winter ranges in lower mountain valleys and foothills.

Pronghorn (Antelope): The pronghorn, the only North American horned animal that annually sheds its horns, is not a true antelope, but a unique North American species without equal anywhere else in the world. True antelope have permanent, unbranched horns. Those of the American pronghorn are branched

or pronged, and they are not permanent. The outer sheath or "horn," composed mainly of hair, is shed every fall. Both sexes have horns, but those of the does are much smaller.

Pronghorn are prairie animals able to run at speeds of 70 mph, the fastest game animal in North America. They represent one of the greatest success stories of North American conservation. When Columbus landed on the East Coast of the continent in 1492 it was estimated that more than 40 million pronghorns roamed the West. By 1925 only 25,000 pronghorns survived, their ranks descimated by the same wastrels, market hunters, and competing domestic livestock that nearly killed off the American bison. Today there are more than 500,000 pronghorns, and in the Northwest only Alaska, British Columbia and Washington do not offer hunting seasons. Wyoming is by far the best antelope hunting state with success running more than 90 percent. Eastern Montana is the best region in the Northwest.

Pronghorns are generally tan in color, with two white bars across the throat, and additional white markings on the rump, lower sides and underparts. When alarmed, pronghorns erect the long, white hairs on the rump, making it highly visible. Average weight for both sexes is about 110 pounds.

The rut occurs from August through September, and kids, usually twins, are born the following spring. Pronghorns are found in the open prairie, and grasslands where sagebrush and forbs form the majority of their diet. They have excellent long-range vision, and are incredibly curious animals.

Bison (Buffalo): Bison, once nearly eradicated, are hunted in a few Western states, including depredation hunts in Montana near Yellowstone National Park, and special herd reduction hunts in Arizona, South Dakota,

Utah, Colorado, the Delta Junction region of Alaska, and the Northwest Territories. Private ranches also sell buffalo hunts in Wyoming, Oregon, Arizona and South Dakota. They are massive animals. Bulls weigh up to a ton and cows to 1,200 pounds.

The impressive head and shoulders of the bison are covered by a blanket of thick, shaggy hair that extends down the forelegs. Short, black, curved horns are present on both sexes. There are two races of bison, or "buffalo" as they are commonly but erroneously called. American bison are not related to the true buffalo of Asia. The name appears to have been imposed by French voyageurs who described them as "les boeufs," which translates to beef or steer.

The largest of the two species are the nearly black wood bison of northern Alberta and the

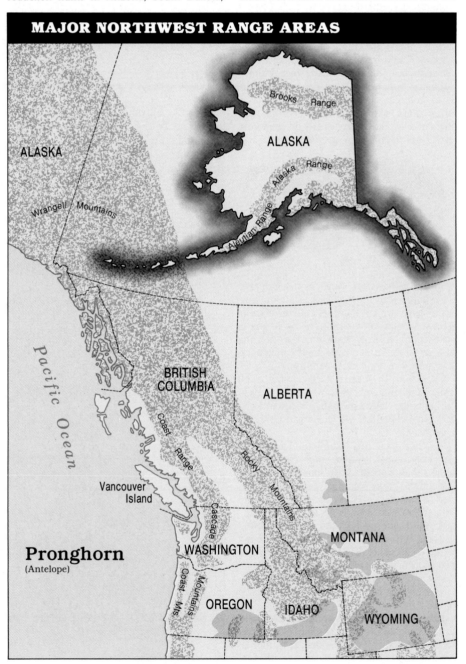

MAJOR NORTHWEST RANGE AREAS

Brooks Range
ALASKA
ALASKA
Alaska Range
Wrangell Mountains
Aleutian Range

Pacific Ocean

BRITISH COLUMBIA
ALBERTA
Coast Range
Rocky Mountains

Vancouver Island

Cascade Mountains

Pronghorn
(Antelope)

WASHINGTON
MONTANA
Coast Mts.
OREGON
IDAHO
WYOMING

wood bison is native to the northern mixed-wood zone. The Plains bison is mainly a grasslands animal. Originally distributed over much of the West, bison may now be seen in parks. Some small herds are raised commercially on private ranches. It has been estimated that between 30 and 60 million bison once roamed the plains country. Today, the combined herds are estimated at between 30,000 and 50,000 animals.

Large Carnivores

Wolf: Wolves are the largest of the wild dog family, and may weigh up to 130 pounds, rarely larger. The fur is commonly gray with dark shading, but varies from near black to almost white. Coats are long and dense, and ears are thickly furred. Large feet aid in traveling over snow. The wolf is distinguished from the coyote by its larger size, broader face and less pointed muzzle.

Wolves are social animals found in packs numbering from two to over 20. Mating usually occurs in February or March. In May, the female retires to a well-hidden den and gives birth to a litter of five to seven pups. Both

Northwest Territories. Wood bison bulls frequently exceed 2,500 pounds. Some have been weighed at 3,000 pounds, earning the wood bison the title of world's largest hooved animal. The more common Plains bison is slightly smaller, but still extremely formidable. They can measure 6 feet high at the shoulder, up to 11 feet long, and weigh a ton. They are generally lighter colored than the wood variety and prefer the open plains and sagebrush prairie country. Despite their bulk, bison are agile and can reach speeds of 30 mph.

The rut occurs from July to September and the calves are born nine months later. The

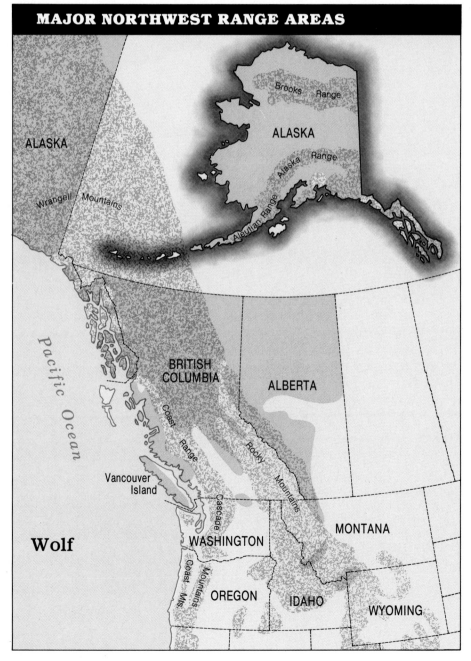

MAJOR NORTHWEST RANGE AREAS

parents, as well as other members of the pack, bring food to the young until they are about 4 months old and ready to participate in hunts. Moose, deer, elk and caribou are the main food of wolves, but their diet may include beaver, hares, fish and some plant material.

In North America, wolves once ranged from Mexico to the high Arctic. As the continent was settled, their range was greatly restricted, and numbers declined substantially. In the Northwest states wolves are rare, and the majority are reported in Montana. Occasionally a wolf will be reported in Idaho and Washington. They are extinct in Oregon. Wolves are plentiful in the mountain forests of British Columbia, Alberta and Alaska.

Coyote: In size, coyotes are between the wolf and fox — adults weighing 22 to 50 pounds. They are usually gray to reddish gray with black markings on the back and tail. Underparts are light. Ears are long and the

a coat of dense fur, long legs and a pointed nose. The fluffy tail is as long as the body and tipped with white. Although normally reddish in color, there are two other common color phases — cross and silver. The cross fox is

generally red with black markings on the back that form a patch or cross. The silver fox is black with white-tipped hairs. All three color phases may occur in a single litter.

Mating occurs in March. In May, four to nine pups are born in a den. Family units hunt together until fall, but throughout the winter foxes are generally solitary. Primarily a "mouser," a fox eats other small mammals, as

muzzle is slender and pointed. The tail is bushy and is usually carried low and close to the hind legs. Coyotes mate in February or March. For a den the female enlarges a rodent, rabbit or badger hole. Young are born in April or May in litters of five to seven pups. Both parents help feed the young until they are about two months

old. The family unit then leaves the den and hunts together until fall, when the group splits up, with individuals hunting alone or in pairs. Coyotes seldom hunt in packs, but occasionally several may gather at carcasses or other communal feeding sites.

Nighttime coyote howling can be heard nearly everywhere in the Northwest, ranging from residential neighborhoods in urban Seattle, to the Arctic. Coyotes are opportunists. Hares and mice are the most important prey species, but the carrion of livestock and other large mammals is often the most important food source in some areas, especially in winter. Blueberries and other fruits are also used.

Long considered a pest by many landowners, the coyote has thrived despite repeated attempts to eliminate it. Today, it is still the most numerous member of the wild dog family. According to Indian legend, coyotes will survive long after mankind. They are hunted, often by calling, and trapped primarily for their pelts.

Red Fox: The red fox is the smallest native member of the dog family; adults weigh from 7 to 11 pounds. It has a slim, graceful build,

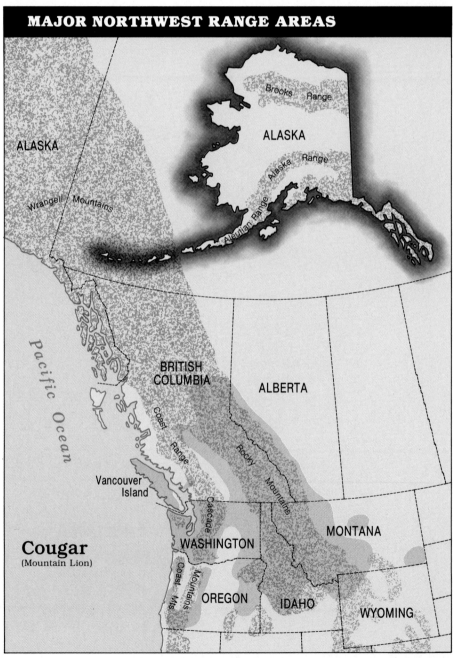

MAJOR NORTHWEST RANGE AREAS

Brooks Range

ALASKA

ALASKA

Wrangell Mountains

Aleutian Range

Alaska Range

Pacific Ocean

BRITISH COLUMBIA

ALBERTA

Coast Range

Rocky Mountains

Vancouver Island

Cascade Mountains

WASHINGTON

MONTANA

Cougar
(Mountain Lion)

Coast Mts.

OREGON

IDAHO

WYOMING

well as birds, eggs, insects, grass and fruit. Since the red fox is a wary animal and hunts at night, it is seldom seen. It is a fairly common resident of the mixed-wood and foothills ranging north to southeastern Alaska and south to Mexico. Areas of patchy bush interspersed with openings are its preferred habitat. Fox are not as common in the West as the Midwest and East regions.

Cougar: Cougars are the largest of North America's wild cats. Adult males average from 140 to 160 pounds and females weigh from 90 to 110 pounds. From nose to tip of tail, a large cougar may be as long as 10 feet. Adults vary in color from yellow through reddish brown to gray, with a light belly, chin and throat. They have short black ears and a long, rounded tail tipped with black.

Cougars, often called mountain lion or panther, do not have a specific breeding season. Although most kittens are born in late winter or midsummer, young can be produced at any time. Two to four kittens are born in a well-hidden den, commonly a cave. The female

raises the young, the kittens remaining with her for about a year. Deer are the cougar's main food, but it also takes other large game animals, as well as small rodents, hares and birds.

This alert, secretive animal hunts mostly at night and is rarely seen. It is rarely found far from dense cover. In the Northwest cougars occur mainly in the mountains and foothill zones. They range as far north as central British Columbia, and the largest concentration is found on Vancouver Island.

Lynx: Lynxes are about half the length of cougars and weigh 18 to 30 pounds. It is higher at the rump than the shoulder giving it a sloped appearance. The long dense fur is frosted-gray in color with a few dark spots. They have tufted ears, and a black tip on the short tail. Mating takes place in March, and three to four kittens are born in May. The den is usually a rock cavity hidden in dense spruce woods. Food is brought to the den until the kittens are two to three months old. At that time they join their parents in hunts. The lynx is highly dependent upon the snowshoe hare for food. When hares are scarce, lynx are forced to travel great distances in search of alternative foods. At this time they may take rodents, birds, carrion, deer fawns or lambs of mountain sheep.

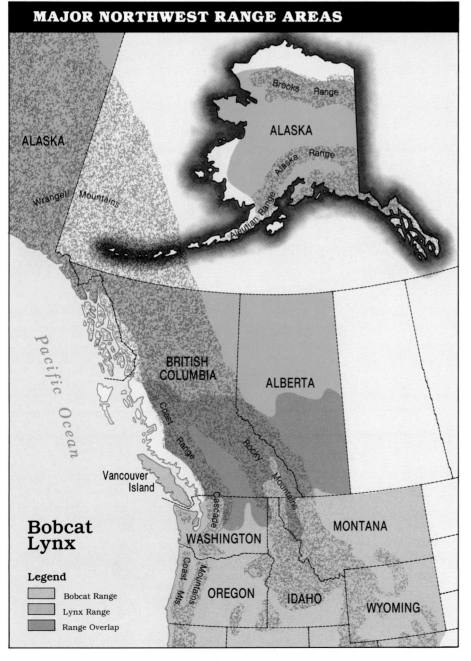

MAJOR NORTHWEST RANGE AREAS

Brooks Range

ALASKA

ALASKA

Wrangell Mountains

Aleutian Range   Alaska Range

Pacific Ocean

BRITISH COLUMBIA

ALBERTA

Coast Range

Rocky Mountains

Vancouver Island

Cascade Mountains

MONTANA

Bobcat Lynx

WASHINGTON

Coast Mts.

Coast Mountains

OREGON

IDAHO

WYOMING

Legend

	Bobcat Range
	Lynx Range
	Range Overlap

Lynx prefer forest with a thick undercover of shrubs and deadfall. They are common in mixed-wood foothills and mountains. A few lynx roam Washington, Idaho and Montana but the majority are north of the Canadian border.

Bobcat: The bobcat is very similar to the lynx and may easily be confused with it. Generally, the bobcat is smaller and more slender than the lynx. A bobcat weighs from 15 to 25 pounds. The coat is brownish with well-marked dark bars. Its feet are smaller than those of the lynx and its ear tufts and chin ruffs are much reduced. The tail is slightly longer and is marked by several dark bands.

Adults mate in February or March, and litters of two to four kittens are born in April or May. Dens are often natural cavities like a hollow log in a secluded thicket. Although excluded from the den when the young are born, the male sometimes brings food after the kittens are weaned. Kittens remain with the female until midwinter when they leave to hunt on

while the sow is in winter hibernation. Cubs are tiny at birth, 9 to 12 ounces, but grow rapidly, and weigh about 5 pounds by the time they emerge from the den in April. Boars do not share in the raising of young, and may attack and devour their own progeny. Cubs

remain with the sow, sharing the den during the second winter. The following spring the cubs leave to forage on their own. Except during the breeding season, and sows with cubs, black bears are basically solitary. They will attack man if provoked or defending cubs

their own. Otherwise, bobcats are solitary hunters. Hares and rabbits make up the bulk of their diet followed by various rodents, insects and some vegetation. They may also take pronghorn kids in spring and ealy summer.

Bobcats are found throughout a wide area of the western United States, extending into Alaska. Unlike the deep forest preference of lynx, bobcats prefer dry regions with sparse woods, open rocky hillsides, and brushy coulees.They respond well to predator calls, and are highly prized for their fur.

Black Bear: The black bear's long hair varies from shiny black to blond, and brown is a common color phase. Adult males or boars weigh from 200 to 500 pounds, and adult females or sows weigh from 100 to 300 pounds. In contrast with the grizzly, the facial profile is a straight line and black bears lack a pronounced shoulder hump. The claws of the feet are shorter than the grizzly's and make less of an imprint in tracks. They are also much more numerous in the Lower 48 states, especially in Washington, Idaho and Montana, where good numbers can be found in nearly every wooded, mountainous area.

Black bears reach breeding maturity at 3½ years, mating in June and July. However, development of the embryo is delayed until the fall. One to four cubs are born in February

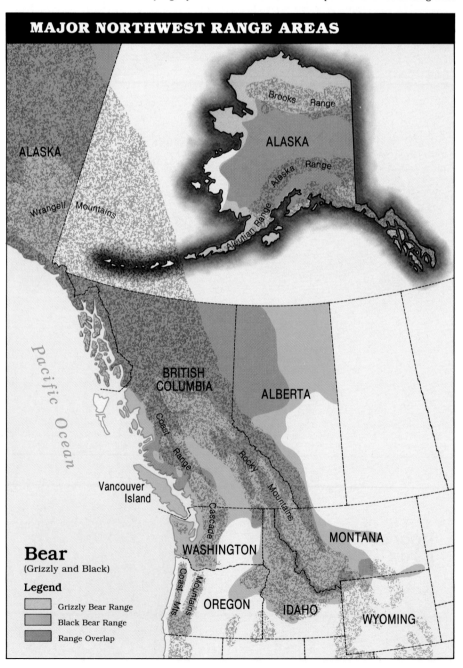

MAJOR NORTHWEST RANGE AREAS

Bear
(Grizzly and Black)

Legend
- Grizzly Bear Range
- Black Bear Range
- Range Overlap

but are generally shy and will flee whenever possible.

The diet of black bears may include leaves, berries and roots, as well as fish, mice, ground squirrels, or young deer, ants, honeybee grubs and honey. They also scavenge on carrion and human refuse. Black bears are common in open forests throughout the mixed-wood foothills and timbered mountains.

Grizzly Bear: The grizzly bear is the largest and most powerful of the carnivores, common in the mountainous regions of British Columbia, Alberta and throughout Alaska, but rare in the Lower 48 states. Adults weigh from 300 to 1,000 pounds; sows average about 110 pounds lighter than boars. Grizzlies vary in color from tawny brown to black. Often the hair is sun-bleached giving it a "grizzled" appearance. In profile, the snout rises sharply into a broad "dished" face. There is a hump

of long hair on the neck and shoulders. However, this hair may be shed for a period in late spring and summer. Claws are long, curved and obvious in tracks.

Grizzly bears reach breeding maturity by the age of six or seven years. Like black bears, they mate in June or July, and the embryo does not develop until fall when bears den up for their winter dormancy. One or two cubs are born during the winter. At birth cubs weigh only 12 to 24 ounces, but grow rapidly to about 33 pounds by the time they leave the den in April. The sow aggressively protects her cubs from all real or possible threats, including grizzly boars which may attack and kill undefended cubs. Cubs remain with sows through the second winter, but leave her before she mates again.

Like black bears, grizzly bears are omnivorous (eat both plants and animals). The diet of a grizzly bear includes roots, grasses, berries, insects, fish, ground squirrels and mice. They readily eat carrion, and occasionally kill deer, moose, elk or even black bears.

Grizzly bears prefer open country, and are found in the foothill, mountain and alpine zones. They once occupied the prairie and parkland regions, but settlers eliminated the species from most of the areas. The largest concentration in the Lower 48 is in Yellowstone and Glacier national parks. Remnant populations are found throughout the Rockies in northern Montana, with a few grizzlies reported in the Selkirk Mountains of Idaho and Washington, and the northern Cascades of Washington.

Grizzlies are neither rare nor endangered in Canada. In recent years their numbers have been increasing as a result of restricted hunting seasons. The Alaskan brown bear (Kodiak), is the largest subspecies of grizzlies. Various subspecies of grizzlies can be found from sea level to above treeline in the mountains.

Fur Animals

Small Weasels (Ermine): The **least weasel** is the smallest living carnivore, preying throughout the Northwest from the mountains to the plains. The least weasel is one of the

predators most beneficial to man, preying on moles, mice and shrews. They also eat insects. In winter, they are completely white. They may give birth to three to five young during any month of the year. The short-tailed weasel's smaller size, white feet and northern distribution distinguishes it from the **long-tailed weasel.** Mating usually occurs in July or August and four to eight young usually arrive in April or May. The long-tailed weasel inhabits grasslands and prairies. Although its range includes the United States and Mexico, only northern populations turn white in winter when they are recognized as ermine.

River Otter: The most aquatic of "land" mammals, the otter is well adapted to fishing in cold northern waters, with webbed feet, a

thick layer of insulating fat under short, dense fur. They are relatively common along the coast and in some foothill rivers of the Rockies. In the winter their tracks may be found along frozen streambeds where they search for ice-free holes to hunt fish, clams and other aquatic animals. River otters may be 4½ feet long and weigh 25 pounds. Because of their size

and habits, otters have few natural enemies. Mating usually occurs in February; one to four kits are born in late April, often in an abandoned muskrat den.

Fisher: Although known as "fisher cat," "Pennant's cat" and "Pecan," this animal does not fish nor is it a cat. The Chippewa Indians knew it best and called it "Tha-cho" or "Big Marten." Both marten and fisher live in the same areas and are similar in appearance. The fisher is darker and larger than the marten, reaching 12 pounds and 35 to 50 inches in length. It is possibly the swiftest and most agile of the weasel family. While the marten can overtake the red squirrel, the fisher can overtake the marten and can outrun the snowshoe hare. Their diet varies from small birds, rodents, lynx, fox, raccoon and porcupine to young deer and bighorn sheep. They are nocturnal hunters and are active all year. Due to their agility, both on the ground and in trees, fisher have virtually no natural enemies. Mating occurs in April, a week after the female has given birth to two or three young.

Mink: The mink is a semiaquatic weasel, valued for its fur, that dines on muskrat, fish, ducks and other small birds and rodents. It hunts at night and is seldom seen far from watercourses in the mixed-wood, foothills and prairies. Mink weigh about 2 pounds and are up to 30 inches long. Mink use musk to mark their territory; although the musk smells worse than that of a skunk, it cannot be sprayed for defense. Mating generally occurs in March and five to six young are born in May, usually in an abandoned muskrat den.

Marten: The marten is the most arboreal member of the weasel family, spending much of its time hunting in trees. Its long, bushy tail and distinctive buff chest patch allow easy identification. Marten reach a weight of 3½ pounds and average 25 to 30 inches in length. They live in the wooded foothills and densely timbered mountains, and may travel for miles without touching the ground. They commonly hunt for red squirrels and can match their prey's every move in a high-speed treetop chase. They also eat rodents, grouse, insects, eggs and occasionally nuts or fruits. The marten's only natural enemies are the equally

agile fisher as well as lynx, great-horned owls and wolves. Mating occurs in July or August and litters of three or four young arrive the following March or April.

Black-footed Ferret: These large weasels are now one of the rarest of North American mammals. Twenty-four inches long and weighing 2 pounds, they have a buff body, black feet and a black face mask. The ferret is dependent upon prairie dog colonies for food and shelter. The extinction of the prairie dog in areas led to the extinction of the black-footed ferret, in the same areas. A few ferrets are found in Wyoming, Montana, Idaho, Washington, Oregon and Alberta.

Rodents

Woodchuck (Groundhog): The woodchuck is a member of a group of large ground-dwelling squirrels, called marmots. Marmots have robust bodies with broad heads, short powerful legs, strong flattened and curved claws, and tails that are about one-fourth the length of the body. The dense, woolly fur of the woodchuck is a grizzled dark brown on the upperparts, and reddish brown on the underparts. The bushy tail is dark brown to black. Adult woodchucks weigh about 7 pounds.

The woodchuck is usually a solitary animal, although pairs may share the same underground den in summer. Mating occurs in March and April. Litters of four to five young are born in May. Young emerge from their burrows in late June and are weaned shortly afterward. Woodchucks usually enter hibernation in late September.

Woodchucks eat green vegetation, insects, and young ground nesting birds. Woodchucks occur in the mixed-wood, parkland and foothills east of the Rocky Mountains where woodlots are broken by pastures and meadows.

Hoary Marmot (Whistler): The hoary marmot is the largest of the marmots, weighing about 13 pounds. The fur of the upperparts is grizzled gray and brown, and the underparts are gray. Hoary marmots live in colonies depending on mutual protection from predators. If one member of the colony detects danger it will give a long, shrill whistle which is passed along by other members of the colony. After the warning the entire colony disappears into rocky burrows. The chief predators of this large rodent are golden eagles,

and grizzly and black bears. Grizzly bears occasionally tear up a portion of a rock slide in search of marmots hiding in their burrows. Mating occurs soon after emergence from hibernation in May. Litters of four to five young are born in June, and the young marmots emerge from their burrows in late July. Hoary marmots enter hibernation in late August.

Hoary marmots eat a variety of green vegetation in alpine meadows. They occur almost exclusively in the high mountain, alpine regions.

Yellow-bellied Marmot (Rockchuck): The yellow-bellied marmot is similar in size to the eastern woodchuck, fabled for its winter-spring prognostications. The fur of the upperparts is grizzled buff brown in color, and the underparts are brownish yellow. The bushy tail

is grizzled brown. Yellow-bellied marmots are more colonial than woodchucks. Many family groups may live together in their rocky burrows. Mating occurs after emergence from hibernation in April. Litters of four to five young are born in May. These marmots enter hibernation in mid-August.

Yellow-bellied marmots eat green vegetation that grows on or near their rock habit. They live at low elevations in talus slopes on mountainsides, and in rock piles under cliffs.

Snowshoe Hare (Varying hare): The snowshoe hare is the most widely distributed lagomorph, occupying all forested regions from treeline in the Arctic to the treed coulees and river bottoms of the prairies. Adults weigh about 3½ pounds. The snowshoe hare has exceptionally broad hind feet, and large ears. In summer, its fur is grizzled reddish or grayish brown on the upperparts, and white on the underparts. In winter, its coat turns completely white, except for black on the tips of the ears. The large hind feet develop thick, stiff hairs that

that are used for grasping objects, and large hind feet that are partially webbed and used for propelling the animal through the water.

Muskrats spend most of their life in water, in family groups, each group occupying a portion of a pond containing a house, feeding areas, and canals through cattails and other pond vegetation. Each family defends its portion of the pond from other muskrats.

Mating may occur several times during the period from March to September. Litters of three to seven kits are born about a month after mating. Kits are weaned in about a month and are expelled from the home lodge to fend for themselves. Young are able to breed the following year. Muskrats eat pondweeds, small animals, including freshwater mussels, frogs, salamanders and small fish. Muskrats are found in all regions except alpine.

Pika: Pikas are small lagomorphs, with no apparent tail, and short, rounded ears. They are the smallest, but heartiest wildlife in the high mountains, living in burrows below the snowpack during the winter. They do not hibernate. Pikas weigh about 5½ ounces and have

a long, dense fur similar to that of rabbits and hares. The upperparts are brownish gray, peppered with black, and the underparts are grayish white. Pikas inhabit rock slides in the alpine regions of all Northwest mountain ranges. They have a "bleating" call. Pikas eat plants and grass. In late summer, they begin collecting large quantities of vegetation. Each pika piles the vegetation into a "haystack" located within its territory in the shelter of the rock. The vegetation dries and provides the pika with winter food.

Porcupine: Porcupines are large, dim-witted rodents weighing up to 22 pounds, with a thick tail, short powerful legs and long curved claws well suited for tree climbing. The unique coat is composed of rows of dense, brown undercoat with yellow-tipped guard hairs. These alternate with rows of loosely attached quills from 1 to 2½ inches long. The quills taper to a sharp and stiff point that is covered with microscopic barbs. Contrary to popular folklore porkies cannot throw their quills. They will slap an enemy with the quilled tail or roll into a protective ball with quills extended when attacked. The quills are hollow, reducing weight, increasing body insulation and providing buoyancy when the animal occasionally swims. Porcupines are solitary animals,

act as snowshoes allowing the animal to "float" on top of the snow, instead of sinking in it. Breeding season starts in March and may continue into summer. Litters of about four young are born to each doe (female) about a month after mating. Young are precocial, being born with long hair, and eyes open. They are able to leave the doe's simple above-ground nest a few days after birth. Does may breed several times during the year, some having as many as four litters. This fecundity is a major factor in the large population changes that occur over the years. In summer, showshoe hares eat a variety of grasses and forbs. In winter, they eat the buds, bark and branches of shrubs and small trees.

Muskrat: The muskrat is the largest member of the rat and mouse family in North America. Adults weigh about 3 pounds and are valuable furbearers. Its dense waterproof, chestnut to dark-brown fur has been the mainstay of many trapline incomes. Unlike the much larger beaver, the hairless tail of a muskrat is narrow and flattened laterally. It acts as a rudder when the muskrat is swimming. The muskrat has short legs, and small forefeet

except during mating season in November and December. Usually only one porcupine is born to each female from mid-May through July. The porcupine, a North American rodent, gives birth to precocial young — the young are born covered with hair and quills, with eyes open, and they are able to move about soon after birth. The quills are flat and limp at birth but soon dry and stiffen. In summer porcupines feed on green leaves of forbs, shrubs and trees. In winter they feed on the inner bark, twigs and buds of trees. Porkies are found throughout the Northwest from the highest peaks to the most desolate deserts.

White-tailed Jackrabbit: Although commonly called a jackrabbit, this lagomorph is a hare, having longer hind legs and ears than the cottontail, giving birth to precocial young, and changing its color in winter. Adults weigh about 7½ pounds. In summer, the coat is a grizzled brownish gray. In winter, the coat changes to pure white, except for black-tipped ears. Mating occurs in April or May, with litters of about four young being born a month later.

The white-tailed jackrabbit occurs in the prairie, sagebound foothills, and grainfields bordered by thickets. In summer, it eats a variety of green vegetation, including grasses, alfalfa and grains. In winter, it browses on the buds, bark and branches of shrubs and small trees.

Cottontail: The cottontail rabbit is smaller than the hares, weighing about 2½ pounds. It has shorter hind feet and ears, and the ears lack the black tips of the hares. The fur is a grizzled brown on the upperparts with gray on the sides and rump, and white on the underparts. The top of the tail is gray, but it is usually the white

Upland Birds

underside that is shown. Cottontails do not change color in winter. Mating may occur as early as February, with litters of two to seven young being born about a month later, naked and blind. Does may breed three or more times a year. Cottontails are sparsely distributed in the coulees, river bottoms and brush of the prairie.

Beaver: The beaver, Canada's national emblem, is the largest North American rodent, adults averaging 44 pounds, some as large as 80. The beaver's flat, scaly tail serves as a rudder when swimming, as a prop when standing, as a lever when dragging logs, and as a warning device when slapped on the water. (The belief that the tail is used as a trowel for mud is a myth.) The digits (fingers) and claws of the forepaws are long and delicate to aid in the handling of wood. Those of the hind foot are broad with webbing of skin between the toes to propel the animal through the water.

Blue Grouse: The slate-gray color, solid black tail, and large size (up to 21 inches long) of the blue grouse are distinctive characteristics. Hens are stippled with light brown but are otherwise similar in color to cocks. Blue grouse occur only in the foothills and high mountains. Contrary to most wildlife that migrate downhill from the mountain peaks in winter, blue grouse migrate up the mountain when the snow flies. They spend their winters in high coniferous forests near timberline, where conifer needles and buds make up about 96 percent of their winter diet.

In spring, blue grouse move down to lightly wooded mountain valleys or foothills. Choosing an open area, the cock sets up a territory, strutting and hooting to announce his presence and attract hens. Yellow-to-orange eye combs are enlarged, and tail feathers are fanned. White-

The rich, deep fur of the beaver have been prized by furriers for centuries. The long and dense undercoat provides excellent insulation; and the long guard hairs that grow through the underfur form a rich reddish-brown outer coat. Beaver ponds are usually occupied by one family of beavers. The average colony contains one pair of adults, about four young of the year (kits), and young from the previous year (yearlings). Mating takes place in January and February, with young being born from April through June. Young do not assist in the work of the colony until their second summer. They become adults in their second winter, and are driven from the colony to start a dam and colony of their own. Beavers eat the bark of poplar, willows, cottonwood, and other trees and shrubs. In summer, they also eat pondweeds, water lilies and cattails. Beavers occur in all life zones except the alpine.

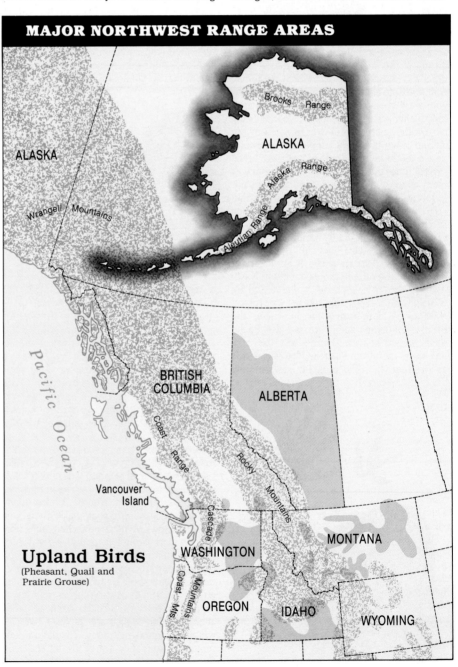

MAJOR NORTHWEST RANGE AREAS

ALASKA

ALASKA

Brooks Range

Alaska Range

Aleutian Range

Wrangell Mountains

Pacific Ocean

BRITISH COLUMBIA

ALBERTA

Coast Range

Rocky Mountains

Vancouver Island

Cascade

Upland Birds
(Pheasant, Quail and Prairie Grouse)

WASHINGTON

Coast Mts.

MONTANA

OREGON

IDAHO

WYOMING

based neck feathers are raised revealing bright yellow or purple skin patches. After mating, the hen chooses a nest site, often at the base of a tree or under a log. She lays from five to 10 eggs that are buff-colored, and finely spotted with light brown. Incubation takes about 25 days. When hatched, the brood leaves the nest with the hen. In late summer, large family groups disperse and individual or small groups of birds then make their way up to the forests of their winter range.

Gray (Hungarian) Partridge: The gray partridge, known in some areas as Hungarian or Hun, is a small bird, only 12 inches long. Both sexes are nearly identical, but the adult

male has a distinct, horseshoe-shaped chestnut patch on its breast. Breast patches of females and immatures are broken and less distinct. In flight, chestnut tail feathers can be seen clearly. A native of the bush plains of Europe and western Asia, the species was introduced to the Northwest in the early 1900s. It is now well established in the prairies and parklands, east of the coast mountain ranges.

In spring, the cock attracts a mate with a call that sounds like the creaking of a rusty gate. The hen builds a nest in grass or low bushes. Ten to 20 olive-colored eggs hatch in about 25 days. The hen and her chicks remain together throughout the summer, feeding on grain, seeds, leaves and berries. Mortality is high, and only about eight chicks will survive to the fall. At this time coveys of 10 to 20 birds are formed. The covey remains together all winter, dispersing in spring as the birds pair off and mate. The gray partridge seems well suited to winters, using windbreaks and straw piles for shelter, and grains and other seeds for food.

Sharp-tailed Grouse: When flushed, sharp-tailed grouse usually fly long distances. In flight their white wings, breast and tail are conspicuous. They are about 18 inches long, and are distinguished from hen pheasants by their narrow, pointed, tail feathers with white edges.

Sharp-tailed grouse are scattered in areas of suitable habitat. They favor brush and aspen groves in the parkland zone and edges of forest clearings near grainfields. Favorable winter habitat consists of wooded areas where tree buds are available, and grassy areas which supply seeds.

Each spring, cocks move to traditional "dancing grounds" to perform a breeding ritual. They fan their tails, and shake them while they

are strutting in circles with their wings out-stretched. Their large purple neck sacs inflate, and the birds utter low, cooing and popping sounds.

Hens are attracted to the dancing grounds where breeding occurs. They lay about 12 olive-brown eggs in nests hidden in tall grass. Incubation lasts about 24 days. After hatching, the brood moves to open grassy areas to feed, and to stands of trees to roost on hot days. In eight to 10 weeks the broods disperse. Cocks again move to dancing grounds in the fall, where young birds "display" and compete. In November, sharp-tailed grouse flock, wintering in large groups.

Ruffed Grouse: The name ruffed grouse refers to the ruff of black feathers on each side of the bird's neck. The birds are about 17 inches long. Ruffed grouse are found in mixed-wood forests in all life zones except the treeless alpine. In fall hunting seasons they are usually found in brushy creek and river bottoms where there is a good cover of alder or aspen trees. On the prairie they can be found in farm woodlots and treed coulees. Seeds, leaves, fruits and berries are principle foods in spring and summer. Poplar and willow buds make up the bulk of their diet in winter.

In the spring the cock attracts hens by strutting on a "drumming log" with ruffs flared,

wings trailing and tail fanned. Occasionally he beats the air with his wings, making the low drumming that is a familiar sound. After mating, the hen usually chooses a nest site under or near a fallen log. She lays from eight

to 14 buff, unspotted eggs. Bushy sites are chosen as brood rearing areas, and families may be found together until fall. Family groups disperse before winter as the ruffed grouse is basically a solitary bird. However, in late winter afternoons and early mornings, two to eight birds may be found together roosting in trees and feeding on buds.

White-tailed Ptarmigan: The white-tailed ptarmigan differs from the willow ptarmigan by having all-white tail feathers. In winter both sexes are entirely white except for their black eyes and bills.

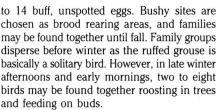

White-tailed ptarmigan are about 13 inches long. They occur in or near the alpine zone of the Rocky Mountains, and occasionally in the higher peaks of the Cascade Range, generally north of Mount Rainier. They are protected in the Northwest states, but are plentiful and heavily hunted in Canada and Alaska. Berries, leaves, flowers and seeds are eaten in spring and summer. Buds and twigs of willow and alder are their sole winter foods.

After mating in spring, the hen nests in open meadow. Her summer coloration blends well with the vegetation and rocks of that habitat, making her difficult to see by predator and man. The four to eight eggs, colored buff and finely spotted with brown, hatch after a 23-day incubation period. Broods stay together until autumn when the birds begin to move down to winter grounds below timberline.

Spruce Grouse: When flushed, this small, 15-inch-long grouse will often flutter into a nearby spruce tree where it will sit, and depend only on its coloration for protection. It is

251

commonly called fool hen for this apparent lack of fear of man. Cocks and hens are very similar, but hens are barred with more brown on the back. The cocks have red combs above the eyes that are usually hidden by feathers. The tail of the cock is black, tipped with pale brown. Franklin's grouse, a variety of spruce grouse, has no brown tip. It has white spots on the sides of the base of the tail. Found throughout coniferous forests of the Cascade, Coast and Rocky mountains, spruce grouse feed almost entirely on conifer needles in winter. In spring and summer they also eat insects, leaves and berries.

In spring, the cock sets up a territory in a forest opening. As part of his display to attract a hen, he struts about, eye combs inflated and tail feathers erect and fanned. He flutters from the low bough of a tree to the ground, producing low drumming sounds that end with a sharp wing-clap just before landing. Hens build nests of leaves and grass, often in moss under spruce trees. The clutch consists of six or seven eggs, mottled light and dark brown. Eggs hatch in about 21 days. Chicks remain with the hen throughout the summer.

Ring-necked Pheasant: The bright bronze colors, white neck band, flaming red cheek patch and long tapered tail feathers of the rooster ringneck makes this bird easy to identify. Males may be as long as 36 inches. The hen is smaller, with a short, pointed tail and drab mottled brown feathers.

The ring-necked pheasant is a native of southern China. They were first successfully introduced in 1881 when Owen H. Denny shipped 21 ringnecks from Shanghai, China, to his brother's farm near Corvallis in Oregon's Willamette Valley. From that brood stock, ringnecks have expanded their range to 37 states and most of southern Canada to become the most popular upland game bird in North America. The birds found the Northwest's dense agricultural cover, irrigation ditches, abundant berries and nearby grainfields ideal habitat. They soon became common in irrigated agricultural areas of the prairie and parkland zones.

In spring, the cock establishes a territory where he crows and beats his wings, warning other cocks of his presence. His feathers become a nearly radiant mix of bronze, green, blue and white and the scarlet red cheek patch

enlarge. Roosters establish territorial rights and will fight other roosters to the death to maintain those rights. After breeding, however, roosters commonly share the same areas. A rooster may attract a harem of up to 10 hens. Nests are usually concealed near fields, often in ditches, or fence rows with dense cover. Six to 12 buff eggs are incubated for 25 days. Chick mortality is high, and populations are supported by release of hatchery-raised birds. In the fall, pheasants move to areas with thick cover near stubble fields or other food sources.

Sage Grouse: Sage grouse are the largest native grouse. Males may be up to 30 inches long, hens are slightly smaller. Both sexes have black bellies, long, pointed tail feathers and white underwings that "flash" when the birds take flight. Their habitat of sagebrush and arid grassland is limited. In spring and summer, they eat leaves; but as the seasons progress, they become increasingly dependent upon sagebrush for food. By winter, it makes up over 90 percent of their diet. Sage grouse numbers are decreasing in direct proportion to the amount of sagebrush acreage converted to agricultural land.

Each spring, cocks gather at dawn to perform breeding rituals on their "strutting grounds."

With olive-colored neck patches exposed, eye combs swollen, tail feathers fanned, and wings lowered, they strut and stamp their feet, uttering a low cooing sound, rustle their feathers, squeak their wings and pop their air sacs. Hens are attracted by this ritualistic performance. After mating the hens move away to nest and lay a clutch of eight or more olive-buff eggs, spotted with dark brown. Eggs hatch in about 27 days and the hen with her brood moves to nearby grasslands to spend the summer. In fall and winter several broods may flock on the wintering grounds of the sagebrush plains.

Willow Ptarmigan: The black tail of the willow ptarmigan distinguishes it from the white-tailed ptarmigan. In summer willow ptarmigan have more white on their wings than white-tailed ptarmigan. At this time the cocks are easily distinguished from the hens by their reddish-brown heads, backs and breasts. In winter both sexes are entirely white, except for their black tails, eyes and bills. Willow ptarmigan are about 16 inches long. Legs and toes are completely feathered.

The breeding population of willow ptarmigan occurs in the mountains and parks. Here birds spend the summer in the alpine zone or just below timberline. In winter they move to lower valleys. They are confined almost exclusively to the country north of the United States/Canada border. They range as far north as the Arctic. These birds breed on the arctic tundra and migrate south to winter.

Upon arrival on the breeding ground, a cock establishes a territory from which he excludes all other males. He displays plummage and makes a variety of boom and hoot sounds. His mate stays within the territory and incubates seven to 10 yellow-brown eggs in a nest hidden under a bush. Eggs hatch in about 22 days and the young remain with the hen, feeding on insects and plants. Adults eat leaves, berries and seeds, but only few insects. As fall approaches willow ptarmigan flock in preparation for migration to wintering areas.

Greater Prairie Chicken: This is the true "prairie chicken," also called the pinnated grouse for the "pinnae," or long feathers on the sides of its neck. Both sexes are about 18 inches long, and are barred and spotted with brown, black and white. They have a small crest on the top of their heads. In the spring the cock "displays" to attract hens by raising his neck pinnae, exposing large, orange-yellow sacs of skin that he inflates. He drops his wings, stamps his feet and gives a low, booming call. This is the "booming display," once a common early morning sight on the prairies in the spring.

Prairie chickens prefer grassy plains with scattered patches of brush. As settlers turned the prairie into grainfields, the prairie chicken was unable to adapt to the changes. It is now considered extinct in most areas. The last recorded sighting in Alberta was in 1972 near Mountain View.

Diving Ducks

Redhead: A large duck, redheads are 20 inches long, and weigh 2½ pounds. They range from coast to coast with the bulk of the ducks in the Central flyway. The rounded head and upper neck of the male redhead is reddish chestnut, with the lower neck, breast and upper back brown black. The abdomen area is white, and the back, wings and sides are white barred

throughout. They build nests of reeds lined with moss in rushes and reeds over the water, and deposit eight to 14 eggs of a cream, or buff color. They feed upon vegetation which includes leaves, sedge weeds, roots, bulbs, and also various insects.

Ringneck: A small to medium-size duck of 17 inches, weighing about 2 pounds. The male ringneck's head, neck and breast are black with a purplish irridescence, and a thin collar of brown. The back and wings are brownish black with a gray speculum. The beak is a slate blue with a white base and a white band near the tip which is probably the best identifying feature. (Scaup have about the same coloration but lack the bill ring.) The female ringneck is brownish, darker on the back and wings with white underparts. A distinctive white ring encircles the eye. These birds winter in

southern British Columbia, western United States and Central America and are usually found in flocks. They are late-season migrants. In spring, a nest of grass, reeds and rushes lined with down is built in a marsh or on the edge of a slough, and six to 12 olive-buff eggs are laid therein. Food consists essentially of pondweed and various aquatic insects.

Ruddy Duck: A small, stout duck, 15 inches long, weighing only 1⅓ pounds, ruddys have a thick body, short neck and large head. On the male, the crown is black with large white cheek patches and a bright blue beak. The rest of the body is a reddish brown becoming black

with black. The tail is brown black. The female's head and neck are dull red brown, with white on the chin. The upper breast and sides are brownish, and the back and wings are dark brown. They winter from southern British Columbia to Mexico and the West Indies, and during the breeding season are distributed

near the rump and tail. The underparts are grayish white irregularly striped with chestnut. The female is a dull brindle-brown color with whitish cheeks and a darker tawny crown. They winter from the northern United States to Central America. Usually found in pairs and rarely in flocks. Early migrants. The nest, usually over water, is built on reeds just inches above water. They lay six to 10 large creamy-white eggs. Food is mainly pondweed and aquatic insects.

Lesser Scaup: Commonly called bluebills, these late-migrating divers are 17 inches long, weigh just under 2 pounds and are extremely fast flyers. A black head, glossy in appearance

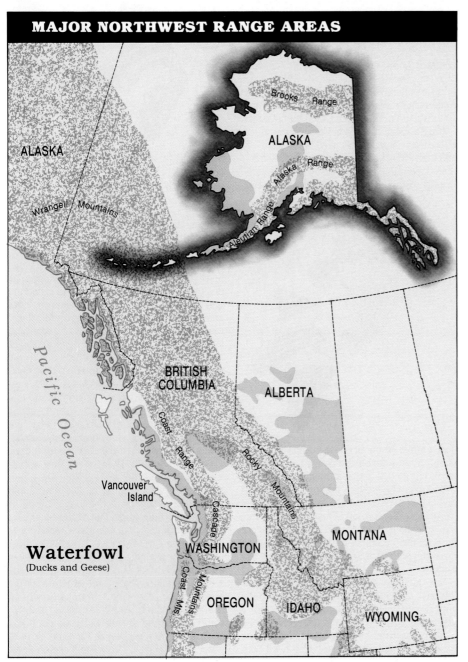

MAJOR NORTHWEST RANGE AREAS

ALASKA

Brooks Range

ALASKA

Alaska Range

Wrangell Mountains

Aleutian Range

Pacific Ocean

BRITISH COLUMBIA

ALBERTA

Coast Range

Rocky Mountains

Vancouver Island

Cascade Mountains

MONTANA

WASHINGTON

Waterfowl
(Ducks and Geese)

Coast Mts

OREGON

IDAHO

WYOMING

with a purple irridescence helps in identifying the male of this species. The back is gray with a black rump and tail, and it has white underparts. The female has a wide white band around the base of the bill and is basically brown in color with white underparts. They winter in the southern United States and Central America, and during the breeding season they are widely distributed throughout the Canadian Arctic and Alaska. They nest on dry ground and lay eight to 12 olive-buff egg on a nest of grasses and leaves lined with down. Food consists of roots and aquatic insects. Travel in large flocks, often erratic and compact. Wind whistling over their wings when decoying, sounds remotely like a fast aircraft. Easily decoyed on large rivers or windswept lakes.

Surf Scoter: Up to 20 inches long, and weighing more than 2 pounds, these sea ducks are commonly called skunkheads for the white

patch on the male's crown. They fly along the coast in loose flocks, just above the waves. A late migrater. Two small patches of white appear on the forehead and on the nape of the male. The beak is very heavy at the base and marked with red, orange, black and white. The legs are red or orange. The female is a drab brownish color with the abdomen mottled light and dark gray. There is a vague white patch on the ear. The legs are slightly tinged with yellow. They nest on the ground on islands. The nest is constructed of reeds and grass lined with down, and five to eight cream-colored eggs are laid. They feed on plant life, snails and insects. Found almost exclusively on salt water, but occasionally stray as far inland as northwestern Alberta. Hunting popularity is minimal in the Northwest.

Canvasback: Considered the king of the divers, canvasbacks are large ducks, stretching out to more than 22 inches and weighing up to 3 pounds. The head is sharply tapered, compared to the round head of its smaller lookalike, the redhead. Big water birds, "cans" fly with rapid, noisy wingbeats and are the fastest of all North American ducks. They migrate late in fall, usually waiting for ice to push them south.

The male's head and neck are dark reddish brown and the lower neck and upper breast are black as is the rump and tail region. The rest of the back is white, finely barred with

black, producing the canvas gray effect. The side and underparts are white. The iris of the eye is red. The females are mostly brown with a tinge of red on the head and chest. The sides, back and wings are gray brown. The rest of the underparts are grayish white mottled with brown. They winter in the southern United States and Mexico and breed mainly in north-central Alberta. Their nests are bulky massses of reeds over shallow water, in which seven to nine pale-olive eggs are laid. They feed on underwater roots, plants, wild celery, shrimp, shellfish and pondweeds. Excellent table fare.

Bufflehead: The smallest diving duck, buffleheads (sometimes called butterballs), are less than 15 inches long and usually weigh less than 1 pound. They are easily decoyed, and usually travel in pairs or small flocks of a half-

dozen birds. Frequent on lakes and rivers, and often dives underwater instead of flushing when alarmed. They float high on the water, with a bouncy corklike motion. Unlike most divers that need to run across the water to get airborne, bufflehead can launch straight up like a puddle duck. If one bird is dropped, it is not unusual for the others in the flock to land on the water with it, or to circle back within a few minutes.

The drake is basically white, with black on the back and primaries. The head has a puffy appearance, because of long feathers, with a green and purple sheen and a large V-shaped white patch from the eye across the top of the head. The female has a dark gray head with

a white cheek patch behind the eye. The body is brownish gray with white underparts. They winter on the Pacific and Atlantic coasts and occasionally on the Great Lakes, and during breeding season they are distributed throughout northern and central Alberta. They nest in the hollow cavities of trees and stumps and lay nine to 14 eggs of a creamy-white or buff color. Their food consists of plant seeds, fish and aquatic insects. Not highly prized on the table, but can be delicious if the oil gland is removed before cooking.

Common Goldeneye: Commons, along with their blue-headed cousins the Barrows, are about 19 inches long. The common goldeneye is the smallest of two, weighing about 2 pounds, while the Barrow will weigh 2¾ pounds. Barrows, predominately a western

bird, are less wary than the common goldeneye, although both decoy well and generally fly near the water. They are often found on rivers. Both are late to migrate, arriving in most hunting areas late in the season, after most puddle ducks have left. Commonly called whistler because of its wing-whistling sound in flight, the common goldeneye is a medium-size duck with a white body, a black back and black forewings. The distinctive feature of the male is an iridescent green head which is puffy in appearance. It has an oval white spot between the eye and bill and the wings have large white areas. The eyes and legs are yellow. The female's head and neck in both species are chocolate-brown with the underparts white. They winter on the coasts and throughout the United States. They nest in the holes of hollow trees or stumps and line the bottom of the cavity with down and feathers where eight to 12 grayish-green eggs are deposited. Their food consists of aquatic insects, snails, shrimps, small fish, seeds and tubers.

Greater Scaup: These divers are almost identical to the lesser scaup. They are generally larger, weighing up to 2 pounds, and measuring nearly 19 inches long. The bill is a distinctive blue color. The head of a greater is more rounded than the lesser, and shines with a green iridescence. They have more white in the primaries, and the back has fewer and heavier black bars. The female has the same coloration, shape and structure as the lesser scaup. They winter from the Northwest south to northern South America, and are sometimes found on salt water amidst flocks of scoters. They nest on dry ground close to water, laying eight to 12 olive-buff eggs in a nest

of grass and leaves lined with down. Their diet consists of various aquatic plants, small fish, snails and insects. They travel in flocks ranging from a half dozen to several hundred birds, and often raft on large reservoirs or lakes late in the hunting season. Good on the table, and exciting to decoy. Occasionally found on large rivers, but prefer large open lakes. The lesser scaup is more likely to be found on small ponds and marshes.

White-winged Scoter: A sea duck, white-wings are large birds, reaching a length of 22 inches and a weight of 3½ pounds. They winter on open coastal waters and attract minimal hunting pressure on the West Coast. The male is entirely black with a white

speculum and a white crescent under the eye. The bill has a prominent knot at its base and an orange tip. The legs are red. The female's color is more brownish fading to gray on the underparts, with a white speculum. The bill and legs are brownish black. They winter along both coasts as far south as California. Occasionally nest as far inland as Alberta. The nest is a depression in the ground, lined with grass and down, in light woods or prairie. The eggs number from six to 10 and are pinkish buff in color. Food consists of aquatic insects and most underwater plant life.

Puddle Ducks

Mallard: The most popular and widespread of our waterfowl, mallards, are the largest puddle duck, measuring up to 24 inches long,

and weighing nearly 3 pounds. The male mallard has an iridescent green head and upper neck separated from the chestnut chest by a white ring, earning the nickname greenhead. The back and wings are brownish gray with an iridescent purple speculum bordered front and back by white. The underparts and sides are light gray, the tail feathers are gray with white borders, and the upper and under tail coverts are black. The legs are reddish orange and the bill is yellow. Northern birds are generally recognized by the bright orange, almost reddish color of the legs. The female mallard is brown, streaked with black. Her throat and foreneck are buffy and the underparts are buffy gray spotted with brown gray. The male in eclipse plumage is similar to the female. This species nests throughout most of North America, and winters from

southern Canada to Panama. They feed on grasses, grain, seed, snails and various surface aquatic plants. The nest is on the ground, made of grass, dead leaves and lined with down. Eight to 12 buffy-green eggs are laid. Can be called into decoys, but can be exceptionally wary especially late in the season. Found mostly on creeks, rivers, sloughs, small lakes and marshes. Feed heavily on grains and often hunted from pit blinds in fields.

Pintail: Often called sprig, pintails are large streamlined puddle ducks, measuring up to 2 feet in length but weighing only about 1¾ pounds. They are found through North America, but are most numerous in the Pacific flyway. They are among the first ducks to

migrate south. They have a distinctive long neck and pointed tail feathers. The male pintail's head and upper neck are dark brown, with the color extending down the neck as a dark stripe bordered with white. The wings are gray with heavy black striped borders, and the speculum is iridescent green. The female's head and neck are buff, striped with brown except on the throat. The upper parts are brownish black, and the speculum is grayish brown with a green edge in front. Pintails are widely distributed and winter in the southern United States, Central America and the West Indies. They build a nest on the ground of grass and reeds lined with down, and lay eight to 12 olive-buff eggs. These ducks are very plentiful and can be seen in grainfields along with mallards. Their food consists of grain and other seeds, as well as aquatic animal life and pondweed. The drakes have a sharp whistle while the hens have a course quack sometimes confused with a mallard. Fairly easy to decoy on water or in grainfields.

Baldpate (Wigeon): A medium-sized puddler, measures 21 inches long and weighs 1¾ pounds. Appear to be most numerous along the coast areas. They are nervous birds, quick to take alarm and fly in a bunched flock, twisting and turning. Prone to rafting during the day and flying inland to feed in marshes, ponds and fields. The male's head and neck are speckled black-and-white except for an iridescent patch behind the eye and a white crown that is its namesake. The back, sides and breast are reddish brown with the sides and breast barred with black. The speculum is black with a small spot of green, and a white patch is conspicuous at the front of the wings. The

female's head and neck are speckled grayish brown-and-white and the back is barred with light and dark browns. The breast and sides are brown and the underparts are white. The wing is similar to the male's, but the white patch is marked with gray. These birds winter from the middle United States south to Central America and in the breeding season they are widely distributed. They build nests of grass and weeds on dry ground near water and lay eight to 12 cream-colored eggs. Their food consists mainly of vegetable matter, including pondweed, grasses and algae.

Wood Duck: The drake is considered one of, if not the most beautiful North American ducks. Not as plentiful in the central and Pacific

flyways as in the Mississippi and Atlantic flyways, they are small, quick ducks, averaging 18½ inches long, and 1½ pounds in weight. The wood duck is small in size with a large head crest iridescent green and purple with white markings. The rest of the upper parts are iridescent green with bronze reflections. The speculum and much of the wing is iridescent green and brown, edged with white in front of the wings. The sides are olive, barred with black and white and the remainder of the underparts are white. The female is a less colorful bird, mostly brown in color with the upper parts a brownish olive glossed with green. The wing is like the male's, but duller, and the abdomen and breast are white with brown sides. They nest in cavities of trees and stumps with the bottom lined with down, in which 10 to 14 buff-colored eggs are laid. Their food consists of vegetable matter and various insects. One of the first ducks to migrate south. Few are found after early November. Small-water birds, they are usually found in pairs or small family flocks in flooded timber, along low rivers, and near ponds. Difficult to decoy, wood ducks are usually bagged by jump shooting or from pass-shooting blinds along rivers.

Cinnamon Teal: The most common teal in the Pacific flyway, cinnamons are small ducks, 16 inches long, less than a pound in weight. The body of the male bird is chestnut in color with a darker brown on the crown, back and tail. The wing coloration is the same as the blue-winged teal. The female is similar to the blue-winged teal but more heavily marked on the sides of the head and chin, with chestnut coloring on the underparts. They breed in southern British Columbia and are fairly scarce east of the Rockies, but some nesting pairs have been seen in the Brooks district. They nest on the ground near water and lay nine to 13

creamy-white eggs in a nest of grass lined with down. Their food consists of aquatic plants, seeds, grasses and leaves.

Black Duck: Rarely found west of the Mississippi flyway, these wary ducks appear much like mallards, measuring 24 inches long and weighing up to 2¾ pounds. Males and females of this species have the same drab coloration, looking much like very dark female mallards, but the purple speculum is bordered

with black only. In the field, no white shows except on under-surfaces of the wings. Eight to 12 buff-green eggs are laid in a ground nest of grass and reeds lined with down, often some distance from water. These ducks tip for food in shallow sloughs during the summer and fly to the grainfields to feed in the fall.

Gadwall: Most numerous in the Central flyway, but not too numerous anywhere, gadwall are large ducks measuring 21 inches long and weighing up to 2 pounds. Sometimes

called gray mallards, gadwall are among the first birds to migrate south in the fall. The head and neck are pale buff streaked and spotted with brownish gray, and the upper back, breast and sides are brownish gray finely barred with wavy lines of white. The inner feathers of the speculum are white, the outer ones are black, and the speculum is bordered in front with a heavy bank of black, in front of which is a large patch of chestnut. The female is a fairly large size, generally grayish in appearance, with white patches on the wing close to the body. The legs are yellow. These birds winter in the

southern United States and Mexico. The nest consists of grass, lined with down, far from water, in which seven to 12 eggs of cream or pale buff are laid. The gadwall likes shallow sloughs which are filled with algae, and feeds on this and other aquatic vegatation.

Shoveler: Scorned by most waterfowlers because of their poor table quality (one-third of the diet is animal matter) shovelers are sometimes mistaken for mallards. They are much smaller, however, measuring 19 inches long and weighing less than 1½ pounds. This duck is easily identified because of its large spoonlike bill, a feature that has earned it the nickname spoonbill. The male has a dark green iridescent head, a white breast with chestnut sides and belly. The shoulders are chalky blue separated from the iridescent green speculum by a white band. The tail and tail coverts are black except for a small white patch at each side of the base. The legs are orange. The female resembles a female mallard

except for the exceptionally large bill. This bird is widely distributed and winters in the southern United States and Central America. Not far from water, a nest of grass lined with down in constructed, and six to 12 buff-olive eggs are laid. These ducks enjoy stagnant algae-filled sloughs where their large bills are used to strain small plants and animals from the water.

Blue-winged Teal: A small, fast target, bluewings are not as plentiful in the Northwest as in the midlands and eastern United States. They are roughly 16 inches long and weigh less than a pound. They are are generally recognized by a high-pitched peeping and quick, twisting flight. They commonly fly low across the marshes, often rocketing past surprised hunters before they can react. They are one of the first ducks to migrate south. The male bluewing's head and upper neck is bluish gray except for a large white crescent between eye and beak and a black crown. The upper parts are spotted brown and the back is brownish black. The tail is black with a distinctive white patch on the side. The speculum is iridescent green and the front of the wing is light blue. The female's head and neck are grayish brown

with a white throat. The underparts are white streaked with brown and the wings are similar to the male's except duller. They winter from the southern United States to northern South America, and in the breeding season they are widely distributed. This species lays eight to 12 buff-white eggs in a nest of grass and down, on the ground near water. They feed on aquatic plants, seeds, grasses and leaves as well as water insects and algae. Often found mixed into flocks of mallards, bluewings often buzz decoys but rarely settle down on the first pass.

Green-winged Teal: Slightly smaller than the bluewing or cinnamon teal, greenwings measure 15 inches in length and weigh only 14 ounces. Common throughout the Northwest and tend to remain in the northern areas slightly longer than their cousins before migrating. The head and neck of the male are chestnut except for an iridescent patch of green extending from the eye down the side of the neck. The breast is pinkish with black spots and the remainder of the underparts are white. The sides are a finely barred gray with the back and wings darker. The speculum is iridescent green bordered in front with light brown and on the sides with black. The female is a grayish-brown color with a white throat and underparts. The wings are similar to the male, but duller. They

winter in the southern United States to the West Indies. During spring and summer they are widely scattered. They build nests of grass lined with down and six to 12 buff-white eggs are

laid. The nest is on the ground near water. Food consists of aquatic insects, plants, seeds and grasses.

Mergansers Sea Ducks

Commonly called fish ducks because of their diet, there are three varieties of mergansers common to the Northwest and all are considered terrible table fare. They are most often found on rivers or in estuary bays. All mergansers are recognized by their narrow, serrated, rapierlike bill compared to the wide, flat bill of ducks.

The largest is the **common merganser,** measuring 25 inches long and weighing

2½ pounds. The head of the male is rounded and dark green and the underside of the body is white. The females have a reddish, slightly combed head. **Red-breasted mergansers**

are slightly smaller in length but weigh about the same. While similar in color to the common, red-breasted have more grayish-brown coloration on the undersides and have ragged crests extending from the back of the head. The smallest is the **hooded merganser,** measuring only 18 inches long and weighing about 1½ pounds. Often seen in pairs or small

flocks. They are black-and-white birds with bronze coloration on the breast and prominent combs rising from the back of the head. Plen-

tiful on small creeks late in the season, especially in the Pacific flyway.

In additon to the whitewing and surf scoters illustrated, Northwest coastal waterfowlers also see several other varieties of sea ducks.

The **common eider** resembles a small goose in flight, measuring 24 inches long and

weighing up to 5 pounds. They are stocky birds alternately flapping and sailing in flight. All eiders have heavy, thick beaks with bold feather coloration, and are passable tablefare. Other eiders include the **Steller's, king** and **spectacled** varieties. They are late migrating birds and are more plentiful in the north coastal regions. Rare more than 50 miles inland from the Pacific, but occasionally follow rivers upstream from their saltwater mouths.

Rare south of British Columbia, **old-squaws** are slim, brightly colored ducks. Generally

about 20½ inches long, weighing 2 pounds, they are smaller than eiders or scoters and fly fast and low to the water. They appear roundish in flight, with sharp, pointed tail feathers. The body is white with small brown areas along the chest and back. They are noisy ducks with a variety of calls, some with a musical quality. The **harlequin duck** is about the same size

as an old-squaw, but less vocal and far more colorful. The males are slate blue in front, striped with white and running to bronze along the flanks. The female is a drab gray with a promient white spot behind the eye. They are most plentiful in Alaska, and rare south of British Columbia. They can be found late in the season along rocky shores and headlands.

Woodlore

Mushrooms,
An Outdoorsmans' Field Guide

By Ethel M. Dassow

Some 7,000 species of mushrooms are known worldwide. Not all of them are found in the Northwest, but some found here haven't been found elsewhere. Some of ours are rare, some abundant. A few species could kill you; more could make you a little (or a lot) sick; some won't hurt you but won't whet your appetite, either. Relatively few species are safe and so tasty that mushroom enthusiasts seek them relentlessly, wherever they grow and whatever the weather.

Mushrooms are fungi. So are lichens, rusts, yeasts and some other growths that don't concern us. No fungi produce their own food by photosynthesis, so they don't need light. Most mushrooms (saprophites) feed on organic leftovers and reduce them for recycling. If they feed on humus they're terrestial; if on wood, lignicolus. A few (parasites) feed on living organisms, usually trees, and may eventually kill them.

Mycology is the branch of botany that specializes in the study of mushrooms, and mycologists are the botanists who study them. Most mycologists are also mycophogists, experts who hunt mushrooms to eat as well as to study. A pot-hunter collects for sport and the cooking pot — though the fascination of fungi can easily turn his sport into an intellectual pursuit. A novice pot-hunter can become a full-fledged mycophogist in 10 to 20 years.

You don't have to be a mycophogist to collect some of the best mushrooms with confidence and eat them with delight. You do have to obey, strictly, the mushroom-hunter's first law of survival:

Never, but NEVER eat a mushroom, or any part thereof, before you know what it is and that mycologists have pronounced it edible.

The second law is: When trying a new species, eat a few bites and wait awhile. Some individuals are sensitive to some mushrooms. (Don't blame the mushrooms! Some of us are sensitive to milk, or wheat, or walnuts.) If you don't get an allergic reaction, eat and enjoy.

Most of a mushroom plant is a fine network of mycelia under the ground or within the host. All that emerges is the fruiting body, and that's what interests the hungry nonscientist. It comes out fully formed and gets bigger by pumping water into itself. (Some species, including the European truffles, live their entire life cycles underground. Hunters for those use trained pigs or dogs to find them by smell.)

Each fruiting body produces millions of microscopic spores, which spread great distances on winds, fur, feathers, clothing, or in digestive tracts of animals, then settle wherever they find habitat to their liking. Many species have spread so far that a Northwest mushroom may be recognized in Nepal or New Zealand, South America or Sicily.

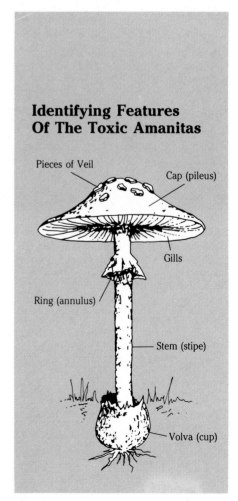

**Identifying Features
Of The Toxic Amanitas**

Pieces of Veil

Cap (pileus)

Gills

Ring (annulus)

Stem (stipe)

Volva (cup)

Photo by Keith Lockwood

Squirrels, elk and deer compete with human mushroom hunters. While the photographer watched, this ground squirrel dismembered a large red-capped **Scaber Stalk,** *Leccinum aurantiacum,* and hung the pieces out to dry for storage. By Joy Spurr

The easy way to identify a mushroom is by show and tell — if there's an expert handy. Just show him and he'll tell you. The experts are almost universally generous with their know-how. (Don't expect them to tell you exactly where to look, however; they don't want competition and you won't, either, when you've prospected good hunting ground.)

If you're on your own, start with the can't-miss species shown and described here, then go on to a good field guide. If your specimen looks like any in the photos, check the characteristics with the descriptions and make sure they all tally. Bear in mind that there's some variation within species, depending upon habitat, light conditions and such.

You'll need to make a spore print to determine the spore color. That's easy. Just break off a piece of cap, put it gills down on a piece of paper — white if you expect dark spores, dark if you expect light, both if you don't know what to expect — then turn a drinking glass upside down over the mushroom scrap and wait. The scrap will be shedding spores, and soon you'll have a clear print.

Some of the best tasting mushrooms (the Prince, the Meadow Mushroom, Shaggymane, Lepiota) may grow in your yard or along the roadsides. Stuff a knife and a couple of collecting bags into your pockets when you go for a walk. Keep knife, bags and a pair of old shoes in your car, in case you spot a mushroom as you're driving. A good mushroom is to get, if, when and where you can.

A foray into the woods takes more preparation. You'll need:

— A large basket or plastic buckets. Better yet, take three buckets, nested, in the brightest colors for easy spotting in case you stray from one. (A knapsack is hard to get things into and out of, and tires your back when you're stooping and bending.)

— Cloth bags, at least one for each species. Old pillowcases do. Old heating pad or bowling ball bags, flannel side inside, do better. If debris goes in with the mushrooms, and some will, it tends to cling to the flannel. Or make bags from old flannel pajama legs.

— A few plastic produce bags for found objects, like antlers, old handmade loggers' climbing spikes, things other people lost, odd growths — you find the darndest things in the woods! Plastic bags aren't good for holding mushrooms. They need to breathe.

— A coffee can or freezer carton, in fall, in case you luck onto some irresistible blackberries or huckleberries.

— Garden cultivator for an arm-extender and climbing grip. Wrap its handle with red adhesive-backed tape so you can spot it easily.

— Knife. A small hunting knife in a belt sheath is ideal but easy to lose. Wrap its handle, too, with red tape. A long-bladed pocketknife on a cord from your belt is harder to use but also harder to lose.

— Whistle, on a lanyard around your neck. Carries farther than voice, in case you're hurt or lost and someone's looking for you. Also helps keep track of your partner. Work out a signal system such as: One blast, "I'm over here. Where are you?" Two blasts, "Come help me harvest these!" Three blasts, "Help!"

— Compass, or an infallible sense of direction (preferably both). You can't see landmarks when you're in the forest, and you may lose the sun. Tune your subconscious to configurations of the ground, changes in vegetation, game trails, stumps, snags, downed and leaning trees. Listen for traffic sounds. If you do get lost, don't panic. Sit, relax, look and listen.

Even veteran woodsmen have to remind themselves to reorient every few minutes. It's also an excellent idea to orient yourself an hour or two before dark. Waiting until the last glimmer of daylight and finding you're a little bit lost can mean a long, unnecessary night in the woods.

— Matches and a votive candle, in case you have to build a fire. (Dead twigs of conifers make good kindling. So do dry cones.) Don't build a fire in dry forest unless you absolutely have to, then clear a wide area of anything that might burn, keep your fire small, and watch it!

— Flashlight.

— Bandana.

— Gloves, flexible cotton-lined plastic or rubber with inside flocking. They keep your hands warmer and drier, and avoid mushroom-stained fingers.

— Shoepacs or boots and wool socks; water-repellent jacket, hooded, or jacket and sou'wester; an extra wool shirt or sweater. Fall or spring weather can get cold and wet in a hurry.

— International orange vest or jacket, especially during hunting season. Or, get that water-repellent jacket in international orange.

— Emergency rations. The eager pot-hunter tends to get exhausted and rubber-legged half an hour from his car. A pint thermos of coffee and some trail food will restore the energy and prolong the fun.

Looks like quite a list, but all of the above (that you aren't wearing) needn't add up to 5 pounds. You'll be using some of the items on every trip. The rest are worth their weight as insurance.

Cook, Freeze or Dry

To wash or not to wash those mushrooms? Some say no, you'll throw out flavor with the wash water; just brush them with a tender touch and figure a little honest dirt won't hurt you. Since pesticides came into our lives, however, you'd risk getting something besides honest dirt. Lawns, roadsides, even national forest lands, may have been sprayed to kill unwanted growth. Better play it safe and wash those mushrooms.

If there's any sign of worms, you have another choice to make. Discard the mushroom, soak it in salted water to draw out worms, or reason that worms are a good source of protein and ignore them.

Mushroom cookery itself is a hobby that can hook you. Most general cookbooks have recipes for the store-bought agarics. They can give you ideas, but there are good mushroom cookbooks. The best are prepared by one or another of the mycology societies (see box, at right), because the contributing members pride themselves on producing the sharing winners. Use the books to learn what to expect of a species, then let your imagination take over. You can do a lot with mushrooms, and they can do a lot for your menu.

Not so incidentally, mushrooms are loaded with vitamins and minerals but shy on calories — about 90 to a pound. True, the butter, oil and sour cream that go well with mushrooms also go to upholster the torso, but you can work that off next time you go pot-hunting.

Freezing or drying mushrooms can extend the pleasures of the palate far beyond the collecting season.

To freeze: Sauté a few at a time (too many, and they'll simply stew) with a dab of onion if you like, and freeze in small cartons.

To dry: Slice them thin, lay slices on a paper towel on a cake-cooling rack, cover with another paper towel, and set them aside for two or three days. Oven-drying is risky, as the mushrooms start to cook at a very low temperature and then rot. A very fast food-dehydrator works well, but others are as risky as the oven. Store in an airtight container with a few peppercorns. They'll keep for years, if you let them.

Recommended Field Guides, Cookbooks

The Savory Wild Mushroom by Margaret McKenny, revised and enlarged by Dr. Daniel E. Stuntz, University of Washington Press, 1971: ISBN (paperback) 951-567, (hardback) 951-559; L of C 78-160288. Best for the Northwest. Now out of print, but copies may still be found in bookstores. A new edition, edited by Dr. Joseph F. Ammirati, released in 1987.

Simon & Schuster's *Guide to Mushrooms*, by Giovanni Pacioni, American edition edited by Gary Lincoff, ISBN 0671-4284-97. (Originally published in Italy; recommended for general coverage.)

Toxic and Hallucinogenic Mushroom Poisonings, A Handbook for Physicians and Mushroom Hunters, Gary Lincoff and D.H. Mitchel, M.D., Van Nostrand Reinhold, New York, 1977.

Wild Mushroom Recipes by the Puget Sound Mycological Society, The Globe Pequot Press, 9533 Palatine Ave. N., Seattle, WA 98103; 178 pages, $7.95. ISBN 0-914718-04-5.

Wild Mushroom Cookery, Oregon Mycological Society Inc., 6548 S.E. 30th Ave., Portland, OR 97202.

The Audubon Society *Field Guide to North American Mushrooms*, by Gary Lincoff, Alfred A. Knopf, Inc., 1981; ISBN 0-394-51992-2; L of C 81-80827.

For information about mycological societies in the Northwest, write: Puget Sound Mycological Society, The Monroe Center, Rm. 104, 1810 N.W. 65th St., Seattle, WA 98117.

Common, Edible Mushrooms

Meadow Mushroom *Agaricus campestris*: Spores purple-brown. Cap satiny-white, smooth and thick, up to 8 or 10 inches across; in larger specimens, cap may split to form an interesting pattern reminiscent of sun-baked clay. Gills first enclosed by veil, delicate pink, aging to purple-brown. Stem white, short, with ring; base may be slender. Flesh of stem and cap pure white.

Grows from late summer into October and, east of the Cascades, often in spring, in lawns, open meadows — never in the woods.

A lovely mushroom, more delicately flavored than its close kin, the commercial white mushroom (agaric). Eat stem and all, raw or cooked. Dries easily, cans or freezes well; whole buttons good for pickling.

All agarics are best used within two or three days, as the gills darken and the flavor gets stronger with age.

The Prince *A. augustus*: Spores purplish-brown. Cap white with soft golden-brown scales, thick, 4 to 15 inches across. Gills first covered by veil, white turning delicate pink to rose to chocolate brown. Stem white, with ring, tapering from bulbous base (no cup). Height to 15 inches. Flesh white, smelling faintly of almond, both stem and cap staining deep yellow to orange-brown where cut or bruised.

Grows from June in wet years, mid-August in dry years, into October, in lawns, flower beds, orchards, on roadsides, near compost piles. Sometimes grows in woods, but best left there as the pot-hunter could easily confuse it with one of the deadly amanitas.

Usually found in groups of several within a few feet, but has been known to grow in dense, convoluted clusters that broke through a 2-inch layer of concrete. Usually comes up several times a season and for several consecutive years in almost the same place. (Yes, that concrete floor got broken year after year. Then the inflorescence appeared in a flower bed, and finally quit showing.)

One of the choicest mushrooms, eat stem and all, raw or cooked. Use, dry or freeze as with the commercial agaric.

Note: The Flat-top Mushroom, *A. placomyces* (or *maleagris*), which often grows in the same area as the Prince, causes nausea in some people. Others find it highly palatable and eat it with no ill effects. The Flat-top is a gray-brown, not a golden-brown, it does not stain where cut or bruised, and it does not smell of almonds. Some persons detect a faint creosote odor from it.

Other species of this genus are edible and good, but less easily distinguished than the Meadow Mushroom and the Prince from allergenic or mildly toxic species, or those with unpleasant flavor.

Shaggy Parasol *Lepiota rachodes*: Spores white. Gills and flesh white, graying with age. Cap smooth, mahogany-brown, shaped like the end of a broom handle; opens to parasol shape, up to dinner-plate size; surface splits to make a white-scaled effect; remnants of veil give a fringed or shaggy look.

Stem bone-white, fibrous, bulbous at base, tapering to slender and joining cap at apex. Except with very young specimens, discard stem. It's tough. Loose, feltlike ring is veil remnant. Height, 4 to 10 inches.

Flesh of stem and cap stains reddish-brown where cut or bruised.

May be found from mid-April to the first heavy frost, most abundantly after the first August rains. Grows in the open, on lawns, roadsides, around outbuildings; often prolific in piles of old lawn clippings.

Wherever you find this species, watch for another inflorescence after the next good rain, and every few days into winter, then again for the next several years.

Over-mature specimens are almost always wormy. Discard them on the spot, or take some to "seed" your own compost pile. Maybe they won't take, but it's worth a try.

A delicious mushroom, compatible with most main-course foods. Keeps at refrigerator temperature for a week or more. Dries well, keeps well when sautéed and frozen.

Warning: *L. molybdites* resembles *L. rachodes* except that it has green gills and it's poisonous. *L. molybdites* has not been reported in the Northwest to date, but you could be the first to find it here. If so, DON'T EAT IT!

Parasol Mushroom *L. procera*: This species differs from *L. rachodes* in that the stem is scaly, the flesh does not stain where cut or bruised, and it's more likely to be found in mixed (deciduous and coniferous) forest. No matter; it's equally edible and some think it's even better. This mushroom is also known as the Tall Lepiota.

White Lepiota *L. naucina*: Spores white. Cap white, sometimes grayish, smooth. Flesh white. Gills, first veiled, white turning pink with age.

Stem white, with ragged feltlike ring (veil remnant) that slides up or down; slender; height, 3 to 7 inches.

Grows in fall on roadsides, lawns, as single or scattered specimens, always in the open.

A tasty mushroom, worth collecting, but be sure there's no cup (volva) at the base of the stem. If there is, your specimen is an amanita and may be deadly.

A gray form of *L. naucina* is allergenic to some people.

Shaggymane *Coprinus comatus*: Spores black. Cap white to grayish, becoming shaggy with fluffy black scales. Gills pink, stem white, with ring, tapering from bulbous base and joining cap at apex. Mature stem tends to fracture vertically. Height, 2 to 12 inches in the open, 18 to 20 inches in tall grass or brush.

Grows from August through a mild winter, on lawns, roadsides, in waste places, often in clay or hardpan such as abandoned roadbeds,

scattered or often in dense patches of up to several hundred. Emerges like a small, compact peg, white, often with pink blush. Develops black scales as it grows taller; as cap begins to open gills "melt" black from the margin upward.

Shaggymanes must be gathered young and cooked within hours or they turn into a black puddle (autodigest). Cut the stem as far down as you can and scrape off the dirt. That bulb is the best part! A delicious species. Slice stem and all, sauté, salt lightly, and serve on toast. (If you wish, thicken with flour, potato starch or arrowroot.) Can't be dried. Sometimes develops a too-strong flavor when canned or frozen.

Inky Cap *C. atramentarius*: Spores black. Gills gray, turning black. Cap dark gray with purple cast, never fully opened. Stem whitish, hollow, brittle. Flesh tannish. Height to 4 or 5 inches.

Grows in fall, usually in dense clusters in lawns or waste places, or in the woods. Another autodigesting species, but slower about it than *C. comatus*. Less choice, too, but worth gathering if found young and used soon.

Warning: The inky cap contains a substance which, though not toxic in itself, reacts badly with alcohol. In fact the substance was developed and used, under the trade name of Atabuse, in treatment of chronic alcoholism before it was known to exist in inky caps.

Shiny Cap *C. micaceous*: Black spores. Cap golden brown with metallic glints, up to 3 inches in diameter but never opens fully. Stem white, hollow. Both cap and stem thin and fragile.

Grows in fall and spring, in clusters, 3 or 4 inches tall, in grass, usually on or near tree roots.

Unmistakably kin to shaggymane and inky cap (also autodigestive), this frail little species has a pleasing flavor, but unless the inflorescence is large and very fresh, it scarcely seems worth gathering.

King Boletus *Boletus edulis*: Olive-brown spores, borne in a layer of fine, spongy tubes on the undersurface of the cap.

Cap tan to brown, dry (not viscous) and very smooth, rounded and then flattening, 3 to 12 inches across. Flesh white. Stem, edible in young specimens, white to dingy, thick, often bulbous at base, upper third veined.

Grows after rain, from August into spring if the winter is mild, under conifers, from sea level to about 3,000 feet.

Considered the best of the boletuses and by some, the best of mushrooms. It may weigh a pound or more, and be so big you'll spot it at the edge of the woods while you're driving at freeway speed. One specimen is worth stopping for, and there'll almost surely be others close by.

Sauté, salt lightly, and serve; use to enhance meat, ragouts and such; slice thin and dry it.

Continued on page 264

Photos by Joy Spurr except as noted

Meadow Mushroom

The Prince (By E. Dassow)

Shaggy Parasol

White Lepiotas

Shaggymanes

Inky Cap

Orange Fairy Cup

Fairy Ring

Fairy Ring

Clitocybe

Yellow Chanterelle

Cauliflower Mushroom (By E. Dassow)

Coral Hydnum

Sulphur Shelf, Chicken of the Woods

All boletuses and species of similar genera *(Suillus, Leccinum)* must be gathered while young and firm, or the worms will have found them first. Worms come up through the stem and spread into the cap. If they haven't infested the whole cap, you may find it worthwhile to break off the good parts.

Use all boletuses soon after gathering, as at least one specimen is sure to harbor worm larvae and they develop fast. In two or three days your whole collection will have become a shapeless mess.

Warning: Never, but never eat a boletus that has red pores or pore mouths. Two of them, Eastwood's and Satan's *(B. pulcherrimus* and *B. satanus),* are poisonous.

Some boletuses stain blue or blue-green where cut or bruised. These are mildly toxic to some people, so should be ignored or tried with caution.

Keeping these restrictions in mind, you're safe in trying other species. There are a dozen or more, growing in much the same habitats, and some are good, some very good. One, Slippery Jack *(Boletus luteus),* cooks into a slimy mess unless the cap surface is peeled off. (It's thin and it comes off readily.)

Fairy Ring Mushroom *Marasmius oreades:* Spores white. Cap pale to dark tan, often with lighter rings; umbonate (bulged center), often with ragged edge, up to 3 inches across. Gills coarse, slightly lighter than cap color. Stem slender, fibrous, lower part lightly streaked with black, 2 to 5 inches tall.

Grows spring through fall, after rains, in lawns, meadows, in ring that expands year after year as it exhausts the food supply. Some fairy rings are said to be miles around and centuries old.

If you have a fairy ring in your lawn, cherish it! (Seems there's no known way to get rid of it, anyway.) Those firm little fungi that come up by the score have a fresh, nutty flavor and a chewy texture not lost in the cooking. They dry easily and reconstitute in mere minutes of soaking. Use in stews, ragouts, casseroles, or with onions to smother a steak.

To gather: Grasp the stem near the base and pull. It should come up with a rootlike tuft at the end. (If it doesn't, discard it.) Pinch off cap with thumb and finger and discard stem. It's tough. Doing this on the spot makes cleaning the cap easy.

Note: The sweat-producing clitocybe, *Clitocybe dealbata (sudorifica),* sometimes grows in fragmented circles on lawns. It's all grayish-white, the mature cap turns up and flutes, and the gills, finer than those of the *Marasmius,* run down the stem. Its stem, and the stems of other "scrap" species that grow in grass, will fail the pull test.

Garlic Marasmius *M. scorodonius:* A mini version of the fairy ring *Marasmius* — brown with white spores and tough stem — grows in fall, in Douglas fir forests. Let your nose guide you to it, and take a few specimens to use (sparingly) in place of garlic.

Yellow Chanterelle *Cantharellus cibarius:* Spores yellow, borne on a network of raised, coarse-edged veins that run partway down the stem. Cap and stem continuous; egg-yolk or apricot yellow (or white, but rarely); comes up as a little yellow button that looks superficially like any of several forest species; matures to a graceful, unmistakable fluted-vase shape. Several stems may fuse into a plant 6 or 8 inches across and almost that tall; may weigh several ounces. Flesh white, smelling faintly of apricot.

Grows from sea level to 3,000 feet or more; most prolific in second-growth forests of the Olympics and the Cascades (seldom, if ever, in primeval forest), occasionally under pine. Has been found throughout the year on the outside coast; most abundant from the first August rain to the first heavy frost. May grow one here, one there. When you spy one, look carefully before you leap. You might step on others hidden in the moss. Often in little enclaves of a score or more — a beautiful (and mouth-watering) sight, especially on a green-moss forest floor.

Slip thumb and finger as far down the stem as you can, then cut below your finger. Don't pull! You might break the stem and waste some tasty flesh (it's all high-quality eating), or pull out some substructure and jeopardize next year's crop.

After the heavy fall rains, when the forest is soggy, chanterelles often grow in patches of salal. You can't see them from above, but get your head down to ground level and look. You may be surrounded by hidden treasure.

This chanterelle will be abundant in an area for several years, then show no more. Best to prospect alternate areas during the height of the season.

With a soft brush or a wad of nylon net, brush off any forest duff before you bag your specimen. Its surface is slightly adhesive and gets more so. Much as you'd rather get more chanterelles now and clean them later, half a minute now could save two or three at home. If you must put it off, lay a dozen or so in a dishpan, run cold water over them, swirl them around, then brush them one at a time and let them drain. Or spread them on a dish drainer outside, spray them with the garden hose, then brush individually and drain.

Chanterelles keep 10 days or so at refrigerator temperature — if they get a chance. Only very old specimens are hosts to worms, and those should be left on the grounds to spread their spores.

Try chanterelles sliced and sautéed in butter with a dab of chopped onion, with or without sour cream. A noble dish! Save some for casseroles, ragouts or whatever. They're compatible with meats, fish, tomato, lemon, cheese, poultry stuffing. A few chopped chanterelles transform an ordinary dish into something special.

To preserve, slice and dry or sauté and freeze. Or, they make a super pickle.

Note: Yellow chanterelles have been abundant in the Northwest, but they may now be an endangered species. They've become

scarce in Europe, where they've been a favorite for centuries, and they're in demand in our East Coast cities. Some entrepreneurs are sending pickers out with rakes, some are taking hundreds of pounds in a day (10 or 12 pounds are a good take for an afternoon pot-hunter), and shipping them off to the East Coast or to Europe. How long the Northwest's chanterelles can survive this ruthless harvest, no one really knows, but our mycologists and home-use gatherers are worried.

Cauliflower Mushroom *Sparassis radicata:* Spores and all, white. One of the coral fungi, the *Sparassis* hasn't the ordinary mushroom cap-and-stem shape. Imagine yards and yards of ribbon kelp, bleached to bone-white and wadded, all the ribbons issuing from a single white mass with a small "root" attachment. A single specimen may be 2 or 3 feet across and too heavy to carry in one trip. Found (but rarely) in fall, in evergreen forest, always close to the base of a tree. It's parasitic; it feeds on live wood.

If you luck onto one of these (and some long-experienced collectors haven't yet), never mind what you came for. Take a careful bearing so you can find the spot again, and cut the plant off at ground level. It should fruit again next fall, and for several years. (If the plant is soft and darkish, it's over-age. Leave it and hope for next year.)

If your specimen has black specks on the tips, they're worms. Trim them off — they haven't affected the rest of the plant — or soak the tips in salted water to draw out the worms. Remember, your first specimen may be all you'll ever get, and for such a choice species, aesthetics can be disregarded.

To use: For a truly noble dish, dredge strips of *Sparassis* in flour, sauté in butter with a dash of onion until tender, than lay strips in a buttered casserole, top with breadcrumbs and bake. Or, saute the floured strips and freeze in meal-size packages for later baking. *Sparassis* dries readily and makes a super seasoning. Crumble it into a powder and use it as you use Bouquet Garni.

Another cauliflower mushroom, *Sparassis crispa,* also fruits in the fall, under pines. It's creamy-yellow when young, darkening some with age. Its ribbons are lobed and fluted, and its flesh is brittle. In flavor it doesn't tie *S. radicata* — but what does?

Coral Hydnum *Hericium coralloides:* Spores colorless. Entire plant white to bone.

Grows from mid-August into winter, on snags, windfalls or stumps in old-growth Douglas fir forest. (It's a lignicolus saprophite — lives on dead wood.)

One of the spine fungi, the coral hydnum looks from a distance like a mass of white lace hanging from its host wood. Starts as a compact plant, branches, rebranches, finally to spine-fringed branchlets. May spread 6 or 8 feet laterally and be 18 or more inches long at its longest.

Continued on page 266

Pine Mushroom

Angel Wings

Oyster Mushroom

Early Morels

King Boletus

Oyster Mushroom

True Morels

Early Morels

Galerina Autumnalis, toxic

True Morels

Panther Amanita, toxic (By Laura Dassow)

Fly Amanita, toxic

Amanita, toxic

If you find one of these — which won't happen often — take what you can use and leave the rest for the next pot-hunter. Remember, the core branches of larger specimens may be fibrous and indigestible. Makes a pleasing dish (try it in place of spaghetti), or an interesting variation of an old standby. Needs longer cooking than most fungi. **Note:** Look-alike species found in the Northwest are *H. abietes*, *H. erinaceus* and *H. ramosum* (or *caput-ursi* — bear's head), all listed in older texts under the genus *Hydnum*. All are nontoxic, so you're safe to gather and try them.

Chicken of the Woods or Sulphur Shelf *Laetiporus (Polyporus) sulphureus*: Spores white, borne in tubes on the lower surface.

A bracket fungus, this one grows like an irregular series of shelves attached laterally to a fallen log or snag (or possibly to a wound in a living tree), sometimes almost covering the entire surface. Fruits from late summer into fall, often for several seasons from the same host.

Flesh white, unchanging when bruised. Musky odor, spongy texture. Underside sulphur-yellow, top bright orange-red bordered and mottled with yellow — a spectacular sight to come upon in a dark forest, or seen from a low-flying plane. A lucky find if you're lost in the woods, as this fungus can be eaten raw. (Older growth has woody texture.)

You won't want to carry out a load of this, but take some and try it sautéed, thickened and seasoned slightly, and served on toast or rice or boiled potatoes.

Matsutake or Pine Mushroom *Armillaria penderosa*: Spores white. Cap white streaked with cinnamon-brown, getting browner with maturity, up to 15 inches across. Gills white, browning with age, first enclosed by heavy veil. Stem white, tall, tapered at base, with soft, thick ring of veil remnant. Even the button of this mushroom is big, like an oversized tennis ball breaking out of the earth.

Grows in fall, sometimes abundantly, under pines or other conifers, at low to medium altitudes on the Olympic Peninsula and in the Cascades.

Matsutake is most compatible with oriental foods, and the most popular species with Japanese pot-hunters. Taken commercially in good gathering years. (Usually available, dried or sometimes fresh, at oriental markets as an import from Japan.)

Angel Wings *Pleurocybella (Pleurotus) porrigens*: Spores white. Cap white, aging to cream, 2 to 4 inches across, attached laterally to its host wood. No stem. Gills white to cream, radiating from attachment.

Grows in fall at the height of the chanterelle season (rarely in spring), always on logs or stumps of conifers. You may come upon dozens or hundreds, strung around like dainty little perches for an audience of elves, their pure white gleaming in the dark, dank forest. They're edible raw or cooked, nice nibbling on

the spot or an agreeable side dish for the table, but it takes a lot to make a serving and they're hard to clean. (They do dry well, and the duff falls off as they dry.) They're worth a try or two, but, to paraphrase Emerson, their beauty is their best excuse for being.

Oyster Mushroom *Pleurotus ostreatus*: Spores lilac. Cap variable, white to oyster-gray or brown, fleshy, up to 5 inches wide, attached laterally with little or no stem. Gills same as cap color, coverging at stem or point of attachment.

Grows in spring, through a damp, cool summer, and in early fall, on deciduous trees or logs (alder, maple, cottonwood). Continues to fruit through the season from the same host wood.

A choice species, the oyster mushroom looks like a larger, coarser, meatier version of the Angel Wing, growing in shelf-on-shelf clusters, and tastes a little like oysters.

Orange Fairy Cup *Aleuria (Peziza) aurantia*: Spores whitish. Cap thin, cup-shape, bright orange inside, soft orange outside. No gills; this is an ascomycetes — bears its spores in tiny asci (singular, ascus) on its paler side and releases them by the millions. No stem, either; it's attached to the ground by a skimpy rootlike structure.

Grows in spring but mainly fall, on disturbed earth such as lately graded dirt roads or where logs have been dragged. When you first come upon an inflorescence of this fungus, you'll think someone has peeled a dozen oranges and scattered the rinds. An oddity, yes, but edible and pleasing. Nibble it raw, or gather lots and sauté them.

Early Morel *Verpa bohemica*: Spores pale yellow. Cap tan to brown, thin, 2 to 3 inches across but never spreads, wrinkled. Stem bone-white, smooth, hollow, usually tapered, up to 8 or 10 inches tall, joined to cap at apex. First of the spring mushrooms, the verpa appears from early March through April (later in higher altitudes) in bogs and along stream banks under cottonwoods, aspens, willows, often submerged by dried leaves. It's well worth searching for. Eat (not raw) stem and all.

Sauté in oil or butter and serve; add eggs, scramble and serve; with larger specimens, cut lengthwise, fill with meat stuffing, bake and serve. Easy to dry. They've a flavor to savor. Some say they're not quite so good as the true morel, but that's debatable.

Smooth-capped Verpa *V. conica (digitaliformis)*: Looks much the same as *V. bohemica*, but is smaller, has smooth cap, and fruits later. The two taste alike and are used in the same ways.

Narrow-capped Morel *Morchella conica*: Spores yellowish. Cap yellowish to brown, aging to nearly black, deeply wrinkled, thin-fleshed, continuous with and longer than the hollow white stem. Height 2 to 10 inches.

Fat-capped Morel *Morchella esculenta*: Spores yellowish. Could easily be mistaken for *M. conica*, but is generally lighter colored and its wrinkles are not so decidedly vertical. The distinctions are irrelevant to the pot-hunter, as both are edible and mouth-watering choices.

Found from April through May and into June in higher altitudes, in old apple orchards, fields, gardens, wood yards, around home burning barrels and (especially *M. conica*) on areas of recent burns. Better take gunny sacks the year after a forest fire. There'll be fewer the following year, and fewer yet or none thereafter.

Warning: Some unfortunate persons are sensitive to verpas and morels, so restrain yourself when you try them for the first time.

Poisonous Mushrooms

Galerina Autumnalis (a killer): Spores rust-brown. Cap dingy yellow-brown, lighter in dry weather; slightly striated margin and (usually) small central knob; slightly sticky; up to 2 inches across. Gills rusty-brown, touching stem. Stem slender, not tapered, white but darkening from base upward with age; usually has thin, hairy white ring.

Grows abundantly, singly or in dense clusters, always on decaying wood (which may be buried), in fall and through mild winters.

This little mushroom looks no-account but contains enough poison to kill you. So do some of its relatives, and some other nondescript little brown mushrooms *(inocybes)*. Shun them all!

Amanitas: Amanitas are another genus to avoid. There's a score of species, some with ominous names like Death Cup, *A. phalloides*, and Destroying Angel, *A. verna*. Not all amanita species are found in the Northwest, and not all are toxic. Two or three are classed as edible and delicious — but the distinctions are not so easily recognized that the novice should try it.

Amanitas emerge like little white balls, with cap and stem enclosed by the "universal veil." The veil breaks as the mushroom grows, leaving the ring on the stem and the stem emerging from the cup (volva), which may be at ground level or, with some species, well below the surface. In some species, remnants of the veil cling as "warts" to the cap. Some of the mushrooms recommended here have rings on their stems, but not one has the cup. Before lifting any whitish mushroom from its growing site, make SURE the stem DOES NOT come out of a cup. Better for the pot-hunter, until he's had years of study and experience, to leave all cupped mushrooms strictly alone.

Panther Amanita *A. pantherina*: Spores white. Characteristic amanita structure but cap and stem are thicker. Cap pale tan to dark brown, with white warts.

Grows in fall, through a mild winter, and in spring, in lawns and flower beds and woods, under or close to conifers.

This species is responsible for most cases of mushroom poisoning in the Northwest, but not because it's hard to recognize. One of its components, mascarine, is hallucinogenic and some foolhardy types gather it to "take a trip." If they get too much they don't come back, because the species also contains ibotenic acid-muscimol, which can be deadly.

Fly Amanita *A. mascaria*: White spores. Classic shape. Cap diameter 2 to 10 inches; from cream-yellow through orange to bright red, kidskin smooth between white "warts." Up to 12 or 15 inches tall.

Grows in spring and summer but mainly fall, in or near woods or brush. Common in the Northwest and Rocky Mountain states; prolific in the coastal forests.

A spectacular mushroom, associated with Christmas in Germanic mythology, *A. mascaria* is said to have affected the course of Asian and probably European history. But that's another story.

If you have to contend with a case of amanita poisoning, and you'll notice strange behavior within half an hour after ingestion, force the patient to vomit and get him to a doctor, fast!

Invisible and undetectable Giardiasis bacteria is spread by the feces of voles, mice, pikas, beaver and muskrats and can be contracted in the most pristine settings, such as this water supply in the Purcell Mountains of British Columbia. By Myron Kozak

Beaver Fever

If the prospect of sipping a cool drink from the clear, quick-running mountain streams is what lures you to the alpine wilderness, you may be in for days of nausea, fatigue and diarrhea.

Many of the prettiest streams are naturally contaminated. One of the most uncomfortable and dangerous diseases which frequently afflicts backpackers and hunters is "Beaver Fever."

The technical term for the disease is giardiasis, an extremely harsh intestinal disease caused by a flagellate which infests some waters. Known as *Giardia lamblia,* the tiny micro-organism, is carried in the feces of some mammals, particularly beaver, however biologists have found that several other animals, especially mouselike voles, are responsible for carry *Giardia*.

Many hikers who see deer and other wildlife drinking from a stream assume the water is safe. Not so. *Giardia* does not affect these mammals in the same way as it affects humans.

Symptoms of beaver fever include diarrhea, gas pains, loss of appetite, abdominal cramps and bloating. Weight loss may occur from nausea and loss of appetite. These discomforts may appear a few days to a few weeks after ingestion and may last up to six weeks. Most people are unknowingly infected and often have returned home before onset of the symptoms. If not treated, the symptoms may resolve on their own, only to recur intermittently over a period of many months. Other diseases have similar symptoms, but if you took a drink from untreated water, you should suspect giardiasis and so inform your doctor. With proper diagnosis, the disease is curable with medication prescribed by a physician.

Giardia can be readily transmitted between humans and animals. Dogs, like people, may become infected with *Giardia*. Unless they are carefully controlled, dogs can contaminate water and continue the chain of infection from animals to humans. Feces can contain the organism and should be buried 8 inches deep at least 100 feet from the nearest natural water source.

There are several ways to treat surface water to make it safe, but the most certain is to boil the water for at least three minutes. Chemical disinfectants such as iodine or chlorine tablets are not considered as reliable as heat in killing *Giardia*, although these products work well against most waterborne bacteria and viruses.

Purifying Wild Water

Health authorities recommend boiling water for five or 10 minutes to make most surface-water safe to consume. But regardless of how long you boil it, some water is going to be brown or green and taste like day-old dishwater.

To help the palatability of water, throw in a few bits of coal embers from your cook fire. Charcoal and embers absorb odor and may remove enough of the offensive qualities to permit drinking.

After boiling with coals, strain the water through a cloth to remove the ash and whatever else may be suspended in the water.

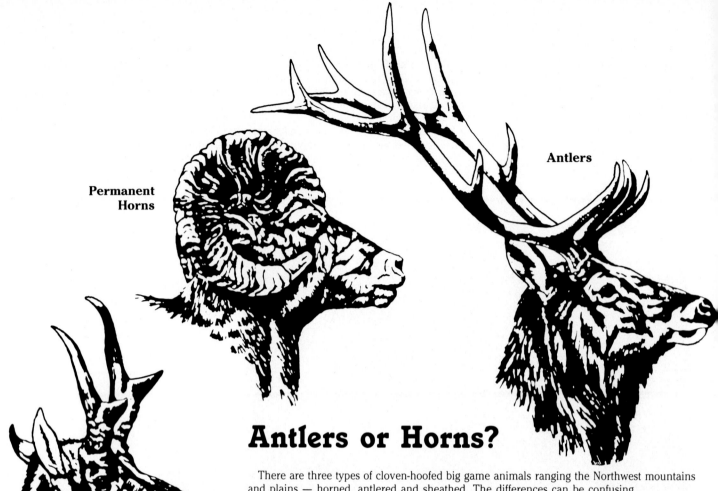

Permanent Horns

Antlers

Shed Horns

Antlers or Horns?

There are three types of cloven-hoofed big game animals ranging the Northwest mountains and plains — horned, antlered and sheathed. The differences can be confusing.

The **deer family** *(Cervidae)* is antlered, but with one striking exception — only the male animals develop antler growth. Included in this family are white-tailed, black-tailed, and mule deer; Rocky Mountain and Roosevelt elk; Shiras, Canada and Alaskan moose; and all subspecies of caribou. Caribou are unique in that females frequently develop antlers, the only member of the deer family that does.

Antlers are composed entirely of bone. They begin to grow in the early spring corresponding with the first leaf buds on browse. As they grow, they are covered with a substance commonly called "velvet" which is a soft, furlike skin filled with tiny blood vessels that feed the growing antlers. While in velvet, antlers are soft and easily damaged and the host animals often stay out of thick, brushy areas. The velvet feeds the antlers throughout summer and into early fall, nurturing tremendous growth, especially in the larger animals like elk and moose. Antler size is believed to correspond directly to the amount of minerals in the soil where the host animal feeds, which is why certain areas produce trophy-class animals year-after-year, while deer in another area just a few miles away rarely grow to trophy proportion.

In the early fall, usually in mid-September, the antlers reach full growth, the blood supply in the velvet dries up and the velvet peels off as the antlers harden. Gradually a seal forms between the antler and blood vessels surrounding the skull, and the antler is shed, falling free much like a deciduous leaf. Most lose their antlers in February and March and regrowth begins almost immediately. Mice and other rodents rapidly devour the shed antlers.

The shape of antlers varies between species and among individuals. Older animals tend to have larger antlers with more tines than younger animals, although in the few animals that survive to extreme old age, antler size can begin to diminish as the animals body siphons off the minerals and nutrients that good antler growth requires.

The second most common family are **horned** animals, including bighorn sheep, mountain goats and bison *(Bovidae)*. Unlike the annual cycle of antlers, horns are not shed. These permanent growths are composed of a hard sheath over a bone core, and grow in a continous stem, never branching. Horn growth continues from an animals first year until its death, increasing in length and massiveness each year. While both sexes have horns, the horns of the male animals are generally larger and more formidable.

Sheathed horn animals are represented by only one species in the Northwest, the pronghorn, a brown-and-white prairie speedster commonly called antelope, although it is not related to the antelope family. The family is known as *Antilocapridae,* and both sexes have pronged, or slightly branched horns. The outer sheath of the horn is composed of thick hair and is shed each year revealing a bone core covered with skin. The horns of the male are much larger than the female. Although they are shed annually, these growth are recognized as horns and are nurtured from within, and not encased in velvet during the growth season.

The antlers of a bull elk grow from the forked nubbins of the young bull at left to the massive velvet-covered rack of the center bull in less than 90 days. After the soft velvet is scraped away in September the antlers of a mature bull take on a whitish cast and may reach up to 6 feet long and 70 pounds.

This remarkable photo (below) captures the split second a bull elk sheds its massive 5-point antlers, made even more rare by the fact that both antlers were dropped simultaneously, at best an infrequent occurrence.

The photographer is Gerry Lamarre, for 17 years a professional wildlife photographer from Castle Rock, Washington. It was taken on a foggy morning Jan. 21, 1984, on the Tule Elk Reserve near Bakersfield, California. Lamarre was tracking the two bulls with a 400mm lens on a motor-driven 35mm camera when the lead bull stopped, then in a sudden twisting motion simultaneously snapped both antlers off the crown. The camera stopped the antlers suspended horizontally a few inches away from the skull before they crashed to the ground.

Lamarre said the bull appeared dazed and stood motionless for several minutes. The second bull sniffed the stumps of the fallen antlers, backed away and bugled, appearing confused but victorious.

By Terry W. Sheely

Using a Compass

By Martin D. Waters

The primary tool of navigation for most sportsmen is the compass. Although the instrument is relatively simple in design, the principal of the compass is rather complicated.

Magnetic north should not be confused with geographic or true north. True north is the northern-most end of the earth's axis and the point at which the longitudes meet. Magnetic north is located approximately 1,300 miles from true north on the northern edge of Hudson Bay in Canada. Because the two are not the same, there is a margin of error to be calibrated, called the declination.

If that weren't enough, magnetic north is not constant. It continually moves, a phenomena of debatable origin. The most commonly accepted theory is that the earth's core, which scientists believe causes the magnetic field, is liquid. The solid crust of the earth spins uniformly, but it's liquid crust moves at a slightly slower rate.

To imagine how this can happen, fill a bucket with water and give it a quick spin. The bucket turns uniformly, but the water inside does not.

The fact that magnetic north moves a little each year should not be a factor when operating a map and compass. If outdoorsmen use recent maps which indicate the date of mapping and the degree of declination, the miniscule movement of magnetic north should not hinder their attempts at orienteering.

There are three basic compass designs. Type A features a circular degree system which increases clockwise (there are 360 degrees in a circle). It also has a needle that operates independently of the base card. The chamber may be filled with liquid to stabilize the movement of the needle. This is the most popular compass in use today.

Hypothermia

The dictionary definition of hypothermia is "subnormal body temperature."

Unconsciousness can occur when the deep body or core temperature drops from the normal 98.6°F to approximately 86°F.

Cardiac arrest is the usual cause of death when the core temperature cools to below 82.4°F.

On land, hypothermia occurs most frequently in temperatures from 32° to 50°F; frostbite can only occur in below freezing temperatures.

In water of 50°F predicted survival time is about 2½ to 3 hours.

Hypothermia is the major killer of outdoor recreationists.

Hypothermia (we used to call it exposure) describes the progressive mental and physical collapse that accompanies the chilling of the vital internal organs of the human body . . . caused by the exposure to cold and aggravated by dampness, wind and exhaustion. Symptoms include uncontrollable fits of shivering, slurred speech and frequent stumbling. Without treatment, the condition may lead to stupor, collapse and death.

On land, hypothermia occurs most frequently at fairly mild temperatures, particularly during wet and windy conditions. It can occur at any time of the year, especially in regions where weather changes rapidly.

Prevention of hypothermia:
- Carry extra clothing in waterproof plastic bags.
- Stay dry. Use waterproof clothing when possible.
- Protect the head area from heat loss.
- Nibble on high-calorie foods.
- Take plastic sheeting and nylon twine for an emergency shelter.
- Don't eat snow. Your body has to warm and melt the snow and a drop in body temperature may result.
- Don't drink alcohol. It causes decreased sensitivity to cold and a lower heat production by the body.
- Do understand hypothermia — its dangers, symptoms and treatment.

Treatment is accomplished by returning the body temperature to its normal range. Move the victim to medical assistance quickly; if this isn't possible, take him to a shelter and bed him down. If he is severely cold, leave his legs and arms alone. Gently remove the clothing from his upper body, place a naked person on each side of him and keep all three well covered by blankets. If the patient is conscious, give him warm liquids *(never alcohol):* if water is available, a warm bath is very effective.

Immersion Hypothermia

Cold water is much more dangerous than cold air, since body temperature is drained away much more quickly.

When on or near cold or rough water, always wear an approved flotation jacket or vest, preferably one that also offers protection from the cold.

If immersion is from a capsized craft:
- Stay with the boat if possible.
- Try to remain inactive (you should be wearing a life jacket).
- Assume a curled-up position, legs together and arms tight against the sides, to reduce heat loss from vulnerable body surface regions.
- Wait for rescue. Don't try to swim to safety unless you are sure you can make it — you cool faster when you swim.

Windchill

Cold is more than a red line near the bottom of a mercury thermometer that measures air temperature. For an outdoorsman it can mean the difference between life and death, or at the least a major comfort consideration.

When dressing for an outing, outdoorsmen must take the wind, as well as air temperature, into consideration because of a factor known as windchill. Wind greatly accentuates the effects of cold on the body. A balmy 40°F day with a 20-mph wind hits the duck hunter with the impact of 18°F weather.

The accompanying chart calculates the actual temperature required by the body, when air temperatures between 40°F and -40°F are multiplied by winds of 10, 20 and 30 mph.

One consideration too often ignored is that windchill can be created on dead calm days by the speed of vehicles. Open boats, snowmobiles and other popular recreational vehicles moving through the air produce the same chill effect as wind blowing against a stationary object.

Chill Factor Table

Temperature (Fahrenheit)	Effective Temperature With Wind Speed of		
	10 mph	20 mph	30 mph
40	28	18	13
30	16	4	-2
20	4	-10	-18
10	-9	-25	-33
0	-21	-39	-48
-10	-33	-53	-63
20	-46	-67	-79
-30	-58	-82	-94
-40	-70	-96	-109

Hypothermia Immersion Chart

Water temperature	Victim will experience exhaustion or unconsciousness	Expected survival time
32.5°F	Under 15 minutes	Under 15 to 45 minutes
32.4° to 40°F	15 to 30 minutes	30 to 90 minutes
40° to 50°F	30 to 60 minutes	1 to 3 hours
50° to 60°F	1 to 2 hours	1 to 6 hours
60° to 70°F	2 to 7 hours	2 to 40 hours
70° to 80°F	3 to 12 hours	3 hours to indefinitely
Over 80°F	Indefinitely	

Boating

The McKenzie
Birth of the Boat Built to Tame Northwest Rivers
By Jim Boyd

If there were a Boating Hall of Fame, the McKenzie River drift boat would deserve a special berth.

Like an Horatio Alger story, its history is one of a little rowboat that made good. Developed in Lane County, Oregon, the McKenzie-type boat is accepted as the ideal craft for fishermen and professional guides who drift down rivers throughout the West in search of steelhead, salmon and trout.

It's an unusual boat. There's even a controversy over which end is which.

Keith Steele of Leaburg, Oregon, one-time president of the McKenzie Guides Association and a builder of wooden McKenzie boats, would get livid when he talked about the bow-stern issue.

A fedeal law required the manufacturer to mount an identification plate on the boat's stern. Despite Steele's protests, however, a Coast Guard officer ruled that the plate must go on the upstream end of Steele's boats. That's the end you can clamp a motor on but Steele maintained it's not the stern.

There's historical justification for Steele's claim.

Until the early 1940s, the distinction between bow and stern was obvious.

The McKenzie boat of the 1920s and 1930s was what's now known as the "square-ender" or the "Kaarhus design." This boat had a pointed bow that faced upstream as the boatman controlled the craft by rowing against the current. The downstream end was a wide, flaring stern.

In rough water, the oarsman would have to turn the boat at an angle so the edge of the stern would slice through the white-water "curlers." These are waves so forceful that they actually sweep up in a curve and splash back upon themselves like an ocean breaker. They are a peril to a boatman — even one with a modern boat — because he can "stall out" at the top of the wave and his boat will flip.

When McKenzie boatmen began running rivers with heavy white water of this type, the "double-ender" boat became popular. With a V-shaped prow on its downstream end as well as its bow, it was better suited to cutting through these treacherous waves.

Finally, the "double-ender" itself was modified. Its pointed upstream-end was sawed off and a small transom was installed so a motor could be carried for use in quiet water. This is the standard "Hindman-type" boat of today.

The development of the McKenzie boat is a classic example of the adage that "form follows function." The boats were made for and by men who earned their living by rowing fly-fishermen and other anglers down the McKenzie River. They had to be light enough to be hauled by trailer and launched in awkward spots. And, in later years, they had to be reasonably uniform so that

groups of guides could stack their boats four and five high on a single trailer for trips to far-off rivers, such as the Middle Fork Salmon in Idaho and the Rogue in southern Oregon.

The McKenzie boat evolved over the years as the product of many minds. But the names of two men stand out. One is Torkel G. "Tom" Kaarhus, a Norwegian who came to Eugene in the mid-1920s and established a reputation as a fine cabinetmaker, boatbuilder and craftsman of snow skis. The other is Woodie Knoble Hindman, a Texan who moved to Eugene in the 1930s and became a boatbuilder and river guide.

Much of the early history of boating on the McKenzie has been lost. But it was construction of what is now the McKenzie Highway that led to the invention of the McKenzie drift boat. The highway dates back to the 1860s when a wagon road was built up the McKenzie Valley and across the Cascades. Hotels and stage houses were built along the route, followed by establishments catering to fishermen.

But there wasn't a road upstream from Lucas Lodge at Agness on the Rogue River. So a long, narrow boat that could be poled upstream through rapids was developed there. Willard Lucas of Eugene, a guide and builder of wooden McKenzie boats, recalls guides poling their boats as late as 1939 or 1940 when he was a boy. "You can't pole a McKenzie boat," he'd say. "They're just too short and tubby. You'd go around in circles."

Boating is the preferred way to fish the McKenzie, especially among fly-fishermen. The river's depth and swiftness precludes wading in most places (typical of many Northwest rivers).

John West, of Nimrod, rowed boats for fishermen for 55 years. He started in 1920, when he was 19 years old, as a guide at the famous Thomson Lodge near Vida. Dayton Thomson, now deceased, is quoted in a 1946 *Register-Guard* newspaper article as saying his father, Carey Thomson, Sr., founder of the establishment, was the first man to take fishermen down the McKenzie in a boat for a fee. It was in 1909, he said, that fishermen started coming to the McKenzie to fish from boats, some of them as long as 22 feet.

West was told the Thomsons hauled their boats upriver in a wagon in those earliest days. But in 1920, the Model T Ford was the popular vehicle, with the boats being hauled behind on trailers.

"Years ago," West once said, "we didn't have boats like we've got now. I'd be afraid to climb into the first boat I ever rowed on the river [then] if it were tied up to the bank."

The bottoms of those boats were constructed of three 1x12 boards, 16 to 18 feet long. The sides were low, with as little as 16 inches of freeboard. And they didn't have the bowed bottom that gives today's McKenzie boat its characteristic bananalike curve.

The boat built for white water.
By Terry Rudnick

Modernizing The McKenzie

McKenzie-style drift boats were created to handle the rock-choked, shallow-bottomed white-water rivers of the Northwest and established a preference dominance that continues today.

They are simple, but subtly specialized craft, designed with high freeboard, minimal draft, incredible balance and maximum stability. A keelless rocker bottom allows the craft to hold nearly stationary in a heavy current while the boatman picks the best route, and the river slides downstream.

They are the favorite boat of white-water river men, guides and fishermen in Washington, Oregon, Idaho, Montana and California, navigating water too shallow or rocky for propeller or jet pump vessels.

While original models were handsomely crafted from wood, today, fiberglass and aluminum are favored because of the durability and minimum maintenance. Specialization has also left its mark on the drift boat industry, producing boats customized or refined for fly-fishing, white-water running, overnight floats, cargo or the back of the pickup truck.

Most of the refinements are confined to interior design. Some drift boats are as short as 10 feet, and others as long as 20. The standard riverboat is 16 to 18 feet long, with a single mid-boat seat for the oarsman and a cross-thwart bench seat, usually equipped with swivel seats, forward for two passengers. A short decking is molded to the frame in front of the passenger seat to support standing fishermen and protect gear.

The boatman's seat is generally made of taut rope suspended above the seat, an innovation that keeps the seat dry, yet firmly holds the boatman when he stands on the oars in heavy water.

Ten- to 12-foot oars maneuver the boat, with the boatman rowing upstream while the boat drifts downstream. Ash oars, once common in the industry, are rapidly being replaced by lighter aluminum with replaceable plastic blades.

Anchors weigh up to 40 pounds and are suspended on a small boom from the upstream end of the boats, the line feeding over a pulley system so the anchor can be released and retrieved without the boatman leaving the seat.

If anything the popularity of the Northwest drift boat is increasing each fishing season, rapidly spreading to other areas of the country. Until the late 1970s it was rare to find a drift boat on a river east of Riggins, Idaho. Today, they are common in Montana, Colorado, Wyoming, and beginning to appear on the white-water rivers of the upper Midwest and East Coast states.

"You'd pull your arms off and not accomplish much," he said of their rowing qualities. "They wouldn't turn too easily.

"At that time [the '20s] there were no real boatbuilders anyplace," he said. "There were people who built boats. They'd build a boat and try it. If it worked, they'd use it. If it didn't work, they'd try something else.

"My brother and I built the first boat shorter than 16 feet long that I ever saw. We decided if we had a wider boat and not quite so long, it would be stable and wouldn't tip much. So we made one 14 feet long and 4 feet across the bottom.

"A few people kind of laughed at us," West noted. "Milo Thomson said it looked like a bathtub with oarlocks on it. but that first year, every time Dayton Thomson got a chance to use it, he took it. Along toward fall, the river was so low there were places a boat wouldn't float. Ours would float over where theirs wouldn't."

Elmer Kensler, a one-time McKenzie River guide recalled that a man known as Grandpa Herbert built curved-bottom boats at his home near there in that decade after the turn of the century. Those boats might be a distant ancestor of today's McKenzie boats — there's no way to tell.

When Kensler bought a drift boat some 20 years later, he went to Tom Kaarhus, Eugene's leading boatbuilder and the man generally credited with developing the first McKenzie boat design.

Kensler speculates that Kaarhus got his ideas either from the seagoing dories of the New England states or from some boat he saw as a boy in Norway.

But that's not correct, according to Kaarhus' son Joe, himself a cabinetmaker.

The elder Kaarhus came to the United States at age 17, first spending a year in Iowa and then moving to Oregon. He spent four seasons fishing for salmon with a hand-line in Alaska and probably repaired and built the 12-foot double-ended boats he used there, his son said.

"I don't think he ever saw a dory," Joe Kaarhus speculated. "All the boats he described to me, the rowing boats he saw in Norway, were round-bottomed, clinker-built. The boat he used in Alaska was round-bottomed."

Joe Kaarhus said his father simply improved upon the flat-bottomed rowing boats he found when he moved to Eugene in 1923. After working on the construction of Pacific Communities Hospital, Kaarhus got a job with the Ford-Nelson planing mill, where he built various types of boats, Joe Kaarhus says. Then, in 1935, he opened the Kaarhus Craft Shop in an old building near the Williams Bakery.

Joe Kaarhus remembered about the development of that early drift boat: "The difficulty with the regular rowboat — the ordinary rowboat that you think of in the '20s or even now that you rent at a lake — is that it hadn't any rocker," he said. "Everyone used the word 'rake' but that isn't correct. We're talking about the bottom of the boat, not the top. It's the rocking chair bottom of the boat that's important. It allows the ends of the boat to be free of the water and makes them maneuverable. So my father came up with the idea to make the boat maneuverable."

According to Joe Kaarhus, his father made another basic improvement. "In a big wave in a rapid," said Joe Kaarhus, "combers would slip over the transom and swamp the boat. So the obvious thing to do was raise the height of the transom, which he did.

"These modifications of the ordinary rowboat were at first gentle and then more and more pronounced," he said, "until now we have the unique shape of the McKenzie River boat which you won't find anywhere else — the closest thing to it is the dory, but a dory is not really similar at all!

"They're superficially similar," Joe Kaarhus continued. "The main difference is that the riverboat has a wide bottom and the dory has a deliberately narrow bottom so that when it's loaded it'll ride deep and have good sea-keeping qualities in the ocean and won't get blown around. The riverboat, at sea, would be at the mercy of the wind — it would get blown around like a piece of thistledown.

"The dory, when loaded — or even with men in it — will have an appreciable draft. The riverboat, on the other hand, is made so that, as one of my Dad's old friends used to say, 'It would float on the dew.' "

According to Joe Kaarhus, his father's original riverboats were of board and batten construction, with every seam covered by a narrow board (the batten). But the invention of waterproof glue in 1934 changed all that. True marine plywood became available in the late 1930s and it was adopted as the standard material for the sides and bottom of the McKenzie boat.

Photos taken in 1940 by George Godfrey, a University of Oregon journalism faculty member and licensed guide, show typical square-ender boats built of plywood.

"They're not built anymore," Joe Kaarhus said, "because there was an obvious improvement by a guy named Woodie Hindman, who became famous for his boats. Woodie was quite a guy — well-loved by everyone."

Hindman is remembered as a fearless boatman and superb camp cook, a skill he learned as chuckwagon cook on the King Ranch before coming to Eugene in the early 1930s.

According to Hindman's wife Ruth, they operated the small Hampton Hotel on 7th Avenue in Eugene until about 1941, when they built a boat shop in Springfield. That came after Hindman had worked for Kaarhus for perhaps a year, Mrs. Hindman says.

"Woodie Hindman, he's a man who could have been an inventor," said Kenny King of Eugene, a guide since 1946. "Some big company could have hired Woodie and made good money just by letting him sit around and think of inventions. There's no one that had the ideas that Woodie had. That's why this boat was developed the way it's developed now."

Traditional wooden style. By Michael S. Sample

Fiberglass modified for fly-fishermen. By Mark Henckel

Sturdy aluminum steelhead drift boat. By Terry W. Sheely

John West isn't so generous.

"Woodie really developed the boat they use now," West agrees. "But he went around and looked at all the boats he could find, every boat he could find he looked at and he examined 'em and took the best points off all of them and put it together and made a boat."

Hindman built Kaarhus-type boats at first. Then came the two changes that revolutionized the design.

Hindman decided to build double-ended boats because of a single incident, says West. "On the Salmon River one trip, the Middle Fork, Woodie got in a bad spot and got turned around and didn't have time to turn his boat around," West explains. "So he turned around and sat down on a bale of hay he was taking down there to an old prospector. He run the boat pointed end first. It run better. So when he come home, he built the pointed-stern boat. That there's where the change comes."

Everett Spaulding, a guide from Lewiston, Idaho, said he was responsible in the mid-1940s for the next change. He had purchased one of Hindman's double-enders but found it didn't suit the kind of guiding he was doing.

"I was boating on the Umpqua River down there from the highway on down to Kellogg and on down toward the ocean there for salmon, trout and steelhead in August and September," he recalls. "And, of course, the put-ins and the take-outs were quite far apart. Consequently, in order to get these fellows enough sea-run cutthroat and steelhead, we'd have to do a lot of rowing through those dead stretches. So I went to Woodie and I told him I'd like to have the end of that boat chopped off. He said, 'Well, you'll ruin it!' and I says, 'I don't care if you do, I want it chopped off!' So we chopped it off and we put a motor on it in order to go through those dead stretches in safe time."

There was one problem, though. Spaulding's boat then was too short. So when Hindman built Spaulding's next boat, he changed the curvature of the bottom to lengthen it and enlarge the carrying capacity. That's when the modern McKenzie boat was born.

After evolving on the McKenzie and then being modified to handle both the treacherous white water of the Salmon and the calm stretches of the Umpqua, Hindman's drift boat was a universally accepted design. Boatbuilders throughout the West now construct drift boats with a McKenzie heritage.

But in recent years, the low-maintenance welded-aluminum boat has gained in popularity over the wooden model, despite the substantially higher price — over $2,000 for aluminum, compared to $800 for a plywood boat. Fiberglass boats are now manufactured, too.

Alumaweld of Medord, for example, lists several models of McKenzie drift boats in its catalog. Willie Illingworth, the original designer says: "The first boat that I built was definitely, more or less, a dead copy of Woodies' boat. But I went through a half-dozen different hull designs — one right after the other — changing the curvature of the bottom, the flare of the sides, the placement of the seats and everything until I got what I felt was the ideal combination as far as feel and everything."

McKenzie guide Dean Helfrich and his brothers continued to buy wooden boats each year from Keith Steele because, according to Helfrich, the Steele-built boat's interior design is more comfortable for paying passengers. Besides, he said, the wooden boats are quieter and less costly.

On the other hand, he admits, aluminum boats are lighter, easier to clean and more durable. So he sees a switch to aluminum. "I would say that approximately half the guides that we work with have gone to aluminum boats now," he acknowledged.

No telling what the next innovation will be.

"It's just a matter of time until these boats will all be plastic. I'm sure of that," says Willard Lucas.

Minesweepers are made of plastic now, he says. Why not drift boats?

(Courtesy of Eugene Register Guard)

Camp Cooking

Game Birds

Roast Duck or Goose, Baked Duck

Wipe the cleaned bird dry and cut away loose fat. Stuff with any poultry dressing, wild rice dressing, or a fruit dressing of soaked prunes and dried apples. Skewer or sew the openings. Place ducks in an open pan in a very hot oven and bake 20 to 25 minutes. Baste every 5 minutes with water and melted butter. Serve rare — pink juice oozes out.

Roast goose in a slow oven (300° to 325°F) until well done, allowing 18 to 20 minutes per pound. For duck, roast in a moderate oven (325° to 350°F) for 1 to 2½ hours. Cover with greased cloth or bacon strips as it roasts to keep the skin moist. Bird is done when legs are loose and skin is nicely browned.

University of Alaska Agricultural Extension Service

Wild Duck Supreme

Dress and clean wild duck thoroughly. Split down the backbone. Soak duck in burgundy wine 2 hours, allowing 1 pint wine for each duck. Turn frequently so all parts are well marinated.

Remove from wine, season well, rubbing salt and pepper inside. Stuff each duck with raw potato, apple and onion. Tie or sew securely. Place in Dutch oven, pour the wine over it, cover and cook in 400°F oven until thoroughly done, basting frequently. To brown the meat, remove cover 20 minutes before taking from the oven.

Remove string and discard potato, apple and onion.

Ruth C. Allman

Duck in the Mud

While you are having breakfast, build up a good campfire in a hollow. Your duck or goose is eviscerated, so wipe out clean with a cloth. Rub the inside thoroughly with salt and a little pepper. Stuff cavity with an apple, an onion or both. Fold the feathers to cover all openings and plaster the whole thing with a coat of clay mud (sand or loam will not do) about an inch thick. Place the bird in the bottom of your fire among the ashes and cover well with wood. Go hunting all day, and when you return for dinner, be prepared for the best duck or goose you ever tasted. Dig it out of the ashes (it should still be hot) and break off the clay.

Kenneth Hughes

Editor's Note: *Many of the uncredited recipes for Camp Cooking were originally published in* The Alaskan Camp Cook, *Alaska Northwest Publishing Company.*

Camp cooking, left. By Robert W. Merz. There is no finer way to start a day in the backcounty than with thick-cut bacon simmered in the smoke of a campfire and coffee brewed in a fire-blackened enamel pot. By Erwin & Peggy Bauer

Mule deer. By Thomas W. Kitchin

Fried or Broiled Upland Birds

Split the cleaned bird down the back and press pieces flat. Brush with oil and sprinkle with salt. Place skin side down and broil 15 minutes, turning once. Place strip of bacon on each bird and broil until bacon is crisp. If desired, baste every 5 minutes with barbecue sauce or sweet pickle juice. Before serving, sprinkle with paprika.

Disjoint larger birds (and rabbits) and fry in fat like chicken. A quick method is to cut meat from the bones in chunks or slices, and dredge with flour, salt and pepper by shaking in a paper bag. Fry in fat 15 minutes, to a golden brown. Pressure-cook bones 10 minutes to make soup or gravy.

University of Alaska Agricultural Extension Service

Grouse Mulligan

 1 grouse
 flour
 salt and pepper
 1 good-sized onion, sliced
 1 green pepper
 1 clove garlic
 1 cup water

Cut up bird, roll in flour and brown in hot drippings. Season with salt and pepper and put into a covered baking dish. Slice the onion, put it, the green pepper and garlic over the meat, add a cup of hot water. Cook at least 2 hours in a slow oven (about 350°F). Add more water while cooking, if necessary. (I dredge a little flour over it once or twice during the cooking.)

This is a good way to use old birds, but young grouse should be fried the same as chicken. If your hunter brings in only one grouse, and it isn't enough for the family, try adding 1 pound veal stew meat, browned and cooked the same as the bird. The veal cuts the wild taste of the bird somewhat, as well as increasing the amount of meat.

Lulu MacKechnie

Game Animals
Cookery

The same principles apply to the cooking of game as to other meats. Cook tender cuts — sirloin, back, ribs, round and shoulder steaks from young animals — with dry heat; broil, fry or roast in the oven. Less tender cuts and meat from old animals may be braised or pot-roasted in a covered kettle or pressure cooker with moisture added.

Wild game fat should be cut away; add lard. With an ice pick or skewer, insert slivers of salt pork into the lean meat, or grease well with oil or bacon fat.

To tenderize less tender meat, cook it or soak it in weak acids such as tomato juice, sour milk, diluted vinegar or lemon juice.

Use the bony and least-tender cuts for stews and soups. A pressure cooker cuts cooking time. Always use 10 pounds of pressure for meat, and cook half as long as without pressure.

Wild game flavor increases with aging or ripening. Some permit meat to hang several weeks to ripen. Those who prefer less flavor can reduce or avoid it by the following methods:

Use, freeze, can or brine meat within a week or 10 days of kill.

Soak meat overnight in vinegar or baking soda solution, or a mixture of oil and vinegar.

Skim and remove the fat and "fell" which contain most of the "off" flavor. Game meats cooked with beef suet or bacon fat will take on the flavor of beef or bacon fat.

Use seasonings, spices, herbs and sauces liberally.

Reindeer, caribou, moose, buffalo (bison) and deer have somewhat similar characteristics and require similar cooking methods. The cuts resemble beef or lamb cuts and may be substituted for beef or lamb in any recipe.

How To Dress Waterfowl, Game Birds

Remove crop and entrails as soon as possible, though feathers may be left on without spoiling the flavor. If not cleaned when caught, birds should be dressed as soon as they arrive in camp. To leave birds undrawn results in poorly flavored meat.

To remove feathers, before opening body cavity, dip in hot but not boiling water and pick most of the feathers. Melt 2 pounds paraffin over hot water. Roll birds in melted paraffin. Dip in ice water. When the wax hardens, peel it off and all the rest of the feathers will come off with the wax. Skin small birds if they are hard to pluck.

Leave birds whole for roasting, but for frying cut apart at the joints. Small birds have so little meat on legs and wings that sometimes only the breasts are served. Other portions may be boiled for soup.

University of Alaska Agricultural Extension Service

Roast Venison

5 pounds venison roast, boned and tied
salt
pepper
garlic salt
shortening
flour

Grease a baking pan. Sprinkle meat with seasoning, rub top with shortening, sprinkle lightly all over with flour. Place in baking pan and sear at 500°F for 15 minutes. Reduce heat to 200°F and roast 50 minutes per pound. This will result in rare juicy and tender meat. If you like it well done, roast a little longer increasing heat to 300°F for the last hour.

Jerky

One of the oldest trail and camp staples, jerked meat is still one of the most popular outdoor "munchies" for sportsmen. It requires no refrigeration, packs easily, satisfies the nagging hungries and has a distinctive, outdoor flavor. Venison makes an excellent jerky, but very lean beef or cured pork can also be used. (Warning: Because of the possible danger of contracting trichinosis never use fresh or uncured pork.)

2 to 3 pounds of very lean steak. Trim away all fat and cut into strips 1 inch thick.

Prepare a marinade of:

¾ cup water
¼ cup soy sauce
Worcestershire sauce to taste
liquid smoke
sprinkle of onion salt and garlic powder
1 teaspoon of black pepper

Marinate the strips in a glass bowl for 3 hours. Blot the strips dry with a paper towel, place them on an oven rack, and oven dry at 150°F for 8 hours. Leave oven door slightly ajar to prevent overcooking. Some cooks prefer to heavily salt the meat after marinating, then wiping away as much salt as possible before oven drying. Some folks prefer to dry their jerky in a smoker instead of the oven, in which case exclude the liquid smoke from the marinade recipe.

Venison Pot Roast in Barbecue Sauce

4 pounds rump, round or chuck moose meat
1 cup tomato sauce
½ cup vinegar
1 tablespoon salt
¼ teaspoon pepper
2 teaspoons chili powder
¼ teaspoon paprika

Brown meat thoroughly on all sides in a heavy kettle or Dutch oven. Mix together the tomato sauce, vinegar, salt, pepper, chili powder and paprika. Pour over browned meat. Cover and simmer gently over low heat, until tender, about 3 hours. Turn meat several times during cooking and add a little water if necessary to keep meat from sticking. Makes 6 to 8 servings.

If moose lacks fat, add 2 tablespoons salad oil to the tomato sauce mixture. For a thicker gravy, remove meat to a serving platter, mix 1 tablespoon flour and 2 tablespoons water to a smooth paste, and stir into the liquid in the kettle.

Teen Cox

Sheep or Goat Stew

2 pounds meat
1 tablespoon fat
1 quart water
½ cup pearl barley
1 sliced onion

Dressing Big Game

Remove all viscera and chest organs. Take out heart and liver with care so as not to break the bile sac, which should be removed carefully from the liver. Discard viscera some distance from carcass to avoid attracting flies.

In a dry climate expose meat to the air to form crust that soon hardens enough to keep out flies. Otherwise, tie cheesecloth over the meat to keep out flies, smear the surface with blood from the body cavity to form a crust that flies cannot penetrate.

Cool meat as rapidly as possible. Cut legs off below knee joint. Remove hide of large animal to hasten cooling and prevent flavor from penetrating the meat. Spread the legs apart, tie them to a gambrell stick, and hoist the carcass several feet off the ground or onto a brush heap.

Cut a large carcass into quarters to hasten cooling and make it easier to carry. Game should not be dragged.

Hang meat to tenderize several days in a cool, airy place protected from sun and rain. If unskinned, hang the head up. The natural direction of the hair keeps out rain and snow.

When meat has cooled and aged, cut up the quarters as for beef or lamb — legs for braised steaks or roasts; back for tender steaks, roasts or chops; shoulder, flank, brisket and shanks for stews, soups and ground meat. If animal is very tender, more leg meat may be used for steaks.

Low in fat content and high in nutrition, venison can provide the centerpiece for the finest outdoor dishes. Venison is the meat from any member of the deer family, which in the Northwest includes mule, white-tailed and black-tailed deer, elk, moose and caribou. The key to delicious venison dishes is careful handling in the field, extended aging, attentive butchering and proven recipes. The appetizing moose roast, above, was the main course at an Alaska hunting lodge. By Dave Engerbretson

Graduated Elements Of A Campfire

1.
Tinder

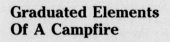

2.
Kindling

3.
Medium Fuel

4.
Warming Fuel

Reflector Wall
(Stump, Boulder, Embankment)

Fire Safety
Ring

2 tablespoons chopped parsley
3 tablespoons chopped celery leaves
2 teaspooons salt
6 medium potatoes
½ cup old-fashioned oatmeal

Heat fat in heavy kettle. Cut meat into 2-inch cubes and brown well in hot fat. Add water, barley, onion, parsley, celery and salt. Cook slowly 1½ hours. Add potatoes and oatmeal and continue cooking until potatoes are tender. Serve with crackers and cheese. Serves 6 to 8.

Louise Juhnke

Roast Bear

Use about an 8-pound roast off the rump of a young bear. Cover with cold water, add 3 or 4 medium-sized onions (sliced), and let soak about 4 hours. Remove from water and wipe dry. Cut 1 small clove garlic into small pieces and, using a sharp knife to make holes, force garlic deep into the meat. Get garlic as near the bone as possible. Season with salt and pepper. Brown in hot bacon drippings. Bake in open pan for 3 hours at 350°F, turning the meat several times while cooking.

Guide Ralph Hall

Pan-Fried Beaver, Muskrat

Disjoint beaver as you would a chicken and remove all fat. Parboil 10 minutes in soda water (1 teaspoon baking soda to 1 quart water), drain and rinse. Cook in fresh water with small chunks of bacon until beaver is tender. Drain again, season with salt, pepper, and thyme, paprika or sage, then brown in hot bacon drippings.

Use only young beaver in this recipe, as large ones have a tendency to toughen.

Vernon Haik

Liver in Onions

½ pound liver
10 slices bacon
6 medium onions
1 cup chopped celery
½ teaspoon salt

Pour boiling water over liver and leave it for 2 minutes. Pour off water, remove the thin skin and chop fine. Dice the bacon and fry until crisp. Remove outer skin of onions and as much of the inside as you can, leaving a firm shell. Chop the onion centers, mix with the bacon, liver, celery and salt, and stuff the hollowed-out onions with this mixture. Place in a Dutch oven, sprinkle cracker or bread crumbs over tops, cover oven and put it on the coals, heaping coals up around the lid. Cook 1 hour. Venison or moose liver may be used in this recipe.

Hazel Wimer

Tongue

To cook a fresh tongue, wash thoroughly, cover with cold water, add 1 teaspoon salt, 1 small onion, dash of pepper, and 1 bay leaf if desired. Quantities are for a large tongue, as of moose. Cook slowly until tender, 1½ hours per pound. Allow to cool, remove skin, bones and any tissue before tongue becomes too cool. Slice and serve hot or cold.

Boiled Heart

Wash hearts thoroughly in salt water, removing blood. Put in kettle and pour on boiling water to cover.
Add:
1 teaspoon salt per quart of water
dash of pepper
1 bay leaf
1 stalk celery, cut in thirds
1 small carrot
1 quartered onion

Bring to a boil, then let simmer until meat is tender. Venison hearts take an hour, others a little longer. Test with a fork. Meat can be cooled in broth, then removed and sliced thin for sandwiches. When broth is cold, remove and discard hardened fat. Strain the broth and use it as the base for hearty soups or gravies, or in recipes that call for bouillon.

Mark Jensen

Fish

Oven-Fried Fillets

2 pounds fillets
1 tablespoon salt
1 cup milk or buttermilk
1 cup browned bread crumbs, cornmeal or crushed cornflakes
4 tablespoons melted butter or other fat

Cut fillets into serving-size portions. Add salt to milk in shallow pan. Dip fish in milk, roll in crumbs, place in well-greased pan, pour on melted fat. Place pan on rack near top of oven and bake at 500°F for 10 to 15 minutes, until fish flakes easily when tested with a fork. Serve immediately on hot platter, plain or with a sauce. Serves 6.

Thelma Rose Lind

This recipe, a variation of the Spencer Hot Oven Method, is also excellent for steaks, or any fish cut not more than 1½ inches thick. The quick cooking at high heat retains the moisture and flavor lost in slower panfrying or baking methods. Less fat may be used, especially when cooking salmon, sablefish or other rich varieties. Greased foil under the fish, turned up slightly at the edges, saves soaking and scrubbing the pan. Lemon, the traditional garnish, should be cut in wedges instead of slices. You can squeeze the juice out of a lemon wedge.

Outdoor Barbecue Salmon

1 white king salmon, 12 to 14 pounds
salt
pepper
garlic salt

Split fish and remove backbone. Season split sides well with the salt, pepper and garlic salt. Place cut side down on barbecue grill. Whe your fire is good and hot, put on some green alder. When you have a nice bed of coals, place the grill about a foot above the coals. When the cut side is nicely browned, about 2 minutes, turn carefully and let cook 3 to 4 hours.

Elsie Calusen

Salmon or Halibut Poached in Sauce

1 small onion, chopped
½ green pepper (chopped), or a little chopped pimiento
chopped celery
1 tablespoon Worcestershire sauce
Fish herbs if desired
salt and pepper
milk

Bring all to a boil in a small amount of water, in a covered frying pan. On top place seasoned salmon or halibut fillets, cover, and poach until barely done. Lift off fish, remove any skin or bone. Add some milk to the sauce, thicken, and serve over the fish.

Baked Salmon

Clean fish and pat dry with paper towel. Sprinkle moderately inside and out with salt. Place on foil-lined baking pan, brush with oil or melted fat. Place 3 or 4 strips of bacon across fish (optional). Measure fish at the thickest part, and allow 10 minutes baking time for each inch of thickness. Bake in a hot oven 425°F. Fish should flake, but do not over-bake; if it seems dry, baste with melted fat during baking. Do not turn fish. Garnish with lemon and serve immediately. Fish may be stuffed with various dressings and skewered shut, then bake as directed.

Halibut Deluxe

Cut about 2 pounds halibut into fillets for serving and place in buttered pan. Sprinkle each piece with salt, pepper and garlic salt. Dilute about ½ can cream of mushroom soup with same amount of sherry and pour over fish. Spread with grated cheese. Broil, or bake at 500°F for 10 minutes. Sauce may be thickened before serving.

Mrs. H.L. Faulkner

Building A Reflector Oven

Some of the finest outdoor dishes are best prepared in an oven, including breads, biscuits, fish and cakes. A lightweight, efficient camp oven can be made in a few minutes and using the reflected heat of an open campfire will produce mouth-watering results.

The reflector oven is made of aluminum foil and sticks. A single, 30-inch strip of foil serves as top and bottom of the oven. Two 10-inch sheets of foil form the sides. Frame the front of the oven with sticks, using two green forked sticks for vertical supports and one green horizontal cross-member stick slightly longer than the foil is wide. The cross member should be roughly 10 inches above the ground, and within a foot of the campfire.

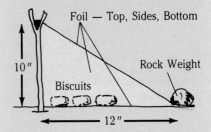

**Reflector Oven
Side View**

Position the leading edge of the single sheet slightly in front of and between the support sticks, extending the excess foil away from the fire. At approximately 12 inches, fold the excess foil up and forward across the cross member. Use a small stone or stick to secure the fold. Position the two side panels to create a triangulated oven with the open end toward the fire.

The most even heat is generally achieved by collecting a pile of hot coals or embers within a few inches of the front of the oven. Open flame should be kept several feet away from the cooking area while the biscuits are browning.

Baked Stuffed Rockfish Rolls

2 pounds (6) rockfish fillets
1 teaspoon salt
dash pepper
1 tablespoon lemon juice
½ cup flour
Favorite recipe, bread stuffing

Sprinkle fillets with salt, pepper and lemon juice. Place a ball of stuffing on each fillet, roll and tie securely with string. Roll in flour and brown in hot fat. Place rolls in a well greased, covered casserole and bake in moderate oven, 350°F., 30 minutes or until fish flakes easily when tested with a fork. Remove string, garnish and serve hot. Serves 6.

Broiled Sablefish (Black Cod)

2 pounds sablefish fillets
1 teaspoon salt
1 teaspoon lemon juice
2 tablespoons butter or other fat, melted

Cut fish into serving-size portions and sprinkle with salt and lemon juice. Place on a preheated, well-greased broiler rack, brush with fat, broil about 2 inches from source of heat for 12 minutes, or until fish flakes easily when tested with a fork. Garnish and serve hot. Serves 6.

Campfire Trout

Another easy way to cook fish either in the field or at home is to use aluminum foil. Place the cleaned trout in the foil with sliced raw onions, two pats of butter, and salt and pepper.

Carefully seal the foil so it is airtight and place in hot coals for about 25 minutes. Cooking in an oven at about 450°F for 30 to 40 minutes works well at home.

Baked Trout

1 large trout
salt and pepper
flour
1 onion, sliced thick
sliced American cheese
1 stalk celery, chopped
top milk or cream
1 tablespoon Worcestershire or steak sauce

Clean the trout, dry it thoroughly inside and out, slit it nearly all the way down one side, season with salt and pepper and dredge with flour. Lay it in a buttered oblong pan, slit side up. Place a layer of sliced onions inside fish, flour slightly, place slices of cheese on top of onions, and celery on top of cheese. Flour slightly to thicken. Season with salt, pepper and sauce and close body cavity with toothpicks. Place remaining slices of onion on top of trout, moisten the top with the milk or cream and pour the rest into the pan beside trout. Bake uncovered in slow oven, allowing liquid to thicken. Baste occasionally and cook until done.

Mrs. James Nolan

Brown Bag Fish

Backpacking fishermen, ever concerned about carrying unnecessary weight into the backcountry, will love this system for cooking fish — preferably those freshly caught from a mountain lake — without a cumbersome skillet.

Lack of frying also enhances the natural flavor of fresh fish, making this technique as popular at roadside campgrounds as in the backcountry. Use whole fish or fillets.

Clean fish (1 per bag). Season with salt and pepper, lemon juice and onion slices. Wrap the seasoned fish in a double section of wax paper and place inside a large, walled brown paper bag. Saturate the bag with water and lay on the coals (not flame) of the cooking fire. Turn the bag and sprinkle with extra water as needed to prevent ignition. In about 10 minutes (or when the bag is hopelessly scorched) remove from the coals and serve. The heat and steam preserves the delicate flavor of fresh fish.

ERWIN & PEGGY BAUER

Cooking On Coals

Cooking in the backcountry, especially in areas where dead wood is at a premium, is best tackled with a small, portable fuel-powered stove. When that is not an option, however, the traditional cook fire is.

Except for hotdogs on a skewer, there is no reason to cook over leaping flames. Coals, preferably from a deep, hot bed burned from large wood chunks, provide a hot, even temperature that is critical for good camp cooking. Cook pots can be hung above the coals, or set directly on top of the embers depending upon the amount of heat needed. Coat the outside of the pan with liquid detergent or wrap in aluminum foil to prevent black soot stains. Expendable coffee cans often work better than conventional cookware.

For skillet frying, position two flat rocks within a few inches of each on the periphery of the fire, then scoop live coals into the space between the rocks. Set the skillet on the rocks above the coals for even heat. If the coals cool before the meal is complete, simply replace them with hot coals from the adjacent fire.

Shellfish

Steamed Mussels or Clams

2 quarts mussels
3 tablespoons olive oil
1 small onion, thinly sliced
4 cloves garlic, pressed (or 1 teaspoon garlic powder)
¼ teaspoon thyme
4 celery stalks, including tops, chopped coarsely
8 ounces dry white wine
½ teaspoon parsley, finely chopped

Scrub mussels and remove threads. Heat olive oil in a heavy pan with cover. Add onion, pressed garlic, thyme and chopped celery. Saute until onion is transparent. Add mussels, pour wine over all and cover tightly.

Cook over medium high heat for 3 to 4 minute. Shake pot briskly to mix. Turn off heat and allow to stand 2 minutes. Open cover and sprinkle with parsley.

Mussels will have opened. Serve with broth from the mussels in 1 cup and drawn melted butter in another.

Clam Chowder

1 cup chopped bacon or ham
½ cup chopped salt pork
2 cups chopped onions
2 cups chopped celery
1 cup chopped carrots
2 tablespoons butter
2 tablespoons flour
1 quart boiling water or ham broth
3 cups diced raw potatoes
salt and pepper
½ lemon
2 quarts coarse-cut raw clams

Braise ham or bacon and salt pork in a heavy pot until half fried. Add onions, celery and carrots, stir occasionally, and braise until vegetables are half-cooked. Pour off excess fat, then add the butter, let it melt, then add flour and when well blended, add boiling water or broth. Allow to simmer 1 hour. Add the diced raw potatoes and seasonings. When potatoes are tender, add the lemon and clams. Never, but never let clams cook more than 12 minutes! Yield: 1 gallon.

While serving this chowder, put a can of allspice on the table for the individual whim.

For variation, add tomatoes or milk. If tomatoes, omit some of the water; if milk, use straight canned milk and add at the very last.

G.S. "Bud" Mortensen

Crab Boil

Use only live, healthy crabs. Crabs are preferably butchered and cleaned before precooking. Use a sturdy, flat-topped table with a sharp, square edge. Hold the underside of the crab on the table edge, keeping the midline parallel with the edge. Grasp the legs and with a slight twisting motion, pull quickly down and away from the back or carapace.

Tear off back. With large crabs a stationary butchering iron or hook may be used to tear off back before breaking in half.

Trim off gills and viscera, being careful not to contaminate meat with viscera, which results in off flavor and discoloration in the finished product. Wash each section thoroughly under running, cold water. Do not soak.

Precooking

Precook in boiling salted water (½ cup salt per gallon of water) for 10 minutes, or steam in pressure cooker at 212°F. (no pressure) for 13 to 15 minutes. Large crabs (king or whole Dungeness) should be cooked 5 minutes longer. Do not overcook, as it tends to cause excessive shrinkage of meat.

If a quantity of crabs is being boiled, change the water frequently to prevent concentration

Hardshell clams, like this mixture of butter and littlenecks, are tender delicacies when steamed and dipped in melted butter. Hardshell clams are plentiful on most gravel coastal beaches. By Doug Wilson

of blood and other coagulated proteins.

Remove from boiling water or steamer and cool quickly by dipping briefly in clean, cold water or spraying for about 2 minutes with cold water. This helps to firm and shrink the meat, making it easier to remove from the shell.

Fruits

Berry Muffins

¼ cup shortening
¾ cup sugar
1 egg, beaten
2 cups flour
4 teaspoons baking powder
½ teaspoon salt
1 cup milk
1 cup berries

Cream shortening, sugar and beaten egg. Add sifted dry ingredients, then add milk and stir until blended. Fold in the berries lightly. Fill greased muffin tins ¾ full, bake 20 to 25 minutes at 350°F.

Marguerite Doucette

Fruit Leather

An excellent trail snack that doesn't require refrigeration and provides plenty of natural "sugar" for energy renewal. A flavorful camp snack or in-the-field pick-me-up. Experiment with different fruit flavors.

4 cups fruit puree (applesauce, strawberry, pear, peaches are popular)
3 tablespoons honey

Spread evenly on a coated (nongreasy) 11-by-16-inch cookie sheet. The mix should be no deeper than ¼ inch. Place in oven and dry slowly at 150°F. In about 6 hours the fruit leather becomes pliable but not sticky and can be peeled from the cookie sheet.

Sourdough

Sourdough Starter

Mix 1 cup flour, 1 cup water, ½ to 1 package (or cake) of yeast in a pint jar. Let stand in a warm place overnight.

Sponge

Empty starter into a bowl. Fill the pint jar with warm water (2 cups), empty it into the bowl, add 2 cups flour and beat to a smooth batter. Let bowl stand in a warm place overnight. Batter should be thin enough to pour. If too thick, add a little warm water.

In the morning, take out ¼ to ½ cup of the sponge, put in clean pint jar, and place in refrigerator or cool place for the next sponge.

A sourdough starter will be good for many years if kept in a cool place and used every week. Never add anything to the starter except flour and water.

To carry the starter or keep it longer than a week, thicken it with flour to form a ball and keep it in the flour or in a covered container. To activate it, thin it out with water.

Sourdough Bread
(Brown)

To 1 cup sourdough sponge add 1 teaspoon salt, 2 tablespoons molasses and 2 tablespoons fat. Mix well. Add 2 cups white flour, or enough to make a stiff dough. Knead lightly. Place in warm, greased loaf tin, let stand ½ hour, then bake at 375°F until lightly browned, about 40 minutes. This is a coarse, heavy bread with a good flavor.

How To Can Salmon

Clean and wash the fish, removing all traces of blood. Cut the cleaned fish in can-length pieces. Leave the backbone, it contains valuable minerals and is made quite edible by processing. Drain the fish for several minutes. Pack into sterilized pint jars or cans until the fish is even with the rim but do not crush it down. Add ½ teaspoon salt. Many persons prefer to skin the salmon before canning. Hold the fish under the hot water faucet one side at a time, allow the water to run on the fish for about a minute, this loosens the skin. Start at the tail end, peel the skin back just enough so you can grasp it with a plier, pull firmly toward the head, using a sharp knife to loosen the skin if necessary. When jars are packed, place them in a pressure cooker, seal the covers, and process for 1 hour and 50 minutes at 10 pounds (240°F) pressure. After cooking, shut off steam and allow the pressure to drop to zero before opening the vent.

Sourdough Pancakes

To 1 cup sourdough (above) add 2 eggs, ¼ cup melted butter or bacon drippings, 1 tablespoon sugar, ½ teaspoon salt, 1 teaspoon soda dissolved in 1 tablespoon hot water. Stir, and watch so it doesn't go over the edge of the bowl. Pour this thin batter onto hot, greased griddle, and when crisp edges curl and top is bubbly, flip over. Serve with blueberry syrup for a real treat.

Outdoor Specialties

Whitefish Pickle

After you've caught your limit of whitefish, here's a delicious way to keep them. The hardest part is deciding whether to go sweet or sour.

Brine

Fillet and skin fish; cut into 2-inch chunks. Make enough brine (1 cup pickling salt to 1 quart water) to cover fish and soak 12 hours or more in a refrigerator. Pour off brine and pickle your fish using one of the following recipes:

Sweet

Cover brined fish with white vinegar; refrigerate for 24 hours. Drain off vinegar. Layer fish in a jar with thinly sliced onions, carrots and celery. Add cool pickling liquor to top; tightly seal and refrigerate for 2 weeks.

Liquor

1 cup white vinegar
½ cup water
¼ to ½ cup sugar
1 tablespoon pickling spice
10 to 15 whole allspice
½ cup white port wine

Bring all ingredients except port to a boil; reduce heat and simmer 30 minutes; cool. Add wine.

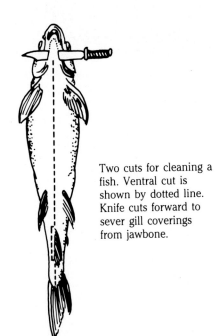

Saltwater rockfish, like these canaries, have delicate, white meat that is excellent baked, fried or battered. By Terry Rudnick

Summer Sausage (Smoked)

3 pounds ground beef
2 pounds ground pork
4 tablespoons salt (noniodized)
3½ teaspoons coarse ground black pepper
1 tablespoon sugar
1¾ teaspoons Modern Cure
½ teaspoon cayenne (red) pepper
¾ teaspoon mustard seed (whole)
⅔ teaspoon black pepper (whole)
garlic to taste (approximately ½ teaspoon minced)

Place ground beef, ground pork and mixed spices in large bowl or pan. Mix thoroughly by hand. When thoroughly mixed refrigerate or keep in a cool place for approximately 12 hours. Stuff casing — tying each casing securely. Smoke at moderate heat for 24 hours or until sausage has the degree of dryness desired. Smoke is not necessary during entire processing period — 4 or 5 panfuls of chips are sufficient in most cases even though total time may take up to 24 hours. Heat should be applied continuously. May be stored in refrigerator or placed in individual plastic bags and frozen until used.

Luhr • Jensen

Two cuts for cleaning a fish. Ventral cut is shown by dotted line. Knife cuts forward to sever gill coverings from jawbone.

Smoked Fish

(for oily fish with a stronger flavor)

2 quarts water
1 cup noniodized salt
½ cup brown sugar
2 tablespoons lemon concentrate or ¼ cup lemon juice
¼ tablespoon garlic powder
¼ tablespoon onion powder

Use small fish or fillet of large. Mix all indgredients and stir until dissolved. Brine fish 4 or more hours. Rinse and dry. Rack and load. Use 3 to 5 pansful hickory, apple or alder chips. Keep in the smoker 4 to 10 hours, depending on the size of fish pieces. (Use this recipe for: cod, bass, pike, tuna types, sturgeon, barracuda, mackerel, eels, squid and octopus.)

Luhr • Jensen

Smoking Wild Game

Brine:

1 pint cider vinegar
1 quart water
1 cup noniodized salt
1 tablespoon black peppercorns
½ cup brown sugar
1 blade mace
2 tablespoons parsley
2 medium onions, chopped
1 medium sliced carrot
1 cup dry red wine

Bring all ingredients, except wine, to a boil. Turn to simmer for 30 minutes. Strain into a large container and add wine. Use immediately. Do not store. Brine meat 3 to 4 days turning often and keeping refrigerated. Place in smoker using 2 to 5 pansful of hickory or cherry chips (depending on the thickness of the meat). Finish cooking on broiler or in the oven. Use this recipe for: venison, elk, moose, bear, horsemeat, antelope, sheep and reindeer.

Luhr • Jensen

Smoking Chicken and Upland Birds

Marinade

¼ cup water
¼ cup soy sauce
¼ cup dry white wine
¼ cup brown sugar
½ teaspoon onion powder
½ teaspoon garlic powder
½ teaspoon ground ginger

Place birds in cool marinade for 6 hours. Rinse and dry on paper towels for 1 hour. Smoke with 2 pansful of hickory or apple flavor chips for 2 to 4 hours. Remove from smoker and cook until done in the oven wrapped in foil. Birds may now be eaten cold or warm and served with a light glaze, sauce or gravy. Use your imagination.

Luhr • Jensen

Ringneck pheasants are the most popular upland bird, in the field and on the table. By Mark Henckel

Index

More Essentials for the Sporting Life . . .

R eaders of *The Northwest Sportsman Almanac* can look to Alaska Northwest Books™ for more outdoor how-to books and for true tales of wilderness adventure.

THE MILEPOST®, THE ALASKA WILDERNESS MILEPOST® and NORTHWEST MILEPOSTS®

Since 1949, *The Milepost®* has served as the "bible of North Country travel" for travelers to Alaska or western Canada. Updated annually, this classic guide gives mile-by-mile information on what to see and do, and where to find food, gas, and lodging. It includes a fold-out "Plan-A-Trip" map and information on customs, air travel, and hunting and fishing. Companion guides, *The Alaska Wilderness Milepost®* and *Northwest Mileposts®,* round out the picture with everything you need to know to discover the glories of bush Alaska (over 250 remote towns and villages covered) and the Northwest (Washington, Oregon, Idaho, Montana, and southwestern Canada). Look for detailed maps, color photographs, and the best information available on parks, historical sites, wildlife areas, and sporting activities.

The Milepost®/546 pages/paperback/$14.95
ISBN 0-88240-214-5
The Alaska Wilderness Milepost®/400 pages/
paperback/$14.95   ISBN 0-88240-289-7
Northwest Mileposts®/496 pages/paperback/$14.95
ISBN 0-88240-278-1

KOOTENAY COUNTRY: ONE MAN'S LIFE IN THE CANADIAN ROCKIES
By Ernest "Fee" Hellmen

Kootenay Country is an easy-reading account of author "Fee" Hellmen's life fishing, hunting, and as a big-game guide in the rugged East Kootenay Valley of British Columbia. Beginning in the 1920s when Hellmen was a boy, this selection of anecdotes chronicles the adventures, dangers and pleasures inherent in a life in the Great Outdoors.

155 pages/paperback/$9.95   ISBN 0-88240-357-5

TRAPLINE TWINS
By Julie and Miki Collins

Identical twins Julie and Miki Collins are trappers in the remote Lake Minchumina region, northwest of Mount McKinley in Interior Alaska. This is their journal of adventurous wilderness living, in which dogsled, canoe and aircraft are their transportation; wild game, garden produce and foraged edibles their food; and furs their cash crop.

215 pages/paperback/$12.95   ISBN 0-88240-332-X

ALASKA BEAR TALES
By Larry Kaniut

Anyone living or traveling in the Alaskan bush knows of the ever-present danger of being attacked by a bear. This best-selling book is a sometimes chilling, always gripping collection of true stories about folks who survived close calls with bears, and those who didn't.

318 pages/paperback/$10.95   ISBN 0-88240-232-3

WILDERNESS SURVIVAL GUIDE
By Monty Alford

Planning is key when you're preparing for a wilderness trek in the North Country. Thirty-eight years of experience with Yukon rivers, lakes and glaciers give Monty Alford the authority to tell you how to build snow shelters, cross icy rivers, build your own survival gear and more.

104 pages/paperback/$9.95   ISBN 0-88240-317-6

COOKING ALASKAN and THE ALASKAN CAMP COOK
By the Editors of *Alaska* Magazine and a host of Alaska's home and camp cooks

Alaska's true mother lode may be the unique meals made from the region's wild fruits and vegetables, mammals and birds, and fish and shellfish. Those who hunt and fish will treasure *Cooking Alaskan* and *The Alaskan Camp Cook* for their many tips on dressing wild game and great recipes for everything from Wiggling Fish Soup to Moose Sausage to Aleut Berry Pudding.

Cooking Alaskan/500 pages/paperback/$16.95
ISBN 0-88240-237-4
The Alaskan Camp Cook/88 pages/paperback/$4.95
ISBN 0-88240-000-2

WOLF TRAIL LODGE
By Edward M. Boyd

In 1957 Ed and Leona Boyd traded a failing Anchorage gas station for a rundown ex-roadhouse and outbuildings in Seward. This is the story of their getaway haven, a place filled with thirty-plus years of moose hunts, bush plane flights, encounters with smart bears, and cliffhangers.

108 pages/paperback/$5.95   ISBN 0-88240-271-4

ALASKA BLUES: A FISHERMAN'S JOURNAL
By Joe Upton

Commercial fisherman Joe Upton has won awards and high praise for his journal of a salmon season in Alaska. In the words of famous author Ernest K. Gann *(The High and the Mighty)*, Upton's photographs and storytelling make *Alaska Blues* "... one of the most unique sea sagas ever written."

236 pages/hardbound/$14.95   ISBN 0-88240-098-3

ALASKA'S SALTWATER FISHES AND OTHER SEA LIFE
By Doyne W. Kessler

Both sport and commercial fishermen will find this an invaluable guide to identifying 370 species of fishes and invertebrates found in the waters of the Alaskan continental shelf. The guide's simplified text and line drawings are complemented by photographs that show the color, form and texture of living sea animals.

358 pages/paperback/$19.95   ISBN 0-88240-302-8

Ask for these books at your favorite bookstore, or contact Alaska Northwest Books™ for a catalog of our entire list.

Alaska Northwest Books™
P.O. Box 3007
Bothell, WA 98041-3007
1-800-331-3510
A division of GTE Discovery Publications, Inc.